KHRUSHCHEV'S COLD WAR

KHRUSHCHEV'S COLD WAR

The Inside Story of an American Adversary

ALEKSANDR FURSENKO AND
TIMOTHY NAFTALI

W. W. NORTON & COMPANY ■ NEW YORK LONDON

For information about permission to reproduce selections from this book, write to
Permissions, W. W. Norton & Company, Inc., 500 Fifth Avenue, New York, NY 10110

Manufacturing by The Maple-Vail Book Manufacturing Group
Book design by Chris Welch
Map on pages 10-11 by John McCausland
Production manager: Amanda Morrison

Library of Congress Cataloging-in-Publication Data

Fursenko, A. A.
Khrushchev's cold war : the inside story of an American adversary /
Aleksandr Fursenko and Timothy Naftali. — 1st ed.
p. cm.
Includes bibliographical references and index.
ISBN-13: 978-0-393-05809-3 (hardcover)
ISBN-10: 0-393-05809-3 (hardcover)
1. Soviet Union—Foreign relations—United States. 2. United States—Foreign relations—Soviet
Union. 3. Khrushchev, Nikita Sergeevich, 1894–1971. 4. Cold War. 5. World politics—1945–1989.
I. Naftali, Timothy J. II. Title.
E183.8.S65F85 2006
327.4707309'045--dc22

2006017576

W. W. Norton & Company, Inc., 500 Fifth Avenue, New York, N.Y. 10110
www.wwnorton.com

W. W. Norton & Company Ltd., Castle House, 75/76 Wells Street, London W1T 3QT

1 2 3 4 5 6 7 8 9 0

CONTENTS

INTRODUCTION

THERE ARE TIMES when the personality of a single human being can rival ideologies, institutions, or social movements as a cause of great international events. The influence of these individuals extends beyond their own cultures, shaping not only other societies but the competition for power among states. In the middle years of the twentieth century the Cold War entered what would be known in retrospect as its most dangerous phase. Five separate crises—Suez, Iraq, Berlin (twice), and Cuba—broke out in succession; each of them seemed capable of producing World War III. For much of that time the world was caught in the grip of intense uncertainty about the future. Leaders and ordinary citizens alike had no sense of how things would work out, whether the two great adversaries, the Soviet Union and the United States, would remain in a limbo defined by no peace and no war or suddenly plunge into a devastating nuclear conflict. There was one leader, however, who stood apart from others in believing in his ability to dictate history.

On January 8, 1962, in a speech that remained secret for over forty years, Nikita S. Khrushchev announced to his colleagues in the Kremlin that the Soviet position in the superpower struggle was so weak that Moscow had no choice but to try to set the pace of international politics. "We should increase the pressure, we must not doze off and, while growing, we should let the opponent feel this growth." He adopted the metaphor of a wineglass that was filled to the rim, forming a meniscus, to describe a world where political tensions everywhere were brought to the edge of military confrontation. "Because if we don't have a meniscus," he explained, "we let the enemy live peacefully."

The United States was the "enemy" that Khrushchev did not want to see "live peacefully." Was the Soviet leader spoiling for war? The wineglass, Khrushchev explained in his characteristically colorful way, was not to overflow, but so long as the Soviet Union was the weaker superpower, it had to practice brinkmanship to keep its adversary off-balance. A dangerous strategy at any time in history, but in the nuclear age this approach was potentially suicidal. Rarely had a single world leader shown this much hubris. Yet the strategy that Khrushchev announced in 1962 was one that he had been practicing in various forms since he had come to dominate the Kremlin's foreign policy in 1955. What made Khrushchev believe he could control the consequences of Soviet pressure tactics? Why was he confident that the United States would understand that the wineglass was not supposed to spill?

President John F. Kennedy, who like the rest of the U.S. government never knew about the January 1962 "meniscus" speech or the strategy behind it, had a very hard time figuring out Khrushchev. All Kennedy had to work with was the abundant evidence of a contradictory man. On the one hand, the Communist Party chief spoke of the need for détente and disarmament. In July 1962 Khrushchev was to agree to the Declaration on the Neutrality of Laos, which eased the U.S.-Soviet struggle in Southeast Asia. At home he was credited with having ended Stalinist repression, releasing political prisoners and speaking out against the blood-splattered previous regime. Yet this same leader gave very tough anti-Western speeches and at times seemed prepared to turn the Cold War into a deadly competition. Endlessly boastful about Russia's weapons of mass destruction, Khrushchev issued ultimatum after ultimatum to force the West to accept his view of how things ought to be in the Middle East, Central Europe, and Latin America.

No amount of intelligence or regional expertise ever gave American leaders in the Cold War enough insight into the Kremlin to feel confident that they knew what was going on in the corridors of power in Moscow. Were there any debates? What were their objectives? Did they ever consider going to war? What role did the personality of the dictator, in this case Nikita Khrushchev, play in the course of events?

Khrushchev left a clue to where some of the answers might be found. "I will have to dictate my memoirs without access to archival materials," he confessed to a tape recorder in the late 1960s.[1] With time on his hands after he was deposed as Soviet leader in October 1964, he set about dictating hundreds of hours of recollections. But the result, though fascinating, was a two-thousand-page tangle of historical truth and self-delusion.[2] The answers lay elsewhere. "In future generations, anyone who is interested in what I have to say can check up on me," Khrushchev revealed on tape. "The facts can be found in the minutes and the protocols of meetings."[3]

Those minutes and protocols—the records of decisions and debates—of the

Khrushchev era, the "meniscus speech" included among them, remained closed in Moscow until the summer of 2003. Despite the opening of many archives in the first years after the fall of the Berlin Wall, the Kremlin's most secret information on Khrushchev was locked away in an archive controlled by the Office of the President of the Russian Federation. Some of this material was shown to the authors in the mid-1990s for a book on the Cuban missile crisis. Although the material was very good, it did not touch on the other East-West clashes of the Khrushchev era, such as the Suez, Iraqi, and Berlin crises. In 2001 a collection of the Khrushchev protocols and minutes of the Presidium of the Central Committee, the top decision-making organ of the Communist Party of the Soviet Union, was transferred from this classified archive to a more accessible archive, where by 2003 it had been fully declassified. The handiwork of the chief of the General Department of the Central Committee, Vladimir Malin, these notes record the debates, decisions, and desires of the Soviet leadership from the year Khrushchev began to shape Soviet foreign policy through crises in Hungary, Suez, Berlin, and Cuba. These dynamic materials depict the hopes and fears of the Kremlin at a time when Western statesmen and journalists assumed that nuclear catastrophe was nigh. Had the CIA been able to steal these materials in 1962, U.S. intelligence and the State Department could have explained to Kennedy the outlines of his adversary's plans.

Using these new materials and others found in Moscow, we attempt in this book to re-create how Khrushchev viewed the Cold War and the strategies and tactics he used to fight it. Using the tools of international or comparative history, we will explore his personal responsibility for the international events that ensued. Between 1956 and 1962 the world witnessed crises in the Middle East, Central Europe, and the Caribbean, yet war did not break out between the superpowers. Why was the world so lucky? Then in 1963, while Khrushchev was still in power, the superpowers reached an accommodation of sorts that seemed to preclude more of these crises. In piecing together the international environment in which Khrushchev operated, we also hope to show the process of action and reaction between the superpowers and the independent actions of smaller players that helped determine the way things turned out.

Unwrapped and declassified, the Khrushchev who emerges was the most provocative, the most daring, and, ironically, the most desirous of a lasting agreement with the American people of any man or woman in the Kremlin. He also was no less cruel or ideological than the other Kremlin leaders who had survived Stalin. Had this complex personality led a small country, his idiosyncrasies would be worthy of some storytelling, but they would hardly be seen as major factors in understanding the course of world events. But Khrushchev stood at the pinnacle of the most powerful adversary ever faced by the United States. The country covered eleven time zones, nearly eight million square miles of territory, with a population estimated at two hundred million. Beyond the Soviet Union, the Kremlin controlled a vast territory of client states. On VE Day in 1945, Soviet armies occupied Poland, Czechoslovakia, Hungary, Bulgaria, Romania, and a third of Germany, including the eastern half of Hitler's capital, Berlin. By the time of Japan's surrender on August 14, 1945, Moscow had added a military presence in Manchuria, the northern islands of Japan, and the northern part of Korea. But it all had come at great cost. No military victor had ever suffered as much as the Soviet Union did in World War II. It is estimated that the Nazis destroyed seventeen hundred Soviet towns and seventy thousand villages, in all about a third of the wealth of the Soviet Union.[4] The human toll remains beyond reckoning. Battlefield deaths, twice those suffered by Nazi Germany, reached about seven million. The civilian loss was even higher, estimated somewhere between seventeen and twenty million people.

Yet what might have turned other civilizations inward seemed to propel the Soviet Union onto the world stage. Within five years of the end of World War II, Russia had detonated its own atomic device, threatened its neighbors, assisted a Communist regime's rise to power in China, and participated in North Korea's invasion of South Korea. This spectacular case of imperial stretch inspired fear and concern that not only was the Soviet Union's political influence worldwide, but its military ambitions were boundless.

Khrushchev was never more than the dark horse candidate to lead this empire. Born to a peasant Russian family in 1894, Nikita Sergeyevich had only four years of formal education before he began a career as a metalworker in the Ukrainian part of Imperial Russia. Following the Bolshevik Revolution of 1917, the far-reaching Communist Party apparatus provided the means of advancement for the ambitious and energetic in the new state. Through a combination of patronage, street smarts, and talent, Khrushchev steadily rose in the party organizations in Kharkov and Kiev before arriving in Moscow in 1929. He distinguished himself by his hard work, the ease with which he learned the details of agriculture and engineering, and his dedication to Joseph Stalin, who by this point had launched the first wave of the great purge. Stalin noticed Khrushchev and in 1938 sent him back to the Ukraine, where he ultimately oversaw the defense and reconquest of that region in the war with Nazi Germany. In 1949, Stalin brought Khrushchev back to the Kremlin to serve as Moscow party chief. He was by now a full member of the Politburo (later Presidium) of the Central Committee and considered one of Stalin's inner circle.

Despite increasing ill health in the early postwar years, Stalin was too paranoid to prepare his lieutenants for the succession. Indeed, in the last months of his life the dictator had sent powerful signals that he was preparing to purge some of the men who were closest to him. When he finally died in March 1953, a few days after suffering a massive stroke at his dacha outside Moscow, the smart money was on others, not Khrushchev, as the heir apparent.

Once it became clear that this would be Stalin's final illness, a group of four formed to lead the country. Georgi Malenkov, the most competent administrator, who was the youngest of the quartet, became the head of the formal government, the Council of Ministers. Clustered around him were Lavrenti Beria, a secret policeman with a menacing pince-nez who was chief of the KGB and minister of the interior; the longtime Politburo member and foreign minister Vyacheslav Molotov; and, finally, Nikita Khrushchev, who became first secretary of the Communist Party of the Soviet Union after Stalin's death. No one was named general secretary, Stalin's old title.

Beria inspired too much fear in his colleagues for any stable power-sharing arrangement to emerge. Either the secret policeman would kill all of them in a single purge, or they would have to eliminate him first. In three months Beria was executed, and Khrushchev played a leading role in the conspiracy that brought him down. For the eighteen months that followed an uneasy alliance remained among the three remaining members of the "collective leadership."

This account begins at the moment in 1955 when Khrushchev stepped out of the shadows of the better-known Molotov and Malenkov and walked onto the world stage. His influence over Soviet strategy grew dramatically, and by the early 1960s the Soviet Union had almost returned to the one-man rule of the Stalin era. In that decade Khrushchev also came to hold a commanding position in shaping world events, locked in a struggle for power with two American presidents, Dwight D. Eisenhower and John F. Kennedy. Ambitious, aggressive, and impatient, Khrushchev intended to leave his imprint on the world. This is the story of how he went about doing it.

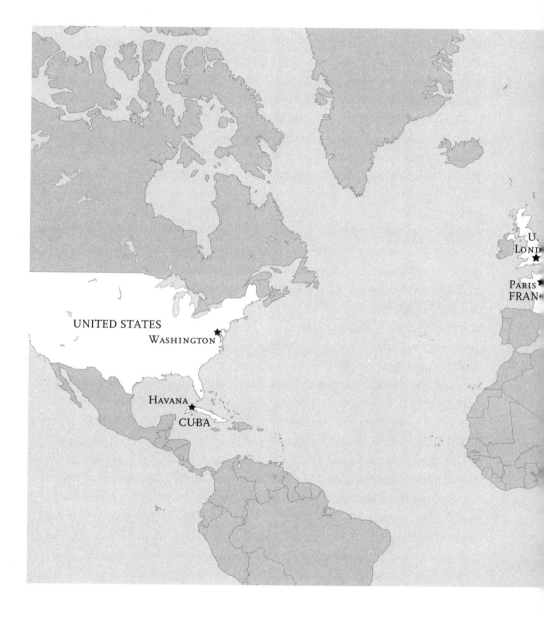

DIVIDED BERLIN

FRENCH

WEST EAST
BRITISH U.S.S.R.

UNITED STATES

U.S.S.R.

Moscow

WEST EAST
GERMANY GERMANY
BERLIN POLAND
Warsaw
VIENNA CZECHOSLOVAKIA
GENEVA Budapest
AUSTRIA HUNGARY
YUGOSLAVIA ROMANIA
SWITZERLAND BULGARIA
LEBANON
ALBANIA Beirut
SYRIA
ISRAEL Damascus
Suez Canal IRAQ
Baghdad
Cairo
EGYPT JORDAN

Pitsunda

AFGHANISTAN

INDIA

CHINA

Beijing

NORTH
KOREA

SOUTH
KOREA

Taipei

Hong Kong

TAIWAN

Hanoi

BURMA

LAOS N. VIETNAM

Vientiane

S. VIETNAM

Saigon

CONGO
Léopoldville

KATANGA
PROVINCE

KHRUSHCHEV'S COLD WAR

INDONESIA

KHRUSHCHEV'S COLD WAR

CHAPTER 1

RED STAR ASCENDANT

RITISH AMBASSADOR Sir William Hayter was bored, but this was not unusual for a Western diplomat in the Soviet Union in the mid-1950s. It was February 8, 1955, the second to last day of a meeting of the Supreme Soviet, the entirely symbolic parliament of the Union of Soviet Socialist Republics, and Hayter was in the diplomatic box with other foreign plenipotentiaries expecting nothing new. Part of the job of being a foreign representative in Soviet Moscow involved attending and then summarizing for a foreign ministry or the State Department the interminable public meetings of Communist officials. With luck you might find amid the ideological blather some new shade of meaning. Today, however, Hayter and the rest of the world were to be surprised by the sudden twinkling of a rising Kremlin star.[1]

Without any warning, after hours of debate on minor matters, a short bureaucrat named Aleksandr P. Volkov walked to the podium and announced that he had a statement to read from Premier Georgi Malenkov.[2] In the two years since Stalin's death, in March 1953, a new "collective leadership" headed by the relatively dapper fifty-two-year-old chairman of the Council of Ministers, Georgi Malenkov, had emerged in the Kremlin. Alongside Malenkov in this troika were two other powerful Kremlin figures: the first secretary of the Communist Party of the Soviet Union (CPSU), Nikita Khrushchev, and Foreign Minister Vyacheslav Molotov. Rumors of tension within the troika had reached Western diplomats, but no one seriously expected the comparatively young and energetic Malenkov to lose his position.

Although all the top Kremlin chieftains were sitting on leadership benches behind the dais, Volkov read the statement as if Malenkov were not in the hall. In his statement, the Soviet premier accepted "guilt and responsibility" for the shortfalls in Soviet agriculture—Soviet farms in 1955 could not produce enough to feed the country adequately—and offered his resignation. "Did I really hear what I thought I heard?" the British ambassador asked his neighbor. Hayter, like the others in the box, had followed the rumors of a rift in the Kremlin but had routinely discounted them. Malenkov seemed clever and, at least among Western observers, well respected. It was assumed he could survive any challenge from Molotov and the lesser-known Khrushchev. But this afternoon it was clear that someone else was in control.

Immediately following the reading of the statement, a resolution accepting Malenkov's resignation was put to a vote. There was no debate. The thirteen hundred or so delegates in the hall raised their hands in approval as if pulled by one puppet master hidden above. In ten minutes the Malenkov era was history. The meeting then broke for a late lunch. The diplomats had just witnessed an unprecedented transfer of power in the Soviet Union. Vladimir Lenin had died in office in January 1924, as had Stalin a generation later. In 1953 Stalin's successors had arrested his police chief, Lavrenti Beria and later executed him, but otherwise the leadership structure remained intact. Now, by a show of hands, the Soviet leadership was being changed.

When the Supreme Soviet reconvened three hours later, a new hierarchy presented itself. The CPSU's chief, sixty-year-old Nikita Khrushchev, nominated Marshal Nikolai Bulganin to replace Malenkov. Bulganin, the fifty-nine-year-old Soviet defense minister, had a white goatee and a good sense of humor, traits that had made him stand out among the stolid and heavyset Kremlin headliners. Khrushchev explained that Bulganin was the choice of the Communist Party's Central Committee. With another show of hands Bulganin became the new Soviet premier.[3]

After Bulganin's election, the sixty-four-year-old Soviet foreign minister Molotov, wearing his trademark pince-nez, severe little mustache, and snarl, approached the lectern to give the first foreign policy speech of the post-Malenkov era. It was a belligerent statement. From the perspective of the British ambassador and the other Western onlookers it was also very disappointing. The ousted Malenkov had spoken publicly of the possibility of peaceful interaction between Moscow and capitalist countries. In his speech, Molotov reverted to the Stalinist line that the peace would only come through the elimination of the hostile Western world: "[T]he lessening of tension in international relations cannot otherwise be achieved than by persistent struggles against the more aggressive circles and their intrigues and consequently this struggle must not only not be relaxed but must of necessity be continued with yet greater persistence, ability and consistency."[4]

From the stage Nikita Khrushchev, a short, stocky man with an almost perfectly spherical bald head and an equally round, chubby face with deep laugh lines and a double chin, applauded Molotov's presentation but remained silent. To the surprise of the foreign diplomats in the audience, he radiated a confidence that suggested he might be the new man in charge.

■

"IT WAS A truly Russian affair," Allen W. Dulles, the director of central intelligence, explained to the president of the United States, Dwight D. Eisenhower, and the National Security Council.[5] Not for the first time Dulles's Central Intelligence Agency had been surprised by the Kremlin. In the decade since the end of World War II and the start of the Cold War, U.S. intelligence had failed to gain any significant insight into Soviet decision making. There was no American agent in the Kremlin or indeed among the elite of any Soviet bureaucracy, and U.S. eavesdropping had not produced any significant breaks into high-level Soviet political communications. The Kremlin was a black box the inhabitants of which became only somewhat known to Westerners when they attended public Communist Party events or turned up at diplomatic functions in Moscow. "Truly Russian" was CIA shorthand for inscrutable.

On February 8 President Eisenhower had first learned about the shake-up in Moscow from his press secretary, James C. Hagerty, who had read about it in wire service reports. The State Department, which was under the leadership of Allen Dulles's older brother, John Foster Dulles, had been of no greater help to the president. Although the U.S. ambassador in Moscow, Charles "Chip" Bohlen, had been among the first Westerners to detect tension within the collective leadership a year earlier, the embassy had not sent any warnings to Washington that major political changes were afoot in Moscow.

Outside the Eisenhower administration the news from Moscow immediately caused deep concern. "The elimination of Malenkov is an unfortunate development for the people of the free countries," said W. Averell Harriman, who had served as Franklin Roosevelt's envoy to Moscow during the Second World War.[6] Truman's ambassador and Eisenhower's wartime chief of staff, Walter Bedell Smith, felt the same way. "I don't like the looks of it a bit," Smith told the *New York Times.* "It certainly doesn't mean that relations with the Soviets are going to be any easier."[7] A limited thaw in East-West relations had occurred since Stalin's death, and most statesmen, diplomats, and journalists gave Malenkov credit for it. In March 1954 the Soviet premier had stated publicly that a nuclear war was unwinnable, completely contradicting Stalin's earlier emphasis on the inevitability of a third world war. Under Malenkov's leadership, the Kremlin had applied pressure to its Chinese ally to accept an armistice to end the Korean War, which had started in 1950, after Stalin had encouraged North Korean leader Kim Il Sung to launch an invasion of South Korea. The

Kremlin had also renounced the territorial claims that Stalin had made on two Soviet neighbors, Finland and Turkey, and ended the USSR's colonial control of the Chinese ice-free port of Port Arthur. At home Malenkov's emphasis on the production of consumer goods and raising the standard of living of individual Soviet citizens had also seemed to presage a more peaceful world. Many feared that this "soft policy" had come to an end with Malenkov's premiership.[8]

President Eisenhower handled the news of Malenkov's political demise calmly, even showing a hint of optimism. Eisenhower, who had attended the U.S. Military Academy at West Point and then became the world's most famous general in World War II, preferred dealing with foreign leaders who had military backgrounds. He assumed that the selection of Bulganin as the new Soviet premier reflected the rising strength of the Soviet Army in Kremlin affairs. "You know," Eisenhower told Hagerty when he received the news, "if you are in the military and you know about these destructive weapons, it tends to make you more pacifistic than you normally have been."[9]

The CIA and the State Department cautioned the president not to consider this moment as the dawn of a Bulganin regime. Nikolai Bulganin, apparently known to Soviet soldiers as General Rabbit, had the reputation of a lightweight. Washington's top Kremlinologists believed he was merely acting as a front for a new strongman, possibly the Soviet party chief, Nikita Khrushchev.[10] Indeed, about the only prediction that the CIA or the U.S. State Department felt comfortable making to President Eisenhower about Kremlin politics in 1955 was that eventually someone had to come out on top. "You can't run a dictatorship," Foster Dulles told a group of journalists, "without a dictator."[11]

■

THE SOVIET UNION was not a one-man dictatorship in 1955, but the political theater of February 8 marked the rise of Nikita Sergeyevich Khrushchev to the position of first among equals in the Kremlin's inner circle and his international debut. From this moment until a different generation of Kremlin peers removed him from office a decade later, Khrushchev was to exercise immense influence over the Soviet Union and its behavior toward the rest of world. Only dimly understood at the time, the era of Khrushchev in Soviet affairs had just begun.

Since September 1953 all Kremlin resolutions had carried two signatures, Malenkov for the government and Khrushchev on behalf of the party. From Lenin's time the Soviet Union appeared to be run by two parallel organizations. The USSR had a premier who chaired the Council of Ministers, which was in effect a cabinet with a defense minister and a foreign minister. The Communist Party of the Soviet Union (CPSU) had its own leadership structure, headed by a Central Committee that was itself directed by an inner circle of about a dozen called the Politburo or, after 1952, the Presidium. Under Lenin and Stalin, the Soviet government functioned as purely an administrative arm of the Communist Party, which held all executive authority in the Soviet state. For sixteen months Malenkov and Khrushchev, however, had governed the country as if the party and the administrative organs were equals.

Khrushchev was too ambitious and disagreed too often with Malenkov on domestic matters for this power-sharing relationship to last. Although they shared a passion for improving the lot of the average Soviet peasant, the two leaders had profoundly different views on how to do it. Malenkov was somewhat skeptical about Marxist economics. By no means a capitalist, he nevertheless understood the importance of higher prices and wages to encourage productivity. He grasped that there were limits on what a planned economy could achieve without financial incentives. The first post-Stalin reform of Soviet agriculture, which Malenkov announced in the fall of 1953, featured higher producer prices for the crops that collective farms were required to sell to the state and lower taxes on private plots for peasants.

Khrushchev preferred to think of the Soviet economic problem as one of production, not of productivity.[12] The Soviet citizen would become better fed not by altering the planned economy but by expanding it. In 1954 Khrushchev championed the Virgin Lands program, which sent three hundred thousand young Communists to the Volga region, western Siberia, and Kazakhstan to till lands that had until then been outside the state agricultural system. Khrushchev was also uncomfortable with Malenkov's belief that the Soviet economy should be reoriented to permit more light industry or consumer goods production. It was not that Khrushchev wanted to deprive the Soviet citizen of appliances or, as Western observers feared, that he preferred to maintain a high level of investment in military production; it was simply a reflection of his doctrinaire approach to Soviet economics that he assumed that all future economic success depended on developing a strong foundation in heavy industry.

■

KHRUSHCHEV ENGINEERED the removal of Malenkov with the support of Vyacheslav Molotov, who had been Stalin's foreign minister between 1939 and 1949 and then regained the post after Stalin died. There was no more senior member of the Presidium than Molotov. Stalin had placed him in the inner circle of the party in 1926, and though Molotov had fallen out of favor by the early 1950s, death had cheated Stalin of the opportunity to purge him. Molotov needed no coaxing to become an accomplice in Khrushchev's plot. He considered Malenkov a "decent fellow" and a superb "manager by telephone," but a featherweight with dangerously naive views on foreign policy.[13]

On January 22, 1955, Khrushchev and Molotov arranged a formal meeting of the Presidium to force Malenkov out. The Presidium was by the mid-1950s regaining its traditional role as the main decision-making body of the Central Committee of the CPSU and therefore of the entire Soviet system. Established at the Eighth Party Congress in 1919 as the Politburo, this inner council had initially included Lenin, four other full members, and three candidate members.[14] At first the Politburo was intended to deal primarily with urgent matters that could not wait to be decided at the two or three plenary sessions (or plenums) of the Central Committee that took place each year, but over time the Politburo met weekly.[15] Although the Bolsheviks looked to Lenin as their leader, he had only one vote in the Politburo, which had a rotating chairmanship and made decisions by majority vote of the full members. Under Stalin this inner council, like all other party organs, had fallen into disuse. For example, in the early Bolshevik period there had been at least one party congress a year to confirm doctrinal changes and determine the composition of the Central Committee; Stalin let thirteen years go by between the Eighteenth and Nineteenth party congresses. The dictator preferred to govern through a kitchen cabinet that he invited to late-night drinking sessions and treated as stooges. Stalin's successors revived the tradition of weekly meetings of the Presidium, which by early 1955 had nine full members, three candidate members, and a permanent chairman.[16]

Since March 1953 Malenkov had chaired Presidium meetings, giving him a slight edge in shaping the collective leadership. Agencies of the Soviet government or Presidium members themselves would propose policies to the Presidium in the form of written resolutions. Sometimes representatives of these agencies were invited to brief the members; often the draft resolutions, which would have been distributed in advance along with any relevant reports, had to speak for themselves. The Presidium chiefs jealously guarded their prerogatives and did not like to admit outsiders. Even the scheduling of sessions was a state secret. Among those allowed into the session, however, an unstructured discussion was permitted, but after a vote, either orally or by show of hands, the resolution would be presented to the rest of the Soviet system as the unanimous decision of the CPSU. Not a hint of disagreement was allowed outside the chamber.

The January 1955 meeting at which the Presidium fired its chairman was civil and orderly.[17] Later rumors spread that at one point Malenkov stormed off.[18] In fact, the event was choreographed, and everyone pretty much kept to the script. Even Malenkov seemed to know the part he was supposed to play. The proceedings began with his admission that he was not up to the job. "I do not meet the requirements," he told his colleagues. "I have been looking for a way out for a long time now."

Khrushchev, the chief architect of the event, remained silent on the indictment. Once every other full member of the Presidium but Bulganin had spoken against Malenkov, Khrushchev moved Bulganin's nomination to replace Malenkov as chairman of the Council of Ministers.[19] On cue Molotov seconded the nomination, followed by longtime Presidium members Lazar Kaganovich and Marshal Kliment Voroshilov. The promotion of Nikolai Bulganin, a notorious drinker but an inoffensive Soviet defense minister, had been agreed to in advance by the key plotters.[20]

Khrushchev took Malenkov's more important post, chairman of the Presidium. Khrushchev believed the Soviet Union should be governed through the Presidium and wanted to control its agenda. His assumption of this powerful position was confirmed without controversy. Molotov did not seem to want any of the spoils or at least did not think he needed to do anything to shore up his own position in the Kremlin elite.

Compared with what might have happened to him under Stalin, the damage to Georgi Malenkov was limited. He lost the top job and the chairmanship, but not his life. In fact he did not even lose his membership in the Presidium. Molotov had wanted him removed, but Khrushchev argued to keep him on the Presidium. Although he said nothing at the time, Khrushchev knew that he would need Malenkov's vote on foreign policy issues, where the two men did not disagree. In concluding these actions, all of which were cloaked in the tightest secrecy, the group had decided to make these changes public at the meeting of the Supreme Soviet two weeks later.

▪

THROUGH THIS secret backroom maneuvering Nikita Khrushchev made himself the most powerful man in a vast and troubled empire. The Soviet Union in 1955 was still having difficulties absorbing the influence and territory that it had acquired in the victory over Nazi Germany. At the wartime conferences of Yalta and Potsdam, the United States, Great Britain, and the Soviet Union had recognized a new order in Europe. Although the Anglo-Americans disagreed with Stalin on how he should use his influence over Eastern Europe, the Western allies were pragmatic enough to understand that the Soviet armies liberating Nazi-occupied Poland, Hungary, and Czechoslovakia, and occupying eastern Germany, Bulgaria, and Romania were intending to do more than denazify these countries. Stalin did not believe he could trust a neighbor unless that neighbor was a fellow Communist.

In the first years after 1945 the Soviets set up Communist regimes under men who had spent the war hiding in Moscow. None of them—Otto Grotewohl and Walter Ulbricht of Germany, Klement Gottwald of Czechoslovakia, or Boleslaw Bierut of Poland—had been popular in their own countries before the war, and now that they were heading war-ravaged countries desperate for the kinds of aid that the West was pouring into its allied states, they were not any more popular. Indeed, there had already been an uprising in the Soviet Union's eastern empire, but it was short-lived. A strike among construction workers in East Berlin on June 16, 1953, had sparked general demonstrations of discontent involving five hundred thousand people in over 560 towns and cities in East Germany. An estimated eighty thousand gathered in the streets of East Berlin the next day to demand the resignation of the disorder. At least twenty-one demonstrators (and possibly many more) were killed and more than four thousand arrested.[21] The situation remained unstable in East Germany, and Moscow had reason to believe that the same set of circumstances could break out in any of the other so-called people's democracies.

There were problems even with the new socialist countries in Europe that were not under Soviet occupation. Josef Broz Tito, the popular Communist guerrilla leader who had liberated Yugoslavia without the Soviet Army, wished to follow a more independent socialist course. By 1948 Stalin had grown impatient with the Yugoslav leader and ordered Soviet intelligence to kill him. Although Tito survived, relations between the two countries did not.

As difficulties grew within the socialist world, the Soviets were observing a gradual strengthening of the Western coalition against it. In 1949 twelve countries headed by the United States formed the North Atlantic Treaty Organization (NATO), an anti-Soviet alliance that continued to grow.[22] By 1952 Greece and Turkey had joined NATO.

■

N IKITA KHRUSHCHEV believed that with his new power came a responsibility to undertake a revolution in Soviet foreign policy. Although he had made a name for himself as an outspoken specialist on agriculture and industry, Khrushchev had developed strong views on how badly Stalin and then Molotov had mishandled foreign affairs. He had just never revealed them.

Khrushchev blamed the Stalin-Molotov approach for the militarized struggle with the capitalists, the lack of much interaction with the neutral developing world, and the weaknesses in the Soviet Union's relations with its socialist allies. Khrushchev's interpretation of Marxism-Leninism made him more optimistic about human behavior than Stalin and Molotov and therefore more of an internationalist than either of them. Although suspicious of capitalists, Khrushchev wanted to believe they were capable of change, and he was convinced that nations—simply put, large groups of people—were invariably more progressive than the few rich men or militarists who might lead them. He believed that if given a chance, all societies would eventually freely choose socialism and then communism. As the world's most powerful progressive power the Soviet Union should be prepared to reach out to leaders and regimes that, though not Communist, were anti-imperialist and anticolonial in outlook. At the same time, Khrushchev shared Lenin's belief, which the Bolshevik leader had expressed near the end of his life, that the socialist world could live in "peaceful coexistence" with the capitalists. Indeed, Khrushchev thought that achieving peaceful coexistence was a necessity if the socialist world was to achieve its potential. His long experience as an agricultural and industrial manager made him more sensitive than Stalin or Molotov to the cost of military confrontation with the West and its effects on the standards of living within the Soviet Union and its Communist allies. His few foreign travels, all of which had been to socialist countries—to East Germany, Poland, and China in 1954—had reinforced his belief that economics was the Achilles' heel of the Soviet bloc.

Khrushchev was convinced that the Cold War had not been inevitable. Although Western, especially American, arrogance irritated him, he assigned most of the blame for the international tension after the collapse of Nazi Germany to Soviet missteps. In 1945 and 1946 Stalin had pressured Turkey to force either the creation of a Soviet naval base on the Mediterranean or at least a renegotiation of the treaty that governed the use of the strait linking the Mediterranean to the Black Sea. Similarly, Soviet efforts to split Iran and transform its northern province into a satellite state had compounded Western concerns that Stalin would not be satisfied with the division of Europe agreed to by the Allied powers at Yalta and Potsdam in 1945.

Khrushchev had personal memories of Stalin's third attempt, and third failure, to rewrite the World War II settlement. By agreement each of the Allies plus the French had been given a slice of Hitler's former capital to occupy and govern. Berlin was a hundred miles inside the Soviet occupation zone, and Stalin was concerned that the Western powers were exploiting their rights to maintain land, air, and rail access to Berlin through Eastern Germany to move soldiers in and out of their sectors. In an attempt to force the Western allies out of the western sectors of Berlin, he ordered Soviet forces to blockade the access roads and rail lines.

Years later Khrushchev claimed the Berlin blockade was a mistake. Stalin had launched the effort "without gauging our possibilities realistically. He didn't think it through properly."[23] Instead of giving in, U.S. President Harry S. Truman launched a massive airlift of tons of supplies to West Berlin. Eleven months later Stalin called off the blockade. Soviet losses included more than just embarrassment over Berlin. As a result of the blockade, Stalin essentially motivated the Western powers to form NATO.

Khrushchev had seen little improvement in Soviet foreign policy since Stalin's death. He had endorsed Malenkov's talk of better relations with the West and the tentative efforts to establish diplomatic and economic ties to the third world, but Molotov had placed severe limits on how far the country could go in either area. On arguably the most important foreign policy question facing the USSR, the future of a divided Germany, Molotov had opposed any practical changes at all in the existing approach. Stalin had pushed for a reunification of Germany on condition that it was neutral and demilitarized. Although Moscow had created a Communist regime in its occupation zone, the protection of East Germany was not the organizing principle of the Kremlin's German strategy. Instead the cardinal point of Soviet postwar policy had been to prevent the integration of West Germany into the Western bloc.

Stalin did not live to realize the bankruptcy of his policy. In the fall of 1954 the Western powers drafted a series of agreements in Paris that, once ratified by all the Atlantic powers, were to bring West Germany into NATO. As of February 1955, these protocols had not yet been ratified, but it looked as if this would happen in May. Molotov, however, had nothing to offer to rescue the policy besides vague and menacing language to the West and the Germans about the effect on international relations.

Khrushchev was not sure he had any answers, but he knew that Moscow had to scramble to try some new tactics to prevent or at least slow down the absorption of the Federal Republic of Germany into NATO. Khrushchev's concern was less the Stalinist worry that as part of NATO the West Germans would somehow prepare an attack on the Soviet Union, than that the direction of European politics would further weaken the socialist East German regime. Every month since the June 1953 uprising an average of fifteen thousand people fled East Germany through West Berlin, a total of about three hundred thousand.[24]

Molotov's insensitivity to the needs of the East Germans was part of his generally callous treatment of the entire Soviet bloc. Khrushchev blamed Molotov for the fact that the Soviet boycott of Yugoslavia endured two years after Stalin's death. Stalin had once boasted to Khrushchev, "I shall shake my little finger and there will be no more Tito," but he had shaken more than his little finger, and Tito was still alive.[25] In the year before Stalin's death a KGB agent under instructions from Moscow had wormed his way into the confidence of Tito's personal staff. Code-named Maks, this agent was Iosif Grigulevich, alias Teodoro Castro, the nonresident Costa Rican envoy to Belgrade. Stalin's secret police wanted Maks to plant a booby-trapped jewelry box that would spray a lethal poison gas the minute Tito opened it.[26] Although the plots against Tito were suspended after Stalin's death, Molotov never stopped hating Tito and continued to obstruct any reconciliation.

■

U NAWARE OF Khrushchev's plans, the Western powers assumed the Cold War was entering a very chilly phase. Molotov's speech at the February 8 event seemed to signal a return to the old Soviet confrontational rhetoric, and with Malenkov gone, it was expected that Molotov's Stalinist ideas would once again dominate how the Kremlin dealt with the world.

The West's expectation reflected less a sense of Molotov's genius than an underestimation of Khrushchev. Whenever diplomats had seen him at receptions before February 1955, he talked loudly and appeared to drink too much. "Khrushchev," recalled British Ambassador Hayter, "seemed to be rather all over the place."[27] The U.S. ambassador, Chip Bohlen, summed up his assessment of Khrushchev in a line he had cabled to Washington in 1954: "[Khrushchev] is not especially bright."[28]

Not all American officials were as dismissive of Khrushchev. The new Soviet star had the grudging respect of the leadership of the Central Intelligence Agency, especially of its director, Allen Dulles, who saw him as a pragmatic realist. As early as April 1954, Dulles had identified Khrushchev as someone to watch. "His [Malenkov's] No. 2 man, Khrushchev interests me enormously," Dulles told the cream of the U.S. officer corps at the National War College. "Unlike most of the leaders of the Soviet Union, he seems to have quite a good sense of humor. Whether that is because he is a Ukrainian or not I don't know, but in any event, there is a fellow to watch. He has a somewhat different mentality apparently than certain of the Soviet leaders with whom we have been dealing."[29]

What apparently drew the attention of the CIA were Khrushchev's public speeches in 1954 blasting Soviet bureaucrats for red tape and incompetence. The agency noted Khrushchev's complaints that in one region of the USSR the salaries of tax collectors amounted to more than the sum of all the taxes they collected. His criticism of the monthly reports that every workshop had to fill out also drew notice. "Scores of workers are sweating over the compilation and propagation of these reports," he apparently said, and "being taken away from useful work."[30]

The CIA chief, who believed that an inefficient Soviet Union was a less threatening Soviet Union, did not think much good for the United States could come out of Khrushchev's reformist instincts. "I think it is a rather dangerous sign," he concluded, "that you have a fellow as realistic as Khrushchev, who apparently has the courage to speak out."[31] Even this praise was tempered by the assumption that Khrushchev was not likely to speak out on foreign policy and, if he did, he would sound much like Molotov.

■

KHRUSHCHEV MADE new policy toward occupied Austria, where forty thousand Soviet troops were still stationed, the first test of his ability to reduce Molotov's influence on Kremlin foreign policy. In 1945 the Allies had restored the independence of Austria, which the Nazis had attempted to erase with the Anschluss of 1938. Austria was then occupied by all four powers. Under Stalin and even Malenkov, it had been Soviet policy to link any future peace treaty with an Austrian government to the reunification of Germany. Khrushchev saw this as a barren approach since the two Germanys were years from reunification. Instead he considered an Austrian settlement a possible first step in a last-minute effort to lure the West Germans into a less confrontational relationship with the Soviet bloc. Perhaps if Austria were allowed to reunify as a neutral, demilitarized state, Germans who were not comfortable with joining the Western military bloc might consider this an attractive alternative.

During their brief political alliance against Malenkov, Khrushchev had managed to convince Molotov to take a new look at the Austrian problem.[32] Embedded in Molotov's stern speech on February 8, and missed by most Western commentators, was the announcement that the Soviet Union would no longer hold the signature of a peace treaty with Austria hostage to progress on settling the future of divided Germany. This actually represented a loosening of the old Stalinist position.

But as Khrushchev well knew, Molotov's support was purely tactical. For him, the offer to Austria was, like so many of his diplomatic offers over the

years, a ploy. Molotov may have feared that western Austria would be integrated along with West Germany in NATO and wanted to dangle an alternative in front of the Austrians.[33] Molotov expected the Austrians to refuse the
Soviet offer, but the negotiations would throw the West Germans and the
Americans off-balance and could easily be dragged out.

Actually Khrushchev had no interest in dragging things out. The talks with
Vienna had to happen soon for there to be any chance to reach an agreement
before the West Germans entered NATO.[34] "Vyacheslav Mikhailovich . . . How
do you feel about signing a peace treaty with Austria?" He asked Molotov in
late February or early March. "How about negotiating a treaty with the
Austrian government?" According to Khrushchev, Molotov resisted with full
force, replying: "Mind your own business. I'm an old politician. I have many
years of experience with such matters and you have only just started down this
path. I was minister of foreign affairs during wartime! I've had all kinds of
meetings and conducted all sorts of negotiations on issues concerning our
country. And now here you come, without consulting me, trying to force your
ideas on me — ideas that are not right, that are harmful to our interests."[35]

Khrushchev then trapped the "old politician." Using his new authority, he
brought the matter to the Presidium, which voted, over Molotov's objections,
to invite an Austrian delegation to Moscow.[36] On March 24 an invitation was
sent to Vienna. The visit, which lasted from April 11 to 15, proved very fruitful
and produced an all but finished treaty.[37]

The first secretary hardly waited to pass this first test before he initiated an
even broader assault on current Soviet foreign policy. On March 12, 1955,
Khrushchev's allies in *Pravda* published an article that signaled Soviet interest in better relations with Belgrade. Marshal Tito, the article suggested,
should "forget the past and come to an agreement with the Soviet Union to
work for peace and international security."[38] This was the start of a major
public relations campaign designed to undermine support for Molotov's
views, though not directed at the Soviet foreign minister himself.

Khrushchev enlisted in this campaign the most famous man in Soviet
Russia, Marshal Georgi Zhukov. In the final months of World War II Zhukov
had been Dwight Eisenhower's equal on the eastern front. As commander of
the First Belorussian Front he had led the advance into Berlin in April 1945 and
had represented the Soviet Union at the surrender ceremony a few weeks later.
Zhukov had come home to as much of a hero's welcome as Stalin would allow.
Standing at Stalin's side atop the Lenin Mausoleum, Zhukov had watched as
unit after unit of Soviet troops threw the regimental banners of the defeated
Nazis at his feet. Within a year Zhukov found himself in the political wilder-

ness, a comparatively lucky victim of Stalin's paranoia, alive but reassigned to the command of the Odessa military district in the southern Ukraine. "It was about the same," observed longtime Kremlin watcher Harrison Salisbury, "as if Mr. Truman had sent Eisenhower to take charge of National Guard training in Oklahoma."[39] Once the old man died, Zhukov returned to Moscow as Bulganin's deputy in the Ministry of Defense. When Bulganin became premier, Khrushchev nominated Zhukov to replace Bulganin as minister of defense, and he was soon promoted to the Presidium.

To increase the pressure on Molotov, Zhukov was approached to give a helpful speech on May Day. The marshal was popular and a trusted ally. No Soviet citizen doubted this war hero's commitment to the security and strength of the motherland. It was a legitimacy that Khrushchev believed he had to borrow for this fight with Molotov. Amid boilerplate references to the Great Patriotic War, there was a phrase that carried enormous importance. "The foreign policy of the Soviet Union," said Zhukov, "proceeds from the wise counsel of the Great Lenin of the possibility of peaceful coexistence and economic competition of states, irrespective of their social or state structure."[40]

Molotov, who received a copy of the speech ahead of time, recognized immediately the immensity of this challenge to his authority in foreign policy. Inclusion of the phrase "the possibility of peaceful coexistence . . . of states" would mean the complete rejection of his confrontational approach to the West. At 5:00 P.M. on April 30, only hours before Zhukov was to give the speech, Molotov distributed a letter to his colleagues demanding corrections in the statement on peaceful coexistence. "He caused a scandal," Bulganin later recalled.[41] Molotov argued that Zhukov's statement was tantamount to endorsing "pacifism." He wanted to make the strengthening of Soviet power, not international détente, the goal of Soviet policy.

Molotov was overruled by the Presidium.

A week later Khrushchev employed Zhukov to signal again that Yugoslavia was the first place where this new policy of peaceful coexistence would be put into practice. In an article published in *Pravda* to mark the tenth anniversary of the victory over Hitler, Zhukov spent some paragraphs extolling the virtues of Tito's fight against Nazi Germany. At the end of the section the Kremlin inserted a political message: "As soldiers who participated in the combined effort of our peoples against fascism, we would like to express the desire that these disagreements (which have arisen between Belgrade and Moscow) would be quickly resolved and that friendly relations would arise again between our two countries."

Molotov tried to have this article stopped. He considered Tito a fascist and hated the idea that he would get the credit for the work of the Communist Yugoslav partisans during World War II. "Trotsky created the Red Army," Molotov argued, "but we don't praise him."[42]

Again, his Kremlin peers overruled him. The article was published unchanged.

Among those peers, Anastas Mikoyan was most helpful to Khrushchev in voting down the Soviet foreign minister. Next to Molotov, Mikoyan had the greatest experience in foreign affairs of any member of the Presidium, having served as Soviet minister of foreign trade on and off since 1926. In 1936 he had traveled to the United States to study food production systems. There he had his first taste of American ice cream, which he liked so much that when he returned, he initiated Soviet production of the dessert. If Khrushchev was "Comrade Corncob" because of his championing of corn production, then Mikoyan was "Comrade Ice-Cream Cone." However, all was not sweetness in Mikoyan's past. He had carried on some of the negotiations with the Nazis that had led to the Hitler-Stalin Pact in 1939, and the next year, after Moscow and Berlin simultaneously invaded Poland, he had been among those who signed the death warrant for forty thousand Polish officers captured by the Soviet Army and later buried in the Katyn Forest. A complex man, Mikoyan nevertheless shared Malenkov's rejection of the inevitability of war, and Khrushchev trusted his judgment in foreign affairs. In the fall of 1954 Khrushchev had invited Mikoyan along with him to visit the People's Republic of China.

When Molotov called Zhukov an anti-Leninist at a Presidium meeting on May 19, 1955, Mikoyan and Premier Bulganin rushed to defend Zhukov and by implication the new policy of peaceful coexistence.[43] "You should never hurl accusations like that—'anti-Leninist,'" said Mikoyan. In the Soviet Union that was a slander akin to Joseph McCarthy's accusations of "anti-Americanism."

"Molotov was like a wind-up toy," Khrushchev later observed. "Once he was wound up and let go, his gears and wheels would turn and turn and turn until all the tension had gone out of his spring."[44] Although Molotov did admit that calling Zhukov anti-Leninist had been a rash thing to do, he refused to budge from his essential disagreement with the direction Khrushchev and his allies were taking the country.[45]

Khrushchev had the votes, however, to initiate high-level negotiations with the Yugoslavs, and Belgrade responded positively to the Soviet suggestion of a visit by a top-level Soviet delegation in May. Molotov tried to sabotage this visit, but he failed. At the two special sessions of the Presidium arranged on the eve of the Yugoslav trip, he opposed almost everything that had been prepared for the delegation.[46] It was in the nature of Soviet rule that the Presidium sign off on the formal instructions given to official delegations, which were usually prepared by the Ministry of Foreign Affairs. It also prepared the "final" communiqués that the Soviets would later recommend to their negotiating partners. Although Molotov headed the ministry, the Presidium had forced the Soviet foreign service to produce non-Molotovian language for these documents. And Molotov despised them. Each time one of these documents came to a vote, the minister of foreign affairs voted against it. And each time the vote ran eight to one against him.

▪

THE TRIP TO Yugoslavia was Khrushchev's first outside the USSR since becoming the principal architect of Soviet foreign policy. The Yugoslavs, however, seemed not to understand the changes in Moscow and treated the Soviet delegation at times as if Stalin and Molotov were still in charge. At the arrival ceremony in Belgrade on May 26, the hosts did not even bother to translate Khrushchev's remarks. "[E]veryone here understands Russian," Tito explained. Khrushchev doubted this was the reason. "I know Ukrainian, but I can't catch everything when an orator speaks Ukrainian rapidly," he later recalled, "and Ukrainian is much closer to Russian than Russian is to Serbo-Croatian."[47] The Soviet first secretary had the distinct impression that not all diplomatic protocol had been observed.

Khrushchev performed very well despite the slights. Although aware that the three representatives of the Soviet Presidium would not be packing white or black tie, Khrushchev's Yugoslav hosts organized a white-tie affair at Tito's Winter Palace outside Belgrade. Khrushchev arrived in a powder blue suit. A bank of cameras and hot lights awaited him as he stepped out of his car. To the surprise of the Yugoslavs and the assembled foreign journalists, who were pressed in so close to the scene that they could have reached out and touched him, the fledgling Soviet leader responded well to the challenge. "He stood there," recalled Edward Crankshaw, the Moscow correspondent for the London *Daily Telegraph*, "[and] allowed himself to be photographed, sweating slightly." To outsiders, Khrushchev seemed to be saying to himself: "What is happening to me? This is clearly a thing I've got to put up with. I will put up with it." He took the scene in stride like "any Western statesman, to the manner born."[48]

But the strain of the trip weighed on Khrushchev. By the end of the formal dinner he was drinking heavily. Becoming very theatrical, he yelled out to the journalists, "Why don't you come and visit us in our country?" When a few of the reporters complained that they had wanted to but had been denied visas, Khrushchev waved his arms and promised them all visas. The liquor continued to flow, and at the end of this very long night Khrushchev had to be carried down the stairs to the car that was to return him to the Soviet Embassy. Mikoyan had wanted to take Khrushchev home hours before, but the Soviet leader wouldn't allow it. "No," said Khrushchev, "you think I am drunk. I am not. You're an Armenian. You can't drink as much as I, but I feel well. I feel very well."[49]

In Yugoslavia, as at home, Khrushchev was at his best when he was outside formal settings, campaigning for socialism. There he showed the sparkle, enthusiasm, and drive that many observers, from whatever culture, found intensely appealing. At one factory stop these traits were on full display. After touring the shop floor, Khrushchev crowded into the factory manager's small office, with Mikoyan, Bulganin, the factory manager, and two journalists. Khrushchev listened intently to the factory manager, who explained the ins and outs of the workers' council setup. When Khrushchev began to speak, it quickly became apparent that he was in charge. He spoke at excruciating length about cement, its properties and its uses and was never interrupted by Mikoyan or Bulganin. Indeed, when Bulganin tried to get the pretty female journalist covering the visit to blush, Khrushchev shot him such a quick and devastating glance that Bulganin stopped and became impassive. "[F]or the first time I realized," recalled Crankshaw, who was the other journalist in the room, "that this was a man of great inner power, who was quite clearly going to have very little difficulty in dominating all his colleagues at home."

Upon their return from Belgrade, it was Khrushchev, not Bulganin, who gave the official report on June 6 to the Presidium.[50] Khrushchev acknowledged that the summit with Tito had not achieved all that had been hoped. On economic and state-to-state issues, the Soviet delegation reached agreements, but on the sensitive issue of the relationship between the Soviet Communist Party and Tito's party a gap remained.

Before the delegation left for Belgrade, Molotov had pressed for them to find out what kind of state Tito was leading.[51] Was it bourgeois or proletarian? The implication was that in the answer to that question was a guide to future relations. For Molotov, a proletarian state by definition had to place the interests of the Soviet Union, the leader of international communism, ahead of its own parochial interests.

Khrushchev and his delegation brought subtle answers to Molotov's question. Dmitri Shepilov, the editor of *Pravda*, who at Khrushchev's request had joined the delegation, replied that Yugoslavia "is not a bourgeois state; it is a people's republic."[52] But it was a people's republic that as yet didn't always agree with Moscow. For all the hours the Soviet delegation spent with Tito and his chief ideologist, Edvard Kardelj, the Yugoslavs had refused to budge on some of their interpretations. For Molotov, this was reason to give up on close relations with Belgrade, but for Khrushchev, Mikoyan, Bulganin, and his longtime patron in the leadership Lazar Kaganovich, this was acceptable. A new doctrine of patient pressure was to replace the rejectionism of the Stalin-Molotov foreign policy. "With confidence," Khrushchev told his colleagues two days later, "we must manage things so that we draw Yugoslavia to our side. Step by step [we must] strengthen our position. We must show confidence and not allow defeatism."[53]

Khrushchev's and Molotov's ideological debate would have implications far beyond the Kremlin's standoff with Tito. If the Presidium followed Khrushchev's lead and dispensed with the tradition of forcing potential foreign allies to jump through ideological hoops, then the number of potential friends for the USSR in the world would more than triple. It was in the developing world in particular that this shift would reap the greatest rewards. In the meantime the trip had put Molotov on notice that whatever his formal position in the government, he was now on the defensive in a struggle with Khrushchev over the future of Soviet foreign policy.[54]

A week after his return from Belgrade, Khrushchev confirmed his achievement at a secret plenum of the Central Committee of the CPSU, a biannual meeting of the three hundred or so members of the Central Committee.[55] He and Bulganin told the stories of Molotov's unwarranted attacks on Zhukov and his uncompromising stand on Yugoslavia.

Khrushchev kept this anti-Molotov diatribe out of the Soviet press, and neither the British nor the Americans had any significant secret or press sources in or near enough to the Kremlin to pick up on either the contest between Khrushchev and Molotov or what it might mean for international security. Khrushchev's next foreign policy initiatives would be of a scale and importance, however, that London and Washington could not miss.

T HE FIRST GREAT power conference since Harry Truman, Clement Attlee, and Joseph Stalin met at Potsdam in 1945 took place against the background of Nikita Khrushchev's effort to wrest control of Soviet foreign policy from Vyacheslav Molotov. On May 10, 1955, France, Great Britain, and the United States invited Khrushchev and Bulganin to meet "at the summit" in Geneva, Switzerland. Four days earlier the formal occupation of West Germany had ended, the Federal Republic of Germany was declared, and it joined NATO as a sovereign state. With West Germany securely within the Atlantic military alliance, the Eisenhower administration had finally agreed to the three-power invitation to Moscow. For two years the British, led by former Prime Minister Winston Churchill, had been pressing Washington to meet with the Soviets, but the U.S. government had resisted so long as there was the chance that a high-level meeting with Soviet representatives might complicate bringing West Germany into NATO.[1]

It would be hard to exaggerate the depth of the defeat for Soviet diplomacy that had made this invitation possible. Stalin had designed, and Molotov had loyally implemented, a policy of encouraging the reunification of a neutral and possibly socialist Germany. In practice, this meant that the Soviet Union would not recognize West Germany as a separate state, and though the USSR would be committed to the support of East Germany, that state was to be considered only a transitional regime before the reunification of the entire country. After Stalin's death and as momentum built in Western Europe for admitting the Federal Republic of Germany into NATO, the Kremlin under Molotov's influence pursued a carrot-and-stick approach. Moscow warned the Atlantic powers that if the West Germans joined NATO, the Soviet bloc would form its own military alliance and the Kremlin would refuse to participate in any four-power summit.[2] If the West Germans rejected the Atlantic alliance, however, the Kremlin promised to support all-German elections with international observers, and a European security system and to welcome normalizing relations with the Federal Republic of Germany.

Khrushchev's last-minute effort to use Soviet policy toward Austria as an incentive to the Germans to reconsider joining NATO had come too late and probably had had no chance of success. The remilitarization of West Germany and its entry into NATO appeared to be popular in that country. The West German parliament, the Bundestag, quickly passed laws to start military training for 150,000 young Germans by 1956 and an additional 250,000 eighteen months later.[3]

The Kremlin's immediate response to West Germany's joining NATO suggested that Moscow would be in no mood for a summit. Arguing in *Pravda* on May 7 that "West Germany [was] being turned into a bridgehead for the deployment of large aggressive forces," the Soviet Union announced its abrogation of the wartime mutual assistance treaties that Stalin had signed with France and Great Britain.[4] It was hardly likely that in the Cold War the French and the British would defend the Soviet Union against an American attack, but Moscow wanted to make a point. The Kremlin also made good on its earlier threat to create an anti-NATO military alliance. On May 14, military representatives from Bulgaria, Czechoslovakia, Hungary, Poland, Romania, and the Soviet Union met in Warsaw to establish the Warsaw Pact treaty organization.

For all of the Kremlin's official truculence, however, Khrushchev did not question his conviction that it was in the long-term interest of the Soviet Union to push for better relations with the West. In his mind, the West German decision was the last in a long line of international events almost entirely brought about by Stalin and Molotov's stupidity. It simply underscored the need for a new approach.

Khrushchev responded by pushing even harder to get the Austrian treaty. Even though it was of little help in keeping West Germany out of NATO, a unified Austria might still play a useful role in the future diplomacy over the German question. At the very least, Moscow would be able to save money by reducing one of its occupation commitments. In early May the Soviets informed their negotiating partners in Vienna that they no longer insisted on maintaining a right to return Soviet forces to Austria in the wake of a collapse of order there. This removed the last real barrier to a four-power agreement ending the ten-year occupation of Austria. The Austrian State Treaty was signed on May 15, 1955.

At the same time, Khrushchev applied pressure to the Soviet Foreign Ministry to come up with a more realistic approach to international disarmament. On May 10, the same day that the summit invitation came from the

Western powers, the ministry announced a plan to reduce international tensions by a phased dismantling of the arsenals of the great powers. Calling for reductions in conventional weapons and the size of each country's armed forces, as well as elimination of all nuclear weapons, the Soviets proposed a two-year schedule to reach these goals, which would include the closing of all overseas bases by the great powers. In addition, as a measure of nuclear disarmament, the Soviets proposed a nuclear test ban, the first time this had been proposed by any nuclear power.[5] At this point in the Cold War the Soviets did not seem to rely as heavily on testing for their nuclear program as did the United States. Since their first atomic blast in August 1949, Soviet scientists had conducted only nineteen nuclear tests, compared with sixty tests by U.S. scientists.[6]

Thus Khrushchev saw the invitation to the summit as a positive development, not as a sign of Soviet weakness. He was eager for a major platform from which he could introduce himself and his new policies to the West. He had met with the press lord William Randolph Hearst earlier in 1955, but in his sixteen years as a full member of the Kremlin's inner circle, Khrushchev really had had few interactions with foreign capitalists. Just as he had thought it important to see Tito as a way of showing the Yugoslavs that Molotov no longer presented the attitudes or objectives of the Soviet Union, so he hoped his appearance at the summit would have the same effect on Eisenhower; Churchill's successor, Sir Anthony Eden, and the French premier, Edgar Faure.

■

THE MAIN FORCE behind American preparations for the Geneva Conference was President Dwight Eisenhower. A popular general whose crowning military achievement was the organization of the successful D-day landings in Normandy, Eisenhower had commanded the Western forces that drove into the heart of Germany in 1945. In the frenetic last weeks of the war he had come under pressure to race the Soviets to Berlin, though Hitler's capital lay a hundred miles inside the agreed-upon Soviet zone and was itself to be divided into four occupation zones. "Why should we endanger the life of a single American or Briton," Eisenhower had wondered, "to capture areas we will soon be handing over to the Russians?"[7] This decision had earned Eisenhower almost as much respect in the Soviet Union as it had dismay the likes of George C. Patton and British Field Marshal Bernard Law Montgomery.

As the U.S. commander in occupied Germany Eisenhower developed some understanding of the Soviets. He spent enough time with Soviet commanders, especially his opposite number in the Soviet Army, Marshal Georgi Zhukov, to escape being one of those who viewed Communists as a unified hostile group. Moreover, on a trip to Moscow in 1945 he had witnessed both the poverty of the average Soviet citizen and the immense destruction wrought by the Nazis. Memories of his interactions with Zhukov and of what he had seen in Moscow forever after served as a check on his accepting exaggerated estimates of Soviet power and the Kremlin's willingness to use it.

Once in the White House, Eisenhower discovered that some fellow Republicans were second-guessing his instincts in foreign policy. The entire first year of his administration had been taken up with a fight over whether hard-line members of Eisenhower's own party would strip the presidency of some of its treaty-making powers. Eisenhower had won that contest, but it had been a real battle, and he had to rely on help from congressional Democrats.[8] No U.S. president had faced such an extensive mutiny from his congressional colleagues since Franklin Roosevelt had pushed through the New Deal.

Eisenhower interpreted Stalin's death, which had occurred less than two months after his inauguration, as a possible turning point in the Cold War, and despite these serious challenges from within his own party, he looked for opportunities to relax Cold War tensions. His motives were not simply humanitarian. Like Khrushchev, an adversary he hardly knew, Eisenhower was concerned about the cost of perpetual confrontation. Unlike Khrushchev, Eisenhower came to this conclusion from a belief in small government and balanced budgets. He was appalled when he saw the amount of money that the United States was spending on defense. During the Korean War the annual defense bill had increased from $13.5 billion to nearly $45 billion per year.[9] Eisenhower's foreign policy strategy, which he called the New Look, was designed to reduce defense expenditures to $35 billion by relying more on cost-efficient nuclear weapons than on conventional forces. To avoid the implication that America was less secure, Eisenhower had his secretary of state, John Foster Dulles, threaten "massive retaliation" with nuclear forces in case of any Soviet attempt to invade the United States or any of its allies. The threat was credible because Eisenhower and Dulles knew that the United States enjoyed a qualitative and quantitative advantage in nuclear weapons. Still, Eisenhower also hoped for some disarmament, which could bring defense expenditures down even more. In the meantime the doctrine of massive retaliation would leave no doubt of U.S. resolve to defend itself.

■

Not every member of the Eisenhower administration looked to Geneva as a welcome opportunity to reduce East-West tension. Secretary of State Dulles had disliked the idea of a summit when Churchill first raised it in 1953 because he did not want to take the pressure off Moscow. Dulles believed the Soviet Union was vulnerable enough that under the right circumstances U.S. policy might force its collapse.[10] "A policy of pressures," he argued, "can increase the gap between their requirements and their resources [and] lead to [their] disintegration."[11] His brother, Director of Central Intelligence Allen Dulles, was less sure that the USSR would collapse anytime soon, but he did believe that the Soviet regime was in trouble. Calling the Austrian treaty "the first substantial concession to the West in Europe since the end of the war," Allen Dulles interpreted the new foreign policy coming out of Moscow as a sign that Soviet leaders understood they were in trouble.[12]

This shared confidence that the Soviets were weak inspired a confrontational approach to the Geneva summit. Why make any concessions now, the Dulles brothers believed, when over time the Soviets were only likely to become more accommodating? As Allen Dulles told a group of journalists on the eve of the summit, "if tensions are relaxed the Soviets get precisely what they want—more time."[13] Foster Dulles, the brother who would actually be taking the trip to Geneva, assumed that at the very least, arguing from strength would score points for the West in world public opinion. Unlike Eisenhower, who was focusing on a possible disarmament initiative, the secretary of state put greater stock in preparing a new German proposal that he was sure the Soviets would oppose and the Western Europeans and democrats around the world would applaud.

Dulles embraced a British idea—in fact the 1954 proposal of Winston Churchill's longtime understudy, Foreign Secretary Sir Anthony Eden—to push for a demilitarized East Germany within a reunited pro-Western Germany. The Eden Plan envisioned all-German elections followed by strict arms control within 150 miles of both sides of the current eastern border of the Soviet occupation zone in Germany. The rationale for this proposal was that the Soviets might accept the dissolution of their East German client state if they were promised that the newly reunified Germany could not pose a military threat to the East. Even if Germany decided to join NATO, the plan stipulated that there would never be NATO troops on the Polish-German border.

Privately Dulles told President Eisenhower that of course, the Soviets would probably never accept the Eden Plan or anything like it. In making this point, he stressed East Berlin's emotional and ideological appeal to the new Soviet leadership. The Soviets, he reported to the National Security Council, "fear the effect of the loss of control over East Germany on the satellites."[14] Nevertheless, the Eden Plan was useful as a ploy. Since agreements were unlikely with Communists, Dulles argued, the goal of U.S. policy should be to appear conciliatory while making proposals that it could be assumed the Kremlin would reject or could accept only out of weakness.

Eisenhower decided to accept the Eden proposal and Dulles's strategy without endorsing the view that an agreement with the Soviets was unlikely at Geneva. He was determined not to let the occasion slip by without making one dramatic attempt to alter the climate of world affairs. Some months earlier Eisenhower had formed a blue-ribbon panel, known as the Gaither Committee, to assess Soviet military power and the United States' ability to defend against surprise attack. The committee reported in February 1955 that U.S. intelligence sources were too weak to draw any firm conclusions: "[E]stimates of the *specific capabilities* and *immediate intentions* of the Soviets have, at their center, only a very small core of hard facts [emphasis in the original]."[5] U.S. estimates were largely based on extrapolations from U.S. defense technologies and assumptions about Soviet manufacturing capabilities. Well aware of this weakness, Eisenhower had been looking for ways to expand U.S. intelligence coverage of Soviet military facilities. One alternative was to rely on a new high-altitude reconnaissance plane being developed by the CIA called the U-2, but U-2 flights would involve violating Soviet airspace, which under international law was an act of war, and Eisenhower worried about the possible consequences. Just before the Geneva Conference, however, Eisenhower was offered a different approach to solving this intelligence problem that involved cooperation instead of confrontation with Moscow. A small group of advisers led by Nelson Rockefeller recommended the reciprocal opening of the skies of both the Soviet Union and the United States to air reconnaissance. By regularly flying planes over each other's territory both countries would lessen the threat of a surprise attack and possibly create some mutual trust. Eisenhower liked the idea a lot and decided to offer it in Geneva. Information about the president's personal initiative, which came to be known as the Open Skies proposal, was tightly held within the U.S. delegation and it would come as a surprise to the Soviets in Geneva.

■

IN HIS INSIGHTFUL biography of Khrushchev, William Taubman returns time and again to Khrushchev's complicated self-image. Proud of his achievements as a self-made man, almost arrogant, Khrushchev was nonetheless painfully aware of his own lack of formal education and his humble background. "I had no education and not enough culture," he lamented. "To govern a country like Russia, you have to have the equivalent of two academies of science in your head. But all I had was four classes in a church school and then, instead of high school, just a smattering of higher education."[16] He was always trying to prove himself, first, to his patron Lazar Kaganovich in Kiev, then to Stalin himself in Moscow. In the Stalin era Khrushchev had given bloodcurdling speeches, and signed many death warrants. He strove relentlessly to leave no doubt that despite the fact that his manner suggested a far less sophisticated man, he was as tough, as smart, as capable as any man.

The Soviet leader thought of the Soviet Union much as he thought of himself. Khrushchev wanted Moscow to be viewed as the equal of the West, yet he was well aware of the Soviet Union's weakness relative to the United States. Despite Soviet successes in testing an atomic bomb in 1949 and a hydrogen bomb only four years later, Moscow's claim to being a nuclear superpower on a par with the United States was little more than posturing. As of May 1955, the Soviet Union had no way of using a nuclear device against any U.S. city. In March 1951 Stalin had established a design bureau in Moscow overseen by V. M. Myasishchev to produce a bomber that could reach the U.S. mainland. To meet this objective, the plane had to have a range, when refueled, of 6,875 to 7,500 miles. A month earlier the U.S. Air Force had authorized production of the first U.S. intercontinental bomber, the B-52 Stratofortress. The first generation of B-52 bomber could fly 7,343 miles when refueled, carrying ten thousand pounds of ordnance at a cruising speed of 523 miles per hour. The new Soviet bomber was intended to keep pace with this new American flying machine.

The Myasishchev-4 (M-4), designated the Bison bomber by NATO, went into serial production in 1954 but was a huge disappointment.[17] It lacked the range to hit American targets because Myasishchev could not devise a reliable method to refuel the plane. At best the M-4 had a combat radius of five thousand miles, too short to reach either U.S. coast from the nearest point of Soviet territory. Despite the Presidium's hopes, the only creatures in the Western Hemisphere threatened by an M-4 attack were polar bears in Greenland.

The Soviet Navy in 1955 also lacked the capacity to deliver a nuclear strike against Washington. Stalin had promoted the development of submarines, but missile-launching craft were still years from production. The Soviet Union had no aircraft carriers.

With no way to deliver a nuclear weapon to the United States, the only way the Soviets could harm the United States was to damage one of its NATO allies. The same year the M-4 emerged as a failure, the Tupoluv design bureau produced the first Soviet bomber that could reliably attack Ankara, London, and Paris. The Tu-16, known to NATO as the Badger bomber, finally made the Soviet nuclear threat credible in Europe, though these planes were vulnerable to NATO's antiaircraft defenses.

For these reasons, conventional forces remained the primary source of Soviet power in Europe. The West estimated that the Soviet armed forces had 175 divisions, or about 4.5 million men, in 1955, though not all were believed to be at full strength and some were deployed in Central Asia and the Far East.[18] By contrast, the United States had 20 divisions defending Europe. In divided Germany, the contest was less one-sided. There 400,000 Western allied troops in West Germany faced 300,000 Soviet troops and an estimated 80,000 East German troops in the German Democratic Republic.[19] Yet in a time of war the Soviets could easily draw on their 2 divisions in Hungary and the 21 fully equipped and well-trained divisions that they kept in Poland and the western USSR.

This conventional advantage held no allure for Khrushchev; he had no intention of starting a war with the West. It also meant less to him because it seemed to mean less to the United States. The Eisenhower administration's policy of massive retaliation bespoke a confidence that the U.S. strategic advantage was sufficient to deter any unwanted Soviet action. It was this confidence that also seemed to have given rise to John Foster Dulles's belief that the USSR could be bullied into concessions. Khrushchev wanted to undermine that confidence. He understood that the Americans intended to negotiate from a "position of strength," and that could only harm Soviet interests.

In preparation for Geneva, Khrushchev tried to alter the psychological climate of the Cold War. From reading U.S. newspapers in translation, he saw evidence that Washington did not understand the deficiencies of the new M-4 long-range bombers and might be vulnerable to some Soviet exaggeration. A controversy had broken out in the U.S. capital in mid-May 1955 over what U.S. Air Force officers believed they had seen at a rehearsal for the Soviet Union's May Day air show. The actual show had had to be canceled on account of poor weather, but at the rehearsal Americans overcounted the number of M-4s in the Soviet arsenal. Because the Americans assumed the plane met all the performance specifications that Moscow had assigned it, the conclusion was that the Soviets had a reliable nuclear attack force that could reach U.S. cities.

The Kremlin watched with glee as a very helpful discussion of Soviet bomber technology subsequently broke into the open in the United States. Led by Missouri Senator Stuart Symington, a former secretary of the air force under Truman with presidential ambitions, some congressmen began decrying a strategic "bomber gap" between the United States and the Soviet Union.

"It is now clear," said Symington, "that the United States, along with the rest of the free world, may have lost control of the air."[20] Despite assurances from the Eisenhower administration that the U.S. Air Force remained ahead of the Soviets, some journalists and legislators began throwing around extravagant assumptions about the capabilities of the M-4. Commentators from both political parties took joy in parsing whether the administration meant that the United States held a lead in total air capability or in what everyone most cared about, the bombers that could reach across oceans.[21]

On May 19, as this controversy was playing out on the front pages of major American newspapers, Bulganin and Zhukov were given the task of preparing a major air show for Soviet Aviation Day on July 13.[22] The country's entire fleet of three or four M-4s was to be flown in wide circles around Tushino Airport to convey the impression that the Soviet Union had at least twenty-eight of them. If this stunt worked, then in Geneva the Western leaders might treat the Soviet Union as an equal and stop trying to play on its weaknesses.

Meanwhile Khrushchev took advantage of a courtesy invitation from Ambassador Bohlen to attend the U.S. Embassy's annual Fourth of July reception. Since diplomatic relations had been established between the United States and the USSR in 1934, no Soviet leader had ever stepped foot inside Spaso House, the beautiful New Empire–style residence of the American ambassador that had been built for a Russian merchant in 1914. The presence of seven of the nine members of the Presidium, led by Khrushchev and Bulganin, was an impressive demonstration of the Soviet desire to change the tone of relations. Khrushchev also wanted to send a message to the Eisenhower administration, especially Secretary Dulles, that he was well aware that Washington believed the Kremlin could be pushed around. He told the gathering that he had read some Western press speculation that the foreign policy moves of the new leadership were being made out of weakness. "Of course, we made these proposals not for the purpose of pleasing somebody," he said. "We made these decisions because they were the right decisions and this is what motivated us."[23] Khrushchev assured his listeners that the Soviet Union was as strong as it needed to be and it just wanted peace.

He backed his words with action. A few days later the Kremlin made an unprecedented offer regarding a recent military incident. On June 23 two Soviet MiG fighters had fired on a U.S. Navy patrol plane over international waters in the Bering Strait. This was not the first time that the Soviet Air Force had attacked a U.S. plane in the Cold War. What was unprecedented was that after Khrushchev's and Bulganin's appearance at Spaso House the Soviets offered to pay half the damages for the incident, which had caused the pilot to bring the crippled plane in for a hard landing on St. Lawrence Island. Seven of the crew had been injured in the incident. Molotov made the offer to Secretary Dulles on behalf of the Soviet government at a UN meeting in San Francisco.[24]

Behind the scenes, Khrushchev also maneuvered to set the right tone within the Soviet government before Geneva. Molotov, who had been flying back from a UN meeting, had been unable to attend the July 4 reception at the U.S. Embassy. When he returned, Khrushchev used a discussion of a new Soviet declaration on the German question to be sure his foreign minister understood that Moscow would have to speak more softly to create a more peaceful world. Molotov had just submitted a draft declaration on the German question for his colleagues' approval. It repeated the stale Stalinist assertion that only a unified, neutral Germany would be acceptable to the Soviet Union. "The declaration is no good," Khrushchev complained. "The language is quarrelsome, [like] a bludgeon." Bulganin agreed: "The document is dry. . . . Comrade Molotov, you did not catch the tone." The draft was rejected, and Molotov had to come up with something better.[25]

Molotov's draft was in response to some incendiary comments made by Foster Dulles. At a press conference on June 28 the secretary of state had goaded the Kremlin. He said that Moscow had "lost interest in the reunification of Germany" and established Soviet readiness to discuss this issue as the litmus test of the new regime's commitment to reducing international tensions.[26]

Dulles had hit on a weak point in existing Soviet strategy. The Soviet Union's rhetorical commitment to all-German elections and reunification made little sense when East Germany's population was less than seventeen million and shrinking and West Germany's population was over fifty million and growing. Khrushchev understood this but as yet had no sense of how to change the Soviet position. His unwavering commitment was to protect East Germany, yet he hoped to use the four-power system to bring about some disarmament in Central Europe.

The public statement that was carried by the official Soviet news agency TASS on July 12 betrayed the muddiness of the Kremlin's collective thinking on what to do next about Germany.[27] It was clearest at the start, where Dulles's views were attacked as wrongheaded. "This matter is being represented in such a way as if the Soviet Union had lost interest in the unification of Germany, and that, allegedly, the Soviet Union sees a threat to its security in the unification of Germany." The Kremlin's reply was simple: "Everyone knows that the Soviet Union has invariably given first place to the question of Germany's reunification." But from here the way forward became opaque. If a united, free, and democratic Germany was not possible in the short term, then Moscow believed that reunification might be achieved on a "step-by-step" basis "in accordance with the establishment of an all-European system of collective security." Nowhere did the Kremlin state how that phased approach could be reconciled with the self-determination of the German people. Also left unstated was the Soviet hope that at Geneva the Kremlin could somehow convince the other occupying powers to accept European disarmament and a twenty-six-nation European collective security agreement, not German reunification, as the best first step toward détente.

Khrushchev had little hope of achieving anything with Dulles but was optimistic that he might find some common understanding with the head of the American delegation. Khrushchev had met Eisenhower only once, in June 1945, when the supreme allied commander visited Moscow, but he thought he had reason to believe that if there were to be any progress toward détente at Geneva, it would be because of Eisenhower. He knew that Marshal Zhukov had worked closely with Eisenhower in occupied Berlin in 1945. Their personal interaction in those early postwar months had been positive and mutually rewarding. Zhukov liked Eisenhower, and when it became apparent that the United States would be including the secretary of defense in its delegation, Khrushchev made sure that Zhukov not only joined the Soviet group but would be afforded opportunities to meet privately with the American president.

■

Nikita Khrushchev's insecurities were triggered immediately upon his arrival in Switzerland on Sunday, July 17. As his official plane was taxiing to the terminal, he noticed that every other leader, particularly President Eisenhower, had flown to Geneva in a much larger plane than his. In 1955 *Air Force One* was a 113-foot-long Super Constellation, a plane built by Lockheed that could carry 60 people and fly four thousand miles. Dubbed *Columbine III*, the presidential plane bore the name of the state flower of Mamie Eisenhower's home state of Colorado. In comparison, Khrushchev's 73-foot, 30-passenger Ilyushin 14 looked, as he later complained to his son, "like an insect."[28] (After his return Khrushchev needled his civilian aircraft designers to provide him with an official plane that befitted a world power. Once they finally delivered the 177-foot 220-passenger Tu-114 four years later, Khrushchev showed his pride not only by flying around in this behemoth, which stood 50 feet off the ground, but by prominently displaying a scale model of the plane on his desk in the Kremlin.)

At the conference, which started in Geneva's elegant Palais des Nations on

July 18, Khrushchev found other ways to puff himself up. Although Bulganin as Soviet premier was the formal leader of Moscow delegation, Khrushchev acted as Bulganin's superior and left no doubt that he expected to be treated as the top man.[29] Khrushchev was quickly and favorably impressed when Eisenhower suggested that all the leaders meet informally for cocktails between the formal working sessions and the dinners. Evidently the American believed in the value of getting to know his Soviet adversaries and would treat them as equals. Khrushchev also noted that Eisenhower put great store in the chance to renew his acquaintance with Defense Minister Zhukov.

But not everything he saw as the conference opened improved Khrushchev's image of the American president. The chairmanship of the meeting rotated among the four delegations. When it was Eisenhower's turn to gavel the meeting to order, Dulles sat at his left elbow. In front of the entire group, Dulles fed Eisenhower handwritten notes, which Khrushchev determined the president was simply reading into the microphone without taking a moment to absorb them himself. "It was difficult for us to imagine how a chief of state could allow himself to lose face like that in front of delegations from other countries," Khrushchev later recalled. "It certainly appeared that Eisenhower was letting Dulles do his thinking for him."[30]

Khrushchev still held hope for the meeting between the two military men. In the early 1960s he would use back channels to express his inner concerns to the Kennedy White House. At this stage he intended to use Zhukov, a man he believed Eisenhower trusted. "[W]e thought their acquaintance," Khrushchev explained, ". . . would lead to an easing of the tension between our countries."[31] The meeting between the U.S. president and the Soviet defense minister on July 20 was to be the most honest interaction between representatives of the superpowers in the first decade of the Cold War.[32]

Zhukov did not mince words. He told Eisenhower of his fears that "dark forces" in the West were attempting to undermine Soviet-American relations, and he blamed these forces for drawing a false picture of the Kremlin as being intent on launching an aggressive war against the United States. On the contrary, Zhukov assured Eisenhower, the Soviet people were "fed up to the teeth with war," and "no one in the Soviet Government or the Central Committee of the Party had any such intentions." The essence of Khrushchev's political agenda, he said, was to improve the Soviet economy and to raise the standard of living of the Soviet people. War would be inimical to that end.[33]

Eisenhower did not debate Zhukov. He agreed with Zhukov's description of the intent of Soviet policy. His "entire experience in Berlin with Marshal Zhukov had led him to place credence" in what Zhukov had told him.[34]

Zhukov then explained why the Soviets had so many armed forces at the ready. Soviet intelligence occasionally forwarded warnings to the leadership of the "readiness of [NATO] to annihilate the Soviet Union from bases located close to the Soviet frontiers." Under those circumstances, Zhukov explained, Moscow had to be prudent. He reminded Eisenhower that they both had seen their countries fall victim to vicious surprise attacks in 1941. Six months before the Japanese hit Pearl Harbor, the Soviets had been invaded by the Nazis. "These armaments," Zhukov explained, "of course, were a burden on the Soviet economy, but [the Soviets did] not wish a repetition of 1941, and no more than the United States could afford to play fast and loose with their security."[35]

Zhukov "urged" Eisenhower to take his word "as a soldier" that the Soviet Union wanted relief from this military standoff. He argued that the two countries "should work very seriously towards a détente." He was hopeful that despite the fact that the United States was "a rich country," America similarly welcomed "a relief from the armaments burden."[36]

Eisenhower responded energetically. Like Zhukov, he assumed that responsible leaders in both countries opposed war. Nevertheless, Eisenhower also believed that the Cold War was as much a psychological phenomenon as a clash of interests. Careful not to seem too disparaging of the U.S. Congress or the American press in a meeting with a Soviet (recent leaks of documents surrounding the Yalta Conference were a reminder that such diplomatic documents do not stay secret for long), Eisenhower tried to explain the role of public opinion in restraining the U.S. government in moving toward détente. He cautioned Zhukov not to expect an improvement "overnight." It would "take some time until the present psychological state of distrust and fear were overcome."

The meeting continued over lunch, where the U.S. president became more expansive. When the Soviet marshal explained that putting an end to the polemics in Soviet and American statements might be a good first step, Eisenhower explained the limits on his presidential power. Khrushchev could control *Pravda*, but as president Eisenhower could control only one of the three branches of government in Washington and none of the press. "What was necessary," Eisenhower said, "were some events or series of events which might change the psychological climate."

Zhukov argued for the simultaneous dissolution of the Warsaw Pact and NATO. In their place he suggested an all-Europe security system. Here the two men did not attempt to resolve their differences over whether to describe a Communist Poland as a free country or one under Soviet military occupation.

Without revealing his hand, Eisenhower tested Zhukov's reaction to the Open Skies proposal. He asked what Zhukov thought of an inspection system "of large installations such as airfields, long-range bombers and guided missile factories [that] could not be hidden." When Zhukov indicated he liked the idea, Eisenhower carefully asked if such an idea would be "politically possible in the Soviet Union." Zhukov's response could not have been clearer. "[I]t would be entirely possible and while its detail should be studied, he was, in principle, in full agreement with the President's remarks." Zhukov said he understood that this inspection would be a guarantee against surprise attack.[37]

Eisenhower emerged from this reunion of wartime friends understandably confident that his Open Skies proposal could be the catalyst that would start changing the psychological climate. What he did not yet know was that in supporting an inspection system that could spot large installations, the Soviet marshal had been speaking for himself, not for his boss.

Khrushchev was furious when he heard the details of Eisenhower's Open Skies proposal at the next day's formal session. It was impossible for him to accept an inspection that preceded disarmament. If he allowed U.S. planes to spy on every Soviet airfield, Washington would quickly discover that his country was a nuclear paper tiger.

The Open Skies proposal created a rift between Zhukov and Khrushchev. The two men disagreed over whether transparency increased or decreased the threat of a U.S. first strike. "The enemy's [military] potential is greater," Khrushchev said. "Whoever has the greater potential is more interested in intelligence."[38] This disagreement did not end at Geneva. It became a source of tension between the two men, as Khrushchev's views on the role of intelligence in disarmament only hardened, even as Soviet power grew.

At the cocktail session following the formal meeting, Khrushchev approached Eisenhower at the small buffet bar. Charles Bohlen, who was interpreting, heard him say, "Mr. President, we do not question the motive with which you put forward this proposal, but in effect whom are you trying to fool?" Before Eisenhower could respond, Khrushchev added, "In our eyes, this is a very transparent espionage device, and those advisers of yours who suggested it knew exactly what they were doing. You could hardly expect us to take this seriously."[39]

The vehement rejection surprised the U.S. president. This had been his proposal, his personal effort to neutralize the combustible mixture of poor strategic intelligence and public anxiety within the highly charged environment in Washington. When Eisenhower tried to dispel Khrushchev's suspicions by pointing to the fact that the surveillance would be mutual, the Soviet leader only promised "to study" the proposal, but he remained obdurate.[40]

Eisenhower's and Dulles's statements at Geneva concerning the German question were no more appealing to Khrushchev because they betrayed an unwillingness to recognize the legitimacy of East Germany as a separate political unit, let alone envision it as an equal partner in a European union. The West insisted that there could be no reduction in military forces in Europe, no collective security agreement, no minimal on-site inspection regime, before Germany reunified.

The conference ended on July 23 with an agreement to convene a meeting in October, again in Geneva, of the four foreign ministers to continue discussing European security. The Western and Soviet sides were no closer together on the central question of whether European disarmament or German reunification should come first. The Soviet position was that disarmament could occur before German reunification, but the Americans, French, and British disagreed. To ensure that the conference ended without rancor, the two sides agreed to have their foreign ministers discuss these two goals simultaneously in the hope of narrowing the gap later.

Despite the lack of movement on both disarmament and the German issue, that the Soviet delegation left in a good mood was a testament to the low expectations that it had in coming to this summit. Instead of seeing a defeat in the absence of any agreement, the Presidium's representatives were delighted that they had been treated with respect by the other great powers and had effectively ended the Soviet Union's diplomatic isolation. At the airport departure ceremony on July 24 Bulganin said that "what has already been done in Geneva is a new step in the relaxation of tension among nations [that] should contribute to the spirit of cooperation that one can already discern."[41] In Moscow Anastas Mikoyan, who was heading up the Kremlin in Khrushchev's absence, told reporters that "the international environment has changed and the weather is good. When the weather is good, everything is good."[42]

The actual weather was not very good for President Eisenhower, who arrived in a downpour at Washington's National Airport on July 24. Fearful of any comparisons to British Prime Minister Neville Chamberlain's return to London from the ill-fated Munich Conference with Adolf Hitler in 1938, Vice President Nixon had forbidden the use of umbrellas at the arrival ceremony.[43] With rain "cascading off" his bald head, a sodden Eisenhower was understandably less exuberant than the Soviets about the new international climate as he spoke into the assembled microphones. He lauded the "many new contacts" formed between East and West but cautioned that "the coming months" would show what it all meant for world peace.[44]

■

Vice President Richard Nixon had rarely seen his friend Foster Dulles so tired. The secretary of state, who flew in two hours after the president, slumped into the backseat of his official car. Nixon rode back to Washington beside him and was the tonic that the older man seemed to need. Dulles easily unburdened himself.

"No one will ever realize what a tremendous burden this conference was to me," said Dulles. As Nixon dictated that night in a taped diary entry, "[Dulles] said the President did a magnificent job but that, of course, it was necessary for him to keep the President advised of all of the curves that might be thrown so that in his extemporaneous remarks he would not make a statement which the other side might pick up and use against us." In Dulles's mind, the president was susceptible to saying the wrong things just because he wanted to make a good impression.

Dulles confessed that he was never sure how well his man would perform in high-level negotiations. In the car with Nixon, the secretary of state revealed that he was relieved that the United States had "not lost anything" in Geneva, with the implication that the president might have committed some harmful faux pas. The conference safely over, Dulles allowed himself the luxury of admitting that there had been at least one possible benefit of the experience: "The President had been exposed to the Communists." In particular, the meeting for which the president had held out such hope—and for which Dulles had shown nothing but polite disdain—was a bust. Eisenhower's visit with his wartime "buddy" Marshal Zhukov, Dulles related, "had not amounted to much except that it was good for the President to meet with Zhukov in this manner and to learn for himself that even a man he considered to be a friend would invariably take the hard Communist line whenever he attended a conference."

■

Following the conference, the American press described it as a good first step. "Geneva was not a third act, but a prologue," said the *Baltimore Sun*.[45] The *St. Louis Globe-Democrat* remarked in the same vein: "[Geneva] did illuminate the road—and . . . if the world will be patient and forbearing, the way is not now quite so long."[46] The *New York Times* editorialized: "We cannot disarm, we cannot wholly trust any agreement with Soviet Russia, until the Iron Curtain is down and freedom is established on Soviet soil. First things must come first—and these are first things. But a third World War would be no solution. A modus vivendi to avoid that frightful tragedy is essential, and we now seem a little nearer to it."[47]

In Moscow Khrushchev decided to continue his peace offensive. Although none of his disarmament proposals had received any detailed notice from the West at Geneva, the first secretary believed that the Soviet position was strategically and tactically wise. In July the Kremlin announced a unilateral cut in the Soviet armed forces of 640,000. In the last five years of his life Stalin had increased the size of the Soviet forces by 50 percent, and Khrushchev intended to bring that number below four million.[48]

A second initiative was even more dramatic. Khrushchev believed that ultimately relations were bound to improve between West Germany and the Soviet Union because of the lure of the Russian market for German capital. As a young man Khrushchev had worked as an administrator of a mine in the Ukraine. The technology used in the mine was made by the German conglomerate Thyssen, and Khrushchev later often referred to this personal experience to make a point of the mutual interests of German capitalists and Soviet Communists.[49] As far as he was concerned, this period of close and beneficial economic cooperation between the countries in the 1920s, known as the Rapallo era after the Italian town where a major agreement between the two governments was signed in 1922, represented a model for how West Germany and the Soviet Union should interact again. The Rapallo Treaty brought German recognition of the Soviet Union and the cancellation of war debts and established preferential trade between the two countries. The fact that Konrad Adenauer's party, the Christian Democrats, received significant support from the big German industrialists who were likely to benefit from renewed trade with Russia was an incentive for Khrushchev to make an effort to cultivate the German chancellor.

Khrushchev's first overture to Bonn had actually preceded Geneva. In early June, almost a month after the ratification of the Paris agreements, the Kremlin had issued a formal invitation to Adenauer to visit Moscow and discuss the possible normalization of relations.

If there was one man who seemed less likely than John Foster Dulles to provide Moscow with a diplomatic opening in 1955, it was the seventy-nine-year-old Konrad Adenauer. In his public speeches, the chancellor proclaimed the Federal Republic of Germany as the most anti-Communist state in Europe, and the KGB agreed that at the very least he was the most anti-Communist leader in Europe. "Adenauer," the intelligence service reported to the Kremlin in 1955, "is a savage enemy of the Soviet Union."[50] A Soviet intelligence source in West Germany had described the chancellor as convinced that "any kind of negotiation with the Soviet Union is akin to a pact with the devil."[51]

In June the Soviets invited him to Moscow anyway. Adenauer waited until after Geneva to say yes. After the date of the visit was set for early September, Adenauer virtually ensured that not much good would come of his visit. He announced in a speech in August that there could be no normalization of relations with Moscow unless the Kremlin agreed to the reunification of Germany and the release of the remaining German prisoners of war still detained in Russia.

The KGB and the Soviet Foreign Ministry were divided over whether there was any hope for a breakthrough. On the basis of its extensive study of Adenauer's past, the KGB was the more sanguine. "The distinguishing features of Adenauer as a politician," it reported to Khrushchev and the other Soviet negotiators, "are caution, dexterity, a demonstrated willingness to compromise, a moderate patience for leading the most difficult negotiations, slyness, a lack of fastidiousness as to means and a persistence as to ends."[52] The intelligence service also had informants telling them that changes in the West German political scene would require this clever man to be more tolerant of dealing with the East, if he wished to remain popular. From the chief editor of the influential *Frankfurter Allgemeine Zeitung*, Khrushchev's agents learned that Adenauer was a victim of his own success. Having presided over the rebirth of the German economy after its destruction in World War II and the integration of the Federal Republic into NATO, he now faced the question of how he intended to use this new power in Europe. This might require him to be a statesman. The Soviet Foreign Ministry had had a hard time getting around the language of Adenauer's August declaration. Molotov's people assumed that he was setting the stage to blame the division of Germany and the international tensions on Moscow.[53]

Of the men in the Kremlin, only Bulganin had met Adenauer before. Bulganin had visited Cologne in the 1920s, when he was a top administrator of the city of Moscow. At the time Adenauer had been Cologne's mayor. Bulganin remembered Adenauer as quite polite, and he had a generally positive impression of the man.

■

THE EISENHOWER administration was unhappy that Adenauer planned to make this trip to Moscow. Although there was no question he was anti-Communist, the West German leader tended to exaggerate the strength of the Soviet Union, which the United States worried might cause him to reach bad agreements with Moscow just to prevent a war. On the eve of the chancellor's trip Dulles wrote to Adenauer to calm those fears: "Let us first of all remember that the present policies of the Soviet Union are born not out of its strength, but out of its weakness; not out of its successes, but out of its failures."[54] The secretary of state pointed out that Moscow realized it could not provide both guns and butter and its citizens wanted more butter. He also told Adenauer that this was not the time to relax the pressure on Moscow. "[T]hey teach the tactics of retreat, in order to gain a respite, and if they now want this respite, which seems to be the case, we have, I think, a possibility of getting the reunification of Germany as the price they must pay. Whether, and how quickly, they will pay that price remains to be seen. But I think there is a good chance that unification, on your terms, can be achieved in a couple of years if we are stout."[55]

Adenauer, however, turned out to be as crafty and subtle as some of Khrushchev's advisers had suggested. In Moscow, he dumped the approach that the U.S. State Department had hoped for. After a few days of frank discussions with Bulganin, Khrushchev, and Mikoyan, the West German revoked the requirement that Moscow had to promise to move ahead on German reunification. When Bulganin offered to repatriate the nine thousand or so Germans still in Soviet captivity, this was enough for Adenauer to approve the normalization of relations. By the end of 1955 the Soviet Union and West Germany had exchanged ambassadors.

Moscow kept an eye on the reaction of its own German allies. Continued nonrecognition of East Germany was one area where Adenauer still refused to budge. Bonn would talk to Moscow but not to East Berlin. Following the Adenauer visit, Bulganin and Khrushchev each traveled to East Berlin to assure the East Germans and the world that Moscow's commitment to German communism remained firm. "If anyone . . . expects us to forget the doctrine of Marx, Engels, Lenin and Stalin, he is making a tremendous mistake," Khrushchev told the East Germans. "Those who wait for this will have to wait until a shrimp learns to whistle."[56]

▪

WHEN THE WESTERN powers outmaneuvered Molotov at the foreign ministers' conference in Geneva in October 1955, Khrushchev was able to hammer the last nail in the coffin of Stalin's German policy. In the weeks before the conference the Western powers had come up with a modified version of the Eden Plan. If Germany were allow to reunify and after elections chose to join NATO, the Soviets would get a demilitarized zone along the former East-West divide in Germany and a collective security treaty—a "treaty of assurance on the reunification of Germany"—whereby NATO would defend

Moscow if any of its members attacked the Soviet Union. Designed to appeal to the German public, this proposal tested the Soviet rhetorical commitment to German reunification and to German self-determination.

Although the foreign ministers met in the same hall in the Palais des Nations that the summit had, the mood could not have more different. There was so much tension that when a press photographer accidentally dropped a camera case, every foreign minister appeared to jump.[57]

Despite this tension, Molotov took the bait offered by Western negotiators. He indicated that he liked the idea of a demilitarized zone in Central Europe, where armaments would be limited and inspected and there would be a ceiling on the number of French, British, U.S., and Soviet troops. However, when the Soviet foreign minister was asked if Moscow would accept the treaty securing this zone as a guarantee that a unified Germany in NATO would not pose a threat to the Soviet Union, Molotov understood that he had fallen into a trap and started repeating long-standing Soviet phrases about the problem of future German remilitarization.

On November 4 the Presidium recalled Molotov to Moscow to discuss the collapsing Soviet position in Geneva. Over an arduous two-day Presidium meeting, the leadership hashed out new language for its German policy. Molotov and the Foreign Ministry went to work on something to take back to the conference table that would permit the Soviets to regain the high ground in the competition for German public opinion.

On November 6 Molotov submitted a new position paper to the leadership.[58] Although its drafters referred to it as a new proposal, it read like the old Stalinist policy on Germany. It stated that the goal of Soviet policy in Germany was the reunification of the country on the basis of all-German elections. To create the possibilities for this, the Soviet Union would propose the withdrawal of all foreign troops from the Germanys within three months and the creation of an all-German council to discuss the details of eventual German reunification. To preserve the "democratic and peace-loving" development of a reunified Germany, Moscow would also demand the rescinding of the Paris treaties—i.e., the removal of West Germany from NATO—so that a united Germany would be neutral and free of all blocs. Molotov made clear that this proposal was purely designed to make gains in the propaganda war. He did not expect the West to accept it.

Khrushchev rejected Molotov's entire strategy and dismissed the proposal out of hand. "We won't do it," he said.[59] "There are too many hidden dangers." Khrushchev was not sure that the West would reject this proposal. "Dulles will maneuver," said Khrushchev out of respect for his adversary. He thought there was a chance that the Americans might test Soviet sincerity by removing all their troops, something that the Soviets were not yet prepared to do themselves. Khrushchev believed that any Soviet mention of withdrawing troops would "disorient" the Germans and threaten the stability of the East German regime.

Molotov tried to rebut Khrushchev by saying that the Soviet Union had to get back on the correct side of this issue. It looked bad for Moscow to seem to be against the self-determination of the German people. "[The West] is in favor of elections," complained Molotov, "while we are against." When Molotov said that there really was little risk involved because the West wasn't really going to go through with its proposals anyway, Khrushchev cut him off. The Soviet foreign minister's cynicism irritated him. Molotov was prepared to risk the future of East Germany in a ploy to defend the old Stalinist position on general elections. "What is the sake of strengthening the NATO front," Khrushchev asked him, "of carrying out reunification for the purpose of having a whole Germany that will strengthen NATO and will be aimed against the policy of peace and the Soviet Union?"

Molotov found he had no allies in this debate. "I doubt the correctness of the proposals offered," said Mikoyan. "I agree with the opinion of Comrades Khrushchev and Mikoyan," added the Soviet president (a purely formal title), Kliment Voroshilov. A telling blow came from Lazar Kaganovich, who shared many of Molotov's views but was closer to Khrushchev on the need to protect socialist regimes. "We will not let them peck the GDR [German Democratic Republic] to pieces and we told them about that," said Kaganovich, "while they keep talking about elections."

Khrushchev led the group in thinking about new tactics. The West had sprung a trap by hinging the success of all disarmament discussions on whether there was an agreement to reunite Germany. If Moscow did not find a way out of its current negotiating strategy, the West would conclude the Soviets could be ignored until they were forced to accept NATO's positions on Germany and European security. "They will raise a cry," said Khrushchev, "that the position of strength prevails. . . . This is wrong." Perhaps it was time to have the Germans settle their differences themselves and for Moscow to stop trying to reach a settlement on Germany at the four-power level. "Every politician of sound judgment," Khrushchev concluded, "understands that in the circumstances where West Germany belongs to NATO, this question is complicated and it is not so simple to resolve it."

The next day the meeting resumed with a speech by Khrushchev outlining the new policy. "Now they wish to speak about elections from a position of strength. We should set up our reasoning against it."[60] He repeated his view that it was time to change the focus of great power diplomacy. It should now be on disarmament and just the development of contacts between the blocs, leaving the German issue to Bonn and East Berlin. The success of the Adenauer visit had reduced the immediate utility of the great power negotiations on Germany for Moscow, and with the establishment of diplomatic relations there were new opportunities for the Soviets to increase their influence in West Germany. Adenauer could not live forever, and there was reason to hope that his successors might turn out to be more interested in developing relations with the East.

In this discussion Khrushchev stressed what he believed to be Moscow's new bottom line in these discussions on the German question: "We wish to preserve the regime established in the GDR." He was also happy to have Moscow's representatives make this clear to the world. As he pronounced the old German policy dead, his Presidium ally Anastas Mikoyan praised its replacement: "Our position is constructive."

In ending Molotov's stranglehold on German policy, Khrushchev had done more than alter the shading of Moscow's language on German reunification. In accepting Khrushchev's leadership on this question, the Kremlin was endorsing the line that however beneficial détente in Europe might be, it could not come at the cost of East Germany. If need be, Moscow would have to be patient, allowing forces in West Germany or in the rest of the West to move Eisenhower, Eden, and the French closer to the view that the best route to détente and disarmament lay in the recognition that there were two Germanys. "The question of European security," said Khrushchev, "can be resolved if both Germanys exist as well."[61]

■

THE NEXT NIGHT Molotov alerted journalists at a huge diplomatic reception in the Kremlin that he was returning to Geneva with new proposals. "I came here with good baggage," said Molotov, "and I am leaving tonight with even better baggage because I have heard many good things here."[62] Once he arrived back in Geneva the representatives of the other three powers learned that Moscow had given up on four-power negotiations of the German problem.

In a one-hour speech Molotov outlined Khrushchev's new policy, and he did it in Khrushchev's language. He attacked the West for trying to deal with the Soviet Union from a "position of strength." West Germany's adherence to NATO was "an insurmountable obstacle" to reunification in the short term, he said, adding that elections now would "provoke a general dislocation" in Germany. He also stressed that the Soviet Union was committed to the survival of East Germany, which faced "a great future since it is moving along the main road of progress which is that of all mankind and since it has strong and loyal friends."[63]

Dulles reacted bitterly to Molotov's speech and called for a recess. This proposal, the secretary said the next day, after conferring with Eisenhower by telephone, "has largely shattered such confidence as was born at the summit conference."[64] The French and the British representatives responded just as negatively.[65] Despite Dulles's effort to show surprise, he had predicted in the summer that the Kremlin would never allow East Germany to die. In what the celebrated American columnist Walter Lippmann called the Geneva gamble, the three Western powers had tried to force the Soviets to accept that its satellite had no future.[66] Apparently Molotov's bosses were not prepared to yield. After a week of inconclusive discussion and some recrimination, the "little Geneva" broke up without any agreement on when it would meet again.

This was a defining moment for both Khrushchev's conduct of Soviet policy and the Cold War. Molotov never regained his influence and would soon be replaced as a foreign minister. A few days after "little Geneva" Moscow announced that it had signed an agreement formally ending the Soviet occupation of Germany and nominally transferred to the East Germans responsibility for defending the borders of the eastern zone.[67] On November 22 West Germans noticed East German troops replacing Soviet soldiers on the frontier.[68] Under the Potsdam Accord of 1945, Moscow had responsibility for monitoring military travel into East Germany and divided Berlin. Although Khrushchev was also eager to hand over this responsibility to the East Germans, Moscow retained it for the time being. With Molotov's loss of authority to Khrushchev, the defense of East Germany became a cardinal point in Soviet policy. Until 1990, in fact, the Soviet Union would not contemplate any security steps that might weaken the existence of its German ally or risk the reunification of Germany within NATO.

For Washington and Moscow the issue was now whether the two governments could live with the status quo in Central Europe. Dulles's policy of forcing Moscow to accept a reunified Germany in NATO had failed. There was a limit to how much Khrushchev would concede to relax international tensions.

Khrushchev and Eisenhower had fundamentally different assessments of the situation in Germany. Eisenhower rejected the notion that the German people in the east were the willing subjects of a Communist regime and had no desire to abandon them. What Khrushchev proudly referred to as the German Democratic Republic, Eisenhower called the Soviet Zone. The future peace and stability of Europe would depend on resolving the tension between those two concepts. Thanks to Khrushchev's energy and ambition, the German issue, which remained a core concern for both Moscow and Washington for the rest of Eisenhower's and Khrushchev's time in power, soon had competition from newer core concerns in geographical regions far outside the traditional areas of U.S.-Soviet rivalry.

CHAPTER 3

ARMS TO EGYPT

"**R**ED BLUEPRINT FOR CONQUEST" read the golden banner headline across a portrait of an unsmiling Khrushchev on the November 28, 1955, cover of *Newsweek*. "Russia's supersalesman, Nikita S. Khrushchev," went the teaser line, "has begun a month-long invasion of Asia's have-not nations, peddling a new line of promises."

For most of 1955 Khrushchev had largely hidden his role in reorienting Soviet foreign policy. The struggles over Soviet policy toward Austria, Yugoslavia, and Germany had taken place behind the opaque walls of the Kremlin. Over the summer rumors had circulated that Molotov might be replaced by Khrushchev's protégé Dmitri Shepilov, the editor in chief of *Pravda*, but this hadn't happened, and the usually dour foreign minister had managed to deflect attention with some uncharacteristic public joking about the speculation.[1] At Geneva Khrushchev had been perceived as the strongest opponent of Eisenhower's Open Skies position, but his overall influence in setting the general Soviet line in foreign policy had not yet been picked up.

It was in the third world that Khrushchev would first come to personify a new and ambitious Soviet approach to the Cold War. "Let us verify in practice whose system is better," he proclaimed on a state trip to India in late 1955. "We say to the leaders of the capitalist states: Let us compete without war."[2] Khrushchev was eager to extend this competition for influence to the developing world, where the dissolution of the great European empires had brought forward a new generation of leaders who were looking for advice, money, and legitimacy.

The event that drew the world's attention to Khrushchev's ambitions in the developing world came in late September 1955, when Egypt's leader, Gamal Abdel Nasser, announced that his country would be buying weapons from the Soviet bloc. Cairo's action reordered the politics of the Middle East and in the minds of Eisenhower, Eden, and the French leadership represented the greatest bid for hegemony over that oil-rich area since German Field Marshal Erwin Rommel's panzers were on the outskirts of Alexandria in 1942. The Middle East was an unexpected place for the Soviets to seek influence. Britain and Imperial Russia had not contested the region in the nineteenth century, and with the exception of Stalin's brief play for a colony in Libya after World War II and some equally short-lived support for the new state of Israel, Soviet regimes had largely stayed clear of the area. The Egyptian decision to buy Soviet weapons signaled a major departure for the Kremlin in a region that was of strategic importance to the United States and Western Europe. Whatever terms Khrushchev might use to try to soften his drive for influence in the postcolonial world, the apparent Soviet-Egyptian alliance represented realpolitik pure and simple. What the West did not understand was that the story could have very easily turned out differently.

■

INITIAL SOVIET EFFORTS to build a relationship with Egypt predated Khrushchev's eclipsing of Molotov. In the months following Stalin's death Soviet diplomats fanned out to the developing world in the hope of establishing diplomatic relations and in search of trade and cultural relationships. There actually weren't as yet many countries to choose from; the explosion of sovereignty in Asia and Africa was still five years away. India, Indonesia, and Egypt therefore received most of the wooing, though Moscow also made an effort with some Latin American republics. Of these first three big partners, Egypt ultimately drew the closest to the Soviet Union. But this was hardly predictable.

In its first phase the Soviet-Egyptian relationship was almost exclusively economic. The catalyst for this limited relationship was the overthrow of the Egyptian royal house in July 1952 by a military junta led by General Mohammed Naguib. A staunch Egyptian nationalist, Neguib was eager to reduce Egyptian dependence on the British, who had exercised influence over the fallen King Farouk, and was prepared to take help from anyone else. In August 1953 Soviet and Egyptian representatives negotiated an economic agreement.[3] Trade negotiations followed in the fall with the result that a barter deal was signed the following spring. Egypt was soon buying as much as 40 percent of its kerosene from the USSR and the Soviet-bloc's Romania. In return the Soviets purchased Egyptian cotton.

When Nasser replaced Naguib in 1954, the relationship with Moscow seemed to stall. Barely thirty-five years old, Nasser had been the brains behind the overthrow of King Farouk. His enormous charisma had created a devoted following among the men who had served with him. Once this charisma was projected to the Egyptian people and beyond, largely through dynamic public speeches broadcast on radio, his following grew into the millions. Nasser brought an expansive political message to his audiences. He dreamed of uniting the entire Arab world in one state and under Egyptian leadership. In a book of his ruminations published as *The Philosophy of the Revolution*, Nasser said, "For some reason it seems to me that within the Arab circle there is a role wandering aimlessly in search of a hero. And I do not know why it seems to me that this role, exhausted by its wanderings, has at last settled down, tired and weary, near the borders of our country and is beckoning us to move, to take up its lines, to put on its costume since no one else is qualified to play it."[4]

Initially Nasser was not that keen to expend much of his charm on the Soviets. He was deeply mistrustful of communists and assumed that the Soviets would use Arab Communists to weaken him and threaten Arab Nationalism. Because of his special interest in the Sudan, where he had served as an officer, he was especially concerned about Moscow's ambitions in that former British colony.

Nasser's principal objective in his first months at the top had been to eliminate Great Britain's remaining influence over Egypt. Britain still had troops in the Suez Canal Zone, and Nasser wanted to negotiate them out of the country. He did not want to give London a pretext to delay negotiations out of fear that he was close to Moscow.

Aware of Egypt's deep financial difficulties—this developing country had few natural resources and few exports yet needed to import vast quantities of industrial goods—Nasser permitted his government to continue talking to Soviet representatives about economic matters. Indeed, Nasser bent their ears to interest Moscow in his great dream of building the Aswan High Dam, a gargantuan project to create hydroelectric power and regulate the flow of the Nile. He hoped the Soviets would consider providing him with financial assistance to undertake this project.

In 1953 and early 1954 Nasser had also informed Soviet representatives that he hoped to equip the Egyptian military with modern weapons. But he was very coy. Although he hinted at perhaps shopping for these in the Soviet bloc, he avoided making a formal request. What he did not tell the Kremlin was that he preferred to buy American weapons. The problem for him was that since 1950 it was the declared policy of the United States to discourage the flow of weapons into the Middle East to prevent another Arab-Israeli war. The United States had joined Great Britain and France in issuing the Tripartite

Declaration, serving notice on the Arabs and the Israelis that they could expect to buy whatever military supplies they needed for internal security and self-defense, but nothing more.[5] Nasser wanted more.

▪

A DRAMATIC EVENT in the summer of 1954, thousands of miles from Egypt, very nearly brought the Kremlin's hopes for a close relationship with Nasser to an abrupt end. The June 1954 overthrow of another young progressive colonel in Central America reinforced Nasser's reluctance to get too close to the Soviet Union.[6] Although it predated Khrushchev's emergence as a major player in shaping Soviet foreign policy, the case of Jacobo Arbenz in Guatemala would remain an enduring object lesson in what could go wrong for Moscow whenever it tried to help a third world regime. This sad tale not only complicated Nasser's relations with the Kremlin before the breakthrough of 1955 but would affect Khrushchev's future relationships with third world leaders, especially in areas where the U.S. was the predominant power.

When Arbenz was elected president of Guatemala in late 1950, Moscow did not consider him a Communist, though the Foreign Ministry knew that some of his advisers were leading members of the Guatemalan Communist Party.[7] The Kremlin had watched with approval as the Guatemalan parliament passed, in 1952, an extensive land reform decree which in the following year permitted Arbenz to nationalize the vast tracts of unused real estate belonging to the two largest firms in Guatemala, the United Fruit Company and the American Railway Company.

Not surprisingly Washington viewed these events differently. Arbenz's land reform stirred concerns in the United States that he might be a Communist. The Truman administration launched the first covert action designed to overthrow Arbenz, but the job was finished by Dwight Eisenhower and John Foster Dulles when they came into office in 1953. Eisenhower shared Dulles's alarm about the susceptibility of the third world to Communist infiltration. Speaking for the new administration, Dulles explained the nature of this threat to Western security:

> On the free world front the colonial and dependent areas are the fields of most drastic contest. Here the policies of the West and those of Soviet imperialism come into headlong collision. . . . The Soviet leaders, in mapping their strategy for world conquest, hit on nationalism as a device for absorbing the colonial peoples. . . . In the first phase the Communist agitators are to whip up the nationalist aspirations of the

people, so that they will rebel violently against the existing order. Then, before newly won independence can become consolidated and vigorous in its own right, Communists will take over the new government and use the power to "amalgamate" the people into the Soviet orbit.[8]

The new administration quickly deemed Guatemala a major battleground in this new war. The covert action authorized by President Eisenhower was designed to undermine Arbenz's support within the Guatemalan Army. Like all armies in the developing world, it was poorly equipped, and its leaders, though some had served with Arbenz for some time, judged his commitment to the army as an institution in modern Guatemala in terms of how well he could equip it. Washington imposed as tight an arms embargo as possible on the country. Timed to coincide with an extensive propaganda campaign that played on military fears of Communist influence, the operation was intended to culminate in a series of small military skirmishes led by counterrevolutionaries that would spark a sympathetic military coup.[9]

Faced with this embargo and aware of the propaganda campaign, Arbenz sought weapons from the Soviet bloc. In the spring of 1954 the Kremlin arranged for Czech weapons to be carried on a Swedish ship, the *Alfhelm*. Although measures were taken to hide the ship's destination from even the captain until he had reached the Caribbean, there was not much that was covert about the Soviet operation. The Guatemalans had to pay for the weapons themselves and the $4.9 million transaction was carried by commercial wire through the Union Bank of Switzerland and Stabank, Prague to the Czech company Investa.[10]

As the Kremlin watched, this arms deal set in motion a series of events that were tragic for Arbenz and Guatemala. The CIA easily picked up news of the commercial transaction and, after mistakenly following a West German freighter, determined the arms were on the *Alfhelm*.[11] At a press conference on May 25, 1954, Foster Dulles denounced the shipment as dramatic evidence of the international Communist conspiracy. The *Alfhelm* quickly became a powerful symbol that created enormous support in Washington to do something about Soviet machinations in the third world. "[T]his cargo of arms is like an atomic bomb planted in the rear of our backyard," said the Speaker of the House of Representatives, John McCormack. "The threat of Communist imperialism," said the *Washington Post*, "is no longer academic, it has arrived."[12]

What was a black eye for the Kremlin turned out to be a terminal condition for the Arbenz regime. The docking of the *Alfhelm* accelerated CIA planning for an attack. On June 18, 1954, a small rebel force invaded a few miles into the country. This force was not designed to overthrow Arbenz—the CIA case officer for the operation called it "extremely small and ill-trained"—and it didn't.[13] What it was supposed to do was to magnify the anxiety fostered by the arrival of the *Alfhelm* and create a sense of increasing disorder that would push the Guatemalan Army to get rid of Arbenz. This it did. Fence-sitters in the Guatemalan Army, few of whom had not been told of the secret purchase from the East, had already started viewing Arbenz as Moscow's puppet. The discovery of the *Alfhelm* helped the United States rally support for a strong response from members of the Organization of American States (OAS), which in 1950 had gone on record opposing the spread of communism or Soviet influence in the Western Hemisphere.[14]

Having provided their enemies with so much fodder, the Soviets found they could do nothing else for their friends. No Soviet service, including the KGB, had a direct line to Guatemala City.[15] The Soviet Navy was incapable of projecting force into the Caribbean, and the Soviet Union lacked any nearby military bases that could sponsor a show of force of any kind.

On June 23, 1954, the Guatemalans requested assistance from the Soviet Union. At the very least they wanted Soviet diplomats to use the UN Security Council to stop the fighting. The next day Molotov instructed the Soviet delegation at the United Nations to express Moscow's "deepest sympathies" for the Guatemalan people and to push for Security Council action.[16] Meanwhile the situation went from bad to worse in the country. On June 25 the Guatemalan foreign minister cabled the Kremlin that jets piloted by rebels had begun bombing Guatemalan cities from bases in Honduras.[17] This disturbing message was distributed to Khrushchev and the other members of the Presidium, who decided to publish the sad correspondence with Arbenz's foreign minister for want of anything better to do for the dying regime.

As the Presidium was deciding it could do little to help the Guatemalan government, Arbenz was telling his cabinet and the leaders of his movement that the army was in revolt. Two days later Arbenz was overthrown by a military that both feared Moscow's presumed influence and wished to avoid Washington's expected retribution.

■

FOR SIX MONTHS after the fall of Arbenz, Nasser avoided the subject of Soviet military assistance. As if the events in Guatemala had not been enough of a reason for caution, the conclusion of the long-awaited military agreement with the British that same summer underscored the folly of risking Western displeasure, at least in the short term. The British agreed to relinquish their military base in the town of Suez at the southern end of the Suez Canal by mid-1956. Nasser did not want to give the British any reason in the next two years to break that agreement and keep their soldiers in Egyptian territory.

Nasser's abstinence did not last long. Two events in February 1955 so shook his confidence about Egypt's destiny in the region that he decided that he could not wait until 1956 to create a modern Egyptian military. That month the British government played midwife to a defense arrangement signed between Iraq and Turkey. Egypt interpreted the pact as both a British effort to retain influence in the region after the Suez base agreement and as an Iraqi bid for dominance. In the modern era Egypt and Iraq had continued the centuries-long rivalry between the civilizations along the Nile and the Euphrates, often by playing one foreign empire off another in an attempt at regional dominance. Iraqi Prime Minister Nuri al-Said lacked Nasser's charisma but not his regional ambitions. A close ally of Great Britain's and friendly toward the United States, Nuri saw the agreement with Turkey as the basis of a wider alliance that would link all pro-Western Arab regimes under Iraqi leadership in the Middle East, precisely what the Kremlin feared.

The British had tried to involve the Egyptians. Before the Turks and Iraq had signed their agreement, British Prime Minister Eden visited Nasser in Cairo in February 1955 in an effort to convince the Egyptian leader to join an anti-Soviet military pact. Nasser, who was too skeptical of British aims to join, told him that if the Soviet Union attacked Egypt, he would request Western assistance, and if the West attacked Egypt, he would turn east for help.

The second event involved Israel. On February 28, 1955, four days after the Turks and the Iraqis signed their agreement in Baghdad, paratroops under the command of a young officer named Ariel Sharon infiltrated Egyptian military positions in the Gaza Strip. The Israeli mission was to damage the bases from which Palestinian commandoes, the so-called fedayeen, were believed to be operating into Israel.[18] The successful attack on Egyptian territory not only humiliated Nasser but played upon his deep suspicion that Israel was an agent of British imperialism. Despite the history of the Jewish struggle with the British authorities in Palestine, Nasser stubbornly believed in the existence of ongoing secret coordination between the British and Israeli governments and he convinced himself that London had ordered the Israelis to attack Gaza. "The western powers are continually using Israel to organize all kinds of provocations against us," Nasser later confided to Nikita Khrushchev. In his eyes, the Gaza attack was payback for his refusal to join the Turkish-Iraqi alliance, the so-called Baghdad Pact.[19]

In Moscow only one event was required in February 1955 to rekindle interest in closer relations with Egypt. The creation of the Baghdad Pact symbolized a tightening of the vise established by the West and its allies all along the periphery of the Soviet Union. Fearing that Turkey and Iraq would soon be joined in the alliance by Saudi Arabia, Yemen, Jordan, and Libya, thus transforming it into a region-wide anti-Soviet bloc, Moscow saw a new mutuality of interests with Arab nationalists, especially Nasser. His dreams of Arab unity were incompatible with the formation of a regional bloc centered on Turkey and Iraq.

To signal their willingness to establish closer relations, the Soviets made a sudden 180-degree change in their policy toward Egypt's neighbor the Sudan. In 1954 Soviet propaganda and the Sudanese Communists had argued against the union of Sudan and Egypt, which Moscow knew was one of Nasser's goals. In February 1955, Moscow began publicly supporting the unity of the Nile Valley.[20]

■

KHRUSHCHEV'S PERSONAL ROLE in this shift in policy toward the Sudan is unknown. In February he was very busy with the formal removal of Georgi Malenkov as Soviet premier. But there is evidence that he soon took a special interest in Nasser. Khrushchev was encouraged when, as hoped, Nasser responded to the policy change by initiating discussions about buying Soviet weapons. But when the Kremlin answered that it could start serious negotiations immediately, Nasser again became elusive. And by May 1955 the news from Cairo was discouraging for Khrushchev. In conversations at the Soviet Embassy, Nasser was alluding to the "risks" involved in acquiring Soviet weapons, a subtle reference to the calamity in Guatemala. Moreover, having just returned from the inaugural conference of the nonaligned movement in Bandung, Indonesia, Nasser was not at all subtle in assuring the Kremlin that he had no intention of joining the Soviet bloc. He told Soviet Ambassador Daniel Solod that he was beginning to fear that strengthening economic and cultural ties between Egypt and the Soviet Union would lead to an increase in the activity of the Egyptian Communist Party, something he considered against the interests of his Revolution. In light of the Communists' anti-Nasser propaganda, which he assumed was directed from Moscow, the Egyptian leader explained to Solod that he had real doubts that the Kremlin truly supported his regime.[21]

Somewhat exasperated, Khrushchev asked Tito during his trip to Yugoslavia in June for his opinion of the Egyptian. Tito advised him to be patient. "Nasser is well disposed toward the USSR," the Yugoslav replied.[22]

Khrushchev understood that Moscow's appeal to Nasser, if successful, would have to be based on the two leaders' shared interest in reducing Western imperial power in the Middle East. Streams of information from the Soviet Embassy in Cairo and via Moscow's official TASS news agency and the KGB detailed Nasser's staunch anticommunism and his preference for U.S. military assistance.[23] Khrushchev was nevertheless optimistic that the two countries and even the two leaders could develop a tight bond. Nasser, however, was stalling because he did not share Khrushchev's belief that close relations between Cairo and Moscow were inevitable. The events in Baghdad and the Gaza Strip served as warnings that Egypt needed to be stronger; but they were not arguments necessarily in favor of looking East for help. Nasser still preferred U.S. military assistance, if he could find away to convince the Americans to circumvent the Tripartite Declaration. The Americans had already been generous with Egypt. In November 1954, Washington had provided Cairo with forty million dollars in economic aid.[24]

In June 1955 the Egyptian leader decided that while keeping the Soviets at bay, he should start playing upon U.S. fears of Soviet influence in the Middle East to force the Eisenhower administration to reconsider its policy on military assistance.

"The Russians have offered me all that we need in arms," Nasser told U.S. Ambassador Henry Byroade on June 9. To add an edge to his little deception— for Moscow had not gotten down to any details with Nasser about a military package—Nasser advised the U.S. ambassador that he had a military mission that was poised to go to Moscow in a week.[25] When he still didn't get a quick answer from the Americans, Nasser chose a dramatic gesture to get President Eisenhower's attention. On June 16 he arrested the leaders of the Egyptian Communist Party and then went back to the U.S. ambassador.[26]

Byroade pushed Washington to give Nasser a reason to believe the United States would sell him weapons. The challenge for Washington was to establish a balance between this policy of cultivating Nasser and the need not to alienate the Israelis and the British. Domestic politics, even more imperatively than Israel's evidently pro-Western orientation, argued for not ignoring Israel. Egypt was an equally sensitive point with the British, who had effectively exercised a veto on U.S. aid to Nasser during the negotiations of the June 1954 Suez base agreement.[27] The product of this dilemma was the Anglo-American Alpha program, an initiative designed to seek a peaceful settlement of the Arab-Israeli conflict through mutual border concessions, massive regional development projects, and economic assistance to both sides.[28] Although Washington and London had been talking about the Alpha program since January 1955, it had yet to be launched.[29]

The day after Nasser jailed the Egyptian Communist leaders, Washington informed Egypt that it was welcome to purchase arms and that its requests would be judged within the framework of the principles of the Tripartite Declaration. If Egyptian requests were "reasonable," Nasser could expect a positive response from Washington.[30]

Nasser submitted a wish list to the Americans on June 30. In all he wanted twenty-seven million dollars' worth of equipment. At the heart of the request were 120 M4 medium tanks, 15 M24 flamethrower tanks, and 26 B-26 jet aircraft. The list was delivered by Nasser's chief of staff, Ali Sabri.[31] Nasser had yet to send a similar list to the Soviets.

The United States responded rapidly to this request. Nasser had firm allies within the administration, including the president. When Eisenhower saw the list of what Egypt wanted, he thought it reasonable. Dulles did not oppose the sale. In fact these events compelled him to work on a general statement of U.S. policy in the region. The administration had promised this statement in 1953 but had decided to wait out the midterm congressional elections in 1954 before approaching such a sensitive political matter.

The problem that the drafters of this general statement faced was that Egypt's long-range goals in the Middle East were incompatible with the realities of the Middle East or U.S. policy there. First, Nasser wanted material compensation for the Palestinian refugees. He did not insist that these refugees had the right to return to pre-1948 Palestine, but he believed they deserved a better life in whatever Arab country in which they had resettled. Nasser's other goal, however, would never be acceptable. As the Egyptian foreign minister explained to John Foster Dulles, "If I wish to go by car from Egypt to Damascus, I would have to have to obtain the permission of Mr. Sharett [the Israeli prime minister]." Egypt wanted the Negev desert to be ceded by Israel to Jordan, "including Beersheba," a town that had been included in the original British plan for state of Israel.[32] No Israeli or American Jew would permit that to happen peacefully.

A still greater problem was that Egypt couldn't really afford to pay for these weapons. At the very least Nasser would need them to be given at a discount. The Egyptian government was hemorrhaging foreign reserves, at the rate of about two million dollars per month. Cairo had only about twenty-four million dollars in hard currency left. In early August, a month after his representative sent the wish list, Nasser himself appeared at the U.S. Embassy to ask for American financial assistance in buying the weapons.

Byroade didn't quite understand the significance of this conversation. In contrast with Washington's reaction to Nasser's June wish list, the administration was slow to respond to his new request. The delay would have severe consequences.

■

KHRUSHCHEV WAS MEANWHILE getting impatient with Nasser. Unaware of the details of Nasser's visits to the U.S. Embassy but no doubt suspicious, Khrushchev decided to send Dmitri T. Shepilov to Egypt to edge Nasser closer to forming a military alliance against the Baghdad Pact. It had been three months since Moscow had made its offer to provide weapons to Egypt, yet not only had the Egyptians not accepted the offer, but Nasser seemed to be intentionally delaying taking the next step. Shepilov, a trusted associate who understood how Khrushchev thought on foreign affairs, would make a perfect representative and observer.

"Dmitri the Progressive," as Shepilov was known by the Moscow elite, was a Khrushchev lucky charm. Having ascended to the editorship of *Pravda* in 1952 at the age of forty-seven, he had been Khrushchev's most important ally in shaping the Soviet press to reflect Khrushchev's rise in stature. It was Shepilov who had written Malenkov's political obituary in January 1955, with a perfectly timed article critiquing Malenkov's approach to economics. Although economics was Shepilov's chosen specialty, Khrushchev decided to groom him for a responsibility in foreign affairs. In 1954 Shepilov was given the chairmanship of the Foreign Affairs Committee of the Council of Nationalities, one of many standing committees on the government side of the massive Soviet bureaucracy. There Shepilov had campaigned against Molotov's worldview, advocating the Khrushchev line of peaceful coexistence and the senselessness of continuing the rift with Tito.

Shepilov's rise accelerated with Malenkov's dismissal. Khrushchev brought Shepilov into the planning of the trip to Belgrade, where he played a role in writing the diplomatic communiqué that the Soviets offered the Yugoslav Communist Party as a possible joint statement of fraternity and solidarity. The Yugoslavs had opposed the joint statement, but this failure had no negative consequences for Shepilov. In early July 1955 Khrushchev rewarded Shepilov for his loyalty by making him one of three new secretaries of the Central Committee of the Communist Party of the Soviet Union, effectively the new Khrushchev team.[33]

■

"**W**E HAD DOUBTS until you visited," Nasser's defense minister, Marshal Abdel Hakim Amer, later told Shepilov.[34] The Shepilov visit, which lasted from July 21 to 29, helped clear the air in Cairo about Soviet intentions. For all his doubts about the Soviets, Nasser was willing to give them a chance to prove themselves. He therefore arranged a very personal visit for Shepilov. The Soviet representative was invited to dinner at the home of Abdel Nasser Hussein, Nasser's father, in Alexandria.

Rumors swirled in Moscow that the younger Nasser had once been a devotee of Adolf Hitler, that there was a portrait of Hitler on Nasser's desk. Shepilov did not find a fascist. What he thought he found was a man with somewhat confused political views. "There was such a soup [of ideas] in his brain, especially at the time of our first meeting," he later recalled.[35]

When Shepilov asked him what his goals were, Nasser introduced a new concept to the editor of *Pravda*: "We would like to build moderate socialism."

"What exactly is that?" Shepilov asked.

"It is socialism without capitalists, without imperialists, and without Communists" was the response.

Shepilov was dismissive. "That kind of socialism doesn't exist."

But Nasser wanted to understand Moscow. He was not about to give up on Khrushchev's envoy. So the men talked for days. "You wrote a book, didn't you?" Nasser asked at one point. Shepilov had written a text on political economy. "Well, is it available in English?" It was, and the Egyptian, who could read English well, wanted a copy to learn even more about Shepilov's thinking.

The Shepilov visit calmed Nasser's concerns about Moscow enough for him to move to the next step in purchasing Soviet weapons. Still having heard nothing concrete from the Americans, Nasser authorized the dispatch of a military purchasing mission behind the iron curtain. These first negotiations were for the supply of Soviet planes. The Egyptians requested jet fighters, the MiG-15s and Nasser asked that these discussions be held in secret.[36]

The Soviets suggested Prague as the location for these meetings. Ironically the Soviets were reviving a Czech back channel that had initially been established to permit secret deliveries of weapons to the Jews in Palestine in 1947 and 1948 before the proclamation of the state of Israel. Now with the shift in the geopolitical needs of the Soviet Union, this system would serve the Arabs. To help shield the group, Cairo also decided not to inform its embassy in Prague of the existence of this delegation. Few Czechs were told of the negotiations either. The Soviets took responsibility for the protection of the Egyptian teams, and Cairo asked Moscow to provide the communications link between Nasser and his representatives in Prague.

▪

N ASSER WAS STILL very uncomfortable with this decision. Communists were his enemies in Egypt and his rivals for authority in the rest of the Arab world. Nasser might well have waited longer to give the United States another chance to help him had it not been for an event in the Sudan in August 1955 that touched on Nasser's deepest insecurities.

Sudan loomed large in the consciousness of Nasser and his fellow revolutionaries. Since the nineteenth century, the British and the Egyptians had contested control over the land that contained the headwaters of the Nile. In 1899 Britain had arranged an Anglo-Egyptian condominium in the region, effectively sharing control with the authority in Cairo. A motherland issue for the Free Officers led by Nasser was the revocation of that condominium to permit the unification of Sudan and Egypt. This goal was related to the regime's extensive plans for the development of the Nile. But it was also linked to the traditional Egyptian claim on the ancient kingdom of Nubia, so redolent of ancient Egyptian power. Personal history also played a role for the young revolutionaries. Two of Nasser's closest allies, the Salem brothers, had grown up in Port Sudan, and since 1954 Salach Salem had been Nasser's deputy for Sudanese affairs. Nasser had had his own Sudanese days. He and his military chief of staff, Marshal Abdel Hakim Amer, had spent the opening years of World War II stationed in the Sudan as lieutenants in the Egyptian Army.[37] It may therefore seem less surprising to reveal that events in the Sudan provided the final nudge to send Nasser into a Soviet arms deal.

Although the new line taken by the Kremlin on this issue after February 1955 should have pleased Nasser, it was contradicted by the propaganda of the Sudanese Communist Party, which continued to attack the Sudanese government for "selling out the Sudan to Gamal Abdel Nasser."[38] Like many world leaders, Nasser couldn't believe that Communists anywhere could act independent of the Soviet party. As recently as June Salach Salem had been instructed to ask Soviet Ambassador Daniel Solod what Moscow thought it was doing in allowing Sudanese Communists to attack the regime in Cairo.[39] Despite the assurances coming directly from Moscow, Nasser had a hard time shaking the view that statements by the Sudanese Communist Party were a better barometer of the Kremlin's real intentions in the region. Then two coinciding events convinced him that his greater enemies lay elsewhere.

On August 19, when armed riots broke out in three southern Sudanese provinces, the government in Khartoum blamed Nasser. It asserted that the organizer of the riots was a longtime advocate of Sudanese-Egyptian union, who had only recently been in Cairo for the celebration of the third anniversary of the overthrow of King Farouk. Nasser had had nothing to do with these riots. Moreover, whatever Nasser initially thought of the events in the Sudan, his assessment was immediately affected by an occurrence hundreds of miles away in the Gaza Strip. Early on the morning of August 22 the Israelis killed an Egyptian officer and at least two enlisted men near Kilometer 95 in the Gaza Strip.

As Nasser had done in February, he linked Israel's latest Gaza raid to a large geopolitical conspiracy. Nasser convinced himself that Great Britain had stage-managed the Israeli attack to distract Egypt from southern Sudan. Because Nasser thought the black residents of southern Sudan incapable of political self-organization, he immediately assumed that the riots that started on August 19 had to have been orchestrated by outsiders. Nasser assumed the Sudanese government would request British intervention to quell the riots, which would allow a de facto division between a pro-Egyptian northern and a pro-British southern Sudan.

A few hours after the Israeli attack in Gaza, Nasser's most trusted adviser, Ali Sabri, met with the Soviet ambassador.[40] Cairo now wanted to speed up the negotiations in Prague. At Nasser's request, Sabri laid out Cairo's conspiracy theory to the Soviets. Nasser expected a British military intervention in the southern Sudan. There were no roads connecting Egypt and the Sudan, and in any case, the northern Sudan was separated from the southern provinces by a marsh. The only way the Egyptian Army could reach the rioters was by air. So desperate were the Egyptians for assistance in the Sudan that Sabri explained Cairo would permit Soviet pilots to fly the MiG-15s and Soviet military cargo planes directly to Almaza Airport in Cairo.

■

WHILE THE PACE of events accelerated in the Middle East, Secretary of State Foster Dulles took his time answering Nasser's request for financial assistance for the proposed U.S. arms deal. Dulles disliked fence-sitters in the Cold War. "He thought it was sinful," recalled Eisenhower's national security adviser, General Andrew Goodpaster. "It was immoral of many of the nations to try to take a neutral stand when truth and right were in jeopardy, so to speak."[41] He was not about to let Nasser dictate how and when the U.S. secretary of state would make his much-anticipated statement on Middle Eastern policy.

Unaware of the dramatic shift in Nasser's assessments of Egypt's immediate interests, the State Department continued working on Dulles's statement.

Not only did Washington miss entirely the deep effect that the riots in the Sudan were having on the Egyptian leader, but the secretary of state was convinced that Nasser could be satisfied with less than a concrete offer of an affordable arms deal. On August 23 Byroade was instructed to meet Nasser to tell him the statement was coming.[42] Byroade went the next day and found Nasser surprisingly passive. A few days later, when he presented an advance copy of Dulles's speech to Nasser, once again the usual Nasser fire was absent. "Had [the] feeling he [was] somewhat confused by general nature of the approach and really did not understand significance of some passages," Byroade cabled. Nasser was not so much confused as distracted and disappointed. He had wanted a response to his request for U.S. economic assistance to pay for the twenty-seven million dollars' worth of weapons. Instead Dulles was sharing a vaguely worded commitment to a general peace agreement in the Middle East.[43]

As Dulles put the finishing touches on his address, Nasser asked for even more from the Soviets. Now convinced that the United States would not subsidize his purchase of M4 tanks, Nasser asked the Soviets for tanks. He also requested a financial aid package to buy all the weapons, the planes, and these newly requested tanks. Despite what he later said publicly, Nasser could not afford to buy any modern weaponry at commercial prices.

In the end, the Soviets got their deal by trying harder to appease Nasser than did the Americans. In early September the Presidium decided to agree in principle to sell Egypt tanks, though the quantity and model remained to be determined. More important, given Nasser's immediate concerns, the Soviets allowed him to buy the artillery pieces and the MiG-15 fighters now and told him that they would accept barter as payment for most of it. After paying for a fifth of the total in Egyptian pounds, Cairo could defray the remaining bill gradually by means of sending rice, cotton, leather, and even silk clasps to the USSR. This remainder was effectively a loan that would increase by 2 percent a year.[44] These were even better terms than Cairo had requested from Washington. On September 12 Soviet and Egyptian negotiators signed the agreement in Prague.

▪

A WEEK LATER U.S. intelligence agents in Cairo picked up pieces of the story from their sources. Sunday evening, September 19, the embassy in Cairo cabled Washington: "[Egyptian] acceptance Soviet arms offer likely . . . Soviet offer said to be embarrassing in size."[45] One person who was not surprised was U.S. Ambassador Byroade. When the State Department responded by asking him to warn Nasser that any Egyptian arms deal with the Soviets "would create most serious public reaction in the US and greatly complicate our ability [to] cooperate with them," Byroade said that this threat lacked the power that it once had.[46] He had said this so many times to Nasser, while promising that an alliance with the United States would be helpful to Cairo, that he was beginning to sound like a broken record. It was time for positive action. Why hadn't Washington responded favorably to Nasser's request in late August for financial assistance so he could buy U.S. weapons? "It is crystal clear that by our unwillingness [to] manipulate a few million dollars we are permitting situation [to] deteriorate to point where chain reaction of nature that will constitute a major defeat for US policy in [the] Middle East . . . is highly probable."

The Soviets partially confirmed the arms agreement with Cairo. Molotov happened to be in New York in the third week of September for the opening of the UN General Assembly. Dulles took the opportunity to sound him out on these reports of Soviets arms sales to Egypt. Although not mentioning Egypt by name, Molotov confirmed that arms negotiations might be going on with Arab countries but that "these conversations should not cause misunderstanding." The matter is being approached "on commercial grounds."[47] With Soviet confirmation—even if tepid—Dulles informed President Eisenhower and conferred with his brother, Allen, about whether to take a positive step to prevent Nasser from going through with it.[48] The secretary of state was very worried. He thought the Israelis might launch a preemptive strike before the Soviet weapons arrived. Also always lurking in his mind was the possibility that once armed with Soviet weapons, the Egyptians might hit at Israel. Dulles approached the British and the French at the UN privately to send a message to their capitals to prepare for the new reality of Soviet involvement in the Middle East.

Dulles conferred with Eisenhower and suggested that this could be stopped only in Moscow. He thought that Nasser had no choice but to take the weapons. His army would overthrow him if he didn't. But perhaps the Soviets could be scared into leaving the Middle East alone. Dulles told the president he would draft something for his consideration.

Allen Dulles thought that his brother was focusing on the wrong people. He doubted Moscow would respond to a protest from the president. The secretary of state and his brother disagreed on the handling of Nasser. Foster said the United States had offered arms to Nasser. Allen wondered if enough had been done. In any case, Foster believed that Nasser could not be turned around on this. Foster did not know what to do, then suggested they wait. Allen agreed briefly, accepting that a few days wouldn't matter. Then he changed his mind and sent a CIA officer to Cairo to speak directly to Nasser.

Although there was no doubt that Nasser's acceptance of MiGs from Moscow was a major turning point, he almost single-handedly built up this event into a revolutionary moment by exaggerating the size of the arms deal. Egyptian sources are very weak on Nasser's thinking at this stage in the relationship with Moscow.[49] On the basis of Soviet information, it appears likely that Nasser was not convinced in September 1955 that the opening to Moscow was anything but a one-shot event. He still wished to establish a close economic and political relationship with Washington. He said as much to Allen Dulles's personal representative in Cairo, Kermit Roosevelt, on September 25. Over the course of this long meeting—three and one-half hours—Nasser played the supplicant, asserting time and again that he thought he might be making a mistake by turning east for his supplies. Even though he had an agreement with Moscow for the delivery of eighty MiG-15s, he wasn't about to end his game of playing the superpowers off each other. Nasser told Roosevelt that the Soviets had already sold him medium bombers, PT boats, and tanks, as well as the fighters and artillery pieces. Nasser claimed that the first shipment was expected in early October.[50]

Like Allen Dulles, Kermit Roosevelt believed that despite the arms deal, Nasser remained "our best hope." In that spirit, he recommended that Nasser make a public statement disavowing any aggressive intent. The CIA officer had not cleared this suggestion before the meeting with the State Department. Indeed, Allen Dulles also knew nothing about it and was later skeptical when Roosevelt reported the conversation to him. Dulles thought it wiser for Nasser to keep the weapons deal secret "in the hope that practical operations under [the] agreement will be less spectacular and possibly disappointing to [him].[51] Nasser liked the idea of a public statement regarding the Soviet deal and used Roosevelt to tell Washington that he wanted to meet with Foster Dulles soon to discuss the secretary of state's peace proposals.

Nasser let the Soviets know the next day that he would be making a speech to announce the Czech sale.[52] Saying nothing, of course, of the fact that the idea had come from the CIA, Nasser had his closest aide, Ali Sabri, tell the Soviet ambassador that in the speech he would explain Cairo's decision to seek weapons from the Soviet bloc as a reaction to the threat from Israel. In response, Ambassador Solod suggested that Nasser not raise Israel and instead focus on the perceived need to strengthen the Egyptian Army. Nasser said he agreed. But he also admitted that he had something else in mind. He would announce his readiness to begin negotiations on reducing Arab-Israeli tension. Direct negotiations with Israel were out of the question, but he hoped for negotiations through Secretary Dulles.

Nasser's comments reminded the Soviets of the work they still had to do with him. He remained very tempted by the American option. Solod discouraged him from working with either Dulles brother. He reminded the Egyptian leadership of how poor the secretary of state's plan was for Egypt. "If you feel it necessary to have an intermediary," Solod suggested to Ali Sabri, "it would be better to turn to the United Nations or to some kind of neutral government."[53]

That night at an arms fair in Cairo, amid a three-hour address, Nasser announced that his regime would buy weapons from the socialist world. Khrushchev's new policy of flexibility in the developing world had just scored its greatest victory.

■

"GUATEMALA, Mr. President, Guatemala." Having just heard the news, the pro-American Egyptian ambassador to the United States Dr. Ahmed Hussein, who was then visiting Cairo, ran excitedly into Nasser's office at 9:00 A.M. on September 28. All he could think of was the *Alfhelm* and what had then befallen Arbenz. As this story was later told, Nasser's reaction was pure resolve. "To hell with Guatemala," Nasser said.[54]

If indeed he ever said that, this was bluster to lift the morale of his inner circle. For Nasser himself worried about the consequences of his decision to buy from the East. He had tried to soften the blow on the eve of his announcement, but even his American advocates Roosevelt and Byroade had warned him that U.S. public opinion, at the very least, would react strongly to the news.

Although not yet trusting the Soviets, Nasser understood their utility and decided to move a little closer to them as he watched the Western reaction unfold. This movement took two forms. First, he decided that he would offer himself as a go-between in Moscow's efforts to seek diplomatic recognition from Saudi Arabia and Jordan. This was good politics because it meant he could monitor what Riyadh and Amman were up to and eventually reap the benefits of any deal that Moscow might strike with them. Egypt would thus become a power broker in the region. The other decision he made was to press the Soviets for some insurance: more military assistance, the existing orders faster, and possibly a deeper rhetorical commitment by Moscow to Egyptian security. Meanwhile he did not privately give up on Washington's reacting to the Czech deal with a massive deal of its own.

On September 29, only two days after his speech, Nasser asked to see

Solod immediately at his private apartment in Cairo.[55] The United States had just informed the Egyptians of the visit of a special representative, George Allen, who would probably wish to see Nasser as soon as he arrived on September 30. Nasser's sources told him that Allen would probably deliver an ultimatum to Egypt. If Egypt refused to break the deal with Czechoslovakia, the United States would encourage Israel to begin military action. Nasser warned the Soviets that Egypt would lose any war with Israel within ten days of its start.

Solod doubted the United States would deliver such an ultimatum. Nasser agreed. But he said that his decision to purchase weapons from the Soviet Union was "a turning point in history not only for Egypt, but for all Arab states. The struggle beginning now will be decisive for Egypt and the Arab world." The struggle against Western imperialism would be "sustained and hard." But Egypt had to go ahead. Nasser said that he had alerted the Egyptian Army to be prepared for "all possible surprises."

This discussion led to the big question: "What would the Soviet position be in the face of this U.S. threat to Egypt?" Nasser asked that Khrushchev be asked whether the USSR could supply the MiGs and the other elements of the September 12 agreement faster. "This would lift the morale of the army, which strongly supports the Czech arms purchase." Nasser stated that the army needed to see these weapons, "especially the planes and tanks."[56] To speed the delivery of aircraft, Nasser asked that they be flown directly to Cairo, by way of Albania or Yugoslavia.

Moscow responded quickly. The Soviet Union would not offer any military commitment to defend Egypt, but it promised political and moral support if the United States threatened Cairo. Solod conveyed this to Nasser directly on October 1.[57] Nasser listened closely to every word. Although he was disappointed, he tried not to show it. Other news proved even more disappointing. Moscow refused to send the planes faster to Cairo. The first shipment would come by boat at the end of October. To save face, Nasser responded that the provision of those planes any faster mattered less to him than making sure the number of Soviet military experts were kept down. Originally Moscow wanted to send 130; Nasser asked that this number be cut to 20.[58]

A few days later Moscow reported that it was prepared to begin additional arms negotiations. Although they would take place in Prague, the Egyptians would have to discuss the purchase of torpedo boats and submarines with the Poles. Nasser preferred to continue discussions with the Czechs, but the Soviets insisted on changing the intermediaries for discussing naval weapons. "Czechoslovakia is a land-locked country," Solod explained.[59] The

Soviets said the Poles would be in Prague, ready for talks, in a matter of days. The Soviets also agreed to Nasser's requirement that not more than twenty trainers and aircraft engineers be sent with the MiG-15s.

Nasser was going to get the weapons, but as he had promised the CIA's Kermit Roosevelt and U.S. Ambassador Byroade, he did not intend to become a captive of Moscow. He had no desire to turn his back on Western assistance, nor did he want Soviet economic assistance if he could help it, given the political dimensions of accepting aid from Moscow. He could not dispel his phobia over letting Soviet citizens enter Egypt. He did not want engineers and economists swarming over Cairo, writing plans by day and engaging in subversive activities with local Communists by night. He didn't even trust the military types that had to accompany the instruction booklets with the MiG-15s.[50]

Nasser also feared that the Soviets would betray him to seek détente with the West. In mid-October, as a new round of arms negotiations began in Prague, Nasser asked if the Soviet Union would trade its new relationship with Egypt for an agreement on Germany. He had heard that the USSR might add its signature to the hated Tripartite Declaration of 1950, the Western initiative to control the arms race in the entire Middle East. Referring to the forthcoming foreign ministers' talks in Geneva, Nasser asked Solod on October 18 if there was any truth to U.S. press reports that a deal was in the works.[61] When the Soviet ambassador said that this Anglo-American propaganda had no basis in fact, Nasser asked that the Soviets make a public statement disavowing any intention of joining the Tripartite Pact. He said this would be necessary to blunt U.S. efforts to discourage Syria and Saudi Arabia from buying weapons from the Soviet bloc. Nasser reported that the United States had just offered weapons, at no cost, to Lebanon. Nasser wanted the Soviets to start supplying other countries in the region. Worried that the Sudanese would otherwise look to the Anglo-Americans, he recommended that Moscow provide weapons to Khartoum. The Egyptian leader also asked Moscow to reconsider its policy toward the struggle for independence in French North Africa. Up to that point the Soviets had been passive, and Nasser, who admitted that Egypt was supplying the rebels, wanted Moscow to start sending material assistance to the Algerian and Tunisian freedom fighters.[62] The Soviets did not respond to any of these requests. For the moment the Soviet Union had penetrated enough into the Middle East.

■

On October 29, 1955, a week after the Soviet ship *Krasnodar* delivered the first cargo of heavy weapons to Egypt, disaster struck the Soviet Navy at home.[63] The 23,662-ton battleship *Novorossisk*, formerly the Italian *Giulio Cesare*, blew up mysteriously at anchor off the southern port of Sebastopol.[64] The incident killed 599 sailors. It was the worst Soviet naval disaster since the summer of 1941, when mines claimed the destroyers *Smely* and *Surovy* and the German Navy sank the destroyers *Gnevny*, *Tuchka*, *Taifun*, and *Tsiklon*.[65] For the Soviet leadership it was a wake-up call.

The tragedy provided Khrushchev with an opportunity to do some house-cleaning in the navy. "Kuznetsov is apparently a dangerous person," he said, blaming the navy chief Admiral N. Kuznetsov, for the disaster. "[And] he is worthless as a commander-in-chief."[66] Khrushchev and Kuznetsov had different dreams for the Soviet Navy. Kuznetsov wanted a navy that could project conventional force, similar in size and capability to the U.S. Navy. Khrushchev wanted to reduce the size of the navy, restricting future procurement to missile ships and submarines, rather than aircraft carriers. The disaster gave him the pretext to purge the navy and place his men in positions of authority.

It is remarkable that as Soviet ships were sending weapons to Egypt and there was pressure from Nasser to assist other countries in the region, Khrushchev was firing admirals in Moscow to ensure that the Soviet Navy remained small. There was no better proof that Khrushchev had only a political and economic strategy in 1955 for dominating the third world than the way he responded to the *Novorossisk* tragedy.

By 1957 the Soviet Navy would be cut from six hundred thousand to five hundred thousand men with 375 warships mothballed; orders for new cruisers were canceled, four uncompleted cruisers in Leningrad were scrapped.[67] In strategic terms, the most important decision involved the future of the Soviet aircraft carrier. Stalin had authorized the building of aircraft carriers in 1938 and 1950, but events had conspired against each attempt.[68] In 1941 the Nazis captured the Soviet shipyards where the carriers were supposed to be built. Stalin's death in 1953 effectively undermined the second push. Current plans had called for the construction of four carriers.[69] Believing that the Soviet Union could not afford aircraft carriers, Khrushchev now scrubbed them. Less interested in being able to project conventional force into regional conflicts, he was prepared to rely in future on the Soviet Union's ability to threaten the use of nuclear weapons.

The unfolding of the discussion of a new Soviet naval doctrine took place against the backdrop of yet another request for military assistance from Nasser. Claiming evidence of increased Israeli activities, in mid-November Cairo requested one hundred MiG-15s, instead of the eighty promised in

September, and five submarines instead of the two promised earlier in the fall.[70] The issue came up at a Presidium meeting on November 16.

■

THE CZECH ARMS deal had become a personal triumph for Khrushchev, and he led the discussion of how Moscow should respond to Nasser. "It would be a risk," he said to his colleagues.[71] But it was a risk worth taking. "We have pursued an independent policy [in the Middle East]," he said approvingly. The risk now was that Moscow might be dragged into a Middle Eastern war. There were rumors of an Israeli preemptive strike to prevent Egypt from absorbing the Soviet arms. Khrushchev opted for a controlled increase in weapons to Nasser. Submarines were out of the question, but the group approved increasing the number of MiG-15s to one hundred. Tanks were also not mentioned. Not long after Moscow would arrange the sale of the tanks Nasser had asked for in August, though not the top-of-the-line T-54s or even the T-34 from the early Cold War period. Egypt would receive the World War II–vintage Is-3. Nasser also eventually received a destroyer or two. "But submarines, we can't give him, not now," said Khrushchev.[72]

One area where Soviet-Egyptian relations did not improve involved the building of the Aswan Dam. During the lengthy visit of an Egyptian economic delegation in the winter of 1954, the head of the delegation, General Hussein Ragab, the deputy minister of defense, asked if the Soviets would help with a large construction project envisioned for the Upper Nile.[73] The Soviet response was vague but encouraging, and the delegation left, having negotiated the bases for a new trading relationship.[74] But by the summer it appeared Nasser had cold feet about asking for Soviet assistance.[75] In financial terms, Nasser was looking for at least one billion rubles or one hundred million Egyptian pounds in credit, which could be given in the form of materials, equipment, and the salaries of Soviet technicians. The Soviets responded cautiously. This seemed like a lot of money, and before they would provide any assistance, they wanted a five- to six-person team to visit the site near Aswan. However, the Egyptian government refused to discuss granting visas to these Soviet engineers. Moscow concluded that Nasser opposed allowing a Soviet team inside his country for fear they would engage in harmful revolutionary activity.

Nasser had always preferred getting Western assistance for the dam project, and after the Czech arms deal was made public, he again maneuvered to exploit Western anxieties about Khrushchev's gains in the Middle East. Knowing how the West would subordinate economic questions to Cold War strategic considerations, Nasser began an ingenious campaign in the fall of 1955 to convince the West that its worst fears about Soviet intentions and capabilities in Egypt were correct.[76] Animating this strategy was his decision to leverage Western fears of the spread of Soviet influence in the Middle East to obtain better terms for Western financing of the Aswan Dam project.

The centerpiece of this strategy was the Egyptian finance minister's November 1955 mission to the West. In London, Abdel Moneim el-Kaissouni told the British Foreign Office that his country could obtain financing from the Communist bloc if it was not satisfied with the offer made by the West. A few days later el-Kaissouni met with World Bank President Eugene Black and his deputy Gardner to discuss World Bank support for the Aswan Dam project.

Nasser timed his next salvo to strengthen el-Kaissouni's pitch. The day after the meeting with Black, Egyptian newspapers published a report based on a declaration by the minister for production, Hassan Ibrahim, that "Egypt received from Poland an offer to finance the high dam. The Egyptian government is studying this offer . . . no decision will be taken until the conclusion of the Minister of Finance's negotiations in the U.S." In the next few days el-Kaissouni met with high-level officials in the State Department. The strategy was working. Secretary of State Dulles announced to the National Security Council during the el-Kaissouni visit that "the Soviets had deliberately opened a new cold war front in the Near East."[77]

But the coup de grace came from London. On November 27, as the Egyptian finance minister was winding up his American tour, Anthony Eden sent a flash cable to Dwight Eisenhower, stating, "Poland will act as a stooge in this case as Czech did for the arms."[78] Eden asked for U.S. financial support to prevent Soviet involvement in constructing the dam. "I am convinced that on our joint success in excluding the Russians from this contract may depend the future of Africa." It would be a disaster for the West, Eden argued, if el-Kaissouni and Samir Hilmy, secretary-general of the High Dam Board, left the United States without conviction that an agreement would be reached.

This was all nonsense. Poland, neither on its own nor on behalf of the Soviet Union, had made no offer of assistance. Without access to Egyptian materials it is unclear to what extent the rumors and false intelligence that flowed to the American and British governments in the fall of 1955 were inspired by Egypt. Eden's warning stemmed from intelligence gathered by an allegedly highly placed British intelligence agent in Cairo, code-named Lucky Break. It seems likely that this was an Egyptian double agent, who supplied deception to trick the British into playing this helpful role in pushing the Americans.[79]

Regardless of the extent of the Egyptian cloak-and-dagger activity, Nasser caught both President Eisenhower and Prime Minister Eden in his trap. It is rare in international history to see cause and effect drawn so clearly. Eden's communiqué had an immediate effect. The next day, November 28, 1955, Eisenhower overcame his advisers' doubts about Nasser and the Aswan Dam, especially those of his Treasury secretary, George Humphrey, and decided to commit the United States to the project. Having no sense of its magnitude, he had not yet decided how much of a commitment to make. But Undersecretary of State Herbert Hoover recommended sending Robert Anderson, a well-respected Texas banker and former deputy secretary of defense, to Cairo to work with Nasser.

In Moscow these events were followed with amusement and slight bewilderment. The Kremlin cabled its ambassador in Cairo, Daniel Solod, to be sure he had never said to anyone that the Soviet bloc intended to participate in building the dam. Solod assured his bosses that he had said nothing and that there was no truth to these assertions.[80] In Moscow the Foreign Ministry decided that Nasser had planted this information to drive a better deal with the West.

The West, for its part, did not consider the possibility that it had been duped by Nasser. Fearful that it was competing with Moscow on the project, the Eisenhower administration on December 1 approved a financial assistance package for it. It was assumed the project would take ten years. The administration decided to support a World Bank loan of $200 million with an additional $200 million from the United States and Great Britain, 80 percent of which would come from Washington. Two weeks later the United States published an official communiqué on the el-Kaissouni visit, which announced U.S. support for the Aswan Dam project. As he boarded the flight from London to Cairo, el-Kaissouni confirmed that the West had committed $420 million to the $960 million cost of the construction of the high dam. Nasser's gambit seemed to have worked.

■

THE CULMINATION of Khrushchev's opening to the third world in 1955 was his five-week, three-nation tour of South Asia with Nikolai Bulganin in late November and December. His goal was less to educate himself about these areas, though he wished to learn about these countries and their populations, than to improve the standing of the Soviet Union there.

In India, Burma, and Afghanistan, Khrushchev encountered countries with different regional and cultural needs. In each case, he saw the opportunity to create strong relations. India was important to the Soviet strategy to increase its influence in the developing world. Khrushchev viewed India thorough an ideological lens, one that inspired him to tell his colleagues in the Kremlin that the situation in India was "Kerensky-like."[81] The implication was that Jawaharlal Nehru was the interim bourgeois leader of a state headed for socialism, the historical role filled by Aleksandr Kerensky in Russia in 1917.

Although he was convinced that India was in a prerevolutionary condition, Khrushchev was in no hurry to see the Nehru era end. He was disappointed by the work of the Indian Communist Party. Moscow's closest allies in the subcontinent were guilty of taking a hard-line sectarian approach to the Nehru government, stressing the overthrow of the elected regime instead of exploiting Nehru's commitment to industrialization, public education, and state property to form an alliance among the population. Flipping through Indian Communist magazines during the trip, Khrushchev found them unappealing and inflexible.[82]

Khrushchev did not want local Communist parties to impede the improvement of relations between the Soviet Union and these regimes. In particular he had high hopes for building very strong relations with India. In mid-December Khrushchev decided that he and Bulganin should return there before heading home to Moscow. The original travel plans had the men ending their tour in Afghanistan. Khrushchev, however, wanted to give a major foreign policy address that would demonstrate to the Indians that he shared some of their priorities in foreign policy. Characteristic of Khrushchev, he did so without seeking any staff support from the Foreign Ministry or even the Central Committee. It was his judgment that Moscow needed to go on record in support of the Indian claims to Kashmir. He also wished to express Soviet approval for the recovery of Portuguese Goa, one of the tiny remnants of the Portuguese Empire located on the west coast of India.

India was not the only place where Khrushchev believed the Soviet Union could make a profitable political investment. When the Burmese leader U Nu had visited Moscow earlier in the year, he had commented on the comfort of the Il-14s that the Russians had lent him for the trip. Khrushchev decided to illustrate his commitment to better relations by making a gift of a plane. Meanwhile Khrushchev and Bulganin intended making an even larger investment in better relations with Mohammed Daoud, the prime minister of Afghanistan.

Throughout the trip the two Soviet leaders kept in contact with the Presidium by cable. During the negotiations with the Afghans the travelers had sent an urgent cable requesting a policy decision on selling arms to this state. Afghanistan in 1955 was a feudal monarchy with no Communist Party to speak of, let alone a progressive united front. The motivation behind the offer was strategic. Khrushchev wanted to build up his relations in the third world and also wanted an additional ally on the Soviet border. Afghanistan fitted both objectives. The recent happy experience with Egypt gave reason to believe that the entire process could proceed smoothly.

In Moscow, however, Kaganovich and Molotov reacted badly to the idea of giving military assistance to a government that besides being non-Communist was a traditional monarchy with no pretense to progressivism. "This sets a precedent," said Kaganovich, fearing that the Soviets would find themselves inundated with requests for aid.[83]

Mikoyan, who chaired the meeting, joined Malenkov in favor of Khrushchev's evident desire to consummate the deal. Neither man made an ideological case for supporting these governments. Their rationale was pure realism: "We should work to attract Afghanistan to our side," said Malenkov. And Mikoyan emphasized the general utility of supporting developing countries: "We will have to render assistance to some states, if we wish to enter into more serious competition with the USA. From the point of view of state interests, it is necessary to render assistance." Malenkov and Mikoyan carried the day for the Khrushchev forces. In mid-December the Soviet government decided to offer Afghanistan a hundred-million-dollar aid package. When Khrushchev got back, he made sure that it included a shipment of arms.[84]

Returning home on December 21, Khrushchev had much to show for his efforts in the third world. Since February the Soviet government had reached trade agreements with Indonesia, India, Burma, Afghanistan, Egypt, and Syria. Of those countries, Egypt, Syria, and Afghanistan were to be the recipients of military as well as economic aid.

These achievements in the developing world capped a remarkable year for Khrushchev. Since January he had supplanted both Malenkov and Molotov, and Soviet foreign policy reflected his priorities. Moscow had reestablished good relations with Yugoslavia, signed a peace treaty with Austria, and opened the diplomatic door to the Federal Republic of Germany. John Foster Dulles's efforts to force damaging Soviet concessions on the German question had failed, with the initiative shifting to Moscow in the pursuit of détente and disarmament. In the months to come, however, Khrushchev came to learn that he could not always control international events as easily as he had in 1955. The initiative might not always stay with him.

CHAPTER 4

SUEZ

I N T H E D I P L O M A T I C revolution that Khrushchev started in 1955, crises or moments of international tension were not expected to be useful for achieving Soviet goals. By the summer of 1956 Gamal Abdel Nasser had set in motion a series of events that tested Nikita Khrushchev's new foreign policy and confronted the Kremlin with its first international crisis since the Korean War. Khrushchev ultimately derived a different, and more dangerous, lesson from surprises in the Middle East.

Nasser and his Egyptian followers had discussed the idea of nationalizing the Suez Canal for a number of years. Although the canal was wholly within Egyptian territory, it was controlled by European shareholders in the Universal Suez Marine Canal Company (Suez Canal Company) under a ninety-nine-year lease that came into effect in 1869. The revolutionaries in the Egyptian Army, the self-named Free Officers, who had overthrown King Farouk in 1952, had vowed to break the lease, which symbolized for them a huge colonial chain around Egypt's neck. But Nasser only decided on July 21, after what one confidant recalled as a long and sleepless night, to make 1956 the year that the lease would finally be broken.[1] The decision was in large part a reaction to the U.S. government's announcement on July 19 that it would not finance Nasser's pet public works project, the huge Aswan High Dam. The decision both surprised and humiliated the Egyptian president, who had expected to reach a deal with Washington.

For six months Nasser had played a high-stakes game with Western bankers and finance ministers to secure funding for the dam project. He disliked the World Bank's financial reporting requirements and worried about other constraints that the United States and the United Kingdom, which was also a party to the dam-financing negotiations, might be able to impose. With these hesitations in mind, Nasser kept pushing for better terms from the West. The Soviets had refused to make a serious offer to help Egypt built the

dam unless Nasser accepted visits from East German and Russian technicians, and in 1956 he considered these terms even more perilous than those
posed by the World Bank, the United States, and Great Britain. In May 1956,
having lost his patience, Nasser decided to recognize the People's Republic of
China in an attempt to increase pressure on the West to come up with a plan
to finance the dam that he could accept. It had been a miscalculation. Nasser
managed only to incur the wrath of the anti-Communist bloc in the U.S.
Congress, which would have had to approve any foreign aid package to Egypt.
Unsure of Nasser's motives and lacking sufficient congressional support for a
massive public works project that would glorify Nasser's regime, the administration decided to back away.[2]

Nasser not only was now eager to strike back at the West with a powerful
gesture but also found himself in need of a way to bring additional hard currency into the state treasury so that he could proceed with the dam on his
own. By agreement with the canal company, Egypt already received a percentage of the Suez tolls. Nationalizing the canal would provide Egypt with all of
the revenue generated by the canal. Nasser decided to announce the nationalization on July 26.

"[T]he West will not be silent," Nasser wrote in a longhand note to himself
as he wrestled with the risks of this move. "Most probably, we will be faced
with military threats that could turn into an actual war, if we don't use our
resources with caution."[3] The British government and a group of middle-class
French citizens were the principal shareholders in the canal. Besides putting
their property rights at risk, the nationalization would likely be interpreted by
the Europeans as a threat to their strategic interests. Of the 122 million tons of
cargo shipped through the canal each year, more than 60 percent was oil.
Indeed, two-thirds of all the oil imported by Europe came via Suez. In calculating the odds of war, Nasser assumed that the British rather than the French
were the more likely to initiate a rash military response. The canal was the
jugular vein that fed Britain's Asian colonies.[4]

Nasser took pains to restrict the number of people who would know about
his plan before he was ready to announce it publicly. Besides his inner circle,
Nasser informed a small group of Egyptian military officers whose job it
would be to occupy the headquarters of the Suez Canal Company in Port Said
after the announcement. The officers were instructed to listen to Nasser's
speech on the radio and seize the building the moment he referred by name
to Ferdinand de Lesseps, the French visionary who had built the canal.

Nasser only brought his cabinet into his confidence a matter of hours
before he spoke. The news stunned the assembled ministers, some of whom

immediately tried to persuade him not to go through with the plan for fear of British and French reprisals.[5] Nasser assured them that he had already calculated the risks and that the British prime minister, Anthony Eden, the key player on the European side, would be too weak-willed to go to war.[6]

After the meeting broke up, Nasser gave his speech, which was broadcast from Alexandria to millions listening on radios throughout Egypt and the Arab world. He spoke with confidence, and there was no masking the bitterness in his voice. He cited every slight ever visited upon the Egyptian people in the modern era. When he arrived at the portion of his speech that railed at foreign financiers, especially the World Bank president Eugene Black, Nasser uttered the command: "I started to look at Mr. Black, who was sitting on a chair, and I saw him in my imagination as *Ferdinand de Lesseps*." At that moment three hundred miles away in Port Said Egyptian commandos occupied the headquarters of the canal company. As this action was taking place, Nasser revealed to his listeners what he had just ordered, "Today, O citizens, the Suez Canal Company has been nationalized."[7] In a bid to take a little of the sting out of this announcement for his Western audience, Nasser promised compensation for the shareholders.[8]

■

NIKITA KHRUSHCHEV was as surprised as Nasser's Arab audience when he learned of the nationalization of the Suez Canal. Moscow had not received any advance warning from the Egyptians. Barely five weeks earlier Molotov's replacement as Soviet foreign minister, Dmitri Shepilov, had been Nasser's guest in Cairo, and though there had been discussions of arms deliveries and economic assistance, the Egyptian president had not alluded in any way to the possibility that he would take on the Western powers in 1956. Nasser was expected to make his first trip to the Soviet Union in August, and the Egyptians had not even suggested Suez as an agenda item.[9]

At the time of Shepilov's visit in June Nasser still believed that he could come to an arrangement with the United States over the financing of the Aswan Dam and had not yet decided to seize the canal. But because the official Egyptian silence had continued even after Nasser had changed his mind, the Soviets were right to believe they had been actively deceived. On the morning before Nasser's speech, Egypt's foreign minister, Mohammed Fawzi, had visited the Soviet ambassador in Cairo and said nothing about the Suez Canal. He had talked instead about the dam project and made the strange request that Moscow pretend that the Soviet Union would help Cairo pay for it.[10] In the week following the U.S. announcement on July 19 that it would not help Nasser build the dam, rumors had swirled in Cairo that Moscow intended to pick up the slack.[11] These rumors were untrue—Moscow remained as dubious of the Aswan project as ever—and its Foreign Ministry spokesmen had immediately denied there was any deal. Through Fawzi, Nasser asked the Kremlin to stop denying these rumors. Although Fawzi had not hinted at any of this, it later became clear to the Soviets that as Nasser prepared to seize the canal, he needed to use Moscow as political cover. He neither wanted the Western powers nor the Egyptian people to suspect that he was nationalizing the canal out of weakness, not strength.

Whatever Nasser's motives for keeping Khrushchev in the dark, his announcement caught the Soviets flatfooted. The Kremlin had no policy prepared for what to do if Egypt took the canal and had hoped not to need one. Khrushchev had made the Kremlin's relationship with Nasser the centerpiece of his strategy of building alliances in the third world and of staking a claim to influence in the Middle East. However, he had not intended to support Nasser's dreams of establishing Egyptian hegemony throughout the region. To discourage any impression both in the West and in Cairo that it did, Moscow had ever since been counseling caution to the Egyptians. Indeed one of Shepilov's objectives in June had been to reinforce the message that Cairo should tread carefully in its foreign policy. Egyptian requests for the most modern Soviet weaponry, the T-54 tank and the MiG-19 jet fighters, suggested to Moscow that Cairo might have aggressive intentions toward Israel. "It is especially important now," the Soviet foreign minister had advised Nasser's minister of war, Marshal Abdel Hakim Amer, "not to allow the imperialists to provoke a military conflict between Arabs and Israelis, which the imperialists would hope to use to improve their position in the Near East."[12] Nasser's decision to nationalize the canal ran completely counter to Moscow's advice.

As far as the Kremlin was concerned, the decision was also exceptionally ill timed. The last thing Moscow needed in July 1956 was another problem. That summer Khrushchev and his colleagues were absorbed by events in Eastern Europe for which Khrushchev felt some responsibility.

Five months earlier, in a keynote address to nearly fifteen hundred Communist leaders from fifty-six countries at the Twentieth Party Congress, Khrushchev had decried Stalin's crimes and launched a purge of Stalinism. "Stalin was devoted to the cause of socialism, but in a barbaric way," he told members of the Presidium before the congress.[13] "He ruined the Party. He was not a Marxist. He erased all that is holy in a human being. He bent everything to his caprices."

The Presidium had debated for two months before deciding to proceed with this speech. Khrushchev vacillated over how critical he should be of Stalin. "We should think carefully about the wording," noted Khrushchev's ally Dmitri Shepilov, echoing his concerns, "not to cause harm."[14] The then Soviet foreign minister, Vyacheslav Molotov, had opposed any attack on Stalin, but even the Presidium's reformers, Khrushchev among them, worried that anti-Communists might try to use these criticisms to undermine the legitimacy of the Soviet bloc. As a result, Khrushchev hoped to restrict knowledge of the speech only to party leaders in the socialist world.

By May, partly thanks to the Eisenhower administration, which acquired a copy from Israeli intelligence and gave it to the *New York Times*, the actual speech was in newspapers around the world and was causing widespread instability in the Kremlin's European empire. What had started out as top-down reform in the Soviet Union, announced by Khrushchev himself, had been transformed by the peculiar conditions in Eastern Europe into a grassroots push for more political freedom and democracy. The movement spread even faster because of the inability of the leaders in these countries, many of whom had been chosen by Stalin, to manage the process that Khrushchev had unleashed. In the first weeks after the Twentieth Party Congress Stalinists in Moscow's client states in Eastern Europe tried vainly to keep a lid on these reformist pressures.

In the summer of 1956 Poland appeared to be closest to a political explosion. Polish leader Edward Ochab, who had described the effect of Khrushchev's secret speech as "like being hit over the head with a hammer," was proving himself to be especially inept at handling the new political environment.[15] In late June the Polish government had overreacted to a demonstration for "Bread and Freedom" in Poznan. Fifty-six workers died and more than three hundred were wounded in clashes with Polish troops.

The situation seemed nearly as volatile in Hungary, where the struggle for reform was taking place within the Communist Party itself. In June Soviet Presidium member Mikhail Suslov had been sent to Budapest to plead for party unity. When that didn't reduce political tensions, Presidium member Anastas Mikoyan followed in July with instructions to force a wholesale leadership change in the country.[16]

■

THE KREMLIN got its first official word from an Egyptian on its new Middle Eastern problem the morning after the nationalization.[17] The Egyptian ambassador in Moscow, Mohammed el-Kouni, painted the situation in alarming colors for the Soviets. "At the moment all [the Western powers] are mobilizing against us," he explained to Foreign Minister Shepilov.[18] Cairo assumed that the war would begin with Israel, though Egypt expected its ultimate enemy would be Great Britain. "Once Israel initiates action from her side," said the ambassador, "the British will embrace her." El-Kouni did not specify what form that embrace would take, but he made clear the further assumption that the British would receive covert assistance from the United States. Referring to the Central Intelligence Agency's role in the overthrow of the Iranian nationalist leader Mohammed Mossadeq in 1953, he warned that "in the past the USA has propagated the illusion that it could accomplish in Egypt what it did in Iran."

Despite these fears, Cairo limited itself to asking the Russians for moral support. "If you [gave this]," el-Kouni explained, "then you would be helping not simply the Egyptian people; but other Arab countries as well who are also waiting for this support." Shepilov, who shared Khrushchev's passion for broadening ties with the third world, promised to forward el-Kouni's suggestions to the Kremlin immediately. Despite the lack of any formal instructions on this point, Shepilov felt confident in adding that "the Soviet government would do all that was necessary so that the measures taken by the Egyptian government in nationalizing the Suez Canal would not lead to unnecessary difficulties for her." This was the answer that Nasser had hoped to receive.

The urgent message from the Egyptian government had no discernible effect on the Kremlin. Khrushchev did not call an emergency meeting of the Presidium to discuss Egyptian concerns, nor were Soviet forces in the southwestern republics of the Soviet Union or in Bulgaria, the closest satellite state to Egypt, put on alert. There was no sense of crisis or imminent confrontation in the Soviet capital. Instead a very comfortable assumption took hold that the Western powers would reluctantly, but inevitably, accept the change at Suez as yet another sign of decolonization.

▪

BRITISH PRIME MINISTER Anthony Eden learned of the nationalization of the Suez Canal late in the evening of July 26, as he was playing host at a state dinner for King Faisal of Iraq and Iraqi Prime Minister Nuri al-Said. Nuri, who was as pro-Western as any Arab leader in the 1950s, spoke for many in the room when he privately told the British foreign secretary, Selwyn Lloyd, "You have only one course of action open and that is to hit, hit now, and hit hard. . . . If [Nasser] is left alone, he will finish all of us."[19] Eden hardly needed any tutoring from the Iraqis on Nasser. He considered himself an expert on the Middle East and had long since become a hawk on Anglo-Egyptian relations. In Eden's eyes Nasser was the "Muslim Mussolini," a vainglorious man who was intent on expansion at the expense of British interests.[20] In 1938

Eden had resigned from the Chamberlain government over appeasement of Italy's flamboyant Fascist dictator, Benito Mussolini, and he was not about to appease Nasser over the Suez Canal.

There was the sting of recent lessons behind Eden's resolve. In recent years Nasser had become a delicate political problem for the British prime minister. In 1954, when he was Churchill's foreign secretary, Eden had taken a risk and negotiated the British military pullout from its base near the canal over the objections of the diehard imperialists along the back benches of his conservative government. From that point on his opponents in the British Conservative Party jumped on Nasser's every move as proof that Eden had misjudged him.[21] As Eden's biographer Robert Rhodes James concludes, this political vulnerability did not lead Eden to seek the approval of the old-line imperialist, but it did make him see Nasser's actions as personal betrayals.[22] The Soviet arms deal in September 1955 had been a shock to Eden. Jordan's decision to fire the British commander of King Hussein's army a few months later, an act associated with Nasser's meddling in the affairs of other Arab countries, came as yet another blow to Eden's policy in the Middle East. The nationalization of the Suez Canal was the last straw.

Eden thought he had no choice but to deal swiftly and harshly with the Egyptian leader. Nasser "stands on our windpipe," he declared to an emergency session of his inner circle that convened after the Iraqis and the other dinner guests had left.[23] Still wearing his formal white tie from the state dinner, the prime minister projected confidence and decisiveness. He had invited the British chiefs of staff as well as the local representatives of his closest foreign allies, the French ambassador and the U.S. chargé d'affaires, to this late-night session to hear his plans. He hoped that the French and the Americans would participate in a coordinated response to Nasser's challenge.

The prime minister was determined to force a reversal of the nationalization. His immediate objective was to shut down the canal and deny Egypt any financial gain. The British subjects who worked for the Suez Canal Company would be encouraged to stay away from their jobs, and he hoped that other nationals would also compel their citizens to walk off the job. Ultimately Eden assumed that the major users of the canal, but not including the Soviets or the Egyptians themselves, would need to meet to discuss how to formally take the canal away from Nasser. Eden did not mince words about what "taking away" the canal might entail. In front of the French and American representatives, he instructed his military chiefs to produce as soon as possible a report on what forces would be needed to retake the canal and how the operation could be implemented.[24]

Eden's belligerence was matched in Paris, where the French government interpreted Nasser's action as yet another blow to French prestige. Since World War II the leaders of the Fourth Republic had witnessed the loss of the Saar, an occupied German province, to West Germany in a plebiscite and German rearmament; the defeat in Indochina; and most recently the start of a bloody civil war in Algeria, the North African colony that was so tightly linked to Paris that it was a fully integrated *departement* of the country. Although the new Socialist prime minister, Guy Mollet, had called the struggle in Algeria "an imbecilic war leading nowhere," he, like the rest of the French political class in 1956, was in no mood to cut and run from North Africa.[25]

The hatred for Nasser was more a product of this political commitment to Algeria than of the French financial investment in the Suez Canal.[26] The Egyptians were arming the Algerian rebels and had offered strong rhetorical support. Many French politicians and military officers believed that the road to victory in Algiers led through Cairo. Many were also convinced that Nasser was not acting alone. The French had seen the machinations of the Kremlin behind their defeat in Vietnam in 1954, and now they considered Khrushchev Nasser's chief inspiration. "It is virtually against France, in effect," noted the chief of the French General Staff, General Paul Ely, "that the Soviet effort to destabilize the Western World is being applied to the maximum."[27]

Once word of Eden's late-night meeting reached Paris, the French rushed to begin planning for joint military action. On July 27 the Mollet government formally decided to use force, if necessary, to break Egyptian control of the canal. This was followed the very next day by the visit to London of a French military representative, Admiral Henri Nomy, with the message that France was absolutely determined to join the British in acting militarily against Egypt as soon as possible.[28] An immediate attack was not feasible. Between them the British and the French had less than one airborne division in the Middle East, while British estimates assumed it would take at least three divisions to capture and hold the canal.[29] A successful attack would require the movement of forces to the eastern Mediterranean. France offered to redeploy some of its forces in Algeria for this operation but understood that even more were required. On its own initiative, Paris began discussions with the Israelis to increase the firepower available for the strike.[30]

▪

NASSER DID NOT evoke the same passions in the Eisenhower administration as he did on the other side of the Atlantic. President Eisenhower and his secretary of state, Foster Dulles, the two principal architects of U.S. foreign policy, mistrusted Nasser but did not feel threatened by him. Unlike the French or the British, the Americans viewed the Nasser problem almost entirely through the lens of their struggle with the Soviet Union. Since April 1956 Washington had undertaken a series of measures, the most dramatic of which was the refusal to help with the Aswan Dam, to break Nasser of his seeming fondness for Khrushchev. "The primary purpose," wrote Dulles, "would be to let Colonel Nasser realize that he cannot cooperate as he is doing with the Soviet Union and at the same time enjoy most-favored-nation treatment by the US."[31] It was administration policy to give Nasser a second or third chance, "to avoid any open break which would throw Nasser irrevocably into a Soviet satellite status and we would want to leave Nasser a bridge back to good relations with the West if he so desires."[32]

Nasser's sudden nationalization of the canal suggested that the Egyptian leader might be irredeemable, but neither Eisenhower nor Dulles was quick to make up his mind. The legal team at the State Department concluded that Egypt was acting well within its rights in expropriating the canal, and the president agreed. "The inherent right of any sovereign nation to exercise the power of eminent domain within its own territory could scarcely be doubted," Eisenhower later recalled, "provided that just compensation were paid to the owners of the property so expropriated."[33] The question mark for Eisenhower was what Nasser planned to do with the canal now that he had it. Would he guarantee that the canal and its ports would remain open to all merchant ships? This was still unclear in late July. Equally uncertain to Eisenhower and Dulles was whether the nationalization was an end in itself or the first step in a series of blows designed by Nasser to undermine the Western position in the Middle East and perhaps to help the Soviets gain ground. Neither man was prepared to accept the French belief that the seizure of the canal was akin to Nazi Germany's remilitarization of the Rhineland in 1936, which turned out to be the first step in Hitler's bid for hegemony. But Eisenhower wanted to keep his options open. Should Nasser not be able to run the canal and refuse internationalization, then the United States would have to consider military action.[34]

In the meantime Eisenhower believed that the worst thing the United States could do was to rush into military discussions with the British and the French. He and Dulles agreed that the solution had to come from a much broader group of states, it would have to involve diplomacy, and any decision to use force would have to await further developments in the Middle East. Domestic politics reinforced Eisenhower's characteristic caution. It was a presidential election year in the United States—election day was November

6—and the president saw no possible political advantage from a Mideast war. An American delegation left the day after the nationalization for London to urge the British to relegate military intervention "to the background."[35]

▪

AUGUST 1 was a great day for Nikita Khrushchev. He was the star of the dedication ceremony for Moscow's Lenin Stadium, the largest sports facility in Europe and one of the largest in the world. He decided to use this occasion to go on record in support of Nasser and Egypt. Since Shepilov's meeting with the Egyptian ambassador, Moscow had provided the requested rhetorical support.[36] The Soviet government used *Pravda* to indicate its recognition of Nasser's right to nationalize the canal, and the newspaper had reprinted the text of Nasser's Alexandria speech on July 28. But there was nothing to suggest that Moscow considered the Suez matter to be a crisis demanding a broad political and diplomatic campaign. No private communiqués were sent from Moscow to Cairo, and Khrushchev had said nothing publicly.

Moscow's initial response had not pleased Nasser, who had expected more from the Soviets. Earlier on August 1 the Egyptian ambassador had delivered a message from Nasser to Khrushchev in which Nasser had pledged to keep the canal open and to provide "free use" by all countries.[37] It seemed that Cairo feared that the Soviet Union's low-key response reflected some skepticism over Nasser's willingness to insulate the canal from politics. There is no evidence that Moscow had raised this matter with Cairo, but Nasser wished to be sure that Khrushchev had no doubts on that score. In handing over the message, his representative in Moscow assured the Russians that Egypt was making every effort "not to give these powers [Britain, France, and the United States] a way or justification to interfere in Egypt's internal affairs."[38]

Cheered on by tens of thousands of Soviet citizens, Khrushchev took the opportunity of the speech to slip in some comments about the developing Suez situation in an effort to calm Nasser. "Nationalization of the Suez Canal," said Khrushchev, "was . . . within the competence of a sovereign government like the Egyptian government." Cautioning the French and the British not to overreact, Khrushchev added: "It must be emphasized Egypt has committed herself to respect free navigation in the Suez Canal and pay compensation to shareholders of the company. Therefore," he concluded, "it is necessary to evaluate this act calmly, soberly considering the new situation and the spirit of the times."[39]

Khrushchev resisted the temptation to grandstand or threaten. Instead he publicly reminded Britain of its successful policy of disengagement in India,

Burma, and, until recently, Egypt itself. And if this were not evidence enough of Moscow's cautious line in this developing situation, Khrushchev identified the Soviet Union as no less an interested party in Egypt's management of the canal. "The Soviet Union, being directly interested in maintenance of free navigation of the Suez Canal and considering the declaration of the Egyptian government that the Suez Canal will be free for all, concludes there is no basis for this display of nervousness and distress in this connection."[40]

Having an incomplete understanding of what was happening in the Western capitals, Khrushchev did not share the nervousness of his Egyptian ally and believed these words to be enough. "We have no evidence," a Foreign Ministry official told the Egyptian ambassador on the day of Khrushchev's speech, "that the Western powers are preparing a military intervention."[41] Soviet intelligence had not detected the bellicose discussions in Paris and London. However, the KGB provided the Kremlin leadership with an interesting window through which to watch how the United States reacted to the developing situation in the Middle East. From at least April 1956, the Soviet had so thoroughly bugged the U.S. Embassy in Moscow that the Kremlin could make copies of virtually every telegraphic message it sent or received.[42] These stolen confidential messages confirmed for the Soviets that the United States was not taking a confrontational position on Suez, and Khrushchev and the Kremlin leadership assumed that no Western military action could take place against Egypt without U.S. participation. Khrushchev did not yet know this, but this rich source of top secret information on U.S. policy toward the Soviet Union ultimately proved an unhelpful guide to developments in the Middle East.

Because of its sensitivity, the Kremlin merely hinted to the Egyptians the source of its confidence. Cairo was told not to discount the possibility that the United States would play a peaceful role in Egypt's dispute with the Western Europeans. "The United States follows a somewhat different line on the Suez question," a Soviet official explained to the Egyptian ambassador.[43] In an effort to be reassuring, Moscow put forward the theory that economic reasons would prevent Washington from embracing British or French extremism. "U.S. oil companies understand," the Soviet official continued, "that there are enormous oil reserves in the Middle East and that any extreme measures taken against Egypt would be bad considering the mood of the Arabs is very fixed."[44]

■

THE MESSAGE that came back from London at the end of July after the U.S. delegation had met with British officials was not what Eisenhower had wanted. The British government and especially Eden were determined "to

drive Nasser out of Egypt."[45] Not only did London seek to reverse the nationalization, but overthrowing Nasser was the principal goal of British action. The
Americans were told that the British had begun planning the invasion of
Egypt, which would take six weeks to set up. To lend some legitimacy to the
attack, the British were planning a conference of the key Western users of the
canal to present Nasser with an ultimatum he could be expected to refuse.

The news from London dismayed the U.S. president. Eisenhower
assumed the Egyptians could be defeated easily but then worried about the
reaction across the Arab world to a British attack before there was any serious
effort at negotiating with Nasser. He foresaw sabotaged pipelines and terrorist attacks against British troops and other Western targets. "The British,"
Eisenhower told his senior advisers, "were out of date in thinking of this as a
mode of action in the present circumstances."[46]

Concerned that his British allies were seriously underestimating the consequences of a war, Eisenhower sent the secretary of state to London with a
proposal for a diplomatic solution. Dulles, who arrived on August 1, brought
an American proposal designed to begin the process of establishing international management of the canal. Instead of a bogus conference, Washington
suggested bringing together all twenty-four original signatories and their successor states to the seventy-year-old international treaty that governed use of
the Suez Canal. In 1888 the principal great powers—Russia, Austria-Hungary,
Great Britain, France, and Germany—had met in Constantinople (now
Istanbul) to draft an agreement to ensure the free use of this strategic water-
way. The British had closed the canal in World War II, but since the war Egypt
had been the principal violator of the Constantinople Convention by its
refusal to allow Israeli ships to traverse the canal.

While assuring the British that it was the U.S. intention to see Nasser weakened and the nationalization undermined, Dulles refused to commit the
United States to any military planning or even to the military option.[47]
Reflecting his differences with Eisenhower, Dulles also explained that the
administration shared the ultimate goal of removing Nasser, but he believed
this could be achieved diplomatically and through the skillful use of world public opinion. The French and the British agreed to the proposed conference, and
Dulles assured them that it would approve a set of resolutions designed to force
Nasser to turn administration of the canal over to an international board that
would set tolls, undertake proper maintenance of the canal, and ensure open
access to all countries. Egypt would be promised a percentage of the tolls, but
its share would be determined by the international board.

Despite his usual hard-line approach to the Kremlin, Dulles believed that the Soviets, whose predecessor government had signed the Constantinople Convention, would have to be invited to this conference; otherwise it would lack all legitimacy. He assured the British and French that the invitation would not imply real consultation or cooperation. The conference could be organized, he explained, so as to "insulate the Russians."[48] The powers would go into the conference assuming what they expected to get out of it, and the Soviets would have no choice but to accept or stay in the minority. The United States also believed that Egypt would have to be invited.

On August 2, Great Britain, France, and the United States jointly issued a statement proposing a conference of all parties to the Constantinople Convention and other nations with substantial interest in the maritime trade carried through the canal. The meeting would begin in London on August 16.

Although temporarily slowed by Washington's insistence at exploring diplomatic options, Eden instructed his military planners to continue preparing for an attack on Egypt. Initially the British military chiefs had planned a September 15 attack after an August 1 ultimatum. Eden wanted them to understand that the London Conference was merely going to alter the timetable of the ultimatum. The prime minister still expected military action in September.[49] He assumed—and hoped—Nasser would reject the conference's demands.

▪

THE FORMAL INVITATION to the London Conference, which the Soviets received on August 3, had the effect of finally attracting serious attention in the Kremlin to the situation in the Middle East. It also prompted Nasser to make his first significant demand of the Kremlin since the nationalization speech. Hours before the Presidium met to discuss what to do about the invitation, Nasser sent word through the Soviet Embassy in Cairo that he hoped the Soviets would refuse to attend. Egypt had no intention of participating in any conference organized, sponsored, or otherwise choreographed by the British and hoped that its close ally the Soviet Union would act the same way.[50] If there had to be an international discussion, Nasser preferred that it be held at the United Nations.

"Maybe Nasser is right," Khrushchev announced to his Kremlin colleagues at their first formal discussion of the Suez question since July 26. "Who is choosing the participants?" He then answered his own question: "England, France, and the USA. We shouldn't go to this. He's right."[51] He also agreed with Nasser that the General Assembly of the United Nations would be a better venue for discussing the nationalization of the canal. Khrushchev wanted to redefine the question, to broaden it, so that Egypt would no longer be the center of attention. The debate should be "not only about the Suez Canal but on other canals and straits."

Khrushchev assumed that the London Conference could be safely boycotted without jeopardizing Egypt. So long as the issue did not become a test of wills between the superpowers, Khrushchev was confident it could be resolved diplomatically at the United Nations. Especially encouraging to him was the evidence that the United States seemed to be acting as a check on the ambitions of its allies. In the meantime Khrushchev believed the Soviet Union had to show self-restraint. On his desk were proposals for a new nuclear test series. He suggested to his colleagues in the Kremlin that these tests be postponed until international tensions had subsided.[52] Khrushchev also wanted Cairo to be especially cautious. The Soviet ambassador was to advise Nasser to reaffirm in public Egyptian neutrality in the Cold War and to resist denouncing the 1954 Suez Base agreement with London, even though it provided for British intervention in the canal in an emergency.[53]

Over the next two days, however, Moscow's confidence in this policy of self-restraint and disengagement eroded slightly. News of what seemed to be British and French preparations for war focused Khrushchev on the need for the Soviet Union to press for diplomatic action. The British were doing so much in the open that the Kremlin did not need spies to see that Nasser's worst fears might actually occur. British newspapers carried reports of naval preparations at Portsmouth. Three British aircraft carriers, HMS *Theseus*, *Bulwark*, and *Ocean*, were due to set sail in the first part of the week. As of Sunday, August 5, the Royal Army's sixteenth Independent Parachute Brigade would be on board the *Theseus*.[54] The army also appeared to be reinforcing its base in Cyprus. The Somerset Light Infantry, the Suffolk Regiment, and two other infantry battalions had been ordered to move there. In Cyprus they were to be joined by the Royal Marines' No. 42 Commando, the Life Guards, and the third Battalion, Grenadier Guards. The War Office would only admit to these being "precautionary military measures."[55]

Nasser was also becoming a concern for Moscow. Ambassador Evgeny Kiselev informed Moscow that Nasser was threatening the United States with a reign of terror if Eisenhower did not accept the nationalization of the Suez Canal. "I told the American Ambassador," Nasser confided to Kiselev, "that the entire canal has been mined and it and all of the Suez Canal personnel could be destroyed within five minutes, if some kind of aggression took place against Egypt."[56] Nasser added that he had also threatened the United States with sabotage against all oil producers in the Middle East, "and especially in Kabul, Bahrain and Aden."[57] If these comments were not enough of a symbol of Nasser's brinkmanship—at least as described by him to the Soviets—the Egyptian leader mentioned that he was considering tearing up the 1954 Anglo-Egyptian accord under which the British had dismantled their military base in Suez.[58]

With the probability suddenly higher that either the British or Nasser might lash out, Khrushchev thought that Moscow had no choice but to involve itself directly as a mediator. Despite having signaled to Nasser on August 3 that the Soviet Union would not send a delegation to the London Conference, Khrushchev now concluded that the Soviets would have to attend. On August 5 he called a special session of the Presidium to discuss sending a team headed by Foreign Minister Shepilov.[59]

Khrushchev took charge of determining how this about-face would be explained to Nasser. At the August 5 meeting he dictated the guts of a letter that laid out his reasoning to Nasser. The Soviet assessment of the political situation "remains as it was," he explained, but because of the receipt of new information, "we are sending our representatives [to London] to foil their military schemes." Khrushchev hoped that in light of British military activities, Nasser would also change his mind about sending a delegation to London. "You might want to send your Minister of Foreign Affairs. But that is up to you to decide."[60] Khrushchev also wanted to shape Indian Prime Minister Jawaharlal Nehru's opinion of the conference. Nehru's standing was very high in the developing world, and it could be expected that as the leader of a former British colony, he would back Egypt's right to nationalize the Suez Canal. The Indians had been invited to the conference but had as yet not decided whether to attend.[61]

The rest of the Soviet leadership blessed Khrushchev's recommendation, but below the surface there was real disagreement over how to prepare for London. Khrushchev, like Eden, had a Nasser problem at home. Many in the Kremlin doubted that Nasser would be able to manage this crisis, but Khrushchev was inclined to support the Egyptian leader. A number of Kremlin insiders and Khrushchev himself believed that Nasser had mishandled the nationalization. His rhetoric had been too strident, and the action seemed rash and ill prepared. Nasser had issued a statement acknowledging the right of all nations to use the canal, but the Kremlin knew that Egypt's policy of not letting Israel use the canal had created international suspicion that the canal would not be insulated from Egyptian politics. Moreover, even if the canal were protected from Cairo's whims, some Kremlin chieftains suspected that Nasser would not be able to administer it. The experience of discussing the Aswan Dam with the Egyptians had left an impression that their ambitions were sometimes greater than their technical competence. Aware of these misgivings at home, Khrushchev understood that he had to make his way carefully through the coming diplomatic engagements.

Six days later the Foreign Ministry circulated first drafts of what Shepilov might say at the conference. It suggested that the Soviet representative make three points: Egypt had a right to nationalize the canal, the users of the canal had a right to expect Egypt to respect the 1888 Constantinople treaty on freedom of passage, and the London Conference was the wrong place to decide how to resolve this problem diplomatically. Forty-five countries used the canal in a significant way, and the three Western powers had invited only twenty-four of them. With the exception of the Soviet Union, the socialist world and some key neutral states had been excluded from the conference to ensure that the body would pass resolutions weakening Egyptian control of the canal. Moscow's goal was to force a second, broader conference at which the Western powers might be outvoted by countries more sympathetic to Egyptian sovereignty.

When the Kremlin met again on August 9 and 11 to review the Foreign Ministry's work, disagreements over Nasser broke out into the open.[62] In November 1955 Khrushchev had acknowledged to his colleagues that arms sales to Egypt were "risky" before pushing for more of them.[63] In light of the recent developments in the Middle East, his colleagues began to reconsider the reward brought by these risks. Malenkov, who remained on the Presidium despite his loss of authority in early 1955, voiced the concern of those who believed that the Soviet Union should not tie itself too closely to Nasser: "We should never be the prisoners of Nasser's political enthusiasms."[64] He complained that there were too many references to Egyptian rights in the proposed statements. In response, Khrushchev tried to shift the discussion away from Nasser.[65] Khrushchev believed the Western powers were inclined to use force because they misjudged Soviet intentions in the region. "Evidently," he explained to his colleagues, "the West thinks the following: we [the USSR] wish to deny them their rights under the [1888] convention, we wish to swallow Egypt to seize the Canal." Khrushchev wanted to defeat these notions by showing that the Soviet Union was seeking a middle road between Egypt and the Western powers. "We understand the anxiety of the English and the French," he said; "we are no less interested [in this matter] than the English. What is needed: freedom of passage." Defense Minister Zhukov came to Khrushchev's assistance in the debate. He accepted that a misunderstanding of Soviet intentions lay behind the aggressiveness that the British and French had been exhibiting in the last two weeks. "They suspect," said Zhukov, "that we want to win a war without having to fight it."

In the days that followed, the KGB provided intelligence that strengthened Moscow's resolve to use the London discussions to persuade the French and the British to find a peaceful solution to their concerns. From a source in the French Defense Ministry, the Kremlin learned of a signed agreement between France and Britain to launch a joint military attack on Egypt in the near future. According to this agreement, French and British forces would occupy the Suez Canal after the London Conference. The source explained that the United States would not attempt to stop the Anglo-French attack. Although the source spoke of a hardening of the British and French position on the use of force against Nasser, it did not rule out the possibility that France would be happy if it could get its way through blackmail and intimidation.[66]

Apparent confirmation that the United States might not be playing the moderating role with its allies that Khrushchev had assumed came from a different confidential source. On the evening of August 13 the KGB reported on U.S. ambassador Charles Bohlen's conversation with Israeli Ambassador Yosef Avidar at the Leningrad airport while the ambassadors were awaiting their respective flights. Avidar told Bohlen, who was leaving to join the U.S. delegation in London, that he and his government were extremely anxious about the situation in the Suez Canal Zone and its long-term consequences. Surrounded by hostile Arab nations, Israel could not last a year if Nasser were to close the canal to all but Soviet warships and those of Egyptian allies. What made this report so startling was not the Israeli's professed anxiety but Bohlen's response, as picked up by the KGB.

"The Canal question is far from decided," Bohlen was reported as saying to Avidar. The U.S. ambassador then explained that Israel could help the West in provoking Nasser into making a mistake. "Israel has the task," Bohlen explained, "of creating in the near future, during the conference, such tension along the Egyptian border that Nasser is compelled to reveal his aggressive intentions toward Israel." This was the pretext the West needed to crush him. "My government is prepared for any kind of struggle with Egypt," Avidar reportedly replied. This information was reported quickly to Moscow by a KGB informant who claimed to have overheard the meeting. By the morning of August 14, Khrushchev, Bulganin, and Shepilov had their own copies to read.[67]

■

KHRUSHCHEV WAS NOT in Moscow to read the KGB report on the Bohlen and Avidar conversation. He had left for the southern Ukraine on August 13 to make a personal tour of the Donbass coal region. In 1956 the Donbass produced 30 percent of all Soviet coal but because of political instability in

Poland, a major source of the coal burned in the Soviet Union, it might now need to produce more. Polish reformers were calling for a revision of the exploitative Soviet-Polish economic relationship. Since the late 1940s the Soviets had forced the Poles to sell them coal at 10 percent of the world price. Coal was Poland's chief export, and with most of it going to the Soviet Union in tribute, Poland could not acquire sufficient foreign currency through trade to cover its purchases of Western machinery and food. Khrushchev's initiation of destalinization had opened the door to the Poles to renegotiate this vestige of the Stalinist era. Still, however sympathetic Khrushchev was to Polish aspirations, he also knew that the Soviet energy industry would have a hard time replacing Polish coal with its own.

While Khrushchev was in the Ukraine, the remaining members of the Presidium reviewed the Soviet agenda for the London Conference. Once again all the leaders agreed that they did not like the draft statements prepared by the Foreign Ministry. Malenkov stressed that there was still too much in the drafts that spoke of Egypt's needs and not enough that explained the Soviet interest in a peaceful settlement of the matter. Malenkov wanted to go a step further, and he returned to an idea he had mentioned at the August 11 session. They could ask Nasser to promise to use some of the Suez Canal Company's reserves to maintain the canal, instead of diverting them all for the Aswan Dam. There had been no encouragement from his colleagues in the earlier session, and Malenkov had no more success this time.

Lacking any strong consensus on how to guide the parties in London to a peaceful settlement, the Kremlin decided for the present time that Shepilov would not carry any formal proposals with him to submit to the conference. Instead the leadership instructed him to give statements that stressed both Egypt's right to nationalize the Suez Canal and Moscow's expectation that the Egyptians would be willing to take some kind of formalized international advice on the administration of the canal. Hidden within the approved language was the suggestion of a compromise, international supervision without international control over the canal. Shepilov was authorized to cooperate with the Western powers, especially the United States, if this would avert a war in the Egyptian desert.

■

As the Soviets prepared for the London Conference, the White House was unsure whether it should take a leadership role in settling the dispute between its Western European allies and Egypt. Subtle differences were appearing between Eisenhower's and Dulles's positions; though both wished to avoid a war over the canal, they disagreed on the best long-term solution to the troubles in the Middle East. Dulles was increasingly convinced that Nasser had to be removed from office, and he saw forcing the Egyptian leader to accept international control of the canal as the first step to making that happen.

Eisenhower, however, was uncomfortable with the hard-line view of the French and the British on international control. He was not prepared to give up on the policy of leaving Nasser a bridge to come back to the West. Better than almost any of his advisers, Eisenhower was able to put himself in the shoes of the leader he confronted. He had his own canal in Panama, and he understood why Nasser had no interest in allowing others to control Suez. As a result, Eisenhower was inclined to accept international supervision of the canal once Nasser rejected international control.

At the last meeting in the White House before the secretary of state left for London, the president expressed his doubts about Dulles's strategy. An all-or-nothing approach bent on achieving international control of the canal would not stabilize the region because Nasser would never accept this kind of international regime.[68] Egypt, after all, had the right to own the canal, and ownership implied a management right.

Despite these concerns, Eisenhower did not rein in Dulles. He had a lot on his mind that August. The Republican National Convention in San Francisco was only a couple of weeks away. Rumors abounded that he was considering replacing Richard Nixon as his running mate. Although Eisenhower wasn't really considering this, it remained a distraction. Perhaps bad health is the best explanation for the president's passive response. Eisenhower was still recovering from a recent attack of ileitis, a painful intestinal disorder, and had suffered a major heart attack the year before, and his energy level was not what it should have been.

∎

DIMITRI SHEPILOV was a refreshing departure from his taciturn and stiff predecessor, Vyacheslav Molotov. This Soviet foreign minister smiled frequently and seemed comfortable with himself. On August 15 Shepilov left Moscow for London. "He appears more like an athlete than a politician," the Reuters news agency observed after he arrived. His clothes were sporty, and unlike the other delegates to the conference, he didn't bother to wear a fedora or a bowler. He did, however, constantly comb his thick black hair, which occasionally fell onto his face.[69]

The London Conference opened at historic Lancaster House the next day. Beautifully appointed, said to be even grander than Buckingham Palace, this former residence of the duke of York was in picturesque Pall Mall, next to the queen mother's official residence. Shepilov's behavior quickly indicated to the British and the other Western allies that more than better grooming set him apart from Molotov. After arriving in London, Shepilov gave a statement to the press in a transit lounge at the airport. Short and sweet, it laid out the principles upon which Moscow sought a peaceful settlement. "In our times international disputes can be settled only through negotiations by the countries concerned being guided by the principles of justice and a spirit of the times." That "spirit" Shepilov defined as "strict observance of . . . full equality between States."[70] In other words, the USSR would not accept any proposed solution that undermined Egyptian sovereignty.

Shepilov's actions in the first few days telegraphed that he would define success in London in two ways. First, he wished to build international pressure to restrain the British and French from taking military action in the Mediterranean. This was the consideration that had prompted Soviet participation in London, and it had to be Shepilov's sine qua non. The other sign of success would be more difficult to pin down. The conference allowed the Soviet Union to demonstrate itself as the protector of young nationalist movements worldwide. There could be no better way to show Soviet commitment to these fragile new states than to be supportive of acts of self-determination.

Shepilov was also breaking the Soviet mold in ways not always appreciated in Moscow. He rewrote the draft statements telegraphed to him from his deputy, Vasily Kuznetsov. Where Kuznetsov had written "we," Shepilov wrote "I."[71] What Moscow found annoying, the Western foreign ministers found dazzling. Not only was Shepilov's manner different, but his words seemed to imply more flexibility in the Soviet position than they had ever heard before. The British foreign secretary, Selwyn Lloyd, told Secretary Dulles that Shepilov had privately agreed that "control of [the] canal could not be placed under one man such as Nasser."[72]

Beyond the idiosyncrasies, Shepilov was faithfully following Khrushchev's line not to give the Western powers any excuse to break up the conference and use Soviet actions as a pretext for an attack on Egypt. A few hours after meeting with Lloyd, Shepilov displayed the same earnest desire to find common ground with Dulles. "I do not intend to argue the correctness or incorrectness of Egypt's action or those [of the] U.K. and France. . . . [The] important thing was to recognize that such situation exists." The Soviet foreign minister praised Washington for sharing Moscow's desire to decrease tension and find a peaceful settlement.[73]

Shepilov hinted that the Soviet Union had sources that suggested a rift between the American and Western European positions. Assuring Dulles that his goal in mentioning the disagreements among the Atlantic partners was "not to drive a wedge" between the United States and its allies, Shepilov added that "if this opinion is true, the U.S. and USSR together might find way out of this crisis."[74] The Soviet foreign minister said that he had heard that the United States was already distributing a draft proposal for internationalizing the Egyptian Suez Canal Company, which administered the canal. Rather than exclude that idea entirely, Shepilov, in the spirit of seeking accommodation, said that "it seemed to him very strict and might have a bad reception in certain areas of the world." Although careful not to encourage Shepilov too much, Dulles said that he shared the Soviet view that the challenge was to find a settlement that reconciled the rights of Egypt as a sovereign country and the interests of countries that had a vital stake in freedom of navigation through the canal. But he refused to budge from the goal of international control of the canal. "[T]here can be no universal confidence in Egypt's ability alone," he told his Soviet counterpart, "to administer [the] Canal operation."[75]

At a meeting later with the British and the French, Dulles assured them that the United States remained committed to using the conference to undermine Nasser.[76] Dulles expected nothing from the formal sessions to come. London, Paris, and Washington had already decided what the conference would conclude. The task at hand was to lobby for a healthy majority among the twenty-two countries represented at the conference. Dulles was eager to ensure that not all of the developing world opposed the U.S.-British-French proposal. "[B]efore it is over," he cabled Eisenhower, "there will be some smoke-filled rooms like Chicago and San Francisco."[77]

The Soviets, however, did not follow the script. The day after the formal start of the conference Shepilov met privately with Dulles to float a compromise proposal. Instead of forcing Egypt to turn the operation of the canal over to an international board, Shepilov suggested the formula of "Egyptian operation with the participation of other countries."[78] The Soviet foreign minister understood that this was a vague proposal, but he wanted Dulles to consider alternatives to the U.S.-British-French position. The Soviet negotiator agreed with the Americans that Egypt had shown political immaturity in the past. Moscow wanted Washington to know that it expected Egypt to permit Israel to use the canal. Shepilov suggested that the language of the 1888 convention be tightened to ensure access to the canal for all states. The Soviet position, however, was that Egypt had to be excused its past mistakes and treated as a sovereign country that would adhere to these new treaty requirements.[79]

Dulles made special mention of the Soviet proposal in a highly secret cable to Eisenhower. But the secretary of state was not interested in working with the Soviets to achieve an acceptable compromise. He believed that accepting Shepilov's proposal would help the Soviet cause with the Arabs and result in "some downgrading of the British and the French." He told the president, "I doubt whether Soviet agreement is worth having at that price."[80] Knowing that Eisenhower was more interested in diplomacy at that moment than he, Dulles added, "I shall do everything possible short of disloyalty to the British and the French to get Soviet agreement."

Eisenhower remained aloof from the proceedings in London. It appears he did not read the full description of what Shepilov actually proposed. This was unfortunate because the Soviet representative was substantially making the same case for modified international participation that Eisenhower himself was making to Dulles. On August 18 and 19 the president sent notes to Dulles to discourage him from signing on to a position that would be impossible for Nasser to swallow.[81] "I see no objection to agreeing to a Board with supervisory rather than operating authority," Eisenhower wrote.[82] He added that he hoped "the results of the conference [would] not be wrecked on the rigidity of the positions of the two sides on this particular point." Although he made no mention of the Soviet proposal, Eisenhower was saying that he liked the idea of establishing an international board to provide advice to Nasser, while leaving the management of the canal to the Egyptian company.

Eisenhower did not insist that these ideas be reflected in the U.S. position at the conference. Dulles persuaded him that Nasser might accept internationalization of the canal, and even if Nasser rejected this first effort at a diplomatic settlement, it was more important for the United States to stand by its Western allies.

With the American position frozen by Dulles, Shepilov curiously did not formally propose the compromise he had privately suggested to the secretary of state. A passivity had also fallen over the Kremlin. Although it was watching the proceedings carefully, Khrushchev was out of the city, and the Presidium did not feel the need to meet to discuss any new instructions for Shepilov.

Fortunately for Moscow, the Indian delegation decided on its own before the end of the conference to propose something that echoed Shepilov's and Eisenhower's ideas about international supervision without control. The proposal was a godsend to Moscow, though there is no evidence that it was behind the proposal. Here a third world country was making the points the Kremlin had intended to make. The canal would remain Egyptian and under Egyptian control.

The Indian proposal made no difference to the outcome of the conference, which had been preordained by the British, the French, and the Americans before any of the other delegates arrived. India lacked the clout of the Western allies to cause any major defections from the supporters of the internationalizing position. On August 23 the chairman of the conference, British Foreign Secretary Selwyn Lloyd, called for a vote on the five-power (Pakistan and Iran signed on with the three-power proposal once some cosmetic changes had been made) and Indian proposals. The five-power proposal received eighteen votes. The Soviet Union, Ceylon (Sri Lanka), and Indonesia joined India in voting for New Delhi's proposal. Great Britain, France, and Dulles got what they wanted. Although the canal would still "belong" to Egypt, the Egyptian government would be expected to delegate to an international board the right to manage it, in return for which Cairo would receive a percentage of the revenues from the tolls. It was decided that a delegation headed by Australian Prime Minister Robert Menzies would present the conference's proposal to Nasser in Cairo in early September.

■

KHRUSHCHEV WAS NOT satisfied with the outcome of the London Conference. Just home from his trip to the Donbass and another to Siberia, the Soviet leader had little energy of his own to devote to the Suez problem. But he was aware of the 18–4 vote in London and the fact that the majority intended to impose the internationalization of the canal on Nasser. It annoyed Khrushchev that the West was allowing its concerns over the efficient management of the canal, which the Soviets shared, to derail any possibility of achieving a peaceful settlement.

He decided to intervene personally. At a dinner reception at the Romanian Embassy, honoring the twelfth anniversary of the entry of the Soviet Army into Bucharest, he took the French and British ambassadors aside to lecture them on the errors of the majority view in London. He stressed that a consultative board was the solution to the problem of reconciling international concerns over the management of the canal with Egypt's sovereign rights. He charged the British above all with pushing for an outcome at the conference that they knew in advance Nasser would reject. Alluding to intelligence he was receiving that pointed to the possibility of an Anglo-French attack following Nasser's rejection of these terms, Khrushchev warned the Western ambassadors. "The Arabs will not stand alone," he vowed, if war broke out.[83]

The only credible military threat that Khrushchev felt he could make was to raise the possibility that the Soviet Union might send "volunteers" to defend Egypt. In 1950 a million Chinese "volunteers" had invaded Allied-occupied North Korea to rid the peninsula of Western influence. Khrushchev said to the foreign ambassadors that if he had a son of military age who could volunteer, "I would tell him to go ahead. 'You have my approval.' "[84]

Khrushchev had new instructions sent to London to toughen the rhetoric that Shepilov was to use at his closing press conference the next day. "Before your departure," he cabled in a message also signed by the chairman of the Council of Ministers, Nikolai Bulganin, "hit these imperialists on the snout!"[85] The period of Soviet conciliation on Suez was over. The Western powers, including the United States, it appeared, had never intended to seek a peaceful settlement.

The next day, in a room filled to overflowing, Shepilov gave a tough speech in front of 175 journalists. He said that his view of Secretary Dulles had changed for the worse. The five-power plan, which he called the Dulles Plan, involved "a flagrant violation of Egypt's sovereign rights" that flowed from "an unacceptable colonialist position."[86] The language was strong but did not come close to expressing Khrushchev's irritation at how the conference had gone.

Khrushchev was still angry when Shepilov reached Moscow. "I had just reached my apartment and put down my valise," Shepilov later recalled, "when I called [Khrushchev]." The Soviet chief told him: "Get over here." When Shepilov reached the Kremlin and they were together, Khrushchev asked, "Now listen, why didn't you follow the instruction that I sent you with Bulganin?" Shepilov replied: "We had already won the battle, and so why ruin relations with them [France, Great Britain, and the United States]?" His ire rising, Khrushchev said, "So now you want to direct foreign policy."[87]

The hectoring of Shepilov continued at a formal meeting of the Presidium a little while later. One after another the members lambasted him for not having been tough enough at the closing press conference. "This voluntarism was wrong and dangerous," stated Khrushchev.[88] "Nothing is to be interpreted; once a directive is given, you should know how to act," Presidium member Mikhail Pervukhin added. Georgi Malenkov even attacked Shepilov for having been too chummy with Dulles at one of their meetings.

This was displaced anger mixed with jealousy. Shepilov had made a good impression in the West and needed to be put in his place. But the main catalyst was the diplomatic defeat that Moscow had suffered at the London Conference. The West had ignored its wishes, and it had only the votes of three countries along with its own to show for its efforts.

The conference was not a fiasco for Moscow. It did represent the first time that the USSR was recognized as a player in the Middle East, and its participation did increase Soviet influence with the Egyptians. For the first time since the dispute had started, Nasser turned to Moscow for foreign policy advice. At the end of August the Egyptian leader called the Soviet ambassador in for a private chat. Knowing that the delegation led by Menzies was due to arrive in Cairo in less than two weeks, Nasser asked for "the opinion and advice of D. T. Shepilov in connection with further steps and tactics." He added, "All Soviet advice would be received positively."[89]

At a Presidium meeting two days later Khrushchev and his colleagues approved a list of policy recommendations for Egypt.[90] Moscow shared Cairo's conviction that despite Western threats, the London Conference proposals had to be rejected. To undermine the Western argument that Nasser had snatched the canal in the hopes of doing damage to other countries, the Soviets suggested instead that he announce the basic principles upon which the canal would be administered. They also suggested the principles. The first was that the Egyptian Suez Canal Company "not be assigned any kind of political function"; the second, that it be "independent in its operational activity of any [governmental] economic organ"; and the third, that it have a "juridical form subject to Egyptian law and operating on the basis of a special administration, in view of its unitary independent budget." They added that Egypt should declare that the Suez Canal Company would guarantee free passage through the canal "on the basis of complete equality for the ships of all flags without any kind of discrimination." In other words, as the price for gaining international acceptance of the nationalization, Egypt would have to accept Israel's right to use the canal.[91]

Moscow continued to have concerns about the proper functioning of the canal under the Egyptians. It suggested that the Egyptian company commit itself to hiring foreign specialists: engineers, pilots, and other technical personnel. Egypt should also say that it endorsed the formation of an international consultative commission on the canal that would allow for international cooperation on technical assistance and on the use of tariffs and their collection before ships exited the canal. Although Moscow wanted the canal company to be separate from this international consultative commission, it suggested that Nasser think hard about how Egypt and the company would link themselves to the United Nations. Moscow thought that in addition to announcing its willingness to proceed along these lines, Egypt should organize a conference in Cairo of countries that used the canal "to discuss the draft of a new convention that would guarantee freedom of passage through the Suez Canal and also the question of the form of international cooperation."[92]

While the delegation headed by Menzies was negotiating with Nasser, the Kremlin did not want the West to have any pretext for a military intervention. Since the middle of the month Moscow had been receiving reports of British and French efforts to undermine the operation of the canal. The British and French governments had asked their citizens working for the canal company as ship pilots to leave their jobs. According to Soviet estimates, of the 280 men who worked as pilots guiding ships through the canal, only 50 were Egyptian. The French, for example, offered their citizens who abandoned the canal thirty-six months' severance pay as well as a pension adjusted to the time worked for the canal company. As a way of helping Cairo keep the canal open and thereby remove any Anglo-French arguments for war, the Kremlin decided on August 30 to send thirty experienced ships' pilots to help fill the holes in the canal administration. It also suggested to Nasser that he formally ask for volunteers from the bloc countries of Poland, Romania, Bulgaria, and Yugoslavia, as well as from India, Greece, and Finland.[93]

As it tried to eliminate any pretexts for a Western attack, Moscow provided some military support to the Egyptians. In the first week of September, as Nasser was meeting with the Menzies delegation, the Soviets sent shiploads of weapons to the Egyptian Army. Meanwhile, by means of the KGB, Moscow provided military handbooks and training films and presumably some military advisers to show Egyptian officers how to use this material.[94]

■

AMERICAN ACTIONS at the London Conference had been disappointing to Khrushchev. By signing on to the declaration of eighteen, the United States effectively endorsed a diplomatic plan that was guaranteed to produce an Egyptian refusal. If Washington was not prepared to stop its allies, then the Kremlin needed to know how seriously to take the anger in Western Europe, especially the determination of Great Britain to harm Nasser.

Khrushchev had some reason to hope that Britain lacked the resolve to participate in any Western conspiracy against Nasser. Since 1951 two former members of the British establishment, Guy Burgess and Donald Maclean, had lived in Moscow. Until they fled their homeland in May 1951, Burgess and Maclean had operated as Soviet intelligence moles in, among other places, the Foreign Office. Now working under the aliases D. M. Elliot and Mr. Frazer, the two former spies served as high-level advisers to the Soviet Foreign Ministry on British politics and politicians. Khrushchev and the Presidium regularly received reports on the meetings that the two most famous Britons in Moscow were having with old friends and British journalists who came to Moscow to see them.[95]

In mid-August Tom Driberg, the deputy leader of the British Labour Party and a journalist, had come to Moscow to see Burgess. Despite the rumblings in the British press that London might strike at Nasser, Driberg had told Burgess that Eden was too weak to attempt to impose his will on Egypt by force: "It was all bluff."[96] Reminding Burgess that "British journalists were usually a good barometer of official decision-making," Driberg assured him that "Fleet Street does not expect a war in the Middle East now." Khrushchev was so taken by this account of the meeting that he asked to see Driberg himself.[97] The British political activist repeated the same story to the Soviet leader at their meeting on August 30.[98] It seemed that despite the hue and cry following Nasser's nationalization of the Suez Canal, at least, Britain, would do nothing.

Events in September deepened the belief in Moscow that a Mideast crisis might be averted. As expected, Nasser refused to accept the proposals carried by the Menzies delegation. However, the day after it left Cairo Nasser called for a new international conference, assuring the world that Egypt was fully prepared to negotiate but not on the terms suggested by the eighteen-country bloc at the London Conference. Meanwhile Foster Dulles suggested a Suez users' association, consisting of all the countries that used the canal, to negotiate with Egypt. France and Great Britain formally endorsed Dulles's plan and called for a second conference in London to approve the suez users' association. From Moscow's perspective what happened next suggested that the British push for war was losing steam. Eden's opponents in the House of Commons started a major public debate on the entire Suez policy, criticizing him for being too belligerent. On September 22 the prime minister surprised the world by calling for the UN Security Council to take up discussion of the Suez problem. The Soviets and the Egyptians had been advocating for this since July, and now, seemingly under political pressure, the British also recommended it. A date was set for talks to begin on October 5.

These hopeful developments in London provoked a policy review in Moscow. Both the Foreign Ministry and the Soviet intelligence community were asked to update their assessments of where the crisis might be going.

The Soviet intelligence community responded with a series of very alarming reports. On September 20 the KGB distributed a report on the measures that France and the British would take in the event of an outbreak of hostilities with Egypt.[99] A few days later the KGB learned of a Western plot to assassinate Nasser that the Kremlin took so seriously that two KGB officers were flown to Cairo to assist Nasser's security detail.[100] The KGB's source is not known, but the warning was grounded in fact. Eden had made it known to his top advisers—and perhaps indirectly to Soviet intelligence—that he supported an assassination attempt if it could rid him of his Nasser problem. "I want Nasser murdered, don't you understand?" Eden had told a senior Foreign Office official on an open telephone line.[101] In early October representatives of the Secret Intelligence Service, Britain's external espionage organization, flew to Washington to confer with the CIA on how the Americans could assist them in overthrowing Nasser. The CIA, however, turned down any participation in an assassination attempt.[102]

Meanwhile the Soviet military intelligence service, the GRU, reported on a significant Western military buildup in the eastern Mediterranean. The Soviet military, which did not discount the possibility that the United States might ultimately assist an Anglo-French assault on Egypt, included the powerful U.S. Sixth Fleet in its tallies of Western strength. But the most significant military deployments observed in the region since August were by the British and the French. Since July 26 the British had increased the number of their troops in the area from twenty-seven thousand to forty-five thousand and the French, who had not had any soldiers there before, now had six thousand. There were three British aircraft carriers patrolling the area, whereas there had been only one in that part of the Mediterranean before. Equally noteworthy was the major increase in Britain's local airlift and sealift capabilities. The GRU detected eight more British transport planes and more than a tripling of British transport ships. Much of this military capability had been put on display in a major exercise called Septex 2 held on September 13 and 14 to train for an invasion from sea and air. In addition, the Soviets noted that as part of a strategy to wear down the Egyptians psychologically, the British had increased the air traffic of their bombers between bases in Great Britain and the island of Malta.[103]

Khrushchev's diplomatic specialists were less alarmist about the situation than were the Soviet intelligence services. The political assessments of the Soviet Foreign Ministry presented a mixed picture of likely scenarios. A crisp analysis of the British political scene in late September informed the Kremlin that Eden led an increasingly divided government in the crisis.[104] The Soviet paper noted that opponents to a military action included Foreign Secretary Lloyd and Eden's political rival, Rab Butler. In Parliament the Tories faced a Labour Party that was solidly opposed to military action, though the party was itself split over whether or not the Suez Canal should be internationalized. The Soviet Foreign Ministry understood that Eden was committed to decisive action but left open the possibility that the opposition was becoming too strong. Evidence for this was that it had been three months since British warships left port headed for the Mediterranean and no attack had followed. It appeared likely that London would not act without some kind of UN sanction.

A similar Soviet study of the French political leadership, however, was much less sanguine. There was still remarkable unity in Paris behind a policy of dealing harshly with Nasser.[105] Soviet analysis identified three reasons for the determination of the French: the anger of French stakeholders from across the party spectrum who had lost their investments when the canal company was nationalized; the role of Jews in French public life, in all parties but especially in the ruling Socialist Party; and a sense that if Nasser prevailed in the Suez, then little Nassers would be encouraged in Algeria, Tunisia, and Morocco. Using the Hitler analogy, the French political elite believed in a parallel between the nationalization of Suez and the Nazi remilitarization of the Rhineland in 1936. Nasser had to be stopped here before the situation got worse.

The Kremlin reached no conclusions over what the French and especially the British intended to achieve at the Security Council discussions that started on October 5. Foreign Minister Shepilov, who headed the Soviet delegation, warned at the UN that the French and British might simply be looking for a pretext for war. He suggested that the Europeans were already prepared to tell their people: " 'You have urged us to appeal to the UN. We have done so, but, as you see, it is powerless. It can do nothing. Other steps must be taken. Egypt is guilty. Crucify it!' "[106]

Nasser had no doubt of London's and Paris's sinister intentions in New York. Anticipating a breakdown in the talks, he spent the first days of October trying to hedge his bets with both Moscow and Washington so that at least one of them would be prepared to come to Egypt's defense. On October 7 Nasser asked Khrushchev via the KGB chief in Cairo whether "in the event of an attack on Egypt, the Egyptian government could count on the Soviets dispatching volunteers and submarines."[107] Meanwhile he sent two of his key aides, Ali Sabri and Mohamed Heikal, to meet with Kermit Roosevelt of the CIA, who was considered a secure back channel to the Eisenhower administration.

Sabri and Heikal told the CIA that Nasser wanted U.S. help to ward off both British military intervention and further Soviet penetration of his country. Cairo was skeptical of British diplomacy, assuming that London's maneuvering in the Security Council was designed to provide a pretext for war. Eden's Conservatives wanted to be able to show the Labour Party that they had done all they could to seek a diplomatic settlement. Meanwhile Cairo argued that Moscow was hungry to play the role of Egypt's savior. Nasser wanted the Americans to advise their British friends not to introduce a hostile resolution in the Security Council. The effect would be a Soviet veto, which would only increase Egypt's debt to Soviet diplomacy. Sabri explained that economic pressures had already forced Nasser much closer to the Soviet Union than he had hoped to be. "He is no longer able," the Egyptian representative explained, "to adhere to his policy of limiting Egyptian trade with the communists to 30% of her trade in any one commodity."

If the Eisenhower administration found that it could not play a helpful role in the corridors at the UN, the Egyptians hoped that at the very least Washington would be willing to share CIA estimates of British intentions in the Middle East. For all his anxiety over what Eden might do next, Nasser had no firm information on which to predict the future course of the crisis. He assumed, wrongly, as it turned out, that the United States had to have a better sense than he did of what their British ally was up to.[108]

Events at the United Nations over the next few days led both superpowers to believe that they could safely ignore Nasser's concerns.[109] By October 12 the foreign ministers of Egypt, France, and Great Britain had reached a tentative agreement on six principles that would govern Egypt's management of the canal. Perhaps because he had not received any reassurance from Moscow or Washington, Nasser had instructed his foreign minister, Mohammed Fawzi, to agree to the French and British demand that Egypt "insulate" the canal from politics. This was exactly the undertaking that Moscow had been urging on the Egyptian government since August. Nasser refused to let Fawzi say whether Israel would again be denied the use of the canal. But Egypt's acceptance of the general policy of letting the use of the canal be handled apolitically satisfied the French and British negotiators. Egypt also agreed to recognize a users' association so long as disagreements between it and the canal management could be handled by arbitration. Although Egypt intended to collect the tolls itself, Fawzi promised that Cairo would negotiate an agreement that set aside a portion for canal improvements. The Egyptians proved so flexible that at one point Shepilov, who had been kept outside the Egyptian-French-British discussions, cabled home his concerns that Cairo might be making too many concessions out of fear of a military attack.[110]

With agreement reached at the United Nations on the six principles, both Washington and Moscow began to assume that war in the Middle East was much less likely. On October 12, in a televised meeting with a group of ordinary Americans organized by the Eisenhower/Nixon campaign, Eisenhower expressed his optimism that war could be averted over Egypt: "The progress made in the settlement of the Suez dispute this afternoon at the United Nations is most gratifying. Egypt, Britain and France have met, through the Foreign Ministers, and agreed on a set of principles on to negotiate; and it looks like here is a very great crisis that is behind us. I don't mean to say that we are completely out of the woods, but I talked to the Secretary of State just before I came over here tonight and I will tell you that in both his heart and mine at least, there is a very great prayer of thanksgiving."[111]

Both Eisenhower and Khrushchev had major concerns that prevented them from giving their full attention to the events in the Middle East. On November 6 Americans would be going to the polls to reelect Eisenhower or to elect his Democratic challenger, Adlai Stevenson. Khrushchev had more than one challenger. The situation in Poland and Hungary had worsened since midsummer, and the Kremlin was spending most of its time thinking about how to avert a breakdown of authority in the Communist states. It was an unusual moment in the Cold War. Neither superpower wanted a crisis, and both Eisenhower and Khrushchev hoped—for their own reasons—that a way could be found for the Western Europeans to resolve their differences with Nasser peacefully.

5

TWIN CRISES

K HRUSHCHEV NEEDED the apparent calm in the Middle East. The pressure to make decisions about Eastern Europe left him with very little time or energy in early October 1956 to devote to Nasser and his problems. This did not reflect a weakening in Khrushchev's enthusiasm for the Egyptian leader. He was still very proud that in little more than a year the USSR had become a factor in the Middle East by forging a relationship with the leading Arab nationalist. But Soviet vital interests were at stake in Eastern Europe, and the steadily deteriorating situation required immediate Kremlin action.

In early October the Polish Communist Party restored the membership of Wladyslaw Gomulka, a popular reformer who had been jailed by Poland's Stalinists. Gomulka was considered anti-Soviet, and his return signaled a dramatic weakening of Polish Communist leader Edward Ochab's authority. These developments caused Moscow, out of renewed concern for the future of Soviet-Polish relations, to end its foot-dragging on some of Warsaw's outstanding demands. Moscow was still paying only one-tenth of the world price for Polish coal, the country's main export. The Poles were desperate for more foreign currency to purchase Western machinery and food.

The reason for Soviet foot-dragging had been pure economics. If the Soviet Union stopped getting Polish coal at a discount, it would have either to pay more for the coal it used or to try to replenish its stocks through domestic production. Khrushchev's summer tour of the coal-producing Donbass region had been discouraging. "The situation is awful," he had reported to his colleagues when he returned to the Kremlin in late August.[1] Despite the situation in the Donbass, which needed expensive improvements to become efficient, with Gomulka's return to prominence in Warsaw Khrushchev thought he would have to give the Poles what they wanted. On October 4 the Presidium revised upward the price that the Soviet Union would pay for Polish coal.[2]

The Kremlin understood that Ochab needed more than the concession on coal to retain control. Political pressure was growing within Poland to lessen its dependence on Russia. In September Ochab had requested that the Soviets withdraw their KGB advisers from the Polish Ministry of Internal Affairs. The Kremlin agreed to this request the same day it signaled its willingness to accept a higher coal price.[3]

Meanwhile in Hungary the situation seemed, if anything, to have deteriorated even more than in Poland. As in Poland, the Hungarian leaders found they could not reform fast enough for the intelligentsia in the street. Moscow had tried to save the situation by forcing the removal of the hard-line party boss Mátyás Rákosi in July. But Rákosi's successor was the weak-willed Ernö Gerö, who was so unsure of himself that he spent half of his short tenure in office outside Hungary, conferring with Tito in Yugoslavia, Mao Zedong in Beijing, and Khrushchev in the Crimea.

Gerö underestimated the extent of Hungarian dissatisfaction with the Communist Party. Consequently the steps he took to calm the situation led instead to an acceleration of political change. In a desperate attempt to buy some legitimacy in the coffeehouses, Gerö permitted the remains of Lazlo Rajk to be reburied in Budapest. Rajk was a Hungarian Communist pioneer who had been executed in 1949 in the wave of purge trials that washed over Eastern Europe just after the war. In the tense atmosphere of 1956 Rajk became a popular symbol of the injustice of Hungary's Stalinist regime. His posthumous return on October 6 touched off the largest political demonstration in Eastern Europe since the Soviets had established their iron rule.

The sight of thousands of Hungarians marching silently but eloquently in the streets of Budapest traumatized Gerö. "The situation in the country is significantly more complicated and acute than I had imagined," he confessed to the Soviet ambassador, Yuri Andropov. "[T]he reburial of Rajk's remains," he said, "has dealt a massive blow to the party leadership, whose authority was not all that high to begin with."[4] In the summer Gerö had described the problem as limited to the Hungarian intelligentsia. Now the discord had spread to a major portion of the country's workers and peasants. Not long after the demonstration for Rajk, the popular Imre Nagy, the Hungarian Gomulka, had his membership in the Hungarian Communist Party restored. Khrushchev now faced a serious challenge in two of his Eastern European client states.

■

As the leaves changed colors on the trees in Washington, the Eisenhower administration watched the events in Eastern Europe with interest but made no serious attempt to assist the democratic forces in either Poland or Hungary. While Eisenhower hoped to avoid any foreign policy challenges before the November election, if there was going to be a problem, he expected that it would be over the Suez Canal, not the future of Poland or Hungary.

The White House received some disquieting intelligence from the Middle East in early October that suggested that the situation was still unstable there. A U-2 flown in early October detected that Israel had recently acquired between fifty and sixty of the French-made Mystère IV-A jet fighters. According to the 1950 Tripartite Declaration governing actions by the three Western great powers in the Middle East, the French were supposed to inform the United States and Great Britain of any arms sales to either the Arab states or Israel. France had admitted to selling Israel twenty-four, not sixty of its top-of-the-line fighters.[5] At least one of America's NATO allies was not telling the truth about its military activities in the region.

Despite this suspicious buildup in Israel, the administration held to the view that tensions were actually decreasing in the region. The British and the French seemed to be negotiating in good faith at the United Nations, and there were no traces of any Soviet, Egyptian, or Israeli misbehavior. By October 10 the CIA was telling President Eisenhower that "deliberate initiation of full-scale Arab-Israeli hostilities [was] unlikely in the immediate future." More dramatically, two weeks later, on October 24, the watch committee set up within the U.S. intelligence community to alert the administration to changes in the Middle East spoke in terms of the "receding danger of hostilities over the Suez Canal."[6]

The U.S. intelligence community would be of little help to American policy makers in unraveling their allies' plans for Suez. The most important decisions by the French and the British were now occurring in secret closed door meetings to which Americans were not invited and at which they did not have any spies.

Even before the start of the Suez discussions at the Security Council, the French had returned to the path toward war with Egypt that they had abandoned at the time of the London Conference. Frustrated by the pace of events in the region and unsure whether the Eden government could be trusted to act, Guy Mollet had turned to the Israelis in late September to design a two-pronged attack with the goal of toppling Nasser. On September 30 a high-level Israeli delegation, led by Foreign Minister Golda Meir and Defense Minister Moshe Dayan, arrived in Paris to confer with their French counterparts. The Israelis were prepared to launch an attack on Egypt with French assistance, so long as they could ensure that London would not go to Jordan's assistance if hostilities also began along the Jordanian-Israeli border. The French, in turn, declined to be involved in a simultaneous attack on Egypt but promised additional tanks and half-track vehicles for the Israeli Defense Force. The two sides set October 20 as D-day for an Israeli attack.[7]

Securing British support remained a precondition for the French to commit any of their forces. In early October the British government was more divided over whether to proceed with military action than at any time since Nasser nationalized the Suez Canal. The protracted diplomacy of the summer and fall seemed to have taken a toll on official support for attacking Egypt. Two prominent cabinet members were now opposed to using force to resolve the issue of the canal. The foreign secretary, Selwyn Lloyd, who was never comfortable with a military solution, now saw real hope in the talks at the UN. In mid-October he believed he had reached an agreement with his Egyptian counterpart on a set of six principles to guide the settlement of the crisis, including the all-important Egyptian promise to insulate the canal from domestic politics. Lloyd's preference for a peaceful settlement of the matter was also shared by the British defense minister, Walter Monckton. He had overseen a revision of the Suez military plan that postponed any possible British landing in Egypt until at least the spring of 1957.

Eden, however, was as committed as ever to war. Egyptian flexibility at the United Nations, which had allowed Lloyd to craft the mutually acceptable six principles, threatened the prime minister's goal of overthrowing Nasser. On October 13 Eden instructed his foreign minister to accept the French suggestion that a poisonous amendment be added to this diplomatic settlement to make it unacceptable to Nasser. The French proposed requiring that Egypt also accept the U.S.-British-French plan endorsed by a majority at the London Conference in August and already turned down once by Nasser in September. Later that day Britain introduced the amended version of the diplomatic deal as a resolution before the UN Security Council. As expected by Eden and the French, the Soviets vetoed the amended Security Council resolution on behalf of the Egyptians, and the entire diplomatic process stalled.

As he was scuttling the UN negotiations, Eden turned to the rank and file of the Conservative Party for moral support. Out of nostalgia for the empire, the party faithful had never wavered in its support for a forceful policy to rid Egypt of Nasser. On October 13 Eden told a cheering audience at the Conservative Party conference, "We have refused to say that in no circumstances would we ever use force. No responsible government could ever give such a pledge."

Information from British intelligence also strengthened Eden's determination. A major assessment dated October 11 had echoed his belief that if Nasser were to get away with keeping the Suez Canal, Britain's position in the Middle East would soon collapse.[8] It was considered only a matter of time before Nasser's supporters in Iraq, Jordan, and the Persian Gulf succeeded in sweeping away any pro-Western governments and increasing Cairo's and Moscow's influence in the region.

On October 14 a French delegation arrived in London to discuss British participation in the Israeli-French plan to attack Egypt and remove Nasser. Eden was no friend of Israel's. He had once sided with Arabists in the Foreign Office who had opposed supporting the establishment of the state of Israel. However, the British prime minister had already made up his mind that he could no longer postpone the war. The French explained the existing plans for a two-country operation and the reasons why Great Britain should turn it into a tripartite attack. They suggested that hours after Israel had launched its attack, the British could join the French in ordering the Egyptians and the Israelis to withdraw their forces from the canal zone. Then an Anglo-French force should occupy the canal zone. The world would be told that the goal was to protect freedom of navigation through the Suez Canal. In fact the French assumed that this coordinated action would bring about the downfall of Nasser and his regime. Despite the misgivings of his foreign secretary and minister of defense, Eden agreed to include Great Britain in the operation.

Eden's embrace of the French strategy broke the last barrier to large-scale military action against Nasser. The British having indicated their willingness to meet with the Israelis, the French invited their allies to meet in Paris on October 21 to discuss the coordinated attack. It was also decided to keep the conspiracy a secret from the United States and, of course, the Soviet Union.

■

K HRUSHCHEV WAS IN Warsaw as the French prepared for the meeting in Paris. The situation in Poland was extremely dynamic. Within days of regaining his membership in the Polish Politburo, the independently minded Gomulka had become the most influential figure in the Polish government. Ochab had been forced to resign, and Gomulka's actions since taking the reins from his pro-Soviet predecessor had transformed Khrushchev's worries into alarm. "Poland might break away from us at any moment," he later recalled thinking at the time.[9] Besides the removal of the KGB men in Polish security, a request that the Soviets had already accepted, the Poles were now demanding the firing of Soviet Marshal Konstantin Rokossovky, whom Moscow had earlier compelled them to appoint their defense minister.

Khrushchev believed that Soviet troops might be necessary to keep Poland in the Warsaw Pact. But he would first lead a high-level delegation to confront Gomulka and the Polish Communist leadership directly. This would be Gomulka's chance to demonstrate his loyalty to the Soviet bloc. If Khrushchev did not get the assurances that he required, his troops would enter Warsaw the next day. In preparation for the attack, two battle divisions were ordered to assume a holding position a hundred kilometers outside the Polish capital city.

On October 19, accompanied by Presidium members Molotov, Mikoyan, Kaganovich, and Zhukov, Khrushchev arrived in Warsaw. Gomulka had refused to issue a formal invitation to the Soviets, an act that Khrushchev later described as "like spitting in our face."[10] Once the Soviets arrived, the Poles had no choice but to meet. Aware of the force waiting in the wings, the Poles then opted to show some deference. Gomulka spoke of Polish-Soviet solidarity and pleaded with Khrushchev to call off the use of Soviet troops. "Everything will be in order here," he said reassuringly," but don't allow Soviet troops into Warsaw, or it will become virtually impossible to control events."

Khrushchev wavered over whether to be satisfied with what Gomulka and the others in the Polish government told him. At first he seemed to think the crisis was resolved and told his longtime ally Mikoyan that upon reflection the use of troops would be a mistake. But no sooner had he arrived back in Moscow late on October 19 than he appeared to have changed his mind. "We've decided our troops should enter Warsaw tomorrow morning after all," Khrushchev told a surprised Mikoyan.[11]

Thanks to some expert delaying by Mikoyan, who was strongly against the use of Soviet troops, the attack on the Polish people did not happen. Mikoyan knew Khrushchev very well. Although he had a penchant for bold and aggressive strokes, the Soviet leader could be dissuaded from acting rashly, if given the chance to take a deep breath and think the matter through. At a Presidium meeting two days later, on October 21, Khrushchev opted to take Gomulka at his word. "We need to display patience," he said.[12] Soviet troops were taken off alert.

■

WHILE CONFLICT was averted in Poland, Israel's prime minister, David Ben-Gurion, arrived in Paris to plan the coordinated attack on Nasser, with whom he had strong grievances. The Israeli leader was eager to put an end to the attacks by Egyptian irregular forces, known as fedayeen, across the border into Israel. He also hoped that military action would open to Israeli shipping the Suez Canal and the Strait of Tiran, both of which fed the Israeli port city of Eilat. His trip, like that of the Secretary Lloyd, was kept secret. The meetings were to take place at a private home in the fashionable suburb of Sèvres, well beyond the scrutiny of the international press or any lucky Soviet or U.S. spies.

Ben-Gurion was uncomfortable about having to rely on the British, in large part because he blamed them for having obstructed the creation of the state of Israel. In an effort to maintain a relationship with the Arabs, the British had deliberately slowed the emigration of Jews to Palestine, which remained under British mandate until 1948. Christian Pineau, the French foreign minister, was insistent that the Israeli leader overlook his past differences with the British. "The English," he said, "are incapable of acting without a pretext."[13] Ben-Gurion understood that he had to provide the pretext as the price for British military participation.

While Ben-Gurion felt discomfort and suspicion, the British representative at Sèvres experienced disgust and didn't mind showing it. Lloyd, who had opposed Eden's decision, behaved in front of the other delegates as if he had a "dirty smell under his nose." It was commonly known that he preferred a peaceful solution to the crisis and was in Sèvres only because Eden had told him to go. When Ben-Gurion asked him why the English didn't just settle with Nasser at the UN, the foreign secretary parroted Eden's thinking: Any diplomatic settlement over the Suez Canal was unacceptable to Great Britain because it meant that Nasser remained in power. Getting him out was Eden's chief objective.

The uncomfortable English gentleman's words satisfied Ben-Gurion. Convinced now that London meant business, the Israelis agreed to the complex French plan. It would begin with an Israeli attack on Egypt, followed by an Anglo-French bombing campaign and an allied landing in the canal zone. The parties quibbled over the length of the delay between the Israeli attack and the intervention by the Europeans. Ben-Gurion wanted almost no gap at all. He had lived in London during the blitz, when Hitler's Luftwaffe bombed the city, and feared the effects of Arab bomber sorties against Israeli cities before the French and British established air supremacy. The British had other concerns and hoped instead for a three-day delay. They compromised and agreed on a thirty-six-hour delay.[14] As the meeting ended on October 22, Israel promised to attack exactly a week later, on October 29.

▪

THE SOVIETS KNEW nothing about these plans. Soviet intelligence had a hard time following the developments in the Mediterranean because Moscow lacked high-altitude spy planes comparable to the American U-2. Through its Syrian ally and from well-informed articles in the British and French press, however, the Kremlin collected some good information about the movements of French and British units in and around Cyprus. Marshal Zhukov presented each member of the Presidium with a special report on those military movements. The GRU, the military intelligence service, had detected French and British reinforcements in the region, but could not provide any sense of Paris's and London's intentions.[15]

Further evidence of how far Moscow's thoughts were from the possibility of a near-term attack came in the Kremlin's preparations for the visit of Syrian President Shukri Quwatly.[16] The visit, which had been planned for some time, was due to begin October 30. In its outlines of Syria's needs, Soviet intelligence made no mention of the possibility of Middle East conflict. Quwatly was expected to request a friendship treaty with Moscow and a huge loan for economic development.

The Egyptians themselves were encouraging the Soviets to believe that the crisis had passed. Even after the collapse of the negotiations with the French and the British in New York, the Egyptian government informed the Soviets that it was no longer concerned about a Western attack on the canal. "It is in large measure settled," Egypt's el-Kouni told the Soviet Foreign Ministry on October 16.[17] The Egyptians were now using terms like "we won" to explain the fact that nearly three months had passed since the nationalization and the French and British still seemed tied up in diplomatic knots.

Nasser was much more concerned about events in Jordan than he was about any Western attack on his country. Criticizing King Hussein as being as inept as King Farouk, the Egyptians worried that Jordan's domestic instability would provoke outside interference from the West or its allies. Nasser's specific concern was that his great regional rival, Nuri al-Said of Iraq would be invited to send battalions into Jordan to protect Amman from an Israeli attack.

The Kremlin was cool when the Egyptians tried to interest the Soviet Union in Jordan.[18] Grateful that the threat of a European war with Egypt had receded, Moscow was not particularly interested in looking for a new source of contention with London or Paris. The Kremlin counseled steady nerves. Cairo was talking about sending a joint Egyptian-Syrian military force to Jordan to bolster the country. Moscow wanted nothing to occur that could give the British a pretext to send more troops into the Middle East. With the Suez Canal lost, London might be considering using Amman as its new strategic center in the region.

As events unfolded, Moscow's understanding of the Suez situation suffered from a lack of any insight into British intentions. Tom Driberg had returned in mid-October to assure Guy Burgess that Eden did not have it in him to resort to force to deal with Nasser. In conveying this information to the Soviet leadership, Burgess had added a note of reserve. He did not think Driberg's optimism was entirely justified.[19] However, with Soviet intelligence unable to detect any evidence to the contrary, the Kremlin, especially Khrushchev, allowed itself to be optimistic about Eden. Khrushchev did not believe that the British would go to war with Egypt. He had convinced himself that the struggle between East and West, which was how he interpreted aggression against his Egyptian ally, would be restricted to political and economic competition in the nuclear age.[20]

■

IN THE WEEK between the secret conclave in Sèvres and the Israeli attack, Hungary so preoccupied Khrushchev that he had little opportunity to test his assumptions about the Middle East. Just as it was gaining confidence in Poland's Wladyslaw Gomulka, the Kremlin lost whatever respect it had for Hungary's Ernö Gerö. Events in Poland had emboldened the leaders of the Hungarian democracy movement to challenge the ineffectual Gerö. On October 22, students at Budapest's Technical Institute published a list of sixteen demands, including the withdrawal of all Soviet troops from Hungary, the nomination of Imre Nagy as Communist Party leader, the organization of national multiparty elections by secret ballot, and the "reconsideration" of the entire Soviet-Hungarian relationship. The next day, amid chants for "national independence and democracy," students tore down the huge statue of Stalin that dominated the city's main square. The revolt radiated outward from the capital, making a mockery of Soviet-style police controls, which had been designed to prevent unofficial public demonstrations. In the eastern provincial center of Debrecen near the Hungarian-Romanian border, students occupied the local party headquarters and the main office of the secret police. Gerö, who was just returning from consultations with Tito in Yugoslavia, was at a loss about what to do.

Khrushchev spent much of October 23 on the telephone with Gerö getting updates on the deteriorating situation in the Hungarian capital. The reports of rebellion in Budapest left no doubt in Khrushchev's mind that it was time for Soviet military intervention. The Soviet Army had already developed plans as early as July for Operation Wave, a military action to crush any street demonstrations in Budapest.[21] In the Kremlin discussion of what measures to take now in Budapest, Mikoyan was again the loudest voice calling for restraint. He believed that Moscow should abandon Gerö and give Nagy the chance as leader to calm the situation. Perhaps Nagy could duplicate what Gomulka had achieved in Warsaw.

Mikoyan's views were ridiculed by the rest of the Soviet leadership. "Hungary is coming apart at the seams already with Nagy," said Molotov.[22] Molotov pressed for the introduction of force. So, too, did Foreign Minister Shepilov, Defense Minister Zhukov, and longtime Presidium members Kaganovich and Suslov. Zhukov and Kaganovich argued that there was no comparison between Poland and the current disorder in Hungary. This time they had to send troops.[23]

Operation Wave began the next day. Moscow had already placed its two mechanized divisions in Hungary on alert when it seemed that the Warsaw Pact was poised to launch a crackdown in Poland. On October 24 thousands of men from these units were sent into Budapest. In addition, portions of a mechanized division in Romania and one in the Ukraine were brought into Hungary to maintain security outside the capital city.[24] To provide reliable reporting for the Kremlin and to test Mikoyan's theories about Nagy's capacity for leadership, Mikoyan and Suslov were also sent to Budapest.

The staggering toll of crushing the Hungarian freedom movement came home to the Soviets on October 28. Suslov, who had by then returned with Mikoyan, reported that on October 24 Soviet forces had opened fire on a group of demonstrators, killing at least 70 of them. Following this massacre, relations between the Hungarians and the Soviet Army reached a new low. The Hungarians began flying mourning flags, and on October 26 a pitched battle broke out between Soviet troops and a large group of armed Hungarian freedom fighters in a section of the capital. The Soviet Army was using tanks as well as infantrymen to crush the revolt. Suslov reported that there had been 3,000 Hungarian casualties, 600 of whom had died. The Soviet Army had itself lost 350 people in battle. Meanwhile Gerö had resigned amid the bloodshed and been replaced by Nagy. Khrushchev's note takers did not write the words "atrocity," "innocent victims," and "war crime" in the official account of the meeting, and it is certain that no one in the room thought to use these words to describe what the Soviet Army had just done in Budapest. Nevertheless, Suslov's report had a chilling effect on the discussion.[25]

Around the room there was scant thirst for additional blood. Following Suslov's report, only the aged Marshal Kliment Voroshilov defended the use of force. "Let's not be in a rush to withdraw the troops," said the Kremlin veteran. "The U.S. intelligence services are working harder than Comrades Suslov and Mikoyan." But Voroshilov was soon drowned out by other leaders calling for a withdrawal from Budapest. Earlier in the day the newly installed regime of Imre Nagy had called for a cease-fire followed by a withdrawal of Soviet troops. Khrushchev held the majority view that this new government should be given a chance. If Nagy could establish control over Budapest, then the Soviet Union would respect a cease-fire and withdraw its troops from the Hungarian capital.

At the end of this long and draining session on October 28, Khrushchev reminded his colleagues they should not lose sight of the propaganda war with the West, especially in the developing world. Soviet moderation now would contrast dramatically with what the imperialists were trying to do in Egypt. "This is politically advantageous for us," said the Soviet leader, who had not completely forgotten Nasser's problem. "The English and the French are stirring up trouble in Egypt. Let's not fall into their camp."[26]

■

A s a temporary cease-fire took hold in Budapest and Soviet troops withdrew from the city, Israel launched its planned nighttime attack on Egypt. On October 29 Israeli planes dropped paratroopers at the entrance to the Mitla Pass in the central Sinai, only forty-five miles from the Suez Canal. Meanwhile Ariel Sharon, then a colonel (and years later the prime minister), led the remainder of the 202 Parachute Brigade across the Sinai to rejoin with this advance force. The Israeli Defense Forces achieved a strategic surprise. The Egyptians had been expecting an Israeli attack on Jordan, not on the Sinai. For days Sharon's force had hugged the border with Jordan to distract Nasser. Israel also achieved a tactical surprise. Two hours before the parachute drop, four Israeli P-51 Mustang fighters had crossed into Sinai airspace to disrupt Egyptian communications. The pilots daringly dropped their planes to an altitude of twelve feet and cut the tops off telephone poles linking the Egyptian commands.[27]

The next day, following the Sèvres script, France and Britain issued their joint ultimatum. The Israeli ambassador in London received his copy at 4:15 P.M., and his Egyptian opposite number ten minutes later. France and Great Britain called on both parties to cease firing and to withdraw ten miles from the Suez Canal. To protect the rights of neutral shipping, France and Great Britain announced their intention to mount a "temporary occupation . . . of key positions at Port Said, Ismailia and Suez."[28] If either the Egyptians or the Israelis did not comply with these demands within twelve hours, UK and French forces would "intervene in whatever strength may be necessary to secure compliance."[29]

■

P resident Eisenhower was not completely surprised when he received reports that Israel had attacked Egypt. For more than a week the White House had been watching the buildup in the region closely. On October 20 the CIA had started daily U-2 flights over the eastern Mediterranean. For a few days there had been some disagreement over whether to interpret Israeli troop movements as preparation for an attack on Jordan or Egypt. But by October 28, with Israeli tanks and armored personnel carriers clearly headed south toward Egypt, not east toward Jordan, the president had become persuaded that Israel was going to attack Egypt.

Eisenhower had also suspected that his French and British allies were making trouble. The spy photographs had revealed an ominous buildup of British and French military assets on the island of Cyprus. As these photographs had been developed and shared with the White House, Eisenhower noticed a dramatic decline in diplomatic messages from the French and the British. The president had been unsure about the extent of their collusion with Israel, but this silence had not been reassuring.

As soon as he learned that Israel had attacked Egypt, Eisenhower informed his advisers that U.S. policy would be to do whatever was necessary to restore peace in the region. By the letter of the Tripartite Declaration of 1950, the United States was obliged to go to Egypt's defense if it was attacked by any of the signatories. France and Great Britain were parties to that declaration, and Eisenhower made it clear that the United States would honor its pledge to Egypt, even at the risk of confronting the British and the French. "In these circumstances," the U.S. president declared, "perhaps we cannot be bound by our traditional alliances."[30] He informed his national security team not to provide any economic support to Great Britain—in particular not to defend the pound sterling in foreign currency markets—if it turned out that the British were colluding with the Israelis.[31] This decision later had dramatic consequences. He also wanted a letter sent to Eden that assured the British that the United States believed it would have to support Egypt if asked under the Tripartite Declaration.[32] Finally Eisenhower wanted the U.S. delegation at the United Nations to table a resolution that day calling for a cease-fire. Some delaying tactics employed by the British and the French late in the day on October 29 postponed discussion on Eisenhower's UN resolution for another twenty-four hours, but his other requests were acted on immediately.

Eisenhower's decisiveness stemmed from a deep concern that only the Soviet Union could benefit from a conflict between the West and an Arab nation. The possibility that France and Britain might have enlisted Israeli assistance for their scheme just increased Eisenhower's pessimism about the effect of the conflict on Western influence in the Middle East.[33] It also increased his anger. He suspected that Paris and London had assumed that he would have to tolerate an attack on Nasser because he needed the Jewish vote in November. American Jews, if they voted as a bloc, tended to vote Democratic, so this assumption was ludicrous.[34] Eisenhower, however, let it be known that whatever the electoral consequences, he planned to oppose this war. "I don't care in the slightest," he told his top advisers, "whether I am re-elected or not. We must make good on our word." He said that though he doubted the American people would "throw him out in the midst of a situation like this." If they did, "so be it."[35]

The French and British ultimatum the next day proved the conspiracy and validated Eisenhower's sense of betrayal. Since late July he had urged French Premier Guy Mollet and British Prime Minister Anthony Eden in every way he knew how not to do anything rash before the election. Eisenhower would probably have looked askance at European aggression in the Middle East after November 6, but he had left no doubt of what his reaction would be up to that time. Eastern Europe was also on Eisenhower's mind. The bloodshed in Budapest on October 24 and October 26 was tragic evidence of what the West had been saying all along about the bankruptcy, moral and otherwise, of the so-called people's republics. London's and Paris's descent into imperial nostalgia over the Suez threatened to undermine the stark contrast that Eisenhower wished to present between the civil West and the brutal East.

■

FOLLOWING THE ISRAELI ATTACK, Cairo expected to hear from Khrushchev, but there was only silence. Early on October 30, before the British and French announced their ultimatum, Nasser's closest aide, Ali Sabri, conveyed a message to Khrushchev through the Soviet Embassy. "With every hour the situation gets worse and is becoming very dangerous."[36] Nasser wanted "unofficially" to request military assistance to help Egypt defend itself against the three armies, Britain, France, and Israel. Sabri added that Nasser was impatient for a response to this unofficial sounding. If Moscow indicated a willingness to support Egypt, a formal request would follow.

Soviet Ambassador Kiselev tried to be helpful to the Egyptians. Although lacking any instructions from Moscow, he asked, "[G]iven the fact that the situation might provoke a third world war, in practical terms, what kind of support does Nasser have in mind?" Sabri had prepared a response: "[T]he deployment of naval vessels close to Egyptian shores would be a major step." He added, "Egypt especially needs the help of an air force." Nasser wanted Sabri to raise the possibility of Soviet volunteers, especially pilots, participating in the defense of Egypt.

Nasser did not wait for the response to repeat this request in a letter to the Kremlin. "The enemy is relying solely on air power," he wrote. "We desperately need air support for our troops." Nasser wanted the Soviet Air Force to intervene on the side of Egypt. He suggested that Soviet volunteers flying MiGs carrying the Egyptian insignia be sent to Egypt. "We will prepare air bases and let you know regarding their location."[37]

Khrushchev ignored both Egyptian requests for Soviet military intervention. He decided to take a chance on Nasser's being able to survive this military crisis on his own. Soviet intelligence believed the Egyptians militarily a match for the Israelis and thought the Egyptians would be in grave danger only if the Western Europeans got involved. Khrushchev clung to the comforting assumption that an Anglo-French attack on Egypt was unlikely. Faced with U.S. opposition to the use of force against Nasser, about which Khrushchev knew from intelligence sources, the British would restrain themselves in Egypt. Soon after the announcement of the Anglo-French ultimatum, Soviet intelligence had reassured Khrushchev that the Europeans were indeed not colluding with Israel against Egypt. Instead the GRU predicted that the British and presumably the French "were preparing to assist Egypt in isolating the Canal from Israel or any other aggressor."[38] Lacking any inside information on Britain's military objectives, and still captive to the portrayal of a weak prime minister provided by Burgess's and Maclean's sources, Khrushchev opted to take the Western powers' ultimatum at face value and let Nasser be protected by the Western Europeans or the United States.

It was uncharacteristic of Khrushchev to abandon an ally in danger. Hungary was the reason for his behavior toward Nasser at the end of October 1956. The Soviet leader was incapable of managing two military crises simultaneously, at least not these particular crises. The problems in Hungary were so overwhelming that Khrushchev concluded he had no choice but to set his Egyptian allies adrift and hope for the best.

The day the Israelis began their attack on Egypt, Soviet troops, including additional units from outside Hungary, were mobilizing for a possible return to Budapest to crush any renewal of the anti-Soviet revolt. On October 30, as news arrived of the Middle East ultimatum from the French and the British calling on both Egypt and Israel to withdraw from either side of the Suez Canal, Khrushchev was agonizing over what to do next in Hungary. Khrushchev revealed his indecision that day to Mao's representative in Moscow, Liu Chiao Chi. "The troops must stay in Hungary and Budapest," was the advice of the Chinese representative.[39] But Khrushchev was not so sure. "There are two options," he explained: "First to use force, second to negotiate a withdrawal of forces."

Throughout October 30 the discussion among the Kremlin leaders involved much more than the decision to use force or not in Hungary. The actions of the Nagy government were calling into question a basic Soviet assumption about the stability of the highly centralized alliance system that the Kremlin had imposed upon Eastern Europe. In both Poland and Hungary Moscow had initially blamed any instability in the streets on the weakness of the local Communists. In Poland the Kremlin had then wondered if Gomulka was encouraging this disorder. But Khrushchev had since been reassured that Gomulka was a true Communist who understood that he needed friendship with Moscow. At this point in the Hungarian crisis the Kremlin did not know what to think about Nagy or the movement that seemed to have brought him to power.

A hothouse environment prevailed in the Kremlin as Shepilov, Zhukov, and Khrushchev began discussing the phenomenon of national communism. "We will have to contend with national communism for a long while," observed a depressed Shepilov.[40] "This is a lesson for us in the military-political sphere," added Zhukov. Stalin had used this phrase to sentence Tito to death. This form of communism implied more differentiation in how socialism was implemented and a more distant relationship with Moscow. For Stalin the phrase had been shorthand for anti-Sovietism. Khrushchev and his associates, however, were not yet prepared to give up on managing foreign Communist leaders who were also strong nationalists.

It will be recalled that Khrushchev in particular had not liked how Stalin dealt with the Yugoslavs and believed that there was more that united Communists than set them apart. On October 30 others of the Kremlin elite shared enough of this basic optimism about fellow Communists that they became very creative in trying to work out the problem of national communism. Ultimately Khrushchev spoke for most in the room when he announced that there should be a complete overhaul of the way Moscow managed its Eastern European allies, which up until this point had been treated like colonies. As of 1956 Soviet troops were stationed in Poland, Romania, and Hungary without any legal basis. In Hungary, for example, this troop deployment was initially justified by an agreement with Budapest that allowed for the Soviet Union to protect the supply lines to its occupying forces in Austria. But the occupation of Austria had ended in mid-1955, and Soviet troops were still in Hungary.

Under the threat of the complete collapse of the Warsaw Pact, the Kremlin began considering how it might reduce its military and security presence in each of the socialist countries. Khrushchev had already permitted the Poles to send its KGB advisers and Soviet officers packing. If the relationship were to become less imperial, Moscow would have to tolerate the same independence in Budapest and start negotiations with Poland and Romania to reduce its troops there as well.

A sense of unreality pervaded the discussion. Despite the fact that by calling for multiparty elections, Nagy was breaking a key unspoken rule for leaders in the socialist bloc, Khrushchev believed that a Soviet declaration of a new style in the handling of the satellites would be enough to bring him and the Hungarian rebels home to the Soviet Union. There can be no other way of explaining this hastily improvised policy than as a function of Khrushchev's belief that other Communist leaders shared his intense devotion to their faith. Nagy might well resent the symbols of Soviet power, but Khrushchev argued that he would not do anything to undermine the existence of a socialist Hungary. This was a test of Khrushchev's assumption that even the most independent socialist regime, such as Yugoslavia and perhaps now Hungary, would ultimately choose to ally itself with Moscow.

A few hours after the meeting ended, Moscow received the first signs of how wrong this assumption about Nagy was. Over Hungarian Radio in the afternoon of October 30, Nagy announced the end of the one-party state in Hungary and called for multiparty elections. The next morning he was to declare his government's decision to remove Hungary from the Warsaw Pact.

Khrushchev's other key assumption on October 30 was that the United States would step in to contain the Western Europeans before they attacked Nasser. For at least a brief moment this assumption appeared validated. Late in the day, just before Britain and France's twelve-hour ultimatum would have lapsed, the United States introduced a resolution at the UN Security Council calling for an immediate cease-fire in the Sinai. For the first time in the Cold War, the Soviet Union found itself on the same side as Washington in a dispute with the Western Europeans. The Soviet ambassador at the UN supported the U.S. resolution. But the British, who as one of the five permanent members had a veto over all Security Council resolutions, used their veto to kill their American ally's proposal. Both the British and the French offered the feeble excuse that the UN was not the proper place to solve the problems of the Middle East. Nevertheless, the Americans were now on record as opposing war in the Middle East.

The events of October 31, 1956, however, overturned Khrushchev's basic assumptions about how to manage the challenges in both Hungary and

Egypt. Two shocking pieces of news hit at precisely the same time. From Hungary came word that despite Khrushchev's expectations, Nagy was now calling for withdrawal from the Warsaw Pact. Meanwhile hundreds of miles away, on the pretext that Israel and Egypt had violated the London and Paris ultimatum, squadrons of British and French aircraft had started bombing Egyptian cities and airfields. Soviet intelligence, which only the day before had assured Khrushchev that Britain would not come to Egypt's aid, now began providing increasingly dire descriptions of the losses to Egyptian weaponry, much of it Soviet made and as yet unpaid for.[41]

These events left the Soviet Union without a strategy to cope with either crisis. The realization that he had so badly misjudged the situations in both Egypt and Hungary left Khrushchev extremely defensive and belligerent. He called the Presidium into session and angrily called for defiance: "If we depart from Hungary, it will give a great boost to the Americans, English and French—the imperialists. They will perceive it as weakness on our part and will go onto the offensive. We would then be exposing the weakness of our positions. Our party will not accept it, if we do this. To Egypt they will add Hungary. We have no other choice."[42] Britain's and France's attack on Egypt upset Khrushchev's calculations in Hungary. A day earlier Khrushchev had been prepared to take a risk that Nagy would quell the revolt in Hungary and resume good relations as a Communist ally of the Soviet Union. Now he could no longer tolerate any uncertainty over Hungary's future in the Soviet Empire. Khrushchev's personal prestige and that of the Soviet Union would not recover if Moscow were to lose two allies in quick succession. Moreover, with the world in crisis, he could ill afford to appear to be retreating in Europe, even if his intention was eventually to restore Soviet power through political means.

Khrushchev decided to deal with the Hungarian problem first and harshly. The previous day's Presidium decision not to use force was immediately overturned, as was the new policy on relations with the socialist bloc. All but Mikoyan, who still hoped to find a peaceful way out of the crisis in Hungary, joined the majority in voting for the largest military assault on European civilians since the end of World War II.

The Presidium discussion was bloodless. It was one of concepts—power, party, stability, and prestige—and not of the fate of human beings. The result, however, was anything but bloodless. The Kremlin ordered the Soviet Army back into Budapest and authorized the use of lethal force against civilians who resisted the reimposition of Moscow's imperial control over the country. It is one of the great tragedies of the twentieth century that the alternative policy toward Eastern Europe was never tested. Eventually the Kremlin might well have determined that there was no choice but to use tanks. Still, who can tell what might have happened in Budapest had the situation been allowed to develop over an additional week or two? Arguably, the Soviet reaction might then have been even more ferocious. But other outcomes might have prevailed.

Regarding Egypt, Khrushchev painfully chose continued inaction. Besides his desperation over Hungary, what may have restrained him was a real fear that Soviet intervention in Egypt could spin out of control. The Soviet Union could not afford to risk fighting a two-front war. Were he to agree to the Egyptian request for Soviet air power, for example, Soviet pilots would soon find themselves firing on the British and the French and perhaps later U.S. pilots.

Khrushchev was not even willing to attempt a sustained political strategy that would at least show solidarity with the Egyptians. Earlier in the day the Kremlin had received an urgent request for some public diplomacy from the Soviet ambassador in Cairo. "Any declaration," Kiselev advised the Kremlin, "would lift the spirits of the Arabs." It was the opinion of both KGB and Soviet diplomatic representatives in Cairo that Moscow's inactivity was harming the Soviet position in the region. They noticed a tendency in the Egyptian press to "exaggerate the peaceful role of the USA in the current events and to hush up our efforts to condemn the Anglo-French intervention and those directed to a liquidation of the conflict." The Soviet ambassador said that Egyptians were criticizing the Soviet Union for getting Nasser to take Soviet advice and, now that Egypt was in this critical situation, for remaining silent. Kiselev wanted Moscow to start an immediate propaganda campaign to attack the United States for its hypocrisy in pleading for peace while apparently allowing its NATO allies to commit aggression against a sovereign state.[43] In response to Kiselev's request, *Pravda* published a statement the next day that blamed France, Britain, and Israel for colluding against the nationalist aspirations of the Arab world but did not suggest a specific response.[44]

For the next three days Khrushchev preoccupied himself with the details of the Soviet-led counterrevolution in Hungary and acted as if he had written off the huge Soviet investment in the Middle East. He flew to the Polish-Soviet border to brief Gomulka, then went to Bucharest to meet with the Romanians and the Czechs and to Sofia for discussions with the Bulgarians. Finally, on November 3, the eve of the Soviet assault on Budapest, he visited with Tito in Yugoslavia. The Presidium met in his absence, but there was no discussion of anything but Hungary. The Kremlin was absorbed with planning the post-Nagy regime. János Kádár, a member of Nagy's government, was secretly in Moscow and would proclaim a new government on the heels of the Soviet advance. In this second Soviet assault on Budapest, which started on November 4, there were twenty-thousand Hungarian casualties, including Imre Nagy, who fled to the Yugoslav Embassy but was later turned over to the Soviets.[45]

■

Moscow LEFT the Egyptians to fend for themselves until after the assault had begun on Budapest. On November 4 the Kremlin issued its first official protest of the Anglo-French military intervention, a toothless call for a cease-fire. Four days into the Western attack, Nasser's military situation was grim. The superiority of Western pilots and equipment had decimated the Egyptian Air Force. The Soviet military estimated that the Egyptians had lost twenty-nine of their forty-eight IL-28 light jet bombers and seventy-six of their eighty-six Soviet-made MiG-15B fighters. Western air attacks on the Egyptian Army were equally successful. On November 2 alone, European planes had destroyed fifty Egyptian tanks and were now systematically destroying Egyptian weaponry. What couldn't be destroyed from the air the Israelis were capturing or destroying on the ground. The Soviets had reports that the Israelis had captured the matériel from two whole artillery battalions in the Sinai after Nasser had abandoned the entire eastern bank of the Suez Canal.[46]

On the morning of November 5, when Khrushchev received reports that eleven hundred British and French paratroopers were landing in Egypt, he did not sink into a deeper depression over the future of his Egyptian ally. Instead he reacted to this development as if it were a personal challenge and once more demonstrated a capacity for dramatic, unpredictable behavior. It is not known for sure why a week into the Mideast war Khrushchev finally chose to act decisively on behalf of his Egyptian ally. A possible explanation is that he had always wanted to do something but that so long as the Hungarian matter was unresolved, he refused to assume the risks inherent in acting in the Middle East. By November 5, however, the crackdown was in full swing in Budapest and Hungarian resistance was quickly collapsing. This freed him to contemplate strong action somewhere else.

Whatever the immediate cause, the result would be a grandiose act of desperation. With the situation dire for Nasser and a Soviet conventional counterattack in the Middle East unacceptable to Moscow, it seemed to Khrushchev that he had to find a way to scare France and Britain into a cease-fire. As he had in the discussion of Poland on October 21, he dominated his Kremlin equals in explaining how this might work. He wanted the Soviet Union to rally the world behind a concerted effort to save Nasser. "We should go to the General Assembly or the Security Council," Khrushchev stated. "We should present an ultimatum and blame the aggressors."[47]

For the first time since the London Conference, Middle East policy was now the main focus of the Kremlin. Moscow shrugged off its earlier passive acceptance of Egyptian despair, and there was a new energy behind Khrushchev's words. He had decided not to give up. But what could the Soviet Union do? It was later said that during Syrian President Quwatly's visit on October 30, Marshal Zhukov had brought out a map to prove to the Syrian leader that there was no way the Soviet Union could defend Egypt. That scene may have been apocryphal, but on November 5 Khrushchev understood there was little in the way of military support that the Kremlin could give. "We would prefer cooperation," he said to his colleagues, "but if not we can send the fleet." As he well knew, the Soviet fleet could not hold its own in a struggle with France or Great Britain. He had been the one who advocated spending less money on a surface fleet so as to be able to invest in future submarines.

A bluff was the only real alternative if Khrushchev wanted to compel the Europeans to accept an immediate cease-fire. From Western newspaper reports, Khrushchev was aware that the West was watching very closely the development of a Soviet medium-range ballistic missile, the R5-m. Once deployed in the European part of the USSR, these missiles could theoretically strike targets in London and Paris. As in the case of the Soviet long-range bomber fleet, Western estimates far exceeded Soviet capabilities. Soviet trials of the R-5m, their first missile to carry a nuclear warhead, had begun as early as January 1955. Although the CIA began reporting in 1956 that the Soviets had this missile, called the SS-3 by NATO, the final stages of development and deployment of this missile would not take place until much later.[48] There were no R-5ms on combat duty in November 1956.[49]

Without any real military options, Khrushchev believed he had no choice but to exploit Western fears of Soviet nuclear capabilities. Nuclear bluff was risky, but Khrushchev was now determined to rescue Nasser. He suggested that the Kremlin send threatening messages to the French, the British, and the Israelis. At the same time, he wanted to explore the possibility of working with the United States to achieve a cease-fire. Washington was saying publicly that it opposed what its allies were doing in the Middle East. Extending the offer of an unprecedented joint Soviet-American intervention for peace would test U.S. intentions. If this offer were rejected, at least Khrushchev would have smoked out Eisenhower's real sympathies and gained a propaganda victory.

The Kremlin unanimously approved the strategy. Telegrams would be sent to the United States and to French and British leaders, as well as to India's Nehru to build support in the third world, and an explanatory communication to Nasser. Although Khrushchev dictated the tone and even some of the phrases, all the messages were prepared to go out under the signature of the Soviet president, Nikolai Bulganin.[50]

At fifteen minutes before 10:00 P.M., Moscow time, on November 5, Moscow radio broadcast Bulganin's message to Prime Minister Eden: "In what position would Britain have found herself had it been attacked by more powerful states possessing all types of modern weapons of destruction?" Bulganin added, "We are full of determination to crush the aggressor and reestablish peace in the East by using force."

In Washington, where it was the early afternoon, Eisenhower expressed concern when he heard about Moscow's threats to the Europeans. Observing that Khrushchev and his Kremlin colleagues "were scared and furious," the president explained, "there is nothing more dangerous than a dictatorship in this state of mind."[51] He did not take seriously Khrushchev's proposal that the superpowers should work together to stabilize the situation in Egypt. His principal concern remained that Moscow should not gain additional influence in the Middle East. The messages from Moscow only caused Eisenhower to redouble his efforts to compel the British and French to accept a cease-fire agreement lest the Soviets be given a pretext for further action.

The French government took the Soviet threat seriously. U.S. Ambassador C. Douglas Dillon was called in to see French Prime Minister Mollet and Foreign Minister Pineau. French and British paratroopers had easily captured the town of Port Said at the northern end of the canal, and Egyptian military resistance was melting away, yet the French government seemed to understand that time was running out on the Suez operation. Paris had every reason to believe that Bulganin's message would mandate some form of response from Washington, and there was every possibility that the United States would want the French and the British out of Egypt. To forestall a hasty American demand, Mollet and Pineau told Dillon that they were ready to accept a cease-fire, perhaps as early as the next day, but under certain conditions. They asked that the UN Security Council resolution be sponsored by the United States, not by the Soviet Union. France also wanted the right to occupy the canal until "it is functioning normally" and was considering calling for "free elections" in Egypt to ensure that the final settlement of the Suez problem would be negotiated with someone other than Nasser. The French were clearly not yet ready to abandon their objectives. They hoped the United States would help them achieve what they could not by force of arms.[52]

Anthony Eden also sensed that the operation was doomed. Although we cannot be certain, it appears that Moscow's threatening message was not Britain's greatest concern on the morning of November 6. The issue of the moment was the possibility of a financial crisis triggered by events in the Middle East. This had come about because of a central flaw in the British operation, the amount of time required to capture the canal and, it was hoped, to cause Nasser's removal. It had been eight days since Israel launched its attack, six days since the start of the air campaign, and two days since British and French paratroopers had landed near Port Said. Over this period foreign currency traders had become concerned about Britain's future oil supply and began dumping their holdings in British sterling. Just two days earlier Nasserist forces in Syria had sabotaged a key oil pipeline that ran through that country, and the Egyptians had begun to sink ships in the Suez Canal, the other main oil route to Britain.

Having assumed that the Americans would reluctantly support any military action against Egypt, the British had never considered how they would manage the economic consequences of the operation. International sales were now placing immense downward pressure on the value of the pound sterling. As part of the international financial system established in the aftermath of World War II, national currencies were pegged to a fixed value by international agreement, and when changes occurred in the demand for its money, a country was obliged to respond by buying or selling either bonds denominated in its own currency or gold reserves. The British were hard pressed to cope with the steep decline of the pound that followed the invasion, but they were confident that the U.S. Treasury would step in to help them defend the pound by buying it up in currency markets. But Eisenhower had already decided to let British currency sink. Every day that the military operation continued, the British were hemorrhaging gold and dollars, hard currency they desperately needed to purchase oil from Venezuela and the other non–Middle Eastern oil producers. By the morning of November 6, it was becoming clear to the chancellor of the exchequer, Britain's finance minister, Harold Macmillan, that without U.S. assistance, the British government could not afford the war. Since that support was not forthcoming, Macmillan concluded that Britain had to end its little Egyptian war.[53]

Macmillan had been a strong hawk. He had also allowed himself to become entangled in the web of misconceptions that guided Eden's policy toward Suez. He too had believed that when push came to shove, the United

States would back its allies. During the Second World War he had been Eisenhower's political chief in liberated Algiers. Just a month before hostilities broke out in Egypt, Macmillan had stopped in Washington to take the temperature of his old wartime comrade on a British assault against Egypt. He left assuming he had Eisenhower's understanding, if not blessing for military action. He was mistaken.

Eden knew the writing was on the wall when Macmillan turned against the action. Calling a cabinet meeting in the morning to decide what to do next about the Suez action, the prime minister curiously relegated to the back burner the problem of how to respond to the Soviets. A veteran Foreign Office diplomat, Patrick Reilly, who was being trained for a future posting as British ambassador in Moscow, was assigned the job of writing the response to Bulganin.[54] Besides having at his disposal a fine set of ideas that the current British ambassador, William Hayter, had cabled that morning, Reilly had no other guidance. It seemed that replying to Moscow was an afterthought in a busy day.

British intelligence was not taking the Kremlin's nuclear threat nonchalantly. Chester Cooper, the CIA station chief in London, recalls a tense meeting of Britain's Joint Intelligence Committee to which he was invited on November 6. The gathered British intelligence chiefs had only one significant question for the American: "Do the Soviets have missiles that could reach London?" When Cooper reported that the Soviets did not, everyone in the room visibly relaxed.[55]

The British cabinet decided that morning to seek a cease-fire in Egypt despite not having achieved its objective. With the decision made, Eden had the Foreign Office summon Reilly to complete the draft response to the Russians. London wanted Moscow to know that it no longer had any reason to be alarmed. The Suez operation was about to end. Reilly was told to bring the draft to 10 Downing Street after lunch.

Reilly, who had been personal assistant to the chief of British intelligence in World War II, had witnessed some dramatic discussions in his career. But on November 6, 1956, he found a listless prime minister and a distracted foreign minister. Eden took the draft and played with it for a while. Scoring a sentence here and a word there, he was like the child pushing an unwanted vegetable from one side of his plate to another. Reilly's immediate boss, Selwyn Lloyd, was even less interested in what Britain ought to tell the Soviets. Reilly later described the foreign secretary as obsessively nattering about how he had to speak to the Venezuelan ambassador that afternoon— about oil, no doubt. Reilly was surprised that he was asked to wait in the room, while Eden placed a call to Guy Mollet. With the support of the cabinet behind him, Eden was asking the French to accept a cease-fire that day.

In Paris the American Douglas Dillon was in Mollet's office suggesting that the French leader call Eden when the call came through. Mollet's subsequent conversation with Eden ended French resistance to an unconditional cease-fire.[56]

For the British and the French, November 6 brought a tremendous anticlimax to the events since Israel launched its attack. The only sound was that of the air being let out of British and French imperial pretensions in the Middle East and the simultaneous inflation of Soviet self-confidence. Delighted by the turnaround and unaware of the backstage role that Washington had played in pressing Eden to stop the war, the Soviets indulged themselves in believing that it was fear of their power, especially their nuclear weapons, that had been central to the demise of the Anglo-French military operation.

For Khrushchev, the Anglo-French collapse and the eventual withdrawal of their forces and those of Israel from Egypt was a satisfying personal victory. It was nearly miraculous that Egypt had been spared. Only a week earlier Khrushchev faced the prospect of losing his key ally in the developing world as the price for restoring order in his Eastern European empire. But events had ultimately moved in Khrushchev's favor. Besides vindicating the risky policy that Khrushchev had been advocating in the Middle East since 1955, Nasser's survival demonstrated the utility of the nuclear bluff for the weaker superpower in international politics. Now it seemed to Khrushchev that he had found in the nuclear bluff an effective way to weaken Soviet adversaries on the cheap. Ironically the problem of Egyptian defense, a challenge that since July 1956 had produced ample evidence of the limits of Soviet power, served to give Khrushchev an inflated sense of what he could do abroad.

6

"KHRUSHCHEY'S COMET"

In late 1956 the CIA assembled some spy photographs on a large briefing board to give President Eisenhower an overhead view of the Suez Canal. Gamal Abdel Nasser had sunk large ships to close the Suez Canal in retaliation for the Anglo-French attack, and now that the war was over Eisenhower had asked to see the damage sustained by the canal.[1]

Eisenhower, who kept a neat desk, did not want the board on his desk or even on an easel beside it. Instead the president asked the startled CIA analyst who had brought the photographs to place them on the floor of the Oval Office. Eisenhower then knelt and on his hands and knees began examining the images. What he saw stirred the famous Eisenhower temper. "Stupid, stupid, stupid!" he muttered as he paused to look at each of the wrecked ships. More than fifty of them were clogging what he knew to be the most important commercial seaway in the world. The president was convinced that Nasser would never have closed the Suez Canal were it not for Anglo-French invasion. For one thing, Cairo badly needed the revenue from the tolls. Indeed, the Egyptians were already working very hard, and very efficiently, to clean up this mess. Despite their efforts, the canal remained closed until April 1957.[2]

The blocked Suez Canal symbolized for Eisenhower the self-inflicted wound that the West had suffered in the Middle East in 1956. Even though the United States had played a decisive role in ending the Suez crisis and as a result had earned the gratitude of many developing nations, Eisenhower was convinced that Khrushchev had emerged the bigger winner. By openly trying to overthrow Nasser, the French and the British had a lost a lot of their remaining influence in the Arab world, creating a power vacuum that the Kremlin was well positioned to fill.

Eisenhower had shown that he understood Egyptian sensitivities about control of the Suez Canal, but he still could not grasp Gamal Abdel Nasser. By 1957 the White House had ample evidence to conclude that Nasser was no more an agent of Communist influence than he was a stooge of the West. He was a political animal who was prepared to bargain with any side in the Cold War to achieve whatever end he thought Egypt needed. Indeed, a careful review of Nasser's actions since 1954 would have shown that in spite of his cooperation with the Kremlin, the Egyptian leader consistently preferred dealing with the United States. In 1955 Nasser had delayed purchasing weapons from the Soviet Union to see if the United States could come close to Moscow's sweetheart deal. In early 1956 his representatives had spent months negotiating millions of U.S. dollars in secured loans to construct the Aswan High Dam before the United States summarily ended these talks. Later, on the eve of the Anglo-French attack, he had sent Washington a secret plea for diplomatic assistance so that he would not have to turn to Khrushchev yet again. And most recently, just after the cease-fire had taken hold in Egypt, Nasser reiterated his commitment to good relations with the United States.[3] Nasser's ideology, if he had any at all, was Arab nationalism.

Yet Cold War concerns so distorted the lens through which the Eisenhower administration viewed the Middle East that the U.S. government convinced itself that communism, with Nasser's assistance, was the main political force shaping the region in 1957. If the United States did nothing, the administration assumed the Soviet Union would rapidly fill the political vacuum created by the collapse of French and British influence. Eisenhower also became convinced that the Soviets wanted to control the oil reserves of the Middle East.[4] The president's anxiety over the future of the region was reinforced by his secretary of state, John Foster Dulles, who was always quicker than his boss to perceive a Soviet challenge and was even less attuned to the mass phenomenon of Arab nationalism.

On January 5, 1957, Eisenhower announced a new political offensive to meet this perceived threat to the Middle East. In a special message to Congress, he formally extended U.S. protection over the entire region. Immediately dubbed the Eisenhower Doctrine, the statement established a U.S. commitment to provide economic and military aid (though not direct military intervention) to "any nation or group of nations in the general area of the Middle East" in light of "the increased danger from International Communism."[5] As Eisenhower later explained, his objective was to demonstrate his administration's "resolve to block the Soviet Union's march to the Mediterranean, to the Suez Canal and the pipelines, and to the underground lakes of oil which fuel the homes and factories of Western Europe."[6] Had the statement been combined with a new initiative to resolve the Arab-Israeli conflict, then it might have been greeted in the Arab world with more approval.

But in so forcefully pursuing the bogeyman of Soviet influence, the United States sent the message that it was departing from its traditional role as honest broker in the region. In the mid-1950s nationalists like Nasser had turned to Washington as a counterweight to Great Britain's imperial pretensions. Now Washington was speaking as if it intended to become Britain's successor in the area. Eisenhower's misunderstanding of the political dynamics in the Middle East soon complicated U.S. policy in the region and handed Khrushchev new opportunities to expand Soviet influence.[7]

■

EISENHOWER AND the U.S. government had made a serious misjudgment about both Moscow's intentions and capabilities. The Kremlin was in no mood for a foreign policy offensive in the Middle East or anywhere else in January 1957. The twin crises of the autumn in Hungary and Egypt had taken a heavy toll on Soviet self-confidence and on Khrushchev's leadership. Despite the Soviet Army's success in crushing the Hungarian revolt and Khrushchev's apparent feat in using the new tactic of nuclear bluff to pull victory from the jaws of defeat in Egypt, his preeminence in the Presidium was now under intense scrutiny. Fortunately for him, his colleagues did not agree on what had gone wrong in late 1956. The old guard eclipsed by Khrushchev in 1955 blamed him for even attempting a political solution with Imre Nagy. Former Soviet Foreign Minister Vyacheslav Molotov had been complaining for two years that Khrushchev was naive in his handling of foreign Communists, like Tito of Yugoslavia, who wanted to be independent of Moscow. When Nagy tried to take Hungary out of the Warsaw Pact and endorsed a call by Hungarian students for a reexamination of relations with Moscow, Molotov felt vindicated. Lazar Kaganovich, a member of the Kremlin leadership since the 1920s, and Georgi Malenkov shared Molotov's concerns.

Khrushchev and his protégés in the Kremlin interpreted the Hungarian incident differently, finding its causes in the failures of socialism in Eastern Europe. None of these men, Khrushchev included, was psychologically prepared to blame the lack of personal freedom under socialism for the fragility of the governments in Eastern Europe. Nor did they hold Western intrigue responsible for the political upheaval in the region, an excuse that would have permitted them to sidestep tough questions about what had happened in October 1956. Instead this group, which constituted a majority in the Presidium, had reached the disquieting conclusion that the Polish and Hungarian governments had brought workers as well as students into the streets by failing to provide their citizens with adequate standards of living.

What made the analysis telling for the Kremlin was that it led to the unspoken but shared assumption that the Soviet Union was not itself immune from political disorder for similar reasons. Barely two weeks after the Soviet troops had put down the rebellion in Budapest, Khrushchev called for an immediate reexamination of the budget for 1957, the second year of a five-year plan announced in 1956. He suggested an emergency investment in Soviet residential housing construction and more funds targeted at raising the material well-being of Soviet workers.[8] The Presidium rallied around the proposal, despite the fact that this infusion of capital would put additional stress on the Soviet budget. Any fiscal qualms were outweighed by the conviction that Soviet standards of living, especially for the industrial working class, had to be improved to forestall political trouble.

The Hungarian effect could also be seen in a hardening of the Kremlin's attitude toward political dissent at home. Khrushchev encountered no opposition when he suggested that the Communist Party begin cracking down on "anti-Soviet and hostile elements" in the USSR.[9] He wanted a subcommittee of the Presidium to reexamine sentencing for political crimes. Since Stalin's death in 1953 the Soviet Union had rapidly dismantled much of the widespread gulag system of concentration camps. Thanks to Khrushchev's policy of destalinization the vast majority of the 2.5 million prisoners of the gulag had already been released.[10] The Hungarian rebellion did not compel Khrushchev to reconstitute the system, but it played on existing concerns that perhaps his act of clemency had gone too far. "We were scared, really scared," Khrushchev recalled later. "We were afraid the thaw might unleash a flood, which we wouldn't be able to control and which could drown us."[11] In December 1956 Khrushchev wondered aloud if some dangerous political opponents who should remain isolated from the general population had been released. "About those we have released from prison and exile," he confessed to the Presidium on December 6, "some don't deserve it."[12] Having seen how the workers had taken up the banner of the Hungarian students, he was eager to prevent disgruntled Soviet workers from finding similar anti-Kremlin leadership at home.

Khrushchev and his old guard critics were of one mind on domestic dissent in 1957. When Khrushchev recommended that the KGB and the Ministry of the Interior be instructed to work harder to root out dissenters, Malenkov and Molotov agreed. Molotov added the grumble that Soviet propaganda had become too weak. He believed it was dangerous to admit that Soviet standards of living were not high. Even Mikoyan spoke up on the importance of strengthening the "party outlook" of the people.[13] Shortly thereafter Soviet soldiers and civilians who were believed to sympathize with the Hungarian reformers started serving sentences in the few remaining camps.[14]

■

CURIOUSLY, IN LIGHT of Washington's assessment of the Kremlin's renewed self-confidence in the Middle East after the collapse of the Anglo-French intervention, the one criticism of Khrushchev that most of the Presidium seemed to share in early 1957 was that he had mishandled the Suez crisis. Both the old Stalinists and some of the younger leaders saw the crisis as a by-product of Khrushchev's eagerness to expand Soviet commitments to Nasser and other Arab states. Even Mikoyan, Khrushchev's friend and political ally, sided with those who believed that Suez had been an unnecessary crisis for the Soviet Union.[15]

Eisenhower's public commitment to fighting communism in the Middle East had the momentary, and no doubt unintended, effect of rallying new support for Egypt in the Kremlin even among those leaders who regarded Nasser as an untrustworthy ally who had dragged Moscow into an unwanted crisis. The Egyptians had recently turned to the Soviets for military assistance at cut-rate prices to rebuild after their losses in the Suez crisis. The cost alone gave Moscow pause. There was also the long-standing Kremlin concern about what Nasser would do with these weapons. Before the nationalization of the Suez Canal, Khrushchev had warned Nasser not to build up his arsenal to the extent that it provoked the more powerful Western powers. However, with Eisenhower's having thrown down the gauntlet, even those who had been wary about providing military assistance to Nasser now supported an arms deal. On January 31, less than a month after the U.S. president announced his new doctrine, Moscow approved a multimillion-dollar package for Cairo.[16]

This was but a blip, however; little more than posturing to show the United States that the Soviet Union was not afraid of the new doctrine. Most of the Presidium opposed any more Middle Eastern adventures. Khrushchev, who wanted to do much more for the Arabs than send them weapons, soon learned that there were limits to how far his colleagues would go to meet the U.S. challenge to the region. Skeptics of Khrushchev's policy were prepared to help the Arabs help themselves, but the consensus in the Kremlin in the wake of the Suez crisis was that it should do nothing to increase the odds that Soviet forces would ever have to fight in the Middle East.

These limits were visible in how the Kremlin responded to the trouble brewing in Syria. Since Soviet-Syrian relations had warmed in 1956, Damascus had worried about Western retaliation. Following the declaration of the Eisenhower

Doctrine, the Syrians became convinced that the U.S. government would soon invade their country. When the Syrians approached the Soviets in March 1957 for a commitment to send volunteer pilots to Egypt or Syria, the Kremlin responded that though it would continue to supply arms to Syria, sending volunteer pilots "might involve negative consequences for both the Arab states and the Soviet Union."[17] Malenkov and Molotov, long skeptical of the relationship with Egypt, led the opposition to expanding Soviet assistance to Syria.

Although disappointed at his colleagues for not strengthening his initiatives in the Middle East, Khrushchev shared the sense that this was not the right time to do anything that might goad the Americans. "This is a dangerous moment," he explained in a secret session in the Kremlin.[18] He made this statement in April 1957 during a Kremlin discussion that he and Mikoyan led on the current international balance of power. Both men believed that because both superpowers were suspicious and still licking their wounds after the events of 1956, the odds of a nuclear war's happening were increasing.[19] Moscow had had its brush with defeat in Hungary. The West had lost in Egypt. Khrushchev and Mikoyan saw the uneasy peace that had held between Moscow and Washington since the end of World War II as more fragile than ever. Under these conditions, Khrushchev believed that the Soviet Union had to redouble its efforts to achieve some form of disarmament.

Khrushchev's subsequent effort to revise the Soviet Union's position at the negotiations of the United Nations subcommittee on disarmament, where the world's largest powers had been discussing the issue since 1955, ran into as much opposition as had his earlier effort to do more to help Syria. The United States had just announced a unilateral cut in the size of its military, which Khrushchev viewed as a hopeful sign. "If the enemy is ready to make real concessions," he argued, "we should not be diehard."[20] But the disarmament issue caused deep rifts within the Soviet leadership. Naturally Khrushchev found himself at odds with Molotov.[21] But increasingly Malenkov, Khrushchev's former ally in the struggle for a policy of peaceful coexistence, was wary of creative approaches to reaching agreement with the West.

Most striking, however, was the form that the disarmament debate took between Khrushchev and the Soviet armed forces. Under the leadership of Marshal Zhukov, the Soviet military staked out a very pro-disarmament position. The reason for this commitment, which differed rather dramatically from the position taken by its counterparts in the Pentagon, who had been vary of Eisenhower's Open Skies proposal, was a judgment about strategic intelligence. Zhukov's military intelligence chiefs could not produce enough information on Western capabilities at NATO's bases in Europe. The Soviets had not been able to develop their own version of the U-2, and spy satellites were still a figment of the imagination. What technology could not provide the Soviet Army, diplomacy might. With strong backing from their military, Soviet delegates at the disarmament talks in London in November 1956 had offered a plan for partial aerial surveillance that covered sixteen hundred kilometers between Paris and the Soviet-Polish border.[22] In this next round of talks the Soviet military hoped to go further, perhaps as far as to allow parts of the Soviet Union to be inspected so as to open parts of the United States to Soviet airplanes.

Unlike in the disagreement over Syria, Khrushchev appeared to emerge victorious from the April 1957 disarmament discussions in the Kremlin. The outcome was a personal defeat for Molotov and Malenkov and a one-sided compromise between Khrushchev and the Soviet military that benefited Khrushchev. The new policy was to accept mutual cuts in the size of NATO and Warsaw Pact armies and to halt all nuclear testing for two years. Khrushchev conceded to Zhukov that for the first time the Soviet Union would offer to open some of its territory to overflights, but he managed to dress it up in a formula that he knew the West would never accept. The portion to be opened was Siberia, which had no missile sites and few strategic airfields. Meanwhile Khrushchev would expect the United States to allow inspections of its western states, where he knew the Americans were planning to station their intercontinental ballistic missiles and which already had many strategic air bases. His concession was in fact no concession at all.

■

K HRUSHCHEV HAD LITTLE chance to savor his victory in changing Soviet disarmament policy. He had won that battle, but a major shift occurring in Kremlin politics suggested that similar victories would be increasingly more difficult. Over the winter and early spring of 1957 the apparent consensus on how to meet Soviet domestic challenges in the wake of the Hungarian crisis frayed. Characteristically responding with a flood of new initiatives to raise the Soviet standard of living, Khrushchev soon found he was testing the patience of even his closest allies in the Soviet leadership. In March 1957 he had to coax the Kremlin into launching a sweeping reform of the way the Soviet Union managed the industrial sector of its economy. Unhappy with the endemic inefficiencies of Soviet industry, Khrushchev decided it was time to decentralize supervision over the factories in the republics. In practice this meant shifting power from Malenkov's and Molotov's allies in the ministries in Moscow to his allies among the regional party elites in the Soviet republics.

Naturally, Molotov and Malenkov opposed this reform.[23] But again, thanks to key votes from younger Presidium members and his staunch ally Mikoyan, Khrushchev carried the day. Had his drive stopped there, he might have negotiated the political shoals of this issue as well as he did the disarmament question, but Khrushchev was too impatient not to push for more changes.

The rural economy was the one bright spot in the Soviet economy in 1957. In the three years since Khrushchev had called for the development of the so-called virgin lands of Kazakhstan and western Siberia, Soviet agricultural production had increased dramatically. Between 1954 and 1956, 137,000 square miles of fallow land—roughly the combined area of Pennsylvania, New York, and Ohio—had come under cultivation.[24] And the yields were excellent. The harvest of 1956 produced a bumper crop both in the established black soil region in southern Russia and the newly developed virgin lands. The returns were 20 percent higher than in 1955 and nearly 55 percent greater than the average in the last years of Stalin's life, 1949–1953. Most satisfying to Khrushchev was the statistic that half of all of the Soviet Union's grain production now came from his virgin lands.[25] The news from the livestock farms was similarly encouraging. Since Stalin's death, meat output was up by 162 percent, and milk by 105 percent.[26] This country of nearly two hundred million people was still not self-sufficient in food, but the gap was narrowing.

Eager for a good story to tell the Soviet people in this period of political uncertainty, in the winter and spring of 1957 Khrushchev embarked on a series of well-publicized victory tours of the winter wheat and cotton areas of southern Russia, the northern Caucasus, Uzbekistan, and Kirghizia. The enthusiasm of the farmers he met when mixed with his own sense of accomplishment formed a bewitching brew. At stops along the way Khrushchev competed with himself to provide ever more colorful and ambitious statements. In the wheat and livestock center of Krasnodar in southwestern Russia, he announced on March 8 that the principal economic goal of the Soviet Union was to "overtake and surpass . . . the most highly developed capitalist countries."[27] A few days later, a little farther north in Rostov-on-Don, he slammed Western imperialists who had so wrongly predicted an agricultural crisis in the Soviet Union.[28] But his most dramatic statement came two months later, on May 22, when in repeating the goal he had laid out for the country in Krasnodar, Khrushchev issued a prediction: "We shall be able by 1960 to catch up with the United States in per capita meat output." Khrushchev was promising almost a tripling of Soviet meat production.[29]

When reported back to Moscow, the catch and surpass pledge pushed his most serious opponents over the edge. Molotov and Kaganovich did not hide

their anger at the first leadership meeting after Khrushchev returned from
Krasnodar. They bitterly reminded him that there was no basis for believing
that the Soviet Union could surpass the United States in meat production anytime soon, let alone within three years.[30] "You talk too much!" Khrushchev
later recalled their yelling at him.[31]

Khrushchev's big political mistake was to engage the prestige of the entire
country without warning the rest of the Kremlin. His actions had annoyed
more than the Stalinists. Even his protégés believed that before setting a
Soviet goal, Khrushchev should confer first with the Presidium and then with
the economic planners at the Central Committee. Like the industry reforms,
the May 22 speech was yet one more reminder of Khrushchev's willfulness
and tendency to go it alone, and dangerously so, if left to his own devices.

Oblivious of the fact that his actions were causing serious disquiet in the
Presidium beyond his stalwart opponents, Khrushchev incautiously mixed
self-promotion with his crusade to lift the morale of the average Soviet citizen.
He decided to have himself awarded a Lenin Prize for the virgin lands program. It had only been two years since the last time that Khrushchev had
received a Lenin Prize, the highest award that the Soviet state bestowed on
one of its citizens. The Stalinist trio of Molotov, Kaganovich, and Malenkov
did not formally oppose the award, but each suggested when the issue was
discussed at a Presidium meeting in April 1957 that probably the timing was
not right. "We do not have the cult of personality," said Kaganovich, "and [we]
should not give a cause [for thinking so]."[32]

Serious preparation to remove Khrushchev began after this inept attempt
at self-congratulation. Predictably, Molotov led the cabal against him. Molotov
had never got over the fact that this upstart had outplayed him in 1955 and
1956, costing him his preeminent role in designing Soviet foreign policy.
Malenkov's and Kaganovich's opposition also stemmed from old slights,
especially the Khrushchev power grab of 1955.

What made the situation dangerous for Khrushchev, however, was that
these three bitter men were soon joined in opposition by other full members
of the Presidium who had actually benefited from the events of 1955 and
1956 but were reacting to the Khrushchev of 1957. These men—Nikolai
Bulganin, Maksim Saburov, and Mikhail Pervukhin—had come to mistrust
Khrushchev, whom they regarded as an erratic, willful man who was allergic
to consensus building. Khrushchev had strong ideas on things about which
he knew something—party work and agriculture, for instance—and strong
ideas on subjects like foreign and military policy that he was just learning
about. Left unchecked, Khrushchev's energy tended toward recklessness. The

nuclear era was just not the right time to have a man with a short fuse atop a superpower.

By June a rough head count showed that a majority of the Presidium agreed that Khrushchev had overstepped his bounds and needed to be demoted from the position of first secretary. Only six votes of the eleven full members were required to overturn the leader, and the conspiracy had eight.[33]

Khrushchev, it appears, was caught off guard by the plot. Although one of the complaints of the anti-Khrushchev group was that his loyal henchman, the current KGB chief, Ivan Serov, had established surveillance over the membership of the Presidium, Khrushchev's first clue that something was up came in the form of an invitation from Bulganin to an unscheduled meeting of the Council of Ministers on June 18.[34] Three days earlier Khrushchev had observed some open criticism of his position during a Presidium discussion of Soviet purchases of machine tools from the socialist bloc.[35] But that was not much of a warning, and he left the meeting unconcerned. In fact the open criticism was a sign of the confidence of the plotters. At one point Voroshilov suggested putting off any decision on the matter "until the next meeting of the Presidium of the Central Committee," which all the conspirators knew as code for the post-Khrushchev era.

At first Khrushchev tried to beg off going to Bulganin's meeting, saying that he was tired and had a meeting in Leningrad later in the day. But Bulganin insisted.

Once Khrushchev reached the Kremlin he found that a formal session of the Presidium had been called without his knowledge. The only topic on the agenda was his future as party leader. Stunned, Khrushchev listened as the conspirators informed him that he would have to cede his prerogative as chair of the Presidium to Bulganin for this extraordinary meeting. Mikoyan, who had not been brought into the conspiracy by the plotters, joined Khrushchev in objecting, but they were voted down.

No Soviet leader had ever survived politically the loss of a no-confidence motion in the Presidium. In January 1955 Georgi Malenkov, the first to suffer this fate, had accepted the outcome and relinquished his positions. Khrushchev, however, refused to resign when the vote went against him on June 18, 1957. He gambled that there was a huge Soviet party apparatus outside the walls of the Kremlin that was beholden to him and that these regional and local officials could keep him in power. Khrushchev had single-handedly rebuilt the party's confidence after the shattering years of Stalinist repression. He had promoted officials from every region, thus cultivating protégés and instilling loyalty even in the men whom he had not brought to

Moscow with him. Thanks to the recent agricultural successes, which had created a better political climate in the countryside, these regional leaders believed that their loyalty had been rewarded. Meanwhile Khrushchev had created good relations with the military by working with Marshal Zhukov to wash away the stain of the Stalin years, during which most of the Soviet general staff had been purged. He had assiduously supported the posthumous rehabilitation of revered civil war veterans like Marshal Mikhail Tukhachevsky, who had been murdered in the 1930s.

Khrushchev called in all these chits at once. The Soviet Air Force put special planes at the disposal of regional party secretaries so that they could fly to Moscow for a special session of the Central Committee. By the end of June 20, 107 of the 130 full members of the committee were in Moscow, and 57 had signed a petition demanding the convening of a plenary session to discuss Khrushchev's future. The signatories supported his position that the Presidium alone could not remove a first secretary of the party.

He knew he had the votes if he could move the decision outside the Presidium. What remained of Malenkov's political base was in Moscow, Molotov was a man of the past, and most of the other members of the conspiracy were political ghosts. There was one painful exception. His protégé the stylish Soviet foreign minister and candidate Presidium member Dmitri Shepilov had impetuously added his name to the conspiracy at the last minute. This was quite a blow to Khrushchev, who had worked closely with Shepilov when the latter was the editor of *Pravda*. As Shepilov become more immersed in foreign affairs, Khrushchev had welcomed his role in bringing Nasser closer to Moscow. If Khrushchev survived this coup, Shepilov would have to go, and his deputy, Andrei Gromyko, would then become Soviet foreign minister.

Khrushchev did not have to wait long to see his analysis proved correct. By June 22 it was all over. The vote in the Central Committee went against the coup plotters, who had no choice but to withdraw their effort.[36]

He showed compassion for his opponents. The four leaders of the plot—Molotov, Malenkov, Kaganovich, and Shepilov—were demoted off the Presidium. But they were neither shot nor arrested. Their principal allies, all of whom eventually recanted their opposition to Khrushchev, suffered less dramatic declines. Bulganin was permitted to stay on the Presidium, but he eventually lost the title of premier or chairman of the Council of Ministers. Pervukhin was shifted from the Presidium to the post of Soviet ambassador to East Germany. The venerable Marshal Voroshilov was too popular with the Soviet people to punish. He was allowed to stay put, though Khrushchev rarely listened to him.

In the aftermath of their miscalculation, two of the old Stalinists, Molotov and Kaganovich, pathetically begged for their lives. Perhaps because they had once planned to kill Khrushchev, both men assumed that he would execute them for their sins. "Comrade Kaganovich," Khrushchev is said to have told one of them over the telephone, "your words confirm once again what methods you wanted to use to achieve your vile aims. . . . You wanted to kill people. You measure others by your own yardstick, but you are mistaken. We adhere to Leninist principles and will continue to do so. . . . You will be able to work and live peacefully if you work honestly like all Soviet people."[37] And Khrushchev kept his promise.

▪

FOR THE WEST whatever meaning the failed coup against Khrushchev might have for assessments of political stability in the Soviet Union was swept away less than four months later. The Soviet Union's unexpected achievement of launching the first satellite into space seemed to change the balance of power in the superpower competition. Instantly a country that could not produce enough meat, butter, and coal to satisfy the needs of its own people had a claim to being technologically superior to the United States.

Sputnik Zemlya ("companion of Earth"), or *Sputnik* for short, started the space age and with it the superpower space race. In the mid-1950s the United States and the Soviet Union each undertook to put a satellite in space sometime during the International Geophysical Year (IGY) of 1957, which coincided with heightened solar activity between July 1, 1957, and December 31, 1958. In early 1957 the chief Soviet designer, Sergei P. Korolev, suggested accelerating the Soviet military program to build an intercontinental ballistic missile, the R-7, and to use it to propel a satellite into space in the fall of that year.[38] It took five failed launches before an R-7 with a dummy warhead blasted off successfully from the Baikonur Cosmodrome in Soviet Central Asia in August 1957. This was itself a great triumph for Khrushchev, who had placed his faith in the future nuclear-tipped missile, although military deployment of the R-7 was still some years away. Korolev, who was more interested in the peaceful exploration of space than in the destruction of any targets on earth, pushed to use the R-7 to place the first man-made satellite into orbit.

Weighing just over 184 pounds, cylindrical with splayed antennas that looked like the popular tail fins on cars of the day, *Sputnik* had no purpose other than to orbit and make a sound. It carried a battery that would allow it to emit a deep *beep, beep, beep* to radio operators in the countries that it flew over. Despite later fears in the West that these beeps were encrypted messages to

Soviet agents, they actually carried no information.[39] Their power would be purely symbolic.

The R-7 carrying *Sputnik* was originally supposed to go up on October 6. There was nothing magical or ideologically significant about that day. The Presidium certainly knew about the forthcoming launch, but because the chance of failure was high, no propaganda campaign was prepared in advance. The Soviet people were not to be told anything about *Sputnik* unless the launch succeeded. At the last moment, Korolev decided to move up the launch two days.[40] A conference on the IGY had just opened in Washington, D.C., and a paper given on September 30 by an American scientist had worried Korolev that the Eisenhower administration might be only days away from sending up its own satellite. On launch day, Khrushchev was scheduled to be coming through Kiev on his way home from his southern retreat at Pitsunda and made no plans to make the long detour eastward to attend the launch at Baikonur.[41]

■

KOROLEV HAD BEEN mistaken to believe that the Eisenhower administration was on the verge of beating them into space. Eisenhower had a very detailed space policy, and it did not include the necessity of being first into space. The U.S. president's ideas about space travel were interwoven with his concerns about intelligence gathering over the Soviet Union. The failure of his efforts to gain Soviet approval of his Open Skies proposal had led to a risky U-2 spy aircraft program that made him uneasy. He could never get over the sense that each U-2 mission constituted an act of war, even if these high-altitude flights were only pinpricks into the sovereignty of Soviet airspace. He longed for the day when spy satellites, seemingly beyond Soviet sovereign airspace, could carry the burden of this surveillance.

Eisenhower's sensitivity to the question of a country's sovereign airspace also affected how he managed the U.S. effort to build satellites. In the mid-1950s the international legal status of space was still undetermined. Theoretically, a country's claim on sovereignty might conceivably be extended into the cosmos, a farfetched notion a decade later, but when Eisenhower approved the first spy satellite program, it was still possible that the nations of the world might carve up space as they had Earth's atmosphere. Eisenhower wanted to prevent that from happening and hoped instead to establish the principle that a nation's satellite could orbit over another country without its permission.

The president believed that it would be easier to sell this idea that space vehicles could freely orbit Earth if the first U.S. satellite project was both open to public scrutiny and presented as having peaceful purposes. He assigned this public satellite initiative to the U.S. Navy, which called it Vanguard and kept it at arm's length from the army and air force's secret efforts to build an intercontinental ballistic missile. It is now believed that had Eisenhower let the army's rocket specialists, who included the notorious Wernher von Braun, who had built V-2 rockets for Hitler, manage the program, a U.S. satellite could have been propelled into space in 1956.[42] The decision to make Vanguard public also had the unintended consequence that millions of Americans quickly came to believe that the United States would be the first to put a satellite into space. By early 1956 *National Geographic* magazine had already crowned Vanguard "history's first artificial earth-circling satellite."[43] If there was any talk of a space race with Moscow, it usually involved the conviction that the Soviets would take second place.

On Friday, October 4, 1957, the popular cultural milestone was supposed to be the premiere episode of a new situation comedy, *Leave It to Beaver.* The White House was not expecting any major international development. The president had left for his farm in Gettysburg, Pennsylvania, intent on playing his fifth game of golf in a week. Then came the beeps. The R-7 carrying the Soviet satellite took off from Baikonur just after 2:00 P.M., eastern standard time. Every ninety-six minutes and seventeen seconds *Sputnik* orbited Earth, and by evening in the U.S. Northeast, ham radio operators were hearing its sound. Just after 8:00 P.M. those without ham radios got to hear the sound for the first time as the National Broadcasting Company aired a *Sputnik* tape on its radio network.

While American scientists immediately hailed *Sputnik* as an achievement for humanity, the media and many citizens saw it as the opening shot in a new and frightening phase in the Cold War. What the *New York Daily News* called "Khrushchey's Comet" not only called into question the supremacy of American science but also suggested that *Sputnik* would be the first in a series of Soviet military achievements.[44] Senate Majority Leader Lyndon Johnson, who was at his Texas ranch on October 4 and had walked outside in the hope of seeing the shiny tin ball, called for immediate hearings on the threat posed to U.S. security. "Soon they will be dropping bombs on us from space," said Johnson, "like kids dropping rocks onto cars from freeway overpasses."[45]

The White House tried unsuccessfully to allay these concerns. Being first in space had never been a litmus test for Eisenhower, who remained confident that the military's scientific team would provide him with ICBMs and a reliable spy satellite soon.[46] At a press conference he told the American public that there was no reason to fear because the Soviets had "put one small ball in the air."[47] His chief of staff added that *Sputnik* was no more than "one-shot in an outer-space basketball game."[48] But what was later recalled as "a wave of unreasoning hysteria" would not go away.[49] Within a year Eisenhower had signed bills strengthening the teaching of science and foreign languages in schools and universities and he had authorized Wernher von Braun's team to enter the space race. On January 31, 1958, *Explorer 1* was placed into orbit by an army Jupiter missile.

The public reaction in the United States and throughout the world, where *Sputnik* was hailed in all languages, was intoxicating for Khrushchev. The Soviets were now touted as being ahead in rocket science, something they had only dreamed of before. If that were not enough to please Khrushchev, because of *Sputnik*, the Americans were second-guessing themselves, complaining about their own weaknesses. The initial reporting on *Sputnik* in *Pravda* had been restrained. But after watching the excitement abroad, the Kremlin decided to give the achievement banner treatment in the October 6 edition. Khrushchev also invited Korolev to a meeting of the Presidium on October 10. After hearing the rocket designer's report on *Sputnik*, the Presidium voted to award him the Order of Lenin. There was no grumbling about this Order of Lenin's being undeserved.[50]

■

THE CELEBRATION over *Sputnik* hid from public view a messy settling of scores in the Kremlin. A matter of hours before *Sputnik* was launched, Marshal Zhukov, the Soviet defense minister, had left Moscow on a previously scheduled three-week tour of Albania and Yugoslavia. His departure was the cue for Khrushchev to set in motion the removal of this popular World War II hero from the Presidium. For three years the two men had been political allies against the hard-line Stalinists. In 1955 Khrushchev had enlisted Zhukov in his struggle to undermine Molotov's opposition to a policy of peaceful coexistence with the West. Most recently Zhukov had helped Khrushchev keep his job by instructing Soviet military transports to ferry Central Committee members to Moscow so that they could vote to overturn the Molotov, Kaganovich, Malenkov, and Shepilov coup attempt. But by October 1957 Khrushchev wanted him out on charges of trying to usurp the role of the Communist Party in Soviet national security.

Although the immediate catalyst for this crisis remains muddy, the origins are clear. Despite their agreement on the threat posed by Molotov and an acquaintance that stretched back to the Ukraine, where Zhukov had been military commander when Khrushchev was regional party chief, these two Kremlin stars had irreconcilable views on the role of the party in the Soviet military. Since becoming a candidate member of the Presidium following the Twentieth Party Congress in early 1956, Zhukov had worked to diminish the position of the political officers, the old political commissars, in the military. Responsible for ensuring the ideological reliability of the officer corps, the commissars represented party control of the military, and the marshal's lack of respect for them as an institution was troubling to men like Khrushchev who put the CPSU first. Zhukov also raised suspicions by allowing to pass into disuse defense councils at the republic level, which were staffed and dominated by the local party elite. There were rumors that among the troops he liked to deprecate the party's representatives, likening them to old cats "that have lost their flair." Moreover, in his public speeches the defense minister seemed to be intentionally vague about the subordination of the military to the party.[51]

Zhukov had seemed especially cocky after his apparent rescue of Khrushchev's political career in June. In August the marshal had tried to reopen the disarmament debate that he had lost in the spring. At that time the Kremlin had decided to offer the West an aerial inspection plan that it knew the Americans could not accept, and Zhukov remained convinced that Moscow should pay the price of limited aerial inspection to open U.S. military facilities to Soviet cameras.[52] He pressed Khrushchev to reconsider his opposition to the idea. Zhukov was also increasingly vocal about his differences with Khrushchev over how to reform the military in a period of budgetary difficulty. In late 1955 the two had disagreed over how to spend money on the Soviet Navy. Whereas Khrushchev wanted to concentrate on improving the submarine fleet, Zhukov wanted to save the aircraft carrier program.[53] After the coup attempt Zhukov expressed uneasiness about Khrushchev's intention to reduce the size of Soviet forces in Germany without reaching some kind of political arrangement with the West, and he opposed any budget cuts that threatened his goal of increasing the standard of living of Soviet soldiers.[54]

Khrushchev was not the only member of the Kremlin leadership to have noticed that Zhukov seemed to be over-asserting himself. Besides his policy initiatives, the marshal raised concerns because he seemed to be going out of his way to cultivate public support for himself. He had recently thrown the support of the Soviet Army behind the making of a movie about the Battle of Stalingrad that highlighted his historical role. He had even commissioned one of the nation's preeminent portrait painters to produce a canvas of him as the savior of Mother Russia, astride a white horse against a background of the burning Reichstag.[55]

Khrushchev and his allies placed a sinister construction on reports that Zhukov was now creating his own personal guard. Without Kremlin approval Zhukov's intelligence branch had organized a special school to train guerrillas and saboteurs. Memories of the corps of bodyguards loyal to Stalin's former intelligence chief Lavrenti Beria were fresh in the party leadership, and they had no wish to see Zhukov establish a similar private army.

Politically stronger after the failed coup attempt against him, Khrushchev did not believe he had to tolerate Zhukov. Once the Soviet defense minister had left the capital, Khrushchev invited Zhukov's principal rival in the military, the head of the Main Political Directorate of the army, General A. S. Zheltov, to slander Zhukov in front of the Presidium.[56] Zheltov, the army's chief political commissar, alleged that Zhukov mistrusted the party's representatives in the military. "If you were to hang red beards on the political workers and give them daggers," Zhukov had reportedly said to Zheltov in an apparent allusion to the Mongol hordes that had swept through Russia in the Middle Ages, "they would slaughter all the commanders." Zheltov complained that Zhukov had placed so many restrictions on him that he could not take inspection tours of the troops without the marshal's approval.

Two days later special meetings were convened for junior officers in Leningrad and Moscow to discuss the accusations against Zhukov. A special conclave of all of the living marshals of the Soviet armed forces was also assembled to prepare the way for Zhukov's removal. Presidium members attended these events.[57]

On October 25, the eve of Zhukov's return to Moscow, the Kremlin officially decided to remove him once he returned.[58] The very next day, just after he arrived in the Soviet capital, Zhukov was called to the Kremlin to be formally told of the charges against him.[59] At this dramatic meeting the war hero denied the accusations, calling Zheltov's central criticism "wild." He did admit to "some blunders" on his part in how he managed his public image, but it was too late. "I consider him dangerous in the leadership of the ministry," said Bulganin. "A regime of terror has been created," added Mikoyan with a dramatic flourish. Brezhnev captured the fears of the Presidium, which seemed less concerned about Zhukov's personal ambitions than the long-term consequences of letting him reduce the role of the CPSU in the Soviet military: "The policy is aimed at a rift [between the army and the party]." Khrushchev brought the vilification to an end: "The drama with Zhukov is difficult for me now. . . . Why cut the threads connecting the party with the army?" Khrushchev's resolution that Zhukov be removed immediately was passed unanimously. The decision was to be publicized on the radio that day to prevent any effort at resistance by Zhukov's allies in the military. In Zhukov's stead the group chose Marshal Rodion Malinovsky, who had been reluctant to join Zheltov in criticizing Zhukov.[60] Although Malinovsky had also been a formidable military commander in World War II, Khrushchev had worked with him and believed he could be controlled.

Khrushchev moved quickly to alter those foreign policies that reflected Zhukov's influence. First, he called for a vote to pull the Soviet Union from the London disarmament talks, which had remained in session throughout the first ten months of 1957. Khrushchev had shared Zhukov's commitment to the talks and still worried about the possibility of nuclear war, but he did not share Zhukov's view that the Soviet position needed to change. Instead he wanted to force a change in the Western conditions for disarmament by dramatically walking out. The most recent Western proposals, given to Moscow's representatives on August 29, had not closed the gap remaining between the two sides.

The Kremlin and the White House had reached an understanding on a very modest cut in the size of their respective armed forces from 2.8 million soldiers, sailors, and airmen to 2.5 million and even that all nuclear testing should be halted for between ten months and two years. But each side continued to impose preconditions that made it impossible to proceed from these shared goals to signed agreements.[61]

On the Soviet side, Khrushchev refused to accept a cut to 2.5 million unless it was agreed ahead of time that it would be followed by a second cut to 1.3 million. As for a nuclear test ban, it was the Americans who imposed the unacceptable precondition. At the urging of his advisers Eisenhower, who wanted a test ban, insisted that the United States would not support a test ban without a simultaneous ban on the production of fissionable materials. In other words, superpower nuclear stocks would have to be frozen at their current levels.

Khrushchev had a greater objective than simply forcing some tactical changes. He intended to kill Eisenhower's Open Skies proposal once and for all.[62] With Zhukov gone, he could rescind the Soviet offers made in November 1956 and April 1957 to open part of Eastern Europe and the USSR to U.S. airplanes.[63] These had been domestic concessions to Zhukov and were no longer necessary.

Khrushchev's tougher disarmament policy made the Foreign Ministry and Anastas Mikoyan uneasy. Deputy Foreign Minister Valerian Zorin, who had been the Soviet delegate at the London talks and was representing the ministry while Foreign Minister Andrei Gromyko, Shepilov's replacement, was at the United Nations, called the recommendation premature, but lacking a vote in the Presidium could do nothing to stop Khrushchev's allies from ratifying this suggestion.[64] Also on the losing end was Mikoyan, who ultimately decided not to fight Khrushchev on this matter. The Soviet Union could return to the disarmament issue later.

With his victory over the old Stalinists and Zhukov, Khrushchev had hopes that he could finally control the Soviet Union's Middle Eastern policy. The Syrian government had just signed a trade agreement with Moscow, and there were indications in the fall of 1957 that the United States was encouraging Turkey to invade Syria in response. On October 10, while Zhukov, who might have objected, was on his final foreign trip to the Balkans as Soviet defense minister, Khrushchev had pushed for a commitment to help Syria.[65] He proposed that Soviet forces be mobilized in the southern republics to deter Turkey from invading Syria. The Presidium approved the request, and when Turkey did not invade, Khrushchev believed he had scored a little personal triumph.

But a month later Khrushchev was to learn a crucial lesson when he tried to exploit his success to push the Soviet Union too far too fast. For all his success in escaping political death in June and in removing Zhukov in October, he was still not alone at the top. Although the era of the nasty debates with Molotov and Kaganovich were over, the Presidium still contained men with independent minds. Moreover, even with the removal of Zhukov the basic conservatism of the Soviet armed forces, which was resistant to expanding defense commitments into the third world, remained.

This hard little lesson came when Khrushchev suggested a Soviet-led military alliance in the Mediterranean modeled after the Baghdad Pact. In mid-November he outlined a plan for the Presidium that would involve giving security guarantees to Egypt, Syria, Yugoslavia, and Greece. But he didn't get it. Mikoyan refused to support the idea, as did the senior military officers whom Khrushchev had brought to the meeting especially to hear the idea. Despite having been handpicked by Khrushchev to succeed Zhukov because he was reliable, the new defense minister, Rodion Malinovsky, also thought it a bad idea to proceed with this arrangement now. The chief of the general staff, Marshal V. D. Sokolovsky, then effectively threw cold water on the plan by suggesting that Nasser, Moscow's key ally in the region, would probably not support it. The Presidium did not formally kill the proposal; it was simply sent to the bureaucrats in the Defense and Foreign ministries and was never heard from again.[66]

These Presidium debates over Soviet policy in the Middle East had taken place in a newly appointed room in the Kremlin. To dramatize his authority after the failed coup, Khrushchev had moved the Presidium meetings from the room where they had long been held to a room adjacent to his suite of offices in a building near the imposing Spassky Gate, which opened onto Red Square. A large oval table that could accommodate forty to forty-five people dominated the new meeting space, and the fact that Khrushchev's own office was next door was a reminder of who had the most powerful voice around that table.[67]

■

THE YEAR 1957 had witnessed the end of the old guard in the Kremlin. What was to follow remained unclear. At best, from Khrushchev's perspective, the Soviet Union was an incomplete dictatorship. There was no question that all future policy initiatives would come from him. This had largely been true since 1955, but now there was less negotiating that had to be done. Nevertheless, if his proposals were too dramatic, as was his call for a Soviet Baghdad Pact, he could count on some opposition.

While the rest of the world had caught glimpses of the major political events of the year in Moscow, all the policy debates had remained hidden from view. The United States had no way of knowing what new Soviet policies Khrushchev's political victories would bring to the fore. Since October 1957 there had been changes in Soviet foreign policy, the most noticeable being the withdrawal from the London disarmament talks, but they had hardly been dramatic. What remained to be seen was what kind of statesman this more powerful Khrushchev wished to become.

CHAPTER 7

COUP IN IRAQ

ON JULY 14, 1958, Khrushchev awoke to the news that his almost single-handed three-year effort to increase Soviet influence in the Middle East had brought a happy result. At 5:30 A.M. a group of army officers had entered the royal palace in Baghdad and executed the royal family. Prime Minister Nuri al-Said had fled the capital. The new regime, led by Brigadier General 'Abd al-Karim Qasim, proclaimed a republic with a neutralist foreign policy, ending Baghdad's alliance with Great Britain and the West.[1] It was not that Khrushchev was surprised. He believed that the rise of Qasims and Nassers was inevitable as Western power receded from the developing world. It was just that he had not expected a revolution in Iraq so soon.

Gamal Abdel Nasser, his closest friend in the region and who had just visited Moscow, had not given the Soviet leader any reason to expect the sudden implosion of the pro-Western regime in Iraq. Indeed, the message from Cairo had been quite the opposite. In their meetings in April and May the Egyptian leader had complained about the slow progress of his policies in the Arab world, singling out the role of conservative Iraq as an obstacle. "The imperialist powers," he predicted, "will by all means create difficulties for us and organize provocations . . . using for these purposes Israel, Iraq and Jordan."[2] At best Nasser predicted a tough slough in Baghdad between the forces he supported, the forces of Arab nationalism, and those supported by Great Britain. Nasser had not dared predict a nationalist revolution anytime soon.

Khrushchev's own sources were not telling him much more. Qasim was not completely unknown to the Soviet Union before the Iraqi brigadier general rearranged the politics of the Middle East. Moscow knew that sometime in 1956 Qasim had reached an understanding with the leadership of the Iraqi Communist Party.[3] He and his followers in the Iraqi Army would conspire with the Communist Party to remove the Feisal dynasty and the conservative Nuri government. The Kremlin was even told that Qasim considered himself a Communist.

But the information was too fragmentary to produce any firm conclusions about Qasim. The Iraqi had never approached any Soviet representative to ask for assistance. So, hearing the news in Baghdad, Khrushchev chose to doubt that this was a direct victory for communism, though the revolution was undoubtedly a step closer to a more progressive regime.[4] Khrushchev's recent experience with Nasser, a man friendly to Soviet power but not to communism, was reason enough to be skeptical of this new Arab nationalist star. In February, Nasser had amalgamated Syria with Egypt to create the United Arab Republic (UAR). The former Syrian government had been friendly toward the Soviet Union, even tolerating the activities of the local Communist Party. All that changed with the unification of Damascus and Cairo.[5] The head of the Syrian Communist Party, Khalid Bagdash, had had to flee the country briefly, fearing for his safety in a new regime dominated by Egypt. The same might occur in Iraq. There was already talk that Qasim wanted to make Iraq a member of the UAR.

Whether or not Qasim was good for Iraqi Communists, Khrushchev understood immediately that this surprise development in Iraq was a boon to Soviet strategic interests. The revolution challenged the Western position in the Middle East and represented a test of the Eisenhower Doctrine. Besides serving as the headquarters of the Baghdad Pact, Iraq was one of only two Arab countries to have hailed the president's doctrine in 1957. "Can we imagine a Baghdad Pact without Baghdad?" Khrushchev mused. "This consideration alone," he added, "is enough to give [John Foster] Dulles a nervous breakdown."[6]

Dulles's suffering a nervous breakdown was not, of course, Khrushchev's real concern. The news from Baghdad brought a different worry. The United States might not accept the new situation in Iraq without some sort of struggle. Eisenhower's so-called doctrine consisted of a pledge to assist any Middle Eastern country that was the victim of aggression from "international communism." Even though Moscow was not actually playing a decisive role in the domestic politics of any Arab state, Khrushchev had reason to believe that Eisenhower had committed himself to launching a U.S. military intervention if a Middle Eastern country shifted away from the West.

Khrushchev could draw some confidence from the fact that his initial testing of the Eisenhower Doctrine had been successful. In October 1957 the Soviets had mobilized along their southern border to prevent Turkey, a U.S. ally, from attacking Syria in retaliation for Damascus's decision to sign a trade pact with the Kremlin.[7] When Turkey did not invade, Khrushchev saw this as proof that if threatened with Soviet military action, U.S. allies and perhaps even the United States itself might leave Moscow's allies in the Middle East alone.[8]

Even so, Khrushchev saw no reason to use Iraq to provoke Eisenhower if he could help it. The revolution was also a challenge to existing Soviet policy. Should Iraq be given the same treatment as Egypt and Syria, two states that the Kremlin had vowed to defend? Khrushchev hoped to avoid a situation in which the Kremlin had to make that decision. From his experience in the fall of 1957, when he had unsuccessfully tried to gain the Presidium's support for a Moscow-led defensive alliance in the region, he knew that it would take some work to get his colleagues to extend Soviet military obligations to Iraq.[9]

Khrushchev had another reason for taking a wait and see approach to the situation in Iraq. The revolution happened just as he was trying to manage an urgent problem in a different part of the world. Soviet negotiations with the People's Republic of China over military assistance and future joint planning had hit a major snag. Soviet statements and Mao Zedong's characteristic suspicion had combined to produce strong and bitter resistance from Beijing, and Khrushchev expected that within the next few days he would have to meet personally with the Chinese leader, perhaps even in Beijing.[10]

■

I n Washington the news from Iraq was greeted with alarm and some despair. "The Arab world is in a period of revolutionary ferment," concluded the CIA in a line that also captured the tumult in the Eisenhower administration.[11] It was broadly assumed that Qasim was a Nasser stooge or at the very least had been helped into his present position by the Egyptian special services. Washington also saw the hand of the Kremlin in the Iraqi Revolution. Eisenhower expressed the view of most officials when he stated that the dramatic events unfolding in the Persian Gulf were "fomented by Nasser under Kremlin guidance."[12]

The loss of Iraq was particularly troubling to the administration. Since 1954 Washington had been content to build on the anti-Soviet regional defensive organization established by the British in cooperation with Turkey and Iraq. The choice of Baghdad as the administrative home for this alliance signaled Western assumptions that Iraq was stable enough to serve as a pillar of resistance to Nasserism and communism in weak Arab states.[13] Now with the apparent disappearance of this regional pillar, it seemed possible to Washington that Arab nationalists would be inspired to finish off the established regimes in Jordan, Lebanon, Kuwait, and possibly Saudi Arabia. The only credible counterforce appeared to be Western resolve to assist those established regimes to hold back the Nasserist tide.

Foster Dulles called President Eisenhower at 8:29 A.M., Washington time, on July 14 with the news that because of events in Baghdad, the government of Camille Chamoun in Lebanon was calling for U.S. military assistance. Lebanon had been the only other Arab country to have publicly embraced the Eisenhower Doctrine.[14] Chamoun headed a weak pro-Western regime. Although grateful to the Central Intelligence Agency for engineering the overwhelming success of his parliamentary faction in the 1956 elections, he was not an easy client. In assuming the presidency in 1952, Chamoun, who led Lebanon's slim Christian majority, had promised supporters and opponents alike that he would serve only one term. He had proved an unpopular leader, and as evidence mounted that he had no intention of leaving office when his term was up, the country slipped into civil war, with Chamoun's most vocal opponents the country's large Islamic population. For months Washington had been trying to convince him to step down for the good of the anti-Nasserist and anti-Communist cause in Lebanon.

Before the Iraqi Revolution, Chamoun's intransigence had presented Washington with unpalatable alternatives. In a desperate bid to hold on to power, the Lebanese president had asked for U.S. military assistance in May. Although there was no great desire to protect Chamoun, the fear that Lebanon might fall to Nasserism or, worse, to communism was enough to prompt serious contingency planning for U.S. military intervention in Lebanon. As far back as the Turco-Syrian tension of October 1957, the chiefs of staff began drafting plans for a joint Anglo-American intervention to assist Lebanon and Jordan.[15] Despite having ordered this contingency planning, President Eisenhower was not particularly happy that the United States had to look at military options to stabilize Lebanon. But he believed he had no choice. Intercepted communications between Syria and the leader of the main rebel group in Lebanon indicated that Nasser was deeply involved in arming and financing the opposition to Chamoun.[16] As the crisis heated up in the spring, grumbling directed at the troublesome Lebanese could be heard in the Oval Office. "How can you save a country from its own leaders?" Eisenhower had exclaimed at one point in frustration.[17]

With the surprising turn of events in Iraq, however, Eisenhower no longer needed any convincing to initiate the first military intervention of his presidency. The Lebanese request provided an opportunity to demonstrate American commitment to the region, "to avoid the crumbling of our whole security structure."[18] The issue was no longer the right way to handle Chamoun; Eisenhower now feared that Iraq was the beginning of a wave of defections to the anti-American side. "Jordan can't stick," Eisenhower warned, sensing that if Lebanon went, then Israel's eastern neighbor, the Hashemite kingdom of Jordan, would be the next to fall under a Nasserist government.

At a hastily convened midmorning meeting of the National Security Council on July 14, Eisenhower's preferences for direct U.S. action in Lebanon became policy. He told his advisers, "[W]e either act now or get out of the Middle East."[19] He was emotional about the challenge his government was facing, resorting to very powerful analogies to explain why there was no choice but to proceed with a show of force in Lebanon. He recalled the mistaken appeasement of Hitler at Munich in 1938. He also equated an unfavorable outcome in the Middle East with the greatest defeat yet suffered by America in the Cold War, Mao's victory in China in 1949. "To lose this area by inaction," he said, "would be far worse than the loss in China, because of the strategic position and resources of the Middle East."[20]

His advisers did not need any persuading. Even before the president announced his determination to organize a show of force in Lebanon, Allen Dulles had painted an ominous picture of the situation in the region. Although the CIA had no firm evidence that Nasser had "spearheaded" the coup, there was no doubt that the new government was led by "pro-Nasser elements" in the Iraqi military. The prospects for any pro-Western resistance were dim. The Iraqi crown prince was confirmed dead, and King Feisal and Nuri al-Said had disappeared along with forty-eight Iraqi military officers, who had been "retired." In Jordan, where the government had recently unraveled a Nasserist plot against him in the army, King Hussein had announced that with the disappearance of his cousin King Feisal of Iraq, he was assuming the leadership of the Arab Union, an Iraqi-Jordanian organization set up earlier in the year as a rival to Nasser's Egyptian-Syrian union, the UAR. In the Gulf the coup had roiled the sheikhdoms. King Saud of Saudi Arabia was threatening to seek an accommodation with Nasser if the West did not intervene to overthrow the new regime in Iraq. Meanwhile there was evidence that Kuwait might also fall. The CIA director reported that the Kuwaiti leader was in Damascus, the Syrian capital, for talks with Nasser, perhaps as a first step to joining the UAR. While the U.S. national security team agreed that a U.S. military intervention would stir anti-Western feelings in the Middle East, there was a strong consensus that the costs of inaction were greater than enraging the Arab public.

What Eisenhower didn't yet know was how far the United States would have to go to stabilize the situation. He had no immediate plans to do anything other than to order U.S. forces to deploy to Beirut.[21] But as he admitted to his national security team in the morning and explained to the congressional leadership later in the day, he knew that there was probably more work to be done in the region. The possibility of the sabotage of oil wells by the new Iraqi regime and that day's news about the teetering of Kuwait and Saudi Arabia raised the specter of losing NATO's principal source of oil. Eisenhower thought it nearly inevitable that the new Iraqi regime would seek to ruin Western interests in the Persian Gulf once it had consolidated its position. If it looked as if this were about to happen, the United States might have no choice but to move beyond Lebanon.[22]

There was no real consensus among Eisenhower's advisers on what to do after Lebanon. Khrushchev had been right to assume that Secretary of State Dulles would be especially alarmed at the turn of events. Together with Vice President Nixon, Foster Dulles hoped that the revolution might yet be overturned in Baghdad. Nixon leaned a little more toward a military solution than did Dulles, who wanted to see if there were any credible pro-Western Iraqi leaders left before giving up on a form of countercoup sponsored by U.S. intelligence. But both thought it inescapable that the United States would have to prepare for joint military operations with the British to occupy Kuwait and the oil fields of eastern Saudi Arabia in order to protect Western interests in Middle East.[23] The president's military advisers were initially more cautious. Having seen what had happened to the French and the British in the Suez crisis two years earlier, they did not want the United States to be embroiled in an unpopular neocolonial war in the Persian Gulf. Chairman of the Joint Chiefs Nathan Twining advocated a combined military strategy that limited the United States to Lebanon, while other countries undertook their own military interventions. The British could go into Iraq and Kuwait, as these were their area of special interest. The Israelis would be encouraged to go into the West Bank, and the Turks into Syria. The U.S. military's apparent reluctance to engage in small conventional conflicts annoyed the secretary of state. "All they think about is dropping nuclear bombs," Dulles told Nixon, "and they don't like it when we get off that."[24]

One area where the secretary of state and the military agreed was over what could be expected from the Soviets in this crisis. Neither the State Department nor the Pentagon was concerned that wider military intervention in the Middle East would provoke the start of World War III with the Soviet Union. There was a pervasive sense of confidence that the United States was ahead in the strategic arms race with Moscow. No one in Washington could explain why, but it seemed that Khrushchev had decided not to build huge squadrons of long-range bombers, and the Soviets were apparently encountering difficulties in translating their *Sputnik* success into a credible intercontinental ballistic missile force. As a result, it was assumed that Moscow would have no choice but to tolerate a show of U.S. power in the Middle East. "[O]ur military advisers," Dulles explained to Congress, "believe we now hold a considerable superiority which the USSR would not want to challenge. . . . So, it is a probability that if we act decisively and promptly, they [the Soviets] may figure that Nasser has gone too fast. They may withdraw before their prestige is engaged and general war risked."

Eisenhower shared his advisers' confidence that the Soviets were very unlikely to use military force in the region.[25] For Eisenhower, who was particularly sensitive to Nasser's and Khrushchev's success in appealing to the Arab world, the struggle for popular opinion in the region was a more significant reason to limit any U.S. military intervention. There had to be a clear, moral rationale for the use of U.S. power in the Middle East. Although he worried about Western access to Persian Gulf oil, he was reluctant to make that the basis for any enlargement of the intervention beyond sending troops to Beirut. Besides this important foreign consideration, he was conscious of a preeminent domestic factor that argued for a disciplined reaction to the evolving and still-confused situation in the Middle East.[26] Eisenhower believed that existing agreements with Lebanon and the fact that Chamoun had requested this assistance provided all the authority he needed to send the U.S. Marines into Lebanon the next morning, but he did not have the necessary congressional approval for any major move beyond Beirut.

The British tested Eisenhower's restrained approach to the evolving crisis. Throughout the day on July 14 the president received word that London wanted to take military action against the Qasim regime. The British were already thinking of sending forces to Jordan, both to strengthen the backbone of its Jordanian ally and as a first step to Baghdad. And they didn't want to act alone.

Harold Macmillan, the former chancellor of the exchequer who had replaced the disgraced Anthony Eden as British prime minister after Suez, made the pitch for joint operations in a telephone call to President Eisenhower that evening. The events in Baghdad had been even more threatening to the British than to the Americans. In the words of the historian William Roger Louis, the revolution signaled "the virtual end of the British Empire in the Middle East."[27] It had been Eden who had orchestrated the Baghdad Pact in the first place, and although Macmillan had indeed been the beneficiary of Eden's mistakes—

notably the debacle in Suez—the new prime minister shared Eden's intense dislike of Nasser. In 1956 Macmillan had argued vehemently that the British had no choice but to remove Nasser: "If not, we would rot away."[28] Two years later he shared Washington's conviction that Nasser was the puppet master behind the Qasim regime. At stake for Britain was not just imperial prestige. Access to cheap oil was essential to the British economy, and the events in Iraq threatened their interests in the Persian Gulf. As the news from Baghdad reached him, Macmillan began to worry about Kuwait. "Kuwait with its massive oil production," the prime minister wrote in his diary, "is the key to the economic life of Britain—and of Europe."[29] Kuwait provided one-half of all of Britain's oil and one-third to one-half of the profits of British oil companies. Kuwaiti oil was priced in sterling, thus propping up the British currency and aiding British banks.[30] The shock to the British financial system by the loss of these assets would be incalculable.

Despite these high political and economic stakes, one mistake Macmillan was determined not to make was to initiate any deep British military engagement in the region without an ironclad commitment that the United States would support him. "If we do this thing with the Lebanese," Macmillan explained obliquely to Eisenhower (because he was on an unencrypted transatlantic telephone line), "it is only really part of a much larger operation, because we shall be driven to take this thing as a whole. . . . I'm all for that as long as we regard it as an operation that has got to be carried through."

Eisenhower's response disappointed the British leader. He refused to give Macmillan the guarantee of support the British leader needed to widen the war. "If we are now planning the initiation of a big operation that could run all the way through Syria and Iraq," the president said, "we are far beyond anything I have [the] power to do constitutionally."[31] He also refused to hint that it was his expectation or even his hope that the United States would eventually participate in an attack on Syria or Iraq.

After he set down the receiver, the president turned to his secretary of state, who had witnessed Eisenhower's half of the call in the Oval Office. The conversation had clearly bothered the president. At one point Macmillan had referred to the possibility that Nasserists would destroy the oil pipelines through Iraq and Kuwait, a nightmare scenario that had also worried Eisenhower all day. "Then we are really at war," Eisenhower told Dulles as he recalled the conversation, adding plaintively, "[but] then what do we do?" Eisenhower knew he had left the British leader with the sense that the U.S. military would just stop in Lebanon, forcing the British to clean up the rest of the mess in the region. This image of the United States not pulling its weight frustrated the American leader, but Eisenhower thought he could not give the British the blank check they were looking for. He would have to see how events played out in the Middle East before seeking additional authority for more interventions.[32]

■

THE MORNING LANDING of a U.S. Marine battalion in and around Beirut was well publicized in the world press on July 15. Neither the press nor Soviet intelligence, however, could tell Khrushchev if the marines' arrival in Lebanon foretold a broader attack. "We are playing chess in the dark," Khrushchev admitted to Nasser two days later.[33] As much as Khrushchev did not like the fact that U.S. troops were in Lebanon, as long as they did not go any farther, he believed that the landing itself did not represent a challenge to Soviet interests. His primary concern was the protection of revolutionary Iraq, which he now considered the front line of Soviet influence in the region. If he let Iraq go, what would happen to Egypt and Syria?

The problem was that Khrushchev did not have a viable military card to play if the West indeed attacked the Qasim regime. The Soviet military was in no better position in the summer of 1958 to defend a strategic ally in the Middle East than it had been during the Suez crisis of 1956 or the Turco-Syrian tensions less than a year earlier. Once again Khrushchev's 1955 decision to limit expenditures on conventional forces, particularly surface ships, was pinching his options in far-flung military crises. The Soviet Navy lacked the aircraft carriers necessary to project power quickly into the region.

The immediate alternative was to resort to political theater yet again and threaten the Western powers with war if they used force against Iraq. But Khrushchev suspected that his Kremlin colleagues might not be prepared to extend a defensive umbrella over Baghdad. A modified version of his 1957 Syrian strategy, which balanced these foreign and domestic considerations, seemed more appealing pending future developments in the region. On July 16 Moscow declared that "the Soviet Union cannot remain indifferent to events creating a grave menace in an area adjacent to its frontiers, and reserves the right to take the necessary measures dictated by the interests of peace and security."[34] Meanwhile last-minute maneuvers by Soviet forces in the Caucasus and the Bulgarian Army were ordered to put some teeth into the public statement. Preparations were also made to announce recognition of the Iraqi regime by the entire Soviet bloc. Finally, the Kremlin decided to send President Eisenhower a special private message that intentionally expressed Soviet interest in Iraq.

Although Khrushchev had the protection of Nasser's regime at the back of his mind, the Egyptian leader himself was not consulted in the first round of Soviet decision making in this crisis. Vacationing in Yugoslavia at the time of the coup, Nasser had scrambled to establish a line of communications to Khrushchev. As a first step, he had wanted Moscow to recognize the Qasim regime "as quickly as possible."[35] On July 15 Nasser's deputy Marshal Amer had brought a message to the Soviet Embassy in Cairo. The Egyptian government believed that not only Soviet recognition but that of the entire Soviet bloc, "including the People's Republic of China," would be helpful to Qasim.[36]

When he heard nothing from Khrushchev, Nasser began to worry that Moscow might not do enough to protect Iraq. When he learned a day later of the U.S. decision to send marines into Lebanon, he thought he had to confer in person with Khrushchev. His immediate concern was how to get himself to Moscow to discuss the evolving situation in the Middle East.[37]

The Yugoslav ambassador in Moscow approached the Kremlin on the morning of July 16 to ask whether Nasser would be welcome if he made a quick trip to the Soviet Union. Khrushchev convened the Presidium to discuss the matter, and the leadership decided to dispatch a Soviet Tu-104 airplane that very night to Belgrade with instructions to pick up the Egyptian leader and his entourage for a secret early-morning flight to Moscow.[38]

▪

LONGCHAMPS WAS A trendy lunch spot in Georgetown. On July 17, Yuri Gvozdev, the Soviet military intelligence (GRU) officer masquerading as a commercial attaché in the Soviet Embassy, had asked Frank Holeman, the chief of the *New York Daily News*'s Washington operations and the president of the National Press Club, to lunch there. Holeman and Gvozdev had been meeting off and on since 1955. Holeman liked to "swap lies" with Soviets in an effort to see what he could learn from them and had a reputation in the local GRU office of being unusually close to Vice President Richard Nixon. The Russians had spotted Holeman as an interesting point of contact in the early 1950s, when he had defended their right to be members of the press club. Gvozdev was Holeman's second GRU contact. His first had been Georgi Bolshakov, who had gone back to Moscow in 1955 and later returned to play an extraordinary role as a back channel in the Kennedy years.[39]

Gvozdev had a message to deliver to Holeman. "War is close," he said. The Kremlin knew that the international press would soon pick up evidence of the military "exercises" in the Caucasus and Bulgaria. But the Soviet leadership wanted to send a clear message directly to the White House. "Any United

States or British move toward Iraq will mean war," Holeman noted in listening to Gvozdev. Moscow did not want Eisenhower to think that this was an idle threat. Gvozdev had been instructed to tell the Americans that the Soviet Army could react as quickly as could the U.S. Army. Gvozdev also raised the possibility of Russian "volunteers" being airlifted into the Middle East. If that weren't enough to deter Washington, he observed that any superpower clash over Iraq would not be contained within the Middle East. "If [there is] war," Gvozdev warned, "[then] Russians will ignore European bases and attack the United States directly."[40]

The Soviets lacked any trusted unofficial link to Eisenhower or Foster Dulles. Perhaps that was why they chose to send the message through the vice president. Nixon was well known to Khrushchev. "He occupied a special position among American political leaders," the Soviet leader later recalled. "We considered him a man of reactionary views, a man hostile to the Soviet Union. In a word, he was a McCarthyite."[41] The Soviets could not have chosen a better channel to the vice president than Holeman. Nixon considered few journalists his friends. Holeman of the *New York Daily News* was an exception.[42]

Having first been used by the Russians in early 1958 to tell the White House of Khrushchev's interest in a summit, Holeman clearly loved the intrigue that ensued. Whenever he had some news from a Russian contact, he left a tongue-in-check message for Nixon's longtime secretary, Rose Mary Woods: "This is Frank Holeman, Boy Spy." That July morning, however, Holeman didn't joke around about Gvozdev's latest message. Since Nixon was out of the office, Holeman conveyed to one of the vice president's aides the gist of Gvozdev's statements. He stressed that he was sure this came from the Soviet leadership.

When Nixon returned after lunch, he instructed that copies of Holeman's message be sent to both the Dulles brothers and J. Edgar Hoover. The private warning through the Soviet intelligence officer reinforced the more public warnings reaching Washington that same day. From Moscow came the official Soviet press agency (TASS) announcement that Soviet land and air forces, approximately twenty-four divisions, would begin maneuvers in the Transcaucasian and Turkestan military districts, on the borders of Turkey and Iran. A few hours later Belgrade added to the tension by reporting on its government radio station that Bulgarian land, sea, and air forces would start maneuvers the next day, with Soviet Marshal N. S. Skripko of the Soviet Air Force in command.[43]

∎

As Washington absorbed the Soviet leadership's initial efforts to stabilize the situation in the Middle East, Khrushchev was attempting to manage another dimension of the crisis. Nasser, who arrived in Moscow on July 17, wanted Khrushchev's word that the Kremlin would stand by Egypt's new ally.

The two leaders ultimately spent eight hours together, with Khrushchev doing what he could to reassure Nasser that Moscow's wait and see attitude toward the situation in Iraq was evidence of steel nerves, not neglect. "The people with weak nerves," an aide to Nasser heard Khrushchev say, "will go to the wall."[44] At the same time he wanted Nasser to understand that resolve was not the same thing as recklessness. "We are now involved in a game that is being played at a very high speed, and in which everyone has to act quickly, without being able to judge what the other players are going to do."[45] Moscow would recognize the Iraqi regime and then rely on bluff, as it had in protecting Syria in 1957. Nasser, however, wanted more of a commitment than this.

After word of Nasser's dash to Moscow had leaked out, Western diplomats heard rumors, probably spread by Egyptian sources, that Nasser had made the trip to prevent Khrushchev from overreacting.[46] The Soviet leader, said these sources, was so incensed at the U.S. intervention in Lebanon that he was considering a threat to deploy Soviet volunteers in Iraq, as he had threatened to do in Egypt during the Suez crisis. In reality, these roles were reversed. It was Khrushchev more than Nasser who had reason to be concerned about an overreaction by his ally. Even before the Iraqi Revolution, Nasser had come to the Soviet leadership with an extravagant shopping list for Soviet weaponry. In May 1958 he had asked for Soviet intermediate-range ballistic missiles and medium bombers, a request that Khrushchev was quick to deny.[47] Amid this new crisis, Nasser asked again for Soviet missiles. "Your country is too small for such military systems," Khrushchev replied. He was astonished that his Egyptian ally would present such a provocative request when Moscow's expressed goal was to prevent Western military intervention in the region. "If the need arises for these weapons to be used," Khrushchev told Nasser, "then it would be better to launch them from our territory. [And] you can be assured that if aggressors start a war against your country, then we will help you by means of these rockets from our territory."[48] Khrushchev was not much more forthcoming when Nasser also asked for Soviet military assistance to the new Iraqi regime, whose army he described as ill equipped.[49] He told Nasser that Moscow would consider giving the Iraqis some low-tech weapons, something that Egypt had already pledged to do, but that was all the military assistance he would promise to Baghdad for the time being.

Khrushchev stressed that Qasim, who was an unknown quantity to him, should not inadvertently provide the West with a pretext for an attack. He advised Nasser to preach caution to the Iraqi. It was the Soviet view that Qasim needed to announce that he would maintain all of Iraq's treaty commitments. For the time being at least, Baghdad should stay in the Baghdad Pact and not threaten the oil wells.

Moscow recognized the Iraqi revolutionary government the next day, and the same day Khrushchev received a telegram from Qasim indicating that Iraq wished to restore diplomatic relations, which had been cut by the previous regime.[50] Qasim also issued a public promise to protect Iraq's oil wells and ensure the flow of oil exports. It appeared that Nasser had been in touch with Qasim to coach him on how to reassure Khrushchev and bring the Soviets to his side.

■

I N WASHINGTON the successive warnings from Moscow did not have the hoped-for deterrent effect. Soviet actions merely confirmed for the hawks in the administration that the Kremlin was limited in terms of what military assistance it could provide to its Middle Eastern ally in response to the movement of U.S. troops into the region. Dulles told congressional leaders on July 18 that Soviet military intervention in the Middle East was unlikely.[51] Dulles thought a "dramatic gesture" by the Soviets, perhaps a large arms shipment to Cairo, but nothing directly threatening to U.S. troops in Lebanon, was a possibility.

Washington did not stop planning for a possible military move against Iraq. On July 15, the same day as the landing in Lebanon, Eisenhower had ordered the embarkation of elements of the First Marine Division, stationed in the United States, for deployment in the eastern Mediterranean or the Persian Gulf.[52] The next day he approved an additional recommendation from the Joint Chiefs for the movement of a marine battalion from Okinawa in the Pacific to the Persian Gulf.[53] He did not change these orders after Moscow's public warning on July 16 and the private warning through the Soviet agent Gvozdev the following day.

The Kremlin's public statements also had no appreciable effect on British plans. Following a formal request from King Hussein on July 16, London decided to deploy twenty-two hundred paratroopers and a guards brigade to protect the Jordanian regime.[54] In meetings with Secretary of State Dulles and President Eisenhower the next day, British Foreign Secretary Selwyn Lloyd again requested U.S. military assistance so that these could be joint operations in Jordan.[55] In the meantime, as insurance against trouble in Kuwait, the British government ordered reinforcements moved from Aden on the Arabian coast to the Persian Gulf.[56]

In spite of these war preparations, Anglo-American views on the utility of military power in Iraq were very much in flux, but the cause was less what the Russians were saying than word of new developments in Iraq. Qasim was effectively rooting out his enemies and establishing firm control in the country. By July 16 London and Washington had learned the sad fate of Nuri al-Said, the key to most official hopes for a counterrevolution. Dressed in woman's clothing, he had been captured and then executed. As early as July 17 the British foreign secretary was cautioning Foster Dulles that "if the new Government of Iraq obtain[ed] effective control of the country it would be out of the question to consider re-conquering the country from the military standpoint."[57] In the judgment of both governments there was no real resistance movement around which to organize a military intervention.

For Washington and London there then came a startling shift in Iraqi statements. On the day of the revolution Qasim's group had vowed to leave the Baghdad Pact. Now there was talk coming out of Baghdad that it might stay in. On July 15 Qasim met with both the U.S. and British ambassadors. He told the U.S. ambassador, "[W]e Iraqis wish for good relations with the United States."[58] Similarly, he promised Sir Harold Caccia, Viscount Hood, Her Majesty's representative, that "not even friendship with any Arab country shall interfere with [Anglo-Iraqi relations]," adding that there would be "no steps to damage British trade."[59] Even more comforting was the public announcement of July 18, the day after Khrushchev and Nasser had their summit in Moscow, that the new regime was committing itself to a stable oil supply. "In view of the importance of oil to the world economy," Qasim announced, "the Government of the Iraqi Republic wishes to declare its anxiety to see the continuation of the production and flow of oil to the markets where it is sold, because of its importance to national wealth and the national and international economic and industrial interests."[60] To counteract Western fears of sabotage, he added that his government had taken "all necessary steps" to protect oil wells, pumping stations, and other oil-related facilities in Iraq.

The vow that Iraq would protect the oil wells reassured the British that if hopes of overthrowing Qasim proved futile, then it might be possible to do business with this regime after all. Macmillan's fears had been fueled by suspicions of a link between Qasim and Nasser. But in light of the somewhat moderate things being said by the regime, the British began to reassess the nature of this revolution and its leader. Having dubbed him the "Iraqi Cassius," the diplomats in Baghdad were now describing Qasim to the Foreign Office as a "highly trained staff officer, extremely popular, [who] regularly kept Ramadan but without distinctly fanatical leanings."[61] Reacting to this new information, Macmillan cabled Foreign Secretary Lloyd, who was still in Washington conferring with the Americans, that there was "quite a chance . . . from the character of the men and some of their first statements that they may turn out to be more Iraqi nationalist than Nasserite."[62]

Washington was less impressed with Baghdad's apparent change of heart and continued to consider military options.[63] What finally ended American talk of an invasion was word on July 18 that the UAR had signed a mutual defense agreement with Iraq, rounding out Qasim's rapid consolidation of his authority and ensuring that any U.S. incursion into Iraq would spark a much larger conflict.[64] That very night Foster Dulles told the French ambassador that now "it was not possible to alter the status quo in Iraq by military means."[65] He made the same point to the British.[66] This shift in policy occurred in spite of the fact that in recent days the prospects of a successful invasion seemed to have become even brighter. On their own initiative, Jordan and Turkey had jointly offered to commit forces to invading Iraq.[67] But with the Qasim regime firmly in control of Iraq, the Eisenhower administration stopped exploring the invasion option. It would not be right, the president explained, for the United States "to get into the position of supporting Kings against their own people."[68]

■

IRONICALLY, AS LONDON and Washington were decisively moving away from the idea of a military overthrow of the Qasim regime, Nikita Khrushchev became convinced that a Western attack on Baghdad was imminent. Late on July 18 or early on July 19, Moscow time, Khrushchev probably received something—a piece of intelligence, a flash of insight, or maybe just TASS or foreign press reports—that significantly raised his anxiety level about the possibility of an attack by Western forces or their allies on Iraq. It is not wholly out of the question that Soviet military intelligence had detected the movement of the U.S. Marine unit coming from Okinawa or of the British force from Aden to the Persian Gulf, though the source seems more likely to have been a leak about the intentions of Iraq's neighbors. Just before midnight on July 16, the Turks passed official word to the Americans that fearing Soviet intervention in Iraq, Jordan, or Syria, the governments of Pakistan, Iran, and Turkey were requesting U.S. preemptive action.[69] A day later, the same day Nasser visited Khrushchev, the Turkish and Jordanian governments notified both the British and the Americans that they were prepared to invade Iraq with Western backing. The Turks also told the French, whose foreign ministry was infiltrated by Soviet intelligence.[70] London and Washington jointly turned down the offers from Amman and Ankara once they abandoned their own hopes for an immediate counterrevolution.[71] But Moscow at that point would not have known of this Western caution.

The evidence from Lebanon and Jordan also indicated to Khrushchev a hardening of the Western position in the region. The U.S. contingent in Lebanon had risen to eight thousand with two additional battalions disembarked late on July 15 and July 16. The British had slightly more than three thousand in Jordan. There was also something in the news that Khrushchev later admitted to having bothered him in this critical period. On July 17 the Soviet military newspaper *Krasnaya Zvezda* carried a comment from the commander of the U.S. Sixth Fleet, Vice Admiral Charles Brown, that the United States was "ready to land forces immediately at practically any point in the Mediterranean."[72] American bravado always annoyed Khrushchev, and this statement came at a particularly bad time for him. "If he were a citizen of the Soviet Union," he declaimed, "he would be tried or . . . put into a mad house."[73]

In light of these developments, Khrushchev convened an unusual Saturday meeting of the Presidium on July 19 to discuss what to do next. Sensing that the meeting would be a turning point in the Soviet handling of the crisis, he invited a stenographer into the proceedings. Ordinarily the chief of the Central Committee's General Department, Vladimir Malin, took notes pertaining to decisions, occasionally preserving the substantive discussion, but this time the meeting also produced a transcript that could be rapidly turned into speeches, letters, and action memorandums. Khrushchev believed that time was of the essence. Soviet warnings up to this point had not worked, and who knew when the Americans, the British, or their allies would strike?[74]

Khrushchev's mood was explosive. Dictating the guts of an angry letter to President Eisenhower, he intentionally used the most hurtful analogy available to get the former Allied commander's attention. "Mr. President," he dictated, "you started the aggression. Now you wish to conduct an aggression, as you claim, of a local character. But Hitler, when he attacked Poland, also considered that he was starting just a local conflict. He thought that they would finish off Poland and then, one by one, they would finish off France and afterward the

Soviet Union. This is how he acted, but this led to a world war and catastrophe for Germany." Khrushchev stressed that as veterans of World War II he and Eisenhower did not have the right to forget the lessons of that conflict.[75]

Despite his anger, the Soviet leader was not prepared to threaten nuclear war over Iraq. Instead he proposed that Moscow send a direct appeal immediately to Macmillan, the new French president, Charles de Gaulle, who had returned to power in June 1958 after a twelve-year absence, and India's Nehru as well as to Eisenhower to participate in a Middle East summit with him under the auspices of the UN Security Council.

He also hoped to enlist world public opinion. The Soviet leader was reasonably confident that Dwight Eisenhower personally did not want world war but was not entirely sure that the old military hero could control the hawks like Dulles and Nixon around him. Khrushchev advocated a major propaganda campaign by international labor unions to hamper any Western attempts to use force against Iraq.

Khrushchev wanted to end the letter to Western workers with the customary Marxist flourish, "Workers of the world, unite." But his ideology chief, Suslov, who was showing a little sensitivity to what did and did not sell in Great Britain and the United States, gently suggested that the line might not be helpful. Other Presidium members endorsed expanding the target audience beyond the international proletariat to include writers, students, and women. So too did the Kremlin's veteran troubleshooter in foreign affairs, Anastas Mikoyan, who mentioned that anything that smacked of Communist ideology in the appeal would be twisted by American leaders to make standing up for nonintervention an impossible political position. The line was purged, and letters for progressive constituencies in addition to international labor were prepared.

There were additional recommendations for softening the rhetoric in the letter to Eisenhower. Khrushchev dismissed outright the suggestion of a sentence reminding the leaders and the world that the USSR had no designs on the wealth of the Middle East. "The entire world knows that we have no material interests [in the Middle East]," he snarled. There would be nothing apologetic in the letter. "It must be written from a position of strength. . . . It is necessary to say here that we make this appeal because we cannot be indifferent," he said, "but we don't want to resolve this question by means of war." Another suggestion, which came from Mikoyan, Khrushchev did take. "For the sake of compromise," said Khrushchev, "I don't insist on [the reference to Hitler]."

Just when Khrushchev believed he had laid out the strategy for dealing with the crisis, an unexpectedly heated challenge rose from a Stalinist ghost in the Kremlin. Echoing some of the concerns hinted at by the military in the fall of 1957, the grand old man of the Soviet Army, Marshal Voroshilov, declared that he did not like the direction the Soviet government was about to take in the Middle East. "I think that we should avoid using expressions that have a somewhat threatening tone," he argued, "that [for example], 'we cannot remain neutral.'" Referring to the Soviet government's two previous statements on the Mideast crisis, Voroshilov warned about the declining value of repeated threats.

Voroshilov was not a Kremlin heavyweight, and probably never had been. Despite his popularity with the average Soviet citizen, his reputation among his colleagues was that of a dimwitted political general who had been no better in the field. Many historians later blamed him for the disastrous Soviet showing in the Finno-Soviet War of 1939 and 1940 and for mistakes committed in his later defense of Leningrad against the Nazis.[76] Voroshilov's political sense was no better. He had sided with Khrushchev's opponents in the June 1957 coup attempt and managed to get back on Khrushchev's good side only by helping him remove Marshal Zhukov four months later.[77] Just recently Voroshilov had again gotten himself into trouble by admitting at a reception at the Finnish Embassy in Paris that the Soviet Union welcomed the inauguration of Charles de Gaulle as president of France. The comment offended the French Communist Party and required several diplomatic letters and a firm Presidium reprimand to set things right.[78]

Despite the flaws of the messenger, Voroshilov's message revealed the concerns of some in the Kremlin that embracing progressive regimes in the Middle East might provoke a war with the United States. No one supported Voroshilov, but as he prodded Khrushchev, it became clear that neither the Soviet leader nor anybody else in the room wanted to go to war with Washington. All were acting out of the belief that the only way to protect Soviet interests in the Middle East was to threaten a war that neither side wanted.

KHRUSHCHEV: If we don't repeat [this threat of using force], they will take it as our backing off.

VOROSHILOV: If we are going to repeat it, then we should prepare somehow. We have declared that we cannot be indifferent; this means that we will have to intervene.

KHRUSHCHEV: That's not correct.

VOROSHILOV: This is disadvantageous for us.

KHRUSHCHEV: This is exactly what they want; they are saying, "Go ahead, act, the Russians will not act."

VOROSHILOV: Well, they are not heeding our statements; they will continue with the same policy, which means we should be thinking about what to do next. We should not go to war.

KHRUSHCHEV: We aren't talking about declaring war, we are talking about a letter. What should we say to them? "We beseech you, If you do swallow up the Arabs then be careful not to scratch your throat." But this is what [the letter] would convey. Then it would be better not to write the letter.[79]

At this point Mikoyan, who also believed it was in the interest of the Soviet Union to defend the new anticolonial regimes in the third world, came to Khrushchev's defense. He was convinced that there was a debate going on in the Eisenhower administration over whether to intervene in Baghdad and that its outcome hinged on an assessment of Soviet willingness to go to war to defend Iraq. To influence the outcome in a way helpful to Soviet interests, Mikoyan argued, the Americans "should feel fear." But Voroshilov would not give in. He was convinced that the West was determined to invade Iraq to overturn the revolution. So, by repeating this pledge not to be on the sidelines, the Soviet Union was putting itself into the position either of having to fight a war it didn't want or of having to back down ignominiously. Khrushchev rejected this logic: "We will have to repeat it, or they will take advantage of us if we are silent."

When Voroshilov still wouldn't give up, an exasperated Khrushchev asked him, "You don't read documents: What did the commander of the [U.S.] Sixth Fleet say?" To Voroshilov's reply, "He [Vice Admiral Brown] threatens that he has enough power," Khrushchev asked, "What did he say that for [?]: In order to scare us." Voroshilov realized that he had been boxed in. "But we are not afraid," he replied. "[So]," Khrushchev said in resting his case, "we should say that."

Khrushchev insisted on getting the letters out to the Western leaders as soon as possible. "It would be good to have it done by two o'clock," he said, "but it would be better if could be done by ten minutes to two." He was going to recommend July 22 for a conference of the six leaders in Geneva. There was no time to lose if there was any hope of arranging this meeting, so he instructed that the letters be transmitted by Moscow Radio. This was an unorthodox means of delivering a sober diplomatic message. Generally the West expected only propaganda from Moscow Radio, and there was a risk that these letters would receive similar treatment. Nevertheless, Khrushchev believed that Washington was still considering an attack on Iraq. "History," he wrote to Eisenhower, "has not left us much time to avert war."[80]

■

AS THE MIDDLE EAST crisis neared the end of its first week, John Foster Dulles was gloomy. The Iraqi revolutionaries had consolidated their hold on the government. The fates of Jordan and Kuwait hung in the balance, and among the Arab weakling regimes only Lebanon's seemed momentarily stable. The threat of the Soviet fist gloved in Nasserism remained. The European reaction to Khrushchev's letter of July 19 only increased Dulles's despondency. The rambling letter, which was also broadcast in almost identical versions addressed to de Gaulle and Macmillan, had created a stir among Washington's allies. The British public, in particular, was clamoring for a summit to head off a superpower clash. It was frustrating that Khrushchev was so successful at a time when the Soviet Union was so weak.

Dulles tried to get British officials, who shared the concerns of their public, to keep the larger picture of the Cold War in mind. Over drinks at his residence Dulles mused with the British ambassador, Lord Hood, over the state of Soviet insecurity. In recent months U.S. spy planes had proved that despite fears of a bomber gap favoring the Soviets, the opposite was true. The Soviets had made a strategic blunder by not building enough long-range bombers. Given that they also lacked long-range missiles, the Soviets could not fight a war with the Americans and win. Dulles began to speculate on what this opportunity could mean for Washington. "We would probably not have another such chance. But probably we did not have the nerve to take advantage of the probabilities." Dulles lamented that no one in Washington was prepared to go to war with Moscow, despite this being "our last fair chance." He added, "Our successors, a decade from now, might pay the price."[81]

Eisenhower didn't share either Dulles's gloom or British alarm. By July 20 the crisis seemed to him to be less threatening. Having encountered little armed resistance from any of Chamoun's opponents, the United States experienced light casualties in Lebanon, and negotiations were proceeding to ease Chamoun out of office.[82] Nothing in Khrushchev's letter of July 19 altered the president's confidence. The Soviets seemed to have accepted the U.S. presence in Lebanon. Instead it appeared that Khrushchev's main concern was an Anglo-American attack on Iraq, something that both governments had already ruled out anyway. Given all these excellent signs, there was no reason for the White House to give Khrushchev the summit he wanted. It would achieve little in the way of positive results for the United States or its regional allies, while providing a marvelous opportunity for the Soviets to rain additional criticisms on U.S. policy.

On July 21 the administration decided to encourage the Soviets instead to use the Security Council at the United Nations to settle their quarrel. The United States would be prepared to discuss the Middle East there but saw no need for a special meeting of the great powers plus India. Khrushchev did not see the letter, which was turned over to the Soviet ambassador on the evening of July 22, until July 23.[83]

As he awaited a response from the Americans, Khrushchev encouraged the Kremlin to consider ways of strengthening the Iraqi regime. Nasser had warned that the Iraqi Army was in poor shape, but up to now Khrushchev had not considered doing anything to help Qasim's force that might provoke a hostile Western reaction. On July 25 the chief of staff of the Soviet armed forces, V. D. Sokolovskii, and the chairman of the State Committee on Foreign Economic Relations, S. A. Skatchkov, submitted a plan to outfit two Iraqi infantry divisions with Soviet equipment.[84] It was to be done on a crash schedule with everything in Iraqi hands in a month's time. The bill of lading would include fifty armored personnel carriers, one hundred tanks, and a massive amount of Soviet artillery pieces, rifles, machine guns, and ammunition. The Soviet Union lacked a border with Iraq, so Cairo was asked if this matériel could be off-loaded at the Syrian port of Latakia and conveyed by land to Baghdad. The Kremlin approved the plan the next day, though it encountered some unexpected reluctance from Nasser, who suggested that the weapons come from Soviet stockpiles already in Egypt.[85] "There are disagreements within the Iraqi regime," Nasser explained, over whether to turn to Moscow for military assistance.[86] The Iraqis did not want, he added, "that the USA, England and the Baghdad Pact should know about the military deliveries from the Soviet Union."[87] Moscow detected in the Egyptian reluctance that it was Nasser who worried about the consequences of a direct relationship between the Kremlin and Qasim.[88] Egypt, it seemed, hoped that Iraq would soon join Syria in the United Arab Republic and did not want anyone to encourage too much independent action by Baghdad. Iraq, as it turned out, agreed to take Soviet military assistance directly.

As the manner of sending Soviet assistance to the Iraqi Army was being settled, Khrushchev was distracted by a challenge in a different part of the world.[89] Sino-Soviet relations, which before the Iraqi Revolution Khrushchev had expected to be his main foreign policy concern in July, refused to stay quietly in the background. His effort to draw China into a new defensive alliance was backfiring.

To a large extent, Khrushchev's difficulties with Beijing were as much an unintended consequence of his new cost-cutting military doctrine as were his current anxieties in Iraq. Believing nuclear-armed submarines would be a more cost-effective way to defend worldwide Soviet interests than aircraft carriers, Khrushchev faced the problem of how to deploy Soviet submarines in the Pacific. The Soviet far eastern port of Vladivostok would be vulnerable to a NATO blockade in the event of war. Khrushchev turned to Mao to see if China would offer the use of its ports, at least in wartime. He also hoped that Mao might permit Moscow to establish radio stations along the Chinese coast to maintain contact with the Soviet Pacific fleet.[90]

In the crush of events surrounding the Iraqi situation, however, Khrushchev had mishandled Chinese sensitivities. On July 15 the Kremlin received a letter from Mao requesting assistance in expanding and modernizing the Chinese Navy.[91] For months Soviet military advisers in China had encouraged the Chinese leadership to request Soviet military aid. The advisers were not simply trying to do their best for China. Khrushchev's efforts to restructure the Soviet Navy had set off a battle at home, which had contributed to Marshal Zhukov's downfall in 1957, and the Soviet advisers were trying to bring the Chinese in on the side of those still arguing against Khrushchev's drive for a smaller navy.[92]

It was no surprise to Khrushchev that Soviet military representatives were complicating Sino-Soviet relations. Khrushchev's relations with the military were strained, and he had come to mistrust the advice his military men were giving him.[93] Joking with Nasser in May 1958, he had warned that military officers never met a new weapons system they did not like and generally exaggerated threats to get the procurement they wanted.[94]

Khrushchev's mistake was that instead of following through with an initial plan to send a private letter to Mao, which would have been drafted by the ever-cautious Mikoyan, he had decided on his own to send an oral message through the Soviet ambassador, Pavel Yudin.[95] Whatever Yudin told the Chinese leader managed to annoy Mao, who got the impression from the ambassador that Khrushchev thought he could speak to him as if he were Moscow's vassal. What was supposed to be a Khrushchevian plea for Chinese assistance in achieving his goals for the Soviet Navy, Mao interpreted as a Soviet demand for Chinese involvement in a joint Sino-Soviet Pacific fleet that would be controlled by the Kremlin.

On July 22 Yudin sent to Moscow a desperate message that Mao opposed the request as an "expression of Great Russian chauvinism." Mao had a bad habit of referring to Soviet acts as Russian acts, something that always annoyed Khrushchev.[96] Now Mao was demanding a summit to discuss this insulting idea of a "joint Sino-Soviet" navy, to complain about the behavior of some of the Soviet advisers in his country, and to discuss the many wrongs committed by the Soviet Union in China.

What had become overwhelmingly clear was that not only had Mao misunderstood Khrushchev's objectives, but he seemed to see this request as a covert effort by the sneaky Russians to reclaim some power over China. Historian Chen Jian has argued that even were it not for Mao's paranoiac tendencies, he was especially sensitive in 1958 to what he perceived as challenges to his twin concerns of Chinese sovereignty and his personal authority as revolutionary leader. Like Khrushchev, he had just launched a major reform drive. That summer Mao unveiled the Great Leap Forward, a broad set of radical measures to accelerate Chinese industrialization and dismantle the traditional rural economy.[97]

Khrushchev was surprised by what had come of his initiative with the Chinese, but he initially believed he had to turn down Mao's request for an immediate face-to-face discussion. There were daily developments in the Middle Eastern situation. "We are for a meeting, but the circumstances do not permit one," Khrushchev instructed the Soviet Foreign Ministry to write to Mao.[98] Having just received Eisenhower's suggestion to resolve the Iraqi crisis within the framework of the Security Council, Khrushchev clung to his hope of a summit meeting perhaps now in New York. He knew from intelligence sources that despite American reluctance, the French government at least was applying pressure for some kind of summit meeting of the great powers.

Khrushchev changed his mind four days later after trading two more letters with Eisenhower.[99] Convinced now that an early summit in New York on the Middle Eastern question was unlikely, Khrushchev thought he could divert his attention to Mao.[100] Using the special high-frequency telephone link that Moscow maintained with its key embassies, he called Yudin in Beijing on July 28 to arrange an immediate meeting with the Chinese leader. He proposed beginning the talks on July 30 and asked the Chinese to decide if this ought to be an official or unofficial visit.[101]

Mao was out of the capital when the call came through. He had a meeting scheduled in Beidaihe, a town 250 miles east of Beijing, for the next day. The Chinese premier, Zhou Enlai, and an aide met with Yudin. Once Zhou understood the Soviet ambassador's request, he knew that he needed Mao's approval before any definitive answer could be given to Khrushchev. He left the Soviet Embassy to contact the Chinese leader. An hour later he returned with Mao's answer: The Chinese would welcome Khrushchev on July 30.[102]

The summit Khrushchev got in July 1958 was a difficult affair. Mao refused to accept Khrushchev's explanation that Yudin had misunderstood the point of the oral message. Khrushchev tried hard to explain how his military reforms would improve the Soviet Union's ability to protect its allies, including China. He recalled the success he had had in brandishing intermediate-range missiles, which could destroy Britain and France, at the time of the Suez crisis. "When we wrote letters to Eden and Guy Mollet during the Suez events," he told Mao, "they immediately stopped their aggression." Khrushchev said that "now that we have intercontinental missiles, we are also holding America by the throat." Adding insouciantly, "And they thought America was unreachable," he explained that this was the key to saving the new progressive regime in Iraq.[103]

Mao was keenly interested in how Moscow was handling the threats to Iraq. Besides being a test of the Soviet Union's willingness to defend an ally, the Iraqi crisis provided insight into the willingness of the United States to accept changes in the developing world that went against its own interests. Mao was more optimistic than Khrushchev that the West would back down. Beijing had joined Moscow in recognizing the new republic of Iraq on July 17, adding its own warning that "the time when aggressors could rely on gunboats to conquer a nation had gone forever."[104] But Mao doubted that an Anglo-American attack on Iraq would happen. He was convinced that London and Washington understood that the next step would be general war. While Khrushchev agreed in theory, he was less convinced of his ability to deter the United States in the Middle East.

Mao's prediction proved to be insightful. Throughout the period that Khrushchev was in China the Americans and the British were considering whether to recognize the Qasim regime. The British were eager to do it.[105] Now convinced that Qasim, who seemed in no hurry to have Iraq join Nasser's United Arab Republic, was primarily an Iraqi nationalist, Macmillan argued for Western recognition of Iraq as part of a strategy of driving a wedge between Baghdad and Cairo. The Americans were more reluctant to press ahead with recognition, in part because of an unwillingness to court Turkish and Iranian disappointment. But ultimately the Eisenhower administration agreed with London that there was no way to avoid dealing directly with Qasim. Just before his last meeting with Mao on August 3, Khrushchev learned that the United States and Great Britain had recognized the Iraqi regime. "[T]hat is one more bitter pill for them to swallow," said Khrushchev with satisfaction.[106]

Mao was as pleased as Khrushchev to hear that his prediction had been borne out. The Chinese leader had very selfish reasons not to want this crisis over Iraq to have continued much longer. He worried that in a summit, especially one held at the United Nations, Khrushchev might be tempted to trade favors to ensure the survival of Iraq. Mao had his own plans to stir up trouble with the Nationalist government in Taiwan, which was occupying a handful of small islands close to the Chinese coast. He did not want the Soviets to promise peace in the Chinese strait to get peace in the Middle East.

Moscow's apparent diplomatic success in the Middle East softened the mixed results of the Mao-Khrushchev talks in Beijing. In the end, Khrushchev secured radio stations for the Soviet submarine force, an essential element of the new strategy. He did not get Chinese support for port facilities, however. The best he could get was a Chinese promise to open up ports from Tianjin (Tientsin) to North Vietnam's Haiphong at times of war. More important, Khrushchev left with a sense that the Chinese still accepted his basic approach to world affairs.

▪

K HRUSHCHEV RETURNED home from Beijing to celebrate his victory in the Persian Gulf. Convinced that the United States had fully intended to invade Iraq, he believed that his policy of public and private threats had stayed Eisenhower's hand. Moscow, which had not known anything about the Anglo-American decision on July 18 to shelve plans to attack Iraq, interpreted London's and Washington's recognition of the Iraqi regime as the end of the threat of U.S. intervention. Khrushchev was now no longer interested in a Middle Eastern summit.

"We are now in the second phase of the struggle in the Near and Middle East," Khrushchev announced at a formal meeting of the Presidium the next day.[107] "Phase one of our strategy was to protect Iraq in the early going of its revolution," he said.[108] Phase two was now to consolidate this geopolitical gain.

Khrushchev no longer believed that a summit meeting with Eisenhower and Macmillan was necessary. "What was the goal when we suggested a summit?" he asked. "To prevent war in the Middle East and not to permit the destruction of Iraq." To remind his colleagues why Iraq lay at the center of this crisis for Moscow, Khrushchev continued: "The destruction of Iraq is an attack on our policy from the point of view of the prestige of our country. The destruction of Iraq is then the destruction of Egypt and Syria; it would be a reversal for the national self-determination movement in the Arab world."

With the war scare over Iraq now past, Khrushchev established the organizing principle of the next phase of the struggle. "Now there remains one thing to do: the removal of the forces from Lebanon and Jordan." He did not believe that he needed to go to New York or to Geneva to achieve that goal.

Nor did he think that this was a matter that required the presence of Eisenhower, Macmillan, or de Gaulle. Recalling what Mao had said to him, Khrushchev wondered if he really wanted to go to the Security Council at all. "Given the alphabet, would that mean I would have to sit near Chiang Kai-shek?" When he was told that his seat would be two over from that of the representative of Taiwan, he said, "[T]hat would be a bad spectacle and a bad role [for me] in this spectacle."[109]

However, Khrushchev did not need the Chinese to tell him that a Security Council discussion structured around the problem of removing U.S. troops from Lebanon was not the one he wanted or needed at this time. It was Soviet policy to seek better relations with the West through high-level negotiations, but a summit would have to wait until the Americans were ready and a broad agenda, covering topics from the future of the Germanys to disarmament, could be mutually agreed upon. "Why would we go to a meeting with Eisenhower now?" he exclaimed. "To rant that he's a son of a bitch? That we already know and there would be little else. The basis for us to meet now is very narrow, really only enough for insults."[110]

Khrushchev was extremely happy with the way events had unfolded in the Middle East. He explained to his colleagues on August 4 that Moscow could not be sure which direction Qasim's regime would take in the future. There could be no guarantees that Baghdad would continue to take Soviet advice or to maintain good relations with Iraq's Communist Party. Yet he was impressed that Qasim had followed Moscow's recommendation, conveyed through Nasser, that he reaffirm all previous Iraqi obligations. Indeed, Baghdad did not formally leave the Baghdad Pact for another six months. In late August Qasim deepened Khrushchev's sense of accomplishment by deftly signaling to Moscow that though he was not a Communist, he was prepared to work with the Iraqi Communist Party. "I am not among those people who fear Communist propaganda," he made a point of informing the newly arrived Soviet ambassador.[111] In the same conversation he also signaled a level of trust with Moscow. Admitting that he lacked an intelligence organization, he requested that the Kremlin "inform him in a confidential manner on the intrigues of the colonialists and their accomplices, both within the country and beyond Iraq's borders."[112]

It turned out that the Soviet leader did not have to go to New York or anyplace else to obtain the removal of the Western troops from Lebanon. From the start the U.S. intervention had been unpopular in Lebanon. In fact the U.S. ambassador in Beirut, Robert McClintock, had all but waded out from shore to prevent the first contingent of U.S. Marines from landing. With the passing of the moment of greatest tension, Chamoun finally agreed to step down, and the leading Muslim candidate, the army chief of staff, General Fuad Chehab, was selected to replace him.[113] The British had had an easier deployment in Jordan, but once U.S. troops started leaving Lebanon, Britain decided its men should go home too. On October 25 the last U.S. and British soldiers left Lebanon and Jordan respectively. Khrushchev thought he had achieved phase two.

The Iraqi crisis was a defining moment for the Soviet leader. From his perspective, the use of high-pitched warnings had brought great success. The fate of Iraq was an essential component of his policy of weakening American power in the Middle East, and he was convinced that the United States would probably not permit the destruction of the Baghdad Pact without a fight. It was this conviction that lay behind his exaggerated fear of a U.S. military adventure during the summer of 1958. Yet however distasteful to Washington, a revolution had taken hold in Iraq. There had been no Anglo-American intervention, and the Baghdad Pact was dead. For the second time in eighteen months, Khrushchev believed that fears of Soviet power had prevented the much-stronger West from destroying one of his new allies in the third world.

Until the release of his Kremlin notes and minutes in 2003, Western policy makers and scholars did not understand the significance for Khrushchev of what he viewed as the Iraqi crisis of 1958. At the time in Washington and London, where Khrushchev's policy seemed to be judged by his inability to orchestrate a summit, the outcome of the summer tensions in the Middle East was deemed a major personal defeat for the Soviet leader. News that he had met with Mao during the crisis, which leaked to the West in August 1958, only intensified the belief that he had backed down from his calls for a summit out of weakness. It seemed to Western foreign policy watchers that Khrushchev had essentially been browbeaten by the Communist Chinese, who did not want the Soviet leader to dignify a session in New York with Chiang Kai-shek.

The West completely missed the enormous self-confidence that Khrushchev drew from the survival of the Iraqi Revolution. Instead of sensing the feeling of triumph in the Kremlin, Western analysts began predicting Khrushchev's political demise because Eisenhower and Mao had thwarted his dreams for a great power summit. A seasoned Western diplomat, described as "not given to rash predictions," told the *New York Times*, "This may even be the end of an era."[114] Indeed, it was, but not in the way that anyone in the West was predicting.

CHAPTER 8

"A BONE IN MY THROAT"

NIKITA KHRUSHCHEV emerged from the 1958 Iraqi crisis convinced of two things: first, that the West, which had fully intended to destroy the progressive Iraq regime, had backed down under Soviet pressure, and second, that pressure was the only language the West understood.[1]

This was indeed a one-sided view of what had happened. Just as Khrushchev never did understand the complex of reasons that had led to Britain's and France's 1956 decision to halt their military intervention in Egypt, so he could not quite grasp that Soviet policy had little to do with Eisenhower's reluctance to invade Iraq in the summer of 1958. But perceptions are king in international politics, and Khrushchev perceived the outcomes of both crises as huge personal successes for him. Having exaggerated the threat to his position at the start of the Iraqi crisis, he now felt exaggerated relief when his position was preserved.

"History is on our side," Khrushchev had already told Nasser in May.[2] Now that the events of the summer confirmed in his mind that circumstances in the developing world were turning in his direction, he could afford to take some additional risks to consolidate these gains. The first of these involved support for Egypt's Aswan Dam project. For two years Soviet officials had advised Khrushchev that the USSR could not afford to provide this aid, and as late as Nasser's 1958 visit the Kremlin had refused to offer its support. But the toppling of the Feisal regime in Iraq and the subsequent disruption of the Baghdad Pact had delighted Khrushchev. Signing an Aswan agreement would be his way of thanking Nasser and solidifying the Soviet-Egyptian relationship. In October 1958 Nasser's military chief and deputy, Marshal Amer, was invited to Moscow to conclude the Aswan negotiations.[3]

If Khrushchev's inflated sense of accomplishment had resulted only in a Soviet commitment to a vast public works project in the Egyptian desert, the West might not have needed to pay any attention to the lessons that the Soviet

leadership had learned from events in Iraq. But Khrushchev's perception of success in the Middle East had far-reaching implications for his handling of foreign
policy problems elsewhere.

For the rest of the world, especially the United States and the nations of
Western Europe, 1958 came to be remembered less for the short-lived tension
in the Middle East than for the start of a new round of East-West clashes over
the future of divided Germany, especially the lonely NATO outpost in West
Berlin. Historians have come to view each of the Berlin episodes as a distinct
crisis.[4] The new material from the Kremlin confirms that Khrushchev
launched three separate pushes for his way in Germany. The first of these
occurred in November 1958.

The presumed victory in Iraq had something to do with Khrushchev's decision to risk a confrontation with the West in the autumn of 1958. As we shall
see, so too did knowledge of the imminent deployment of Soviet nuclear
weapons to East Germany as part of the "new look" strategy adopted by the
Kremlin in 1955. That Khrushchev chose to make this stand at this time over
Germany reflects the roles played by two other men, both Germans, who
helped set the stage for November 1958.

■

THE WIZENED West German chancellor Konrad Adenauer was a skilled
magus who liked to tell the story of how as a schoolboy he had orchestrated
one of the largest cheating conspiracies in his secondary school's history.
When a classmate found the answers to the annual German and Latin exams,
the future chancellor came up with a scheme by which all twenty-one students in the class could use these answers without getting caught. Reasoning
that the authorities would be suspicious if all of them turned in perfect or
near-perfect papers, the young Adenauer mandated that each boy make a certain number of errors on the examination, depending on his grades to that
point. They were never caught. In fact the graduating class of 1894 was her-
alded as the most accomplished of the fin de siècle.[5]

By the fall of the 1958 the Soviet leadership had had to acknowledge that for
nearly two years Adenauer had been employing his ample talents as a dissem-
bler to play a much more dangerous game with Moscow. At some point in 1956
or early 1957 Adenauer had come to the conclusion that the Federal Republic of
Germany (FRG) needed to acquire nuclear weapons to be a fully sovereign
nation. As part of the agreements that made possible the declaration of an independent West Germany in 1955, however, Adenauer had forsworn the acquisition or development of nuclear weapons by a future West German army. This

decision had been very popular with the West German people and been a prerequisite to the Soviet decision to normalize relations later that year.

Adenauer's ideas about military power, however, were constantly in a state of flux. In the early postwar years he had thought it possible to build a sovereign West Germany without a military. Then came the Korean War, which seemed to confirm for him worst-case scenarios about the Kremlin's willingness to use force to achieve the spread of communism.[6] West Germany's bid to join the North Atlantic Treaty Organization followed as a result. By the end of the 1950s perhaps in reaction to Khrushchev's use of nuclear bluff in the Suez crisis, Adenauer believed he had to take German self-defense one step further. In May 1957 the West Germans formally asked the United States for tactical nuclear weapons, those with a short range that could be used by infantry on a battlefield. With tactical nuclear weapons the West German Army, the Bundeswehr, would not need any other nation to defend itself. West Germany would be in control of its own security, the most essential prerequisite of sovereignty.

The German chancellor chose to keep these thoughts about the need for nuclear weapons secret from the German people until he had renewed his parliamentary majority in the elections scheduled for the fall of 1957. West German public opinion was still solidly against nuclear armaments, and he could not risk letting this become an issue in the election. Instead he campaigned hard on the promise of "no new experiments," cleverly painting his chief rivals, the Socialist Party (SPD), as dangerous tinkerers with the status quo.[7]

Adenauer was especially proud of how well he managed to deceive the Soviets. In April 1957 he had arranged a meeting with the Soviet ambassador in Bonn to deny that his government then possessed nuclear weapons or had even asked for nuclear weapons from the United States. "The Soviet ambassador never asked me whether I would request nuclear weapons in the future," the old man later said self-approvingly to Secretary of State Dulles.[8] A month after this meeting with the Soviet ambassador, Adenauer formally requested "the most modern and effective weapons," a euphemism for nuclear-capable armaments, from the United States.[9]

Despite the KGB's excellent sources in West Germany, it was not until the spring of 1958 that Khrushchev began to take seriously the possibility of a West German nuclear arsenal. And only then because Adenauer intentionally revealed his objective. Following his reelection, the chancellor sensed that he could move ahead with obtaining nuclear weapons for the Bundeswehr. Although his margin of victory was not large and he needed to govern through a coalition with the small Free Democratic Party, Adenauer believed he had sufficient power to press on with his ambitions.[10] After a false start in January 1958, Adenauer in March was able to shepherd through the Bundestag a law permitting the acquisition of nuclear weapons. The debate was long and rancorous. At one point an SPD deputy compared Adenauer's Christian Democratic Union (CDU) with the Nazi Party, causing government benches to empty in disgust. But Adenauer got what he wanted. He said that though he hoped for better relations with the Soviets, "Germany's first task is security in [the] Federal Republic."[11]

Even with seemingly clear signs that the chancellor was leading the charge for nuclear weapons, Khrushchev found it hard to believe that Adenauer was the force behind the Bundestag debate. Although he considered Adenauer clever and a formidable opponent, Khrushchev couldn't help assuming that a man of his age—eighty-two—lacked the willpower necessary to mastermind all of these political games. Thus Khrushchev blamed the nuclear strategy on the West German minister of defense, Franz Josef Strauss, whom he described as the Hitler to Adenauer's Hindenburg. Moreover, it seemed to Khrushchev that Adenauer was too wily a politician to be pushing the nuclear option. He assumed that Adenauer actually wanted better relations with the Soviet Union.[12] His motivation, thought Khrushchev, was not due to any personal desire on the part of the chancellor, who was devoutly anti-Communist. Instead Khrushchev believed that it was German public opinion that compelled Adenauer to deal with the Kremlin.

Consequently, when word reached Moscow in late March 1958 that the chancellor had won the Bundeswehr debate, the Soviets responded with a public offensive directed primarily at the West German people. Foreign Minister Gromyko warned the West Germans on March 31 that their government had fallen under the same conservative leadership that had permitted Hitler to come to power in 1933, while the Supreme Soviet addressed a similarly solemn letter to the Bundestag.[13] Behind the scenes the Soviets tried to enlist the help of the SPD. Soviet representatives leaked drafts of Moscow's diplomatic protests to the SPD leadership ahead of time to sharpen public debate on the CDU's new foreign policy.

The final maneuver was aimed directly at the old man. Using the excuse of some languishing cultural and trade agreements, Moscow arranged for Mikoyan to be invited to Bonn in mid-April 1958. Although younger than Khrushchev, Mikoyan had been a member of the Politburo, or Presidium, ten years longer, and Germany had been an area of great interest to him for a long time. As commissar for foreign trade in the 1920s Mikoyan had played a major role in making work the so-called Rapallo arrangement, named for the Italian town where Soviet and German diplomats had met to discuss military and economic cooperation. Mikoyan ultimately signed many of the documents establishing the economic relationship between Weimar Berlin and Moscow.

The goal of Mikoyan's mission in 1958 was to establish some kind of rapport with Adenauer and to assess the reasons and the individuals behind what seemed to be a dramatic shift in West German policy. The Kremlin still believed in the Adenauer who in 1957 had stated his personal opposition to acquiring nuclear weapons.

The Mikoyan mission to Bonn failed. Not only did the Soviet effort to put a thumb on the scales of public debate come to nothing, but Mikoyan found himself yet another Soviet victim of Adenauer's cleverness. In the sessions with Khrushchev's representative, the West German chancellor admitted that he had indeed changed his mind since 1957. Now he intended to acquire the U.S. Matador missile, which could carry nuclear as well as conventional warheads.[14] This should have been a devastating blow to Soviet assumptions, but Adenauer somehow persuaded Mikoyan, and through him Khrushchev, that the decision to buy U.S. nuclear weapons could be revisited if there were any progress on general disarmament among the great powers.

What made Adenauer's performance especially masterful was that he managed to convince the Soviets not only that he was a reluctant player in the drama of West German rearmament but that despite the fact that the Bundestag had authorized him to make West Germany a nuclear power, nothing bad was going to happen. The Kremlin decided that despite the failure of its attempt to alter the Bundestag vote through public diplomacy, there was no need to reappraise Soviet policy toward West Germany. Curiously, in trying to manage Adenauer at this stage, the Soviet Union apparently did not consider making any overtures to the United States, without which Bonn could not acquire nuclear weapons in the near future. Moscow, which apparently knew nothing about Adenauer's May 1957 request for tactical nuclear weapons, probably assumed Eisenhower would give Adenauer the Matador missiles if he formally asked for them. Yet the Soviet policy of preventing that from ever occurring was directed primarily at altering West German behavior.[15] And as the war clouds gathered in the Middle East that summer, the Kremlin felt it could afford to take a wait and see approach to Adenauer.

▪

K HRUSHCHEV'S PATIENCE with the West Germans would have been even greater had it not been for the difficulties he was having simultaneously with his East German allies. Events in East Germany in 1958 magnified the

danger to Moscow posed by Bonn's nuclear dreaming. The economic dispar-
ity between the two Germanys was growing, with East Germany becoming
ever weaker. The East German leadership had launched its own version of
Khrushchev's catch and surpass campaign in July 1958, with West Germany
as the means of comparison. Rather than energize the East German population, these efforts had created political unease. With West Berlin available as
an escape route, upward of twelve thousand people were leaving East
Germany every month. These were many of the best-trained East Germans,
the engineers, doctors and other professionals that the Berlin government
could not do without.[16]

One very forceful German lay behind East Berlin's failing economic campaign. Walter Ulbricht was almost a generation younger than Adenauer, but
he had been a player in German political disputes since the 1920s, when he
served as a functionary in the German Communist Party. Having fled from
the Nazis in 1933, he spent the next twelve years in Moscow, where ultimately
Stalin tapped him to be the first secretary of the Party of German Unity
(SED), the Communist Party in the Soviet zone of occupation.[17] Ulbricht, who
wore a distinctive white goatee, had the great distinction of being almost as
thoroughly disliked by Communists as by capitalists. He was viewed as pushy,
arrogant, and doctrinaire. But Stalin had liked him, and Khrushchev had
decided to tolerate him.

Ulbricht had very nearly lost his job in 1953, when the SED's attempt to
foist half-baked collectivization schemes on the Soviet zone led to riots in East
Berlin. Once again in 1958, he faced the consequences of mass dissatisfaction
when he tried to tighten controls on the East German economy to make it
more efficient. Instead of being deterred by domestic troubles, Ulbricht
reacted by trying to force an acceleration of negotiations with the West over
the future of Germany. He assumed that treaties that confirmed East
Germany's eastern borders and closed the escape valve through West Berlin
would consolidate the SED's control over the former Soviet occupation zone.

As of September 1958, Ulbricht was sending signals that the East German
regime was eager for additional protection from Moscow. He did not hide his
concerns about Bonn's drive for atomic weaponry. The new weapons could
not reach Moscow, but they could inflict damage on fellow Germans in an
accidental war. Beyond this medium-term issue, there was the immediate
problem of the growing inequality of the two Germanys. Parity was the best
that East Germany could hope for in its rivalry with its larger and more popu-
lous capitalist brother. But with the drain of some of its best citizens and the

growth in political, economic, and now military might of the other Germany, a sense of urgency was developing among the East German leaders.

■

IN THE FALL of 1958 Khrushchev left it up to the Soviet Foreign Ministry to manage the German problem. In September 1958 a stultifying exchange of notes took place between the two Germanys and the occupying powers. The two sides were arguing over whether to start discussing a peace treaty between each Germany and the occupying powers before or after the formation of an all-German commission that was itself designed to prepare a peace treaty. When all the diplomatic rhetoric was stripped away, the issue came down to the fact that the West Germans, who wanted East Germany to disappear, hoped for all-German elections. Even in the unlikely event that all adults among the seventeen million in East Germany voted Communist, Ulbricht would be defeated. The East German leaders understood this very well. They tied the survival of a Communist Germany to a treaty system that guaranteed the equality of the two Germanys. In their eyes, the first step to that goal would be for Moscow to sign a pact with East Germany that declared a formal end to World War II and permitted East German soldiers and police to replace their Soviet counterparts along the borders of West Berlin and West Germany.[18]

Following this exchange of notes, which only served to confirm the gulf separating the official positions of Bonn and East Berlin, Ulbricht turned to Moscow for help. He believed the Kremlin had been too passive in dealing with both Adenauer and the deteriorating situation within East Germany. Ulbricht initially found support at the Soviet Embassy in East Berlin. The former Kremlin heavyweight Mikhail Pervukhin, who was now in virtual exile as Soviet ambassador to East Berlin after his participation in the failed June 1957 coup against Khrushchev, added his voice to Ulbricht's call for some Soviet movement toward signing a peace treaty with East Germany. In early October Pervukhin met with Ulbricht, who called on Moscow to support this initiative. In reporting this conversation to the Kremlin, Pervukhin agreed with the East German leader.[19]

Unlike the East Germans and the Soviet ambassador in Berlin, the Soviet Foreign Ministry saw no reason for haste in dealing with the German question in October 1958. It was quietly understood that the East Germans should be mollified and that the Westerners who had been acting up lately ought to be contained. But there seemed to be no particular crisis brewing, nor was there any pressure at that moment from the Kremlin for action. There was time before West Germany would acquire nuclear weapons, if that ever happened. There was also time to manage whatever economic difficulties were experienced by East Germany. So in an effort to keep everybody busy and out of trouble, the Soviet Foreign Ministry settled on an elegant nonpolicy. According to a draft prepared for consideration by the Kremlin, the Soviets were to invite France, Great Britain, and the United States to a four-power conference on resolving the German question.

"This recommendation," the Germanists argued in their brief to the Presidium, "would undermine the principal argument used by the West against preparing a peace treaty with Germany: namely, that the fundamental prerequisite of negotiations on such a treaty is the formation of an all-union Germany government."[20] In forwarding this modest proposal to his Kremlin bosses, Foreign Minister Andrei Gromyko explained that it was certain the West would reject it. He regarded this rejection as useful, although not to move the German problem any closer to solution. No one in the ministry thought that a possibility. No, this tactic's appeal was that it "would draw attention to the problem of the preparation of a peace treaty and the formation of a German federation at the expense of the Western idea of all-German elections."[21]

Sometimes foreign ministries are a step or two ahead of their political masters. Sometimes they are a step or two behind. At this time and on this matter the Soviet Foreign Ministry was so out of step with Nikita Khrushchev that they might as well have been providing policy guidance to Dwight Eisenhower. Khrushchev, as the world was soon to discover, was tired of playing games with the West over Germany.

■

THE PRINCIPAL REASON why Khrushchev did not take a more active part in handling the German leaders in September and October 1958 was that domestic problems did not leave him much time for foreign policy. All fall, but especially in October, he was leading a complex discussion on what shape Soviet society should take into the mid-1960s.[22] Since the 1920s the Kremlin had produced five-year plans for the domestic economy and social programs. For the first time in Soviet history, it decided to prepare a seven-year plan, requiring even more complicated estimates and raising even more management issues. Reflecting Khrushchev's desire to achieve the lofty goals announced as part of his 1957 crusade to catch and surpass America, the plan was to be ambitious not only in its chronological sweep but also in the improvements to Soviet living standards that it promised. The Kremlin hoped to increase the supply of food and consumer goods, to build more housing and more preschools and kindergartens, and to complete the massive northern Crimean canal, designed to irrigate the Crimean agricultural region and provide fresh water to southern Ukrainian towns. Khrushchev was preoccupied with the details of the seven-year plan; the discussion at the top included everything from projected levels of national milk production and the need for more sugar refineries to the high cost of inputs in building apartments. The Soviet system relied on the Kremlin to set all these targets and then to use a combination of coercion and flattery to see that they were met by thousands of bureaucrats throughout the country.

Although these Kremlin discussions of future achievements tended to take on aspects of fantasy, especially as discussion centered on the production of wheat in 1965, even Khrushchev felt the need to acknowledge limits. He believed the USSR could not go as far as some of his colleagues wished in lifting some of the burdens of Soviet life, especially those carried by women. A commission of the Central Committee had recommended phasing in a thirty- to thirty-five-hour workweek. Soviet citizens, who were required to work on Saturdays, put in at least forty-two hours a week. Complaints about the long workday were on the rise, particular among women, who predominated in the fields of education and medicine. The Kremlin's sole woman member, Yekaterina Furtseva, not only wanted a shorter workweek but thought the government should increase family allowances to allow women to have more children.[23] Khrushchev had his doubts that the country could afford these worthy goals.

By early November Khrushchev was impatient to settle the main planks of the party's new economic program. The seven-year plan would not be announced until the Twenty-first Party Congress in January, but he appears to have set a personal goal to end discussions of the outlines of the plan before the forty-first anniversary celebrations of the Bolshevik Revolution on November 7. The next regular Presidium meeting was scheduled for Thursday, November 6. At that meeting he would have to disappoint Furtseva and those who supported a shorter workweek and more family assistance. He not only worried about the cost of these initiatives but had ideological qualms about any assistance that was made directly to individuals. He preferred distributing money to communes, communities, and club organizations. He did not want people to become wards of the state. Instead he hoped that through these social organizations, people would become self-sufficient. But the bottom line for him was that in 1958 Moscow could not afford any experiment that supported a higher birthrate or shorter workdays, not if the USSR was to catch up with the United States anytime soon.

■

THE FOREIGN MINISTRY'S unimaginative suggestion for dealing with Germany landed on Khrushchev's desk just as he was grappling with how to explain the limits on what the Soviet Union could provide its own citizens in the short term. He was so busy that he could have pushed the German problem to one side, as he had done in the summer, when Iraq appeared to be threatened, but he didn't.

Instead he decided to take the greatest foreign policy gamble to that point in his career. The collision of his mounting German frustrations with his domestic troubles had raised the temper of this emotional man. New archival evidence suggests that though Iraq had increased his foreign policy swagger, a dramatic development in the Soviet nuclear posture played an important role in the timing of his explosion.

In contrast with the disappointing news about the Soviet economy, Khrushchev was doubtless receiving at the same time some encouraging progress reports on the highly secret Operation Atom.[24] In March 1955 the Kremlin had approved a plan to deploy medium-range ballistic missiles, the R-5M, which had a range of 1,200 kilometers, or 750 miles, to the far eastern and transcaucasian regions within the USSR as well as to East Germany and Bulgaria outside the country. This first generation of medium-range ballistic missiles lacked the range to strike Paris and London if only stationed in the European portion of Russia, Byelorussia, or the Ukraine. Operation Atom had run into difficulties, however, chiefly because of production bottlenecks in the inefficient Soviet defense industry, and deployment deadlines were repeatedly missed. Moscow eventually decided to drop the Bulgarian deployment, but as Khrushchev knew in the fall of 1958, the East German deployment was finally taking place.

In the summer of 1958 the Soviet Army had built special bases north of Berlin, which included housing for troops to guard and service the missiles and storage facilities for the nuclear warheads. It is not known if Khrushchev was given a date for when these missiles would become operational, but they reached these bases in late November or early December 1958. What Khrushchev could confidently expect in early November was that the Soviet Union was about to acquire a real nuclear threat to London and Paris, rather than the hollow boast that he had been using since 1956. Although he did not tell Ulbricht about Operation Atom, he did hint that he was increasingly confident of the correlation of Soviet and American forces. "The more the Western powers know that there is a balance in the area of atomic weapons and rockets," Khrushchev told the East German leader, "the better for us."[25]

■

MOSCOW WAS LOOKING more festive for the forty-first anniversary of the Bolshevik Revolution than it had looked for the fortieth. Western journalists remarked on the number of colored lights, a rarity in Soviet shops. Max Frankel of the *New York Times* noticed that though some were arranged in decorative daisy chains, most were strung to represent graphs showing industrial progress.[26] Only the regular Thursday Presidium session on November 6 separated most of the Kremlin bosses from the three-day holiday weekend. It is not known if any of them expected the early festivities that Khrushchev had planned for them. Unfortunately, though Malin was in attendance to take his notes, Khrushchev did not invite a stenographer to what was, in retrospect, one of the most important Kremlin meetings of his era.[27]

He led off with a discouraging discussion of what the Soviet government could and could not do to help the country's workers. He explained to Furtseva and her supporters Anastas Mikoyan and Averky Aristov, that the issues of the workweek and family assistance would have to be reexamined. It was too late for these reforms to be included in this version of the seven-year plan. This was a painful admission by Khrushchev that the dream of a better life for Soviet citizens was not yet attainable. It simply cost too much.

Khrushchev then moved to unveil his foreign policy surprise. He had decided to ignore the Foreign Ministry's proposal for the next diplomatic phase in the discussion on a German peace treaty. He wanted a bold initiative. He was tired of diplomacy, tired of the rhetorical games over this or that procedure to signing a peace treaty, and though it had not happened, he assumed that it was only a matter of time before Washington provided Adenauer with nuclear-tipped short-range missiles. "What remains of the Potsdam Accord?" Khrushchev asked, referring to the arrangements for governing Nazi Germany confirmed by Harry Truman, Joseph Stalin, and British Prime Minister Clement Attlee in a Berlin suburb in August 1945. He listed Western violations of the postwar settlement. "They attracted Germany into NATO, they are giving her atomic weapons." His conclusion was that nothing remained of the agreement. "Is it not the time to begin rejecting the Potsdam Accord?" he asked. He was prepared to announce this declaration to the world and suggested that the right opportunity was only a few days away. The following Monday, November 10, he was scheduled to give a speech at a Soviet-

Polish friendship rally that the Polish leader Wladyslaw Gomulka was expected to attend. Although the focus of the event would be Soviet-Polish relations, which had again become rocky in recent months, he thought this would be a reasonable forum in which to announce a formal end to the Second World War.

With a few lines in one speech, the Soviet leader would effectively renounce the entire basis for European stability since 1945, and Khrushchev left no doubt among his colleagues that he understood at least some of the implications. He wanted plans drawn up for the immediate removal of Soviet military personnel from East Berlin and East Germany. He would sign a peace treaty with the East Germans that would make them responsible for their own borders. One important consequence of the peace would be that if Americans wished to visit their political island of West Berlin, they would have to get permission from the East Germans to cross East German territory, by air or by land.

There was no reason to believe that the West would allow this to happen without some kind of fight. What would the reaction of East German soldiers be if the Americans and the British, as they doubtless would, decided to strengthen their contingents in Berlin in the wake of the chaos created by the Soviet removal of all rules governing the area? The postwar settlement permitted the Allies to move troops at will into West Berlin, and as of November 1958 there were already eleven thousand NATO soldiers in the city.

Khrushchev had not requested any analyses of this proposal in advance. The Foreign Ministry had done its work using a different set of assumptions, and there was no preliminary military planning. Rodion Malinovsky, the Soviet defense minister, had not even been invited to attend the Presidium meeting. Khrushchev simply presented the renunciation of the postwar European settlement as his wish. This was enough for his acolytes, who enthusiastically endorsed the idea. Suslov, Brezhnev, Kozlov, and Kirichenko chimed in their support. Only Gromkyo and Mikoyan spoke in less than positive terms, and Gromyko's concerns were only minor quibbles. Gromyko, who was not a member of the leadership of the CPSU, had to agree with his boss, but he did mention that this idea would have to be discussed in advance with the East Germans. The Soviet foreign minister also thought that there should be some clarification of what the Soviets intended to do in the absence of the Potsdam Accord. In the hands of a skilled debater, that concern could have been telling, but Gromyko, who "was afraid of Khrushchev to a degree that was indecent," was only soliciting more instructions from the Kremlin.[28]

Mikoyan's dissent was unmistakable and telling. He understood immediately that Khrushchev was talking about the future of Berlin. "How far are we to go with this?" he asked, fearing the West would say that Khrushchev was after Berlin. Adding, "I have doubts," Mikoyan argued that he didn't think Khrushchev should renounce the Potsdam settlement anytime soon.

Mikoyan had identified the most dangerous element of Khrushchev's proposal. World War II had left Hitler's great capital city of Berlin in an anomalous position. The Allied powers had competed to see who would occupy the city, a symbol of the victory over nazism. In the immediate aftermath of the Allied success in Normandy in the summer of 1944, Winston Churchill had begun a campaign to convince Supreme Allied Commander Eisenhower to make a dash to Berlin to end the war sooner and cut off the Soviet's advance from the east. Eisenhower preferred deploying Western troops along a broad front to occupy as much of the western portions of Germany as possible and was not convinced that racing the Soviets to Berlin would bring the war to an end any faster. As a result, forces led by Field Marshal Georgi Zhukov reached the city first in late April 1945, causing Hitler to take his own life and that of his wife, Eva Braun, in his subterranean bunker. Even before Zhukov captured Berlin, the Allied leaders at Yalta had decided that they would jointly administer the occupied city. Churchill, Stalin, and Roosevelt did not bother with the logistical details of how the French, British, and American sectors of Berlin, which lay a hundred miles inside the Soviet zone, would be provisioned. Those decisions were to be made as needed by the local military commanders.

East-West relations were so good in the afterglow of the victory that when Marshal Zhukov assured Western generals in late June 1945 that "Western forces could travel to the city unhampered," nothing further was thought to be needed to guarantee road and rail travel to Berlin.[29] The potential for accidents in unregulated airspace, and not a concern about politics, did, however, produce a more formal system for air travel. A four-power air security office was established in Berlin, and in September 1945 an agreement was signed that specified the three air lanes, or corridors, that Western planes could use to fly across the Soviet zone to the western sectors of Berlin.[30]

These arrangements went untested for three years until June 1948. Mikoyan, who had been in Moscow at the time, recalled the international crisis that ensued when Stalin tried to throw the Western powers out of the city. Angry at a series of Allied decisions to coordinate the economies of their occupation zones, Stalin closed all land and water routes to West Berlin, as the British, American, and French sectors had come to be known. Forced to rely on the air corridors, which were guaranteed by the September 1945 agreement, the Western air forces mounted an unprecedented airlift to keep the residents of West Berlin alive. In March 1949 Stalin ended the blockade without getting anything in return from the West, and from that moment onward Mikoyan understood that the Western powers had invested their prestige in the survival of West Berlin, home to 2.2 million people in 1958, and the access routes that guaranteed that survival. Khrushchev's proposed obituary for the Potsdam Accord would effectively cancel the 1945 agreements on access to West Berlin and cause Washington, London, and Paris to assume that a new Berlin crisis was at hand.

Before his colleagues in the Presidium, Mikoyan phrased his opposition carefully to avoid a direct confrontation with an obviously determined Khrushchev. He recommended that the Kremlin not be hasty in trying to resolve the German question. "Why not wait until after the elections in West Germany?" he said, trying to buy time. West Germans were not going to the polls until December.

Although the Khrushchevite bloc—the youngest members of the Presidium who had benefited from Khrushchev's patronage—spoke up in favor of the first secretary's sweeping proposal, Mikoyan thought he had carried the day. The Presidium did not issue any formal instructions on November 6, and there was no vote that day on the German question. That should have been it for a while. It was a matter of Soviet practice that policies had to be formally endorsed by the Presidium if they were to take effect.

But Khrushchev interpreted the outcome of the meeting very differently. He left the session with the endorsements of his men ringing in his ears. Brezhnev and Kozlov had shouted in approval, "We must start!" while Kirilenko of the Ukraine had exclaimed, "Let's light a fire under them." Confident he could bring the entire Presidium around, Khrushchev told Gromyko to reassemble his German experts to prepare a speech for the rally on Monday. Word was also leaked to the East German ambassador, Johannes König, that Khrushchev's November 10 speech would bring "something new."[31] However, Foreign Ministry officials were not permitted to tell their East German colleagues any specifics about the speech.

Although Khrushchev did not yet know it, in circumventing Mikoyan and the traditional Presidium process, he had set in motion a crisis that would test his hold on power. His longtime colleague Anastas Mikoyan, had left the meeting assuming that no decision had been made. He would not soon let Khrushchev forget his mistake.

■

SHORTLY BEFORE leaving for Moscow's Sports Palace on November 10, Khrushchev decided to make his Polish visitor the first Eastern European ally to learn the details of what he was about to say. He told Gomulka that he was preparing to withdraw the Soviet mission from West Berlin and to have the American, British, and French missions expelled from East Berlin. He left no doubt that he was eager to have all Soviet responsibility for overseeing the checkpoints pass to the East Germans. It would be up to them what they did with the access routes. Gomulka grasped immediately, as he later put it, that Khrushchev wished to "liquidate the western part of Berlin."[32]

In laying out his decision to move dramatically to revise the system put in place by the Potsdam Accord, Khrushchev emphasized that he understood the risks. He expected that the Cold War would become as tense as it had been in 1948, when Stalin blockaded West Berlin. This time he suspected that the Allies would refuse to accept East German controls, and all rail and auto transit would stop. "Some form of blockade will result, but we have enough foodstuffs. We will also have to feed West Berlin. We do not want to, but the population will suffer from it."[33]

Khrushchev assured his Polish guest that despite the crisis that would ensue, he did not expect war. "There will be tensions, of course . . . there will be a blockade. They will test to see our reaction. In any case," he explained, "we will have to show a great deal of cold blood in this matter." He told Gomulka that he believed the risks worth taking because the situation of West Berlin was intolerable: "West Berlin is there to be used as an attack base against us." Yet Khrushchev believed that nuclear weapons made a world war over Berlin unlikely. Although the Soviet Union could not yet launch a missile strike against the United States, it had developed missiles that could hit U.S. allies. Fudging the distinction between these two things, Khrushchev boasted to Gomulka, "Today America has moved closer to us; our missiles can hit them directly."[34]

His speech that day was longer and less direct than his talk with Gomulka. But the message was clear. "The time has obviously arrived," he announced, "for the signatories of the Potsdam Agreement to renounce the remnants of the occupation regime in Berlin and thereby make it possible to create a normal situation in the capital of the German Democratic Republic."[35] The Potsdam Accord was "out-of-date." Now that the United States and its NATO partners were prepared to allow West Germany to develop a military that was more powerful than the armies of Britain and France combined, there appeared to be nothing in the Potsdam Agreement for Moscow. The only part of it that the Allies still observed governed their occupation rights in West Berlin, and Khrushchev saw no reason to let those rights continue. "Who profits from such a situation?" he asked rhetorically. Not the Soviet Union, was the implicit response. As a result, the USSR planned to hand over to the

East Germans those functions that it still provided as one of the four victors of World War II. East German soldiers would patrol the corridors that led from West Germany through East German territory to West Berlin and check the visas of visitors into the city. East Germans would also replace the Soviet officers who coordinated air traffic control for the greater Berlin region. Ultimately it would be up to the East Germans whether to permit access through their airspace or territory to West Berlin.

■

INITIAL WESTERN REACTION to the Sports Palace speech was muted. Despite the shrill, indignant language, Khrushchev had never said when the Soviet Union would remove its representatives from the four-power headquarters that oversaw Berlin or when it would transfer its responsibilities for border control of the Soviet zone to the East Germans.

The Eisenhower administration did not see any need for a major response. Instructions went to a lower-level State Department official in Washington to reaffirm the U.S. commitment to West Berlin and reject Khrushchev's assessment of the condition of the Potsdam Accord. The French and British said even less. Meanwhile in Moscow the three main Western ambassadors feverishly tried to parse Khrushchev's statement to see if there was any indication of what could come next. The British ambassador Sir Patrick Reilly focused his attention on getting a better translation of the speech, which had been broadcast over Moscow Radio. He knew that London wanted to know whether Khrushchev had been speaking in the future tense or just the subjunctive.[36]

The calm lasted only two days. Although Khrushchev had not officially terminated Soviet participation in the occupation of Germany, the Soviet military stationed there had apparently received permission to harass Western military movements into and out of West Berlin. By right, the forces of the four occupying powers could move men and weaponry into their sectors of Berlin without declaration to the other occupying powers. At 1:00 P.M., Berlin time, on November 12 the Soviets showed that change was in the air by stopping three U.S. Army trucks that were leaving West Berlin by the Babelsberg checkpoint at the southwest corner of the city. The Soviets insisted on inspecting the vehicles before allowing them to proceed. In accordance with U.S. policy, the commanding officer of the contingent refused to permit inspection. The standoff was broken eight hours later, when a platoon of U.S. tanks arrived at the scene. Once the Soviets realized that the U.S. Army was prepared to use force to retrieve a minor convoy, they released the men and their trucks.[37]

The border incident changed the attitude at NATO headquarters in Paris and among the U.S. Joint Chiefs of Staff. It now seemed what many considered a purely political gesture by Khrushchev might have a military component. Both General Lauris Norstad, the supreme commander, allied powers, Europe, and General Nathan Twining, chairman of the Joint Chiefs, recommended the preparation of a military motorized unit to move from West Germany, along the autobahn corridor through East Germany to West Berlin, as a way of demonstrating the continuing Western Allied commitment to the divided city.[38]

Foster Dulles had a different reaction to the Babelsberg incident. He did not want a show of Western Allied military resolve at this point in the crisis. His view of the strategic implications of Soviet moves in and around Berlin was fundamentally different from his view of the situation in the Middle East. In July he had been disappointed by the Joint Chiefs' unwillingness to consider some kind of military operation to help the British in the Persian Gulf. Here he thought that the U.S. military was moving too fast to consider a military reaction to Khrushchev.[39]

■

WHAT THE WEST did not know was that Khrushchev's speech had also left the Kremlin in disarray. The Babelsberg incident did not reflect the thinking of the entire Soviet leadership, and any Western efforts to parse the November 10 speech or to discern what was happening on the ground in Berlin would be in vain. No intelligence service or foreign ministry, no matter how wise or well informed, could have predicted what the Soviet government would do next. Khrushchev's decision to start a crisis over Berlin had brought a challenge to his leadership from a most unlikely quarter.

The November 10 speech had infuriated Khrushchev's longtime ally Anastas Mikoyan. "It was," Mikoyan later recalled, "a most flagrant violation of party discipline."[40] Mikoyan considered himself more of an expert on international affairs than Khrushchev, who had, in Mikoyan's view, very simple ideas about the world. In particular, Mikoyan thought he understood Germany better than Khrushchev did. Mikoyan's reputation may have been somewhat tarnished by the poor assessment of West Germany's nuclear ambitions that he had brought back from his April 1958 visit with Adenauer. Nevertheless, he believed that Khrushchev's proposed policy presented even more dangers to Soviet security than anything Adenauer had yet done.

Little is known about how Mikoyan began his intrigue, but almost immediately after the Sports Palace speech, it became clear to him that if he wanted to stop Khrushchev from turning Europe upside down, he would have to work fast. On November 14 Khrushchev used a speech to new graduates of Soviet military academies to signal to the West that the Soviet Union was planning to make "definite proposals" on Berlin. A document, he said, was being prepared.[41]

Mikoyan could count on little help in his effort to revise the new German policy. One possible ally was Gromyko, whose German team had drafted the original proposals on November 3 before having to rush out a Khrushchevite speech a few days later. But when Mikoyan approached him, Gromyko showed that he was unwilling to challenge Khrushchev. Another possible sympathizer was the Soviet president, Voroshilov, whom Khrushchev had not bothered to purge after the failed coup in June 1957. The old marshal had been quick to question Khrushchev's risk taking over Iraq in the summer but had remained silent on Berlin at the November 6 session. The sole female member of the Presidium, Furtseva, might also be helpful. She and Mikoyan were allies in the fight for reducing the length of the workday and a few other social reforms that Khrushchev had abandoned as too expensive. She too had remained silent on Khrushchev's Berlin proposal, but she had even less political sway than Voroshilov. All she could bring was one vote.

The new Khrushchev men were of even less use to Mikoyan. Ten of the sixteen full members of the Presidium had been elevated since 1955 and felt various degrees of gratitude to Khrushchev. Leonid Brezhnev, Averky Aristov, and Frol Kozlov, in particular, owed their positions to Khrushchev and were unlikely to mount a challenge to his foreign policy. In any case, they were even more ignorant than Khrushchev in matters of international affairs. The Presidium's chief ideologist, Mikhail Suslov, was a dark horse for Mikoyan. Clever and ruthless, Suslov had endorsed the Berlin policy, but perhaps his mind could be changed.

Despite these odds, Mikoyan decided he had no choice but to try to head off Khrushchev's potentially disastrous Berlin policy. He knew that a direct challenge against Khrushchev would probably fail, so in good Soviet style he worked instead to undermine Khrushchev's authority by an indirect attack.

For years Mikoyan had been trying to remove the chairman of the KGB, Ivan Serov, a man whose fingerprints were all over the terrible years of the 1930s. With destalinization, the Soviet regime had made a promise to the people to curb the more terrorist tendencies of the secret services. Having Serov in place as the chief of the KGB belied that policy. Well before the Berlin debate, Mikoyan had tried to convince Khrushchev that it did not look good for the regime to continue entrusting Soviet security services to someone as odious as Serov. He had gotten nowhere. Serov was one of the few individuals Khrushchev trusted in Moscow. The two had formed a bond when Khrushchev was Stalin's viceroy in the Ukraine and Serov was his chief of security. A persistent rumor in the Kremlin and among the inner circle of Soviet society was that at Khrushchev's instructions, Serov had personally overseen the destruction of Stalin-era archives that implicated them for crimes in the Ukraine.[42]

In the closed world of the Kremlin, Mikoyan understood that by applying pressure on Serov, he could remind Khrushchev that there were limits to his power. But being an accomplished intriguer, Mikoyan also understood that he could not pin his hopes on the Serov ploy alone. Khrushchev had made himself vulnerable among his colleagues by his harsh treatment of the fallen Nikolai Bulganin. The amiable former chairman of the Council of Ministers had been edged out of the Presidium as punishment for siding with the conspirators who had tried to fire Khrushchev in 1957. Mikoyan decided to play as well on that to slow the drive toward a new Berlin policy.

The Presidium had decided in October that as part of the public campaign before the Twenty-first Party Congress, the Kremlin would "reveal more widely the essence of the Anti-Party Group [the 1957 coup plotters]." Khrushchev and his supporters wanted the Soviet people to understand that his opponents had doubted their own wisdom, productivity, and energy. But the Presidium had not decided to use this campaign to destroy Bulganin. It was Khrushchev who decided to use the public campaign to link Bulganin to the men who conspired to overthrow him in 1957.[43] Mikoyan knew that this act of unnecessary political cruelty was a sign of overreaching by Khrushchev that could also be used to undermine his hold on foreign policy.

■

IN THE CIA's inside language, closed societies were hard targets for the purposes of intelligence collection. Within the Soviet Union the Kremlin itself was the hardest target of all. At an off-the-record dinner with several journalists on November 18, Allen Dulles mentioned being puzzled at the public attacks on Bulganin that the agency was picking up in Moscow. Other than that, Dulles knew nothing about the struggle that was going on over the shape of Berlin policy or his opposite number's future at the KGB.[44] But because he assumed that Khrushchev would not risk war to get the Western powers out of West Berlin, the CIA chief was not too worried. James Reston, who attended the select gathering for the *New York Times*, noted that the key to Dulles's lack of concern was the belief that "the Communists knew that a serious effort to block our traffic into West Berlin would merely unite the West and lead to trouble for the Communists."[45]

The three key Western ambassadors in Moscow shared the CIA director's view that Khrushchev was completely in charge of Berlin policy, though they were less sanguine about how far he would go. In the days following Khrushchev's speech, the recently arrived U.S. ambassador, Llewellyn Thompson; the British ambassador, Sir Patrick Reilly; and the French ambassador, Maurice Dejean, shared notes on what they thought was happening. They had no idea that Mikoyan was working behind the scenes to undo the damage of Khrushchev's pledge to junk the Potsdam Accord. What they did understand were the pressures behind Khrushchev's outburst. At the very minimum, Khrushchev wanted to bolster the status of the GDR "in the face of the growing strength of the Federal Republic."[46] His major aim was to force a high-level summit where "re-unification, if discussed at all, would be discussed on his terms." London shared the view of the ambassadors. For good measure, the analysts at the British Foreign Office correctly surmised the role of the nuclear debate in altering Soviet assumptions about the near-term consequences of their German strategy. "The prospect of nuclear armament of the Federal Republic was," British diplomats informed their prime minister, "what may be giving a sense of urgency to Khrushchev's effort at loosening the Western hold on the Federal Republic."[47]

■

THE NEXT PRESIDIUM meeting on November 20 brought a qualified victory for Mikoyan over Khrushchev. The fragmentary records that we have of this meeting barely hint at how Mikoyan rallied the group to derail Khrushchev's ten-day-old Berlin policy.[48] In the days before the meeting Mikoyan appears to have used the issues of the treatment of Bulganin and the future of Serov to enlist the support of Mikhail Suslov and Yekaterina Furseva for a reappraisal of Khrushchev's recent handling of the German question. Once the meeting started, Khrushchev unexpectedly found himself having to defend Serov and the recent public campaign against Marshal Bulganin.

With Khrushchev caught off guard by this criticism, Mikoyan moved to reconsider the Berlin policy. He later recalled dominating the proceedings by giving a long speech on the need to uphold the Potsdam Agreement.[49] As a result, the "plan" that the Foreign Ministry had worked out in connection with the rash promise in Khrushchev's Polish speech was voted down by the Kremlin.

Khrushchev's proposal for unilaterally ending the Potsdam Accord was dead.

And now there was nothing to replace it. As of November 20, despite public statements by Khrushchev and a promise to the Poles that the Potsdam Accord was over, the Soviet Union had to scramble to decide what it would be saying to the West and to the East Germans when asked what its new policy was.

Within hours of the Presidium meeting, Gromyko and his Germanists conceived a two-pronged approach to replace the Khrushchevite diktat on Potsdam.[50] First, the Foreign Ministry would work on a new note to the Western powers that indicated both continued Soviet support for the Potsdam settlement and Khrushchev's demand for change in the status of West Berlin and in the relationship between the occupying powers and the two German successor states. Second, the men decided to see what a back channel approach to Adenauer might bring.[51] Despite mounting evidence that the old fox had deceived them on the nuclear issue, Soviet foreign policy specialists believed that perhaps something could be achieved by communicating privately with the West Germans. Older members of the Foreign Ministry recalled the years of cooperation between the Soviet Union and Germany in the 1920s. Although this was by no means Khrushchev's or Ulbricht's goal, there was still some belief in the ministry in the possibility of one day achieving a unified, neutral, possibly Communist Germany. At the very least it was hoped that by evoking that goal of a neutral Germany, Soviet officials might prod the West Germans into finding a way out of the Berlin deadlock. Before the day was out, Gromyko recommended to the Kremlin that the Austrians be used to pass a special message in this spirit to the West German ambassador, Hans Kroll.[52] It is unclear if Khrushchev knew who Kroll was at that point, but that ignorance would not last long.

▪

B ORN IN 1898 in Deutsch-Piekar, Hans Kroll grew up in a small town a mile away from the border between Wilhelmine Germany and Imperial Russia. As a young boy he fished on the river that divided the two empires. The first words of Russian he learned were shouted by fishermen on the other shore. Years later Kroll recounted these boyhood memories to explain the almost mystical concept of Russia that he developed early on and the drive that led him to learn as much about that country as he could.[53]

Kroll joined the German Foreign Ministry in the difficult years after the defeat in World War I. He himself had been badly wounded fighting the Allies in France. After his recovery he worked for the commission that oversaw the plebiscite in his native province of Upper Silesia, which would determine whether it would join the newly independent Poland or stay with the

much-diminished Germany created by the Versailles Treaty. Despite a majority vote for staying with Germany, the people of Kroll's province were forced
by the victorious great powers to accept a division of their region. The experience traumatized the young Kroll. "This was a clear breach of a promise," he
wrote, "an offensive deceit of the population of that area and a mockery of
self-determination."[54] It also propelled him into the German foreign service,
where at twenty-two he became the youngest attaché. Three years later Kroll
was sent to the German Embassy in Moscow.

He served two years in Moscow in the 1920s and soon acquired a solid
command of Russian, working with Russians and Volga Germans as a representative of the German Foreign ministry's foreign trade division. These were
the years of the Rapallo Agreement. In 1923 the Weimar Republic and the
Soviet Union had signed treaties establishing cooperation. Both pariahs of
the international system, the countries saw value in very close cooperation,
despite differences in political ideology. Germany was eager to circumvent
the restrictions on the size of its military established by the Versailles Treaty,
while Moscow was interested in expanding trade. Even though a very junior
diplomat, Kroll was invited to witness the lively discussions between the
German ambassador and the leaders of the Bolshevik Revolution, many of
whom spoke German. Despite the worldliness of some of the Bolsheviks, the
differences in outlook between Moscow and Berlin meant that this was not an
easy relationship. Nevertheless, Kroll came to understand the advantages for
Germany of a good relationship with the East. This sense of the value of an
Eastern policy never left him. Thirty years later it drew the attention of
Konrad Adenauer, who thought that Bonn needed in Moscow a representative
who spoke Russian and might also have the ability to get the Soviet leadership
to speak frankly.

■

ALTHOUGH NOT in formal session, the Presidium chiefs approved the
Foreign Ministry's suggestions of drafting a new note to the other occupying
powers and making the secret approach to the West Germans through the
Austrians.[55] On November 22 Gromyko went himself to the Austrian ambassador, Baron Nicholas von Bischoff, to ask this special favor. He wanted the
Austrian to understand that Moscow doubted the West Germans would interpret a direct approach as anything other than propaganda in these tense times.
As an alternative, the Kremlin hoped to use Bischoff, who was a "respected
channel." Gromyko asked that the question, Why is West Germany taking
nuclear weapons from the United States? be the first that Bischoff put to Kroll.

The Austrian was also to raise the issue of West Germany's unwillingness to have relations with East Germany. Finally, Gromyko pressed on Bischoff the most important message he had. "Convey to your colleague the West German ambassador," said the Soviet note that Bischoff was handed to read confidentially, "that the conclusion of a peace treaty with Germany could lead to the resolution of the entire German problem." Bischoff said he would carry out this service. Promising not to inform his embassy or anyone else, Baron von Bischoff wasted no time in contacting Hans Kroll.[56]

A couple of hours later the two were having lunch together. Bischoff reported to his German colleague what the Soviet foreign minister had told him. He even exceeded the Soviets' instructions. He had prepared a personal handwritten note, which he handed Kroll, beseeching Bonn to take advantage of this opportunity for direct negotiations with Moscow to prevent a conflict in the heart of Europe. Kroll agreed that a peace treaty with Moscow was "the first step" that would open the way to future moves toward peace and stability in Central Europe. He promised to fight "like a lion" for a German peace treaty. However, he did not indicate any divergence of opinion from that of his government. Instead he believed that the West German position on having the four powers settle the issue first was already quite nuanced in that it allowed for East and West German "experts" to participate in any peace commission. It was Kroll's personal view that these experts would interact and thereby create the bases for reunification.[57]

As Gromyko's initiative was working its way to Adenauer, the Soviet Foreign Ministry put finishing touches on the new diplomatic note. Neither Khrushchev nor Mikoyan got all that he had hoped for, as the note reflected a position in the middle of their divergent opinions. Potsdam was put on life support, rather than executed. Although the West would be told that Moscow considered the occupation zones null and void, Moscow promised to wait six months, until late May, before acting on this situation unilaterally. It is hard to imagine an ultimatum as a compromise position for any government, but this is what the Kremlin was left with after Khrushchev's initial proposal for a more radical approach had been rejected.

The most significant change was not in the timetable for action. It was in the new proposal that Moscow would make on the future of West Berlin, something that Khrushchev had originally intended to leave to the East Germans. The new diplomatic note proposed that with the ending of the occupation regime West Berlin become a demilitarized free city, in effect a city-state linked neither to NATO nor to the Warsaw Pact. Free cities did not have a tradition of lasting very long before being gobbled up by their neighbors. This had been the fate of prewar Danzig and postwar Trieste. But the Soviet Foreign Ministry came to believe that this proposal would satisfy the Western commitment to a non-Communist West Berlin while assuring that NATO forces would have to leave the city.

Khrushchev probably had a hand in drafting the free city proposal as the Foreign Ministry was scrambling to create a new German policy. A former Soviet diplomat later claimed to have witnessed the meeting in the second half of November at which Khrushchev unveiled his idea. Characteristically Gromyko was about to read a draft diplomatic note when Khrushchev stopped him cold. "This doesn't matter," intoned the Soviet leader, "listen to what I have to say—the stenographer is taking notes. If it coincides with what you have written there—good—and if not, throw your notes into the waste basket." He then outlined his free city idea. When he came to the end, he was so pleased with himself that he slapped his knee and exclaimed, "Ha, they will really be thrown in the West, they will say, Khrushchev, that son of a bitch, has now thought up a 'free city.'"[58] Whether this anecdote is accurate or not, Khrushchev immediately embraced the idea of proposing a free city of West Berlin. He was convinced that the West would view this as a serious concession to its interests.[59]

It is even more likely that Khrushchev was directly involved in the decision to limit the ultimatum to six months, rather than a year or longer. He was certainly keeping an eye on the progress of Operation Atom as he reluctantly put his stamp on the revised diplomatic strategy for Germany. Sometime in late November or early December Soviet missile troops, members of the Seventy-second Engineering Brigade, were transported to the bases north of Berlin. The missiles themselves were not yet in East Germany, but they and the nuclear warheads were expected to arrive early in the new year. The entire complex, which was to include twelve R-5m missiles with three-hundred-kiloton nuclear warheads, would be operational by May 1959.[60]

There is good reason to believe the Presidium never formally reconsidered Operation Atom in light of the debate over Khrushchev's German strategy. Malin, who later noted with care the decision to place nuclear missiles in Cuba, left no record of any Presidium discussion of this deployment in November or December 1958. Nor has evidence of a Presidium resolution to proceed with the missile deployment turned up in the top secret Kremlin files for Berlin in 1958. Historian Hope Harrison, the preeminent scholar of Soviet-East German relations, could not find any evidence in East German files of this deployment or that Ulbricht was ever told about it.[61] The deployment proceeded along the lines of the 1955 decision, which assumed the Soviet Union did not require East German approval because of its occupation rights.

In 1958 the Operation Atom deployment reflected Khrushchev's thinking about the political role of nuclear weapons. A year earlier he had revealed to his colleagues a curious belief in the possibility of using threat to achieve peace. In an otherwise gray discussion of a Soviet disarmament proposal, he had used an odd turn of phrase to explain why the tougher the proposal, the better. "The purpose," he said "is to give a rebuff, to steer to détente."[62] For most statesmen, the concepts of rebuff and détente were mutually exclusive. Not for Khrushchev. This was peasant logic. Scare your opponent enough, and he will give you what you want. As Khrushchev gave his preliminary approval to offering the free city concept as a concession to the West, he understood that the Soviet military was prepared for a tough standoff if diplomacy failed.

The Presidium did not wait to hear from Ambassador Kroll or Chancellor Adenauer directly before approving the new note with the reference to a free city of Berlin on November 24.[63] It had been two weeks since Khrushchev had vowed to announce a new policy, and there was a sense that something had to be sent to the West. Approval of the note meant that Mikoyan and Gromyko had bought some time for diplomacy. The goal of these negotiations was first to create a free state of West Berlin, which would be demilitarized and guaranteed by the United Nations. Eventually West and East Germany might be able to draw this city-state into a loose confederation that would allow each of the components to retain its existing political character.

The unintended consequence of this policy compromise was that it left the Soviets in a much weaker position than they had been when they used pressure tactics to keep the Turks out of Syria in 1957 or the Anglo-Americans out of Iraq just four months before. Those threats had been designed to deter immediate military intervention altogether. Here the Soviets were attempting to use the threat of action in six months to compel the West to make concessions to Soviet power right now. If the Western allies sat still, the Soviets faced an unpleasant choice between taking military action themselves or backing down.

The note, ultimately sent on November 27, was the unloved product of a Kremlin power struggle, the result of a disagreement between Mikoyan and Khrushchev over the appropriate risks to take to force the West to accept Khrushchev's conception of an acceptable German settlement. This hastily conceived compromise strategy proved to be a major burden for the Soviets in the coming years.

Word of the dramatic meeting on November 24 eventually leaked out to Marshal Bulganin, who was no longer permitted to attend. He knew of Mikoyan's opposition to Khrushchev's rash Berlin initiative and of course was sympathetic to Mikoyan's position on his own status in the Soviet hierarchy. Seeing Mikoyan in the corridors after the meeting, Bulganin called out, "You won!"[64]

■

EISENHOWER WAS BRIEFED on the Soviet note only a few hours after it was received by his ambassador in Moscow. It was the morning of November 27, and the president was relaxing at his farm near the Civil War battlefield in Gettysburg, Pennsylvania. He took the news calmly. It was really much better than he had expected. Three days earlier Secretary of State Dulles had reported high tension in military circles in Washington. "[E]veryone is stirred up," he wrote, "the JCS [Joint Chiefs of Staff] want to do something fast and quick and [General Lauris] Norstad wants us to fight our way through."[65] The Pentagon had feared that Khrushchev's next step would be action, a more forceful version of the Babelsberg incident on November 14. Although there was a deadline, this new diplomatic note spoke of negotiations. After the briefing Eisenhower called Dulles and received the good news that the British had also steadied their nerves. The prime minister had repudiated a think piece that had been circulating in the British Foreign Office after the Babelsberg incident that called for early recognition of the German Democratic Republic. The memo had come to the attention of the Americans and worried them almost as much as the uncertainty of Khrushchev's next move.[66]

As for Khrushchev's suggestion of turning West Berlin into a free city, Eisenhower told the secretary of state that he was not opposed to the concept in principle so long as it applied to all of Berlin, including the Soviet sector, which was now the capital of the German Democratic Republic. Eisenhower didn't say it, but he assumed Ulbricht and Khrushchev would never agree to that. Dulles shared the presidential calm. Neither man thought that any emergency action was required. Khrushchev had given the allies six months. The tension might eat away at him as much as it would them.[67]

Adenauer was also not worried by the Soviet note. He had already decided to reject the back channel approach through Kroll. He and Kroll had agreed that domestic factors had compelled Khrushchev to take this risky step. They assumed the Soviet leader was very keen to present a Western summit on Berlin as a trophy at the party congress in January. Why, Adenauer wondered, should Bonn help him out?[68]

A few days later Adenauer used Kroll to tell the Soviets that the November 27 note had destroyed any chance for fruitful discussions between Bonn and Moscow. The Soviet proposals regarding a free city of West Berlin were "100% unacceptable." As long as Khrushchev insisted on this change in the status quo, the chancellor saw no way out of this problem.[69]

■

E ISENHOWER'S AND Adenauer's sangfroid hurt Khrushchev at home. In refusing to exhibit any fear, they were denying him the chance to achieve the changes he wanted in Central Europe short of war. Since no one in the Kremlin, including Khrushchev, wanted war, the six-month ultimatum was already beginning to look like a sure loser.

Even though Mikoyan shared paternity for this new Berlin policy, he emerged strengthened from the struggle with Khrushchev and was not harmed by the Soviet Union's sudden international embarrassment. Within a week of the November 27 note Serov was gone. After one of Khrushchev's key young allies, a post–June 1957 addition to the Presidium, Nikolai Ignatov, overplayed his hand trying to protect Serov, the remaining support for the KGB chief collapsed, and Khrushchev had to accept the inevitable on December 3.[70]

He was a poor loser. The day of Serov's dismissal Khrushchev showed anger during a meeting with visiting U.S. Senator Hubert Humphrey. Describing Berlin as "a bone in my throat," Khrushchev assured the American that the Soviets intended "to cut this knot which spoils relations between the four powers."[71] Eager to continue the pressure on Washington, Khrushchev wanted Humphrey to convey two messages to Dulles and Eisenhower: "Don't threaten me," and, equally important, "what are your counterproposals?"[72]

The Soviet leader was doing more than posturing for a visiting American legislator. He was not convinced that diplomacy would work without a period of extreme tension. Despite Mikoyan's revolt and the toning down of the political challenge, Khrushchev had not reversed the decision to send nuclear missiles to East Germany. In December 1958 the Soviet Army deployed the twelve R-5 medium-range ballistic missiles in East Germany. The deployments were done in secret—indeed, it is not known how many of the Presidium members in 1958 were informed of them—though presumably Khrushchev intended at some point to let the Western world learn of this new nuclear threat in Eastern Europe.[73] They would be pointing at London and Paris at the moment the ultimatum expired.

Mikoyan knew about the 1955 decision to deploy nuclear weapons to East

Germany, which had been approved by the Presidium members of that time, but it is not clear if he was kept informed of the actual progress of Operation Atom. If he had been, he almost certainly would have opposed the idea as unnecessarily provocative. In December 1958 he was working hard to undermine the Berlin ultimatum and avert any crisis with the West. On December 17 the Soviet Foreign Ministry handed U.S. Ambassador Thompson a note, requesting visa assistance so that Mikoyan could make an "unofficial visit" to Washington as a guest of the Soviet ambassador, Mikhail Menshikov.[74] Mikoyan was not in the habit of making private visits to capitalist countries, nor was Menshikov a friend of his. The Kremlin wanted Mikoyan to reduce the tension caused by Khrushchev's maladroit treatment of the German problem by conferring with the Eisenhower administration. Seeing the value of a trip by this high-level Kremlin leader, Washington agreed.

To make sure the administration got the message, the next day the journalist Frank Holeman heard once more from his Soviet intelligence contact, Yuri Gvozdev, who had sent messages to him during the Iraqi crisis a few months earlier.[75] The Soviet said that some positive comments Richard Nixon had made on a recent trip to London about the Soviet Union's participation in the Second World War had been noticed by the Kremlin. Would Nixon be interested in visiting Moscow? Holeman thought he heard Gvozdev say that Moscow "would bid very high for [a visit] in terms of constructive proposals on Berlin." The journalist thought he was getting "the straight dope." After Khrushchev's November 10 speech, at a time when Holeman thought things looked very bleak, the Soviet intelligence agent had told him, "[D]on't worry about Berlin; there is not going to be any war over Berlin." This time Gvozdev hoped for an answer in twenty-four hours, but Washington decided not to send a formal response. Apparently any future visit by the vice president would depend on how Mikoyan conducted himself in the United States.

The Kremlin's policy toward Berlin was completely incoherent and potentially dangerous. Khrushchev had designed the Soviet response to the Suez and Iraqi crises, and the logic of Soviet actions reflected his own theories of what might work. But this policy on Berlin was a compromise that satisfied no Soviet policy maker. And now, with evidence mounting that the November 27 note was insufficient to force Western concessions, there were no particularly creative ideas in Moscow available to induce the West to come to the negotiating table. To those who did not know about Operation Atom, it seemed that the momentum that Moscow had gained following the Iraqi coup had been squandered. To those who did know about the missile plan, it was not clear how the appearance of twelve medium-range ballistic missiles north of Berlin could be incorporated into a workable political strategy. Khrushchev's hope seemed to be that the general unease created by the ultimatum, eventually strengthened by the missiles in East Germany, would force the West to embrace the concept of a free city of West Berlin. That was a lot to hope given the history of NATO's commitment to West Berlin since Stalin's blockade. Mikoyan certainly thought so. Hopeful of fixing the mess, he headed to Washington, D.C.

9

KHRUSHCHEV IN AMERICA

A YEAR THAT BROUGHT a major reversal of Khrushchev's tactics in the Cold War began with the arrival in the United States of his chief foreign policy critic. Anastas Mikoyan had not been to America since 1936, when he was the first high-ranking Soviet official to visit the country. At that time he had come ostensibly on a mission to study U.S. canneries, though everyone knew that he was there to feel out what the U.S. government and the American people thought of the Soviet Union and Joseph Stalin.[1] The 1959 trip was equally unprecedented, though this time Mikoyan's primary intent was not to learn something about America or Americans. As the first member of the Soviet elite to visit the United States since Stalin's death, he was coming to lower the level of tension between the superpowers while explaining why Berlin was very important to the Kremlin.

The general importance of the trip was not lost on the Eisenhower administration, though no one in or around the White House grasped the significance of Mikoyan's having made the trip himself. Neither the State Department nor the CIA, which lacked any spies or listening devices in the Kremlin, knew of the power struggle that had preceded the visit or that Mikoyan had been the leader of the faction that produced the watered-down version of Khrushchev's Berlin policy.

Having worked hard to soften Khrushchev's position, Mikoyan now hoped to soften Western interpretations of Soviet intentions. The Eisenhower administration provided him with excellent opportunities to do so. He was given private meetings with both the president and the secretary of state, at which Mikoyan presented a remarkably candid outline of the thinking behind Soviet foreign policy. Soviet leaders, he explained, were realists. He cited as an example the Kremlin's relationship with Nasser, which he insisted could not be explained by ideology. Moscow was well aware that Nasser imprisoned

Communists. Nevertheless, the Soviet Union and Egypt shared enough interests to make the relationship work.

For all his success at the end of 1958 in blunting Khrushchev's aggressive policy on Berlin, Mikoyan was not an independent actor. He had to operate under instructions from the Presidium, and he carried with him a Soviet aide-mémoire on Berlin that reflected the compromise position reached at the end of November. But he did what he could to telegraph to his hosts that there were some people in the Kremlin who had more patience for discussion on Berlin than Khrushchev. He stressed again and again that Khrushchev's November 27 note was not an ultimatum, though he acknowledged that he could not single-handedly remove the deadline.

In making this attempt to move beyond polemics to settle the Berlin problem, Mikoyan lacked a feel for U.S. attitudes on the Berlin issue. Although he represented the Kremlin doves on Berlin, there were rigidities behind his tactical flexibility that limited how much common ground he could achieve in discussions with any American leader. He rejected the idea that East and West Berlin should be treated alike. In his mind East Berlin belonged naturally to East Germany, whereas West Berlin, because of its geographical position inside the territory of East Germany, could not belong to West Germany. Thus he could assert that the East Germans were within their rights to claim the Soviet zone of Berlin as their capital, while Adenauer had no right to control the combined former U.S., British, and French zones of that great German city. At the same time Mikoyan lacked any sense of the depth of Washington's commitment to West Berlin. A long-time critic of Stalin's misdeeds in international politics, he understood that the legacy of the 1948–1949 Berlin blockade complicated the resolution of the Berlin question. But Mikoyan did not grasp that the free city concept would be interpreted by U.S. leaders as tantamount to abandoning the residents of West Berlin.

So Mikoyan arrived with a confusing message for his American hosts. No, there was no ultimatum. Yet when he was pushed on how long the Soviets might wait for a resolution, his answer was disappointing: He urged the Americans to take seriously the need for bilateral negotiations and argued that six months "was a reasonable amount of time for a negotiation." To Americans that sounded an awful lot like an ultimatum, even if the melody was more pleasing.

Consequently, Eisenhower and his foreign policy team found Mikoyan affable enough but were not favorably impressed by his visit. "I had hoped that he was prepared to talk constructively," the president later recalled; "it was not so." Mikoyan's efforts to reveal what lay behind the zigzags of the Soviet Union's Berlin policy seemed pointless.[2] Some were even less impressed with the man. Eisenhower son's, John, who by the end of his father's second term had become an important confidant and adviser, characterized the second most powerful member of the Presidium as resembling "the man behind the counter in a meat market."[3] The younger Eisenhower also suspected that this ordinary fellow had a darker agenda. "Presumably," he later wrote, "[Mikoyan] had been sent to begin muddying the waters."[4]

The reception in Moscow when Mikoyan returned three weeks later was very different. Khrushchev overcame his frustration with the foreign policy debate over Berlin and hailed the visit as "useful" and "to our advantage."[5] He believed that much had been accomplished. First of all, a representative of the Soviet Union had been treated with respect by the Americans. The visits to the White House were unprecedented for a member of the Presidium. In the Kremlin, where the understanding of how a free press functions was never strong, they were equally impressed that U.S. newspapers had covered the event closely and seemed to trumpet Mikoyan's efforts to start serious negotiations on Berlin. Yet on the big issues the Americans had promised nothing. At best there seemed to be some interest in Washington in a foreign ministers' meeting, but Eisenhower remained firmly against a summit and did not waver in his commitment to the status quo in West Berlin.[6] Nevertheless, the Soviet leadership convinced itself to proceed on the assumption that diplomacy might work.[7]

"The question of a summit hardly needs to be forced now," Khrushchev announced to a full session of the Presidium after Mikoyan's return.[8] If the West suggested it, Khrushchev was prepared to allow the Soviet Union to participate in discussions at the foreign ministerial level, which he expected would ultimately "legitimate the idea of concluding a peace treaty with the GDR." Mikoyan was now allowed to do something that he had clearly wanted to do throughout his American odyssey but for which he had lacked formal authorization. Khrushchev suggested that a press conference be arranged that afternoon at which Mikoyan could hint that the May 27 deadline might be extended.[9] If there was to be an actual settlement of the German question, Khrushchev of course intended to negotiate the terms himself, but Mikoyan had earned the right to be the one to formally soften the ultimatum.

Khrushchev's comments to his inner circle after Mikoyan's return suggested that he was sorting through his thinking on the Berlin crisis, to separate demands that were a matter of principle from those that could be dropped.

In the wake of the Mikoyan visit Khrushchev began developing some ideas for potential concessions that might make a negotiation more appealing to the West. He was now prepared to assure NATO that Western troops could stay in West Berlin, so long as there was no buildup in either their size or their complement of weapons.[10] This was an important change from the draft peace treaty that the Soviets had distributed to London, Paris, and Washington in January; it had said that all foreign troops would have had to leave the Germany within one year of the conclusion of the treaty.[11]

The survival of the German Democratic Republic was the irreducible minimum for Khrushchev. Its survival, he believed, depended on establishing formal borders in the east, which then reflected the great powers' decisions at the end of the world war but lacked the force of a treaty commitment, and on eliminating NATO's ability to violate East German sovereignty. Of all the annoying elements of the current situation in Berlin, what irritated the Soviet leader the most was the Western allies' postwar right to fly into West Berlin without East German permission. No solution to the German problem would be acceptable if it let the three allied air corridors stand. Khrushchev was very sensitive to the issue of overflights. He hated the fact that American spy planes flew over the Soviet Union because these flights revealed the weaknesses in Soviet air defenses and invited attack from the West. Similarly the allied flights into West Berlin opened East Germany to surveillance. Yet even here Khrushchev indicated to his colleagues some willingness to negotiate a controlled form of air access. If Western planes first landed at GDR airports, where the passengers could have their visas checked, then these planes could continue on to West Berlin.

Khrushchev believed that these concessions would bring some movement from Allied negotiators over the future of Berlin and the two Germanys. Why would NATO oppose them? Unless the West wanted to have West Berlin as a staging area for a forward attack on the Soviet Union or was determined to hand Berlin to Adenauer for some reason, Khrushchev believed that his proposals would satisfy Western concerns about the future of its enclave. Underestimating the symbolic importance to the Western powers of secured access to West Berlin, Khrushchev assumed that all he needed was an appropriate venue at which to make these proposals.

▪

IN THE SPRING of 1956 Khrushchev and Bulganin had made a colorful trip to the United Kingdom, their first goodwill visit to a NATO country. As they were about to leave London, the two Soviets had invited then British Prime Minister Eden to make a return trip to Moscow. The Suez crisis had intervened, costing Eden his job, but the invitation still stood for Eden's successor, Harold Macmillan, who was eager to make the trip. Facing a stiff electoral challenge early in 1959 and British public concerns about the implications of the Berlin troubles, Macmillan believed that he needed the trip. As Mikoyan was finishing up his tour of the United States, the prime minister sent word to Moscow that he thought the time was right to visit.

The timing of Macmillan's request gave Khrushchev the chance to try out some of the possible compromises on West Berlin that he had been mulling over. Moscow responded positively to the British, and the visit was arranged for the middle of February.

Macmillan's eagerness to see Khrushchev was not greeted favorably in Washington. President Eisenhower was worried about the damage the Briton might do in Moscow. So too was Secretary of State Foster Dulles, who had been diagnosed with terminal cancer but remained at his post as long as he was physically able. The Americans recalled how inconsistent Macmillan, as chancellor of the exchequer, had been during Suez. At the start of the crisis he had shown bravado, telling Dulles at one meeting in August 1956 that "if we should be destroyed by Russian bombs now that would be better than to be reduced to impotence by the disintegration of our entire position abroad."[12] But ultimately it was Macmillan who started the cabinet revolt against Anthony Eden when it became clear that the British public and the U.S. government would not back the Anglo-French military intervention. Sensing that the British leader was so eager for political success in 1959 that he might be tempted to indicate a weakness in the Western wall of defiance on Berlin, Dulles went to London in early February to encourage resolve.

Macmillan was indeed already considering proposals that could be made to the Soviets on behalf of all the Western allies. At his meeting with Dulles he suggested that NATO might offer a "thinning out" of troops in Central Europe, a proposal that was similar to suggestions that the Soviets had been making for some time. He also made comments indicating that the United Kingdom might consider some form of recognition of East Germany. Although already going too far for either Dulles or President Eisenhower, Macmillan would at least stop short of proposing an allied withdrawal from West Berlin.[13]

Dulles's visit to England did little to settle U.S. concerns that NATO's unified front on the future of Berlin was in danger of dissolving once Macmillan reached Moscow. Completely unaware of the changing mood in Moscow—the U.S. government had missed the significance of Mikoyan's comments at the January 24 press conference—and thoroughly dismissive of Macmillan's abilities as a standard-bearer for NATO, the U.S. government moved decisively to undercut the British prime minister's little summit. On the eve of Macmillan's trip, it issued a harsh diplomatic note to the Soviets that reaffirmed that the Western powers "have no choice but to declare again that they reserve the right to uphold by all appropriate means their communications with their sectors of Berlin." This diplomatic message was Washington's formal response to the draft peace treaty that the Soviets had distributed in January. It signaled complete disagreement with the Soviet position without suggesting any alternatives. As far as Washington was concerned, the Communists had only themselves to blame for the tensions in Central Europe. Both "the persistent and flagrant denial to the East Germans of human rights and fundamental freedoms" and the Soviet Union's "intention unilaterally to abdicate certain of its internationally agreed responsibilities and obligations in regard to Berlin" were the main causes of all the trouble there.[14] As a sop to international opinion, the Eisenhower administration did suggest that talks take place among the foreign ministers of the big four.

If Washington's objective was to torpedo any chance for substantive discussion between Macmillan and Khrushchev and make the Soviet leadership more intransigent, its diplomatic note did the trick. The note so infuriated Khrushchev that he dropped any idea of trying out any of his Berlin concessions on the visiting Briton. Khrushchev's pride was by now the main factor driving his choice of tactics to achieve his objectives in Berlin. If he felt confident that the West respected him and that he might succeed in securing his irreducible demands, then Moscow's line softened. Conversely, if he felt he was being humiliated, the line would harden despite the cost in terms of international instability. The U.S. refusal to respond to the lengthy draft treaty with any proposals for alternative scenarios to resolving the West Berlin question fed Khrushchev's frustration with relying on traditional diplomacy. He had wanted to pursue a wholly confrontational attitude in November, but Mikoyan had persuaded him to try diplomacy. Now, with the U.S. note essentially saying *nyet*, Khrushchev's desire for a fight intensified.

The Macmillan visit, which was supposed to be the next step in the diplomatic resolution of the Berlin crisis, was now a potential embarrassment for both political leaders. Khrushchev convened a special Saturday meeting of the Presidium only hours before the prime minister's arrival to cancel the planned concessions and initiate a new harder line.

At the meeting Khrushchev found himself once again disagreeing with his own Foreign Ministry and with Mikoyan.[15] He refused to entertain the ministry's suggestion that Moscow respond positively to the U.S. offer of a foreign ministers' meeting. If Moscow sent the proposed reply, he argued, the Western powers "will believe that the Russians are retreating." Why agree to their conference when there was nothing in the note to indicate that there was going to be any movement in the Western position? Khrushchev warned his colleagues that "the West wants to freeze the question at its current level." He said; "They are dragging us into an *aventura*," meaning that the West was pushing Moscow to make a provocative act.[16]

Khrushchev's new proposal was that there be either a summit that involved the leaders of all four great powers from World War II, where the leaders could discuss the unacceptable situation in Berlin and direct serious attention to preventing the militarization of the two Germanys, or nothing. To his colleagues, Khrushchev revealed a sense of urgency about the consequences of waiting any longer to solve these issues. Recent trends in U.S.–West German relations, including the possibility that the Bundeswehr might acquire nuclear weapons, suggested the fragility of the four-power settlement that had ended World War II. How long until the West sought to eliminate East Germany through a combination of economic, political, and perhaps even military means? "All we want to do is to secure the status quo," Khrushchev repeated. This could not be done by means of a foreign ministers' conference or a summit with Macmillan alone. For new initiatives to appear there was no better forum than a heads of government summit. Anything less would offer the West a chance to delay dealing with the question to allow the situation on the ground to continue shifting in its favor. To get the West's attention, Khrushchev believed the Soviets had to threaten military action. "If you wish to force your way through, using all appropriate means . . . we will answer with all appropriate means."[17]

But Khrushchev lacked sufficient Kremlin support in 1959 to provoke a direct military clash with the United States over Berlin, even for the purposes of bluff. Mikoyan came to the defense of the Soviet Foreign Ministry and pleaded successfully for a more conciliatory reading of the U.S. note. "I agree with what the Foreign Ministry has said," said Mikoyan. "[The Western powers] have made some concessions to us." He added that if the Soviets did not accept talks among the foreign ministers, "they will claim that the Russians are trying to avoid negotiations."[18]

Mikoyan's intervention prevented Khrushchev and his allies from engineering an immediate Presidium decision on what to do next about Berlin. Instead the Foreign Ministry was given three days to draft a new reply to the U.S. note. Meanwhile Khrushchev would have to entertain his British guest and Macmillan's visit had the potential to tip the balance in favor of either Mikoyan's or Khrushchev's preferred approach to Berlin.

▪

ALTHOUGH HAROLD MACMILLAN had no idea that he was arriving in the midst of a Soviet foreign policy storm, he was arguably the best-prepared Western leader to navigate through it. His foreign policy team, unlike Dulles and the U.S. State Department, had grasped the essence of Khrushchev's desire for consolidating the Soviet position in Eastern Europe as a step toward demilitarizing the Cold War. It was Her Majesty's representative in Moscow, Sir Patrick Reilly, who had written that Khrushchev's "chief ambition [was] not the extension of an empire, but to be able in his lifetime to 'declare Communism' in the Soviet Union [i.e., celebrate the realization of the economic and social potential of communism], with its corollary of overtaking the United States in gross production."[19] Meanwhile the roots of his drive for disarmament lay in this goal, not in any superficial grab for favorable propaganda or attempt to divide NATO. Khrushchev did not want "his handwork" obliterated in a nuclear confrontation. For the British, this fact created a zone of mutual interest between East and West in seeking agreements on ending nuclear tests and reducing nuclear arms stockpiles.

The British also understood that as long as the Soviets insisted on comparing themselves with the Americans, they would be laboring under an enormous inferiority complex. Macmillan was quick to sense that Khrushchev personified that complex. However, this insight did not mean that the British always acted with tact. For some unknown reason Macmillan thought it wise to arrive in Moscow wearing a high white fur hat, which he had dug out one of his closets. The last time he had worn it was in 1940, when he had visited Finland as a well-publicized observer of the Finno-Soviet War, a war Moscow would rather have forgotten.[20]

It is not clear if the fur hat meant anything to Khrushchev. Notwithstanding advice from Mikoyan and the Soviet Foreign Ministry to be conciliatory, he had decided to be churlish with his guest. In Macmillan's presence, Khrushchev gave a speech at a public event denouncing the Western approach to the Berlin question and announcing that he would not accept a foreign ministers' meeting to solve the issue. A private lunch with Macmillan the next day dissolved into an angry exchange between the leaders. Khrushchev stirred the pot by demanding that Macmillan explain Western stubbornness on West Berlin. The Briton's efforts to outline the thinking of his NATO partners, with whom it had to be said he did not always agree, only angered Khrushchev more. He railed at Macmillan, accusing a unified West of conspiring with Adenauer to liquidate East Germany. When Khrushchev vowed to push ahead with a peace treaty with the GDR, Macmillan lost his temper. "If you try to threaten us in any way," the usually composed Briton exclaimed, "you will create the Third World War. Because we shall not give in, nor will the Americans. . . ." At this Khrushchev was now on his feet, shouting, "You have insulted me!"[21]

On February 26 Khrushchev announced that he had decided not to accompany Macmillan, as he had intended, on a trip to Kiev and Leningrad. He blamed this decision on a sudden need to have a tooth filled.[22] Despite the flimsy excuse, Macmillan did not rush home. He continued his visit, giving Khrushchev a chance to calm down. Behind the scenes Mikoyan and the Foreign Ministry effectively persuaded Khrushchev to leave the door open to a foreign ministers' conference if that was all that Moscow could get from the West.

When Macmillan returned to Moscow, he was met with smiles. The British leader might well have thought he was dealing with a manic-depressive regime. Khrushchev had sent him a cable before he left Leningrad telling him that his toothache had passed because "the dentist had used an excellent and newly designed British drill!"[23] In Moscow Macmillan learned that he would be allowed to make an uncensored broadcast over Soviet television, a first for a Western leader. While they did not reach any agreement on Berlin, the two leaders agreed that the abolition of nuclear weapons and an interim nuclear test ban agreement were of mutual interest. A few days after Macmillan returned home, the outcome of the backroom debate in Moscow became public. The Soviets issued a statement that pushed for a summit but accepted a foreign ministers' conference were a summit to be impossible at the present time. Even more significantly, a few weeks later Khrushchev announced a six-month extension of the ultimatum. Meanwhile Operation Atom, the stationing of a dozen Soviet medium-range ballistic missiles in East Germany, was completed as all the missiles became operational. Moscow was now able to launch a nuclear attack on Paris and London, but Mikoyan had too effectively contained Khrushchev for the Soviet leader to exploit this new power in 1959 to renew his brinkmanship and press for a complete rupture in East-West relations until the problems of Berlin was solved.

■

THE NEXT FEW MONTHS saw an unusual amount of East-West diplomatic activity. In May 1959 the foreign ministers of France, the United States, Great Britain, and the Soviet Union convened in Geneva to discuss a settlement of the Berlin question. Observers from East and West Germany were invited to witness the proceedings. At issue for the West was whether the Soviets would acknowledge that the Americans, British, and French had a right to be in West Berlin. Meanwhile the Soviets pushed the Western powers to accept negotiations between East and West Germany, to undertake steps to limit the use of West Berlin to destabilize East Germany, and to acknowledge that the situation was abnormal and needed to be fixed. Meanwhile in the United States Foster Dulles, one of Khrushchev's staunchest opponents, had succumbed to cancer at age seventy-one. In April Dulles had been replaced by Christian Herter, a former governor of Massachusetts and congressman, who despite a low-key personality was ardently committed to active international diplomacy.

Khrushchev seemed to be gripped by uncertainty over how to proceed in the wake of Dulles's death and the opening of negotiations in Geneva. At times he screamed at any and all who suggested that there was hope for diplomacy, while at other times he grasped at what could best be described as straws in an effort to convince himself that he could champion a diplomatic approach.

One such straw came into his grasp just before the formal start of the foreign ministers' conference. A Soviet representative, presumably the KGB representative with the delegation, cabled that there appeared an opportunity for successful negotiations on "a narrower basis."[24] Available Soviet records leave unclear whether the KGB had learned this from a spy within a Western delegation or was using one of its own men to undertake back channel feelers with Western diplomats. In any case, Soviet intelligence had picked up indications that the West might agree to reduce the size of its eleven-thousand-man contingent in West Berlin. Even though there did not appear to be any concrete basis for this reduction, Khrushchev was encouraged and wanted to take advantage of this possibility.

On May 24 Khrushchev suggested to his Kremlin colleagues that the KGB be used to convey to the West that if they agreed to a troop reduction, the Soviets would reduce and then withdraw their own contingent in East Berlin. The current occupation regime in West Berlin would then be allowed to remain for one to two more years, during which time the Soviets would promise not to sign a peace treaty with East Germany.[25]

Nothing came of this KGB-sponsored diplomacy; but the fact that Khrushchev pursued it revealed that underneath the bluster was a leader who hoped for a diplomatic settlement. The Soviets did not need the KGB, however, to pick up that some members of the Western delegations were indeed considering reducing the size of their contingents in Berlin. British Foreign

Secretary Selwyn Lloyd mentioned in an open session that the troops could be reduced to eighty-five hundred or perhaps seventy-five hundred.[26] The proposal did not go anywhere because the United States delegation, led by Secretary Herter, refused to agree.

At the first formal meeting of the conference Foreign Minister Gromyko presented a draft agreement on West Berlin that permitted the presence of small numbers of Western troops once West Berlin became a "free city," so long as these could "in no way be considered as occupation of territory."[27] A week later he explicitly linked an immediate reduction of Western troops with a one-year suspension of the Soviet threat to sign a peace treaty.[28] The Soviets stipulated four preconditions in all. Besides the reduction of Western troops to a "symbolic number," the West had to agree to end all "hostile propaganda against the GDR and other socialist countries" and all espionage and subversion launched from West Berlin. Finally, it had to agree not to station any nuclear weapons or missiles in West Berlin.

Eisenhower's response was immediate and direct. The new Soviet proposals were "a clearly unacceptable challenge to our position in that city," he wrote to Khrushchev on June 15.[29]

In response, Khrushchev tried something new.[30] In the 1950s it was Kremlin practice to send open letters to U.S. presidents, which were published almost immediately in Soviet newspapers. But Khrushchev wanted to indicate some flexibility with Eisenhower and open the way for a real bilateral discussion. So he composed the first private letter ever sent by a Soviet leader to the White House. He used this unusual method to underscore the honest concerns behind his impatience to see the start of real negotiations on West Berlin. Chancellor Adenauer had made known that West Germany wanted these discussions over Berlin to drag on for years. "In this time," Khrushchev explained to Eisenhower, ". . . the policy of militarization of West Germany and the policy of preparation of war would be continued." He ended the letter in somewhat dulcet tones. If the foreign ministers' conference did not succeed, perhaps a summit would be more successful. In any case, he told Eisenhower that the Soviets wanted to meet the West halfway on establishing a timetable for agreement.

The next day Khrushchev told the East Germans, who were in Moscow for high-level talks, that he was confident that the discussions with the West were moving in the right direction. He was pleased that the Western powers were at least prepared to discuss the future status of Berlin and to have observers from East Germany in the room as they did so. Khrushchev sensed that it was only a matter of time before the West gave Moscow and East Berlin what they wanted, and he wanted to prepare the East Germans for the Kremlin's deci-sion to drop the ultimatum completely. "Let's not give a time period," Khrushchev told Ulbricht. "A year or a year-and-a-half—this isn't a key issue for us."[31] He also wanted Ulbricht to understand that a resolution would probably take a heads of government summit, so there was only so much that East Germany should expect to be achieved at a foreign ministers' meet-ing. "[N]ot one self respecting prime minister will allow his foreign minis-ter," he told Ulbricht, "due to prestige considerations, to sign an agreement on concrete issues."[32]

In a meeting with visiting American governors on July 7, Khrushchev indi-cated his interest in visiting the United States and seeing President Eisenhower.[33] If the Americans agreed, Khrushchev would be the first Soviet leader ever to visit the United States. The year 1959 was already shaping up as the most active period of face-to-face meetings between Soviets and their American counterparts up to that point in the entire Cold War. As Khru-shchev met with the state governors, Soviet Presidium member Kozlov was at the end of his own extensive ten-day tour of the United States. Kozlov had had a pleasant, though unproductive, meeting with President Eisenhower at the end of June.[34] Khrushchev had hopes that he would have more luck if given the chance.

The *Washington Post* picked up the story of Khrushchev's comment to the U.S. delegation, and Eisenhower was asked about it at a press conference the next day. "This was the first I had heard of Khrushchev's statement," Eisen-hower later recalled.[35] The president was intrigued by the idea. Once the press conference was over, he called his new secretary of state. "The Khrushchev statement," Eisenhower said to Herter, "might possibly provide a device to break the stalemate."

Khrushchev's initiative had caught the president in a reflective mood about the Cold War. Just before that morning's press conference, Eisenhower had made a very difficult decision. The CIA wanted presidential approval to send a U-2 spy plane into Soviet airspace. In March 1958 Eisenhower had dis-continued U-2 flights after the Soviets protested a U-2 mission over the Soviet Far East.[36] When Eisenhower approved the U-2 project in 1954, he had been assured that the planes would be able to fly unnoticed into Soviet territory.[37] Since 1956, however, the United States had known that the Soviets could detect these missions, though they still lacked the capability to bring these high fliers down. The flights continued in large measure because Foster Dulles had convinced a skeptical Eisenhower that the Soviets would never protest these flights. "To do so," Dulles had observed with acerbity, "would make it necessary for them to admit also that for years we had been carrying on flights over their territory while they, the Soviets, had been helpless to do anything about the matter."[38] It took the Soviets until 1958 to begin their protests of U-2 flights, but once they did, Eisenhower had believed he had no choice but to call a halt to these missions.

Eisenhower had taken the Soviet protests very seriously. He believed that an unauthorized Soviet airplane in U.S. airspace would be an act of war and expected Khrushchev to react the same way. Sixteen months had passed since the last U-2 flight, and his intelligence and diplomatic advisers were now telling the president that he needed to revisit the prohibition. Concerns were rising in Congress and throughout the intelligence community about the pace of Soviet strategic missile development. Herter believed that the potential intelligence harvest from a series of U-2 missions that could document Soviet missile launch facilities outweighed the diplomatic costs if one were shot down. The CIA's desire for the missions was equally clear. Reluctantly Eisenhower concluded that his country's ignorance of the state of Khrushchev's strategic arsenal was too high. He approved a single U-2 mission that morning.[39]

Khrushchev's surprise proposal of a state visit to the United States was a breath of fresh air for Eisenhower on a day when he was feeling the burdens of leadership in the Cold War. In rescinding the prohibition on U-2 flights, the president had told his inner circle that "we are getting to the point where we must decide if we are trying to prepare to fight a war, or to prevent one."[40] In his conversation with Herter after the press conference, Eisenhower expressed a preference to tie a Khrushchev visit to some kind of summit, probably in Quebec, Canada, where Roosevelt and Churchill had conferred twice during World War II. This newfound interest in summitry was a sign of how seriously the president took that morning's U-2 decision. He believed that it was not enough to take risks to acquire intelligence but that he needed to take risks to try to improve relations so that these dangerous U-2 flights might become less necessary. He had tried summitry in 1955 and been disappointed. He had avoided meeting Khrushchev over Iraq in the summer of 1958, and once the Kremlin laid down its Berlin ultimatum in November of that year, Eisenhower became firmly opposed to any summit with the Soviet leader. It would be humiliating, he thought, for a president to meet his Soviet counterpart under threat of an ultimatum. But now Eisenhower believed it was time to let Khrushchev have his summit.

Over the next two days Eisenhower worked with Herter on an invitation to Khrushchev. Kozlov, who was due to leave the United States on July 12, could be used to carry a secret message to Khrushchev. A text was drafted that invited Khrushchev to the United States but still bore vestiges of Eisenhower's long-standing reluctance about a one-on-one meeting with him. The White House believed it was sending a qualified invitation to Khrushchev: If the foreign ministers' conference produced some kind of positive result and the Berlin ultimatum was removed, then the Khrushchev visit should be scheduled together with a summit in Quebec. However, the State Department doubted that the invitation was qualified in any meaningful way.[41] Sure enough, when Khrushchev received the invitation, he concluded that Eisenhower had invited him without any conditions. Finally, one of his initiatives had borne fruit.[42] He was going to visit the homeland of his great adversary.

■

Eisenhower did not face any public opposition to his decision to be the first American leader to invite a Soviet leader to the United States. A survey sponsored by the State Department found that most newspaper editors and commentators expressed support for the visit.[43] The most vocal opposition came from veterans' groups, the Roman Catholic Church, and hard-core conservative columnists, who believed that the invitation bestowed untoward legitimacy on a Communist dictator. Despite general approval of the visit, few Americans expected any breakthroughs.

For Khrushchev the three-week trip, scheduled to begin September 15, was going to be as much about show as it was about substance. It was a great achievement of Soviet socialism that the United States, its most formidable adversary, would treat a Soviet leader with the full pomp and circumstance accorded any visiting head of state. Khrushchev's pride was also mixed with some fear. He could not help expecting some kind of effort by the Americans to humiliate him—a "provocation," as he termed it. Evidence of this fear, and of his own government's inability to prepare him for the trip, came when the State Department reported to him that the president very much wished him to visit Camp David. What almost every American or Western European who read newspapers knew apparently stumped the Soviet Foreign Ministry. Neither Ambassador Menshikov nor the Americanists in Moscow had any idea what or where Camp David was.

Faced with an invitation to this unknown place, Khrushchev immediately conjured up the specter of a visit to an American internment facility. "One reason I was suspicious," he later recalled, "was that I remembered in the early years after the Revolution, when contacts were first being established with the bourgeois world, a Soviet delegation was invited to a meeting held someplace called the Prince's Islands. It came out in the newspapers that it was to these islands that stray dogs were sent to die. . . . I was afraid maybe this Camp David was the same sort of place, where people who were mistrusted could be kept in quarantine."[44] Once his advisers described where he was actually being invited, the presidential retreat in the Cacoctin Mountains of Maryland, Khrushchev was delighted and, he later recalled, a little ashamed: "It shows how ignorant we were in some respects."[45]

Khrushchev wanted to arrive in style. Nonstop transatlantic travel was still in its infancy, and the Soviet turboprop Tu-114, which Khrushchev had ordered in 1955 after the embarrassment of arriving in Geneva in the smallest plane of any of the participants in the great power summit, was one of the few airplanes that could do it. The problem for Khrushchev's bodyguards in the KGB was that the plane was only in its experimental phase, and there was evidence of flaws in the design. Microscopic cracks had been discovered in the fuselage of the single operational plane during its first long-distance flight in May 1959. Nevertheless, Khrushchev insisted on using that aircraft. He wanted the world to see that Soviet technology could be world class. In June he had forced his dauphin, Frol Kozlov, to use the TU-114 to fly to the United States for his visit. Now Khrushchev would do the same.

Sergei Khrushchev, who accompanied his father on the U.S. tour, recalled later that the plane should never have been certified to fly. The designer, Andrei Tupolev, made a show of his confidence in the plane by suggesting that his own son, Nikolai, accompany the Khrushchevs. Despite the grandstanding by Khrushchev and his aircraft designer, there was enormous concern that something might happen during the flight, and the reason would not be CIA mischief but Soviet incompetence. The Soviet merchant marine sent instructions to Soviet trawlers and cargo ships in the Atlantic to stand guard to rescue the Khrushchev delegation in the event the plane went down.[46]

Precautions were also taken onboard the aircraft. The Soviets built a special compartment where the wings met the fuselage to accommodate a team of Tupolev engineers during the flight. Armed with instruments that looked curiously like stethoscopes, they spent the trip listening for the development of any cracks and watching a bank of red and green sensor lights that might indicate some other system failure.

Although in the end not life-threatening, the trip was a misery for the Khrushchevs. The plane's turboprops created a huge amount of noise, which prevented all but the hardiest sleeper from getting any rest during the twelve-hour flight. Khrushchev spent the time reading and fussing about. When he wasn't sending cables to all the foreign leaders whose countries the Tu-114 flew over, he was thinking about the country he was about to encounter.

Before leaving the Soviet Union, Khrushchev had had a final chance to size up his American hosts. Vice President Richard Nixon arrived on July 23 for a ten-day visit. Nixon was ostensibly in the Soviet Union to open an exhibition of U.S. science and technology, but the future Republican nominee for president was also eager for a stage to show that he could stand up to "Mr. K," as journalists jocularly referred to Khrushchev. The Soviet leader respected Nixon but disliked him enormously. Khrushchev believed that with Foster Dulles gone, Nixon was the new leader of the faction in the Eisenhower administration that had sought to thwart Eisenhower's efforts to reach détente with Moscow. Nixon, for his part, considered Khrushchev "a man of great warmth and totally belligerent."[47]

The two men held the famous debate on their respective political systems in the model U.S. kitchen at the U.S. exhibition in Moscow. Nixon spoke of the benefits of living in the United States, while Khrushchev denounced an electric juicer sitting on the counter in the kitchen exhibit to make a general argument about what the wasteful luxury of the model kitchen said about the United States' ability to meet the needs of its citizens. The two politicians seemed to enjoy the give-and-take thoroughly.[48] For the vice president, however, the visit had at least one moment of discomfort and possible danger. Secret Service officers assigned to his detail discovered a high level of radiation in and around the vice president's bedroom in the U.S. Embassy. Nixon was informed but decided to stay in the room anyway. His Secret Service detail devised a different plan. The officers sat in the bedroom and at the top of their voices started cursing the Soviet Union for attempting to poison the vice president of the United States with radiation. The next day the levels returned to normal. The reason for the radiation and whether it was connected with a malfunctioning Soviet listening device were never explained.[49]

■

KHRUSHCHEV'S ARRIVAL in the United States started out as comically as the flight over had been. At fifty feet off the ground, the Tu-114 was at the time the world's tallest airplane, although the reason was not the Soviet love for the gigantic. To sustain itself over long distances, the plane had enormous propellers that acted like huge vacuum cleaners, sucking in birds and everything else that had the ill fortune to come too close. Because Soviet airfields were notoriously dirty—even those used by the Soviet Air Force could never be swept clean of debris—Tupolev had placed the engines as high off the ground as possible.

What was convenient for engines was inconvenient for passengers. As the airplane taxied along the tarmac at Andrews Air Force Base, the grounds crew realized that they did not have a ladder tall enough to accommodate this airship. Khrushchev and his party would have to descend using the emergency escape ladder in the back. "Therefore," Khrushchev later recalled, "we had to leave the plane not in the formal, dignified way called for by protocol, but practically climbing down using our hands and legs."[50]

Khrushchev was a little unsure of himself as he stepped onto U.S. soil for the first time and was greeted by President Eisenhower. He had performed well in India and the United Kingdom, but now he was in the country he had eyed with envy and contempt for so many years. Before the trip Khrushchev's representatives had insisted that he be treated as a visiting head of state, despite the fact that the president of the Supreme Soviet was still Kliment Voroshilov. One of the usual rituals for a visiting head of state was the reviewing of troops on the tarmac. Khrushchev found it hard to keep up with the long and lanky Dwight Eisenhower. Ambassador Llewellyn Thompson's wife, who had never seen Khrushchev outside the Soviet Union, watched bemused as his quick and short strides intensified the impression that he was finding the whole thing trying and uncomfortable.[51]

On the advice of Mikoyan, Khrushchev had decided to bring his family with him: his wife, Nina Petrovna; son, Sergei, and daughters, Rada and Julia. Under Stalin, Kremlin families had remained hidden. As a result, there was so little known about them in the West that when Khrushchev became first secretary of the CPSU, there was some speculation that he was married to a relative of Molotov's. The U.S. press still had no idea of his children's names, and for several days, because the two daughters were so shy, could not determine which was Rada and which Julia. There were even some untrue reports that all the children were from Khrushchev's first marriage. The eldest, Julia came from his first marriage to Yefrosina Ivanovna, who had died in 1919, while Rada and Sergei were his children with his second wife.

He had brought more than his family and a very big plane in an effort to impress the Americans. During the first part of the trip he was scheduled to give a major address to the United Nations. The text of the speech included an announcement of a Soviet initiative to achieve "general and complete disarmament." This was not a new proposal; the Kremlin had announced something similar in 1955. What was important was that Khrushchev announced he was willing to be more patient in the negotiations over the future of Berlin if he could achieve a relaxation of international tension through arms reductions. The man who had been eager to wash his hands of international agreements in November 1958 had come around enough nearly a year later to give them another try. Regarding Berlin, Khrushchev knew he had to lift the ultimatum, which had never really been his preferred strategy. He had wanted to cancel unilaterally the set of informal four-power agreements that allowed the militaries of the United States, France, and Great Britain to be stationed in West Berlin and to have unfettered access to their bases. Mikoyan and others had convinced him that it was better to find a diplomatic solution that involved the Western powers, an argument that had produced an ineffectual attempt to bully the West. Khrushchev intended to explain the thinking behind his urgent attempts to persuade the Americans to recognize the existence of three Germanys: a Communist East, a non-Communist West, and a capitalist but nonaligned West Berlin.

Khrushchev worked hard to set the right tone in the opening moments of his trip. He made pilgrimages to honor two American presidents whom he admired. Accompanied by U.S. permanent representative to the United Nations Henry Cabot Lodge, who would be with him throughout his stay, Khrushchev visited the Lincoln Memorial. He hailed Lincoln's great achievement in ending slavery and then, in a theatrical gesture, bowed from his waist in the direction of the reflective Lincoln.[52] Khrushchev later visited with Eleanor Roosevelt in Hyde Park, New York, and placed flowers at the grave of Franklin D. Roosevelt, the last American leader to have had good relations with Moscow.

For a while it seemed as if Khrushchev were imbued with the spirit of Hyde Park. On September 15 he hinted to his American hosts that the Soviets would be prepared to wait a little longer on Berlin. "Believe me," he told President Eisenhower at their first meeting, "we would like to come to terms on Germany and thereby on Berlin, too. We do not contemplate taking unilateral action."[53] The ultimatum was not fully lifted, but Khrushchev was signaling that it would be. At the United Nations two days later he announced the Soviet program for complete and general disarmament. With those two items out of the way, Khrushchev was eager to see the rest of the United States. He was to return to Washington on September 25 and expected by then that the administration would have some substantive responses to his initiatives.

Khrushchev had a short meeting with Eisenhower before leaving on his grand tour that produced a small but unexpected victory. The president pleased the Soviet leader by characterizing the Berlin situation as "abnormal." For months Soviet diplomats had used that word to explain a situation that had to be corrected. Eisenhower's word choice did not represent any concrete concession by the Americans, but it suggested that Khrushchev's strategy of going straight to Eisenhower, bypassing all the professional anti-Communists around him, might be working.

Not all went well, however, in those first few days. Khrushchev found it a lot harder to explain himself to the U.S. press. At the National Press Club in Washington, D.C., he was asked to explain what he had meant when he vowed, "We will bury you," to a group of Western diplomats in Moscow in November 1956. "We will bury you," was a Russian proverb that meant, in effect, "I shall outlast you" or "I shall live so long that I shall be able to attend your funeral." It captured Khrushchev's belief that the Soviet system would outlast capitalism. But many in the West had interpreted the phrase to mean that Khrushchev intended to cause the death of the United States, something altogether different. His effort to clear up this confusion in Washington seemed only to make matters worse.

Khrushchev and his family were having a hard time adjusting to more than just the questioning of a free press. They were baffled by the crowds that lined the streets of Washington and New York to look at them. Neither cheering nor screaming, these people were largely just silent, as if in the presence of Martians.

One of Khrushchev's principal goals in coming to America, perhaps his most important objective, was to meet Americans and to let them meet him. "I do not have horns," he said to an audience in New York City. He wanted Americans to substitute whatever misconceptions they had about him and the Kremlin with the reality, as he saw it.

Yet he came to believe that a wall had been built between him and the American people to prevent this from happening. Not convinced that he needed so many policemen around him and a closed limousine, he blamed Ambassador Lodge, his personal escort for the tour, and the State Department, which oversaw the logistics of the tour, for acting as if they were intentionally trying to insulate U.S. citizens from an infectious creature.

■

THE TRIP NEARLY ENDED prematurely in California. Khrushchev, who had been on his guard for any attempts at provocation, experienced a stream of them in Los Angeles. They started with the first local dignitary assigned to meet him. Victor Carter, a movie mogul who headed Republic Studios and the City of Hope, a California hospital, had fled years before from Rostov, a town in southern Russia. When Carter announced that he was Jewish, Khrushchev assumed he was in the presence of a class enemy. By Czarist decree, Jews could not live in Rostov unless they were wealthy merchants. Privately, Khrushchev wondered how to interpret the fact that the U.S. government had selected an emigrant from Russia to be beside him. Throughout the remaining twenty-four hours of his stay in Los Angeles, Khrushchev ascribed every untoward event to the evil genius of the Jewish merchant's son.[54]

The next annoyance came when the Khrushchev party was informed that they would not be visiting Disneyland. They had set aside time in the late afternoon for the visit, but just as the family started lunch, the Soviet leader learned that the Los Angeles police believed the visit would be too risky. Khrushchev's children were naturally disappointed, and he himself reacted badly to the news, less because of a desire to see Mickey Mouse, about whom it is safe to say he knew nothing, than the feeling that he was again being hemmed in by his hosts.

On September 19 at Twentieth Century-Fox, where the family was being treated to a sumptuous lunch, Khrushchev complained loudly that he and his family had not been allowed to see Disneyland. "Is there some kind of cholera or launching pad out there?" he asked. "You have policemen so tough they can lift a bull by the horns, yet they say it [Disneyland] cannot be securely guarded."[55] Khrushchev's disappointment marred what was an unusual gathering of Hollywood royalty.[56] "This is the nearest thing to a major Hollywood funeral I've attended in years," quipped one guest. Among the 350 people packed into the Café de Paris, Twentieth Century-Fox's studio dining room, were Judy Garland, Edward G. Robinson, Sammy Davis, Jr., Gregory Peck, Gene Kelly, and Rita Hayworth. At the head table Khrushchev's wife, Nina Petrovna, sat between Frank Sinatra and Bob Hope with the always debonair David Niven just opposite.[57] "She's absolutely lovely," Niven purred to the press about the first lady of the Soviet Union. Sinatra's comment was equally characteristic: "She swings pretty good English, too . . . and I'm not using my jazz talk, either."[58]

After the luncheon Khrushchev and his party were escorted to the Stage 8 area, where a special balcony had been built to allow the group to observe the filming of a dance number from Fox's *Can-Can*, a star vehicle for Sinatra, Louis Jourdan, and the young Shirley MacLaine. Rather than be amused by the display of bloomers and energetic behinds, Khrushchev decided that the whole spectacle was intentionally humiliating. He became annoyed when a studio publicity photographer tried to get two of the women to lift their skirts on either side of him. A diplomatic incident was averted when the women themselves refused to play along.

Khrushchev's State Department escorts were not happy with the entire Can-Can episode, but the greater challenge to the success of his visit came later in the day. The mayor of Los Angeles, Norris Poulson, was a conservative lightweight who seemed intent on having a highly public debate with Khrushchev. Poulson was due to speak at a dinner meeting of the Los Angeles world events forum. At the cocktail party beforehand, Ambassador Lodge was able to get a hold of an advance draft of the speech. In the opening lines there was a mocking reference to Khrushchev's by now famous "We will bury you" assertion.

Lodge believed Khrushchev had calmly answered the question in Washington but felt sure if the mayor of Los Angeles raised this issue again over dinner, Khrushchev might very well blow up. When Lodge asked Poulson to drop the reference, the mayor refused. "The speech has already been written and distributed," said a determined Poulson. "It is too late to change it."[59]

The result would have been comedy had it not involved the world's second most powerful man. After the Los Angeles mayor said, "We won't bury you; you won't bury us; we will live together in friendship," Khrushchev retaliated. He interrupted the mayor and announced to the startled audience that it had taken him only twelve hours to fly to the United States, and it would take him ten hours to return, flying directly to Vladivostok in the Soviet Far East from California. Calling out to Tupolev's son who was sitting in the audience, Khrushchev asked, "Isn't that so?" Khrushchev felt he was on display, like the big bear at a Russian circus, and as such was being taken advantage of by Americans.

When Khrushchev got back to his hotel, he gathered the entire delegation in one of the suites and started ranting. "How dare this man [Poulson] attack the guest of the president of the United States?" Khrushchev yelled. He made it known to his family, his advisers, and their wives that he was seriously considering canceling the remainder of the trip. He did not want to go to San Francisco, the next stop on their itinerary, or anywhere else without an apology from the U.S. government. His tirade was so intense that Gromyko's wife thought to run to the bathroom to find him a sedative, but Khrushchev shot her a knowing glance. "I was giving vent to my indignation for the ears of the American accompanying us," Khrushchev later recalled. "I was sure that there were listening devices in our room and that Mr. Lodge, who was staying in the same hotel, was sitting in front of a speaker with an interpreter and listening to our whole conversation."[60]

At 2:00 A.M. Gromyko went to Lodge's bedroom to deliver a formal complaint, just in case the FBI's listening devices weren't working. The Soviets could have picked a number of things to complain about but decided to highlight a woman who had stood on a street corner with a black flag and a sign saying DEATH TO KHRUSHCHEV, THE BUTCHER OF HUNGARY. The Soviet leader believed that she had to have been there because Eisenhower wanted her there. Lodge tried his best to explain that because the United States was a free country, this woman had a right to her views, however inconvenient they might be to the White House or State Department. He also passed on his regrets for the misbehavior of some of the Americans Khrushchev had met. Gromyko took the explanation and went back to his room. The trip had hit rock bottom. Lodge went to bed thinking that the Khrushchev visit "was becoming a horrible failure." He believed major changes had to be made to rescue it.[61]

■

THE NEXT MORNING Lodge moved to change the character of the Khrushchev See America tour. If Khrushchev agreed, Lodge would alter the Soviet leader's security so that he could interact with more ordinary citizens. In a moment of inspiration, Lodge came upon the idea of treating Khrushchev as if he were a political candidate. The Soviet delegation was scheduled to take a train to its next destination, San Francisco, and Lodge thought that there should be some whistle stops along the way. He also decided to let Khrushchev mingle with the press on the train. To this point reporters had been kept far away from the leader.

Khrushchev had begun the day in a dark mood. He had hoped his nemesis, Mayor Poulson, would take the trouble to see him off with a parting statement at the train station. It was not to be. A lone microphone stood by the platform, but there was no mayor. Once he realized that he had seen the last of Poulson, Khrushchev quipped to Lodge that the mayor of Los Angeles "[had] tried to fart but shit in his pants."[62]

Lodge's new approach worked magic on Khrushchev's mood. "I felt that you had kept me under house arrest for six days," Khrushchev told him. He roamed the train to greet members of the press. To entice the Soviet leader to stop in his car, one enterprising journalist had brought on board a large bottle of vodka, which he left open on a table next to him. Khrushchev decided to walk right past the open bottle—after years of complaints from his wife he was trying to be abstemious—but his characteristic gregariousness was on full display.[63] At Santa Barbara and San Luis Obispo he eagerly left the train and plunged into the crowds on the platform. Khrushchev loved the exposure and these Americans were not afraid to smile at him. One person, in particular, had a deep effect on the first secretary. At one of the two stops Khrushchev pressed so hard into the crowd that he lost his Lenin Peace Prize medal, which he wore proudly on his jacket. A member of the crowd found it and, rather than keep the gold medal as a souvenir, handed it to Ambassador Lodge, who passed it back to Khrushchev before he had even discovered it was missing. "The incident pleased me very much," Khrushchev later recalled, ". . . the fact that the person returned it to me made me respect these people."[64] The U.S. trip had taken a new turn. Insofar as Khrushchev was concerned, it was about to get much better.

■

THE IOWAN ROSWELL "BOB" GARST had promised "to leave no stone unturned" to make Khrushchev's visit to his farm the highlight of the Soviet leader's trip.[65] As a group the farmers of Iowa had been among the first Americans to seek better relations with Khrushchev's Russia. America's granary was overflowing with surpluses, and Iowans were eager to find a market for their wheat and to test the one-world idealism of their native son, and former vice president, Henry Wallace. Four years earlier, after Khrushchev had been quoted as exhorting Soviets to create an "Iowan corn belt" of their own, an influential journalist in Des Moines editorialized that any agricultural experts Khrushchev sent to the American Midwest would be welcome. Moscow agreed and established an agricultural exchange.[66]

Although the Garst farm was not on the official list of farms that the Soviet delegation was to visit on that first agricultural exchange, Bob Garst ultimately made the greatest impression on the Soviets of any American farmer. Garst had first come to the attention of the American public in 1948, when his friend the celebrated writer John Dos Passos wrote a *Life* magazine profile of Garst entitled "Revolution on the Farm."[67] Dos Passos described the persuasive farmer as a man who spoke in a manner "between that of a lecturer explaining the solution of a problem at a blackboard, and a lawyer pleading with a jury."[68] During the Great Depression Garst had been in the forefront of the movement to increase the use of nitrogen as a fertilizer, especially in the production of corn. As a result, by the mid-1950s U.S. farmers were facing the problem of massive surpluses in the American breadbasket.[69]

Garst was more than just a salesman for Iowan wheat and corn. He sensed that East-West relations could be improved if Americans helped the Soviets solve some of their problems. In 1955 he made his first trip to Eastern Europe and the Soviet Union to see Soviet agriculture firsthand. Having already heard of Garst through his reading of the reports sent back from Iowa, Khrushchev arranged to meet this energetic missionary for the American way of farming. Khrushchev no doubt had seen a little of himself in Garst's gruff confidence and boundless interest in producing corn. A number of return visits by Garst followed, and the men struck up a lively correspondence about agriculture. In the 1950s Khrushchev wrote to Garst more often than he wrote to Eisenhower.

Khrushchev came to trust Garst and invoked the American farmer to his Kremlin colleagues in support of this or that agricultural method.[70] In June 1958 Khrushchev had sent a Soviet delegation to spend three months at the Garst farm planting crops, chopping hay, and feeding cattle.[71] When these men returned home, they became stars of Soviet agriculture. "They [have] studied under Garst," Khrushchev later boasted before his Presidium buddies, "they didn't go in vain, they really studied well."[72]

In recent years Khrushchev had come to understand nuclear weapons and submarines, but agriculture remained one of his central concerns. When his relations with Cabot Lodge improved on the train in California, Khrushchev opened up about the importance of agriculture to him. Perhaps the most significant intelligence the Soviet leader imparted to his American hosts came in a confession to Lodge of the weakness of the Soviet standard of living and Moscow's need to find a way to provide its citizens with the very necessities of life. The Soviet Union, Khrushchev explained, was like "a hungry person who had just awakened and wanted to eat. Such a person would not wash his hands before eating. . . . Therefore, the Soviet Union was not trying now to develop the production of any sophisticated consumer goods; it was simply trying to satisfy the basic needs."[73]

Now it was Khrushchev's turn to visit Garst, and the farm provided the catalytic moment for his U.S. trip. What Khrushchev saw in Coon Rapids, Iowa, on September 23 raised his own expectations for what he should be able to do in the Soviet Union. In just one example, the farm had a very efficient open pen system for feeding the livestock, whereas in the Soviet Union, Khrushchev later noted acidly, "we provide each cow with a stall, each one is allotted with a fork and a knife. . . . What kind of idiocy is this!"[74]

Khrushchev's pride seemed a little bruised after the visit to the farm. As he so often did when he felt bested by someone else, he responded by bragging.[75] In the car on the way back to Des Moines, he began talking about a new Soviet airplane, a turbojet with a maximum speed of 640 kilometers and a payload of 14 metric tons. "It can land on dirt fields," Khrushchev said, in reference to the Iowan fields he saw passing on either side of him on the highway. Afterward on the flight from Des Moines to Pittsburgh, he invited his American hosts and their wives to his compartment in the plane for some drinks. He couldn't stop talking about Garst. He had loved how the farmer had tried to kick the *New York Times*'s Harrison Salisbury after losing patience with the journalists hounding the two men but had lost his footing, nearly impaling himself on a stalk of corn.[76]

The trip to the farm put Khrushchev in a different frame of mind for his next round of discussions with Eisenhower. These meetings, which were to dominate the last few days of Khrushchev's trip, took place at comfortable Camp David. The tone was civil, at times friendly. From Eisenhower, Khrushchev heard nothing that he hadn't before. The U.S. president did hint in one of their conversations on Berlin that he thought that Roosevelt and Truman had erred in placing the West in so exposed a position in the middle of East Germany; but he left no doubt that despite this difficult situation, he would do nothing that conflicted with existing U.S. policy in the region.

Khrushchev took the initiative anyway. He wanted Eisenhower to know that he had decided to discard his strategy of diplomacy by ultimatum. The November 1958 ultimatum on Berlin had been a dead letter since Mikoyan's return from the United States earlier in the year, and even though Khrushchev indicated in their earlier conversation that the ultimatum was not absolute, the threat of a renewed ultimatum had remained. With a gesture that showed Khrushchev could be a diplomat when he wanted to be, he took Eisenhower into his confidence. He admitted that he had tried to force a settlement in 1958 out of a sense of exasperation at the "high-handed" behavior of the United States. At the time he had judged the situation as steadily deteriorating, and there seemed to be no avenue available to settle the matter through diplomacy. Khrushchev proposed that if Eisenhower admitted that the United States opposed a permanent continuation of the present state of occupation, then the Soviets would not insist on any deadline in the negotiations over Berlin. Given that it was established U.S. policy to pursue the eventual reunification of the two Germanys, Eisenhower could easily agree to that.[77]

The leaders also reached another point of understanding. Khrushchev revealed to Eisenhower his ever-present concern about the cost of arming his country. He asserted that for the Soviet government, disarmament was a more important matter than Berlin. Eisenhower, who had hoped this was the Soviet position, agreed readily. After the rescinding of the Soviet ultimatum on Berlin and Khrushchev's acknowledgment that disarmament was a more important matter for discussion between the two leaders, Eisenhower agreed to a summit of the four occupying powers sometime before the end of the year.

Despite this apparent meeting of the minds, Khrushchev felt somewhat disappointed in Eisenhower. The Soviet chief had come to Camp David empowered by the Presidium to negotiate an agreement if he could, but it appeared that the U.S. president was either unwilling to talk or incapable of talking about specifics. When asked for the U.S. position on disarmament, Eisenhower would say only that his experts were studying Khrushchev's UN speech on "general and complete" disarmament. Efforts to draw the president out on his own preferences came to naught. In the end Khrushchev concluded that the sixty-nine-year-old Eisenhower was tired, like "someone who had just fallen through a hole in the ice and been dragged from the river with freezing water still dripping from him."[78] Nevertheless, he had learned what he needed, and he had been treated better by the U.S. government than he had expected to be treated.

Having spent nearly five years in the Soviet Union, Ambassador Thompson understood the effect of this American adventure on Khrushchev. "I am convinced," he wrote, "that Khrushchev was deeply impressed with the richness and strength of the United States, both in material and human terms." In particular, Thompson singled out the visit with the Garsts. "The comparison between a small Iowa farm community and a similar community in the Soviet Union," he wrote, "must have been very striking indeed."[79] Thompson was right about the effect of the trip. It emboldened Khrushchev to take ever-greater risks to achieve the Soviet society and international order that he dreamed about.

▪

WITHIN THIRTY-SIX HOURS of returning to Moscow, Khrushchev flew to Beijing, where he intended to do some missionary work on behalf of a new American policy. Relations between India and China were reaching a boiling point over a border dispute, and Khrushchev wished to discuss the possibility of war in South Asia in the context of what he had achieved in the United States. Mao was to be the first of Khrushchev's socialist allies to see the effect that the U.S. visit had on him.[80]

The Soviet leader carried a message from Eisenhower to the Chinese leadership. Recently two CIA pilots had been downed over China. Although the first to admit that the fate of these men was a matter of Chinese domestic policy, Khrushchev believed that the Americans should be released. He stressed the importance for China of contributing to Soviet efforts to reduce tensions and improve international relations. Mao was dumbfounded by the spectacle of his socialist ally pleading on behalf of capitalist spies.

But Khrushchev wanted to make a point. He sensed that a relaxation of international tension, a condition vitally important to his plans for Soviet domestic regeneration, was near at hand. He did not want his Chinese ally to do anything that might undermine this relaxation. In this vein he mentioned his concerns about events in Southeast Asia. He had heard that the North Vietnamese military wished to increase its military support of the Communist Pathet Lao faction in the civil war in neighboring Laos. He and Mao agreed that this was not the time to widen any war in that landlocked country.

Meanwhile an event at home reminded Khrushchev of the necessity of pushing forward with his domestic reforms. In late September a riot broke out over wages and food prices at the metallurgical factory in Karaganda, a town in Kazakhstan. The Presidium managed the crisis despite Khrushchev's absence, and by early October the situation was stable and men were in jail.[81] But Khrushchev and the Kremlin understood that there was no time to waste. Fresh from his successes in America and the Far East, Khrushchev would very soon propose the most audacious reform of his career. Not only the Soviet Union but the Cold War itself would take a new turn.

CHAPTER 10

GRAND DESIGN

I N THE WAKE of Khrushchev's trip to the United States, the Cold War entered a period of rapid and dramatic change. In retrospect the late fall and winter of 1959–1960 might well have seen one of the great pivots in that fifty-year war, easily on a par with events in 1946, the year the U.S.-Soviet struggle first took front and center on the world stage, and 1972, when Washington and Moscow reached a strategic détente. Only with the release of the Kremlin leadership documents is it now possible to understand the extent to which Khrushchev tried to create an opportunity for reducing the level of international danger and limiting the enormous economic burdens of defense budgets. Not until Mikhail Gorbachev would a Soviet leader again initiate as bold an effort to end the Cold War.

Once he returned to Moscow on September 28, 1959, Khrushchev didn't waste any time in signaling to party apparatchiks and the Soviet people that he believed a corner had been turned in the Cold War. Standing as tall as his five-foot frame allowed, and with more energy than he should have had after an exhausting transatlantic flight, he announced nothing less than a new era in superpower relations. "I can tell you in all frankness, dear comrades, that as a result of my talks and discussions of concrete questions with the U.S. president," Khrushchev informed a crowd of officials at Moscow's Vnukovo Airport, "I have gained the impression that he sincerely wishes to see the end of the cold war. . . . I am confident," he added, ". . . that we can do a great deal for peace."[1] As he left the rostrum, Khrushchev surprised some in the audience by crying out, "Long live Soviet-American friendship!"

The change in Khrushchev's statements was a matter neither of propaganda nor of good manners, a trait rarely associated with him at any time. Something profound had happened to the Soviet leader's assessment of the struggle with the United States. "I am pleased with my U.S. trip," Khrushchev had told a group of American businessmen a few days before leaving New

York. "It seems to me that the American people want to come to an agreement and live in peace." Before the trip he might have gone on to say that the desires of the American people were bound to be thwarted by Wall Street. But he was no longer convinced of that view, as he had been. Although admonishing himself not to "dig into souls," he seemed hopeful that at heart most American businessmen preferred peace over war profits.[2] For Khrushchev, who believed that the corporate world drove political decision making in the West, this new conclusion had widespread implications.

In cities from New York to California, the Soviet leader had observed a standard of living for ordinary people almost beyond his comprehension. It was one thing to look at a mock-up of an American kitchen at an exhibition designed to promote the virtues of the United States, as he had done in 1959 with the visiting Nixon at his elbow. It was something else to see row upon row of middle-class houses along the train route from New York to Washington. What Khrushchev had to admit was that the Americans had succeeded in providing to their workers a lifestyle that he had imagined possible only under full-fledged communism. The trip had not made him a capitalist by any means; instead its effect was to stir his competitive spirit.

Khrushchev had always understood that the Soviet Union had to become more efficient for its citizens to live comfortably. Even without the shock of seeing the United States, he had ample evidence at home that things were not going well. Instead of the gains mandated by the seven-year plan, 1959 had brought a drop in labor productivity, by one estimation from 7.2 to 2.7 percent. News from the farms was even worse. Agricultural production actually shrank by 4.1 percent in 1959.[3] Lacking any sense of the role that market forces had played in America's postwar boom, Khrushchev assumed that solving the problems of the Soviet economy lay in wiser Kremlin decisions and better people to implement those decisions. In his first weeks back home, he seized on any and all visible signs of inefficiency in Soviet life and dramatized them to make his point. Having noticed that in major U.S. cities the mayors spent money cultivating lawns instead of large floral arrangements, Khrushchev began questioning the wisdom of maintaining acres of greenhouses to line Moscow's main boulevards with flowers. If the rich Americans didn't need them, why did Soviet citizens?[4] Similarly, he had noticed that New York City had many fewer lampposts than major Soviet cities. "Why do we waste electricity to produce light our cities don't need?" he asked.[5] If the famed New York urban developer Robert Moses did not think that there had to be two lampposts on every block, why did Moscow city authorities believe otherwise?

There was a direct connection in Khrushchev's mind between this drive for a more efficient Soviet Union and talk of better relations with the United States. Khrushchev had long feared that the race to keep up with Washington in military firepower would bankrupt his country. "If we are forced into doing this," he told his son, Sergei, "we'll lose our pants."[6] In 1958, during Nasser's first state visit to the Soviet Union, Khrushchev had warned the Egyptian leader not to believe what military advisers said about the defense needs of the country. "You give them twice as much as they asked for and the very next day they will tell you that it is not enough [to defend the country]." Khrushchev believed that arms races corroded a country's ability to provide for its own citizens, and if any general or admiral tried to argue otherwise, he advised Nasser, "[y]ou should pour cold water on them."[7]

■

KHRUSHCHEV'S INCREASING confidence in U.S. intentions in foreign policy and his desire to match the Americans in economic achievement were necessary ingredients in determining his next great initiative, but what made the moment ripe for him was a breakthrough in Soviet nuclear technology. Within three months of his return from New York, Soviet nuclear scientists gave him an unprecedented opportunity to test how far he could go in cutting the Soviet defense budget. Six and a half years after the Kremlin had authorized its development, the first Soviet intercontinental ballistic missile, the R-7, was prepared to go into service at two launch facilities in Plesetsk. Although the missile had been used to put *Sputnik* into space in October 1957, the R-7 had needed more engineering before it could be outfitted with a nuclear warhead and brought into the arsenal. The first successful launch from Plesetsk took place in late July 1959, and now the Soviet military reported that it was prepared to station two R-7 missiles, each of which carried a three-megaton nuclear warhead, at both launch facilities.[8] Although the force was tiny in comparison with the U.S. arsenal, it had symbolic meaning. The Soviet Union finally had the ability to launch a nuclear missile attack on the United States.

Khrushchev hoped that only a few nuclear weapons of this kind would be necessary to reach rough parity with the United States. In 1958 Soviet military planners had presented him with plans for the creation of a vast system of intercontinental ballistic missile bases, which would have assured him complete parity with the expected U.S. nuclear forces of the 1960s.[9] But he had turned down that proposal, trusting instead in the logic of what might be called minimum deterrence. Why waste money on a program that the

Soviet Union could hardly afford when no sane leader, he believed, would ever risk war with the USSR so long as it had a few nuclear missiles? There is no evidence that Khrushchev had a particularly sophisticated view of what a sufficient deterrent would entail, but he had a sense that he needed only enough rockets to make any U.S. president fear the potential cost of a nuclear exchange. "Missiles are not cucumbers," he liked to say, "one cannot eat them and one does not require more than a certain number in order to ward off an attack."[10]

Armed with news of Moscow's new nuclear deterrent, Khrushchev moved fast to alter his government's approach to the Cold War. There was some grumbling in the Presidium and the Central Committee about the lack of preparation for the party plenum scheduled for late December, but Khrushchev wanted the government's agenda to accommodate yet one more topic. Military strategy was added to the schedule for a Presidium meeting on December 14. Concerned about how his colleagues might respond, Khrushchev opted not to spring his new plan for the military as a complete surprise. A few days before the meeting Presidium members received a lengthy memorandum describing what he had in mind and why.[11]

■

KHRUSHCHEV CHOSE a December morning to discuss his vision of the Soviet future. "Each citizen," he said, "each resident of the Soviet Union, should more and more and in full measure be provided for; his needs should be satisfied at the expense of public service."[12] Khrushchev believed that the weak Soviet economy stood in the way not only of a better life for Soviet citizens but also of achieving the classless political system that Marx and Lenin predicted under communism. "When we have created the material foundations for communism . . . it will become clear where there is freedom, and where there is no freedom," Khrushchev told his colleagues on December 14.[13] But in the wake of his recent trip to the United States, he felt compelled to discuss how far the Soviet Union was from achieving that utopia.

In this secret session among his closest associates, Khrushchev admitted what he would almost never allow himself to say anywhere else. Throughout his American tour he had boasted of the overwhelming superiority of the Soviet political system. But behind the walls of the Kremlin he acknowledged that he did not fully believe this anymore. What he had seen in the United States convinced him that the Americans were much closer to the type of democratic society that he expected under communism. He was struck by the fact that Americans had found a way to ensure a peaceful transfer of power from one president to another. He also thought Moscow could learn from the newly ratified Twenty-second Amendment to the U.S. Constitution, limiting U.S. presidents to two terms of four years. "When we have communism, it will not be possible that a person will sit at a post forever . . . [I]t is impossible to use a person until he is worn out."[14] Khrushchev warned. "If the bourgeois and capitalists are not afraid, that their foundations will be destroyed because after two terms the elected president changes, then why should we be afraid? What, are we not certain of our system or less certain than these bourgeois, capitalists and landowners?"[15]

What frustrated Khrushchev was that the USSR was so many years away from undertaking those political reforms. He believed his system could not survive a free vote or regular transfers of power so long as the Soviet standard of living was low. The Soviet people could not possibly believe in the superiority of communism over capitalism so long as they were ill fed, poorly sheltered, and underemployed and the citizens of the West enjoyed a higher standard of living. When Khrushchev suggested term limits for Kremlin leaders, he was thinking of generational change, pumping fresh blood into the system, not a replacement of Communist party members by Western liberals or conservatives. Khrushchev believed, until the country reached a higher level of economic performance, Moscow could not risk granting American-style democracy to its people. "The further we go in the elevation of the economy," he explained, "the deeper and the stronger will be the basis for democratization."[16]

Khrushchev did not offer his Kremlin colleagues any specific plan for improving the Soviet economy. He asked only that the economic planners be instructed to prepare detailed statements of goals for each step in the drive toward full-fledged communism, which in effect meant a U.S.-style standard of living in the Soviet Union. Khrushchev tossed out the figure of fifteen to twenty years to accomplish this radical transformation of the Soviet economy. In 1957 he had pledged that at least in the production of meat and milk the Soviet Union would catch and surpass the United States by 1970. But now, as then, he really had no idea how long catching up would take. Still, he did believe it was possible. In the meantime he wanted the Kremlin to send a series of signals through all levels of Soviet society that Moscow took this goal seriously and would expect to make systematic progress according to some well-defined list of milestones.

The few concrete proposals Khrushchev did have in mind for improving the Soviet way of life concerned reducing the cost of the Cold War so that more money could flow into the civilian economy.[17] Following the Presidium's discussion of Soviet political goals, the country's most powerful military men were ushered into the Kremlin hall to join the meeting. Khrushchev was very comfortable with his military commanders, all of whom he had handpicked. Gone were the troublesome Marshal Vassily Sokolovsky, who had expressed doubt about Khrushchev's approach to the Middle East, and the wrong-thinking Admiral Nikolai G. Kuznetsov, whose dreams of a massive three-ocean navy would have bankrupted the state. Khrushchev's new military elite was anchored by men who had fought alongside him in World War II, Marshals Rodion Malinovsky, Ivan Konev, and Andrei Grechko. Beside them was a new generation of military men who owed their promotions to Khrushchev, Marshal Kyrill Moskalenko, Marshal M. I. Nedelin, and the great architect of the Soviet war machine Marshal Dmitri Ustinov. With these men present Khrushchev outlined an audacious new Soviet military strategy designed to win the Cold War without a single shot being fired.

Desperate to shift the superpower struggle away from an arms race toward a contest of political ideas and economies, Khrushchev believed it was time to take a huge risk to achieve a major disarmament agreement with the United States. Earlier in the year the Soviet government had authorized the parallel development of two intercontinental ballistic weapons systems, the R-9 and the R-16. Both missiles were lighter and thinner than the bulky R-7 that had put *Sputnik* into orbit. Khrushchev had been looking for a missile that could be placed in underground silos to protect it from a U.S. attack. On the drawing board the R-16 had the added advantage of using a solid fuel, which meant it could be prepared for launch faster than a liquid-fueled missile and also would be more stable. The only problem was that the deployment of the R-9 and the R-16 systems was as much as six years away, and although not as expensive as conventional weapons, they were still a burden on a failing economy.

The Soviets faced a stark choice. Already far behind the United States in nuclear firepower, Moscow had few military options for keeping pace with Washington in the short term. Even though the U.S. rocket program had barely caught up with the Russian program, U.S. bombers with nuclear weapons were stationed at NATO air bases in Europe only hours away from Moscow. Eisenhower already had the capability to deliver a crippling strike on the USSR with one order, whereas Khrushchev was years away from achieving that. As he looked forward, the situation was not likely to get better. It was known from open sources that the United States had also invested in long-range nuclear missiles and in missiles that could be launched from submarines. The missile gap favoring U.S. power would probably widen before the R-9 and the R-16 could be deployed.

Constrained by the Soviet economy and his own ideas about how to achieve better living standards in the near future, Khrushchev did not opt for a crash rearmament program or even an acceleration of the development of the next generation of missiles. Instead he decided to gamble on a diplomatic strategy that would head off a costly arms race with the Americans. His plan was to announce at the party plenum in January a dramatic unilateral cut in the Soviet armed forces. He suggested cutting between 1 and 1.2 million soldiers, about a third of the active Soviet military. The Western powers had always complained that the enormous Soviet Army posed a constant threat to the security of Central Europe and to Germany in particular. Now he would show Washington, London, and Paris that Moscow had no military designs on Bonn.

The Presidium adopted Khrushchev's strategy of unilateral disarmament after hearing nothing but praise from his handpicked military chiefs. Defense Minister Malinovsky blessed the troop cuts and assured the Presidium that the general staff had already worked through these numbers and could do it.[18] The chief of the Warsaw Pact forces, Marshal Konev, also applauded the cuts, underscoring the fact that the nuclear revolution made this disarmament possible without harming Soviet security. Equally enthusiastic support came from the younger military men. To show his commitment to building a nuclear missile force, Khrushchev planned to create a separate branch of the Soviet armed forces for nuclear weapons, and he wanted Marshal Nedelin to command this force. Not surprisingly, Nedelin expressed delight at Khrushchev's new strategy and the cuts in conventional forces. So too did the man selected as his future deputy in the Soviet rocket forces command, Kirill S. Moskalenko.[19] The two had served together in an antitank brigade in 1941 and had grown to appreciate the cutting edge in Soviet military technology. "Nikita Sergeyvich," Nedelin said in front of the Kremlin bosses, "your proposal is not only necessary but overdue." Moskalenko chimed in that Khrushchev's proposal was "courageous and responsible before the nation and history. The peace initiative is in our hands." Nedelin's future assistant then proceeded to list conventional weaponry that could also be considered obsolete, including the T-34 tank and much of the army's artillery.[20]

The entire Soviet leadership understood that Khrushchev was forcing the country to take a huge strategic risk. The effect of these decisions would be to create a Soviet window of vulnerability. Even the nuclear enthusiast Moskalenko had to admit that the USSR was still two years from having a reliable retaliatory capability in case the United States launched a first strike. By having placed some limits on rocket development and production and by not increasing expenditures on Soviet conventional forces, Khrushchev ensured that in the early 1960s the Soviet Union would be far weaker than the United States. He would have the few missiles he thought he needed to be a great power, but he would not have anywhere near the capacity to ensure a nuclear retaliatory strike in the event the United States launched its missiles, bombers, and submarines first. Secrecy would be essential to ensure Soviet safety during these difficult years. Not only would he have to hide Soviet vulnerability, but he would have to find a way to use disarmament negotiations to soften the U.S. advantage in the correlation of forces.

For Khrushchev there was also a political risk inherent in his plan. The memorandum distributed before the meeting barely masked his concern that this approach made him vulnerable to political attack for being too soft on the United States: "Perhaps I cannot foresee everything. But it seems to me that these proposals of mine, if we implemented them, would not cause any damage to our country and would not threaten our defense capabilities vis-à-vis the enemy forces, but would rather enhance our international prestige and strengthen our country."[21] In the meeting itself Khrushchev spoke of the need for a campaign to sell this plan to the military commands in the field and to the various military committees in the Kremlin.[22] He expected opposition, especially from among the ranks of those who would lose their jobs and older retired military officers. To steel the determination of his military men and colleagues and perhaps to hide his own insecurities, the Soviet leader vowed no mercy for these military hawks. "[Let's] knock the bragging out of them . . . expel [them] from the party, act on the offensive."[23]

▪

Dwight Eisenhower probably would have flashed one of his trademark grins had the CIA been able to report that Khrushchev now wanted to "knock the bragging" out of Soviet military hawks. For years Khrushchev had been the biggest braggart of them all about the alleged military superiority of the Soviet Union. Since *Sputnik* those claims always involved the rate of production of missiles that could reach the U.S. mainland. In February 1959 Khrushchev had reported to Communist Party officials from across the USSR that "serial production of intercontinental ballistic rockets has been organized."[24] Then, in November 1959, he had told journalists that "now we have such a stock of rockets, such an amount of atomic and hydrogen weapons, that if they attack us we could wipe our potential enemies off the face of the earth. . . . [I]n one year, 250 rockets with hydrogen warheads came off the assembly line in the factory we visited."[25]

President Eisenhower had seen through these claims. "They also said that they invented the flying machine," he told a group of journalists with tongue in cheek, "and the automobile and the telephone and other things." For Eisenhower it was essential not to become an alarmist on the subject of Soviet power. "If we react violently to every new development such as *Sputnik*," he later advised the Kennedy administration, "then we're licked."[26] From his long military service, Eisenhower understood how much militaries cost, and he refused to let fear force the United States to overspend just because Moscow had been the first to fire a long-range missile. What mattered was whether the Soviets had the actual missiles to back up these claims. Everything he had seen from the CIA and other sources failed to prove to him that they did.

Eisenhower had a fine grasp of the trade-off that his adversary faced. In early 1959 he had taken time to look closely at Khrushchev's seven-year plan and the demands that it would make on the Soviet economy.[27] The CIA pointed out to him that the Kremlin's projected rates of economic growth were unrealistic. Labor productivity was "a big problem," and apparently Moscow could not acquire the fertilizer and machinery that would make Soviet agriculture efficient enough to satisfy the plan.[28] The only way for Khrushchev to achieve greater food production would be to redirect investment to agriculture and increase labor productivity or to increase the number of workers. Eisenhower understood better than anyone in his administration that it would be impossible for the Kremlin to pursue this domestic agenda while simultaneously building the huge nuclear force predicted by Washington doomsayers and bragged about by Khrushchev.

The president's cool response was in no way representative of public attitudes in the United States toward national security. Despite the positive aspects of the Khrushchev visit, nerves first frayed by *Sputnik* remained sensitive to evidence of U.S. military vulnerability. For many Americans, even those friendly to Eisenhower's defense posture, the entire balance of power in the late 1950s hinged solely on the number of intercontinental ballistic missiles (ICBMs) in each country's arsenal. The administration had opened itself to criticism by deciding as a cost-cutting measure to try to leapfrog missile technologies. The military had purchased fewer Atlas and Titan missiles in favor of waiting for the solid-fuel Minuteman, a more efficient ICBM, to be developed. The deployment of the first Minuteman was not expected until 1962, leaving a few years when it was feared the Soviets would have many more missiles than the United States. The White House's decision not to buy more Atlas missiles had been especially controversial with the Convair division of the General Dynamics Corporation, the primary contractor for the

Atlas, which wasted no opportunity to try to influence the public debate and compel lawmakers to overturn Eisenhower's penny-pinching.

The wisdom of waiting for the Minuteman missile seemed to rest on how many missiles the Soviets were expected to have by 1961. Eisenhower's problem was that his critics were vocal and influential and professed to have the answer to this all-important question. Within the government, the air force's Strategic Air Command (SAC), which was responsible for the country's fleet of intercontinental bombers and ICBMs, was leading the fight for additional appropriations for Atlas, Titan, and Minuteman missiles. SAC believed that by 1961 the Soviets would have 150 ICBMs, exactly the number needed to destroy all thirty SAC bases in the United States as well as twenty other key military and civilian targets, including Washington, D.C. SAC made a point of letting influential hawks, such as the syndicated newspaper columnist Joseph Alsop, know these calculations. In a letter to his friend retired General Lucius D. Clay, who had directed U.S. operations during the Berlin blockade, Alsop wrote approvingly that senior members of the SAC staff "do not think, and I do not think[,] that it is at all certain that the national estimates are wrong. They only believe, as I most firmly believe[,] that there is a considerable margin of possible error which gives one chance in three, or four, or five of the dreadful result I have described."[29]

The loudest voice on Capitol Hill warning of a missile gap belonged to Senator Stuart Symington, a Democrat from Missouri. The former secretary of the air force in the Truman administration, Symington was positioning himself as a hawk for the presidential nomination of his party in 1960. When the Eisenhower administration tried to temper the public and congressional overreaction to *Sputnik*, Symington had charged that it was irresponsibly choosing a balanced budget over national security. "What do you do with a government," he had said in September 1959, "which decides that money is more important than security?"[30] In Senate hearings that same fall he had confidently predicted that by 1962 the Soviets would have three thousand ICBMs, punctuating this groundless prediction with "Let that be on the record."[31] As it turned out, the record showed that Senator Symington was off by a mere 2,938. No friend of Moscow, Symington had cracked during the Khrushchev visit that Truman would have been impeached by Congress had he dared invite Stalin to America. "Why is it today that many of us think Mr. Khrushchev's visit may be helpful?"[32]

Symington was by no means the only Democratic presidential contender to sense the political utility of warning about a missile gap. All the major candidates spoke as if it were a given that between 1960 and 1964 Soviet nuclear missile stocks would significantly outnumber the U.S. arsenal. Senate Majority Leader Lyndon Baines Johnson, of Texas, fanned fears of a missile gap to show his command of foreign policy issues.[33] Senator John F. Kennedy, of Massachusetts, also raised the specter of a U.S. window of vulnerability. As early as mid-1958 Kennedy had warned that the United States was fast approaching that period "in which our own offensive and defensive missile capabilities will lag so far behind those of the Soviets as to place us in a position of great peril."[34]

Eisenhower could be excused if he felt a sense of déjà vu at this ill-informed debate over Soviet missile capabilities. Four years earlier almost the same groups had been arrayed to debate whether the Soviets had more intercontinental bombers than the United States. The alarmists had been proved wrong but deftly managed not to be discredited. They rescued themselves by arguing that Khrushchev had unexpectedly decided to invest resources in building up missiles and not bombers.

The U-2 spy plane had played a role in exploding the myth of the Soviet bomber gap in 1956. But as of 1959 U-2 surveillance flights were not producing enough intelligence on Soviet missile production and deployment to settle the missile gap debate. All U-2 flights over the Soviet Union had been halted in 1958 because of Eisenhower's concerns about the diplomatic risks of violating Soviet airspace, and in mid-1959 the president had approved only one flight. Meanwhile spies and intercepted Soviet communications were equally unable to provide enough detail to paint the complete picture. As a result, for two years U.S. intelligence analysts had been admitting to policy makers that they could not explain what was going on in Khrushchev's rocket program. They had heard his boasting, but when they sent U-2s to photograph test sites or to pick up the electronic signals emitted by missile test flights, the numbers did not correlate with the huge program Khrushchev seemed to be talking about. It had taken the United States 115 missile test flights to achieve a production rate of six ICBMs per month.[35] Yet between the summer of 1957 and May 1958 the CIA had detected only six Soviet tests, and the pace did not pick up significantly through the remainder of 1958 and 1959. Without anyone on the inside of the Soviet missile program or within shouting distance of the Kremlin, the CIA did not know of Khrushchev's decision to leapfrog the R-7 program in favor of the R-16 and R-9.

Although the U.S. intelligence community lacked good information on the size and capability of the Soviet strategic missile arsenal, it was expected to issue an annual estimate of that arsenal to assist the Pentagon in budgeting American missile production. In the 1950s and 1960s the director of central intelligence supervised what were called national intelligence estimates

(NIEs) on Soviet military power, and CIA officials were the principal drafters of these estimates. In Eisenhower's second term the agency offered what it considered the middle ground between the exaggerated predictions of the U.S. Air Force about the size of the Soviet rocket force and the smaller projections of the U.S. Army. In 1958 that median estimate was that the Soviets would have ten R-7s by the end of 1959, one hundred a year later, and a grand total of five hundred sometime in 1962. Although the resulting NIE cautioned that these figures were selected "arbitrarily in order to provide some measure of the Soviet capacity" and "d[id] *not* [original emphasis] represent an estimate of probable Soviet requirements or stockpiles," they became the benchmark for discussions of near-term Soviet capabilities. Taking this middle road was considered the sane response to the "Sky Is Falling!" approach of SAC, Joe Alsop, and the Democratic hopefuls.[36] But even this moderate estimate far exaggerated Soviet capabilities.

▪

As KHRUSHCHEV had hoped, he grabbed the Eisenhower administration's attention with his announcement of unilateral troop reductions at a public meeting of the USSR Supreme Soviet on January 14, 1960. The announcement impressed Eisenhower as serious and positive. Not all of the president's advisers agreed. But Eisenhower was confident that Khrushchev was trying to lessen international tensions. When Director of Central Intelligence (DCI) Allen Dulles downplayed the significance of the speech at a meeting of the National Security Council (NSC) on the same day of the speech, Eisenhower contradicted him. "[This was a] very tough speech," the president insisted, "especially from the military point of view."[37] In Eisenhower's eyes, Khrushchev's dramatic move was an act of real disarmament that was consistent with the ideas that the Soviet leader had described at Camp David. It had to be viewed as a constructive first step.[38]

Within a week the CIA came around to the view that Khrushchev's initiative was an act of significant disarmament. From its monitoring of public speeches by Kremlin officials in the wake of the Khrushchev's announcement, the agency detected significant opposition within the Soviet military. At least 250,000 officers were about to be retired early, and many were displeased. At the NSC meeting on January 21, DCI Dulles went even further. He informed the president that they were possibly witnessing a sea change in the Cold War. Khrushchev's decision to push ahead with these deep conventional cuts, he argued, "seems to exclude general war as a deliberate Soviet policy." Khrushchev's statement also forced the agency to revise downward its estimates of the Soviet Army's size. For three years the intelligence community had refused to accept published Soviet numbers for its conventional forces, which it considered too low. But given the data the agency had acquired in and around Khrushchev's speech, it appeared that he was cutting 1.2 million from a smaller base than had been assumed. Moscow could not hope to occupy Europe with a force this size.[39]

There was a significant difference between Eisenhower's and the CIA's hopeful interpretation of Khrushchev's proposed action and the conventional wisdom outside the White House. The Soviet announcement had no perceptible effect on the intense public debate over the supposed missile gap. In fact some of the other sections in Khrushchev's January 14 speech may actually have hurt his case. In announcing the troop cuts, he had reaffirmed his belief in nuclear deterrence and boasted of the Soviet Union's superior missile technology. A careful reader of his speech would have also seen that he was now saying that a successful first strike was impossible in a world where both sides had missiles and bombers. A careful analyst might also have understood that the language was designed to smooth any domestic feathers ruffled by this surprise unilateral cut. But the missile gap lobby in the United States looked past that and ignored the conventional cuts altogether. More impressive to them was the successful launch four days after Khrushchev's speech of an R-7 with a dummy warhead that traveled more than seven thousand miles from Soviet Central Asia to a point in the Pacific just south of Hawaii. This test, the first of its kind, occurred on the eve of a major congressional debate concerning the 1961 defense budget.

Chairman of the Joint Chiefs Staff Nathan Twining and the defense secretary-designate Thomas Gates ran into a chorus of suspicion on Capitol Hill when they tried to downplay the existence of a missile gap in testimony on the 1961 defense budget. They explained that even if the Soviets had more ICBMs than the United States, the United States retained more nuclear firepower on long-range bombers and submarines than the Soviet Union. There might be a missile gap, but there was no deterrence gap, and it was the latter that spelled the difference between peace and war.[40] Nevertheless, congressional assumptions would not be set aside that easily. Expressing the view of many powerful lawmakers, the chairman of the Armed Forces Committee, Senator Richard Russell of Georgia, told Eisenhower's defense team, "I can't accept the statement that there is no missile gap. I think there is."[41]

A Democratic Congress could be expected to be skeptical of a Republican administration. The real problem for Eisenhower was that like his adversary Khrushchev, he faced dissension in his own military. Only four days after

Khrushchev's speech, General Thomas S. Power, the head of the Strategic Air Command, had delivered a speech at the Economic Club of New York that contradicted the administration's statements.[42] He had spoken of a future in which the Soviets "might accumulate enough missiles to destroy this nation's retaliatory missiles and bombers before they could be fired or take off." He had then given a number that defined what the Soviets needed to achieve a successful first strike capability: "With only 300 ballistic missiles the Soviet Union could virtually wipe out this country's entire retaliatory capability in thirty minutes." Power had called for strategic bombers to be kept aloft at all times to be able to retaliate, in case Khrushchev launched first. At the time the U.S. Air Force estimated that fifty bombers would have to be in the air at any given moment to ensure U.S. security. Incoming Defense Secretary Gates tried to downplay Power's estimate. It "is unrealistic," he told Congress, but he did not persuade many people.[43]

From Khrushchev's perspective the most unnerving development in the missile gap debate that he saw played out in U.S. newspapers was the start of a highly influential series of articles by Joseph Alsop that seemed to wrap all the prevailing missile gap lore together with a bow. Over six columns starting on January 23, Alsop laid out the case for believing the Soviets were well ahead in missile development.[44] He built his argument on Power's premise that with 150 ICBMs and 150 intermediate-range missiles firing on European targets, the Soviets could destroy all of NATO's nuclear weapons. He then set out to explain that if the Soviet missile factories were as efficient as the factory that produced SAC's Atlas rockets, then Khrushchev would have 150 ICBMs in ten months. Alsop charged the Eisenhower administration with playing Russian roulette in refusing to accelerate the arms race because of lack of firm proof that the Soviets had as many missiles as they could have. "[N]o intelligence service on earth can be absolutely certain that the closed Soviet society, using all the resources of the Soviet economy, has not produced a number of weapons equal to a mere ten months of capacity production in a single American factory."[45] In the absence of certainty about an enemy's capabilities, Alsop believed that one had to assume the worst about both his capabilities and his intentions. Unfortunately for the country and the world, Alsop's thesis proved to be more persuasive than President Eisenhower's calm.

■

ALSOP'S COLUMNS and other U.S. press reaction disappointed and angered Khrushchev, who received daily translations of the most important columns and articles. He suspected the administration was behind the bad reviews of his Supreme Soviet speech. "It is not the journalists who write it themselves," Khrushchev said, "but the journalists write about what the government thinks."[46] What stood in his way was the inability, or unwillingness, of the U.S. government to accept that he wanted disarmament, not war.

The campaign of alarmists like Alsop helped Khrushchev see the corrosive effect that three years of his own nuclear bluster had on his ability to do business with the United States. Had he not claimed that the Soviet Union could make missiles "like sausages"; had he not boasted of the capability to set the major U.S. cities afire? Of course this was nonsense; as of January 1960, the United States led the race in all the nuclear systems categories, even in the prestigious missile race. While Joe Alsop spoke of a Soviet force of 150 ICBMs, Khrushchev knew that he had only 4 and that the United States already had twice as many.

So, Khrushchev felt he had to devise an imaginative way to undermine the popular U.S. perception of Soviet missile capability. He would offer to destroy all Soviet intercontinental ballistic missiles. "They blame us for advocating cuts in conventional forces," he told his colleagues in the Presidium a few days after the Alsop series was published. "Now let's call for cuts in an area where they think we are ahead."[47] How could Alsop and the missile gap alarmists continue to discredit the idea of disarmament if the Soviet Union offered to get rid of its ICBMs?

Throughout the early Cold War the United States had questioned if the Soviets were sincere in their pleas for disarmament. Stalin and Molotov were accustomed to making proposals for propaganda purposes alone. In early 1960 Khrushchev was different. He believed that now that he had some ICBMs to give away, he could talk about the destruction of all strategic delivery systems. This would undermine talk of a missile gap in the United States and perhaps lead to better relations between the superpowers.

The idea had come to Khrushchev from the French. In the fall the French representative at UN-sponsored disarmament negotiations in Geneva, Jules Moch, had raised this possibility in general session. It is not clear whether Khrushchev happened to remember that or perhaps was inspired by some intelligence from within the French government, still a fertile field for Soviet espionage. The fact that the idea was French opened some intriguing possibilities. In late December 1959 the Western powers had invited Khrushchev to a summit of the big four in Paris in May. Khrushchev himself was planning a visit to France in March. If played right, this Soviet proposal could be wrapped in the tricolor before delivery to the Western powers at the summit.

The Soviet leader unveiled his strategy at a Kremlin meeting on February 1, 1960. "Our most sacred dream" is what Khrushchev called the dismantling of the Western military alliances: the North Atlantic Treaty Organization, the Southeast Asian Treaty Organization, and the Central Treaty Organization. He saw these organizations as aggressive military obstacles to his goal of transforming the superpower struggle into an economic and political competition between the two different systems.

His strategy was simple. As he explained it to his colleagues, he wanted to force the West to accept disarmament by offering them something that proved he was sincere. He also wanted to offer them something that both sides could accept.[48] If Khrushchev had his way, the Soviet Union would soon be dismantling its nuclear weapons, its fleet, and its aviation. The victory of world communism did not need this high-tech weaponry.

Khrushchev's hand had grown much stronger in the past year, and the Presidium readily endorsed his disarmament proposal. The only disagreement arose over when and how Khrushchev should announce it. His ally Leonid Brezhnev thought he should save it for his Paris meetings with de Gaulle in March. Gromyko, who seemed to be no fan of this idea, asked that the Kremlin wait to see if the world embraced Khrushchev's earlier call for general and complete disarmament. Khrushchev's military advisers did not seem to care when he made the announcement so long as it was done at home, apparently to avoid the impression that it had been imposed upon him by the West. Khrushchev left the gathering without making up his mind. The one place he thought he didn't want to make the announcement was at the summit in May. He seemed to want to do it sooner.

His immediate problem was that the missiles he would offer to dismantle were very vulnerable. Soviet missile engineers were only now building silos or "hardened" positions for the next generation of intercontinental ballistic missiles, the R-16s and R-9s, which were expected in a few years. In the meantime it was essential that the United States not discover the exact locations of the few missiles he had. With only four R-7s to defend the entire country, Khrushchev could not accept any inspection regime before disarmament. Once the United States and the Soviet Union had dismantled their rockets, there would be no danger in letting NATO see the launchpads at Plesetsk and Tyuratam. Khrushchev meanwhile hoped that the advantages of disarmament would compel the United States to take a risk of its own before it got a full inspection.

■

DISARMAMENT WAS ALSO on Dwight Eisenhower's mind in early February 1960. At the time he was locked in discussions with Great Britain over how to make a realistic proposal to ban all nuclear testing. The British were eager to move as quickly as possible to enact a test ban. Eisenhower also was eager for one. Since 1958 the world's three nuclear powers—Great Britain, the United States, and the Soviet Union—had observed a morato-rium on all atmospheric testing. This came largely in response to interna-tional concerns about the health hazards of testing. Japanese fisherman caught in the downdraft of a U.S. nuclear test at Bikini Atoll in March 1954 were later found to have developed cancer. Concern became even more wide-spread when strontium 90, a radioactive particle found in nuclear fallout, was detected in milk throughout Europe.

Eisenhower had no plans to violate the atmospheric testing moratorium between the United States and the Soviet Union. However, he was not pre-pared to sign a treaty that formalized the moratorium unless it was verifiable. It was just as important to him that the United States be able to monitor Soviet compliance with the moratorium as it was that the U.S. intelligence community be able to count Soviet missiles accurately. On the morning of February 2 the president told Secretary of State Herter that there was "scarcely any proposal in the field of disarmament equitable to the two sides that he would not accept if it can be inspected."[49] For Eisenhower inspection was the key. He did not fear a world without nuclear weapons. What concerned him was the possibility that the Soviets would cheat to gain an advantage over the United States.[50]

Had either the CIA or the KGB been powerful enough to discern the think-ing of its adversary, the Kremlin and the White House would have discovered that in February 1960 the two most powerful men in the world were on the same wavelength. Khrushchev and Eisenhower believed in the need to elimi-nate nuclear weapons, and both shared the view that if there had to be nuclear missiles for deterrence, they could remain few in number. Eisenhower sum-marized his thinking in a press conference on February 4: "What you want is *enough* [emphasis added], a thing that is adequate. A deterrent has no added power, once it has become completely adequate for compelling the respect of any potential opponent for your deterrent and, therefore, to make him act prudently."[51] Not until the Reagan-Gorbachev summit in Reykjavik, over a quarter century later, did the Soviet and U.S. leadership come this close to deep cuts in nuclear weapons stockpiles. By 1986 the arsenal of each country had reached nine thousand warheads; in 1960 the number was only ten.

A week after he had introduced to his Kremlin colleagues his new thinking on disarmament, Khrushchev tried to convey it to Eisenhower. He took advantage of the Moscow visit of the U.S. ambassador to the United Nations, Henry Cabot Lodge. Lodge, who had been Khrushchev's touring companion on the trip across the United States in September, was doing some unofficial advance work for President Eisenhower's expected visit in June. This last was a by-product of the Camp David summit, at which Khrushchev had extended an invitation to Eisenhower to visit Moscow.

During the American tour it was to Lodge that Khrushchev had made some of his most extreme boasts. But in an unguarded moment in California, he had also revealed that all was not well with the Soviet economy. Now, less than half a year later, the Soviet leader was even more forthcoming and was prepared to admit how far his country was behind the United States. When Lodge mentioned how impressed he was with the state of Soviet housing, Khrushchev brushed aside the compliment: "[W]e have much to do before getting ahead of you." But the most telling comment came when Lodge mentioned that the Soviets had already surpassed the United States in quite a few fields, strategic rockets being one of them. Khrushchev said point-blank, "No, we're not, not really."[52]

The American national security community was incapable of absorbing the implications of Khrushchev's candor. Lodge reported his comments to the State Department, but they failed to produce even a ripple in Washington. As far as Eisenhower was concerned—if he even learned of this exchange—there was nothing new in what Khrushchev had told Lodge. The president already believed that the United States was way ahead. So too did the Republican front-runner, Richard Nixon, who in private sessions with Eisenhower and Allen Dulles agreed that the gap was phony. The problem was that publicists and military lobbyists had created a poisonous atmosphere in which debate over real threats to the United States was impossible. Too many powerful people—Democratic presidential candidates, air force generals, military contractors, "national security" columnists—stood to gain from the existence of the "gap" for it to be defeated by logic alone.

■

FLU KEPT KHRUSHCHEV from visiting Paris in March, when he had hoped to test Western interest in his still-secret nuclear disarmament proposal. He rescheduled the trip for late March and early April. Once he arrived in Paris, Khrushchev played the French president, Charles de Gaulle, very well.[53] As he had explained in the Kremlin in early February, he would use French disarmament proposals to his advantage. He let de Gaulle raise "his" scheme for eliminating nuclear delivery vehicles in conversation and then accepted them. The French had no interest in any conventional disarmament. They had thousands of men under arms in Algeria and some men stationed in tropical Africa and Laos, and they retained a commitment to defend West Germany from Soviet attack. France, which had just joined the nuclear club by testing a nuclear prototype in the Sahara on February 13, 1960, was so far behind the superpowers that nuclear disarmament would benefit it immediately. The French did not yet have any strategic bombers or missiles.

Khrushchev also used this preliminary visit to Paris to set the stage for discussing Berlin at the summit scheduled for May. Although his new strategy for peace revolved around nuclear disarmament, his mind never strayed too far from the German question. He shared with de Gaulle his concept of an interim agreement. He intended to give the West an additional two years to reach some kind of agreement on the future of West Berlin, and he explained to de Gaulle that the West had to understand that this concession represented the limit of his patience on the issue. If that old crank Adenauer survived the two years and prevented any agreement, the Soviets would make good on their threat to end the three-power occupation of West Berlin with the stroke of the pen.

Khrushchev revealed to de Gaulle that his bottom line on Berlin remained the same. West Berlin would have to become a free city-state. It could not, through a plebiscite or any other means, join the Federal Republic of Germany as a *Land*, or province. The West would have to pull its troops out of West Berlin. The defense of the free city-state would become the responsibility of the United Nations. All access to West Berlin, via land or air, would have to be negotiated with East Germany.

The Khrushchev visit to de Gaulle had the expected effect. It inspired intense consultation by the West as it prepared for the formal presentation of these Soviet proposals at the summit. De Gaulle acted as the messenger, visiting first Macmillan in London, then Eisenhower in Washington. At each stop, de Gaulle explained that the Soviet leader had accepted the French disarmament proposal.[54] He also spoke of the possibility of a two-year interim agreement on Berlin, which would postpone another crisis over Berlin until at least 1962.

The British were delighted with what they viewed as new Soviet flexibility. Macmillan believed that in his comments on Berlin, Khrushchev was returning to a position that had nearly been agreed to at the foreign ministers' meeting in Geneva in 1959. "Perhaps Mr. Khrushchev was prepared to agree to such an arrangement," the British prime minister suggested to his French visitor, "provided he negotiated it himself."[55] If anything the British leader was even more encouraged by what the French president told him about the new Soviet position on dismantling nuclear delivery systems. At the moment

the British faced difficult choices as they set about modernizing their strategic nuclear forces. It was very expensive to remain a real player in the nuclear
game. De Gaulle said that he hoped that at the summit the parties could agree
to the principle of establishing limits on the number of strategic bombers and
missiles in their arsenals and then follow that up by establishing a permanent
committee to study the problem. "This would be a great advance."[56]

■

MEANWHILE PRESSURE was building in Washington to disprove Joseph
Alsop's and Stuart Symington's claims of a missile gap. No one in the U.S.
intelligence community had spotted the 150 launch sites Alsop alleged existed
in the Soviet Union. CIA analysts, who were just completing their annual
review of the Soviet missile program, admitted that they had "no direct evidence of Soviet ICBM deployment concepts" or of "the intended nature of
operational launch sites."[57] However, U.S. intelligence had identified eleven
areas where ICBM deployment might be happening. Little other than fragmentary photographic intelligence and the presence of long rail lines
explained why these locations were selected.

The alarmists in the intelligence community, led by the U.S. Air Force,
believed that unless and until all eleven locations had been photographed,
very little could be said about the future deployment of Soviet ICBMs.
Intelligence analysts were especially eager to photograph the north-central
portion of Russia. In 1959 U.S. intelligence had collected evidence of a new
ICBM facility near Plesetsk, along the railway line between Vovodnya and
Murmansk. The CIA considered two ways of photographing the northern
area.[58] A U-2 flying from Greenland could enter Soviet airspace near Novaya
Zemlya, then go far enough south to photograph Plesetsk before returning.
The other idea was more ambitious. U-2s had never flown right across the
Soviet Union. Up to that time all flights went halfway into the country and
then turned around. The proposed Operation Grand Slam would start in
Pakistan and photograph the Soviet Union on a diagonal from the Central
Asian republics to Murmansk on the Gulf of Finland.

President Eisenhower was lobbied hard in late 1959 and early 1960 to use
the U-2. General James Doolittle of the President's Board of Consultants on
Foreign Intelligence Activities urged him to send as many U-2s as he could
over the Soviet Union; so too did Allen Dulles, who believed that one reason
the CIA was not doing a better job of estimating Soviet missile development
was the president's reluctance to exploit the U-2.[59] Since the beginning of

the year Eisenhower had approved two flights. Under this pressure he approved one more at the end of March. In giving in, he asked his intelligence advisers not to let this intelligence program undermine his efforts at superpower diplomacy. "[I] have one tremendous asset in a summit meeting," he said. ". . . That is [my] reputation for honesty. If one of these aircraft were lost when we were engaged in apparently sincere deliberations, it could be put on display in Moscow and ruin [my] effectiveness."[60]

Eisenhower left it up to the CIA to choose between the Greenland flight or Operation Grand Slam. The agency's deputy director for plans, Richard Bissell, who had supervised the development of the U-2, and his team subsequently decided to attempt to do the longer flight. Soviet air defenses were quite strong in the north, so a flight that entered from the northern USSR would incur greater risks. In late March and early April, when plans for Grand Slam were assembled, it was assumed that Soviet radars in the south could not track an incoming U-2. By the time Soviet radar picked up Grand Slam in the north, the plane would be heading home.

Just after making his decision, Eisenhower welcomed Prime Minister Macmillan to Camp David. The president was upbeat about the possibilities for some agreement in Paris. The four-power summit was now scheduled to begin on May 16. He had an idea of offering the Soviet Union a guarantee that the Oder-Neisse Line would remain the eastern boundary of East Germany. He believed that if Khrushchev were assured that a resurgent Germany could never take back the sections of Prussia that had been transferred to Poland at the end of World War II, the Soviets might become more conciliatory toward the Western position in Berlin. When Macmillan indicated that he was prepared to consider how they could establish a free state of West Berlin, Eisenhower said he could not agree to that, given that he thought an independent West Berlin would soon be swallowed up by the East. Instead he hoped that Khrushchev would follow up on what he had said at Camp David in 1959 and again, more recently, to de Gaulle in Paris by promising a two-year standstill on the Berlin matter. Regarding disarmament, Eisenhower was trying to devise an inspection plan that the Soviets might accept. What he had in mind was a variation on his call for open skies in 1955 that would divide the United States, the USSR, and Europe into zones and permit Khrushchev to accept inspections in stages.[61]

Bissell had been instructed to complete the U-2 flight before April 19, but bad weather intervened. Meanwhile a U-2 flew over Kazakhstan and part of the Urals on April 9 before returning safely home. When the Soviets did not protest this flight, it strengthened assumptions in Washington that they would swallow more U-2 fights. Bissell requested and got a delay for Operation Grand Slam. Eisenhower ordered that "one additional operation may be undertaken, provided it is carried out prior to May 1. No operation is to be carried out after May 1." The White House understood that the Soviets would be particularly offended by a violation of their airspace on May 1, their most important national holiday. However, the order was so carelessly phrased that Bissell understood the instruction to mean that if need be, he could send a U-2 over the Soviet Union on May Day.[62]

CHAPTER 11

THE CRASH HEARD ROUND THE WORLD

L ENINGRAD WAS SPORTING new colors in May 1960. That year the traditional blood-red banners with Marxist-Leninist haiku celebrating May Day had some unusual competition. There were greens and newly painted yellows on some buildings, and along the main railway line to Moscow, new fences were sprouting. Russia's second city was undergoing a face-lift in preparation for a special American visitor, a man whose military exploits in the Second World War had earned him a place in Soviet hearts. Now president of the United States, Dwight D. Eisenhower was expected to arrive on a state visit in mid-June.

No American visitor of any kind, however, was expected that spring in Povarnia, a village near Sverdlovsk in the Ural Mountains. But at about 11:00 A.M., local time, on May 1, villagers heard an explosion, and in the upper sky an orange and white parachute appeared with what looked to be a man hanging from it. Home for the May Day holiday, P. E. Asabin was startled by the sound and ran out to the street, where he was in time to see a column of dust rise and then fall on the village. As he started talking to a neighbor about this strange noise, Asabin observed that many people were running out of the village toward something. Then, not more than ninety feet away, he could see a man in a parachute coming toward him. "I ran immediately to his side and caught up with him, just as he landed."[1]

V. N. Glinskich also saw the mysterious parachutist. Glinskich was at work on the collective farm, spreading manure using one of the fancy, by Soviet standards, automatic dung distributers, when he heard the bang. "Then I suddenly glimpsed in the sky," Glinskich later told the KGB. "High up I could see some kind of balloon. . . . When the balloon fell closer, then it became clear to me, that this was a parachutist."[2]

There were some official watchers that day too. At the command dispatch point of the Sverdlovsk civilian airport in Koltsovo, two KGB officers, Captain V. P. Pankov and Lieutenant I. A. Ananeyev, witnessed the morning show. Concerned that this was some kind of enemy paratroop action, they called the chairman of the local collective farm, M. N. Berman, with an order that the stranger be detained. Moments later the two KGB men were off on their motorcycles toward the nearby village.

Meanwhile a gaggle of townspeople reached the parachutist. At first they assumed he was a Soviet. "*Fsyo v poriatke?* [Is everything okay?]," they asked as a few tried to help him out of his parachute, radio helmet, and flight suit. But the pilot or spaceman or whatever he was couldn't understand them. As it became clear that he wasn't Russian, the wonder turned to suspicion and fear. One of the villagers saw a holster with a pistol and, on the parachute harness, what seemed to him like a Finnish hunting knife. Another saw another parachute, this one red and white, descending from even higher up in the sky. Using sign language, the villagers asked the soldier, "How many are you?" The alien put up one finger. This brought some relief. But the villagers decided to act before the authorities arrived. The man was pushed into the back of a car, a two-cylinder Moskvich, and driven over to the house of Berman's driver, who could take the stranger in the collective farm's service car to see the boss at headquarters.[3]

Captain Pankov and Lieutenant Ananyev were already at the headquarters of the collective farm when the stranger arrived. A nurse took a look at the man. He had a slight abrasion on his right leg, but aside from an elevated pulse, he seemed normal. Then the KGB took over. Pankov and Ananyev had no experience interrogating strange parachutists. But there was a procedure for this, as there was for almost everything in the KGB. The villagers had brought along the man's helmet and overalls. The helmet had radio gear installed, so the man must have been a pilot of sorts. Oddly the overalls told more. Stitched into the side was a leaflet topped by an American flag and an inscription in several languages, including Russian: "I am an American and do not speak your language. I need food, shelter, assistance. I will not harm you. I bear no malice toward your people. If you help me, you will be rewarded."[4] Once they filled out all the paperwork on the American pilot, the KGB men had to take this fellow to Sverdlovsk, the nearest city where there was a major KGB center with an English-speaking interpreter.

In Sverdlovsk, Francis Gary Powers finally met someone who could speak at least broken English. He gave his name as he was required to do, as if he were a prisoner of war. The KGB interpreter was fascinated by a pin that he had found in the one of the pockets of the overalls that the villagers had taken from Powers. "What is this needle for?" "It is an ordinary needle, used for ordinary things." The Geneva Convention said nothing about describing suicide devices.

▪

KHRUSHCHEV DID NOT yet know who Francis Gary Powers was, but the illegal flight of his U-2 spy plane over the USSR had been on the Soviet leader's mind from the moment he awoke on May Day. Ordinarily the first secretary's family accompanied him to Red Square for the traditional parade, but this year the routine had been broken by a telephone call from Malinovsky at 5:00 A.M.[5] The Soviet defense minister told Khrushchev that less than half an hour earlier a foreign plane had been detected crossing north into Soviet territory from Afghanistan. Having been severely reprimanded by the Presidium for not shooting down the U-2 that had violated Soviet airspace on April 9, Malinovsky was determined that this U.S. spy plane would not get away. He ordered a halt on all civil air traffic over most of the Soviet Union to facilitate the pursuit.[6]

Khrushchev tried to conceal the developing story from his family, telling them only that he would have to leave first for the Kremlin, and they were to follow later in another car. Subdued and preoccupied, he ate his breakfast without saying a word. His son, Sergei, knew not to ask what the matter was: "A great deal could happen in our vast country that we were not supposed to know at home."[7] But Khrushchev could not hold the secret long. Walking to his car with Sergei, he said, "They flew over again." "How many?" his son asked. "Like before—one. It's flying at a great height. This time it was detected at the border, at the same place."[8]

From the initial reports, Khrushchev knew that the U-2 was already near Tyuratam, the site of three of the country's now five ICBM launchpads. When asked by his son before leaving the residence whether the Soviet air defense command would catch this intruder, Khrushchev did not show his customary optimism. What he found so infuriating was how well, and how easily, the American spy planes revealed the weaknesses in Soviet defenses. "[The Soviet military chiefs] claim that they'll shoot it down—unless they miss," Khrushchev replied. "You know perfectly well that we have only a few T-3s [high-altitude interceptor jets] there and that missiles have a small operational radius at that altitude. It's all up to chance."[9]

As Khrushchev's limousine sped off to the Kremlin, it seemed as if the Soviet military would confirm his pessimism. Because of the national holiday, there weren't many T-3s available to scramble, and some of the Soviet air defense missile sites that Powers passed on his way north were not even manned. But around Sverdlovsk Powers flew over two battalions armed with the Soviet Union's new S-75 surface-to-air missile (SAM).

Soviet commanders ordered the first battalion to fire on the intruder. Two missiles jammed while being launched, but one was fired successfully. Exploding just behind the U-2, it caused the fragile plane to break apart. In the confusion, the second SAM battalion also fired a salvo, hitting one of the MiG-19s pursuing the U-2 at a lower altitude and causing the death of a Soviet pilot. It was the red and white parachute of that mortally wounded airman that Powers and the townspeople of Povarnia had seen in the sky.

Khrushchev was already standing on the balcony of Lenin's Tomb reviewing the colorful waves of May Day celebrants when he received news of the capture of the American pilot. The commander of Soviet air defenses, carried by the newfound pride of his service, rushed to the platform. Marshal Sergei Biryuzov was still dressed in his combat uniform, rather than the full-dress uniform he would have worn for the May Day celebration. This breach in protocol caused a minor stir in the Kremlin family section behind the dais, where the Soviet elite strained to read meaning into Biryuzov's unusual appearance.[10]

Khrushchev was delighted to hear that this time the American intruder had not gotten away. Immediate instructions were sent to Sverdlovsk to bring the pilot to Moscow. The chairman of the KGB, Aleksandr Shelepin, and the procurator general of the USSR, R. A. Rudenko, who had represented the Soviet Union at the Nuremberg war crimes trial, were to conduct the interrogation themselves. Powers was to be held and questioned at the dreaded Lubyanka, the KGB's headquarters just north of Red Square.

▪

"BILL BAILEY didn't come home." Richard Bissell, the CIA's deputy director for plans, had dreaded ever hearing those words, agency code for a missing U-2. At least, Bissell believed, he did not have to worry that the Soviets would learn very much from this mishap. The skin of the U-2 was so fragile, and it was flying at so high an altitude, that the plane and its pilot would have been destroyed if the plane had gone down. As he had told President Eisenhower, the odds were one in a million that the pilot could survive the event.[11] However, it was a shame to lose Powers. In four years with CIA he had flown more U-2 flights over the Soviet Union than any other pilot.

There was a plan on the shelf to deal with a failed mission. Four years earlier Bissell had developed the false story to be put out if a U-2 were ever lost over hostile territory. The National Advisory Committee for Aeronautics (reorganized as the National Air and Space Administration [NASA] in 1958) would issue a public statement that it had lost contact with a U-2 conducting high-altitude weather research. At the time Bissell proposed this cover story, two of President Eisenhower's closest scientific advisers—Edwin Land, the owner of Polaroid, and James Killian, the president of the Massachusetts Institute of Technology—had raised objections. In their view it would be better for the United States to own up immediately to this high-level espionage as a regrettable requirement of the Cold War. The White House, however, accepted Bissell's plan, which by 1960 had become standard operating procedure.[12]

The plan was silent on what to do if the pilot survived. This was a curious oversight because U-2 pilots had survived crashes during training. In December 1956 a U-2 pilot suffering from high-altitude sickness had flown his plane too fast, causing it to disintegrate at a very high altitude over a test ground in Arizona. The pilot managed to eject the plane's canopy and was sucked out of the cockpit at twenty-eight thousand feet. He parachuted to safety.[13] There were other stories of pilots surviving malfunctions, but none had been shot down. Perhaps the oversight also reflected an assumption that no U-2 pilot would allow himself to be caught alive.

Eisenhower learned of the plane's disappearance on the afternoon of May 1. He was at Camp David and received the news by telephone. The president was told simply that the U-2 was overdue. More than anyone in his administration, he dreaded hearing this kind of news. He felt completely responsible for the U-2 flights. He approved each individually, and he had never found the decision easy to make. Twice he had imposed moratoriums on these flights because of his concerns that they were too provocative. Now he faced a potential failure just before the long-awaited superpower summit. It would be hard to imagine a more inopportune moment.

Even though it was possible the plane had gone down, Eisenhower had reason to hope the Soviets would not be able to learn much about the mission. He had been assured that the fragility of the U-2, which was really more of a glider than an airplane, made it impossible that the pilot and the sensitive equipment aboard would survive impact. "This was a cruel assumption," Eisenhower later acknowledged, "but I was assured that the young pilots undertaking these missions were doing so with their eyes wide open and motivated by a high degree of patriotism, a swashbuckling bravado, and certain material inducements."[14]

▪

Detailed interrogation of Francis Gary Powers began immediately after his arrival in Moscow on May 1. The prisoner was led from his cell into a large room with a long table.[15] There were about twelve people there, though only two mattered. The setting was stark and forbidding, but Powers at least could be thankful that his questioners abstained from any kind of torture, including the nonlethal but nevertheless annoying tactic of shining a bright light into a prisoner's eyes. The KGB report on his first interrogation concluded that he had "answered all questions." The authors of this book are the first scholars to have had access to the official Soviet interrogations of Powers. In fact Powers said very little of consequence and nothing proscribed by the CIA's policy for captured pilots. He had been instructed in training that were he to be captured he was "perfectly free to tell the full truth about their mission with the exception of certain specifications of the aircraft."[16] True to these guidelines, Powers admitted he was a civilian working for the CIA but concealed from his captors the cruising altitude of the U-2, the number of times he had overflown Soviet territory, and the names of his superiors at the CIA. The needle was one thing he was prepared to talk about. He now admitted that it was indeed unusual. "It contains a very active poison. A prick from this needle brings instant death," he told his interrogators. Powers added that this was specially given to him "in the event of atrocities or torture, but he was never to use it on anybody but himself."[17] He was being truthful. Indeed, pilots had the right not to bring the suicide device on their mission, and they were told that the use of it, under any circumstances, was optional.[18] Powers decided to break his silence on the needle because his situation was already bad enough without accidentally causing a death in the KGB.[19]

The hard questioning began two days later, on May 3.[20] The KGB chief, Shelepin, asked Powers how he had been able to maintain radio contact from a high altitude. The question bothered Powers. As he well knew, the U-2s were outfitted with radios, but the pilots had strict instructions on when to use them. When the pilots reached cruising altitude and were about to enter enemy airspace, they were expected to click their radio switch to signal that the mission was a go. Then they were to maintain absolute radio silence until they landed at a friendly base.[21] Powers had followed procedure on May 1. He had maintained radio silence even during those harrowing moments after he heard the explosion near his plane.

Powers feared that if he answered the question honestly, it would lead to other questions that might enable the Soviets to figure out that the U.S. government had no evidence that he had survived the attack on his aircraft. Powers believed that the Soviets would be much less likely to kill him if the Kremlin assumed that Washington thought he was still alive. For the first time since his ordeal began, Powers dropped the façade of cooperation. "I don't believe I can answer that question," he said, "it would not be in my self-interest."

The interrogators pushed him. "But it is in your interest to answer it."

Powers still refused to answer, but he perceived an advantage to exploit in his interrogators' interest in the radio question. Perhaps he could use this issue to force the Soviets to announce publicly that he was alive, thereby ensuring he could not be held indefinitely or killed without international knowledge. "My mother is very sick," Powers replied. "If I do not answer the question, your government might report in the press that I am still alive, and this would be very welcome to me."

Powers's performance worked. Shelepin and Rudenko were now convinced that the American pilot was indeed hiding something important. Powers's U-2 had initially zigzagged away from one of the SAM sites protecting Sverdlovsk, and the Soviets suspected that the CIA had been able to warn him about this site in flight. Shelepin and Rudenko pressed Powers for more details: "When would you answer this question?"

Powers stalled, deciding to hold off on any further discussions about deals. "I don't know . . . ," he replied. "It seems to me that it would be more to my advantage not to answer than to answer this question."

The KGB chief and the chief prosecutor were perplexed by his stubbornness. "We insist that you answer this question," they said. If a deal was not possible, then he might yet be bullied into talking. "If you don't answer then it is not only not in your interest but it would be damaging to you." Powers would not give up. "I would prefer not to answer," he said.

Powers's display of nerve in the Lubyanka coincided with the release of the prearranged cover story in Washington. On May 3, NASA issued a statement that a joint NASA-USAF Air Weather Service mission had apparently gone down in the Lake Van area of Turkey. "During the flight in eastern Turkey," said the release, "the pilot reported over the emergency frequency that he was experiencing oxygen difficulties."[22] The deception was transparent to the Soviet authorities, but it was to have a side effect never imagined by the CIA's Bissell. The reference to an "emergency frequency" increased the KGB's impatience at getting the captured U.S. pilot to divulge what he knew about the U-2's communications capabilities.

■

For all the satisfaction at Powers's capture, this unwanted American guest had arrived at an awkward time for Khrushchev. Within two weeks the Soviet leader was expected to travel to Paris for the long-awaited summit of the four powers that had defeated Nazi Germany in 1945: the USSR, the United States, Great Britain, and France. Since his January announcement of unilateral cuts in the Soviet military, Khrushchev had tried to choreograph his moves with maximum effect on this upcoming summit meeting, having made a trip to France in the spring to involve Charles de Gaulle in a plan to get NATO to accept limits on nuclear delivery vehicles.

At home Khrushchev was already busy maneuvering to consolidate support for his ambitious domestic and foreign agenda. The Supreme Soviet, where Soviet leaders traditionally gave something akin to a state of the Soviet Union speech, was due to meet in the first week of May. For months the Central Committee had been preparing the presentation of the next phase in Khrushchev's push to improve the Soviet standard of living. Khrushchev was now prepared to risk some of the measures that Presidium members Mikoyan and Furtseva had argued for unsuccessfully in 1958. He would announce a cut in the workweek from forty-eight hours to forty-two hours. Spending on consumer goods by the government would increase. At the same time, the Soviet state would "abolish" income taxes, though an increase in payroll taxes would weaken the effect of this tax cut.[23] This was the domestic complement to his international détente policy. If he could reach some kind of general settlement with the United States to demilitarize the Cold War, then he could afford to reorder spending priorities at home.

In recent weeks support for his policy of unilateral disarmament had eroded somewhat. While he was in France in late March and early April, the Kremlin received an anonymous letter, apparently from a Soviet military commander, that criticized the January troop cuts.[24] Khrushchev, who could have just as easily buried the letter, instead took it as a potentially dangerous sign of rumblings in the Soviet officer corps. He opted to deal directly with this infection of dissent before it spread. At the very first Presidium session after his return on April 3, Khrushchev had the letter read aloud.[25] Then he defiantly attacked the political education of Soviet military commanders, who by their dissent were showing insufficient loyalty to the leadership of the Communist Party. He ordered that this education be improved and that the government consider setting up a reporting system to monitor what commanders were saying.

The anonymous letter had at least one fan in the top leadership of the Kremlin, Marshal Voroshilov, who insisted on showing his sympathy for military critics of Khrushchev's efforts to cut defense spending.[26] "Is it correct for us to reduce allotments for the construction of [civil air] shelters?" Voroshilov had asked at a Presidium meeting in late April in defiance of Khrushchev's proposed defense budget. This comment had been reported to Khrushchev, who had been absent from the meeting.[27]

■

THE NEWS ABOUT Powers did not initially provoke Khrushchev to alter his strategy for the Paris summit. The Soviet leader still clung to an almost mystical belief in Eisenhower's personal desire for peace. At a New Year's Eve party a few months after his return from the United States, Khrushchev told the U.S. ambassador, "If only [Eisenhower] could serve another term, he was sure that our problems could be solved."[28] Khrushchev perceived the American president as being nearly alone among his advisers in this regard. Until the death of Foster Dulles in May 1959, Khrushchev had held out little hope that the genial Eisenhower would get his way. Now that the president seemed to have the upper hand in Washington, Khrushchev believed that the hard-liners around Eisenhower were doing whatever they could to derail the summit. He also suspected that Allen Dulles, the director of central intelligence, had intentionally ordered the U-2 mission to disrupt the improvement of relations between Eisenhower and him. The Soviet leader was not about to give the American spy chief the satisfaction of letting that happen.

Khrushchev's concerns about the importance of Eisenhower's personal engagement in the summit extended to the composition of the U.S. delegation. In April the president had alerted Khrushchev that were the conference to last more than a week, he would have to leave for Lisbon to honor a previous commitment to the prime minister of Portugal. In his place the delegation would be headed by Richard Nixon. Khrushchev disliked Nixon, whom he associated with Foster Dulles's approach to the Cold War. Khrushchev believed that somehow the United States would define its interests differently if Nixon rather than Eisenhower was heading the delegation. Khrushchev assured the French that he did not intend to hang around Paris to negotiate with the U.S. vice president. "I don't respect Nixon," he told the French ambassador in Moscow.[29]

Khrushchev convinced himself that he could exploit the U-2 incident to strengthen Eisenhower's hand against the hawks around him. On April 28 he had used the occasion of a speech in Baku celebrating forty years of Soviet rule in Azerbaijan to warn the world that recent U.S. actions were complicating preparations for the summit. With the American pilot Powers in Soviet custody, he now had even better proof of the Eisenhower administration's apparent schizophrenia. Khrushchev planned to reveal enough about the U-2 mission to embarrass hard-line American cold warriors without pushing the president so far as to endanger the summit.

As the interrogations of Powers began at Lubyanka Prison, Khrushchev decided that the French, his future hosts, should be the first Westerners to get an inkling of his new worries about Washington. Meeting with the French ambassador, Maurice Dejean, on May 3, the same day as the U.S. announcement of the lost weather mission, Khrushchev warned the ambassador that "he had real reason to doubt the desire of some of the leaders to find a solution to the problems under discussion."[30] He did not reveal that reason but used the conversation to outline his concerns about the machinations of those in the United States who did not want to pursue détente. In a message dated April 30, de Gaulle had suggested that perhaps some of the meetings in Paris should be held behind closed doors.[31] At the meeting with the French ambassador, Khrushchev couched his rejection of secret sessions in terms of not wishing to give Western hawks any opportunity to ruin the summit. Secret discussions, he believed, would shield the opponents of détente from international public opinion. Thus, he concluded, the summit "could be reduced to zero."

Khrushchev also mentioned to the French that he would be sharing his assessment of the international situation with the party leadership during the session of the Supreme Soviet scheduled to open on May 5. "My report will establish, in an incontestable manner, that there are people who do not wish a détente and who instead are seeking a return to the cold war." He added: "At this moment, I cannot reveal the evidence I am talking about."

Two days later, as Khrushchev had told the French he would, he released some of the evidence to the Supreme Soviet. In the midst of a three-and-one-half-hour speech outlining his domestic reform package, he reported that on May 1 a U.S. plane on a mission of "aggressive provocation aimed at wrecking the summit conference" had violated Soviet airspace and been shot down.[32] Observing that this action was only the latest sign that the "imperialists and militarists" around Eisenhower were gaining strength, Khrushchev expressed his confidence that the president still wanted the upcoming negotiations to succeed though he faced a tough task in controlling his own administration. The Soviet leader singled out the new American secretary of state, Christian Herter, Assistant Secretary of State C. Douglas Dillon, and Vice President

Nixon as representatives of the harder line. He referred to the possibility that Nixon might replace Eisenhower at the Paris talks as "leav[ing] the cabbage to the care of the goat."[33] Saying that disarmament and a "peaceful settlement with Germany, including the question of West Berlin," were the "vital problems of the day," Khrushchev indicated that he still intended to go to Paris, though he held out less hope that anything would be accomplished there.

Khrushchev spoke from a position of strength. The day before, the Presidium had approved a series of leadership changes that he had designed to increase his influence in that body.[34] Brezhnev was chosen to replace Marshal Voroshilov as Soviet president, a purely ceremonial post, but one that Brezhnev later used to acquire his own power. Voroshilov was to be removed from the Presidium in July. Khrushchev also removed two former protégés, Nikolai Belyaev and Aleksei Kirichenko, from the Presidium. He blamed Belyaev for recent agricultural failures in the "virgin lands" of Kazakhstan. Kirichenko's reappointment to the Soviet embassy in Czechoslovakia had been arranged a few weeks earlier, but any hope that he could retain a seat on the Presidium was dashed. Meanwhile Khrushchev added three new allies as full members of the Presidium: Aleksei Kosygin, Nikolai Podgorny, and Dmitri Polyansky.

In his speech to the Supreme Soviet, Khrushchev never mentioned Francis Gary Powers. In fact he said nothing about the fate of the pilot of the downed American plane. For the moment Khrushchev preferred to let Washington tangle itself in its own lies.

■

THE FIRST LEAK to Washington that Powers might be alive came from a most unlikely source. Jakob Malik was a veteran Soviet diplomat who was as uninformative to foreign diplomats as he was trustworthy to the Kremlin. But perhaps drink or age got to him at a reception at the Ethiopian Embassy that followed Khrushchev's Supreme Soviet speech. In response to a question from the Swedish ambassador about the fate of the pilot, Malik responded, "I don't know exactly. He is being questioned." No one as yet suspected the American pilot was alive. Malik realized his mistake immediately and tried to explain away his gaffe. In reporting this incident to the Soviet Foreign Ministry later in the day, he explained that there was little reason for anxiety that the Swedish ambassador would tell the Americans. "He is neutral, after all."[35]

U.S. Ambassador Llewellyn "Tommy" Thompson, who had been within earshot of the conversation at the reception, did not need the Swede to give him a special report. At 7:00 P.M., Moscow time, he cabled the first intelligence the administration had that Powers was still alive. Thompson was not 100 percent sure—he could not have been—that Malik was telling the truth. In his dispatch home he mentioned the "possibility" that Powers was alive.[36]

A few hours before the cable arrived, Eisenhower had convened the National Security Council to discuss how to maintain the cover-up. The talk at the NSC was about what Khrushchev had said in his speech on the plane's having been shot down. No one as yet was prepared to contemplate that the pilot or any incriminating piece of the plane could have survived.[37]

Eisenhower's instincts were to stick with the NASA cover story and not say any more. Secretary of State Herter and his other advisers pressed him to authorize a new statement that would show that the United States—despite Khrushchev's bluster—stuck by its original (and false) explanation. "I accepted the recommendations of my associates," Eisenhower later recalled, and the United States headed further along the murky road of international deceit.[38] Officials at the State Department announced that the president had authorized an "inquiry" to determine how this plane managed to violate Soviet airspace. The department also stated that the plane mentioned by Khrushchev might be the NASA science plane whose "pilot reported difficulty with his oxygen equipment. It is entirely possible," the statement added, "that having failure in the oxygen equipment, which could result in the pilot losing consciousness, the plane continued on automatic pilot for a considerable distance and accidentally violated Soviet airspace."[39]

After Thompson's cable entered the bureaucratic bloodstream in the afternoon, the administration still had a hard time believing that Powers could have survived this crash. Nevertheless, the State Department reflexively prepared a diplomatic note requesting information on Powers's condition. It was to delivered to the Soviets the next day.

▪

POWERS KNEW NOTHING of the drama in Washington. In Moscow his interrogations continued, eleven hours a day, every day. Shelepin returned on May 6 to put more pressure on Powers. By reiterating in its May 5 statement that a U.S. pilot had reported oxygen difficulties, the State Department had unknowingly hardened the KGB's belief that the U-2 pilot must have maintained contact with his base. Once again Shelepin put the question to him. Again Powers refused to answer. "Your silence does not help your situation," the KGB chief responded.[40]

As he had the very first time he had been asked about the U-2's radio capabilities, Powers brought up the medical condition of his mother, who he was sure would be saved by news that her son was still alive. This time Shelepin decided to make a direct offer to him: "If you honestly answer this question, then you will be given the chance to write your mother a letter." Powers refused to give up what he believed was the last card that he had to play: "Give me the chance to write my mother a letter and to receive an answer and I will answer all of your questions."[41]

■

THE OFFICIAL "INQUIRY" from the State Department about Powers's condition and word from insiders of Jakob Malik's mistake prompted Khrushchev to reveal finally that Powers was alive and under arrest. At the closing session of the Supreme Soviet on May 7 he told his audience and the world what had actually been found in Sverdlovsk on May Day, squeezing every ounce of drama out of the story. To a chorus of "shame, shame," Khrushchev unfurled photographs alleged to be from the film in Powers's cameras. To a chorus of "bandits, bandits," he produced the needle that had been dipped in poison for the U-2 pilot to commit suicide. In describing the foreign currency and gold that Powers had carried along on his flight to bribe his way home, Khrushchev made fun of the CIA's precautions: "Why was all this necessary in the upper layers of the atmosphere?" He had an answer: "Or maybe, the pilot was to have flown still higher to Mars and was going to lead astray Martian ladies?"[42]

■

NEWS THAT POWERS was alive stunned Washington. Eisenhower was both surprised and angry. Khrushchev had mentioned many details in his speech about the U-2 program, especially the highly classified detail that flights actually took off from a secret airfield in Pakistan and not from Turkey. Eisenhower assumed Powers had "started talking as soon as he hit the ground."[43]

Commenting on Khrushchev's revelation, the U.S. ambassador in Moscow advocated admitting to the act of espionage without suggesting that the president had personally authorized the mission. "This would preserve for us," Thompson argued, "[the] great asset we have in the regard which Soviet and other people have for [the] President."[44]

Initially Washington took Ambassador Thompson's advice. In response to this latest Khrushchev performance, the administration formally acknowledged that the U-2 had been on an intelligence mission but that the mission was unauthorized: "As a result of the inquiry ordered by the President, it has been established that insofar as the authorities are concerned, there was no authorization for any such flights as described by Khrushchev." As the administration had hoped, the world press reported this statement as if President Eisenhower himself had not authorized intelligence missions over the Soviet Union, thus giving the impression that the CIA had acted alone, as some kind of rogue element in the federal government.[45]

Washington's allies reacted with grave concern about the effect of this incident on the forthcoming summit. Publicly the British and French leaders showed support for the American president. Privately they castigated him. "The Americans have created a great folly," Prime Minister Macmillan confessed to his diary. The British leader had very good reason to be annoyed. The Paris summit had been his idea. He believed in the power of face-to-face meetings to shape high politics in a positive manner. He was also no stranger to the problem of balancing espionage and diplomacy. The British, who received U.S. spy planes on loan, were participants in the top secret USSR overflight program. Macmillan had suspended these flights weeks before the summit and had been told that the Americans would do the same.[46]

Macmillan wanted to minimize the consequences of the American mistake. He sent word to Eisenhower that Washington should take a leaf from the British book in such matters. In the meantime the British government steadfastly refused to acknowledge any intelligence activities. In fact the country's foreign intelligence service, the Secret Intelligence Service (SIS), had no formal legislative existence. Macmillan wanted Eisenhower to say nothing.

The president was unhappy with the way his administration's official explanation of the U-2 affair was developing. He disliked the implications of what his ambassador in Moscow and the British prime minister were suggesting. How could he let the world think that U.S. airplanes could violate Soviet airspace, an act of war, without higher authorization? In the nuclear era, when millions of people could be destroyed by solitary planes carrying hydrogen bombs, an unauthorized flight was inexcusable.

He ordered the State Department to correct the record. On May 9 Secretary of State Herter retracted the earlier characterization of the flight as unauthorized. In its place, the secretary announced that such flights, while violations of international law, were necessary in the real world of Cold War politics. The administration's new position was that the president had authorized the U-2 operations in general, though not this flight in particular. The Soviets had refused to accept President Eisenhower's Open Skies proposal in 1955 and so had reaped the U-2 program as one of the consequences. Herter made no mention of the role of U.S. public opinion in pressing a reluctant

Eisenhower to pursue the U-2 overflights so dangerously close to the summit. Both the international press and the Soviets interpreted Herter's statement to mean that the United States was determined to continue its policy of overflights of Soviet territory.

■

THE KGB'S EFFORTS to break Powers continued in spite of Khrushchev's dramatic announcement. To keep the pressure on him, the pilot was not told that the world knew he was alive. But after two more days of Powers's repeating that he would not discuss the U-2's radio capabilities unless he was in open court or had received evidence that his parents knew he was alive, Shelepin concluded he would have to switch tactics. On May 10 Powers was shown the front pages of *Izvestia* and the *New York Times* of May 8, which had reported on Khrushchev's statement that the U.S. pilot had survived the crash. The interpreter read from *Izvestia* Khrushchev's comment: "We also have the pilot, who is alive and kicking." He read as well from some regional U.S. newspapers, one of which quoted Powers's father saying, "I'm going to appeal to Mr. Khrushchev personally to be fair to my boy. As one coal miner to another, I'm sure he'll listen to me." This broke the tension in the room. Hearing his father's voice in those words, Powers began to cry.[47]

Powers then said he was ready to answer the one question that had obsessed his captors since the beginning of this ordeal. Although he still had no intention of telling the whole story to the KGB, he now thought he could risk a useful half-truth because there would be an international scandal if the KGB killed him during the interrogation. "There were no radio communications of any kind from the moment of my takeoff to the moment when I was shot down," he said, carefully covering up the radio signaling all U-2 pilots did before entering Soviet airspace. "I was capable of contacting my base only a half hour before landing," he added. "In fact, the radio on the U-2 had only a 400 to 500 mile range." The range of the radio on the U-2 was actually much greater, the reason why radio silence had to be maintained, but the Soviets did not need to know that.

"You didn't radio in when you were shot down?" Shelepin responded incredulously.

"I didn't even have the opportunity to send any kind of signal," replied Powers.

"Why didn't you tell us this earlier?" asked the KGB chief.

"If you knew that I did not have any contact with my base and that the people of my service did not know what had happened to me," Powers explained coolly, "then you would probably not have published that I was alive and what had happened to me."

This truthful response evoked unexpected candor from the KGB chief. "The issue is not with you," said Shelepin. "The matter is that the USA committed an aggressive act." He then explained that he believed Powers's flight was a deliberate provocation to scuttle the summit due to begin in only a few days. "Why else were you sent?" asked Shelepin.

Powers's response was curt and patriotic. "I don't know why I was sent. There must have been good reasons." He then proceeded to offer the same rationale that President Eisenhower later gave in his first public defense of the flight. Powers recalled that he had once read in the newspaper that there were fears that the Soviet Union was planning to attack the United States. When his interrogators explained that it was difficult to differentiate between an intruder on a spy mission and one on a bombing run carrying thermonuclear weapons, Powers explained that he refused to accept that his government was taking unnecessary risks. It needed this intelligence.

■

In spite of Secretary Herter's statement, Khrushchev continued to believe that the U-2 flight had been orchestrated by one of Eisenhower's opponents in Washington. He might have thought differently if he had heard Eisenhower himself admit to sending the spy plane, but since that hadn't happened, Khrushchev intended to go ahead with his policy of demilitarizing the Cold War in 1960. Preparations continued for the long-awaited official visit of Soviet air chief, Marshal Konstantin Vershinin, to the United States. Vershinin was due to leave on May 14 for Washington, where he would be the guest of the Pentagon. In the same spirit Khrushchev let the Foreign Ministry proceed with its preparations for the Paris summit. He made no effort to redraft any of the summit proposals that had been under review since early April.

Khrushchev was beginning to wonder, however, whether he had selected the right partner in Eisenhower. His uncertainty about the degree of the president's complicity in the U-2 flight was on display two days later, when he and Marshal Biryuzov went to view the wreckage of the U-2 plane, which the Soviets had put on public view in Gorky Park. To the journalists at the park, Khrushchev lamented the difficult pressures on the well-meaning American president from the hard-liners around him. He singled out Secretary of State Herter for attack: "Far from feeling guilty and ashamed of aggressive actions, he justifies them and says they will continue into the future."[48] But for the first time Khrushchev was clearly finding it difficult to hold to his policy of not attacking Eisenhower personally for the outrage. "I was horrified to learn that the President had endorsed the acts," he said in response to a question about whether the State Department's May 9 statement had affected his opinion of Eisenhower. He still spoke of the importance of a successful summit and alluded to a future Eisenhower visit to the USSR, but a new tentativeness had crept into his words. "I am a human being and I have human feelings. I had hopes and they were betrayed . . . you must understand that we Russians always go whole hog: when we play, we play and when we fight, we fight."[49]

The Presidium gathered the next day, May 12, to place its official stamp on the instructions and proposals that Khrushchev and the Soviet delegation were to take with them to Paris. No stenographic account from that meeting seems to exist. Later there were rumors that the Presidium was split over whether Khrushchev should go.[50] But Mikoyan did not recall this as an episode in the story of Khrushchev's struggle with the Foreign Ministry, and it was not cited in the bill of particulars against him when he was overthrown in October 1964.[51] Instead what is known is that the Presidium endorsed the entire package of proposals and draft negotiating instructions that Gromyko's team had been preparing for over a month.[52]

Indeed, Khrushchev was authorized to show flexibility on general housekeeping matters in Paris. If his Western counterparts refused to commit to a negotiating agenda, he was to let this pass. The goal was to foster a discussion with the powerful people who made decisions for the West. With regard to the U.S. delegation, the instructions had both sweet and sour elements for Eisenhower. Khrushchev was to remind the president of the fruitful discussions they had during his visit to America: "Negotiations between the USA and the USSR," he was supposed to say, "have exerted very good influence on the international situation and, as hoped by the Soviet Union, could lead to a very good start in the direction of the establishment of general relations and cooperation between our countries."

Khrushchev would have one demand for the Americans: The Kremlin expected the United States to undertake measures to stop all future intrusions into Soviet airspace. "The Soviet people hope not only to live in peace, but in friendship with the American people."[53] Ending the U-2 flights was a prerequisite.

While clearly the product of a sincere effort to achieve a successful summit, the instructions on Berlin displayed a crude understanding of how to achieve results at a summit. In discussing how to handle these proposals in Paris, the Presidium did not provide for any fallback positions. Instead it decided that the negotiations on this point "should be conducted in such a way to leave no doubt among the Western powers in the Soviet Union's deter-mination to complete a German peace treaty in order to liquidate the rem-nants of the past war, in particular the occupational regime in West Berlin."[54] The West would be offered the two-year interim agreement. As Khrushchev and the Foreign Ministry envisioned it, the interim agreement would not be a device to permit four-power negotiations in a calmer environment but merely a two-year postponement of what Khrushchev had hoped to achieve by fiat in 1958.

On disarmament, the Soviets had something more to offer. They were going to push hard for the dismantling of nuclear delivery devices in the first phase of general and complete disarmament. On the issue of inspections, Khrushchev was open to some form of on-site verification by foreign observers of the destruction of ICBMs and intercontinental bombers. Although the proposals were still very vague, they were less likely to be dis-missed out of hand by the Western powers. Something might indeed come out of them.

■

In THE DAYS before he left for Paris, Eisenhower had some idea of what Khrushchev might propose at the summit. The United States had known since early April to expect that the Soviet leader might use the meeting to spell out what he had meant by an interim Berlin agreement in his conversa-tions with de Gaulle. After the Soviets submitted their final proposals to the French on May 9, they had been translated into English for the president.[55] The French had also briefed their NATO allies on the Soviet interest in the French proposal for eliminating the means of delivering nuclear weapons. At NATO meetings in late April and early May the Western powers had dis-cussed what this arrangement might mean in practice. Of all the participants, the American delegation was most hostile to the idea. Secretary of State Herter called the French interest in this proposal "embarrassing to the West" and believed that the Soviets would find a way to cheat, rendering the whole concept of mutual disarmament very risky without an elaborate international inspection body.[56]

Eisenhower was neither optimistic nor pessimistic about what could be achieved in Paris. He was not as dismissive of nuclear disarmament as his new secretary of state, but he planned to continue to insist on verification and wondered if Khrushchev would ever go along. On Berlin, Eisenhower saw lit-tle room for negotiations. He just wanted the Soviets to accept the status quo. Change might be possible around the edges, perhaps involving a reduction in strength of allied contingents in West Berlin. With his approval, the State Department had started speaking of German self-determination instead of German reunification. In other words, if the Soviets thought that a change was required in the Germanys, then there should be an all-German vote or at least an all-Berlin vote. The United States was convinced that in either case the German people would vote for liberal capitalism, not Marxism-Leninism.

The U-2 affair distracted Eisenhower from his preparations for the summit. Instead of calmly weighing the arguments that he was receiving from the British and his own Soviet expert in Moscow about how to handle Khrushchev, he was preoccupied with reestablishing his leadership over national security. In his memoirs the president argued that he believed he had an obligation to take responsibility for this act. "To deny my part in the entire affair," he argued, "would have been a declaration that portions of the government of the United States were operating irresponsibly, in complete disregard of proper presidential control."[57] As supreme allied commander during World War II Eisenhower had made some difficult and controversial decisions. He had never shirked responsibility for deciding whether to proceed with the Normandy landings, to give gasoline to General George Patton's Third Army, or to try to beat the Russians in a race to Berlin.

On May 11 Eisenhower used a press conference to remove any doubt that he had authorized the Powers mission. Press conferences were difficult for this president. He never seemed able to get through one without getting tangled in his own syntax. Sometimes he did it intentionally. Before a press conference in 1955, Eisenhower had assured his press secretary, James Hagerty, "Don't worry, Jim . . . I'll just confuse them."[58] Sometimes the slipups were unintentional. Now, on May 11, Eisenhower spoke unusually clearly. "No one wants another Pearl Harbor," he said. Because of the secrecy in Khrushchev's Soviet Union, the United States had to resort to espionage. It was a "distasteful but vital necessity."[59] Otherwise how could the United States keep track of those military forces that are "capable of massive surprise attacks"? Eisenhower wanted to reduce secrecy in international affairs because he knew how incompatible it was to security. For this reason he had made his Open Skies proposal in Geneva in 1955 and planned to renew that offer to Khrushchev in Paris. In the meantime he was not about to be apologetic about the need for espionage.

Ten years later, as a pensioner, Khrushchev recalled how angry he had become when he learned that the White House had refused to stick with its denial of responsibility for authorizing Powers's mission. "A long as President Eisenhower was dissociated from the U-2 affair," Khrushchev recalled, "we could continue our policy of strengthening Soviet-US relations, which had begun with my trip to America and my talks with Eisenhower."[60] The president made that impossible at his May 11 press conference.

Eisenhower's statement put Khrushchev in a corner. Building up the prestige of the Soviet Union—in other words, U.S. respect for its power—was as essential to his program of constructing socialism as achieving détente in Europe and trade with the West. Yet the U.S. president's words suddenly made superpower détente and Soviet prestige appear to be irreconcilable concepts. "Here was the President of the United States," Khrushchev recollected later, "the man whom we were supposed to negotiate with at the meeting in Paris, defending outrageous, inadmissible actions!"

■

KHRUSHCHEV MAY HAVE learned of Eisenhower's statement before the Presidium meeting that approved his instructions on May 12, but he didn't allow it to alter his careful strategy for the summit. The first sign of the explosion to come was the announcement the next day that Marshal Vershinin would be postponing his trip to the United States. But it was not until May 14, the very day he was supposed to go to Paris, that Khrushchev revealed to his colleagues how upset Eisenhower's embrace of the U-2 incident had made him.

At Vnukovo Airport, Khrushchev hastily assembled Malinovsky and Gromyko for an impromptu discussion with Presidium members who had come to see the delegation off. Khrushchev's foreign policy aide, Oleg Troyanovsky, recalled that this took place in a glass-enclosed VIP lounge not far from the plane.[61] Once aboard the Il-18 for the flight to Paris, Khrushchev announced that he had effectively thrown away his prepared script. With his aides huddling around him, he said that he wanted his speech for the next day rewritten. His staff would have to prepare it quickly once they arrived in Paris, so that it could be sent back to Moscow for formal approval by the rest of the Presidium.[62] Khrushchev would insist on an apology from the United States as the price for his participation in the summit. If he didn't get it, the Soviet delegation would leave Paris without divulging any of its proposals on disarmament or Berlin.

In Paris the delegation moved into the Soviet Embassy. The group was in a mild panic. The new speech needed to be completed and approved in a hurry and then translated into French and English. Gromyko's deputy moaned to those who had time to listen, "What a situation, what a situation."[63] Khrushchev was now prepared to sacrifice the summit to get an apology from the Americans for the U-2 affair. He wanted Eisenhower to swallow his words and retract his defense of overhead reconnaissance: "A sovereign state cannot let the American president get away with his perfidious statement."[64] He also expected the United States to punish those "directly guilty of the deliberate violation" of Soviet airspace and to declare that "in future it will not violate the state borders of the USSR with its aircraft." Khrushchev still believed that Allen Dulles had been solely responsible for Powers's mission. All he wanted was for Eisenhower to admit this. In hammering out this new position, Khrushchev wondered if there were any way he could compel the president to apologize. Then he thought: "[W]e couldn't possibly offer our hospitality to someone who had already, so to speak, made a mess at his host's table."[65] He would threaten to withdraw the invitation he had given Eisenhower to visit the USSR in June. "We were charged up with explosive ideas," Khrushchev later said.[66]

The next morning Khrushchev handed a copy of his six-page declaration, including the demand for an apology from President Eisenhower, to his host, French President Charles de Gaulle. Implicitly he wanted the French leader to pressure his American counterpart to give in, to allow the negotiations to continue. He stressed that the Americans were seeking to live by a double standard in international politics. "The United States has on more than one occasion declared that if Soviet planes appeared over U.S. territory, the United States would start a nuclear war against the Soviet Union. Why is it, then, that when the situation is reversed they do not expect the same reaction? What is this unilateral right that they claim?"

Khrushchev expected some sympathy from de Gaulle, who was himself chafing at U.S. power. As he had explained to the Presidium in February, when he first presented his French strategy, Khrushchev knew that ultimately the French position alone would not determine whether there was a détente.[67] However, he had worked hard to bring de Gaulle into his camp, above all by planning to associate the Soviet disarmament proposals with the French strategy of destroying nuclear delivery vehicles. The summit was in Paris, and de Gaulle would assuredly not want a failure. Yet despite good reasons to expect the contrary, the French president refused to play into Khrushchev's hands. After listening to the Soviet leader's explanation of his new demands, the Frenchman showed absolutely no sympathy. All nations spy, said de Gaulle, and the issue of the U-2 was a matter between the United States and the Soviet Union. He did not want Khrushchev to lose sight of the big picture. The summit was designed, de Gaulle reminded him, to push ahead on the larger questions of international politics. If the Soviets thought they had to leave Paris, that would be unfortunate, but it would be up to them to decide what they needed to do.[68] After meeting with de Gaulle, Khrushchev went to see Macmillan, to warn that the summit was in trouble if the Americans did not admit their mistake. The British prime minister also expressed the wish that Khrushchev not allow the U-2 incident to undermine this significant opportunity to improve international relations.[69]

■

 EISENHOWER ARRIVED in Paris on May 15 to reports of Khrushchev's last-minute insistence on an apology. At meetings with the French and the British leaders at 2:30 and 6:00 P.M., Eisenhower discussed the meaning of the Soviet demand. He was firmly against giving an apology, even at the risk of losing the state visit to Moscow.[70] He did not believe that it would come to that, however. He shared the hope of his Western colleagues that Khrushchev would back down if told that the alternative was a failed conference. None of the participants held out much hope for a breakthrough on Berlin. All agreed that an interim agreement that specified an agreement within two years was tantamount to a new Soviet ultimatum and was unacceptable. But the three Western leaders believed that enough progress could be made in the area of disarmament to persuade Khrushchev to stay.

For all their confidence that disarmament was the right subject to discuss with the Soviets, the Western leaders could not agree on how to respond to Khrushchev's interest in eliminating bombers and missiles. As Khrushchev had planned, the French were sympathetic toward the Soviet position. De Gaulle not only saw real possibilities for an arms control agreement that limited nuclear delivery devices but also believed that an arms control agreement would take the stinger out of Khrushchev's threatening policy toward Berlin. In private talks with the French and the Americans, Macmillan was a little more helpful to Khrushchev. He was worried about a collapse of the summit. Unlike de Gaulle, Macmillan thought the United States should consider apologizing for authorizing the U-2 flight.

■

MONDAY MORNING, May 16, the long-awaited summit began. The French had picked an elegant venue for these discussions, but the events of the previous day cast a pall over the proceedings. The leaders and their closest advisers were escorted to the second floor of the Élysée Palace. Khrushchev shook hands with Macmillan as he entered but did little more than acknowledge the presence of Eisenhower and the American delegation. For Khrushchev, it was a matter of only signaling, "Okay, we see you."[71]

Khrushchev delivered the first address. Uncharacteristically, he stayed on message for forty-five minutes, avoiding the temptation to stray from his text. "In a situation like this I knew I couldn't speak off the top of my head. Every word had to be exact. . . ."[72] He repeated the three demands that he had outlined for the French and the British the night before. If they were not met, Khrushchev vowed, he would leave Paris, and Eisenhower would no longer be invited to visit the Soviet Union in June.

Khrushchev believed that these demands could be acceptable to Eisenhower. He convinced himself that as Eisenhower listened to the translation of his text, he turned to Christian Herter and said, "Well, why not? Why don't we go ahead and make a statement of apology?"[73] Khrushchev believed he heard this and repeated this story to others, before consigning it to his memoirs. Eisenhower and Charles Bohlen, who sat nearby, each denied this.[74] It was an interesting sidelight into Khrushchev's psychology that despite all the evidence he had at his disposal, including Eisenhower's own statements, he refused to believe that Eisenhower supported the U-2 policy.

Eisenhower was well prepared for Khrushchev's speech. Although he would not apologize, he pledged that he would satisfy one of Khrushchev's three demands. There would be no more overflights of Soviet territory. He also had something else to promise. As he had signaled in his presummit press conference he resurrected the 1955 Open Skies proposal. This time he suggested using airplanes under the control of the United Nations, instead of Soviet or U.S. spy planes, to perform the surveillance in the hope this might be more acceptable to Moscow.

Eisenhower did not understand the depth of Khrushchev's hatred of the idea of opening Soviet airspace to foreign planes. Neither the State Department nor the CIA had been able to tell him that one of the main reasons Marshal Zhukov had been fired in October 1957 was that he insisted on trying to get Khrushchev to agree to the Open Skies proposal.[75] Allowing U.S. observation of the Soviet strategic forces would undermine Khrushchev's risky plan to restructure the Soviet Union and defend the socialist world despite the Soviet Union's strategic inferiority. How could Khrushchev redeploy assets to the civilian economy if the United States knew how very weak he was? The Americans feared he had 150 intercontinental ballistic missiles, or would have very soon, whereas he had about 4 and expected a mere handful more in 1960. The United States, which already enjoyed a huge lead in strategic bombers, already had 12 ICBMs.

There was an awkward moment after Eisenhower spoke. "Nobody knew what to do," Khrushchev later recalled. Then the U.S. delegation left, and the day's meeting ended. Khrushchev's motives and actions from that point on became increasingly erratic. Having staked so much on Eisenhower, he found that he had no real strategy once it became clear the president would not apologize.

Khrushchev sent a bizarre cable to his Kremlin colleagues to sum up the session. It was defensive and affected a hollow, optimistic tone. "The situation, as it has developed here, demonstrates once more the wisdom of the line we have taken. The NATO allies of the U.S. though they are trying to save American face are striving for our participation in the summit."[76] It was true that the French and the British wanted the Russians to keep negotiating. But there was no evidence that they would work on his behalf to bring about an apology from Eisenhower. Khrushchev's cable seemed to be saying that success was possible, but it is doubtful that he really believed it.

After dinner, Macmillan, the leader who most wished to avoid having the summit collapse, called on Khrushchev at the Soviet Embassy and asked him to stay. "I cannot say that there is not a cloud in the sky, but if we stayed here another 2-3 days, establishing the bases for extended discussions of the issues, then the meeting could be adjourned and we would leave with the feeling that continuity had been preserved," Macmillan argued.[77] He also tried to downplay the importance of the U-2 for Soviet prestige. Like de Gaulle, he reminded Khrushchev that all countries spied on one another. "There are microphones hidden in every embassy," said Macmillan. "We discover them every day and by evening new ones have taken their place. They are everywhere, even in ink wells. . . . I could show you these devices." Referring to the Soviet Embassy reception hall where he was meeting Khrushchev, Macmillan added for effect, "Certainly such devices are even in this room. So let's not be hypocrites."

Macmillan pleaded with Khrushchev to find a way to stay in Paris, to continue his participation in these important discussions. "I ask you as a friend to pay heed to what I am saying to you. . . . I repeat, I ask you as a friend not to push the matter to a head today or tomorrow, go forward, to cross into the next stage."

Khrushchev indicated that he saw a way out of this mess. He repeated to Macmillan his strong belief that Eisenhower was not really responsible for the U-2 flight, that it was Allen Dulles's idea. The CIA chief had pressured the U.S. president to go ahead with the flight, and now Eisenhower was protecting Dulles. All Khrushchev wanted was for Washington to admit it had been wrong to act so insolently. "The Soviet Union is not Cuba, not Guatemala, not Panama, not Iceland." At the end of the meeting Khrushchev seemed moderately optimistic about the next day. He thanked Macmillan for the opportunity to discuss the summit and then turned plaintive. "I ask you, though, go work on President Eisenhower." Embedded within all this talk, however, was a single line that revealed how very difficult this summit had become for Khrushchev: "I don't believe Eisenhower now."[78] Khrushchev, the man who was so often the captive of strong assumptions, had seen an influential one shattered.

▪

FROM THE START of May 17, Khrushchev acted as if he had already decided that the Soviet delegation and he would have to leave Paris. Before Macmillan had even had a chance to see Eisenhower, Khrushchev arranged an impromptu press conference on the sidewalk in front of the Soviet Embassy. He said he thought that he would be leaving France very soon. Just the day before, he had assured de Gaulle that he would be making no public statements. Then Khrushchev and Malinovsky headed off in a motorcade of press and embassy personnel toward the battlefield of the Marne. In World War I, Malinovsky had been stationed with imperial Russian troops outside Paris. He wanted to show Khrushchev the little village of Pleurs-sur-Marne where he had once been billeted.

As the Soviets left for the Marne, the Western leaders gathered to discuss their next move. Eisenhower again told Macmillan and de Gaulle that he could not accept the Soviet ultimatum. De Gaulle, in a last gesture to save the summit, suggested that Khrushchev be invited to meet with them at 3:00 P.M. A message was sent to the Soviet Embassy requesting Khrushchev's attendance.

Khrushchev spent the entire morning enjoying his bucolic visit to the village of Pleurs-sur-Marne. The son of Malinovsky's former landlord entertained the party with some bottles of wine and some cheese. Malinovsky and Khrushchev started drinking, and the Soviet defense minister told stories of his time there. "I got the impression," Khrushchev later said, "that the old woman [the wife of the deceased landlord] didn't want to indulge in those memories: she kept an expression of indifference on her face."[79] The drinking continued long enough that Malinovsky also started talking about women he had known. "Malinovsky was a man who loved women, especially beautiful women," observed Khrushchev. As the tales got more colorful, the crowd of French townspeople joining in grew larger. Despite the passage of four decades, Malinovsky could still speak a little French. It was quite a spectacle.

The happy group returned to the Soviet Embassy in the early afternoon. It seems that Khrushchev was given the French invitation at least by 2:00 P.M. Without responding to the invitation, let alone going to the meeting, or calling de Gaulle or Macmillan, Khrushchev decided that the summit was over for him. It is fair to wonder how sober he was at that moment.[80] The cable he sent to the Kremlin was clear, though: "The change in the situation that would have permitted us to stay has not occurred. Therefore we have decided to leave Paris."[81] It was 2:15 P.M. Khrushchev also recommended to the Presidium that the East Germans be instructed to invite him to speak in East Berlin on his way home. He wished to reaffirm his commitment to solving the German problem. It was revenge served cold for Eisenhower's humiliating him over the U-2.

As for the three world leaders awaiting his decision that day, Khrushchev wanted nothing to do with them. He instructed a low-level diplomat to convey a message to the French: "If the question was to discuss what had been discussed yesterday, then the meeting would be acceptable, but not before 5 P.M. because Khrushchev had had no lunch. However, if other questions were to be discussed, then Mr. Khrushchev would not attend."[82] The message was a deliberate fiction. "Mr. Khrushchev" had already decided that he would not attend any meeting. Later that evening he sent word to the French that he would be leaving Paris the next day after conducting a press conference.

When Eisenhower heard of the brushoff from Khrushchev, he was so angry he could not bring himself to say the Soviet leader's name. Khrushchev became "this man." De Gaulle was also fed up with Khrushchev, whose disappearing act to the Marne was the last bit of boorishness the French leader was prepared to stomach. Macmillan, who knew enough not to try to force the Americans to accept Khrushchev's conditions, was intensely disappointed. "The Summit—on which I had set high hopes and for which I worked for over 2 years—has blown up, like a volcano! It is ignominious; it is tragic; it is almost incredible. . . ."[83] In many ways he blamed his old friend Dwight Eisenhower for not exercising good judgment in the weeks leading up to the meeting.

■

THE WORLD'S NEWSPAPERS covered the collapse of the summit as a great calamity. Despite the U-2 affair, expectations had grown in the weeks preceding the event. Now that nothing had come of the meeting, the general disappointment was equally exaggerated.

In Moscow the KGB lectured Francis Gary Powers on how his flight had caused the collapse of the summit. Powers replied that it was wrong to assume he was a patsy in some kind of right-wing conspiracy to wreck U.S.-Soviet relations; "Whoever organized my flight, in my opinion, did not want to disrupt the summit. If they had known that this flight would break up the summit, they would not have done it." When he was asked to condemn the aggressive acts of the American "reactionaries," he politely declined. "If I consider these flights as necessary to protect the security of the United States, I will not condemn them."[84]

In Washington the administration had its own theories about why the summit collapsed. Led by the two longtime Soviet watchers, Tommy Thompson and Charles Bohlen, the U.S. government came to believe that Khrushchev had used the U-2 affair as an excuse to back away from the summit. Many in Washington still could not quite understand the politics of Khrushchev's January announcement of a unilateral cut in the Soviet armed forces. Their thinking was that Khrushchev faced enormous opposition from the military to his plans for a détente and so needed a real breakthrough on Berlin in Paris to shore up his authority in the Kremlin. When it became clear to him in April that the West would not reconsider its opposition to the free city proposal and that it was firmly committed to stationing NATO forces in West Berlin, Khrushchev scouted around for a pretext to call off the summit. The ill-fated Powers mission gave him that excuse.[85]

Eisenhower seemed to share this view of what had happened in Paris. The day after the summit collapsed, he offered this explanation in a letter to the president of Colombia, Alberto Lleras Camargo: "As result of a chain of events within the Soviet Union which is not clear to me at this time, Mr. Khrushchev must have concluded before coming to Paris that progress at a Summit Meeting would be either undesirable or impossible. Accordingly, he embarked on a calculated campaign, even before it began, to insure the failure of the conference and to see to it that the onus for such failure would fall on the West, particularly the United States."[86]

The U.S. government and Eisenhower had missed the real story. Khrushchev had not wanted Paris to fail. He had shared the president's hope that the summit would lead to a period of relaxed international tensions. Indeed, like Eisenhower, he had invested some political capital and personal prestige into the prospect of achieving better relations. Until May 15, two weeks after Powers had parachuted into Russia, the Soviet leader was reluctant to sacrifice all that he had done since December 1959 to achieve a détente.

Yet a détente was not realized. The year 1960 did not become a turning point in the Cold War. Was this all the fault of a single failed spy mission, as the KGB asserted to Powers? In a word, no. A review of what the United States and the Soviet Union planned to say to each other in Paris shows that a dramatic breakthrough would have been impossible on Berlin and unlikely on disarmament. The West was unwilling to give up its protection of West

Berlin, and Khrushchev's views on that city had not evolved since November 1958. On the subject of disarmament, where his views were more flexible, the Russian appeared to be too afraid of U.S. power and intentions to concede to Eisenhower's request for a verification regime, the on-site and overhead inspections, that Washington needed to overcome its deep mistrust of Moscow. Nevertheless, the dynamics of a summit where the Soviet Union would have been treated as an equal might have alleviated the fears of the mercurial Soviet leader. The aftermath of the U-2 incident, however, made this impossible to know.

What the U-2 affair did reveal was the enormous role of reputation in the superpower confrontation. Both leaders allowed matters of personal prestige to dictate their most important decisions in May 1960. At key moments, neither swallowed his pride when doing so would have allowed the embarrassing spectacle of a U.S. pilot in Lubyanka to fade into the background. This was not, however, the fault of grandeur or vanity. In a war fought more on a psychological plane than a conventional battlefield, where a superpower's most potent defense involved deterring an enemy attack before it ever happened, the credibility of each leader carried enormous significance.

Two months after the failure in Paris, Khrushchev again reminded Washington of the importance of prestige. Although U-2 flights were suspended, the United States continued to send reconnaissance flights along the border with the Soviet Union. On July 1 the Soviet Air Force shot down an RB-47 spy plane that had taken off from a U.S. base in Great Britain on a mission over the Barents Sea. U.S. intelligence concluded that the plane never came closer than thirty miles from Soviet airspace. The Soviets argued otherwise. Four crew members died in the attack. The two surviving pilots were captured, and the Soviets refused to return them without a United Nations investigation. They joined Powers in Soviet custody.[87]

Powers stood trial in August 1960 and was sentenced to three years in prison and an additional seven years of hard labor. He was exchanged for a Soviet spy, Vilyam Fischer, alias Rudolf Abel, in February 1962 and set free. Although the U.S. government negotiated for Powers's freedom, he returned home under a cloud. The American people and Dulles's replacement as CIA director, John McCone, believed that he had been disloyal under KGB interrogation. McCone set up a board of inquiry under Federal Judge E. Barrett Prettyman at the CIA to investigate Powers's actions. The board determined that Powers had not been disloyal. The Senate Armed Services and Foreign Relations committees also investigated his actions. But these investigations like the assessments of the Prettyman board were kept secret, thus denying

Powers the opportunity not only to clear his name but to gain public praise.[88] The KGB's records of Powers's actions under interrogation remained closed until the publication of this book.

▪

DESPITE THE TOLL that the U-2 experience had taken on his respect for Eisenhower, Khrushchev did not intend to give up entirely on seeking détente with the West. A few weeks after the failure of the summit, he instructed Soviet representatives at Geneva to present the disarmament plan that he had intended to unveil in Paris.[89] On June 7, 1960, the Soviet Union formally proposed that the destruction of all strategic missiles and bombers be the first step in general and complete disarmament. More important, the Soviets agreed that "all disarmament measures be carried out under strict international control from beginning to end." Foreign inspectors would be allowed on Soviet soil but only after weapons had been destroyed.

Khrushchev also signaled that he continued to be patient about Berlin. He still assumed that it would take a meeting of the great leaders to reach an agreement. Unwilling to risk another Berlin crisis in the short term, he settled into a policy of marking time until Eisenhower's replacement came into office in January 1961. There was little he expected to get out of the remaining months of the Eisenhower regime.

What Khrushchev did not anticipate was that events in three developing countries, in three different regions of the world, would make a six-month pause in the Soviet-American competition impossible.

CHAPTER 12

CASTRO AND LUMUMBA

KHRUSHCHEV SAW NO inherent contradiction in actively cultivating new allies in the third world as he worked to relax military tensions with the West. In February 1960, just days after single-handedly reshaping Soviet disarmament proposals and three months before the Paris summit, Khrushchev had approved plans for a new Friendship University in Moscow to bring young adults from Asia, Africa, and the Middle East to study Marxism-Leninism and the practical arts of agriculture and engineering.[1] Scheduled to open in October 1960, the school was designed to accommodate five hundred foreign students in the expectation they would come from ninety different countries.[2] This was a substantial undertaking. "The university cost us a hefty sum," Khrushchev later recalled, "but it was worth it."[3]

It had been a long time since Moscow had sponsored a special school for foreign Communists. In 1921 the Bolsheviks in Tashkent had established a Communist University of Toilers of the East to promote revolution in India and Central Asia. A few years later the Soviets added the Sun Yat-sen University to train cadres for the revolution in China.[4] Stalin had closed these schools as he turned the energies of the regime inward and moved the USSR away from supporting the international Communist movement. Khrushchev, however, was eager to restore that focus of Soviet foreign activity.

Recent developments had encouraged Khrushchev to pay even more attention to developing ideological allies in the third world. Since 1955 he had championed signing arms deals, providing grants, and sending industrial and agricultural delegations to cultivate the first generation of third world leaders without regard to their political affiliation. Although the peoples of such newly independent countries after World War II as India and Indonesia spoke dozens of different languages, prayed to different gods, and were shaped by different histories, Khrushchev saw them as a cohesive group that could be converted to Marxism-Leninism. Five years into this campaign the results were not as Moscow had hoped. The leaders were turning out to be more nationalistic than progressive and far less pro-Soviet than they should have been in light of the money that the Kremlin was spending on them.

Egyptian President Nasser no longer acted like a dependable Soviet ally. When Iraq refused Egypt's offer to join the United Arab Republic after the Iraqi Revolution in 1958, Khrushchev found himself in the midst of a feud between the Iraqi leader, Brigadier General Qasim, and Nasser that appeared to have wrecked his relationship with the Egyptian leader. Nasser blamed Iraqi Communists, who formed part of the governing coalition, for Qasim's lukewarm embrace of Arab nationalism and assumed Moscow was directing the local Communists. By 1959 Nasser was putting more of his own Communists in jail and both publicly and privately attacking Khrushchev for not having done enough for Egypt in the 1956 Suez Crisis.[5] Complaining about these attacks on Communists, Khrushchev told Egyptian Ambassador Mohammed Awad el-Kouni, "we consider the struggle against imperialism under the banner of Arab nationalism to be a progressive phenomenon in so far as it consolidates the power of colonial and dependent people." El-Kouni replied: "But President Nasser is not an anticommunist, he is only against Arab communists."[6]

Meanwhile Moscow's alliance with Iraq had also gone sour. In August 1958 Qasim had told the Soviets that he did not fear the position of the Communist Party in Iraqi society. Indeed, some prominent members of Qasim's inner circle were party members. His first cousin Mahdavi, the chief justice of the country's revolutionary tribunal, was a Communist.[7] So too were Qasim's personal aide, Colonel Basfi, and the chief of the Iraqi Air Force, General Avkati.[8] By early 1960, however, relations between Qasim and the Communist Party had become sharply antagonistic. He held the party responsible for a series of bloody clashes between Kurdish Communists and government soldiers in northern Iraq in the spring of 1959 that jeopardized his control of the country. Qasim had subsequently outlawed all political parties. In February 1960, just as Khrushchev was announcing in Moscow the formation of Friendship University, the Communists closest to Qasim approached the Soviet ambassador at a housewarming party for General Avkati to share their concerns about the direction in which the country was going.[9] Mahdavi told of a recent meeting with Qasim in which he had warned his cousin that his autocratic ways were strengthening the reactionary forces in the country at the expense of his progressive allies. Qasim's response to Mahdavi had been flippant: "Does this mean you are tired of your job at the tribunal?"

In the winter of 1960 Moscow took this gloomy report from its chief allies in Baghdad so seriously that it turned to its traditional fixer, Anastas Mikoyan, and asked the Iraqis to permit special high-level talks. The Presidium instructed Mikoyan to report back on "Qasim's attitude toward the Communist Party and the willingness of the communists to cooperate with him."[10] Expecting that this conversation would be disappointing, the Kremlin also instructed Mikoyan to tell Qasim that the Soviet Union, his principal supplier of weapons, was "unhappy" with his treatment of the Iraqi Communist Party. As a reminder of the value of keeping in Moscow's good graces, Mikoyan was to bring with him some KGB information on Western plots to overthrow the Iraqi leader. The Qasim regime, however, was so cool to a visit from Mikoyan that it was delayed until April.[11]

■

D ESPITE THESE REVERSES in the Middle East, Khrushchev remained optimistic. His commitment to the Friendship University in early 1960 did not stem from pessimism about Soviet opportunities in the third world. Balancing out the bad news from Cairo and Baghdad were hopeful new developments in parts of the world where the Soviet Union had never before had interests. In late 1958 and 1959, while Khrushchev's foreign policy concerns were primarily Berlin and disarmament, a second wave of national liberation reshaped the map of Africa and brought postcolonial regimes to power in the Caribbean and Asia. The first move to sovereignty occurred in West Africa, where Ghana, the former British colony of the Gold Coast, declared its independence in 1956. The former French West African colony of Guinea followed in 1958. Sékou Touré, the new president of Guinea, turned to the Soviet Union soon after independence. "When I look into the face of the Soviet Union," he had told a visiting Soviet diplomat, "I see a reliable friend."[12]

This new generation of leaders brought Moscow its two brightest hopes for expanding Soviet influence in the developing world. Over the course of 1960 the world came to pay enormous attention to Khrushchev's relationships with Fidel Castro and Patrice Lumumba. The charismatic young Cuban revolutionary and the dynamic Congolese nationalist personified the kind of leader that Khrushchev hoped to see in the third world. Although neither Castro nor Lumumba was a formal member of a Communist Party, both seemed reassuringly comfortable with Marxism-Leninism and, most important, looked to Moscow for guidance.

In the months to come, Khrushchev took risks to help Castro and Lumumba as local events transformed the two nations into hotly contested squares on the Cold War chessboard. The strong ideological affinity between Moscow and these two young leaders added a new dimension of fear for Washington, making these entanglements seem more threatening than any the Soviet leader had made in the Middle East. With dark passions provoked, the administration would soon be actively trying to kill Castro and Lumumba. But before recounting how the Cold War struggle turned so deadly in the third world in 1960, we should examine the origins of Moscow's relationship with these young leaders. In neither case did Khrushchev make the first move.

■

THE CUBAN REVOLUTION began in 1956, when Fidel Castro led a band of guerrillas calling themselves the July 26 Movement into the mountains of Cuba, where they mounted sporadic attacks against the regime of Fulgencio Batista. Following the lead of the Cuban Communist Party, the Partido Socialista Popular (PSP), Moscow at first took little notice of this struggle. The local Communists, who believed that revolution should come through a political uprising of the urban working class, seriously underestimated Castro and doubted the revolutionary potential of Cuba's vast population of agricultural workers. When it became clear, however, that Castro's movement was capturing the Cuban public's imagination and wearing down the Batista regime, the Cuban Communists rallied to his side, and Moscow followed. In December 1958 the Kremlin organized a small covert operation to ship surplus World War II–era German rifles to the revolutionaries, using a company in Costa Rica.[13]

Soviet assistance, however, played no role in the outcome of the Cuban Revolution. Castro's forces reached Havana before the weapons did. On New Year's Eve 1958 Batista fled the country, and the next morning a new Cuban government led by the July 26 Movement was declared.

Over the course of 1959 Fidel Castro gradually introduced himself to the Soviets. Moscow already knew something about his younger brother, Raúl. In his early twenties Raúl had attended a youth congress in Bucharest, Romania, and joined the youth wing of the PSP upon his return.[14] According to Raúl's wife, Vilma Espín, Raúl discussed this decision with his older brother, who was attending the law school at the University of Havana at the time. Fidel advised Raúl to "go ahead" and join the party in 1953. Fidel was already a Marxist, but he told Raúl that he could not follow him into the PSP. According to Espín, Fidel believed his fledgling political career would be doomed if he were a party member.[15] The Soviets, on the other hand, were never sure how much Fidel knew of his brother's work with the PSP and doubted that Fidel was a Marxist-Leninist.[16] Instead, Fidel appeared to be a revolutionary who intended to put his own stamp on a social revolution in his own country. In a word, Latin America's first Fidelista. He needed neither party nor ideological guidance from abroad. In part, the Soviets got this view from the Cuban Communists. The PSP's leaders told Moscow that Raúl was much closer to the PSP than Fidel. Indeed, the Cuban Communist leaders reported that Raúl and Ernesto "Che" Guevara, an Argentine-born Communist in the inner circle of the revolution, had kept their Communist membership a secret from Fidel, despite their intense loyalty to the man.[17]

Moscow's first inkling that a special relationship with Fidel Castro and his regime was possible came in April 1959, when Raúl Castro sent a representative on a mission to Moscow to request Soviet assistance in creating a Marxist-Leninist cadre within the Cuban Army.[18] The Kremlin obliged the Cubans by sending seventeen Spanish republican military officers who had taken refuge in Moscow at the end of the Spanish civil war in 1938.[19] The next step came a few months later, when the Cubans approached the Poles for military hardware. The Kremlin reviewed all weapons sales by its satellites to nonbloc countries, and in late September 1959 it approved the Polish request to send some Soviet bloc tanks to Havana.[20] The first Soviet representative to visit Cuba after the revolution, the KGB's Aleksandr Alekseyev, reached the island a few weeks later.[21] When the Cubans approached the Czechs in January 1960 to request weapons from them, the Kremlin agreed.[22] The next month Presidium member Mikoyan visited Cuba in a major public display of friendship to open a Soviet exhibition in Havana. Mikoyan was passionate about what he found there. "I felt as though I had returned to my childhood!" he reported to the Kremlin. "[Fidel] is a genuine revolutionary—completely like us."[23]

Fidel Castro initially imposed limits on Cuba's relationship with Moscow. At his first meeting with the KGB's Alekseyev in October 1959, he had explained how his fear of U.S. retaliation shaped his approach to the Kremlin. "For Nasser it made sense," Castro told Alekseyev in explaining why Cuba would not be requesting weapons directly from Moscow. "First of all, American imperialism was far from him, and you are next door to Egypt. But us? We are so far. . . . No weapons. We do not ask for any."[24] Castro also believed that the real threat to his regime was economic, not military. "All U.S. attempts to intervene are condemned to failure," he said confidently to Alekseyev at a later meeting, in February 1960. "The only danger for Cuban Revolution is Cuba's economic weakness and its economic dependence on the U.S. which could use sanctions against Cuba. In one or two years, [the] U.S. could destroy the Cuban economy. But never, even under mortal danger, will we make a deal with American imperialism. And under these circumstances, the USSR could play a decisive role in the strengthening of our revolution by helping us economically."[25] Castro also wanted to limit what the Cuban people knew of his dealings with Moscow. Anticommunism was deeply ingrained in Cuban society, where the Roman Catholic Church remained a strong institution, and Castro did not want to restore open relations with the Soviet Union until he was more confident of the domestic reaction.

Despite Castro's caveats, Khrushchev had reason to be optimistic about the potential for sturdy ties between the Kremlin and Cuba. The thirty-two-year-old Castro seemed to be a true revolutionary and reliably anti-American.

■

ON APRIL 18, 1959, three months after Castro's triumphant arrival in Havana, a tall Congolese activist named Patrice Lumumba entered the Soviet Embassy in the Guinean capital of Conakry. At the time the Congo was still a Belgian colony, and Moscow knew nothing about Lumumba and very little about his homeland.[26] The night before, a Guinean official had introduced the Soviet ambassador to Lumumba, and the two set an appointment for the next day. "The struggle for the independence of the Congo," Lumumba explained to Ambassador P. I. Gerasimov, "is progressing."[27] He was the founding leader of the Mouvement National Congolais (MNC), a grassroots organization that demanded Congo's independence from Belgium. Born in 1925, Lumumba had only a primary school education because the Belgian colonial administration did not offer public secondary education to blacks. In his early twenties Lumumba had gone to work in the post office in Stanleyville, and eventually he started writing pamphlets for the local branch of the Liberal Party of Belgium. While in prison in 1956 for allegedly embezzling funds on the job, he wrote a political tract, Le Congo, terre d'Avenir: est-il menacé? [The Congo, Land of the Future, Is It Threatened?]. After he was released later that year, Lumumba's political activism became more intense and more radical. In October 1958 he played a major role in establishing the MNC, which advocated independence.

Lumumba hinted strongly to Moscow's representative in April 1959 that he was pro-Soviet, if not a Communist. He asked for permission to make a secret visit to the Soviet Union, explaining that once he returned from Moscow he would be in a better position to "expose the anti-Soviet propaganda that the colonial powers are now increasingly disseminating in Africa."[28] To keep the trip a secret from the Belgians, the Guineans had already promised to allow Lumumba to leave from Conakry if the Soviets agreed.

Lumumba also asked for Soviet financial assistance. He lacked the funds to distribute his own propaganda throughout the vast territory of the Belgian Congo. If his message could get out, he assured the Soviet ambassador, it would undermine the "anti-Soviet fabrications" of the Belgians.[29]

The meeting with the Soviet ambassador was not Lumumba's only effort to seek Communist assistance in 1959. Two weeks later he left for Brussels to meet with the leaders of the Belgian Communist Party, whom he saw as natural allies. His conversations with Albert de Coninck, the secretary of the Central Committee of the Belgian party, created great optimism among the Belgian Communists, which they communicated to Moscow. "The Congo," de Coninck explained to the Soviet officials at the embassy after his meeting with Lumumba, "presents the most favorable conditions for the spread of Marxism of any country in Africa."[30] As evidence, he pointed to the colony's large—by African standards—urban population. Compared with 10 percent in French West Africa, 26 percent of the Congolese population lived in towns or cities. De Coninck also celebrated the fact that the party Lumumba led was the strongest in the Congo and "practically stands at the forefront of the national-liberation movement." Although not formally a Communist, Lumumba "supports progressive positions." This was a codeword among Communists for someone who was politically reliable.

The Belgian Congo was a potentially rich prize. A vast empire in Central Africa that stretched from the mouth of the Congo River on the western coast of the continent for twelve hundred miles into the interior, it had more mineral wealth than any other country in Africa. The colony produced 9 percent of the world's copper, 49 percent of the world's cobalt, 69 percent of the world's industrial diamonds, and 6.5 percent of its tin.[31] During the Second World War the Congo had been the source of almost all of the financing of the Belgian government-in-exile, and since 1945 its mining output had almost doubled.[32] Moscow had no particular interest in acquiring these resources, but this mineral wealth meant that once it was independent, the Congo had a good chance of prospering and might thereby become a useful Soviet ally.

In January 1960 Congolese negotiators reached an agreement with the Belgian government that independence would be declared on June 30. This would be preceded by the country's first parliamentary election in May.

Lumumba was unquestionably the Soviet favorite in the political struggle for the Congo. In late December 1959 the Kremlin had turned down a blanket request for assistance from representatives of another coalition comprising distinguished Congolese nationalists who were not allied with Lumumba.[33] Moscow suspected the ideological commitment of these nationalists, and Khrushchev preferred to take his chances with Lumumba.[34]

▪

WELL INTO THE WINTER of 1960 the U.S. government knew surprisingly little about the extent of the Kremlin's relationship with Castro and cared little about Lumumba. Neither the CIA nor the National Security Agency, which intercepted and decrypted foreign communications, had detected the covert supply of Soviet bloc weapons to Havana that the Presidium had approved in September 1959 and January 1960. Lumumba's contacts with Soviet representatives had been noticed but were largely ignored.

Washington was working hard to understand Fidel Castro. With Cuba only ninety miles off the coast of Florida, the Eisenhower administration had followed the Cuban Revolution very closely. For a time after the July 26 Movement took control of the island, the administration was unsure how to handle Castro. The State Department initially recommended engagement. An undercover CIA officer was assigned to spend time with Castro during a tour of the United States that the young leader took in April 1959. Castro made some very reassuring statements to this officer. In fact the visit, which was partially choreographed by an American public relations firm, created widespread support for the rebels without revealing Castro's future revolutionary aims. Castro repeated the mantra "We are not communists," throughout his stay.[35] He was so convincing that even Vice President Nixon, who had a private meeting with Castro in Washington, D.C., described him as an anti-Communist who cavorted with the PSP out of sheer naiveté.[36]

Despite this initial positive evaluation, by the end of 1959 the U.S. government had turned against Castro. Fidel Castro's October 1959 nomination of his brother, Raúl, to lead the newly created Ministry of the Revolutionary Armed Forces provoked a series of high-profile military defections in Cuba that created deep concern in Washington. The defectors revealed that Raúl was employing veterans of the Spanish civil war to train a Marxist cadre within the Cuban armed forces. The White House knew that Raul was a hard-core Communist, as was Che Guevara, but had not been sure of their influence and that of the PSP over Fidel. These changes in the Cuban military seemed to presage a Communist takeover. In early November President Eisenhower decided that the United States had no choice but to remove the Castro regime. "There is no reasonable basis," explained the

State Department in a memorandum clarifying the issue for the president, "to found our policy on a hope that Castro will voluntarily adopt policies and attitudes consistent with minimum United States security require- ments and policy interests."[37] Consequently, argued the State Department, "the prolonged continuation of the Castro regime in Cuba in its present form would have serious adverse effects on the United States position in Latin America and corresponding advantages for international commu- nism." President Eisenhower agreed.

Within a month of this change in U.S. policy, Allen Dulles and the CIA prepared proposals for bringing an end to the Castro regime. The agency even called for "thorough consideration [to] be given to the elimination of Fidel Castro." In formally recommending assassination as an option, the agency stated: "None of those close to Fidel such as his brother Raul or his companion, Che Guevara, have the same mesmeric appeal to the masses. Many informed people believe that the disappearance of Fidel would greatly accelerate the fall of the present government."[38]

Eisenhower, however, did not believe it was time to force the issue. Despite his suspicions of Castro, the president set the CIA's plans to one side. As of early 1960, the White House was watching to see what direction events took on the island.

■

THE EISENHOWER administration also adopted a wait and see approach to the Congo, though this was less because of high-level uncertainty than because of a general lack of concern about the Belgian colony. Washington had only a vague opinion of Patrice Lumumba, and the president and his top foreign policy advisers were not at all engaged in thinking about the Congo's political future. By early 1960 Washington had received reports that Lumumba was receiving money from the Soviets, but those following the issue were not sure whether this was proof of ideological commitment or rank opportunism.

Lumumba actively sowed some of this confusion. In late February 1960 he met the U.S. ambassador in Brussels after consultations with the Belgian gov- ernment. "[A] highly articulate, sophisticated, subtle and unprincipled intelli- gence," wrote Ambassador William Burden in describing Lumumba for the State Department.[39] Lumumba, who arrived half an hour late and kept the meter running in a taxi left standing outside the embassy, struck Burden as thoroughly opportunistic and extravagant. "[He] would probably not meet the famous definition which was given a century ago of the honest politician as one who, when bought, stayed bought."[40]

The Congolese was indeed playing a game. He tried to convince the Americans that the Soviets had approached him first, not the other way around. Complaining to Burden about the Kremlin's pressure on him, Lumumba wove a fanciful story of a stream of invitations to visit Moscow, all of which he "had turned . . . down because he believed that these influences from the East were very bad from the point of view of the Congo."[41] Lacking any contradictory information, the U.S. ambassador did not reject Lumumba's denial out of hand. "It seems clear that if Lumumba is receiving any specific support from the East, he is perfectly prepared to betray these supporters to the fullest extent that suits his purposes." When Lumumba asked for an invitation to visit the United States, Burden endorsed the idea in a cable later sent to Washington.

Lumumba's meeting with Burden did not spark any action by Washington, and there was no subsequent invitation to visit the United States. The administration had not yet decided that the Congo was a contested spot in the Cold War.

▪

CASTRO WAS THE FIRST of Khrushchev's new allies to increase East-West tensions. On March 4 *La Coubre*, a Belgian ship bringing French weapons to the Cuban Army, blew up in Havana Harbor, killing more than a hundred aboard the ship and along the shore. This tragic and mysterious explosion set off a chain of events that committed Khrushchev and the Soviet Union more deeply than ever to Cuba and brought a strong reaction from the Eisenhower administration.

The blast shook Castro's assumptions about the security of his regime. Although he admitted that he didn't have any "juridical proof," he told the KGB's Alekseyev, "I am absolutely certain that the United States blew up the ship."[42] He assumed that the CIA had been behind the attack. On March 5 he publicly blamed the United States for the tragedy, a charge that Washington immediately denied in a statement to the press.[43] Indeed, although U.S. intelligence later did engineer quite a few explosions in Havana, there has never been any credible evidence to link it to *La Coubre*.

Castro's conviction that Washington was responsible eliminated his reluctance to request military assistance directly from Moscow. He now assumed that the destruction of *La Coubre* was just the opening salvo in a war against his regime. "The Americans are deciding on extreme measures," Castro confided to Alekseyev at a private lunch on March 6. "Could [Cuba] count upon the help of the USSR with supplies of goods and weapons in the case of a blockade or [U.S.] intervention?" He asked Alekseyev to send an immediate cable to Khrushchev inviting the Soviet Navy to send submarines to assist Cuba. "We have here very many caves and all are unoccupied," he added as a suggestion for a secret port. Despite this request, the explosion did not eliminate all of Castro's inhibitions in dealing with Moscow. There was still no Soviet Embassy in Havana, the reason why Alekseyev was the key link between the regimes. Castro told Alekseyev that he considered it premature to reestablish formal diplomatic relations. He wanted his government's alliance with the Kremlin kept confidential until he was certain that the Cuban people would not overreact.

Khrushchev acted quickly when he received a report on Alekseyev's meeting with Castro. To that time he had not been in direct communication with Castro, but on March 12 he sent a personal letter to the Cuban leader, offering both advice and weapons.[44] Reflecting his general optimism about a coming détente with the United States (the ill-fated Paris summit was still two months, away and Francis Gary Powers had not yet set off in a U-2 over Russia), Khrushchev cautioned Castro not to assume the worst about the Eisenhower administration. "In spite of the difficulty and growing tension of the situation, the USA is today content to restrict itself to measures designed to further the favorable development of international relations, and will under no circumstances cross the line to undertake an open intervention against Cuba." Khrushchev's opinion reflected the assessment of the KGB, which had collected information indicating that the Eisenhower administration would attack Cuba only if provoked.[45] What would provoke it? The KGB suggested either an attack on the U.S. naval base at Guantánamo, on the eastern tip of Cuba, or the establishment of a Soviet missile base anywhere on the island.

Although Khrushchev did not share Castro's new fears about an imminent U.S. attack, he was prepared to sell the Cubans whatever weapons they believed they needed. The letter invited Castro to request arms shipments from Czech or Soviet manufacturers and said nothing about price. The Cubans had paid for the Soviet bloc weapons they received previously. This time they would not be expected to. The letter closed with an invitation for the Cuban leader to make his first visit to Moscow.

"Could you write down the Spanish translation for me?" asked Castro excitedly when Alekseyev read a hasty translation of the letter a few days later in Havana. Castro could not have been happier and told the Soviet representative that this letter would be placed in a box of keepsakes that he had stashed away in the mountains. With the letter came an odd Soviet offer to pay Castro for the "rights" to his speeches. Initially the honoraria were a few hundred U.S. dollars, but by 1961 Castro would be receiving eight thousand U.S. dollars for a set of his speeches.[46] This was just a little bonus for Castro to use as he wished.

▪

CASTRO'S PUBLIC REACTION to the explosion also removed any remaining doubts in Washington. Although the administration had been discussing the removal of Castro since November, there had been little urgency to implement this policy. Castro's campaign to associate the administration with the *Coubre* incident accelerated U.S. activity against Castro. "The Country Team is of the unanimous opinion there is no hope that US will ever be able to establish a satisfactory relationship with the Cuban government as long as it is dominated by Fidel Castro, Raul Castro, Che Guevara and like-minded associates," wrote the U.S. Embassy in Havana on March 8 after canvassing the opinion of the local CIA representative as well as those of the resident diplomats.[47]

The White House's high-level advisory group, including the president's national security adviser, Gordon Gray, met to discuss Cuba the same day the report from the embassy arrived in Washington.[48] An NSC meeting, chaired by the president, was scheduled for the next day. The advisory group accepted that the United States could not live with Castro but suggested four reasons why a U.S. military invasion was inadvisable: the lack of any alternative to Castro, the concern that an attack would solidify Castro's government, the need to coordinate with Latin American countries, and the effect on world opinion. As an alternative to invasion, the group suggested economic and diplomatic measures against Castro's regime.

The discussion at the NSC on March 10 was more bellicose. The U.S. military believed that Washington had to consider an invasion. The navy, in particular, feared that Castro would try soon to close the U.S. base at Guantánamo. In a paper prepared for the meeting, the chief of naval operations, Admiral Arleigh Burke, argued that should covert action "fail to bring a solution in time . . . the United States [should] be prepared to take military measures."[49]

Despite the rising concerns, expressed alarmingly by his military advisers, Eisenhower refused to rush to solve his Castro problem. He dismissed any immediate threat to Guantánamo and assured his team that if any of the ten thousand U.S. citizens in Cuba were "in danger," he would order an intervention. Instead he wanted his advisers to think about an alternative to Castro. He did not want to topple the regime in Havana without having a favorable replacement in the wings. Otherwise, he warned, "we might have another Black Hole of Calcutta in Cuba."[50]

The effect of these discussions was a renewal of administration interest in covert solutions. On March 16 the 5412 Committee of the NSC, which oversaw the planning of covert action, discussed specific plans for "the replacement of the Castro regime with one more devoted to the true interests of the Cuban people and more acceptable to the US in such a manner as to avoid any appearance of US intervention."[51] Responding to Eisenhower's concerns at the NSC meeting, the group stressed that the first objective was to create "a responsible, appealing and unified Cuban opposition to the Castro regime."[52]

Assassination plans were frozen. At the moment the administration was merely entertaining schemes to embarrass Castro. The CIA plotted to spray with LSD a cigar that an agent could hand him minutes before he was to give a major public speech. It also worked on a depilatory powder that would make his beard fall out; captured perhaps by the legend of Samson, the CIA believed that Castro's personal charisma would disappear with his whiskers. The agency took this ludicrous notion seriously enough that it looked around for appropriate agents so that the next time Castro went abroad, a hotel attendant could be recruited to dust the Cuban leader's shoes with the powder when they were left outside his suite to be shined overnight.[53]

■

I N T H E W E E K S after *La Coubre* Castro took a series of steps to radicalize the Cuban Revolution and bring his relationship with Khrushchev into the open. In May, Cuba established formal diplomatic relations with Moscow, allowing the Soviets to open an embassy in Havana. That month Castro also informed U.S. oil companies operating in Cuba that they would have to refine the three hundred thousand tons of crude oil the Soviet Union had promised to sell Cuba. He expected the U.S. companies to say no, and on June 10 the Cuban government nationalized the refineries.[54] When Cuba's foreign-owned electric utilities refused to operate using Soviet oil, Castro nationalized them too.

Castro was not yet free of his fear of the United States. Although he had no precise knowledge of the CIA's plotting, it did not take him long to develop cold feet about the extent to which he was publicly identifying his regime with Moscow. In late spring 1960 Castro began to notice an increase in opposition to his regime. Some counterrevolutionaries had taken up guns and were going into the mountains as his July 26 Movement had done in the mid-1950s. Statements by U.S. officials had also become sharper of late.

In this climate Khrushchev's invitation to visit Moscow was unhelpful. At first Fidel thought he might just send his brother, who was expected to leave in the spring of 1960 on a tour of major Eastern European capitals and

Beijing. But by late June Fidel thought that even a visit from Raúl would be too dangerous for his regime. "At this time, when an intervention is being prepared," Castro told Alekseyev on June 24, "Raúl's visit would be seen by our enemies as evidence of a new orientation of Cuba under the military assistance of the USSR."[55]

The postponement of Raúl Castro's visit came at an awkward time for Khrushchev. The great wave of decolonization had increased Sino-Soviet tensions. The Chinese disapproved of Moscow's cautious approach to the social movements in Africa and the Caribbean. Mao and his colleagues believed that the Kremlin's aversion to using violence as a political tool was causing it to miss opportunities to spread the gospel of socialism. This disagreement spilled out into the open just at the moment that Castro postponed his brother's visit. In early June 1960, at a meeting of international trade unionists in Beijing, the Chinese and their allies—the Burmese, North Vietnamese, Sudanese, Somalis, Argentines, Ceylonese, Japanese, and Zanzibaris—had raised doubts about Khrushchev's leadership of the international Communist movement. They berated Moscow for not being revolutionary enough, for promoting a doctrine of peaceful coexistence that appealed to bourgeois nationalists more than to Communists and weakened the possibility for revolutionary activity. Khrushchev answered his critics in Bucharest two weeks later. It was not enough to read Marx, he declared. "One must also correctly understand what one had read and apply it to specific conditions of the time in which we live, taking into consideration the situation and the real balance of forces."[56]

Khrushchev saw significant value in a public visit by Raúl Castro in July, and the postponement worried him. The Soviet leader, who doubted that a U.S. military invasion of Cuba was either imminent or likely that summer, regarded Castro's explanation as a poor excuse. Moreover, the latest Soviet information was that Raúl intended to go ahead with the other stops on his planned foreign tour, including Prague. Khrushchev wondered if the postponement might actually be linked to the events in Beijing or Bucharest. Reports had come to the Kremlin that Raúl and some of the other Cuban revolutionaries were somewhat attracted to Beijing's more radical line. Khrushchev decided not to waste time in removing any doubts, his own or those of the Chinese, that Cuba viewed Moscow as its principal socialist ally.

The KGB predicted more U.S. covert action but assured the Kremlin that the Eisenhower administration was no more likely to launch a military attack on Cuba now than it had been months earlier.[57] Assuming that the risks were low and the potential benefits high, Khrushchev chose a public forum to reassure the Cubans that their security was a vital Soviet interest. Before a group of Soviet teachers on July 9, he announced that the Soviet Union would defend Cuba with nuclear weapons, if need be. He said: "It should be borne in mind that the United States is now not at such an unattainable distance from the Soviet Union as formerly. Figuratively speaking, if need be, Soviet artillerymen can support the Cuban people with their rocket fire should the aggressive forces in the Pentagon dare to start intervention against Cuba. And the Pentagon could be well advised not to forget that, as shown at the latest tests, we have rockets which can land precisely in a preset square target 13,000 kilometers away. This, if you want, is a warning to those who would like to solve international problems by force and not by reason."[58]

This extraordinary statement—the first time the Soviet Union had rattled its nuclear missiles in defense of a third world nation since the Suez crisis in 1956—achieved the goal Khrushchev set out for it. Fidel Castro was so appreciative that he decided to let his brother go to the Soviet Union.

Raúl Castro arrived in Moscow on July 17 for what turned out to be a warm and productive visit. The young revolutionary was eager to express his brother's and his own gratitude for the Soviet diplomatic support. They were convinced that Khrushchev's July 9 statement had altered U.S. calculation and forestalled an attack.

Khrushchev had some advice for the Cubans. Despite his disappointment at the recent collapse of the four-power summit in Paris, he still doubted that Eisenhower would invade Cuba unless provoked. His greater worry was that the Cubans might somehow trigger a U.S. counterstrike. "We don't want war," Khrushchev cautioned Raúl, "and you don't need war."[59]

When Raúl asked, "Do you think the U.S. can arrange intervention under the banner of Organization of American States, as it was in Korea under the banner of United Nations?," Khrushchev responded, "It is not a real possibility now; it is an absolutely different situation [today]." Khrushchev, however, did not want the Cubans to believe that he was intending to limit Soviet military assistance to Cuba. "If it [is] useful for you," he said, "we can give you more."[60]

The meeting had its light moments. To demonstrate how committed the Cubans were to building a socialist society, Raúl spoke of himself toiling day and night. In response Khrushchev threw out a half-mocking taunt: "Don't work all night. You will make stupid mistakes if you do."[61]

Khrushchev thought the visit had achieved all that he had hoped it would. Cuba had become a very strong ally. A clerical change at the KGB signaled this new confidence. In August 1960 the code name for the Castro regime file was changed from YOUNGSTYE (Youngsters) to AVANPOST (Bridgehead).[62]

▪

KHRUSHCHEV'S MEETING with Raúl Castro coincided with major developments in the Congo, which soon placed the Soviet relationship with Lumumba at the center of an international storm. Khrushchev did not attend the independence ceremony on June 30, but the events that followed had important consequences for the Soviet Union. In May, Lumumba's party won the largest number of seats in the country's first election. Congo became a parliamentary democracy with a prime minister, the head of government, and a president as the head of state. Lumumba became the country's first prime minister, and Joseph Kasavubu, a fellow nationalist but not a member of Lumumba's party, became president.

The deal struck between Belgium and the Congolese nationalists left a thousand white Belgian officers in charge of Congo's twenty-five-thousand-man army, called the Force Publique, on the day of independence.[63] Belgian nationals were also kept in posts in the new government's civil service. This deal quickly unraveled. Within days of independence the Congolese Army collapsed. Black noncommissioned officers mutinied, declaring they were unwilling to serve under white officers. With the army paralyzed, disorder spread throughout the huge territory. Many of the hundred thousand Europeans living in the Congo at the time of independence fled out of fear. They included the civil servants, who had not had time to train Congolese replacements. The Belgian government reacted by sending troops on July 10 to protect the remaining foreign community.[64] The independence accord stipulated that Belgium could not redeploy troops to Congo without the permission of the new sovereign government, yet Brussels sent troops anyway.

The next day the situation in the Congo became even more confused. With the support and encouragement of the Belgians, a Congolese soldier named Moise Tshombe declared the independence of the copper-producing province of Katanga. The province, the source of one-half of Congo's exports, was by far the country's richest region. A day earlier Tshombe had invited the Belgian government to send paratroopers to the provincial capital of Elisabethville. Eager to defend the Union Minière du Haut Katanga, a Belgian company that enjoyed a monopoly over copper production, Brussels also sent forces to Katanga.

With the Force Publique in disarray, Lumumba and Kasavubu jointly requested intervention by the United Nations on July 12. It was an unprecedented request by a sovereign state. The UN had never before been asked to send troops into a civil war. The two leaders explained that international intervention was required to prevent "acts of aggression" by Belgian troops against Congolese citizens. They asked that membership in the UN contingent be restricted to soldiers from neutral countries. Stressing the urgency of the situation, Lumumba and Kasavubu threatened to appeal to the countries associated with the nonaligned movement founded at the Bandung Conference in 1955, including India and China, if the UN did not act "without delay."[65]

Kasavubu did not share Lumumba's interest in close ties with Moscow. However, the next day he agreed to send a joint message to Moscow asking Khrushchev "to watch hourly over the development of the situation." They added: "We may have to ask for the Soviet Union's intervention should the Western camp not stop its aggression against the sovereignty of the Republic of the Congo." Soviet Foreign Minister Gromyko distributed copies of the telegram to all members and candidate members of the Presidium.[66]

■

As of early July, Khrushchev had no desire to involve the Soviet military in an intervention in Africa. The Congo presented a major logistical challenge to any intervention because it lacked a major port near its principal cities, meaning that all military assistance would have to be airlifted. Khrushchev preferred a political solution anyway. It served Soviet interests to let the UN restore order. Moscow's favorite was already Congo's prime minister, and the international community was coming to his rescue. On July 13 the Soviet delegate at the UN was instructed to support a Security Council resolution calling for the formation of a UN force for the Congo and the immediate withdrawal of Belgian forces from the country. The resolution passed that night, 8–0, with Washington and Moscow on the same side of the discussion. Both superpowers were asked to contribute weapons and food to the UN force.[67] On July 15 Khrushchev sent word to Kasavubu and Lumumba that he regarded the UN intervention as a "useful thing."[68] In this telegram, which the Kremlin made public, Khrushchev also warned the Belgians and their allies: "If aggression were to continue in spite of this [UN] decision, the Soviet Government declares that the necessity would arise for more effective measures."[69]

Advance elements of the UN force began arriving in Congo the same day as Khrushchev's telegram. As soon as the Security Council passed the enabling resolution, UN Secretary-General Dag Hammarskjöld moved quickly to organize a military force that initially numbered four to five thousand men, largely recruited from African countries.

Kasavubu's and Lumumba's appreciation was short-lived. They soon were disappointed to learn that this force would not deploy to the secessionist region of Katanga. Determined to avoid involving the UN in any civil wars, the Secretariat refused to be drawn into the conflict between the Congolese government and Tshombe's forces in Katanga.

■

The Eisenhower administration knew that its interests in the Congo were different from those of the Soviet Union. On the day the Congo became independent, the CIA described its new government as having a "leftist tinge" and warned that it was vulnerable to Communist influence.[70] The agency, which may have been receiving information from the Belgians, asserted that five of the ten members of the cabinet were "inclined toward communism." It added: "Lumumba himself appears to be neutralist in attitude, with a Leftist and opportunistic bent."[71]

As chaos spread throughout the country, the administration sensed it might be witnessing the creation of a second Cuba. The U.S. Embassy in Léopoldville baldly drew the parallel between Lumumba and Castro: "The most serious effort is centered in Leopoldville where they [the Soviets] are well on their way to completely capturing Lumumba and followers like they took Castro in Cuba. Believe pattern very similar but this one is easier in some ways; Congolese are totally disorganized, they are political children and only pitiful few have faintest idea where Lumumba is taking them."[72]

Washington had an opportunity to get a better sense of whether Lumumba was another Castro when, on July 23, he flew to the United States at the invitation of the administration. The Congolese prime minister decided to leave his country in a desperate attempt to get the UN to help him fight Katangan separatism and to encourage the Americans to increase the pressure on their Belgian allies to leave the Congo. He planned to spend a few days at the UN before visiting Washington.

Lumumba made his case to the UN in New York. He visited with Secretary-General Hammarskjöld and various ambassadors. He also made time to see Soviet Deputy Foreign Minister Vassily Kuznetsov.[73]

President Eisenhower did not make time to see Lumumba, but the Congolese leader was given half an hour on July 29 with Secretary of State Herter. Lumumba left a bad impression on the Americans. Herter's deputy, C. Douglas Dillon, who attended the meeting, later recalled that Lumumba struck him as "a person who is gripped by this fervor that I can only describe as messianic . . . he was just not a rational being."[74] Lumumba's request for

U.S. assistance, which included a plane that he and Kasavubu could use to get around the Congo, fell on deaf ears. The administration wanted all support for the Congolese government to go through the UN lest it establish a precedent that the Soviets could use to outbid Washington.[75]

Lumumba next went to Ottawa, and the Canadian government was as unhelpful as the U.S. government. Frustrated by the lack of success, Lumumba went to see the Soviet ambassador in Canada, A. A. Aroutunian. A few days later, when he reached New York for more lobbying at the UN, Lumumba followed up the talk with Aroutunian with a second conversation with Kuznetsov.[76] Afterward Lumumba flew to Western Europe to continue his search for allies in the fight against Brussels and Elisabethville.

The threat of Soviet intervention propelled the UN to take one of the steps that Lumumba had requested. On August 1 Moscow issued a public statement that "[i]n the event of the aggression against the Congo continuing . . . the Soviet government will not hesitate to take resolute measures to rebuff the aggressors who . . . are in fact acting with the encouragement of all the colonialist powers of NATO" and appointed a Soviet ambassador to the Congo. The next day Hammarskjöld declared that the UN force would enter Katanga Province on August 6. For some time the secretary-general had been telling the U.S. government that the UN had to go into Katanga to deny Moscow a pretext for military intervention.[77] The Kremlin's statement made the argument for him.

■

IN THE FIRST WEEK of August Khrushchev decided to abandon any hope that the UN could manage the situation and pursue instead a unilateral approach to the ever-worsening Congo situation. Lumumba's comments to Soviet representatives on July 25, July 31, or August 1 may have been the catalyst. On August 5 Khrushchev sent a letter to Lumumba—and pointedly not to Kasavubu—that promised that "the Soviet Union is prepared to give and is already giving the Republic of Congo comprehensive support and assistance."[78] He added that Soviet military assistance might be necessary. "The difficulties of your struggle are clear and known to us. We know that the imperialists are mounting every possible intrigue against your young government. They do not have an aversion to use any means to achieve the success of their insidious aims. In their arsenal of subversive action is not only sabotage and economic diversion but the organization of plots and terrorist acts of every kind, which will require special vigilance on the part of the people and government of the Congo." Khrushchev assured Lumumba that in an effort to strengthen his government, he would receive the "friendly and disinterested help of the Soviet government." He also assured him that the Soviets sought a united Congo and viewed the Katangan separatists as part of a Western conspiracy.

The Soviet leader's determination to do something bold in the Congo hardened a few days later, when he learned that Ghana wanted the Kremlin to intervene. On August 6, when UN forces did not enter Katanga as the secretary-general had promised, President Kwame Nkrumah asked the Soviet chargé d'affaires in Accra for assurances that in the event of the outbreak of general war in Central Africa, Ghana could count on secret tactical assistance from Moscow.[79]

▪

As MOSCOW was preparing its response to Nkrumah, Hammarskjöld reported to the UN Security Council that on the advice of Ralph Bunche, his personal representative in the Congo, he had decided to postpone the entry of UN troops into the secessionist province because of the likelihood the Katangans would attack them. He still wanted to send them in, but he wanted the consent of the secessionists and Belgium, which was increasingly acting as Katanga's ally and protector.[80] In response to the secretary-general's initiative, the Soviets proposed a new Security Council resolution that drew a clear distinction between his and the Kremlin's approach to the crisis. Whereas Hammarskjöld continued to look for a diplomatic way to restore order in Katanga without in any way tipping the balance toward either Tshombe or Lumumba, the Soviets wanted UN troops to enter the rebellious province and "put an end to acts directed against the territorial integrity of the Republic of Congo."[81] Moscow knew that it did not have the votes for this resolution. On August 9 it withdrew this resolution in favor of a compromise proposed by Ceylon (now Sri Lanka) and Tunisia, which demanded the "immediate" withdrawal of Belgian forces from Katanga and the deployment of UN forces to the province, while reaffirming that UN troops could not participate in the civil war between the Congolese government and Tshombe.[82]

With the United Nations unwilling to defend the unity of the Congo, the Kremlin stepped up its support for the central government in Léopoldville and its allies. On August 11 the Presidium approved a letter from Khrushchev assuring Ghana that it could count on receiving Soviet weapons if they were needed in the Congo conflict. More important, Ghana received a promise "to give the African people not only symbolic assistance but real help in this struggle."[83] The same day a Soviet Il-14 transport plane arrived in the Congo as a personal gift to Patrice Lumumba.[84]

Lumumba had meanwhile returned to Léopoldville from his extended trip to the United States and Europe. Although the UN's August 9 resolution was disappointing, he was emboldened by Khrushchev's letter to apply even more pressure on the UN to defend the principle of a united Congo. On August 14, a day after appealing for unity in a speech to the Congolese people, Lumumba issued a series of demands in a letter to Hammarskjöld, who was back in the Congo. The central government wanted Congolese troops, not the UN, to guard Congo's airports, it wanted African and Congolese troops to be sent to Katanga and all non-African UN troops to be removed, and it wanted all weapons captured by the UN in Katanga be turned over to the government. Over the next twenty-four hours, although Lumumba and Hammarskjöld both were in Léopoldville, they communicated by letter. Five letters passed between them, and Lumumba's became increasingly angry. At one point he charged that Hammarskjöld, a Swede, was not impartial because of the dynastic ties between the Swedish and Belgian royal families. The secretary-general's response was to return to New York, and relations between the men were ruptured.[85]

At this point Lumumba formally requested Soviet military assistance. Although Lumumba claimed that Kasavubu had agreed to make this request to Moscow, the Congolese president later denied it and soon used the government's turn to the East against his prime minister. Khrushchev had been expecting a request, and on August 20 the Kremlin agreed to send cargo planes to the Congo. Five days later the Soviets requested permission from the Greek government to overfly its territory and refuel in Athens. The Greeks, who told United States about the Soviet request, agreed so long as they could inspect the cargoes.[86] On August 28 ten Il-14s took off from Moscow for Léopoldville, via Athens, with foodstuffs for the Congolese people.[87] Soviet military assistance took a different route. Four days later five AN-12 cargo planes left Moscow for Conakry, Guinea, filled with weapons and ammunition for the Congolese.[88]

■

WITH KHRUSHCHEV'S direct involvement in the Congo conflict, fears that it had become a second Cuba bubbled over in Washington. Throughout July the U.S. government had continued to hope that the UN could stabilize the situation and prevent the Kremlin from increasing its influence. There had also been a debate over Lumumba's politics. "Despite charges by the Belgians and his Congolese opponents that Lumumba is a communist," concluded the State Department's Bureau of Intelligence and Research in late July, "we have nothing to substantiate this allegation."[89] The news in August that Soviet cargo planes were flying to Congo settled the debate about Lumumba.

The news also had an impact on a much broader discussion in the administration. Coming on the heels of the apparent Soviet gains in Cuba, the summer's events in the Congo suggested that the third world was nearing a tipping point that required more energetic U.S. action if the entire region was not to be lost to communism. Eisenhower had told his foreign policy team on August 1 that the world was in "a kind of ferment" greater than he could remember "in recent times." "The Communists," he added, are trying to take control of this and have succeeded to the extent that students in many cases are now saying that the Communists are thinking of the common man while the United States is dedicated to supporting outmoded regimes."[90]

On August 18, 1960, the administration began seriously preparing for the removal of the prime ministers of both the Congo and Cuba.[91] At a morning meeting of the NSC the president said that Western troops might have to intervene in the Congo under the UN flag. "We should do so even if such action was used by the Soviets as the basis for starting a fight."[92] Eisenhower was convinced that Lumumba was on the Soviet payroll, and the council discussed rumors that Belgian Communists or Soviet advisers were writing his cables and plotting strategy. The chairman of the Joint Chiefs requested that the White House consider overt and covert measures to keep a Congolese airfield and one port out of Soviet control, predicting that "the covert activities of just a few Communist infiltrating such essential facilities" could "threaten the Free World's essential South Atlantic sea routes."[93] The Joint Chiefs presented no evidence for this, nor had they ever previously described the sub-Saharan region as a U.S. vital interest. But such was the emotional pitch that August in Washington. Formal planning for covert action to unseat Lumumba began after this meeting.

That afternoon the CIA updated the president on the progress of the anti-Castro planning. For months the administration had been watching developments in Cuba with dismay, reacting to them with more and more active planning but no action. Most recently, on July 21, the CIA had sent a message to the head of its station in Havana: "Possible removal top three leaders [Fidel, Raúl, and Che] is receiving serious consideration at HQS."[94] The next day the same officer was told, "Do not pursue. . . . Would like to drop matter."[95]

The change in Washington's mood in August inspired renewed planning by the CIA, which now offered a three-point initiative, involving the creation of an opposition, black propaganda (covertly distributed false rumors and assertions concerning the regime), and paramilitary training of a shock force of Cuban émigrés. Most of the discussion concerned the third point. As out-lined by Richard Bissell, the agency's King Midas, who had turned the U-2 program around in the 1950s, this involved the training of five hundred exiles in Guatemala for infiltration into the Cuban mountains. They would be intro-duced into the country in groups of seventy-five, dropped and supplied by air. over several months these units would make contact with the thousand or so rebels estimated to be actively fighting the regime on the island. Because Bissell was not completely confident that the paramilitary infiltration and the development of a resistance following infiltration would be enough to topple the regime, the agency had begun thinking of a backup émigré invasion of the Isle of Pines to establish a base from which a government-in-exile recog-nized by the United States could operate.

It was in this climate that the administration instructed the CIA to begin looking at how to kill both Patrice Lumumba and Fidel Castro. The U.S. gov-ernment had considered political assassination as a tool of foreign policy once before. Between 1952 and 1954 the CIA had investigated ways of murdering key Guatemalan officials, including President Jacobo Arbenz. According to an internal CIA study, "some assassins were selected, training began, and tenta-tive 'hit lists' were drawn up."[96] The State Department under Presidents Truman and Eisenhower was aware of this planning. The Eisenhower admin-istration found a different way to remove Arbenz, however, before the CIA ever received a formal order to use this particular tool.[97]

It is one of the conundrums of the Cold War that it was the democratic West and not the Soviet Union that considered the use of political assassina-tion as a means of increasing its influence in the third world. There is no evi-dence that the Presidium in the Khrushchev era ever contemplated killing Tshombe or Kasavubu or the leaders of the Cuban exile community, let alone the leaders of pro-Western developing countries like Tunisia and Thailand. This difference may reflect Khrushchev's innate optimism about Soviet prospects in the region, as compared with the deep pessimism of Dwight Eisenhower and even that of his successor, John F. Kennedy, about U.S. prospects in the third world.

In August 1960 the CIA, opened contacts with members of the Mafia to plan a hit on Castro.[98] The Mafia had its own reasons for wanting to elimi-nate the Cuban leader: He had closed its casinos in Havana. The planning against Lumumba, however, was more urgent, and the CIA received much clearer instructions from the White House. On August 25 the subcommittee of the NSC responsible for planning covert action recommended that "plan-ning for the Congo would not necessarily rule out 'consideration' of any particular kind of activity which might contribute to getting rid of Lumumba."⁹⁹ Eisenhower had already sent word to this group through his national security adviser that he wanted "very straightforward action in this situation." On August 26 Allen Dulles reported to the CIA chief in Congo that "we conclude that [Lumumba's] removal must be an urgent and prime objective and that under existing conditions this should be a high priority of our covert action."¹⁰⁰ The CIA station in Léopoldville was authorized to spend up to a hundred thousand dollars to "carry out any crash programs."

■

HAVING VOLUNTEERED to risk a minor intervention in Africa, Khrushchev decided to go himself to the United Nations to rally the support of the Afro-Asian countries for Lumumba's cause and the Soviet Union. The new General Assembly session was scheduled to begin September 20. The Soviet leader decided to go by ship. The creaky Tu-114 that had brought him across the Atlantic in 1959 was undergoing repairs, and no other aircraft in the Soviet fleet could take him nonstop from Moscow to New York City. The trip on the steamer *Baltika* would take ten days, so he intended to bring along several East bloc leaders to allow for some conferences on the way over.

As Khrushchev was preparing to leave the Soviet Union in early September, the situation worsened in Congo. Secretary-General Hammarskjöld had lost his patience with Lumumba and told the Americans that he must be "broken."¹⁰¹ The UN leader, who now shared the dire opinion of the Eisenhower administration, had become convinced that the situation in the Congo could not be stabilized until Lumumba was out of the way. Hammarskjöld "is clearly looking forward to forcing issue with Lumumba," the US ambassador to the United Nations Henry Cabot Lodge had reported, "but wants latter to create the situation."¹⁰²

Equally worried was President Kasavubu, who insisted that he had not been consulted on Lumumba's request to Khrushchev for Soviet military assistance. On September 5 Kasavubu dismissed Lumumba on the grounds that his handling of relations with the Soviets suggested he was trying to turn the Congo into a dictatorship.

Kasavubu's action caused both a constitutional crisis in Congo and an international crisis between the Soviet Union, which supported Lumumba, and those countries that did not.¹⁰³ The Congolese president had the right under the constitution to fire the prime minister. However, the elected Congolese Parliament voted on September 9 to annul Kasavubu's decree against Lumumba and on September 14 called for a cabinet shuffle, retaining

Lumumba as prime minister but dropping some of his allies.[104] Meanwhile, afraid that the Soviets might try to intervene to restore Lumumba, the UN's local commander ordered the closure of the country's airports and shut down Léopoldville's only radio station after allowing Kasavubu to make a public announcement of Lumumba's dismissal.[105]

Khrushchev was furious when these events in the Congo were reported to him, and he lost any remaining trust in the leadership of the UN. After having argued for two months that it could not intervene in the domestic affairs of the Congo, the UN was now siding with Kasavubu against Khrushchev's ally. The Soviets refused to recognize Lumumba's firing and continued with plans to assist the Congolese Army in attacking Katanga. On September 5, 6, and 7 Soviet transport planes, piloted by Soviet citizens, flew an estimated 450 Congolese soldiers south from Lumumba's headquarters in Stanleyville in the northern Congo in likely preparation for an attack on Tshombe's forces.[106] Moscow permitted Soviet pilots, at some risk to their planes, to take off and land from the grasslands near the airports that had been closed by the UN.[107]

Khrushchev sailed for the United States on September 9 and had to monitor the developments in Central Africa from the ship. "All the way across the Atlantic on our way to New York," Khrushchev later remembered, "we had kept in close touch with our Foreign Ministry about the situation in the Congo, sending and receiving coded messages between our ship and Moscow."[108] Meanwhile, although Khrushchev refused to abandon Lumumba, the Soviet government did place a temporary halt to the use of Soviet planes by the Lumumbists.

On September 14 Lumumba suffered an even more dramatic blow orchestrated in part by the U.S. government. Lumumba's former personal secretary, Joseph Désiré Mobutu, whom he had promoted to a leadership position in the Congolese National Army, staged a coup against him. Mobutu seized power, pledging that the country's elected leaders would be replaced by nonpartisan, nonsectarian professionals until the end of the year, by which time the constitutional crisis could be resolved. "This is not a revolution," said Mobutu; "it is a truce."[109] In early September, after Kasavubu had proved unable to remove Lumumba, the U.S. Embassy in Léopoldville began intensive discussions with Mobutu, who had been trained in the United States, to encourage him to take action against the Lumumbists and the Soviet bloc.[110] On September 16 Mobutu's forces chased the elected representatives out of the parliament building in Léopoldville, and the next day he ordered the Soviets and the Czechs to close their embassies. Although Mobutu was criticized by Kasavubu for being "insolent," he was allowed to remain president.[111]

Mobutu's coup and the subsequent expulsion of Soviet diplomats sharp-ened Khrushchev's anger at Hammarskjöld and the UN. "I spit on the UN," Khrushchev said in reaction to the unceasingly bad news from the Congo. "It's not our organization. . . . That good-for-nothing Ham is sticking his nose in important affairs which are none of his business. . . . We'll really make it hot for him."[112] The Soviet delegate at the UN, Valerian Zorin, received instructions to charge Hammarskjöld with colluding with the Americans to remove Lumumba from power.[113] But Khrushchev was determined to do more. He wanted Hammarskjöld's resignation and thought it time to elimi-nate the secretary-general position altogether. "On the ship's deck the thought came to me," Khrushchev explained a month later to his colleagues in the Kremlin, "about the structure of the United Nations."[114] Believing the future of the UN was at stake, he concluded that a troika of representatives from the three worlds—capitalist, socialist, and neutral—should jointly run the organi-zation. While deciding to raise the pressure on the UN, Khrushchev neverthe-less decided to reduce the immediate risks for the Soviets in the Congo conflict. Moscow ordered the Soviet pilots and planes, whose missions in sup-port of the Lumumbists had already been suspended pending developments, to return with its diplomats.[115]

Events at the UN in the days before Khrushchev arrived in the New York showed that he faced a tough campaign to rally majority support for reform-ing the UN's leadership structure and reversing its policy in the Congo. In response to Zorin's charge, Hammarskjöld had appealed for a show of confi-dence from the delegates. He got it in a resolution proposed by the Ghanaian delegation. Accra supported Lumumba but had no interest in allowing the Congo to become a battlefield in the Cold War. Passed by a unanimous 70–0 vote on September 18, the resolution affirmed that Hammarskjöld should take "vigorous action" to implement Security Council resolutions and declared that no state should send arms or military personnel into the Congo except as part of the UN mission. Only the Soviet bloc, France, and South Africa abstained. Not one of Khrushchev's new allies in Africa or Asia had opposed the resolution.[116]

■

WASHINGTON WAS NO MORE confident of the outcome in the Congo than was Khrushchev. The administration did not believe that Mobutu alone could effectively contain the threat from Lumumba. On September 16 Lumumba delivered himself into the protective custody of the United Nations. He was given UN guards and allowed to walk around Léopoldville.

On September 24 Allen Dulles reaffirmed Washington's desire to "eliminat[e] Lumumba from any possibility of resuming [a] government position."[117] Two days later the CIA sent its science adviser, Dr. Sidney Gottlieb, to the Congo with a collection of poisons to use against Lumumba. It was believed possible to gain access to his home and put the poison in his toothpaste.[118] Lawrence Devlin, the CIA station chief in Léopoldville, was told that the order to kill Lumumba had come from Eisenhower. When Devlin asked if Gottlieb had actually heard the president say these words, Gottlieb said no but explained that Bissell, the CIA's influential deputy director for plans, had assured him that the president had issued the order.[119]

■

THE STEAMER *Baltika* with Khrushchev and his delegation on board arrived in New York Harbor on September 19. Khrushchev had not told the Americans how long he planned to spend in New York. There were rumors that he would ring in the New Year in the city famous for its street party in Times Square. Unlike in 1959, the administration did not throw out any red carpet for him. Khrushchev had mentioned his interest in meeting President Eisenhower to the international press, but the president did not respond with an invitation.

In his speech to the General Assembly four days later, Khrushchev blasted the Western powers for their machinations in the Congo. He denied Lumumba was a Communist and warned the West not to celebrate its victory over him too soon. Then he attacked the leadership of the United Nations. Calling it "one-sided," he outlined his troika proposal.[120]

Hammarskjöld refused to resign. In a calm but firm speech on September 26, he defended the office of the secretary-general. "This is a question not of a man," he said, "but of an institution."[121]

Between sessions, Khrushchev met with world leaders to solicit support for restructuring the UN. He spent a lot of time with President Nasser of the United Arab Republic and the Ghanaian leader, Kwame Nkrumah. Both men received Soviet military assistance and were pro-Lumumba, yet both disappointed Khrushchev. Ultimately, with one important exception, none of the Soviet Union's third world allies—India, Ghana, Guinea, the United Arab Republic—supported Khrushchev's call to replace Hammarskjöld with a troika. Guinea's Sékou Touré was the most publicly critical of Hammarskjöld, but like Nkrumah, he only endorsed a compromise plan to ensure that Hammarskjöld's three deputies represented each of the three world groupings.

Nkrumah presented Khrushchev with the most interesting paradox. On

Nikita Khrushchev, Georgi Malenkov, and the Presidium listen to Alexandr Volkov reading Malenkov's surprise resignation speech at a meeting of the Supreme Soviet on February 8, 1955. Flanking Khrushchev in the front row are Malenkov and Kliment Voroshilov to his left and Nikolai Bulganin and Lazar Kaganovich to his right. (© *Bettmann/CORBIS*)

[In the foreground from left to right] Defense Minister Marshal Georgi Zhukov, Foreign Minister Vyacheslav Molotov, First Secretary Khrushchev, and Premier Nikolai Bulganin attending the great power summit in Geneva in July 1955. (© *Bettmann/ CORBIS*)

Yugoslav leader Josef Broz Tito (in white coat), Khrushchev, and Egyptian leader Gamal Abdel Nasser outside the Soviet consulate in New York City during the opening of the United Nations General Assembly in September 1960. In 1955 Tito first encouraged Khrushchev to be patient with the independent Arab leader. (© *Bettmann/CORBIS*)

President Eisenhower with John Foster Dulles on August 14, 1956, just before the secretary of state leaves for the London Conference on the Suez question. *(Dwight D. Eisenhower Library)*

In the third week of October and in early November 1956, the Soviet armed forces opened fire on Hungarian demonstrators in Budapest. The attack in November was largely provoked by the Anglo-French intervention in Egypt, which crystallized a sense in the Kremlin that its international influence was under siege. *(Dwight D. Eisenhower Library)*

There was no socialist leader who tested Khrushchev's patience more than East Germany's Walter Ulbricht (at the flower-laden rostrum). The two leaders are pictured in August 1957 in East Berlin, a little more than a year before Khrushchev launches the first of three Berlin crises designed to save Ulbricht's troubled state. (© Bettmann/CORBIS)

The new Iraqi prime minister Brigadier General 'Abd al-Karim Qasim (on the right) and his vice-premier and eventual murderer, the Ba'athist Colonel 'Abd al-Salam Arif, following the revolution that toppled the pro-British monarchy on July 18, 1958. (© Bettmann/CORBIS)

While still concerned that the West would attempt to overthrow the Qasim regime in Iraq, Khrushchev visits Mao in Beijing to discuss closer defense cooperation in late July 1958. *(© Bettmann/CORBIS)*

Anastas Mikoyan flies to the United States in January 1959 to hint to Eisenhower that there is real flexibility behind the Kremlin's November 1958 Berlin ultimatum. Standing directly behind Eisenhower is Llewellyn Thompson, who would serve as U.S. ambassador to the Soviet Union for both Presidents Eisenhower and Kennedy. *(Dwight D. Eisenhower Library)*

Khrushchev visiting Eisenhower in September 1959 at Camp David, which
Eisenhower had named after his grandson. When invited to this presidential retreat
north of Washington, D.C., Khrushchev had at first wanted to decline, fearing that
this was "where people who were mistrusted could be kept in quarantine." *(Dwight
D. Eisenhower Library)*

Shortly after his release from Soviet prison in 1962, Francis Gary Powers, whose U-2 was shot down by the Soviets on May 1, 1960, appears before the U.S. Senate. (© *Hulton-Deutsch Collection/CORBIS*)

Accompanied by KGB Havana station chief (and future Soviet ambassador) Aleksandr Alekseyev, Anastas Mikoyan meets Ernest Hemingway in February 1960 during the first visit by a Soviet Presidium member to Cuba. *(Collection of Aleksandr Fursenko)*

Meeting the "son of a bitch:" Khrushchev and John F. Kennedy shaking hands on June 3, 1961, on the steps of the U.S. Embassy in Vienna at the start of their two-day summit. *(John F. Kennedy Presidential Library)*

Khrushchev and his wife, Nina, join the youthful Kennedys at a formal dinner given in their honor by the Austrian President Adolf Scharf (center) at Schönbrunn castle on June 3, 1961. *(John F. Kennedy Presidential Library)*

President Kennedy meets in the Oval Office with Souvanna Phouma, the prime minister of Laos, on July 27, 1962. Four days earlier the Soviet Union and the United States had joined eleven other nations in signing the Declaration on the Neutrality of Laos in Geneva. *(John F. Kennedy Presidential Library)*

A Communist, who was initially considered by Moscow to be more trustworthy than his brother Fidel, Defense Minister Raúl Castro visits with Khrushchev in early July 1962 to discuss the shipment of Soviet missiles to Cuba. At the time of this visit, Khrushchev begins to connect the issues of Cuba and Berlin. *(Collection of Aleksandr Fursenko)*

Kennedy meets with Soviet Foreign Minister Andrei Gromyko in the Oval Office on October 18, 1962. Two days earlier Kennedy, who would say nothing about this to Gromyko, had been informed of U-2 photographs showing Soviet medium-range ballistic missiles in Cuba. Seated beside Gromyko is Soviet ambassador Anatoly Dobrynin. *(John F. Kennedy Presidential Library)*

Anastas Mikoyan meets with President Kennedy on November 29, 1962, on his way home following a difficult month-long visit to Cuba. *(John F. Kennedy Presidential Library)*

Roy H. Thomson meeting with Nikita Khrushchev, Saturday afternoon, February 9, 1963, at the Kremlin. When receiving two watches as gifts from Thomson, Khrushchev joked, "Thank you very much. It looks like some infernal machine that the Capitalists have dreamed up to blow up the Communist world. I will tell my wife to try them on first." *(Roy Herbert Thomson Archives)*

Khrushchev invited Fidel Castro to visit the Soviet Union in April 1963 to bury the hatchet following the Cuban missile crisis. Here Castro is pictured with Anastas Mikoyan, Nikolai Leonov, a KGB officer and longtime friend of Raúl Castro, and Soviet ambassador Alekseyev in Moscow. *(Collection of Aleksandr Fursenko)*

On June 26, 1963, President Kennedy visits West Berlin accompanied by West German mayor Willy Brandt (center) and the chancellor of the Federal Republic of Germany, Konrad Adenauer (far right). The leaders are on a platform by Checkpoint Charlie at the Berlin Wall. Only weeks earlier Adenauer had sent his secret message to Khrushchev. *(John F. Kennedy Presidential Library)*

Kennedy is seated near Vice President Lyndon B. Johnson (in the pith helmet) during a demonstration of tactical nuclear weapons at White Sands Missile Range in New Mexico on June 5, 1963. In less than six months, Johnson would be Khrushchev's new chief American challenger. *(John F. Kennedy Presidential Library)*

August 6 the African leader had asked for secret Soviet military assistance, now at their meeting in New York he privately told Khrushchev that "there is no other path for Africa except socialism," but in the General Assembly he refused to support the attack on Hammarskjöld.[122]

Fidel Castro was the lone exception among Khrushchev's third world allies. The two met for the first time at the Soviet consulate and quickly established a personal rapport. The Cubans then demonstrated their friendship by following the Soviets in voting against Hammarskjöld's Congo policy and in calling for UN restructuring.

Although Khrushchev could not gain enough votes for his UN proposals, his energetic diplomacy did affect Hammarskjöld's handling of the Congo operation. The UN informed its team in the Congo that Lumumba would have to be a part of any political settlement. When the United States asked the UN to allow Mobutu's forces to arrest Lumumba, the secretary-general refused. Instead he wanted Lumumba kept in "cold storage" under UN protection until a political settlement involving all of the parties could be reached.[123] When Mobutu's troops appeared with an arrest warrant at the house where the UN was protecting Lumumba on October 10, the Ghanaian soldiers guarding Lumumba as part of the UN force told them to leave.[124]

Disappointed by the secretary-general's sudden reluctance to pursue Lumumba, the United States accelerated its own efforts to eliminate the deposed prime minister. The CIA considered both using Congolese agents in an assassination attempt and deploying "a commando-type group" to remove Lumumba from UN custody. Devlin, the CIA's station chief in Léopoldville, did not want to use the poison sent to him from headquarters and threw it into the Congo River.[125] Instead he cabled Washington on October 17 to recommend that headquarters send "soonest high powered foreign make rifle with telescopic scope and silencer. Hunting good here when light's right."[126]

▪

K HRUSHCHEV WAS the center of attention throughout his three weeks in New York. The day before he left, he ensured that this became an indelible impression. While listening to a Filipino diplomat chastise the Soviet Union for its colonial behavior in Eastern Europe, Khrushchev began pounding the desk with both fists. Figuring he was not making enough noise, he then slipped off one of his loafers and began pounding with it. An embarrassed Gromyko, who looked as if he were "about to plunge into a pool of icy water," removed his shoe and gingerly accompanied his boss as if shoe drumming were a traditionally acceptable form of protest at the United Nations.[127]

A buoyant Khrushchev flew back to Moscow on October 13 on a Soviet plane. Although none of his African or Asian allies had endorsed his proposals for reforming the UN, he told the Presidium two days later that he had made the case effectively. He had no doubts about his campaign against Hammarskjöld. Indeed, he informed his colleagues that henceforth "[w]e will not agree to any disarmament if the structure of the UN does not get changed."[128] He also brooked no questioning about Soviet policy toward Lumumba and the Congo. "The Congo [policy] is to our advantage," said Khrushchev. "It discredits the imperialists and discredits the UN." If his colleagues disagreed, they stayed silent.

■

For ALL HIS optimism in these Kremlin discussions, Khrushchev knew that both his third world champions were vulnerable. Lumumba was now in the opposition, not in the government, and under a kind of house arrest. Castro was still in power, but he had a dedicated enemy in Dwight Eisenhower.

Only days after Khrushchev's return to Moscow, the Kremlin began receiving information from the KGB that Eisenhower might be preparing a military attack on Cuba to boost his vice president into the White House. Nixon was caught in a tight election against the Democratic challenger, John F. Kennedy. "Acts of sabotage and terrorism are being prepared," Aleksandr Alekseyev, the KGB resident in Havana, had reported a month earlier, and the reports continued.[129]

In anticipation of internal trouble Castro had already launched a crackdown on the island. In August he had purged his own security service, and on October 1 the Cubans initiated a block surveillance system similar to one devised by the East Germans that encouraged neighbors to spy on one another. Castro had learned more recently that he might also face another challenge, this one launched from abroad. Communists had observed the training by the CIA of Cuban émigrés, who Castro assumed might be used in a full-scale military invasion. Moscow shared his concerns and launched a propaganda campaign to deter a U.S. attack.[130] On October 14 *Pravda* asserted that "there are more and more facts which show that the territory of Guatemala is being turned into a bridgehead of aggression against Cuba."[131] Starting on October 18, *Izvestia* and *Pravda* warned Washington not to attack. On October 25, at the UN, Zorin denounced U.S. efforts to train Cuban émigrés in neighboring

Latin American countries to remove the Castro regime. That same day the Cubans deployed thousands of militiamen along the southern coast of the island, where an invasion force from Guatemala might land. On October 27, 1960, Cuban forces were placed on the highest military alert.[132]

Khrushchev responded by restating his July threat to use nuclear weapons to defend the Castro regime. This time, however, he believed that the threat to Castro was real. The TASS news service released on October 29 a transcript of an interview Khrushchev gave to a Cuban journalist in which he warned the United States not to force him to make good on his "symbolic" threat to use nuclear weapons.[133]

The tension over the Caribbean lasted another ten days. When John F. Kennedy won a razor-thin victory over Richard Nixon on November 8, the Soviets and Cubans relaxed. The feared preelection attack had not happened.

Whereas Khrushchev could believe he had protected Castro, he was not able to save Lumumba. In November the Soviets lost a crucial diplomatic battle at the UN when the United States successfully lobbied to seat a Congolese delegation led by Kasavubu. The vote went 53–24 (19 abstentions) against the Soviets and their friends, with the margin of victory coming from the former French colonies in West Africa.

When Lumumba learned of Kasavubu's victory in New York, he looked for an opportunity to rally his own forces. Taking advantage of a thunderstorm, Lumumba escaped from his UN guards on the night of November 27. His flight worried Mobutu and his Western allies. Were Lumumba to reach Stanleyville, where the bulk of his supporters were forming a resistance to Mobutu and Tshombe, he could set up a secessionist government and request Soviet military assistance. While Mobutu's forces launched a manhunt, the CIA sent a contract killer, a European with a criminal record, to Stanleyville with orders to murder Lumumba. Meanwhile UN headquarters ordered the UN force to step aside and allow events to take their course.

Although Lumumba's name was well known throughout the Congo, his image was not. As he and his men traveled the seven hundred miles to Stanleyville in a convoy, they were repeatedly stopped by tribesmen who did not believe that this figure in sports shirt was the "savior" Lumumba. "You are a liar. We know Lumumba well. He always wears suits and glasses. But you?" one village headman reportedly said to Lumumba.[134] These delays did not worry Lumumba, who took time to give long speeches in the villages along the way. A spectator at one of these speeches tipped off Mobutu's force, and the hunt narrowed. On December 2 Lumumba was captured in view of a contingent of UN troops from Ghana. When the troops requested permission to rescue Lumumba, New York stuck to its position of neutrality. Lumumba disappeared into Mobutu's custody.

■

THE FIRST ELEVEN months of 1960 had taught Khrushchev some hard lessons about the perils of establishing new allies in the third world. He assumed the United States had connived with Hammarskjöld to neutralize Lumumba and had a lot of evidence that Washington was trying to overthrow Castro. There could be no doubt that the administration was at least determined to deny Moscow any and all of these new allies. If Moscow wanted to continue winning new allies, Khrushchev understood that political and economic competition might not be enough. He had to be prepared to take some military risks. Southeast Asia, an area that previously he had left to the Chinese and the North Vietnamese, would be the proving ground for this new form of the strategy of peaceful coexistence.

13

SOUTHEAST ASIAN TEST

Thε coup of August 9, 1960, was a surprise to all but the Second
Battalion of the Royal Lao Army and its commander, Kong Le. Kong had
duped the United States, the main foreign supporter of the Lao Army,
into helping him. A week earlier, at Kong's request, U.S. military advisers had given the battalion training in a nighttime takeover of the capital. The
explanation given by Kong Le and his men was that they needed to know this
in case it was ever attempted by the Communist Pathet Lao.

Only twenty-six years old, this young commander professed no wish to be
the generalissimo of Laos. Once the coup succeeded, he threw his allegiance
behind a former Lao prime minister, Souvanna Phouma, and called for a return
to a foreign policy of genuine neutrality. Kong Le was no Communist, but he
considered himself an anti-American nationalist. Whereas in Egypt Nasser had
initially been able to reconcile a desire for better relations with the United
States with strong nationalism, this was more difficult for nationalists in
Southeast Asia, where since 1954 the United States had been seen as the principal imperialist power. Kong Le clearly blamed the United States for having
brought the Cold War into Lao politics. The major task facing the Laotian people, he said in the months after the coup, was to "drive away the Americans."[1]

■

The coup in Laos, a country that had never before attracted his attention, fitted a predictable and welcome pattern for Nikita Khrushchev. Once
more an anti-imperialist leader had emerged to lead a nationalist movement
in the third world. Yet in August 1960 Khrushchev was much too preoccupied
with the nationalists in the Congo and Cuba to take much notice of this development in Laos.

At a conference in Geneva in 1954 the Soviet Union, along with China,
Great Britain, and the United States, had formally dismantled the French

Empire in Indochina. Vietnam was split in half pending a general election that never happened. Meanwhile Laos and Cambodia were given their independence. Laos, the "land of a million elephants," had no more than three million people. Poor, landlocked, and with no important economic resources, it had significance solely because of its location. Sandwiched between Vietnam in the east, China in the north, Cambodia in the south, and Thailand in the west, Laos became a contested borderland as North Vietnam vied for unity with South Vietnam and Thailand sought to prevent Communist influence from penetrating further into the interior of Southeast Asia.

Much to the disappointment of Moscow's Asian allies, in his five years at the helm Khrushchev had shown very little interest in the successor states of the former Indochina. It was not that he had an aversion to Southeast Asia. He had visited Burma and even Indonesia but had never bothered to stop in North Vietnam, let alone landlocked Laos.[2] Khrushchev was physically uncomfortable in the tropics. "I found the climate almost unbearably hot, damp, and sticky," he later said about his trip to Indonesia. "I felt like I was in a sauna the whole time. My underwear stuck to my body, and it was almost impossible to breathe."[3] But it wasn't the weather that kept him from Hanoi or Vientiane. Indeed, he had made a second trip to Southeast Asia in early 1960. His discomfort stemmed from Vietnamese politics.

Khrushchev liked and respected the Vietnamese leader Ho Chi Minh. "I've met many people in the course of my political career," he recalled in his memoirs, "but Ho Chi Minh impressed me in a very special way. Religious people used to talk about the holy apostles. Well, by the way he lived and by the way he impressed other people, Ho Chi Minh was like one of those 'holy apostles.' He was an apostle of the Revolution."[4] Ho remained friendly to the Soviet Union until his death in 1969, and he visited Moscow a number of times while Khrushchev was in power. But as the Vietnamese leader grew older, Moscow found itself at odds with the next generation of leaders, who tended to share Beijing's views on Khrushchev and the revolutionary potential in Southeast Asia.

As was the case in China, the Vietnamese leadership had become suspicious of Khrushchev during the Twentieth Party Congress, especially after his introduction of the doctrine of peaceful coexistence. Initially, the Vietnamese had supported the doctrine. Anastas Mikoyan, the first Presidium member to visit North Vietnam, went to Hanoi in 1956 and discovered that so long as Ho was in control, support for the policy was secure.[5] But Ho entered a form of semiretirement in 1958. Vietnamese newspapers began calling him Uncle Ho, and he restricted his official functions to giving advice, mainly on foreign policy. By 1959 North Vietnam had embarked on a more revolutionary path. At the Fifteenth Plenum of the Vietnamese Communist Party, the Vietnamese replaced peaceful coexistence with a strategy to achieve unification: "The fundamental path of development for the revolution in South Vietnam is that of violent struggle."[6]

For Moscow Laos was indistinguishable from the Vietnamese problem. The leaders of the Democratic Republic of Vietnam, the North Vietnamese, identified the political future of Laos with their own struggle for the reunification of Vietnam under Hanoi. Before 1945 there had been a single Communist Party of Indochina under the leadership of Ho Chi Minh. The Vietnamese formed not only the leadership of the Communist Party but most of the rank and file as well. As Moscow well knew, there was not much of an indigenous Lao Communist Party. Nationalist feeling in that country centered on the king of Laos. Vietnamese comrades, however, pushed ahead with creating a Lao party after Geneva. As the Vietnamese admitted to the Soviets, most of the members of the Lao party in the beginning were in fact Vietnamese.[7]

Moscow had provided little assistance to the People's Party of Laos, or Pathet Lao, since its foundation in March 1955. Although led by a dedicated Communist, Prince Souphanouvong, who enjoyed the support of the Vietnamese and the Chinese, the Pathet Lao was too small and politically unimportant to warrant any great investment by Moscow. Instead Khrushchev chose to demonstrate Moscow's commitment to his policy of patient, political transition by dealing with Souphanouvong's half brother, a dedicated neutralist, the Laotian prime minister Souvanna Phouma.

Moscow had first dealt with Souvanna in 1956. In response to his call for a neutral Laos foreign policy, the Soviets had tried to establish diplomatic relations in the summer of 1956. Representations were made to the Laotian government through its representative in Bangkok.[8] An exchange of notes ensued, with both sides indicating an interest in negotiating the establishment of diplomatic relations. The matter went so far that Moscow sent a formal recognition of the independence and sovereignty of the country.[9] A week after this message, Soviet tanks entered Budapest. Then the discussion abruptly stopped. From November 1956 through July 1957 the Laotians exhibited diplomatic cold feet.

When the dialogue resumed from the Laotian side, Vientiane suggested the establishment of relations but resisted letting the Soviets establish an embassy in the country. Pleading the inability to afford an embassy in Moscow and wishing to avoid an unequal diplomatic relationship, the

Laotians suggested that the Soviets accredit their ambassador in Paris as ambassador to Moscow. The Soviets agreed and proposed that their ambassador in Cambodia act as the Soviet representative to Laos as well. Moscow produced a joint communiqué, and then again there was silence from Laos. This silence lasted three years.

The United States had watched the Soviet-Laotian negotiations with concern and worried about Souvanna Phouma's politics. In 1957, Souvanna and Souphanouvong had signed a public agreement permitting the political wing of the Pathet Lao, the Neo Lao Hak Sat, to participate in the general elections in 1958. The administration opted not to wait to ratify the result. Shortly after the election, in which several Communist deputies were elected and brought into Souvanna's cabinet, a U.S.-backed political faction forced his resignation and formed a right-wing government.

The emergence of Kong Le and the restoration of Souvanna in August 1960 provided Khrushchev with a second opportunity to show the Chinese and the Vietnamese that working with progressives and neutrals could bring about the peaceful transformation of Laos into a socialist country. One of the new government's first acts was to resume the stalled negotiations with Moscow over diplomatic recognition. In September the Souvanna government informed Moscow through the Soviet ambassador in Cambodia that it wished to conclude the negotiations on diplomatic relations.[10]

■

ALTHOUGH MOSCOW's allies in the region considered Kong Le's mutiny a mixed blessing, they were pleased to see that this might bring Moscow and its financial resources into the region. The North Vietnamese offered themselves to the Russians as tutors to understand the players in Laos. Hanoi was not unhappy that Moscow quickly restarted the diplomatic negotiations with Souvanna that had stalled in 1957. But the Vietnamese wanted the Soviets to understand that at best, Souvanna was a temporary solution. As an anti-Communist neutralist he was very dangerous from Hanoi's perspective because he would place limits on efforts by Communists within his own country to take control. North Vietnam's ambassador to Beijing warned his Soviet counterpart that Souvanna was "just like [Burmese Prime Minister] U Nu and [Cambodia's King] Sihanouk in his anticommunist leanings."[11] They told Moscow that he was "unstable."

The Vietnamese hoped the mutiny would finally stir Moscow to show some real interest in their protégé, the Pathet Lao. Hanoi seemed to have hopes of tapping the Soviet Union as a source of assistance to the Pathet Lao.

In the past Moscow had refrained from providing any significant amount of assistance to the Communist forces in Laos.[12] Hanoi was not shy to take credit for the fact that a Laotian Communist movement existed at all. "The Vietnamese have played the leading role in the revolutionary struggle of the Indochinese people," the North Vietnamese bragged to Moscow. Ho Chi Minh had been agitating for revolution as far back as the Versailles Conference that ended World War I. In Laos there had been no revolutionary movement to speak of between 1930 and 1945. It was only after the August 1945 revolution in Vietnam that a Laotian nationalist movement developed. With the help of the Vietnamese the Pathet Lao had emerged as an independent army fighting the French. "This army, which grew and strengthened, had many Vietnamese members who helped in the organization of political work and the preparation of cadres," said Chan Ti Bin, a North Vietnamese official sent to explain the realities of Laos to the Soviets.[13] Meanwhile a people's party, established along Marxist-Leninist lines, had developed on the basis of a united front organization, known as the People's Patriotic Front of Laos, the Neo Lao Hak Sat.

The Vietnamese tried to stoke Khrushchev's competitive urges by detailing how much money the United States was devoting to the small kingdom. Hanoi estimated that between 1955 and 1960, Washington provided $169.6 million. Most of this money went to pay the salaries of the Lao military and the civil servants of the Royal Lao government. During this period the Lao Army grew from twenty-five thousand to thirty-two thousand with a militia of five thousand. There were one thousand French soldiers stationed in Sena and another detachment of four hundred military advisers with the Lao Army under a French lieutenant general.

An excellent barometer of Khrushchev's lack of interest in Laos was that unlike the Congo, nothing about events in the Asian country was important enough to interrupt his games of shuffleboard aboard the steamer that was taking him to the opening of the General Assembly session in September 1960. It is impossible to know for sure, but this may have been studied indifference. Khrushchev was increasingly concerned about the Chinese, who seemed to be standing behind the more militant Vietnamese.

That summer Khrushchev's relations with China deteriorated further. There was nothing new about Sino-Soviet tensions. Relations between the countries had been steadily worsening since 1956, and time had failed to heal the wounds caused by Khrushchev's drive for destalinization and peaceful coexistence. As the years passed, Mao increasingly saw himself as the victim of Khrushchev's efforts to improve relations with the West. When Khrushchev temporarily discarded his policy of applying pressure on the Western powers over the status of Berlin in mid-1959, the Chinese were told that Moscow could no longer proceed with helping Beijing build its own nuclear bomb, as it had promised in October 1957. The Communist Party of the Soviet Union, which informed its Chinese counterpart of the cancellation, could not have made the link to détente any clearer. "[I]t is possible that the efforts by socialist countries to strive for peace and the relaxation of international tensions would be jeopardized," the Soviet party explained, if this agreement were to continue and the West found out.[14] Khrushchev's visit to Beijing in September 1959, coming right on the heels of his triumphant trip to the United States, did not help matters. Bubbling over with optimism about the potential for better relations with Washington, Khrushchev managed to enrage his Chinese hosts, who had invited him to participate in a commemoration of the victory of the Chinese Revolution.[15]

In the summer of 1960 for the first time the strain seemed to have caused a visible tear. The Chinese and Soviet delegates traded insults at the Third Congress of the Romanian Communist Party in Bucharest in June 1960. That was enough for Khrushchev. "We took great care never to offend China until the Chinese actually started to crucify us," Khrushchev later recalled. "And when they did start to crucify us—well, I'm no Jesus Christ, and I didn't have to turn the other cheek."[16] In July 1960 the Soviets announced that they would be withdrawing all their advisers from China. Diplomatic relations continued between the Communist giants, but fraternal relations seemed to be at an end.

■

UNLIKE THE KREMLIN, the White House took Laos seriously as an area of Cold War conflict. The Eisenhower administration had not liked Souvanna in the 1950s, seeing his neutrality as far left–leaning, and it still did not like him. In the first days after the coup Washington hoped for Kong Le's removal and the preservation of the dependable anti-Soviet policies of the U.S.-supported Prince Somsanith government. This did not happen. Kong Le announced a provisional government of forty men, which included the chieftains of the Pathet Lao. He had hoped to include Lao's former prime ministers, Souvanna Phouma and Boun Oum, but they declined, preferring to wait for a decision by the National Assembly. In short order, the Lao Assembly passed a vote of nonconfidence, dissolving the Somsanith government. The king nominated Souvanna Phouma as prime minister, and on August 17, 1960, Kong Le transferred power to him.

With this political failure in Vientiane, the administration was divided over what to do next. The U.S. ambassador, Winthrop Brown, believed that the United States had to compete for Souvanna's support. Washington had to be prepared to offer him a wide range of political, military, and economic assistance in return for a pledge that he would not establish relations with Hanoi, Beijing, or Moscow and that he would not repeat the mistake of 1958 by bringing members of the Pathet Lao into his cabinet. The State and Defense department were more concerned about preserving the Royal Lao Army as a viable force first to contain and then to destroy the Pathet Lao. Washington's favorite, General Phoumi Nosavan, commanded this army, and he was already mounting operations against Pathet Lao villages in the northern province while the Americans were debating one another.[17]

Eisenhower was among those who were most alarmed by the situation in Laos. This contrasted sharply with the cool head that he had displayed during the missile gap debate earlier in the year. Perhaps because the president knew less about the developing world than he did about the strategic balance, any perceived Soviet gains in the third world touched an exposed nerve. In what became a famous metaphor, he compared Laos to a piece in a game. "[T]he fall of Laos to Communism could mean the subsequent fall—like the tumbling row of dominoes—of its still-free neighbors, Cambodia and South Vietnam and, in all probability, Thailand and Burma. Such a chain of events would open the way to Communist seizure of all Southeast Asia."[18]

Washington really had no clear idea of what was happening in Laos. In the words of an administration staffer, the problem of intelligence there was "a question of gathering data on the basis of two men who met on a jungle path in the middle of the night."[19] Eisenhower later recalled that "we studied intelligence reports day-by-day and sometimes hour-by-hour."[20] But this did little to clear the fog in what the president described as "this mysterious Asian land."[21] A general pessimism about the strength of communism—or the weakness of liberalism—in Southeast Asia led to a tendency to opt for worst case assumptions, even in the absence of hard data. As of October, Eisenhower and his team believed that "Souvanna Phouma was either an accomplice or a captive of Captain Kong Le who, himself, was an accomplice of the Communist Pathet Lao."[22]

■

THE SOVIETS also had no idea what was going on in Laos in October, but there was some hope they might find something out. Moscow's appointed ambassador, Aleksandr Abramov, the current Soviet ambassador to Cambodia and a former envoy to Israel, arrived in Laos on October 13, 1960. He had been nominated as ambassador five days earlier. One of his missions was to send Moscow a deeper assessment of the character of both Souvanna and Kong Le. A useful source of information was the Indian ambassador in Vientiane, Patnom. According to the Indian diplomat, Kong Le was the most popular man in Laos.[23]

The Indian also reinforced the Vietnamese view that the U.S. aid program in Laos had been a political failure. Few Lao villagers benefited from the assistance. He told Abramov that of the thirty to thirty-two million dollars in aid, twenty-five million went to the army, an additional three and a half million went to pay for the activities of the U.S. team in the country, and one and a half million was allocated to pay off the Lao budget deficit.

Kong Le asked to see Abramov within a few days of his arrival. He wanted the Soviet diplomat to meet with representatives of the Neo Lao Hak Sat, the political wing of the Pathet Lao. Abramov was careful not to. Having not yet met with the king, he lacked official blessing as an ambassador to the court. Moreover, he worried that any meeting with the Pathet Lao, but especially one that came before he had seen Souvanna, would confuse the neutralist and the king about the nature of his mission.

When Abramov finally met Souvanna on October 27, the Lao leader wasted no time in telling him that the Laotians needed fuel "as much for military as civilian purposes." They needed airplane fuel and diesel for automobiles. The government was building a road to the Burma-Lao border that was scheduled to be completed by December, but in the meantime Souvanna hoped the Soviets would provide fuel supplies by air.[24]

■

MOSCOW'S PASSIVITY in Laos continued. The Kremlin waited to hear from Souvanna again before doing anything about his request for aid. There is also no evidence that Moscow stepped up aid to the Pathet Lao. Meanwhile the neutralist government's hold on power began to deteriorate rapidly. On November 14 the government garrison guarding the royal capital of Luang Prabang joined the antigovernment forces led by Phoumi Nosavan. Souvanna tried to project an air of confidence, telling reporters, "[W]e are taking steps to retake Luang Prabang."[25] But privately his doubts were mounting. When Luang Prabang fell to its ally, Washington dropped its pretense of neutrality. On November 15 it advised the Laotian prime minister not to try to retake his own capital. "It . . . seems to us that such an open use of force would further exacerbate the situation," announced the State Department's spokesman; "it would lead to further divisions and might facilitate additional communist gains."[26] Instead it was Washington's intervention on behalf of the rightists that was to be the greatest catalyst for Communist gains. Even though he knew Phoumi Nosavan was supported by the United States, Souvanna had requested a continuation of U.S. military assistance for the Royal Lao Army. Privately Washington told Souvanna not to expect any more U.S. military assistance, leaving him few options to maintain a semblance of control over his country. On November 17 his government announced it would recognize the People's Republic of China and send "goodwill missions" to Hanoi and Beijing.[27] The following day Souvanna took members of the Pathet Lao into a coalition government. The Lao government and the Pathet Lao then issued a joint announcement that Laos had accepted aid from Beijing and Hanoi.[28]

Abramov, who was still Soviet ambassador to Cambodia, was back in Phnom Penh in the midst of planning Prince Norodom Sihanouk's state visit to Moscow when he received word that Souvanna Phouma wanted to meet with him in Vientiane as soon as possible. Souvanna had sent his request on November 19, and by November 22 Abramov was back in Laos.

The next day, November 23, Souvanna Phouma described a bleak situation to the Soviet ambassador.[29] As the result of a blockade established by the Thai government with U.S. blessing, the Lao economy was "completely disorganized." He estimated that many thousands of tons of food intended for his citizens were rotting at the port of Bangkok. The official capital was now without sugar, lard, and milk products.

Besides requesting airlifts of food, Souvanna wished to broach a more sensitive subject. His army lacked sufficient supplies to carry on the war with Phoumi Nosavan because the United States was now refusing to provide any military assistance to the Royal Lao Army. Souvanna explained that sometime before, a list had been sent to the U.S. military mission of necessary supplies for three infantry battalions and two airborne battalions. Abramov noted: "Souvanna said this list represents the maximum and the Lao government would be happy if the Soviet government gave us 1/2 or even 1/5 of what is on the list." Souvanna added, "We need . . . pistols, automatics, machine-guns, mortars, grenade-launchers, machine guns, light artillery and ammunition for all of this." Souvanna also did not mince words about when it should arrive: "All of this is needed as soon as it can be brought here."

Souvanna explained that the loss of Luang Prabang had been "a great misfortune to the country," and he had received reports that the military situation might get worse. Phoumi Nosavan was receiving U.S. military assistance and U.S. dollars. As a result, Souvanna revealed that he was trying to form a government of national unity, with representatives from his group, the Pathet

Lao, and even Phoumi Nosavan's "revolutionary committee." Souvanna explained that he had talked to his half brother about how this was the only way to avert a wider war. "Without the foreign intervention," Souvanna said, "there would be no division in the country." Souphanouvong and other members of the Pathet Lao leadership had agreed to the proposal for a government of national unity.

The meeting with Abramov pleased Souvanna. The Soviets reaffirmed their agreement to provide food and fuel to Vientiane, and Souvanna left the meeting believing these would arrive by an emergency airlift "within three or four days." He did not know if he would be receiving any weapons. Although the meeting had been private, he had announced his intention to request economic and "perhaps" military assistance from the Soviets at a press conference a few hours before he met Abramov.[30] The Laotian did not want to poison any future negotiations with Phoumi Nosavan or the United States by acting in a sneaky manner. Following the meeting, Souvanna told the press that the Soviets had agreed to airlift milk, floor, sugar, and 220,000 gallons of gasoline to Laos very quickly.[31]

▪

E VEN BEFORE Souvanna announced he would be getting Soviet assistance, the Eisenhower administration had been looking for reasons to unleash its allies on the Laotian right. The defection of the garrison at Luang Prabang had changed the military situation on the ground in Phoumi Nosavan's favor, and Souvanna's subsequent decision to bring the Pathet Lao into his government and recognize Red China provided a welcome excuse to let Phoumi Nosavan launch an all-out attack on the neutralist government. Washington was not impressed with Souvanna's announcement on November 20 that he would be broadening this government to include supporters of Phoumi Nosavan, seeing this as purely a tactical move. On November 21 President Eisenhower ordered U.S. representatives in Laos to "take the wraps off Phoumi right away." The State Department quickly instructed the commander in chief, Pacific (CINCPAC) to forward CIA payments to Phoumi Nosavan's forces, to give him necessary air support, and to "remov[e] any military restraints hitherto imposed by us on Phoumi."[32]

Phoumi Nosavan had been waiting for Washington to give him a green light to attack Souvanna's forces, and he wasted little time in taking advantage of his new opportunity. On November 30 he launched an assault from his headquarters at Savannakhet on the border with Thailand, a hundred miles south of Vientiane.[33] His strike force was small by U.S. and Soviet standards, consisting of only three battalions with some tanks, but in the Laotian conflict it was frighteningly large.

The situation quickly unraveled in Vientiane. On December 2 several hundred demonstrators friendly to the Pathet Lao denounced Souvanna's efforts to create a broad coalition that included Phoumi Nosavan. "The choice is yours," a beleaguered Souvanna announced from the steps of the National Assembly, "peace or war. If you want war you can have my resignation."[34] Meanwhile Souvanna asked Phoumi Nosavan for a cease-fire and sent a message through the U.S. ambassador to ask Eisenhower to stop assisting Phoumi Nosavan so long as he continued the fighting.[35]

Despite the perilous situation of Souvanna and his Pathet Lao allies, the Kremlin lacked a sense of urgency about events in the country. The promised Soviet food and petroleum supplies were expected by the end of November. On December 3 the Soviet Embassy in Vientiane announced that the first shipment of petroleum products would arrive that day. Abramov hurried to the airport to discover that the plane, which arrived several hours late, was carrying only pilots "on a familiarization run."[36] The first Soviet supplies finally arrived two days later. Five Il-14s brought merely forty drums of oil.[37] On December 6 Abramov formally announced the start of the Soviet airlift of petroleum. "The Soviet Government and people always accord assistance to their friends who find themselves in danger," he said at the Vientiane airport in front of Soviet pilots and their World War II–era planes, some of which had just been used to ferry assistance to Lumumba's forces in the Congo.[38]

Abramov's words had moved him far ahead of Soviet policy. In Moscow, Khrushchev was still taken up with what he considered far more important matters to make any real investments in Laos. Representatives of eighty-one Communist parties came to Moscow for a special meeting ostensibly to discuss the international situation but in fact to manage the Sino-Soviet dispute. The Kremlin got around to considering Souvanna's request for military aid only on December 7, the day after the delegations had left Moscow. Abramov, still shuttling between Vientiane and Phnom Penh, was immediately instructed to tell Souvanna that his request had been approved. The Soviets promised light weapons for the Royal Lao Army's three infantry battalions and two airborne battalions. But Moscow did not pick up on the need to send the weapons quickly. The instruction to Abramov was that delivery would be made in December and January. Moscow also requested overflight permission from Beijing and Hanoi to deliver these weapons directly to Laos.[39]

The Vietnamese greeted the news that Moscow was finally going to do its part in Laos with some disappointment. Soviet weapons were to go to

Souvanna's government and not to the Pathet Lao. It would be up to Souvanna to determine what was shared with the Pathet Lao. The Vietnamese, who expected an armed struggle between the Pathet Lao and Souvanna once Phoumi Nosavan was defeated, saw Moscow's policy as shortsighted.

■

IN SPITE OF the preferences of his Vietnamese ally, Khrushchev had decided to view Laos as a testing ground for a more flexible and muscular form of the peaceful coexistence strategy. Recently in Cuba and the Congo, the Soviet leader had learned that he had to take real risks to defend ideological allies in the developing world. In Laos he would build upon those lessons but apply the policy differently. Moscow would continue to support its ideological allies but over the objections of the local Communists, it would also forge a tactical military alliance with the neutralists. The reasons were complex. Believing that the United States held a decisive military advantage in the area, Khrushchev rejected the optimism of the North Vietnamese and the Chinese that violent revolution could succeed in the region regardless of Washington's preferences. The Soviet strategy would instead be to buy some time to allow the Pathet Lao to become politically dominant in Laos. Accordingly, Khrushchev wanted the Lao Communists to join in the neutralists' united front, which would be armed by Moscow and strengthened by international agreement. "The fundamental task with regard to Laos," the Soviet Foreign Ministry wrote in an early 1961 position paper, "is to struggle for the liquidation of the sources of international intervention in this region and the neutralization of this country."[40]

The promotion of Souvanna Phouma became the centerpiece of the Soviet strategy in Laos. He had international credibility, and his vision of a neutral, nonaligned Laos was the right one for the medium term. Since the United States would provide weapons to Souvanna's enemy, Moscow was determined to match that military assistance to ensure that the neutralists won. Thus could Khrushchev make a point to Washington, Beijing, and Hanoi.

■

WHEN ABRAMOV finally received word on December 10 that the Kremlin had agreed to send weapons, it seemed as if this help would arrive too late. With Phoumi's forces only fifty miles from Vientiane, there was panic in the air. The day before, the situation had forced Souvanna to declare that the capital, with its population of 110,000, would be not defended. On December 9, Souvanna's minister of information, Quinim Pholsena, had requested Soviet assistance in flying to Hanoi to hand deliver a letter from Souvanna to Ho Chi Minh that requested immediate military assistance. Abramov provided his plane, and Pholsena received promises of Vietnamese support.[41] Three days later Pholsena, supported by Kong Le's troops, who had rushed to Vientiane for the last stand against Phoumi, established a provisional government to replace the collapsed Souvanna regime. Souvanna had already left the capital.

Pholsena was very pro-Soviet, but his elevation did not alter Khrushchev's handling of the situation. The Soviet leader made no public comments about Laos. Soviet spokesmen decried U.S. support for Phoumi Nosavan's "aggressive" actions, but the Kremlin chose not to warn Washington about the consequences of this policy.[42] Modest military support was Moscow's only response to the emergency. The first of the Soviet military deliveries arrived on December 12, when Kong Le's forces received a shipment of howitzers.[43]

The Soviet artillery pieces did not come in time to prevent the fall of Vientiane. On December 20 Abramov and the remaining members of Souvanna's government had to leave the city or face capture. By the end of the month the Soviet airlift of military supplies had begun to tip the balance in favor of the neutralist government. Using Hanoi as the central staging area, six Soviet Li-2 transports carried supplies to Kong Le's forces and the Pathet Lao in the eastern part of the country, nearest the border with North Vietnam. On December 31 the resupplied Lao forces launched an offensive, causing alarm in the White House and relief in the Kremlin. In under a month Kong Le and the Pathet Lao had retaken Vientiane and pushed Phoumi's U.S.-backed forces out of central Laos.

In early January the Soviets met with the Poles, the Vietnamese, and Souvanna to discuss the situation. The Poles, who with Canada and India constituted the international control commission that monitored the 1954 Geneva settlement, said that "the resolution of the Laos question now depends on the military situation."[44] Moscow wasn't so sure, and Khrushchev decided to associate himself with efforts by the Cambodian leader, Prince Sihanouk, to open an international conference on the crisis as soon as possible.

The turnaround in Laos pleased Khrushchev. Soviet military assistance had been more effective at rescuing an ally than it had been in the Congo that summer. Nevertheless, he must have been aware that by delaying military assistance until Vientiane was on the verge of collapse, Moscow had almost misplayed its hand. At one point in December the Chinese representative in Hanoi had told his Soviet counterpart that Moscow had to "drop all the political nuances and do what it could to send arms to Laos."[45] Fortunately for the Kremlin, the conflict involved such small numbers of people and weaponry that, even late, the Soviet military airlift was able to prevent a complete collapse of the Communist and neutralist forces.

As 1961 began, Khrushchev felt the need to formalize the lessons he had learned in the developing world in 1960. On January 6 he delivered a widely quoted speech on the problem of revolution in the third world. While not at all recanting his commitment to peaceful coexistence, he allowed that at certain times military action might be required to ensure the success of national liberation movements. With specific reference to the civil wars in Vietnam and Algeria, Khrushchev introduced the term "sacred war" to describe these violent struggles. Given all that he had invested in his politically based approach, this was a big concession for Khrushchev. What he now hoped was that this concession would not mean Soviet involvement in many future small wars.

The Soviet leader did not have long to savor the praise this statement produced before events in the Congo reminded him of the chronic weakness of the Soviet position in the third world.[46] Patrice Lumumba had remained in the custody of the Congolese Army chief, Joseph Mobutu, since his arrest on December 2. In mid-January the Kremlin was elated by news that Lumumba had provoked a mutiny among the soldiers holding him and had escaped. Four days later, January 17, optimism turned once again to anger. Lumumba had been recaptured by Mobutu's forces and sent to the headquarters of Moise Tshombe in secessionist Katanga Province, home base of the one man in the Congo who hated Lumumba more than Joseph Mobutu did. Lumumba was never again seen alive. When Khrushchev learned of Lumumba's assassination, he ordered that the Friendship University be renamed in his honor. The Soviet leader still believed the future held great promise for socialism worldwide, but the struggles of the present worried him.

▪

AS HE LEFT OFFICE, Dwight Eisenhower had no sense of how vulnerable Nikita Khrushchev felt in the third world. On the contrary, the president seemed annoyed at the fact that he was bequeathing Soviet gains in Cuba and Laos to his successor. Despite recent successes in the Congo, Eisenhower was still seized with the fear and alarm that had spawned the CIA's assassination plans in August 1960. Lumumba was gone, but Eisenhower decided to leave to his successor, John F. Kennedy, the question of what to do about Fidel Castro.

In a farewell meeting with the president-elect on January 19, Eisenhower also made a point of stressing the importance of Laos. The outgoing president believed that the future of the entire region hinged on the fate of this tiny country. "It is the cork in the bottle," he said. Little known to the American people, the civil war in Laos had been elevated to a new level of importance in December 1960, when the Soviet Union began its airlift from Hanoi to the left-leaning government forces. For the Eisenhower administration Khrushchev's move presaged a new offensive, suggesting that the Soviets had decided to pick up the cudgels in a fight led to that point only by its socialist allies North Vietnam and to a lesser extent the People's Republic of China.

The new president brought some knowledge of his own to the Laos problem. Kennedy had visited Southeast Asia as a young congressman in 1951. On this extensive tour, which involved stops in Indochina, Japan, India, and Korea, he had done a lot of listening. He had returned energized by seeing nationalism in action and deeply concerned about the inability of even his fellow Democrats to appreciate that nationalism not only was here to stay but, if properly encouraged, could be a force for good in the developing world. Following the bitter debate in Congress in the early 1950s over who had "lost" China to Mao Zedong, in which Kennedy had been as much a partisan of the "we could have prevented it" line as any other congressman, U.S. legislators shied away from even appearing to support any neutralist movement that might have the potential to turn Communist.[47] First as representative and later as a senator, Kennedy took a more nuanced line on policy in the developing world, ultimately publicly supporting decolonization as well as anticommunism in both Indochina and Algeria.[48]

Now on the verge of the presidency, Khrushchev's future adversary had not yet decided what his policies would be in either Cuba or Laos. What he did know was that more often than not inflexible policy ideas or awkward diplomats had failed to make the friends for the United States that they should have. Like the Soviet leader, Kennedy understood that across the former European empires, "the fires of nationalism so long dormant . . . are now ablaze. . . . Colonialism is not a topic for tea-talk discussion; it is the daily fare of millions of men."[49] Kennedy expected the third world to be a principal focus of the Cold War for his administration.

Khrushchev, however, had his own idea of where the Cold War was headed. Hopeful that his more muscular approach to defending young postcolonial allies would deter future crises in the third world, he looked to focus Kennedy's attention on areas of more central concern to the Kremlin.

CHAPTER 14

"HE IS A SON OF A BITCH"

KHRUSHCHEV SAW the political victory of the young John F. Kennedy in November 1960 as an important opportunity to push his national security agenda. Soviet Ambassador Mikhail "Smiling Mike" Menshikov hinted to almost anybody with a plausible link to Kennedy that Khrushchev was eager to resume the process of relaxing international tensions largely abandoned after the Paris summit.[1] The Soviet Union sent a strong signal of its hope for better relations with the incoming administration by unconditionally releasing two RB-47 pilots it had detained since July 1960. And it seemed clear to the foreign policy community in Washington that the Kremlin was brushing aside any potential concerns about John Kennedy's razor-thin victory margin, immediately treating him as a leader with a mandate to change the Cold War.

It was an indication of how much he disliked Richard Nixon that Khrushchev greeted the Democratic victor so eagerly. From everything Khrushchev had learned about Jack Kennedy, he had little reason to harbor high hopes for this particular American politician. On the campaign trail, Kennedy had criticized the outgoing administration for failing to meet the Soviet challenge vigorously enough. "I don't want to be the President of a nation perishing under the mushroom cloud of a nuclear warhead," Kennedy had told crowds of American World War II veterans like himself in the final weeks of the campaign. "But neither do I wish to be the President of a nation which is being driven back, which is on the defensive, because of its unwillingness to face the facts of our national existence, to tell the truth, to bear the burdens which freedom demands, a nation which may be declining in relative strength, and with the world coming to an end as T. S. Eliot said, 'Not with a bang, but with a whimper.'"[2]

On the two issues that mattered most to Khrushchev, disarmament and the German question, Kennedy during the campaign seemed to take positions that were tougher than those of his rival, Nixon. Kennedy assured voters that the priority of his administration would be to build up U.S. strength—accelerate missile development, expand conventional forces, restore America's international prestige—before starting another round of talks with Khrushchev. He made repeated promises to defend West Berlin's security and Western access to the city. Moreover, though he assured his audiences that the next U.S. president would have to negotiate with Khrushchev on Berlin, at no point in the campaign did Kennedy offer a diplomatic plan for solving the problem.[3]

Another source of potential disappointment for Khrushchev was Kennedy's repeated criticism of Soviet gains in the third world. "[T]he great struggle in foreign policy in the next decade will not take place in Western Europe and will not be directly between the Soviet Union and the United States," said the candidate. "The great test will be which system travels better, which system solves the problems of the people of Latin America and Africa and Asia."[4] Among the places where communism had already traveled, Kennedy was most concerned about Cuba. "Castro is not just another Latin American dictator—a petty tyrant bent merely on personal power and gain. His ambitions extend far beyond his own shores. He has transformed the island of Cuba into a hostile and militant Communist satellite—a base from which to carry Communist infiltration and subversion throughout the Americas."[5] "[T]he United States," Kennedy added, ". . . can hardly close its eyes to a potential enemy missile or submarine base only 90 miles from our shores."[6]

The main biographical information on the new U.S. president available to Khrushchev also argued for caution. Born in Brookline, Massachusetts, in 1917, Kennedy was a child of privilege. A graduate of Choate and then Harvard, he gained an unusual political education when President Franklin Roosevelt appointed his father U.S. ambassador to the Court of St. James's. In London Joseph P. Kennedy courted notoriety with statements suggesting that the British would wilt under the pressure of fighting the Nazis and advocating that the United States stay out of the European contest altogether. Joe Kennedy seemed to worry more about the threat from Stalin than about anything Hitler could do to America. Kremlin staffers pointed out to Khrushchev the possible effect that the elder Kennedy might have on John Kennedy's views on foreign policy. Both the Foreign Ministry and the KGB, in their biographical sketches of the new president, pointed out Kennedy's strident rhetoric in the campaign and awkwardly tied it to the notorious anticommunism of his father.[7]

The Foreign Ministry did describe John Kennedy as "a typical pragmatist" but was much less sanguine about the prospects for successful negotiations on any of the issues that mattered to Khrushchev.[8] "[O]n relations between the USA and the USSR," Khrushchev was informed, "Kennedy's position . . . is quite contradictory." The KGB saw a little more liberalism than pragmatism in the new leader. Khrushchev's key foreign spies had concluded that Kennedy was from the liberal Adlai Stevenson wing of the Democratic Party, which believed in seeking diplomatic compromises wherever possible to reduce Cold War tensions, thus making it more likely that Kennedy would consider innovative approaches to bilateral problems.[9] Although the KGB and the Soviet Foreign Ministry disagreed on the extent to which the son shared the severe views of the father, analysts in both institutions noted that Kennedy accepted the fallacy of the missile gap and was unlikely to engage in any worthwhile negotiations before he had built up U.S. military power.

Buried in these papers, which Khrushchev may or may not have read, was a nugget that suggested some interesting corridor gossip in and around the Kremlin. Although the KGB was not yet ready to put on paper its verdict on the new president's leadership abilities, the Foreign Ministry was prepared to characterize him as "unlikely to possess the qualities of an outstanding person." There was a sense among some in Moscow that this scion of a wealthy American family, who lacked serious legislative or executive experience, was a lightweight.

It would have come as a surprise to many Western cold warriors, but this was not the kind of adversary that Khrushchev welcomed. He wanted a strong-minded pragmatist who could stand up to the forces of militarism and reaction, which he assumed were rampant in Washington. The experiences of 1960, culminating in the U-2 incident, served to reinforce his belief that U.S. foreign policy was inherently unstable. Khrushchev still believed that Eisenhower was a man of peace whose good instincts had been undermined by the CIA and the Pentagon. If John Kennedy were a strong leader, Khrushchev would expect him to tame these forces and negotiate in good faith with Moscow.[10] Essential to this view was the Soviet leader's belief that his own proposals, whether regarding Western access to Berlin or superpower disarmament, were eminently reasonable.

In late November at the Kremlin Khrushchev outlined his strategy for dealing with the new president for the East German leader Walter Ulbricht. The Soviet leader intended to solve the Berlin problem in early 1961 at a summit with Kennedy. In a departure, Khrushchev would seek a one-on-one meeting, not a four-power gathering, and planned to offer the Berlin "concession" originally prepared for Eisenhower, an interim agreement on West Berlin with a fixed time limit, after which West Berlin would become a free city without any occupation forces or special access routes for NATO forces. If Kennedy proved unwilling to negotiate a reasonable agreement, then the Soviet bloc would again resort to an ultimatum.

Khrushchev's decision to force the Berlin issue early in Kennedy's first year in office came as a surprise to Ulbricht, who hadn't been warned that the Soviets were considering another ultimatum.[11] The bruising experience of the 1958 ultimatum had made the German skeptical of Khrushchev's resolve. "Among our population," said Ulbricht, "there is already a mood taking shape where they say you only talk about a peace treaty, but don't do anything about it. We cannot act the same [way we did]. . . ."[12] Khrushchev assured him that things would be different this time. "[I]f there is not an interim agreement, then we will sign a peace treaty with the GDR and let them see their defeat." Khrushchev was confident that though this push would result in a period of tension, it would not spark a world war. "Of course, in signing a peace treaty," he said, "we will have to put our rockets on military alert. But, luckily, our adversaries still haven't gone crazy; they still think and their nerves aren't bad."[13] What Khrushchev refused to predict was whether a crisis would occur. Perhaps Kennedy would agree to their demands.

A day or so after Ulbricht left the Kremlin, Khrushchev received an encouraging top secret message from Washington. On December 1, 1960, the president-elect's brother and victorious campaign manager, Robert F. Kennedy, granted a thirty-minute interview to a KGB officer working undercover as a Soviet journalist. It is doubtful that Robert Kennedy knew for sure that this journalist had special access to the leadership; the future U.S. attorney general probably had just assumed—rightly, as it turned out—that most Soviet journalists were spies. Using the KGB man, Robert sent a message to Moscow on behalf of his brother. The president-elect, Robert said, "was seriously concerned about the situation in Berlin and will strive to find the means to reach a settlement of the Berlin problem. However, if in the next few months the Soviet Union applies pressure on this question, then Kennedy will certainly defend the position of the West."[14] Khrushchev wrote Ulbricht a few weeks later to explain that the Americans were rethinking their Berlin policy, as he had hoped.[15]

■

KENNEDY CAME to office intending to pick up the pieces of the diplomatic process that had exploded with Francis Gary Powers's plane over Sverdlovsk. For all his tough talk in the campaign about the Soviet challenge, Kennedy's ultimate goal was to engage the Kremlin and reduce the dangers of the Cold War. "We arm to parlay," he had also said frequently in the campaign, invoking Winston Churchill.[16] Kennedy believed that Eisenhower had fumbled the handling of the U-2 affair, thereby squandering a real opportunity to establish a modus vivendi with the Soviets that could have reduced the risk of war in Central Europe. "It would have been better," Kennedy told reporters later, "for the President to express regret at the [U-2] crash on Soviet territory rather than putting out a lie, as he did, which was later proved to be a lie before world opinion."[17]

During the ten-week transition between the election and the inauguration, the Kennedy team assembled experts to examine policy on all aspects of the U.S. relationship with the Soviet Union. Ideas for new proposals and strategies to ease the relationship came from these groups. It was suggested that the United States and the Soviet Union increase cultural exchanges, there were proposals that trade between the two countries be expanded beyond the sales of crab meat, and there were recommendations of possible cooperation in space.

But no new ideas on Berlin came Kennedy's way. Kennedy had brought Harry Truman's secretary of state, Dean Acheson, out of retirement to consider a way out of the Berlin impasse. Even before this process was over, however, longtime State Department German specialist Martin Hillenbrand expressed the problem for the Acheson group. "We can live with the status quo in Berlin but can take no real initiative to change it for the better," he wrote in January 1961. "To a greater or lesser degree, the Soviets and East Germans can, whenever they are willing to assume the political consequences, change it for the worse."[18] Since 1948, when Stalin first tried to remove the Western allies from West Berlin, the defense of the city and its 2.2 million residents was a touchstone for U.S. prestige in postwar Europe. No president could consider giving it away. Ultimately each of the men Kennedy asked to review the problem reached Hillenbrand's un-Kennedy-like conclusion: "However impelling the urge to find some new approach to the problem, the ineluctable facts of the situation strictly limit the practical courses of actions open to the West."[19]

■

YET ANOTHER POLICY review of immediate significance remained hidden from the Kremlin's view. The final months of the Eisenhower administration brought an acceleration of covert preparations for removing Fidel Castro from office. Despite substantial fears in Moscow and Havana, the administration had never planned an operation to kill or forcibly to remove Castro in a bid to ensure Richard Nixon's election to the presidency. Nevertheless, a team of CIA officers, led by the former supervisor of the U-2 program, Richard Bissell, worked tirelessly to provide an array of covert options to the White House. By the time the guard changed, the specialists had come to believe that a force of about a thousand Cuban émigrés, trained in guerrilla warfare at secret facilities in Louisiana and Guatemala, could deliver a knockout blow against the regime.

A friend of Kennedy's from the Georgetown cocktail circuit, Bissell was likely the first person to have hinted to him that the CIA hoped to get White House approval for something dramatic in Cuba early in the new administration. After a meeting on November 18, 1960, at which Kennedy received his first formal briefing on the Cuban planning, both the CIA director, Allen Dulles, and Bissell came away confident that the new administration would continue what Eisenhower had started.[20] There would be no change in the policy of removing Castro. In February 1961 the CIA completed its program of action, which the Joint Chiefs of Staff then received for their review and ultimately approved. In April Kennedy gave his provisional approval, though he always retained the right to cancel the operation at the last moment.

Although the Kremlin was not completely ignorant about Washington's anti-Castro activities, Khrushchev allowed himself to be lulled into a sense of complacency about Kennedy's intentions. Just as events in Eastern Europe in the fall of 1956 had clouded Khrushchev's analysis of the threat to Nasser in the Middle East, so events at home in early 1961 had a similar effect on the Soviet leader.

The seven-year plan to improve domestic conditions in the Soviet Union, announced with such fanfare in 1958, was failing. The Kremlin had drafted this plan in the wake of fears that the material concerns of Soviet workers would produce a political crisis similar to the one that Soviet tanks had crushed in Budapest in 1956. On his inspection tours around the USSR, Khrushchev saw mounting evidence that the Soviet state was not even meeting the most basic of its citizens' requirements. Dmitri Polyansky, the head of the Communist Party in the Soviet republic of Russia (the largest of the USSR's fifteen republics), had assured him that food supplies were ample in Russia. After Khrushchev discovered this was not so, Polyansky responded, "If one were to remove Moscow and Leningrad from our responsibility, then we could feed ourselves." Incredulous at this stupidity, Khrushchev asked, "But to whom will we give Moscow—Georgia?" In fact the Soviet people were experiencing shortages in meat, milk, and eggs. In peasant markets eggs, when they appeared, were selling for the equivalent of three dollars a dozen when loaves of good Russian bread cost pennies.[21] The Kremlin would have to sell twenty-three tons of gold in London, the equivalent of twenty-six million dollars, to buy European butter because it could not produce enough of its own.[22] A joke was heard along the lines of people waiting to buy food: "What nationality were Adam and Eve?" The answer was "Russian." To the question "Why?" came the answer "Because they were both naked, had only an apple to eat, and thought they were in paradise."[23]

Khrushchev understood all too well that his people were not living in paradise, and the problem was not simply the availability of butter. In the weeks after the Hungarian revolt, Khrushchev had warned his Presidium colleagues that housing was as politically important to the survival of the Soviet regime as was food. Consequently, in 1958 the Kremlin had promised two million cubic meters of new housing. By early 1961 housing starts had fallen so far short that Khrushchev decreed that all new apartment buildings would be built higher than the standard five stories to try to catch up with demand. Even this Band-Aid solution proved unworkable. Khrushchev had to rescind the order when he received the news that the USSR lacked the raw materials to build elevators for taller apartment buildings.[24] Kremlin bosses were soon huddling to decide how they would fudge the numbers for all aspects of the seven-year plan, so that the gap between promise and reality would not appear as huge as it actually was.[25]

Khrushchev marveled at how easily his subordinates were willing to accept this sad state of affairs. "Why are we bringing such shit into the bosom of the party?" he remarked upon learning of a regional boss who was promoted after he met his meat quota by slaughtering cows needed for milk production.[26] One party secretary in a town three hundred miles from Moscow insisted on admitting failure by taking his pants down to be lashed personally by Khrushchev. "He repeated this three times," Khrushchev said later, "I couldn't take it anymore and said to him: 'Why is it that you want your pants whipped off to show us your ass? Do you think you will give us some kind of thrill?' What kind of secretary is this?"[27]

For all the humor, Khrushchev felt threatened by these failures. His promise to the Soviet people was that their society would catch and surpass the United States by 1970. These dismal reports from the field caused him to remind his colleagues that the regime had to be serious about achieving the goal of affording its citizens an American standard of living. "Do you remember how Molotov and Kaganovich yelled at me when I announced that we would catch up with America. . . . They got frightened by the call to catch up with America." Khrushchev still believed it possible. But it meant working harder. "What does catching up to the United States mean?" he asked his colleagues in March 1961. "It means hard thinking. Stop all this fussing."[28]

Another annoyance and distraction in the early months of 1961 were China and its strange little ally in Europe, Albania. The xenophobic Albanian regime, led by Enver Hoxha since the collapse of Nazi power in the Balkans, had turned toward China out of fear that Khrushchev and Tito of Yugoslavia were scheming to divide up southeastern Europe. Ideology also played some role. Hoxha had no intention of giving Albanians even the modest liberalization associated with Moscow's destalinization campaign. Tensions between the Soviet Union and Albania broke into the open at the Fourteenth Congress of the Albanian Communist Party in February 1961. Although personally annoying to Khrushchev—reports came to Moscow of Albanians replacing his official portraits in all their public buildings with old pictures of Stalin—the dispute was of almost no consequence to world affairs.[29] However, when Khrushchev suggested breaking all trade ties to the country, Mikoyan reminded him that what really mattered was China, and Mao might overreact if the Soviet Union ganged up on his Balkan friend.[30]

Mikoyan made good sense, and Khrushchev accepted his plea for caution. Besides, the Kremlin's real concern was not Chinese influence in Europe but how Beijing was complicating the picture in Southeast Asia. The Chinese were lining up with the Pathet Lao and the North Vietnamese to press for a revolutionary victory in the kingdom of Laos.[31] The situation had changed dramatically since U.S.-backed Phoumi Nosavan's December 1960 offensive had forced the neutralist prime minister, Souvanna Phouma, and most of the leadership of the Communist Pathet Lao to flee the country. In January 1961 the Pathet Lao's successful counterattack had raised the possibility that Beijing's and Hanoi's dreams might be realized. Even as the Pathet Lao continued to make gains, however, Khrushchev advised both regional Communist powers to seek a diplomatic solution in Laos. Convinced that the Pathet Lao risked U.S. intervention if the offensive continued, he argued that only patient political struggle would bring lasting success in the region.[32]

In March Kennedy helped Khrushchev make this argument. In a meeting with Gromyko, who had flown to the United States to take a measure of Kennedy's views on the situation in Southeast Asia, the U.S. president told the Soviets that Washington now supported the neutralist government of Souvanna Phouma. Kennedy hoped to create a united neutral Laos with a united army and a coalition government, exactly the policy Khrushchev had been advocating to Beijing and Hanoi.[33] Four days later the Soviets gave the

North Vietnamese a copy of those sections of the Russian transcript of the meeting dealing with Laos and asked that they be shared with the North Vietnamese Politburo and the leader Ho Chi Minh.[34] Moscow then issued a public statement in favor of a cease-fire in Laos and privately called on Beijing, Hanoi, and the Pathet Lao to follow suit. Although the Chinese later joined with the Pathet Lao in accepting the cease-fire, Moscow understood that Mao was firmly opposed to establishing a unified Laos under a neutralist government.[35]

In this climate of disappointment at home and dispute abroad, the successful flight of cosmonaut Yuri Gagarin on April 12 came as a welcome distraction for Khrushchev and the Soviet leadership. Although unable to feed or house its citizens properly, the Soviet Union was the first nation to put a man in space. Khrushchev had feared that something would go wrong with the Gagarin flight and had turned down a May 1 date for the mission lest a failure mar the traditional holiday. His space advisers were confident they could succeed, however, and they advanced the schedule to ensure that Moscow would be ahead of the Americans, who were preparing astronaut Alan Shepard to fly in the first week of May.[36]

Khrushchev greeted the news of Gagarin's successful mission by calling for the largest national celebration since the war-ending festivities of May 9, 1945. Four MiG fighters escorted the Il-18 plane that brought Gagarin back to the Soviet capital, and the entire group circled Moscow before landing at Vnukovo Airport. People lined the streets, the roofs, and balconies along the route into the center of the city, and a huge parade in Red Square followed.[37] The Soviet people were hungry for something to celebrate, and public enthusiasm for Gagarin rapidly spread throughout the USSR.[38] Although the scale of these theatrics in Moscow surprised even his family, Khrushchev understood that the celebration helped distract the Soviet people from the grim reality of their daily lives and the apparent bankruptcy of his promises.[39] Given the recent reports he had been receiving of widespread shoddy housing construction, he considered it a bonus that none of the balconies filled with onlookers collapsed during the show.[40]

■

A MID THESE EVENTS the Soviet leadership chose to ignore the increasing evidence of U.S. plotting against Castro. In April a wave of terrorist bombings and suspicious fires occurred in Havana. On April 13 El Encanto, the largest department store in Cuba, was destroyed by arson.[41] The day before, the KGB resident in Mexico City reported that sources in the Guatemalan Communist

Party were predicting that a broader U.S.-sponsored attack was only days away.[42] Since the summer of 1960 Soviet fears of a U.S. military strike against Castro had risen and fallen. Much as in the children's fable of the boy who cried wolf, the value of these alarms had worn down with each subsequent discovery that U.S. Marines were not on their way.[43]

Moreover, Khrushchev had received two signals from Kennedy that made a U.S. attack on Castro much less likely. In March U.S. Ambassador Thompson had traveled two thousand miles to Siberia to deliver a personal note to Khrushchev from the president saying that it was time for a face-to-face meeting and suggesting late May in a neutral European capital. On April 1 Khrushchev had sent his agreement to Kennedy.[44] The date was still uncertain, but Kennedy's willingness to meet was not. A week later the Americans asked to delay the meeting until June and for it to be in Vienna.

The U.S. agreement to a summit was taken as a sign of the new president's respect for Khrushchev. The second signal that confused the Soviet leader came in the form of a statement by Kennedy that seemed to imply tolerance of Castro. The same day that the KGB in Mexico sounded the alarm, the president publicly denied the rumors that the United States was on the verge of attacking Cuba. In response to a question at a press conference, he stated that "there will not be, under any conditions, any intervention in Cuba by United States armed forces. This government will do everything it possibly can, and I think it can meet its responsibilities, to make sure that there are no Americans involved in any actions inside Cuba. . . . The basic issue is not one between the United States and Cuba. It is between the Cubans themselves."[45]

Kennedy's answer not only strengthened Khrushchev's assessment that this White House would restrain itself but also sent a wave of reassurance down the line of the Soviet national security system. On the assumption that nothing would happen in his absence, the KGB resident in Havana, Aleksandr Alekseyev, was permitted to leave Cuba in April for a trip to Brazil. Before leaving, Alekseyev had witnessed the opening phase of the U.S. campaign, a string of attacks by anti-Castro saboteurs in central Havana, that culminated in an invasion at the Bay of Pigs. He later recalled that even he thought that no greater threat loomed: "I had seen the [U.S.] bombings. . . . But why did we not believe that it would be such a large invasion? I don't know. . . . We just did not believe it."[46]

Cuban anxieties subsided somewhat after Kennedy's press conference. Che Guevara, in a meeting with the Soviet ambassador Sergei Kudriavtsev on April 14, said that "the danger of invasion of the country by large beachheads of the external counterrevolutionary forces has now in all likelihood receded."

The Cubans had evidence that the U.S. government had been behind the El Encanto fire. "One of such [small] bombs," Guevara reported to the Soviets, "was found unexploded in the [El Encanto] store building after the fire with a stamp 'U.S. Army.'" But even Guevara believed that though Kennedy was as much an enemy of the Cuban Revolution as Eisenhower had been, the new president was less comfortable with extreme measures. "[T]he tactics are being somewhat changed," Guevara told the Kremlin. At the moment the Cubans believed that the main emphasis of U.S. policy was on diplomatic isolation and economic sabotage.[47]

An intensification of the U.S.-sponsored bombing campaign the day after Che's meeting with the Soviet ambassador, however, put the Cubans back on alert. Explosions in Havana, Santiago de Cuba, and San Antonio de los Baños in the early morning of April 15 caused Castro to announce that this was a prelude to an invasion of the island. On April 16 the Cuban Air Force and Navy launched very visible patrols, though Havana had no real information on when the attack would occur.[48] Meanwhile Moscow seemed not to be expecting any attack.

On the afternoon of April 17, 1961, reports reached Moscow that U.S.-backed Cuban rebels had invaded three beaches along the Bay of Pigs and a Cuban government-in-exile was calling for a national uprising.[49] Khrushchev worried that the CIA's Allen Dulles had staged this provocation to undermine the forthcoming meeting with Kennedy, just as he had dispatched Francis Gary Powers's U-2 flight to ruin the summit in Paris. Unwilling to admit that he had misjudged Kennedy's dislike of the Cuban regime, Khrushchev took solace in KGB reports that pointed to Dulles as bearing the primary responsibility for the Cuban fiasco.[50] For example, the KGB reported from London that officials in the U.S. Embassy were saying that Kennedy now regretted having retained Republicans like Allen Dulles and Secretary of the Treasury C. Douglas Dillon in his administration.[51]

Although the Kremlin was caught off guard and Cuban intelligence did not have detailed warning, weaknesses in the tactical aspects of the CIA's operation doomed it to failure. There was no guerrilla force nearby to fortify the beachhead. The twelve hundred men landed in a flat, marshy region that had only a single road. When dawn broke, columns of Soviet-supplied tanks rolled down that road to defend the beaches. Besides the weakness of the plan, the operation suffered from poor presidential leadership. At the last moment Kennedy had called off an air strike that could have assured that the invasion force enjoyed air superiority. Because it did not, the six planes of Castro's air force were able to sink two of the landing force's ships, one of which carried the brigade's radio equipment and some ammunition. By April 19 the United States had begun to withdraw whatever equipment and fighters it could from the area. More than eleven hundred survivors of the assault remained as prisoners in Cuba.[52]

■

THE BAY OF PIGS invasion ended Khrushchev's complacency about the Kennedy administration. Now the Soviet leader did not know what to think about the young president. Had President Kennedy been behind this attack, or were the hard-liners like Allen Dulles in control? Khrushchev did not immediately make up his mind about what all this meant. On April 18 he sent Kennedy a stinging written protest. But he also had Andrei Gromyko, who delivered the protest by hand to Ambassador Thompson, sweeten the bitter herbs with words indicating his desire that "the differences which have arisen recently would be resolved and U.S.-Soviet relations improved."[53] Khrushchev hoped that Kennedy would signal which direction he intended to take U.S.-Soviet relations.

■

THE BAY OF PIGS fiasco revived Washington's interest in a superpower summit between Khrushchev and Kennedy. The president decided that though he had no real diplomatic concessions to offer the Soviets, he needed to show presidential leadership at a meeting with the Soviet leader. Although not deaf to the chorus of political disapproval, particularly in Western Europe, that followed the failure in Cuba, Kennedy was principally motivated by a concern that in the wake of the failure in Cuba the Soviets had concluded that he was a weak president.

The president's brother the attorney general gave him the opportunity to jump-start the summit. Naturally secretive, Robert Kennedy was the kind of man who found it liberating to work behind the scenes. "It would be extremely helpful if the Attorney General of the United States," wrote his longtime secretary Angie Novella, "would notify his immediate staff of his whereabouts at all times."[54] When Robert Kennedy learned from his press secretary, Edwin O. Guthman, that a former president of the National Press Club claimed a special link to Moscow through a Soviet diplomat, Robert Kennedy wanted to meet this Russian.[55] The journalist was the ubiquitous Frank Holeman, Richard Nixon's longtime press ally, who hoped to make inroads in the Kennedy White House, and the diplomat was his occasional lunch partner, Georgi Bolshakov, an agent of the Soviet military intelligence service (GRU). "My guy wants to meet your guy," Holeman told Guthman before a meeting was scheduled. Later the attorney general and the GRU officer called each other directly.

The Bolshakov-RFK connection became so important to the story of Khrushchev's relationship with John F. Kennedy that its origins are worth some attention. After a few weeks of triangular diplomacy managed by Holeman, the first meeting was set for May 9. Bolshakov's chief at the GRU station in the embassy had already disapproved of any meeting. The big bosses at GRU headquarters did not want Bolshakov to engage in diplomacy. He was in Washington to spy. It remains unclear whether Ivan Serov, whom Khrushchev had partially rescued by shifting him to the leadership of the GRU after Mikoyan successfully provoked his ouster from the KGB in December 1958, talked to his patron about this probe beforehand. In any case, Bolshakov was told not to press on with this meeting. What he did next he did on his own.

The Kennedy brothers also worked outside channels to make this meeting happen. They did not reveal to any of the statutory members of the president's foreign policy team their scheme to sound out Khrushchev's plans before the summit. The president's patrician assistant for national security affairs, McGeorge Bundy, later philosophically described the Bolshakov channel as among "the unsharables" kept between the brothers. Although hired by Kennedy to coordinate foreign policy within the White House, Bundy was cut out of the Bolshakov initiative. So too was Dean Rusk, the new secretary of state. As a result, the country's three most experienced Kremlinologists were left in the dark: Llewellyn Thompson, who had agreed to stay on as Kennedy's ambassador to Moscow; Charles Bohlen, now ensconced at the State Department as chief Soviet specialist in residence; and George Kennan, who had returned to government after an eight-year hiatus to serve as Kennedy's man in Belgrade.[56] Bundy later concluded that the Kennedy brothers had been too clever by half in cutting out all these potential sources of advice just to maintain the secrecy of the Bolshakov channel.[57]

In preparation for the first meeting the brothers discussed the outlines of the U.S. positions on the major issues that separated the two powers. The president was especially eager to focus Khrushchev's attention on securing a nuclear test ban treaty. Since 1958 the superpowers had been negotiating a comprehensive nuclear test ban while maintaining a voluntary moratorium on any testing. From the start, disagreement had arisen over how to make the agreement verifiable, and it had especially intensified as the nuclear powers moved their testing facilities underground. American and British negotiators pointed out there were hundreds of seismic events a year on the vast Soviet landmass, each of which potentially represented an unannounced nuclear test. The U.S. position was that it should have the right to mount a number of on-site inspections a year to verify that these were acts of nature.

The Soviet position on the test ban had hardened over the course of 1960. Kremlin negotiators had never agreed to any on-site inspections, seeing them as U.S. attempts to spy on Soviet territory. In the aftermath of the Congo crisis, Khrushchev had further complicated an agreement on verification by ruling out any role for the United Nations in monitoring compliance. Similar in spirit to his UN reform proposal, he wanted the monitoring to be controlled by a troika of countries representing each of the two blocs and the neutral world. Not fully trusting even the third world, Khrushchev also insisted that the troika had to be unanimous for any inspection to occur.

Kennedy was certain he could not give in on letting the Soviets veto an inspection of a suspicious event on their territory, but he was confident he could get the number of on-site inspections down to something Khrushchev would accept. JFK was a strong advocate of a test ban.[58] He also did not want to resume testing in part because a test ban would symbolize a rare foreign policy achievement for his fledgling administration.

Kennedy had a second important proposal to make. In late April his administration had seriously considered sending U.S. Marines into Thailand to shore up Souvanna Phouma's position in Laos, and the president did not want the Soviets and their allies to push the United States that close to intervention again. If possible, at Vienna he wanted to formalize the understanding that he seemed to be reaching with Khrushchev over neutralizing a united Laos.[59]

At his first meeting with Bolshakov on May 9, Robert Kennedy rolled out the president's thoughts on the outlines of a test ban deal amid pleasantries about better relations and the possibility of a neutral Laos.[60] The president, he reported, would be prepared to accept a limit of ten on-site inspections per year and an international commission to monitor compliance with the treaty, so long as neither side had a veto over its operations. The attorney general expressed his brother's impatience for a real achievement in Vienna: "The President does not want to repeat the sad experience of Khrushchev's meeting with Eisenhower at Camp David and hopes that this forthcoming meeting will produce concrete agreements."

The Kennedys expected the Kremlin to move fast once Khrushchev understood that the U.S. president had become personally engaged in reaching real agreements before the start of the summit. They hoped that after Bolshakov's report had been absorbed in Moscow, the diplomats of each country would be assigned to work through the details of a test ban agreement, which could be signed when the two leaders met in three weeks. But the Bolshakov communiqué had come absolutely out of the blue for Khrushchev, whose thoughts were still on setting a date for the summit. On May 12, possibly without even having read Bolshakov's report on his meeting with Robert Kennedy, Khrushchev signed a letter to President Kennedy calling for a summit in June or July. The letter said nothing about achieving a test ban but mentioned optimism about progress in Laos before stressing that the problem of West Berlin "urgently require[d]" a solution.[61]

Once Khrushchev finally digested the report from Bolshakov—he did not know the GRU officer, though his son-in-law, Aleksei Adzhubei, was acquainted with him—he was disappointed. Kennedy had said nothing of interest about Berlin, the main reason Khrushchev had wanted to meet in the first place. He had little interest in achieving a test ban agreement at Vienna. On the contrary, his military chiefs were advising him that after a delay of two years it was time for the Soviet Union to resume nuclear testing. Despite the fears of some in the U.S. intelligence community, the Soviets had not violated the test ban moratorium. Soviet generals appealed to Khrushchev's interest in curbing the costs of the Cold War with arguments that testing would make the Soviet nuclear arsenal more efficient. Although Khrushchev liked that argument, it did not completely neutralize his unwillingness to be the first to break the moratorium. World public opinion would turn against the first superpower to resume atmospheric testing, which was believed to spread harmful radioactive ions. Unlike the United States, the Soviet Union could not yet do any of its testing underground.[62]

With Kennedy determined to make the test ban the focus of the summit, Khrushchev realized there was nothing much he could offer in his reply through the back channel. The only exception would be a kind word on Laos. Khrushchev asked that the message go back that he was pleased to hear Kennedy confirm the policy on a neutral Laos that he seemed to be following since March. Otherwise, the foreign and defense ministries were to produce boilerplate responses on the test ban and the Berlin question to encourage the Kennedys to come back with something more creative.

Gromyko's Germanists had to juggle preparing these talking points for Bolshakov with completing a few think pieces for Khrushchev and the delegation to take with them to Vienna. The Soviet Foreign Ministry had learned the hard way the pain of being caught off guard by the country's mercurial leader. Once in 1958 and twice in 1960 Khrushchev had changed the country's entire approach to a major foreign policy problem at the last minute, without any warning to his foreign policy staff. Perhaps in the expectation that he was about to do the same again, as of mid-May the Foreign Ministry had prepared far less for the Vienna meeting than it had in the months before the abortive summit of May 1960.[63] Gromyko and his people were watching what Robert Kennedy had to say in these secret talks with as much anticipation as Khrushchev.

Meanwhile, as if he had needed more pressure, Khrushchev was receiving information that hardened his resolve to focus the summit on Berlin. Ulbricht sent word in mid-May that he could not wait much longer to do something about the flood of East Germans leaving the country through West Berlin. In April 1961 twice the number of refugees signed in at the registration center in West Berlin as in the same period a year earlier. This was largely because East Germany's economic woes had increased dramatically. An attempt to lift wages and reduce the number of hours in the workweek had failed in the East German parliament. With industrial production down and export income declining, the regime could not afford these luxuries. So the number of people voting against socialism with their feet was increasing. As Ulbricht himself had to reluctantly accept, "it is not possible for a socialist country such as the GDR to carry out peaceful competition with an imperialist country such as West Germany with open borders."[64] The Soviet ambassador in East Germany, Mikhail Pervukhin, warned Moscow that even though this might complicate "the struggle for a peace treaty," the East Germans wanted to close the sectoral border between East and West Berlin now. Perhaps the summit could be used, Pervukhin suggested, to reach at least a provisional agreement on Berlin, which would precede a general settlement of the German question.

∎

W HEN ROBERT KENNEDY met again with Bolshakov on May 21, this back channel scheme began to take a very negative turn. The attorney general was as disappointed in Bolshakov's message as Khrushchev had been when he heard the gist of the May 9 meeting. Nevertheless, Robert Kennedy came armed with one more offer to make on the test ban. Washington would accept a troika of inspectors but no veto. Kennedy impatiently called Bolshakov two days later, hoping for better news from Moscow. "Please hurry the response to the issues raised," he said.[65]

Khrushchev had set progress on Berlin as the test of American statesmanship, yet now he could see from the GRU report on the meeting in Washington that President Kennedy wanted to talk about practically anything else but Berlin. In response to Bolshakov's statement about the need for a peace treaty, Robert Kennedy had said on behalf of his brother, "The President will discuss this subject with Khrushchev in Vienna, but only to discuss it and not to seek any kind of agreement at this meeting."[66] The attorney general's effort to sugarcoat the White House's inability to come up with anything new on Berlin only increased Khrushchev's frustration. The president, Robert Kennedy added on May 21, "understood the importance of resolving the German question, but this was a very difficult problem, which had historical roots and for any resolution of it the US government would need time."[67] Khrushchev believed he had already waited long enough.

The Kennedys were clamoring for a response, so Khrushchev decided to give it to them himself. Taking advantage of the visit of some American figure skaters, Khrushchev invited Ambassador and Mrs. Thompson into the Kremlin's box at the rink. He would give Washington one last chance to understand that Berlin was the main obstacle to better relations. If Kennedy truly wanted détente, he would have to come to Vienna with concessions on Berlin.

The ice rink discussion was the toughest any U.S. envoy had had to sit through in years. Khrushchev relentlessly poked and prodded the Thompsons on Berlin. When the U.S. ambassador asked why the status quo could not be maintained for another seven years, the Soviet leader blew up. The status quo was unacceptable to him. Jane Thompson, the ambassador's wife, became so uncomfortable that she came to the assistance of her husband, debating with Khrushchev how long the Soviets could wait for a resolution. Ultimately Khrushchev heard an angry Llewellyn Thompson threaten him: "Well, if you use force, if you want to cut off our access and connections by force, then we will use force against force." Khrushchev responded: "You don't interpret it quite right. We have absolutely no plans to use force. We will sign the peace treaty, and this is how your rights stemming from the conditions of capitulation will end." He added that the United States could count on the Soviets and the East Germans signing a peace treaty after the West German elections in September and certainly after the Soviet party congress in October. He warned that U.S. forces in West Berlin "might have to tighten their belts."[68]

Unfortunately for Kennedy, who needed to know that he was heading into an ambush in Vienna, Thompson discounted much of what Khrushchev was telling him.[69] This longtime Kremlin watcher understood that the Soviet leader had invested a lot of his personal prestige into finding a way out of the Berlin impasse. Thompson had been the ambassador in 1959, when Khrushchev had backed down on Berlin the first time. Having seen that retreat, Thompson now doubted the Soviet leader would provoke a second crisis. If he did, the U.S. ambassador assumed, it would not come until after the party congress in mid-October. It is quite "possible K[hrushchev] will attempt [to] slide over Berlin problem in sweetness and light atmosphere."[70] He couldn't have been more wrong.

▪

IN THE YEARS since the collapse of Soviet power in 1991, with the flood of revelations that so much of the red menace had been made of papier-mâché, it has been natural to question how dangerous the Cold War really was. How close did we ever come to nuclear war? The Central Committee documents of Nikita Khrushchev reveal that starting with the Presidium meeting on May 26, 1961, the world moved closer to nuclear war than at any time since the Soviets tested their first atomic bomb in August 1949. Even if Khrushchev's war talk was the product of a frustrated man, rather than a sign of mental breakdown, the Soviet leader on that day deliberately set in motion the machine of war. In the prenuclear age such a decision had only local consequences. In the Kennedy-Khrushchev era this act of willfulness immediately had global significance.

The May 26 meeting was to be the last Presidium meeting before Khrushchev left to see Kennedy in Vienna on June 3. The Soviet leader planned to travel by train so that he could view progress in the cornfields of the Ukraine. The Czechs had also asked him to make a short stop, and the Austrian Communists were hoping for some time with him, too. Khrushchev's mind was not really on these requests, however. Instead he wanted to set a new, more dangerous course for Soviet foreign policy. It appears that the only warning the other Kremlin leaders had was that Khrushchev invited his stenographer to this meeting on the Vienna summit. Since 1958 he did this only when he intended to announce a new policy.[71] "I attach a lot of significance to the meeting with Kennedy," Khrushchev began, "because we are approaching the moment when we must solve the German question. This is the key issue."

Then Khrushchev let his colleagues know what he thought of Kennedy: "He is a son of a bitch," he said. In the two days since the ice show, the Soviet leader had made up his mind that he had no choice but to seek an early confrontation with the Kennedy administration. The back channel through Bolshakov and the front channel through Ambassador Thompson confirmed that Kennedy was no more prepared to accept Khrushchev's Berlin demands than Eisenhower had been.

"We are not afraid of German aggression. . . . Germany . . . will not start a new war," Khrushchev said; "the most dangerous [country] is America." He blamed the U.S. system of government more than any individual for American misbehavior. The Bay of Pigs and the disappointing back chnnel that followed had convinced him Kennedy was not in control of his government. Kennedy, like Eisenhower, was a captive of the Pentagon and CIA. "That's why we cannot vouch for America. Its decisions are not based on logical principles; rather [it is] governed by different groups and sudden coincidental events. That's why America could easily start a war, even if it is fully aware—according to military circles—of the fact that the situation could grow worse. That's why certain forces could emerge and find a pretext to go to war against us."

Under these circumstances, a patient leader might have suggested a quiet period, building up Soviet strength to meet the dangers of an erratic United States, but Khrushchev was impatient. He announced to his colleagues that he intended to drag the world through the greatest nuclear crisis of the Cold War. Khrushchev did not believe he was choosing war, but he was prepared to take that risk. East Germany, the keystone of the Soviet position in Eastern Europe, would die without an agreement that closed the West Berlin loophole and strengthened its sovereignty. The Soviet demands regarding Berlin, he believed, were reasonable, and the Americans had to be made, even at the point of a sword, to accept them. "[T]he risk that we are taking is justified; if we look at it in terms of a percentage, there is more than a 95% probability that there will be no war."

Khrushchev described how this crisis would begin. The Soviet Union would sign a peace treaty, then turn over control of the air, rail, and road access routes to the East German government. He then revealed how he expected the end game over Berlin to play itself out: "We don't encroach on West Berlin, we do not declare a blockade; [but] we cut off air traffic. We show that we are ready to permit air traffic but on the condition that Western planes land at airports in the GDR, near Berlin. We do not demand a withdrawal of troops. However, we consider them illegal, though we won't use any strong-arm methods for their removal. We will not cut off the delivery of foodstuffs and will not sever any other lifelines. We will adhere to a policy of noninfringement and noninvolvement in the affairs of West Berlin. Therefore, I don't believe that because the state of war and the occupational regime are coming to an end it would unleash a war."

Khrushchev's confidence that he could pull this off stemmed from his assumption that international public opinion and the Western European members of NATO would prevent the United States from using force to defend its position in West Berlin. "[French President Charles] de Gaulle and [British Prime Minister Harold] Macmillan will never side with the Americans in unleashing war in Europe now," Khrushchev told his colleagues, "because the main deployment of nuclear weapons will be in the territory of West Germany, France, and England. They are intelligent people, and they understand this."

In the United States Kennedy's advisers were telling him that Khrushchev faced opposition from hard-liners who disliked his efforts at détente with the West. In truth Khrushchev fathered all the offensive policies directed at the United States and had no one of any consequence pushing him to be more aggressive. After listening to Khrushchev's description of this new policy, only one man in the room stood up to oppose this descent into danger.

Just as in November 1958, when Khrushchev had advocated ending four-power control over Berlin unilaterally, Anastas Mikoyan was the lone voice of reason in the Presidium.[72] Mikoyan believed the probability that war would result from Khrushchev's proposal was much greater than he had predicted. Mikoyan was not convinced that fear of a nuclear engagement would be sufficient to deter the NATO countries from going to war over their rights to West Berlin. "In my opinion," he said, "they could initiate military action without atomic weapons."[73] Essentially, Mikoyan and Khrushchev were disagreeing over the value of nuclear deterrence in a local conflict like Berlin. Khrushchev assumed that the West would be so afraid of the possibility of a general nuclear war that Kennedy would choose not to initiate any military action whatsoever in reaction to a Soviet blockade of West Berlin. Mikoyan believed that the Americans might respond to the Soviet provocation by using conventional weapons. Mikoyan was also not yet ready to discount the character of the new American president. Under pressure, Kennedy might prove a worthy opponent.[74] He mentioned only a 10 percent possibility of war, but this was a rhetorical ploy to prevent Khrushchev from looking like a fool. Mikoyan sought to rally his colleagues around the idea that Khrushchev's proposal would most likely corner Kennedy, with potentially disastrous consequences. He stressed that closing down the air corridors would create "a great aggravation." Perhaps, he suggested, keeping them open would make the fait accompli acceptable to the West.

Khrushchev's anger grew as he listened to Mikoyan. This was not 1958. He was not prepared to compromise with anyone. "Then nothing will change, in fact," he declared. "If only we maintain air communication, then there will be no real changes, except for the legal ones. The Americans will accept what you suggested with pleasure because it maintains their rights."

The unwelcome debate with Mikoyan forced Khrushchev to remind his colleagues why West Berlin mattered. The central issue for him was the defense of the Soviet bloc in general and the protection of East Germany in particular. Nothing that compromised either goal should be tolerated. He did not fear an attack by West Germany, although Konrad Adenauer's drive for nuclear weapons was worrisome, or by the rest of NATO. The main threat to East Germany was internal. Every week thousands of German professionals were fleeing the country through West Berlin. Mikoyan's compromise would not meet the Soviet leader's needs.

"You see," Khrushchev said, "if we maintain air communication, this will make the Germans, the Ulbricht government anxious. He already stresses that it is impossible, we train engineers, doctors, they leave the country and we can do nothing about it, it's true that they are better paid out there; educated people have greater opportunities. This is how it is! Therefore, if we declare this position, then in the first place, our Warsaw Pact allies will sense in this action our inconsistency and uncertainty. As a result, we will shake their confidence in our policy and in the first place in the GDR, and not only Ulbricht's confidence. . . . They will feel uncertainty. . . . We shouldn't do this. It means introducing different legal grounds, but de facto it remains the same, the gates remain open."

Annoyed by Mikoyan's interruption, Khrushchev decided to go a step further. Not only would he force the closure of the air corridor, but he would make his determination known by shooting down any allied plane that attempted to land in West Berlin: "Our position is very strong, but we will have, of course, to really intimidate them now. For example, if there is any flying around, we will have to bring aircraft down. Could they take any acts of provocation? They could. If we don't bring the plane down, this would mean that we capitulate. I think that they will put up with it. . . . This is also a confirmation that if we declare something, we do it. In a word, a policy is a policy. If we want to carry out our policy, and if we want it to be acknowledged, respected and feared, it is necessary to be firm."

Khrushchev did not agree that the West would risk even a conventional war over Berlin. In his eyes, the balance of forces in Central Europe was so unfavorable to NATO that this would not make sense. There was an ecstatic quality to his speech as he made this point. In recent weeks the Presidium had been deciding questions for military assistance to countries as far-flung as the Congo and Laos. Khrushchev was plainly tired of having to find ways to neutralize the U.S. advantage in areas of interest to Moscow. Berlin should be different. Here the Soviets enjoyed a conventional superiority. "These days with regard to conventional weapons . . . these considerations do not concern Berlin. This is a matter of consideration for Laos, for Cuba, for the Congo, even, perhaps for Iran. But [in Berlin] meanwhile we are stronger than they are, and they say, 'The Russians have the advantage. . . .' This means, they will agree. We will present this proposition and insist on it. Then this matter will be accepted."

To ensure that the Soviet conventional advantage was as obvious as possible, Khrushchev ordered his three top marshals—Defense Secretary Rodian Malinovsky, Army Chief of Staff Matvei Zakharov, and Commander of the Warsaw Pact Andrei Grechko—"to thoroughly examine the correlation of forces in Germany and to see what is needed."[75]

At the end of the meeting, a touch of absurdity crept into this high drama. Just as Khrushchev finished his speech on behalf of starting an international crisis, he was asked if the Foreign Ministry should go ahead with preparing gifts for President and Mrs. Kennedy and the members of the U.S. delegation. Knowing the president's taste for fine foods and assuming he liked classical music, Gromyko's team suggested giving him twelve cans of black caviar along with an assortment of phonographic records in leather covers filled with music by Russian and Soviet composers. For Mrs. Kennedy, the Soviets thought that a silver coffee service for six among other gifts might be appropriate.[76] Khrushchev had a mordant response for his diplomats: "Presents can be made even before a war."

■

As Khrushchev rode a train through the Ukraine and Czechoslovakia, Kennedy and his delegation flew to Paris for a presummit discussion with the French president. De Gaulle had hosted the last meeting of an American president and the Soviet leader, and Kennedy was seeking some pointers. De Gaulle's principal advice was that it did not make sense to negotiate on Berlin. It was up to Kennedy to stand up to Khrushchev, so that the Soviets would finally learn to accept the status quo. "It is annoying to both sides that Berlin should be located where it is; however, it is there."[77] De Gaulle did not worry about Khrushchev's ability to retaliate. He reminded Kennedy that the Soviet leader had a habit of issuing ultimatums and then forgetting about them. "If he had wanted to go to war," de Gaulle explained, "he could have already."[78]

De Gaulle found Kennedy very concerned that Khrushchev doubted Western resolve. "[T]he West is not as weak as people think in regard to the Berlin question," de Gaulle told Kennedy, revealing that just recently the Soviets had bought sixty thousand tons of meat from France.[79]

The Kennedy-Khrushchev discussions began the day after Kennedy left Paris. Midmorning on June 3 the two leaders met on the steps of the U.S. Embassy in Vienna. The smiles at that point may well have been genuine, but they did not last long.

After exchanging some pleasantries over Khrushchev's and Kennedy's first brief meeting in 1959 during Khrushchev's visit to Capitol Hill, the opening session dissolved into a fruitless exchange over the possibility of miscalculation in world politics.[80] At its core the disagreement reflected the disparate views of world politics that each leader had brought to the table. Khrushchev knew that the United States could dominate militarily in any part of the third world. Kennedy, for his part, did not understand that in the third world Khrushchev had rarely been the initiator of conflicts. More often than not the Soviets had reacted to opportunities.

The afternoon session went no better. Kennedy had taken stock during lunch and seemed to realize that the discussions had gotten off to a bad start. In the hope of developing some kind of rapport, he asked Khrushchev to join him for a short walk in the embassy's garden, with only their interpreters present. Khrushchev was more than half a foot shorter than Kennedy, so the stroll put additional strain on Kennedy's tender back. But it seemed worth the effort. Kennedy recalled that at the otherwise frosty discussion at the ice rink, Khrushchev had told Thompson that he would be able to speak more openly with the president when the two men were not surrounded by aides.[81]

Kennedy asked how it was that Khrushchev was able to find the time to give lengthy interviews to the journalist Walter Lippmann and to the visiting U.S. senator Hubert Humphrey, both of whom had been to Moscow in the spring.[82] Khrushchev explained that the Soviet system permitted him the time for these sorts of meetings. Kennedy was amazed and pointed out that because of the tripartite nature of the U.S. system, he spent a lot of time persuading, cajoling, and consulting with the various branches of government. "Well, why don't you switch to our system?" Khrushchev asked.

With rapport still elusive, Kennedy suggested the leaders continue the discussion inside but without reconvening the rest of their delegations. Returning to very general themes about what each country was doing to advance its vision of the future in the third world, the president gave the impression of wanting some sort of general meeting of the minds on reducing military tensions in the third world before delving into the specifics of the various problems facing them, especially the test ban and Berlin. Feeling good about how the discussions were going, Khrushchev agreed to devote another few hours to talking about such abstract propositions. There was still another day for the Americans to present him with something new on Berlin, and he was not hopeful that a confrontation could be avoided anyway.

So the two world leaders spent another three hours talking about very little of consequence to Khrushchev. From an Olympian perspective—if that is possible—Kennedy said nothing of which he might later be ashamed. But the conversation played to Khrushchev's strengths. Before long Kennedy found himself having to explain why the United States maintained relations with dictatorships in Spain and Iran. "U.S. policy," said Khrushchev in attributing Fidel Castro and the slain Patrice Lumumba's behavior to simple anti-imperialism, "is grist on the mill of Communists." Unwilling to give up all hope of developing some understanding with Khrushchev, Kennedy refused to counterattack. He never once mentioned Hungary or the riots in East Berlin in 1953.

The two leaders finally got down to specifics the next day.[83] Kennedy, again in search of the human side of Khrushchev that his Soviet experts had told him about, started with some biographical questions about the Soviet leader's childhood.

Khrushchev, who was in no mood for personal recollections, responded with a speech on the magnificence of Soviet iron ore deposits, especially those near his birthplace. Kennedy then switched to Laos, the only area where there seemed to be any semblance of agreement. Had Khrushchev been interested in engaging Kennedy, this was his chance. Khrushchev had his own problems in Laos, where the Chinese, the North Vietnamese, and the Pathet Lao were trying to force his hand away from neutralization. He could have mentioned that the superpowers had a shared interest in seeing that these regional conflicts did not spin out of control. Had he done so, Kennedy would have given him a knowing nod. But Khrushchev didn't. Instead he attacked U.S. policy and its allies like Thailand and Taiwan as if these were the only sources of instability in Laos. He also attacked Kennedy personally when the president tried to pass off the situation in Laos as something he had inherited. Khrushchev disagreed. He had heard that Kennedy himself had ordered the U.S. Marines into the region but that then the order had been rescinded. Kennedy knew this to be untrue, but he also knew that he had come very close to giving that order.

Tiring of the Laos discussion, Khrushchev took the initiative to move the conversation to disarmament, nuclear testing, and Germany, knowing that otherwise their time would run out without their covering these subjects. Before they turned to these matters, Kennedy nailed down the fact that he and Khrushchev agreed that Souvanna Phouma should be supported and that the neutralization of Laos should be achieved. Gromyko and Rusk, who had joined the leaders for this session, were then given instructions to follow up over lunch.

The discussion on Laos turned out to be the brief high point of the meeting. Kennedy would be disappointed in what Khrushchev had to say about the test ban treaty. Years later Robert Kennedy explained his brother's disappointment as having been a by-product of some deception the Kremlin fed to the White House through Bolshakov.[84] Soviet records make the existence of this deception highly doubtful.[85] More likely Kennedy just couldn't understand the basis for Khrushchev's stubbornness. He spoke as if he wanted détente, yet here was a first step, and he was afraid to take it.

Khrushchev spent some time trying to explain that he wanted disarmament, not arms control. He was not about to admit to Kennedy, as he had to Cabot Lodge in a careless throwaway line in February 1960, that the Soviets were facing a missile gap. Instead he explained that he wanted to eliminate all weapons, in stages, and that the United States could have its inspections but not *before* these weapons were destroyed. He characterized the test ban as far less important than disarmament. Indeed, in a world without nuclear weapons the test ban would be a natural by-product. If Kennedy insisted on a test ban, Khrushchev would agree to one, but the Soviet Union had to have a veto on any enforcement mechanism, and in any case, there could not be a significant number of on-site inspections of suspicious seismic activity in the USSR. Khrushchev's one concession was that the Soviet Union would permit three inspections a year. Kennedy was downcast. He had come to Vienna expecting Khrushchev to accept ten on-site inspections and thought the Soviet leader understood that there could be no veto for either party. He told Khrushchev that his proposition was akin to a situation in which Khrushchev and he lived in adjacent rooms and neither could visit except by invitation. "Under such conditions, how could any of the two be certain that nothing suspicious is going on in his neighbor's room?" Khrushchev had no response other than to insist that the United States display the necessary courage to embrace disarmament.

Then came Berlin. For a day and a half Khrushchev had been well behaved. There had been no shouting, and the truculence that he had displayed in the Kremlin had remained discreetly veiled. The veil came off as he handed Kennedy an aide-mémoire that outlined the new ultimatum from Moscow.[86] Khrushchev admitted that his position on Germany would affect U.S.-Soviet relations "to a great extent and even more so if the United States were to misunderstand the Soviet position." He then set out his basic position. The Soviet

Union sought no special advantage in Central Europe. It merely wished to extinguish the last embers from World War II. To do so, it was eager to sign a peace treaty with East Germany that would automatically bring an end to all the institutions of the occupation, including the corridors to West Berlin. Before he took this step, he wanted to reach an agreement with Kennedy personally so that the United States would accept the new situation. But if that proved impossible, he was determined to move ahead with a peace treaty unilaterally. What kind of agreement? Western troops could stay in the free city, but only if the Soviets could also place their own troops there. There could also be an international agreement to protect West Berlin's communications with the world, but no more special-access routes—air, road, or rail—for NATO.

Kennedy tried to explain why Khrushchev's preferred settlement was as unacceptable to him as it had been to his predecessor. "Here, we are not talking about Laos," said Kennedy. He depicted the Western alliance as fragile enough that a decision to abandon occupation rights in West Berlin would lead his allies to regard U.S. commitments "as a mere scrap of paper." He added: "[W]hen we are talking about West Berlin, we are talking about West[ern] Europe."

The president tried to understand why Khrushchev was so insistent on changing the status quo in Central Europe. He told the Soviet leader that he was convinced that the USSR was as powerful as the United States and that Khrushchev wished to improve relations. Then why try to force the United States to abandon the rights that it had won by fighting the last world war? Repeating his concern that the United States would lose its allies if he accepted Khrushchev's position, Kennedy said that he had not become president of the United States "to preside over [the] isolation of his country."

Khrushchev coolly interrupted Kennedy. "So I am to understand that you do not want a peace treaty?" He then added that Kennedy's ambitions seemed to extend to downtown Moscow if what he wanted was to improve the strategic position of the United States. Khrushchev recalled that he had lost a son in World War II, Gromyko had lost two brothers, and Mikoyan had also lost a son. Ending the occupation of Germany would help block the revanchists in West Germany who wanted to reunify their country by force. Khrushchev regretted that Kennedy refused to see the value for world peace of eliminating that opportunity for mischief.

"No further delay is possible or necessary," said Khrushchev. "Will a peace treaty block access to Berlin?" Kennedy asked. Khrushchev said it would. Then he calmly told Kennedy that he could still agree to a six-month interim agreement, the agreement he had hoped Eisenhower would accept in Paris.

The gesture was as meaningless now as it had been then, for as Khrushchev explained, once the six months were up, the Soviet Union would sign the agreement that it wanted with the East Germans regardless. In any event, he told Kennedy that he would sign a peace treaty by the end of the year.

The meeting broke up for the last meal of the summit. It was an unpleasant lunch for Kennedy, who was determined not to have the meeting end on such a sour note. His hopes of a concrete improvement in superpower relations had been dashed. Seeing this as his last chance, he asked Khrushchev to meet with him privately after lunch. The president still believed that Khrushchev's hard-line opposition at home was the source of his obstinate positions. Perhaps he would speak differently alone.

Taking Khrushchev aside, Kennedy stressed that he did not want to travel home with the sword of a Soviet ultimatum hanging over his head.[87] He wanted the Soviet leader to understand the differences for him between a USSR-GDR peace treaty and the loss of rights of access to Berlin. He could accept the former, but not the latter. Khrushchev was equally frank. He told Kennedy that if the United States tried to exercise these rights after a peace treaty had been signed, there would be a military response. He, who had already prepared the Kremlin for this possibility, was deadly serious. Kennedy could see that this was not a bluff. "It is up the United States," Khrushchev said, "to decide whether there will be war or peace. . . . The decision to sign a peace treaty is firm and irrevocable and the Soviet Union will sign it in December if the U.S. refuses an interim agreement."

"Then it will be a cold winter," replied Kennedy. The summit was over.

Khrushchev had seen the effect of his bluntness on Kennedy and was pleased with his own performance. At their final meeting he had observed that the young American leader was "not only anxious, but deeply upset."[88] This impression of a somewhat crestfallen Kennedy was later confirmed by the Austrian chancellor, Bruno Kreisky, who met with Khrushchev just after seeing Kennedy off at Vienna's airport. "The President was very gloomy at the airport," Kreisky told Khrushchev. "He seemed upset and his face had changed. Obviously the meeting did not go well for him." This was exactly the impression that Khrushchev had intended to create. He had hoped to get his way on Berlin, but now that he hadn't, he wanted the U.S. president to be anxious. Khrushchev said as much in response to the Austrian's observation. Kennedy was upset because "the President still doesn't quite understand the times in which we live. He doesn't yet fully understand the realignment of forces, and he still lives by the policies of his predecessors—especially as far as the German question is concerned."[89]

In 1958 Khrushchev had lacked the power in Moscow to launch his assault against the West in Berlin. This time he intended to get his way no matter how hard he had to push. Immediately after Vienna, Khrushchev increased the pressure on the United States and its allies. The next day he went to East Berlin to announce a December 31 deadline for a Berlin settlement. On June 9 TASS published the aide-mémoire on Berlin that Khrushchev had handed to Kennedy in Vienna. On Soviet television a week later Khrushchev repeated the vow to sign a peace treaty by the end of the year. Then, for a speech on June 21 marking the twentieth anniversary of the Nazi attack on the USSR, he donned the dark green uniform of a Soviet lieutenant general and vowed that those who tested Soviet resolve on the Berlin question would "share the fate of Hitler."[90]

When he returned to the Kremlin, Khrushchev pushed his stenographers to produce a clean copy of the minutes of his first meeting with Kennedy. He wanted copies distributed far and wide as a part of the political campaign for West Berlin. "The meetings demonstrated the wisdom of taking a hard line on the Berlin question," intoned a Central Committee resolution passed at Khrushchev's instruction. "There must be no illusions that President Kennedy or the American government are as yet prepared to take steps to improve U.S.-Soviet relations." The distribution list for the usually top secret Soviet document showed both the extent of Khrushchev's self-confidence in his handling of Kennedy and the ways in which he viewed his alliances. Foreign Communist leaders were to receive their own copies. The Central Committee made a point of including Fidel Castro in that list, even though Cuba was not as yet considered a Communist or socialist country. Friendly but not doctrinaire leaders were to be briefed on its contents. Soviet ambassadors in Cambodia, Egypt, Iraq, India, Brazil, Mexico, and Ghana—to name just a few of the eighteen countries listed—were to make appointments to see the foreign leaders to read from the document. Finally, even Tito was to be honored with an oral briefing. He was not considered dependable enough to be given his own copy, however.[91]

Khrushchev's mood was not simply determined; it was dark. The impatience that governed his approach to the new U.S. president now carried over to his treatment of the Soviet Union's domestic problems. Having received additional reports on higher joblessness, theft, and vagrancy, he called in mid-June for a reversal of some of the reforms in the Soviet judicial system associated with the wave of destalinization that he had initiated. His language was crude, bitter, and the most authoritarian since the removal of Kaganovich and Molotov in 1957.

He blamed the increase in civil discontent and crime on too much liberal-ization. The reform of the repressive organs of KGB and the militia had gone so far, he believed, that "everything got focused on the moral."[92] When Roman Rudenko, the chief Soviet public prosecutor, explained that not all thieves were given the death penalty, Khrushchev responded: "Go to hell. . . . Thieves, they're stealing, and you're writing laws for them. What is this? What liberals you've become, what is it that you are expecting—praise from the bourgeoisie when no one gets shot, and all the while they are robbing the workers and the peasants."

RUDENKO: No matter how you scold me, if the law does not provide for the death penalty, we can't apply it.

KHRUSHCHEV: The peasants have a saying: "Get rid of the bad seeds." Stalin had the correct position on these issues. He went too far, but we never had any mercy on criminals. Our fight with enemies should be merciless and well directed.

The tenor of Khrushchev's statements was ominous enough with respect to the average Soviet citizen, but considering the international crisis that he had just launched, this dangerous mood had potentially catastrophic implica-tions. Angry, arrogant, and frustrated, he rammed through in July 1961 a series of changes in the Soviet criminal justice system that increased the use of the death penalty and the size of the police units within the KGB and reversed the mild liberalizing trend that Soviets had been experiencing pro-gressively since 1956.[93]

Khrushchev's determination was plain in other ways. In a speech to the graduates of Soviet military academies on July 8, he announced a one-third increase in the Soviet defense budget and a suspension of additional reductions in the size of the Soviet armed forces planned for 1961.[94] At a time when the entire leadership understood that the Soviet economy was a failure, this repre-sented a dramatic reversal of the grand policy of 1959–1960, Khrushchev's personal crusade to improve the domestic standard of living through demilita-rization and détente. If that were not proof enough that he was preparing for a dance on the brink of war, he was also talking about unilaterally end-ing the test ban moratorium, something he had earlier told the Presidium he would not do.[95]

15

IRON RING

J OHN KENNEDY BLAMED himself for Khrushchev's risk taking. He "just beat [the] hell out of me," the president confessed to James "Scottie" Reston just after the Vienna summit.[1] He was convinced that it was his own failure at the Bay of Pigs that had inspired Khrushchev to push him hard on Berlin. He had been concerned before Vienna that this might happen and had tried to communicate to the Soviets through his brother Robert that they ought not underestimate him.[2] Clearly something had gone wrong. Kennedy wondered if his performance with Khrushchev had made matters worse.[3] Joseph Alsop and the publisher of the *Washington Post*, Philip Graham, were among the close friends invited to listen as Kennedy read aloud from the transcripts of the meetings prepared by the State Department.[4] Like a quarterback reviewing films of a game that he should have won, he scrutinized these exchanges to see whether there was something else he should have said or if perhaps there was something he should not have said at all.

Kennedy took a few days off at the family home on South Ocean Boulevard in Palm Beach after flying back from Europe. He looked bad. He had twisted his chronically weak back in March during a tree-planting ceremony in the Canadian capital of Ottawa. The stress after Vienna had caused the pain to flare up, and White House correspondents noticed in June 1961 that his crutches were out again. Those accompanying him on the flight back from Florida watched as a fruit picker crane was used to lift the hobbling president onto *Air Force One*. Kennedy was also fighting a virus, for which his doctors had increased his daily dose of cortisone.[5] The lack of exercise caused by the bad back and the puffiness attributable to the cortisone made him look noticeably sluggish and fatter.[6]

Kennedy returned to a Washington taut with fear. Headlines blared that a new Berlin crisis was on. Khrushchev's uncompromising aide-mémoire appeared in U.S. newspapers after the Soviets released it, along with what seemed like daily reports of his various statements reaffirming the December deadline. Other evidence that Khrushchev was serious flooded in. In early July the head Soviet negotiator at the test ban discussions in Geneva announced that Moscow considered the talks a waste of time in light of American attitudes.[7] A few days later the Soviet Air Force organized its first major air show since 1956 to show off a long-range four-engine supersonic plane, nicknamed Bounder by NATO.[8] The West had seen Bounder before, but the flyby near Moscow was a reminder of Soviet strategic capabilities. So too was a prominent article in Aleksei Adzhubei's newspaper, *Izvestia*. Referring to an apparently unflattering statement by Attorney General Robert F. Kennedy on the Soviet submarine fleet, the newspaper warned: "[D]o not make any miscalculation, Mr. Kennedy, and do not overestimate your atomic weapons. The United States ceased long ago to have a monopoly on such arms."[9]

A policy debate raged in the White House over how to respond to Khrushchev's new Berlin ultimatum. Kennedy again invited a veteran of Stalin's 1948–1949 Berlin blockade, Truman's former secretary of state, Dean Acheson, to participate in the discussions. Acheson had headed the working group on Berlin for Kennedy's transition, and now the young president asked the old cold warrior to coordinate his administration's responses to Khrushchev.

Acheson rose to the challenge and prodded, pressed, and humiliated the administration's younger hands into offering Kennedy a series of options designed to convey U.S. toughness. He believed that it was Western resolve that had proved decisive in forcing a peaceful end to Stalin's Berlin crisis. Despite the change in Soviet leadership and the recent reforms in Soviet society, Acheson sensed that the lessons of that earlier crisis still fitted the circumstances of the current confrontation. He advocated an immediate conventional buildup in Europe and refused to consider negotiations with Khrushchev before the Soviets understood the nation's determination to defend its interests by force, if necessary.[10]

It was curious that Kennedy had enlisted Acheson's help. As a congressman Kennedy had been very critical of the Truman administration's foreign policy. He joined the chorus of those who blamed Truman for having "lost" China by mishandling Chiang Kai-shek and questioned the president's firing of Douglas MacArthur during the Korean War in 1951. One Kennedy broadside against the Truman administration had caused a Massachusetts paper to editorialize that "the political point of the Kennedy speech is that the Republicans should try to sign him up for a job with their speaking bureau."[11]

Kennedy also did not much like Acheson, whom he found overbearing, arrogant, and not always trustworthy. "[Dean Acheson] thinks that nothing has been done right since he left office," Kennedy confided to the journalist Theodore White in 1961.[12] Nevertheless, Kennedy understood that the institutions that made it easier for the United States to contain Soviet power were in large part the handiwork of this martinet.

Kennedy also shared many of Acheson's concerns. He knew that he could not negotiate at gunpoint. Once again it was a matter of "we arm to parlay." Khrushchev would need to be convinced that the United States was prepared to fight to retain its access to West Berlin. Kennedy was already a devotee of Maxwell Taylor's ideas on the importance of conventional weapons in the superpower contest. A thinking man's war hero who had proved his grit at the Battle of the Bulge in World War II, Taylor had almost single-handedly inspired a public debate over Eisenhower's nuclear policy in the late 1950s. Taylor argued that by relying so heavily on the threat of massive nuclear retaliation, Ike had devalued the currency of deterrence. Taylor advocated instead a more balanced approach to deterring Khrushchev, including building up U.S. nonnuclear forces so that the Kremlin understood that conventional war was still possible in the nuclear age. The fact that Khrushchev kept threatening to alter the status quo in Central Europe was strong proof for both Taylor and Kennedy that the Soviet leader believed the United States was too afraid of the consequences of massive retaliation to fight for anything but its homeland. The remedy was to present him with credible U.S. commitments to defend regional interests abroad with conventional forces.

In mid-July specific recommendations on how to demonstrate U.S. resolve to the Soviets flowed to Kennedy. Most his advisers believed that this was essentially a military crisis like 1948 and not the political crisis of 1958 that Eisenhower had handled so well by doing nothing. Acheson led the group that believed the potential was greater now for a military clash than in 1958. Khrushchev was so bloody-minded now that he might have to be defeated in a localized conventional struggle in Germany. "Khrushchev has, I believe, sensed weakness & division in the West and intends to exploit it to the hilt," Acheson wrote to his former boss, Harry Truman. "It wouldn't take more than an error or two on each side to carry us over the edge into nuclear war."[13] Vice President Lyndon B. Johnson and Assistant Secretary of Defense Paul Nitze joined the former secretary of state in advocating maximum preparations at the earliest possible time. A note of alarmism soon crept into their arguments. The hawks wanted Kennedy to declare a national emergency. Acheson predicted a congressional revolt if he did not declare a national emergency by the end of July. Johnson agreed, arguing that Congress expected a demonstration of presidential leadership. Nitze asserted that without this declaration of emergency now, there would be no hope of having enough soldiers and pilots in place by the end of 1961, when they might be needed for the next Battle of Berlin.[14]

Kennedy had not yet made up his mind whether to embrace the full Achesonian program when he received some unusually good intelligence that suggested that the main threat was more political than military.[15] On July 13 Allen Dulles, who remained CIA director until November, informed him that for some months the CIA and the British had been jointly operating an agent who had remarkable insight into what the Kremlin might be thinking. He was Oleg Penkovsky, an unusually well-connected colonel in the GRU, the Soviet military intelligence service.[16]

Penkovsky was a social friend of Chief Marshal Sergei Varentsov, a member of the Central Committee and a deputy to the Supreme Soviet. On June 25 Varentsov took Penkovsky aside at a party to chat with him about Khrushchev's intentions. It turned out to be much more than gossip. The gist of Khrushchev's May speech to the Presidium had managed to leak out to Varentsov. "Soon after the Party Congress [October 1961] a peace treaty will be signed," he told Penkovsky. "The Soviet government knows that signing this treaty means a certain risk and danger, but they are not worried, because they know that the FRG [Federal Republic of Germany, West Germany] still is not ready for war and needs two or three years more. The U.S., Britain and France, because of this, will not start a big war and will retreat. We also do not want a big war, but we want to force the West to begin to negotiate with the GDR on the procedures for movement along the access routes, the procedure for entrance and exit from Berlin, etc."[17] The mole then repeated this conversation to his Western case officer.

The spy's report alone might not have been that reassuring, but at the same time, and from highly reliable technical sources, Kennedy received information that Khrushchev was playing an extremely weak hand.[18] A U.S. satellite had just produced an unprecedented set of photographs showing the status of the Soviet missile program. After Powers's U-2 had been shot down, the United States had put its faith in the Corona satellite program to determine the size of the Soviet missile threat. Information from the most recent mission revealed that there were no more than two ICBM sites between Leningrad (now St. Petersburg) and the Ural Mountains, with a combined total of eight launchpads.[19]

Kennedy had believed in the missile gap.[20] Despite some contrary indicators and the skepticism of Secretary of Defense Robert McNamara, it was not until mid-July 1961 that Kennedy realized how far the Soviets were behind the United States.[21] Just before the Corona photographs came in, the intelligence community was still advising the president that the Soviets probably had between fifty and a hundred ICBMs.[22] Now he was assured that they had fewer than twenty, enough to destroy New York and Washington, if accurate, but nowhere near the offensive threat that the alarmists had predicted. There was indeed a missile gap, but it favored the United States, and it was enormous. At that moment United States had an ICBM fleet of over two hundred Titan and Atlas missiles, with hundreds of the new solid-fuel Minutemen missiles in development.[23] The brink, it seemed, was a much more dangerous place for the Soviet Union than for the United States.

Some wisdom from Gettysburg reinforced the reassuring information about missile developments in the Soviet Union and the United States.[24] Kennedy had asked for Eisenhower's opinion on the options he was considering and dispatched Dulles and McNamara to brief the former president at the Pennsylvania farm to which he had retired. Dulles and McNamara also brought along the new Corona intelligence. In return Eisenhower gave Kennedy the best advice he was to receive in the crisis. He dismissed Dulles's prediction that Khrushchev would probably test the United States after the West German elections scheduled for September. Eisenhower was confident that the United States was so much stronger than the Soviet Union that Khrushchev would not dare push too far. When McNamara mentioned the appearance of the Bounder bomber, Eisenhower recalled the bomber gap nonsense of the mid-1950s and advised the new defense secretary not to listen to congressional fears. "Congress," he said, "is not capable of exercising sound judgment regarding military programs." The thrust of his advice was that the Kennedy administration should not overreact. Declaring a national emergency, he said, "would be the worst mistake possible" in that it would give Khrushchev the idea that "all [he] has to do is needle us here and there to force us into such radical actions."

Two days later Kennedy made his decision. He chose preparedness over provocation, selecting those elements of Acheson's proposal necessary to demonstrate a willingness to fight a conventional war in Central Europe without causing panic.[25] He would request a massive increase in the defense budget and issue a call-up of some reserve troops and the National Guard, but he would not formally declare a national emergency. He and the Defense Department had wanted six additional army divisions to be in place by January 1962, but Kennedy knew that these deployments would be impossible without a declaration of national emergency, and he did not want to declare one. McNamara had assured him that this drastic call-up could be postponed until early September, and Kennedy hoped that Khrushchev might have given up on his ultimatum by then. In addition, Kennedy signed off on a tepid aide-mémoire that warned Khrushchev to stop trying to force unacceptable settlements down Western throats.

The human and satellite intelligence, as well as the advice from Eisenhower and others, had bolstered Kennedy's natural caution. In Vienna he had warned Khrushchev about the dangers of miscalculation in a nuclear struggle, and he was not about to make that mistake himself. In teeing up the decision for the president, McGeorge Bundy had noted that the country's prominent sparring columnists, Walter Lippmann and Joseph Alsop, both believed that Kennedy would have to take the lead in resolving this problem.[26] Kennedy agreed. He would use a televised speech to the nation on July 25 to request the additional $3.25 billion from Congress for defense, announce the call-ups, and also introduce a new program of civil defense, which was more a public confidence measure than a realistic approach to protecting the country in future nuclear crises.

Kennedy intentionally cut Acheson and Vice President Johnson out of the meeting at which he first tried out his decision.[27] Once he had built consensus among McNamara, Bundy, Secretary of State Rusk, Treasury Secretary Dillon, Maxwell Taylor, and his brother, the attorney general, he subjected his program to formal approval from the entire National Security Council and Acheson. Although he had the firm support of his inner circle of advisers, this had been a very difficult decision for Kennedy. Since Khrushchev's challenge at Vienna the world had been watching how he would react. Kennedy, who could be quite a pessimist, sensed that he did not have a lot of political capital either at home or abroad. "There are limits to the number of defeats I can defend in one twelve-month period," he told his former Harvard tutor John Kenneth Galbraith.[28]

The administration told the European allies the gist of these decisions before Kennedy gave his speech. On July 20 letters from the president were delivered to Adenauer, de Gaulle, and Macmillan. The next day Rusk, who had flown from Washington to Paris, met with the French, British, and West German foreign ministers to discuss what Kennedy intended to do. The White House had not consulted with the Western Europeans before Kennedy made up his mind, but Washington wanted the Europeans to be willing to assist in the crisis that the Americans expected.

■

As WASHINGTON debated its response to the Soviet ultimatum, Khrushchev headed south for his annual vacation at Pitsunda to think about his next step in the Berlin chess match. "[H]ere I work more fruitfully," Khrushchev wrote, "because my attention is not diverted to routine matters of which I have plenty. . . . Here I can concentrate on the main things."[29] His dacha had been built with the leader's comfort in mind. From its large windows and three balconies, he enjoyed a magnificent view of the Black Sea.[30] To allow the portly Khrushchev a little exercise, a pool, a luxury practically unheard of in the country, was set next to the house.

By mid-July, however, there was little tranquility for him to find at this beautiful place. Most unsettling were the reports on the ever-increasing number of East Germans fleeing their country through West Berlin.[31] In the first six months of the year a hundred thousand had left, twenty thousand of them in June alone. Since his ultimatum speeches of late June and early July, the numbers had become even more dramatic.[32] The flow of East German refugees to West Berlin was now the heaviest it had been since October 1955. As Khrushchev had said to the Presidium in May, he knew that a disproportionate number were professionals, who would be difficult to replace.[33] Even harder for him was the fact that these people were seeking better lives in the West because the standard of living in the GDR could not yet compete.[34] "The question of whether this or that system is progressive ought to be decided in political terms," said Khrushchev. "However, many people decide it in the pit of their stomach."[35]

The news that reached the Soviet leader at Pitsunda from the United States was no more encouraging. Kennedy's formal response to the Soviet aide-mémoire on Berlin finally arrived on July 18 and was a major disappointment. Calling the Soviet effort "a document which speaks of peace but threatens to disturb it," the president in a message accompanying the U.S. response advised Khrushchev to reconsider the West's proposals of 1959, which included free elections for a unified greater Berlin.[36] There was no suggestion of negotiations or bold new offers. Washington instead called on the Kremlin "to reconsider its course."

Around the third week of July intelligence reports that reached Khrushchev reinforced the impression that the White House was girding for a protracted crisis. Khrushchev later said that the most influential was one that predicted Washington intended to take advantage of the situation in East

Germany. In 1953 the Eisenhower administration had declined to intervene to help the rioters in East Berlin who had launched a short-lived revolt against the East German regime. But Khrushchev, who was unsure that Kennedy really controlled his own government, gave credence to the possibility that this U.S. government might not be as cautious.[37]

From his protégé Aleksandr Shelepin, the chief of the KGB, Khrushchev learned on July 20 that NATO was preparing to deal with the Berlin matter as a military problem. Soviet sources in some Western European governments were reporting that NATO was united in its determination to prevent Moscow from signing a peace treaty with East Germany that would affect access rights to West Berlin. The KGB predicted that if Khrushchev went ahead with his plan, the West would "be ready to take steps that could threaten the security of the Soviet Union." Evidence had reached Moscow of serious Western military planning to counter any attempt to isolate West Berlin. There was also intelligence indicating plans for political, economic, and other nonmilitary sanctions to put pressure on Moscow to desist.[38]

Khrushchev may have also received hints of the conventional buildup that Kennedy had outlined in his letters to the big three European leaders or that Rusk discussed in Paris with the foreign secretaries. Soviet penetration of those governments was impressive in the early 1960s. In May, for example, the Kremlin had received copies of papers delivered by the French government to NATO that outlined the various countries' positions on the Berlin question.[39] Similarly Presidium members were able to read copies of the West German ambassador's correspondence with Bonn.[40]

Confronted with the rigid U.S. aide-mémoire and the related intelligence, Khrushchev decided that he would have to prepare for a much longer and tougher confrontation than anticipated. He had already canceled some military leaves and reapportioned funds to his Defense Ministry, but the situation in East Germany needed immediate attention. Ulbricht's regime already seemed to be cracking under strain of this crisis, and now it seemed the international tension would probably last through the end of the year.

Khrushchev decided to build a wall through the center of Berlin. This was in part a reaction to a suggestion from Ulbricht. On the eve of the Vienna summit the East Germans had communicated to Moscow that their immediate objective was to close the sectoral border through which so many East Germans were fleeing. This was more important to them in 1961 than a peace treaty.[41] Khrushchev had long understood that this would have to be part of the peace agreement, but he was hesitant to proceed with this step before exhausting his negotiating strategy. He knew that a Berlin wall would be viewed as a provocation by the West and would therefore complicate all efforts to achieve a general settlement. He now thought he could no longer wait for the West to come around to a general settlement.

The decision to build the Berlin Wall was Khrushchev's alone to make. He oversaw all aspects of the Soviet bloc's strategy for settling the German question. Only he could decide to divorce border control measures from the larger effort of isolating West Berlin through a peace agreement. He therefore bore sole responsibility for the many lives that would be inalterably hurt by this decision.

Khrushchev had no moral qualms about separating millions of German families, some of whom, as it turned out, did not see one another for a decade. Although he reluctantly understood their motivations, he was just as dismissive of the thousands of East Germans who educated their children in West Berlin schools and of the tens of thousands of workers who worked for higher pay in West Berlin. They were not as reprehensible to him as the thieves, those he called economic criminals, that he had put to death in the Soviet Union. But the callousness of that recent decision could be seen in his treatment of the Berlin problem. For all his empathy for those who did not live as well as they should under communism, Khrushchev had no human feeling for those individuals who by their actions threatened his plans. It was this authoritarian blindness that prevented him from ever understanding the concept of human liberty.

Instructions were sent to the Soviet group of forces in Germany and the East German Ministry of Internal Affairs to work together on a plan for establishing control over "Greater Berlin," including the boundary between the Eastern and Western sectors. "Exit or entry into West Berlin," the plan specified, "would be outlawed for all citizens of the GDR, except for those with special permits."[42] Approved by the chief of staff of the Soviet forces in Germany on July 21, the plan did not address political matters. On its face, it seemed designed to be part of the measures that would take effect once Khrushchev and Ulbricht signed the peace treaty that would transfer Moscow's remaining responsibilities to East Germany. Of course it could be implemented earlier. All that was required was a political decision to build a wall.

Khrushchev wanted the formal decision to be made by the leaders of the Warsaw Pact in the first days of August. The Presidium had already decided in late June to arrange a meeting of the pact members on August 3 to discuss the Berlin situation. In the third week of July Gromyko drafted an agenda and prepared invitations for the meeting at which closing the Berlin sectoral border would be discussed.[43] Khrushchev insisted on maximum secrecy; any leak to the West might provoke a preemptive strike. Only Ulbricht would be told the reason for the session beforehand. The other Warsaw Pact leaders would be told only when they arrived in Moscow on August 3. Khrushchev wanted the invitations to go out on July 26.[44]

■

THERE WAS A BUZZ in Washington on the morning of July 25. The *New York Times* predicted the speech would be Kennedy's second inaugural address. "This one," observed the *Times'* James Reston, "will inaugurate a new flexible policy, not only for Berlin but for the whole 'cold war' front."[45] Rumors about this speech had been appearing in newspapers for days, and it was expected that Kennedy would meet Khrushchev's threats with counter-measures that demonstrated the resolve of the United States.

Theodore Sorensen, Kennedy's principal speechwriter, took the president's reading copy up to him in the family quarters of the White House that morning and found him propped up in bed with a heating pad supporting his aching back. He was making some last-minute changes to the speech, adding a final, very personal note, in longhand. "When I ran for the Presidency of the United States," he scribbled in his nearly illegible handwriting, "I knew that this country faced serious challenges, but I could not realize, nor could any man realize who does not bear the burdens of the office, how heavy and constant would be those burdens. . . . In these days and weeks I ask for your help, and your advice. I ask for your suggestions, when you think we can do better. All of us, I know, love our country, and we shall do our best to serve it."[46] Sorensen took the changes and had them typed up.

The handwritten addendum was uncharacteristically confessional for a man who believed that leadership required cool detachment. The estimated fifty million television viewers and those listening on radio would be invited to peer through to the insecurities that Kennedy usually hid from almost all but a few family members. From the man who only six months earlier had spoken confidently of "bearing any burden," there would be an admission of vulnerability. Yes, he would bear this burden, but it wasn't going to be easy. No words ever spoken by this president, and there were many more in the crisis-filled years to come, would be as poignant.

Giving the speech proved to be just as difficult as writing it. Although the broadcast had been delayed until 10:00 P.M., when at least children on the East Coast would be asleep, the heat of a July day in Washington still hung heavily that night. Air conditioners in the early 1960s were especially noisy contraptions, and the president's television producers thought they had to turn down the only source of cool air in the Oval Office. Journalists covering the speech described the room as being "like an oven." Television viewers, who had no idea of the temperature their president was enduring, concluded that Kennedy's frequent mopping of his brow reflected tension, thus heightening the effect of the speech.[47] "[West Berlin] has now become—as never before—" Kennedy told the American people, "the great testing place of Western courage and will, a focal point where our solemn commitments . . . and Soviet ambitions now meet in basic confrontation."[48] Then, if there were any doubt that Kennedy was ready for this test, he added, "I hear it said that West Berlin is militarily untenable. And so was Bastogne. And so, in fact, was Stalingrad. Any dangerous spot is tenable if men—brave men—will make it so."[49]

■

"KENNEDY HAS DECLARED preliminary war on the Soviet Union," Khrushchev barked at John J. McCloy.[50] Khrushchev had invited McCloy, Kennedy's special adviser on disarmament, to Pitsunda so that he could respond immediately and personally to the much-anticipated U.S. response. McCloy was well known to Khrushchev as a charter member of the U.S. foreign policy establishment. A former deputy secretary of war under Franklin Roosevelt, McCloy had served Harry Truman as U.S. high commissioner in occupied Germany. But McCloy had not come to the Soviet Union in mid-July 1961 to discuss Germany; he was leading a State Department delegation to discuss arms control when he received the unexpected invitation to see Khrushchev on July 25. McCloy was therefore the first Westerner to experience the heat of Khrushchev's displeasure at Kennedy's Berlin speech.

Although McCloy had no inkling of this, the speech redoubled Khrushchev's determination to install the wall before the Americans made any move. On July 26 Khrushchev instructed the Soviet ambassador in East Berlin to tell Ulbricht that in his judgment "we have to use the tension in international relations now to circle Berlin in an iron ring. This must be done before concluding a peace treaty."[51] Khrushchev explained that the international situation had brought about this 180-degree shift in his opinion on taking a unilateral measure to stop the flow of refugees. This would be a joint operation. "Our troops will create this ring; but your forces will control it," he had his ambassador tell Ulbricht. To ease any concerns the East German leader might have about the Soviet Union's resolve in the especially tense days that were sure to follow the building of a wall, Khrushchev instructed Ambassador Pervukhin to assure him that "we are approaching this question seriously and if this drags us into war, there will be war."

Ever the engineer, Khrushchev was interested in the details of how this barrier would be built. He instructed Pervukhin to send him the plans recently worked out by the East Germans and the Soviet Army and to ask Ulbricht for an estimate of how long the entire operation would take. He also wanted to see what Ulbricht planned to say at the Warsaw Pact meeting.[52] Khrushchev wanted the East German leader to take the lead at the session in explaining to the other leaders why this iron ring was necessary.

Khrushchev received the response from Ulbricht the next day. It was pithy and enthusiastic. "This is the solution!" Ulbricht exclaimed.[53] He went on to assure the Soviet government that once the decision had been made it would take a mere eight days to prepare all the measures required to initiate the closure of the border between East and West Berlin and to tighten the control around all Berlin. Khrushchev was especially concerned about the transit systems—the S-Bahn and the subway—that crossed the sector boundaries. The East Germans assured him that closing those down would take only between four and five weeks.[54] The first day guards would be posted at all the crossing points, and over time they would be replaced by physical barriers.

▪

A FTER McCLOY'S DEPARTURE from Pitsunda on July 26, Khrushchev had spent a few days touring farms in the Ukraine before returning to Moscow on July 31 to see Ulbricht. The East German leader was due to arrive in Moscow before the other Warsaw Pact leaders so that he and Khrushchev could plan their strategy. Although Ulbricht was relieved, his old concerns about the Western reaction to any East German and Soviet provocation had returned. As he had in November 1960, the German worried about a Western economic blockade.

The Kremlin had anticipated this problem.[55] Even before Khrushchev returned to Moscow, Mikoyan and Gromyko drafted a proposal for countermeasures should the West impose an economic blockade on East Germany. They suggested that East Germany retaliate by preventing all nonmilitary transportation from West Berlin to West Germany. This would be "a blow to West German firms that obtained manufactured products from West Berlin but would not interfere with the operation of West Berlin industry or the supply of food to the population."[56] Another suggested form of action came from the KGB chief, Shelepin, who on July 29 proposed a series of measures around the world that "would favor dispersion of attention and forces by the United States and its satellites, and would tie them down during the settlement of a German peace treaty and West Berlin."[57] In particular, Shelepin advocated assisting revolutionary movements in Latin America to distract Washington.

These recommendations, if accepted, would mark a major shift in how Khrushchev competed with U.S. power in the third world. Up to now the Kremlin had not created any national liberation movements and had been reluctant to sponsor revolutionaries who preferred armed rebellion to creating socialism through political subversion. Among the KGB's recommendations was a plan to work with the Cubans and the Sandinista movement in Nicaragua, the Frente Sandinista de Liberación Nacional (FSLN), to sponsor revolutionary movements throughout Latin America. The FSLN was itself to be built up so that it had a credible chance of overthrowing the Nicaraguan dictator Anastas Somoza.[58]

On August 1 Khrushchev and the Presidium accepted the KGB plan to distract the United States by "creating a hotbed of unrest" in Latin America. It was evidence less of new thinking about the third world than of an almost desperate desire to chip away at U.S. resolve in the Berlin crisis. Khrushchev was kept informed of the planning in Latin America. Shelepin reported to him that the KGB was funneling a modest amount of money to the FSLN and exercising influence over the movement through three confidential contacts—PIMEN, GIDROLOG, and LOT. In this way, the KGB gave the FSLN ten thousand U.S. dollars to buy weapons and subsequently recruited twelve Nicaraguan students in Mexico City to train for operations against the Somoza regime.[59]

Khrushchev's main concern remained the situation in Berlin, and on August 3 he met with Ulbricht to discuss it. Not wishing to encourage Ulbricht's slight defeatism, Khrushchev opted to conceal the Kremlin's emergency plans from the East German. Instead Khrushchev merely suggested that once the barriers were up the Soviets and the East Germans would announce in a joint communiqué that this had been done in the interests of the socialist world. When Ulbricht asked that his people be told something before the wall went up to prevent fear of economic strangulation, Khrushchev disagreed. Predicting a mass rush for the exits, he told the East German that the best way to create panic would be to tell the public anything before the barriers were erected. "We have to do this the way we introduced the new currency regime," Khrushchev said, referring to how the Soviet regime had suddenly introduced an East German mark in the early 1950s.[60] He wanted the wall to be built without warning, a sudden fait accompli.

Khrushchev went on to outline his thinking on how this border closing should proceed. Although he wanted the wall to go up secretly, he also proposed to position Soviet tanks along the border with the Federal Republic of Germany behind a wall of Soviet troops. His intention was to send a signal to the Western governments without creating a war scare among the populations of Europe and the United States. He did not want public hysteria; he just wanted to do enough to deter Washington, Bonn, Paris, and London from intervening to prevent the closure of the border. Ulbricht worried that these steps might not be enough. "Perhaps your units will need reinforcements," he said. Khrushchev disagreed. "[T]his would evoke a negative reaction (from the Germans) and as a demonstration [of power] this step would not have any decisive meaning."[61]

Again Khrushchev asked how long this would take. Ulbricht now believed the iron ring could be constructed within two weeks, instead of the eight days he had previously predicted. This was good enough for Moscow. In a moment of generosity, Khrushchev assured the German that it would be up to the GDR to decide the best moment to start the operation. Whenever it decided to go ahead, Moscow would be ready. "The date for the beginning of border control was to be August 13, 1961," Khrushchev later recalled. "We kidded among ourselves that in the West the thirteenth is supposed to be an unlucky day. I joked that for us and for the whole socialist camp it would be a very lucky day indeed."[62] August 13 was a Sunday, and it made sense to launch this operation in the middle of a weekend, when few East Germans would be working in West Berlin.

■

Despite the Penkovsky penetration and the timely visit of John McCloy, the Kennedy administration did not pick up on any of Khrushchev's plans. The Kremlin followed a very strict policy of secrecy about the plan for Berlin, even at the risk of annoying its allies. Moscow stonewalled the nosy Polish leader Wladyslaw Gomulka, who kept asking about the agenda items for the forthcoming Warsaw Pact discussions.[63] The wall operation was also closely held in Moscow. Instructions to the KGB and the other relevant ministries regarding a worldwide propaganda campaign to accompany the unveiling of the wall were not distributed until the last possible moment.[64]

In a message to the Kremlin, Ulbricht insisted on even stricter measures to preserve the security of the operation. Remembering perhaps how quickly copies of Khrushchev's secret speech to the Twentieth Party Congress had reached the West in 1956, he didn't want the Soviet government to prepare any materials for the visiting delegations that could reveal the secret. "In connection with this meeting," he wrote, "we will provide to the representatives of the fraternal parties only those materials that can be published."[65]

The Warsaw Pact representatives gathered in Moscow on August 3 for a three-day session on Berlin.[66] In his speeches Khrushchev prepared the entire group for the building of the Berlin Wall and the expected international tensions that would ensue. "No one can give a guarantee that there will be no war," he told them.[67] Although he did not expect any Western attack, he advised his comrades that the bloc should "strengthen our defense, strengthen our military forces. . . . We must, comrades, show them our will and decisiveness, [or they] will say that we are bluffing and consequently will strengthen the pressure against us."[68] Khrushchev and Ulbricht, who gave his main speech on August 4, both addressed the more likely possibility of a Western economic embargo against East Germany. Moscow and East Berlin hoped that the Poles, the Hungarians, and the Czechs would be able to find a way to reduce some of the pressure on the East German economy were this to happen.

The meetings ended on August 5 with a partial victory for Khrushchev and Ulbricht. Their socialist allies were generous in offering moral support for the wall operation. The pact passed a resolution in support of closing the border. However, each of the Eastern European leaders also reminded the Kremlin that there was a limit to the economic assistance that they could offer East Germany. They had weak planned economies of their own.[69]

Returning to Berlin immediately after the conference, Ulbricht turned to the many preparations required before the border could be closed a week later. On Monday, August 7, he informed the East German Politburo of the talks in Moscow and the decision to close the border on the night of August 12–13.[70] On Wednesday, August 9, he assured the Soviets that all necessary preparations would be completed by Saturday and supplied a timetable for the weekend's events.[71]

Ulbricht laid out for Khrushchev via the Soviet ambassador in East Berlin how he planned to choreograph the night of August 12–13 to minimize the possibility of leaks to the West. He would invite the formal cabinet of the East German government (the Council of Ministers) to his country house outside Berlin at the last possible moment on August 12. Around midnight he would convene this group to approve the Warsaw Pact resolution calling for the closure of the border. As the group was rubber-stamping the decision, East German policemen would form lines along the sectoral boundary and begin unrolling barbed wire, which would have been distributed to them in advance as part of an "exercise." Ninety minutes later, if all went according to plan, an official announcement of the sealing of the East Berlin border would be sent to the GDR's press agency for distribution to the world.[72]

Khrushchev received this report from Ulbricht on August 10, the same day the Kremlin announced that Marshal Ivan Konev, the former commander in chief of the Warsaw Pact forces, who had played a major role in Stalin's military campaign against Hitler, was returning as commander in chief of Soviet Forces in Germany. Khrushchev was responding to Ulbricht's earlier request that something be done to prepare the East German population for the tense days to come. The selection of a war hero like Konev to be in Berlin signaled Moscow's direct involvement in what would be happening there.[73]

The new commander in chief reached Berlin slightly ahead of Khrushchev's statement. A bulldog of a man with the hands and face of a Ukrainian peasant, Konev took some pleasure in surprising the Western liaison officers assigned to his new command. The American, British, and French missions in East Berlin had already been invited to a late-afternoon meeting with Colonel General Ivan I. Yakubovsky, the commander in chief of the Soviet Group of Forces in Germany. Standing next to Yakubovsky when they arrived was the diminutive Konev. "Gentlemen, my name is Konev," he reportedly said with a twinkle in his eyes. "You may perhaps have heard of me."[74] The gathered mission chiefs could only smile.

Konev's appointment was the only public act that any Western intelligence professional could later point to as a possible signal of what was to come.[75] At the time, however, the appointment passed without anyone in the White House or even at the Pentagon suspecting a change in Khrushchev's tactics.

Konev quickly met with Ulbricht to assure himself that the East Germans were indeed ready for the operation. According to the plan created in July, the Soviet armed forces would remain in the background throughout the operation unless the Western powers made a provocative move. There was no mention in the plans sent to the Soviet Presidium in the first days of August of what steps the Soviet armed forces might take if the U.S. Berlin command tried to test the East German police action in the early moments of the operation. In his meeting with Ulbricht, Konev stressed two points: First, the operation had to proceed quickly, and second, the ability of the citizens of West Berlin to move back and forth to West Germany should not be affected by this action.[76]

As Ulbricht met with Konev, the top level of the East German security police received its first briefing on the coming operation. On Friday, August 11 the East German police chief, Erich Mielke, revealed to them the code name for the closure of the Berlin border, Operation Rose, and instructed them to do all their preparatory work "under the strictest secrecy."[77]

▪

E ARLY IN THE morning on August 13, East German police began stringing barbed wire and tearing up roads along West Berlin's twenty-seven-mile border with East Berlin and the remaining sixty-nine miles of border with East Germany. Concrete barriers did not go up for another two days along the line separating the two Berlins, but within the first few hours of Operation Rose police stood in a wall-like formation to prevent any traffic through the historic Brandenburg Gate, once the symbol of a united Germany. Khrushchev's iron ring sliced through 192 streets, thirty-two railway lines, eight S-Bahn (city train lines), four subway lines, and three autobahns.[78] Where a river or lake defined the border between East and West, the East Germans later built submerged barriers, but on this first day special marine patrols were organized. Left untouched were the three railway lines and three highways through East Germany that linked West Berlin to West Germany. The goal of Operation Rose, as Konev had earlier reminded Ulbricht, was to restrain the East German population, not to prevent movement from West Germany to West Berlin.

A formal decision by the East German government preceded this operation. Ulbricht had gathered the GDR's Council of Ministers at his country home in the daylight hours of August 12, earlier than originally planned. As it turned out, they needed the extra time to discuss the plan and only at 11:00 P.M. reached agreement that the wall should go up. The delay caused some awkwardness for Ulbricht when as the ministers were being driven home, they saw Soviet and East German tanks that had already received orders to move in preparation for the construction of the barriers. Besides this somewhat embarrassing hiccup, there were some real difficulties with policemen and railwaymen who, disgusted by the closure of the Berlin border, refused to cooperate.[79]

Soviet military representatives reported back to Moscow that the operation had gone nearly flawlessly.[80] While there had been some popular resistance along the border, its significance was played down. The East Germans seemed to have everything under control, and at no time during the night had Ulbricht's men requested assistance from Soviet forces. Even more satisfying was evidence that not only had the operation caught the West by surprise, but Western troops were staying in their barracks. No alert of any kind had been detected at the NATO garrisons in West Berlin.

▪

K ENNEDY WAS BACK from a Sunday sail off Hyannis Port when he first received reports of the barriers dividing Berlin. The closure of the border was already over eighteen hours old, and he was angry that neither the CIA nor the State Department's representatives in Berlin had given him any warning.[81] But there was really nothing he could do about Khrushchev's wall. Theodore Sorensen later summarized the view shared by the president and his closest associates: The wall was "illegal, immoral and inhumane, but not a cause for war."[82] Much harder to admit was the sense that it might prove to be, in the words of Kennedy biographer Robert Dallek, a "godsend."[83] The Kennedy administration knew that the flight of East Germans via West Berlin—it was estimated that 3.5 million East Germans had already left their homes for the refugee centers in the enclave—posed a daily threat to the stability of Khrushchev's German satellite. In bringing this hemorrhaging to an abrupt end, the wall might reduce the pressure compelling Khrushchev to crusade for a peace treaty. Kennedy's only responses were therefore designed to restate the U.S. commitment to West Berlin. He immediately dispatched retired General Lucius Clay, the hero of the 1948–1949 Berlin airlift, and Vice President Lyndon Johnson to West Berlin to reassure the population of the divided city. A week later he sent a convoy of sixteen hundred troops along the autobahn to show the flag and to reinforce the U.S. occupying force.[84]

Kennedy faced the same moral dilemma as had Eisenhower during the Hungarian uprising of 1956. Now, as then, the U.S. president believed he had to turn his back on the plight of the citizens of the socialist bloc to prevent a wider war. Kennedy had not considered that the building of the wall might be a possible scenario flowing from the Vienna ultimatum. His greatest concern had been, and remained, a Soviet military effort to strangle West Berlin. Although the new wall now seemed to rule out a Soviet military assault into West Berlin, the Western access routes remained vulnerable. Kennedy was not prepared to risk everything by destroying a wall that was being built on East German territory.

Protests in West Berlin underscored the moral implications of the wall. The stunned acceptance of the early morning was followed by waves of protest, especially along the corridors of freshly laid barbed wire separating the two Berlins. Three thousand people gathered by early evening at the western end of the Brandenburg Gate. When they started throwing stones east, the East German police opened water cannons on them from the other side. In the southwestern corner of the city, the East German police lobbed tear gas canisters and then used truncheons to disperse an angry West German crowd that had surged into East Berlin. Meanwhile desperate East Germans, including policemen, tried to crash through or jump over the barriers, which were flimsy in these early hours of the division.[85]

Despite the hurt and fear felt by Berliners, the federal government in Bonn also recognized instantly the utility of the wall. The day after the first barriers went up, Adenauer announced he would not cut trade ties with East Germany. The dreaded economic sanctions would be imposed only if the Kremlin went through with its threat to sign a peace treaty.[86] Even Adenauer's hard-line defense minister, Franz Josef Strauss, appealed for calm among West Germans. "If shooting starts," he said, "no one knows with what kinds of weapons it will end."[87]

■

KHRUSHCHEV WAS RELIEVED by the lack of a forceful Western response. "War might have broken out," he said.[88] Not only had there not been any Western efforts to remove the barriers, but Kennedy, Macmillan, de Gaulle, and Adenauer seemed to have ruled out any immediate plans to penalize the Eastern bloc for this step. The Kremlin's secret retaliatory measures could be kept on the shelf.

■

THE BUILDING of the wall did not end the Berlin crisis of 1961. Neither the Soviets nor the East Germans believed that stanching the flow of refugees had solved the problem. For the remainder of the month of August the Soviet government continued its campaign of psychological pressure on the West in preparation for a treaty showdown. For the first time in nearly twenty years foreign military attachés were invited to observe Soviet army maneuvers. On display were units equipped with nuclear-tipped battlefield missiles.[89] No effort at military posturing was more impressive than the announcement at the end of the month that the USSR planned to break its self-imposed moratorium on nuclear testing. Two days later, after three years of abstinence, the Soviet Union began a nuclear test series at its testing range at Semipalatinsk in Central Asia.

Soviet saber rattling emboldened the East Germans to engage in provocations of their own. On August 22 they announced the establishment of a hundred-meter no-man's-land on both sides of the Berlin Wall. The residents of West Berlin were warned that they might be shot if they approached closer than a hundred meters to the boundary.[90] The next day the East Germans unilaterally reduced the number of crossing points that could be used by the West from seven to one, which became known as Checkpoint Charlie, at Friedrichstrasse.[91]

The Soviets were prepared to accept additional border controls so long as they did not raise the risk of confrontation with the West in Berlin. However, Ulbricht's new policies, neither of which had been cleared ahead of time by Moscow, involved taking rights away from the West. On August 24 the Soviet ambassador and Konev met with Ulbricht to explain why it was wrong to declare a no-man's-land on the Western side of the Berlin boundary. "The establishment of a 100-meter security zone on West Berlin territory and the granting of permission to the police to use force against trespassers in this zone," the Soviets said, "could lead to a clash between the GDR police and the forces of the Western powers." The next day Ulbricht issued a statement rescinding the zone and assuring the West that the agencies of the GDR had "no intention of interfering in the internal affairs of West Berlin."[92] However, he refused to back off his plan to maintain only one checkpoint, and Moscow tolerated this small act of defiance.

■

BY THE END of August Soviet and East German actions were suggesting a policy in flux. All Soviet actions were of course authorized, but Khrushchev was changing his mind. He was back in Pitsunda, where the sunny isolation had again set the wheels of his imagination in motion.

Although Kennedy had responded meekly to the Berlin Wall, the daily reality of the U.S. military commitment to West Berlin was wearing at Khrushchev's determination to sustain this self-made crisis. For all the hints and intelligence that he had received before Kennedy's July 25 speech, Khrushchev apparently was not prepared for the scale of the conventional buildup initiated by the U.S. president. At the meeting with McCloy, Khrushchev had tried to scare him by stressing the Soviet Union's conventional superiority in and around Berlin. "Each division you send to Europe," he said, "we can match with two of our own."[93] From the start of this crisis he had based his confident prediction of a 5 percent chance of war on the assumption that the United States was so outgunned in Berlin that it had no realistic military options to defend its position. The measures laid out by Kennedy in his speech, which had since been implemented by the United States and accepted by Europe, invalidated the basic premise of Khrushchev's Berlin gambit. Mikoyan's prediction of U.S. willingness to engage in a conventional battle, not Khrushchev's assumption that war was impossible in the nuclear age, seemed to have been borne out.

Khrushchev, who was not one to engage in honest postmortems, did not leave to history the exact reasons for his change of heart. But he knew that he had backed himself into a corner.[94] By late August he was looking for an excuse to call off his ultimatum. He still dreamed of a German peace treaty as a capstone of a new European settlement, but the last few months had demonstrated that crude pressure tactics alone were not enough to get the Kennedy administration to yield. A new approach was needed: a few carrots to go with the sticks.

Thousands of miles away Khrushchev's shifting strategy was as yet unknown. Instead a sticky pessimism settled over Washington as the tension dragged into the late summer. Dean Acheson wrote Harry Truman, who served as his father confessor throughout this crisis: "I believe that sometime this autumn we are in for a most humiliating defeat over Berlin. . . . I hope I am wrong, but do not think that there is the remotest chance that I am. The course is set and events are about to take control."[95] George Kennan, another architect of the U.S. strategy of containing the Soviet Union, was equally morose. Returning in August from Belgrade, where he was serving as Kennedy's ambassador, Kennan confided to his friend Arthur M. Schlesinger, Jr., "I do not propose to let the future of mankind be settled, or ended, by a group of men operating on the basis of limited perspectives and short-run calculations. I figure that the only thing I have left in life is to do everything I can to stop the war."[96] Schlesinger, who described these as "strange, moody days," shared the pessimism. "I feel more gloomy about international developments," he wrote to a friend, "than I have felt since the summer of 1939."[97]

CHAPTER 16

"THE STORM IN BERLIN IS OVER"

O N AUGUST 26 the *New York Times* correspondent Cyrus Sulzberger received an unexpected cable at his hotel on the small Peloponnesian island of Spetsai. Yuri Zhukov, a well-placed and engaging Soviet flack, who had been a prominent Kremlin spokesman since the early days of the Korean War, had interesting news for his old friend Cy. If the journalist could make his way to Moscow, Khrushchev might see him. Zhukov suggested Sulzberger arrive in Moscow on September 2 or 3, when the Soviet leader was to return from his Black Sea vacation. Zhukov didn't let on what Khrushchev wanted to talk about, but in August 1961 no one was talking about much else besides Berlin.[1]

A few days later the Soviet ambassador in Yugoslavia informed his American counterpart, George Kennan, that Nikita Khrushchev "enthusiastically endors[ed] further conversations" between the ambassadors on the issue of Berlin.[2] Washington had already tried to use Kennan to communicate to the Kremlin its interest in diplomacy. The day after the wall first started going up, the State Department had authorized Kennan to approach his Soviet opposite number to sniff around for a chance to open a line to Khrushchev.[3] The Kremlin had not been ready on August 14. Now it was.

Meanwhile in Brussels the chargé d'affaires at the Soviet Embassy issued an unexpected invitation to the Belgian foreign minister to visit Khrushchev in Moscow. A short man from a small country, Paul Henri Spaak was nonetheless a respected force in European affairs.[4] Until February 1961 he had been NATO's secretary-general before returning to Brussels to become foreign minister. In late July Spaak had used a roundabout way to communicate to Moscow his belief that a negotiated settlement was possible.[5] Until this moment Moscow had not taken him up on his offer.

A famously short Frenchman received the fourth invitation. In the more fashionable salons of prewar Paris, Paul Reynaud had been known for his "small-man arrogance" and "walking almost on tiptoe to appear taller."[6] In the late summer of 1961 this eighty-three-year-old former French prime minister was due to visit the Soviet Union to close an exhibition of French goods and technology on display in Moscow.[7] The Kremlin's unscheduled approach to Reynaud for a session with Khrushchev was rife with symbolism. It was Reynaud who had resigned in despair when Hitler attacked France in May 1940.[8] This phantom of France's past was about to be asked to help arrange a less dramatic, though significant, Western surrender in 1961.

Khrushchev had decided at Pitsunda to initiate feelers to the West in an effort to jump-start negotiations. The approaches to Sulzberger and Kennan were designed to establish a new back channel to Kennedy. Khrushchev was probing for some change in Kennedy's negotiating position. From Spaak and Reynaud Khrushchev wanted understanding and support. When he set his Berlin strategy, he had expected the Western Europeans to magnify the pressure on the United States to avoid war by accepting Soviet terms.[9] Still convinced they could be used to break America's resolve, Khrushchev decided to court prominent Europeans who had already demonstrated an interest in conciliation.

As his representatives were putting this diplomatic offensive into place, Khrushchev was himself the recipient of a surprising initiative. If a personal message from Khrushchev was a most unexpected thing for Kennan, Reynaud, Spaak, and Sulzberger that summer, its shock value was far surpassed by Konrad Adenauer's private approach to him. On August 29, 1961, the West German chancellor sent a secret message to his Russian counterpart. As interpreted by the Soviet Foreign Ministry, after its delivery by West German Ambassador Kroll, the message read:

> The Chancellor wanted his adversary to know that he fully agreed with Khrushchev that the developing serious situation must be approached soberly, not yielding to emotions. The Federal Republic knows that neither Eisenhower [sic] nor Khrushchev wanted war. But the outbreak of war was possible. The two greatest dangers: when tanks stand opposite tanks, at a distance of just some meters, as is the case now in Berlin, and the even greater danger of an incorrect assessment of the situation. The Federal Republic is convinced that negotiations constitute the sole exit from the situation, which must begin within the shortest possible time. The Federal Republic's position regarding the direction of negotiations fully coincides with the positions of the USA and Great Britain. As is

well known, France occupies a special position regarding the timetable for undertaking negotiations.[10]

The West German leader's public stance was that negotiations with Moscow were dangerous because they were likely to result in Western concessions on Berlin. Through Kroll, however, Adenauer stressed to the Kremlin that there was no reason for the Soviets to wait until the September 17 West German elections to begin negotiations. Moreover, the West German asked Moscow to show its willingness to reduce tensions by releasing the last group of German citizens who remained captive in the USSR.[11] Adenauer's initiative played into Khrushchev's stubborn notion that eventually he could attract Bonn away from Washington. Perhaps this was just a preelection trick by the wily German chancellor. Neverthless, Khrushchev needed all the European help he could get in the negotiations to come.

■

K HRUSHCHEV SPENT five hours with Cyrus Sulzberger on September 5. He gave the journalist enough fodder for a series of front-page articles and then got around to the reason for the meeting. Sulzberger was handed, for Kennedy's eyes only, a private note in which Khrushchev suggested that the two leaders establish "some sort of informal contact . . . to find a means of settling the crisis without damaging the prestige of the United States." All he asked was that Kennedy agree "in principle with the peace treaty and a free city."[12] For the first time he did not demand that Kennedy accept the loss of Western access rights.

■

T HE INITIATIVE fell on fertile ground. Kennedy was also thinking hard about how to negotiate a way out of this crisis.[13] The president faced some unpleasant decisions in September 1961. If he wanted to have six more divisions deployed in Europe by the beginning of the new year, he could not delay declaring a national emergency much longer. The Joint Chiefs and some of his civilian aides continued to interpret his July decision as just a postponement of the inevitable. But Kennedy wondered if those six divisions were really needed after all.[14] Pressure was also building on him to decide whether to resume U.S. nuclear tests. An ever-larger group of Kennedy advisers were saying that in light of the Soviet test series at Semipalatinsk, the United States really had no choice.[15]

Kennedy had already reacted positively to news of the Soviet approach to

George Kennan before Khrushchev even met with Sulzberger. The Kremlin seemed prepared to talk instead of shout, though Kennedy wanted these discussions to take place at a higher level than Kennan and Soviet Ambassador Aleksei Yepishev. Soviet Foreign Minister Gromyko was likely to be in New York later in the month for the opening of the UN General Assembly. On September 3 the State Department instructed Thompson to propose Rusk-Gromyko talks to the Soviets.[16] Thompson was outside Moscow at the time, and it would take him a few days to let Khrushchev know that Kennedy was interested in talking.[17]

In Washington Kennedy sent a strong signal to his advisers that he wanted to give these talks a real chance of success. He ordered Secretary of State Rusk on September 12 to gather a small group of advisers to prepare the government's position for negotiations to end the Berlin crisis.[18] It was a mark of Kennedy's desperation that he assigned a leadership role to the State Department for this initiative. Since the start of the crisis Kennedy had come to refer to American diplomats as collectively "a bowl of jelly."[19] He doubted that in the absence of firm guidance State could come up with something new and creative to offer Khrushchev. "I am talking about a real reconstruction of our negotiating proposals," he exhorted Rusk, "and not about a modest add-on." The formal U.S. reply sent to Khrushchev's June Berlin ultimatum, which Rusk had crafted with the French, British, and West Germans, had been sterile. Kennedy knew very well that German reunification or the reunification of Berlin on the basis of free elections was a nonstarter in any discussion with the Soviets. "These are not negotiable proposals," he reminded Rusk; "their emptiness in this sense is generally recognized."[20]

Kennedy decided to confine this effort to rethink the U.S. position to a very small group. Dean Acheson and Lyndon Johnson, who were inflexible on negotiations, were to be cut out, and Kennedy did not want anybody at the Pentagon to know what he was doing. In the White House only the president's assistant for national security affairs, McGeorge Bundy, and speechwriter Sorensen would know. The president did give them some room for creative thinking. He was prepared to consider turning West Berlin into a free city. But he wanted NATO to be able to protect the city and its inhabitants without Soviet or East German interference.

Kennedy, who knew nothing of Adenauer's personal approach to Khrushchev, expected the West German leader would be the hardest ally to convince of the need for new proposals, especially anything that implied that West Berlin could not become part of West Germany. Once the new negotiating package was ready, he intended to send someone Adenauer respected, possibly even Acheson, to sell it to him. That is, of course, if Kennedy could sell the package to his own hard-liners first.

■

IN MID-SEPTEMBER, just as his meetings with the two specially selected Europeans were to begin, Khrushchev received the news that Kennedy wanted Rusk and Gromyko to meet in New York. The U.S. ambassador had not indicated any new U.S. position, but Khrushchev was encouraged that at least Kennedy seemed prepared to discuss his Berlin demands. He approved Soviet participation in the talks, scheduled to begin on September 21.

Meanwhile events in Germany were a reminder of the risks that both sides were taking in allowing this crisis to continue. Just after 5:00 P.M., Central European time, on September 14 two West German Air Force F-84 Thunderjet fighters crossed into East German airspace near Zlend, seventy-six kilometers southwest of Magdeburg. The Soviet Air Force had standing orders to shoot down planes that violated East German airspace. None of the eight Soviet fighters scrambled, however, was able to intercept the F-84s in the twenty-one minutes before they landed at Tegel Airport in the French zone of West Berlin. The very next day another West German F-84 again violated East German airspace. This violation lasted only four minutes, a less glaring failure for the Soviet Air Force but still unwelcome evidence of the flimsy nature of East German sovereignty nonetheless. These two incidents worried the Soviet military command in Germany and raised some questions in Khrushchev's mind that despite Adenauer's secret message two weeks earlier, the West Germans might be trying to provoke a conflict.[21]

The Russian translation of a timely article by Walter Lippmann in the *New York Herald Tribune* crossed Khrushchev's desk as he was considering the implications of these incidents. Entitled "Nuclear Diplomacy," it was the American pundit's astute observation on the nature of international politics in a world where either of the superpowers had the capability of destroying the other.[22] "We cannot understand the realities of the Khrushchev-Kennedy encounter," wrote Lippmann, "unless we remind ourselves that nuclear war is not just another war as history describes war, but a wholly new order of violence." Khrushchev agreed with this analysis. It was after all the basis of his risky strategy to force the West to accept a new status for West Berlin. The Soviet leader believed that in a world dominated by nuclear weapons, rational men should be afraid to go to war, choosing diplomacy, even surrender, instead.

On September 16, Khrushchev praised Lippmann and the column in front of Paul Reynaud: "This is a man who understands and I agree with a lot of his conclusions. He is certain that today war means suicide."[23] But Khrushchev apparently had not comprehended or preferred not to discuss the tag line of Lippmann's piece. "This being the nuclear age," Lippmann concluded, "it is the paramount rule of international politics that a great nuclear power must not put another great nuclear power in a position where it must choose between suicide and surrender."

Any hopes that the fear of general nuclear war would make his two European guests pliable were quickly frustrated. Khrushchev's three-hour meeting with Reynaud was little other than opéra bouffe. The Frenchman turned out to be an unapologetic white imperialist, more concerned about the yellow peril than nuclear danger. "The first two European wars gave world supremacy to the Americans," said the former prime minister in arguing that Khrushchev had an obligation to stop his saber rattling. "A new war would bring the suicide of the white race, giving China the chance to dominate the world." These comments were not at all helpful to Khrushchev, who wasted no time telling Reynaud that as an internationalist he put class over race. The Soviet leader certainly had his problems with Mao, but he was not about to talk about his Chinese allies in racial terms with this representative of the French bourgeoisie.[24]

The meeting with Spaak a few days later was less strange but no more successful. The Belgian had drawn the Kremlin's interest by telling the Poles that the "proposal of granting West Berlin the status of a free city with certain guarantees of access, as the Soviet Union has declared it would, could bring an agreement by the western countries with him [Khrushchev]."[25] Spaak had thus become the first Western foreign policy maker to endorse the concept of a free city of West Berlin in a conversation with a Soviet bloc diplomat. However, Khrushchev's hopes were soon dashed once the Belgian was in his office and the two discussed specifics. Spaak, while still in favor of a free West Berlin, also wanted NATO to retain its special access routes to the city. Khrushchev left the meetings with Reynaud and Spaak thinking that he had yet to meet a Western European figure who accepted his definition of a free city of West Berlin.[26]

Khrushchev could be forgiven if he believed that he was now giving the Europeans more than he received in return. With Reynaud and Spaak, Khrushchev revealed that he would be prepared to see the United Nations move its headquarters to West Berlin.[27] This admission dramatized his willingness to let a future West Berlin remain independent and even capitalist. Indeed, Dwight Eisenhower had once mused about offering to put the UN in West Berlin, though John Foster Dulles had put a stop to the idea.[28]

Khrushchev had also let slip in the course of his discussion with Spaak that he had no deadline in mind for the start of negotiations, meaning that he might be willing to lift the looming ultimatum in 1961 as he had done in 1959. As Spaak told a special session of the NATO Council at the end of September, Khrushchev was not especially in a hurry. The Soviet leader, he said, "preferred delayed negotiations to a hasty war."[29]

■

I N N E W Y O R K , Rusk and Gromyko began their discussions after a long lunch on September 21. Neither had anything new to say or present.[30] Khrushchev assumed that the ball was in Kennedy's court, and the review of the administration's Berlin policy that Kennedy had initiated on September 12 was still weeks away from completion.

Khrushchev was nevertheless satisfied with this first meeting of the foreign ministers. He noted approvingly that Rusk had said nothing critical about the Berlin Wall. As Gromyko later affirmed to the Central Committee, the "representatives of the USA recognize in [these] talks that the measures of 13 August 1961 correspond to the vital interests of the GDR and other socialist states."[31] Khrushchev presumably also liked the fact that the Kennedy regime had dropped the Eisenhower administration's insistence on only talking about a free city of Greater Berlin that encompassed both the eastern and western halves of the city. Although each side still saw the problem of Berlin differently, the Americans at least were now willing to discuss West Berlin as if it were a separate entity.

With this encouraging news from New York, Khrushchev threw even more energy into creating as favorable a climate for negotiations as possible. Since late August he had been signaling to key socialist allies in areas of particular interest to Kennedy that they should show restraint. In late September he redoubled his efforts to avoid trouble in Southeast Asia and the Caribbean. Aware of U.S. sensitivity to events affecting Laos and Cuba, Khrushchev understood that any provocations there could upset Kennedy's willingness to reconsider U.S. policy toward Berlin.

■

E ARLIER IN THE SUMMER the Chinese had predicted that under U.S. pressure Khrushchev might link his policies toward the third world with his plans for Berlin. During a visit to Moscow in July Chen Yi, the Chinese foreign minister, had expressed a concern that the Soviets would compromise on Laos to get a better deal from the United States in Central Europe.[32] Beijing expected the West to try to blackmail the socialist bloc by linking these international questions and wanted Moscow to avoid the trap. "If we proceed with concessions on Laos," said the Chinese, "then this will lead them to think that we will concede on other international matters." Chen Yi hoped that the Soviets would choose to delink Southeast Asia from the turmoil over Berlin in an effort to gain some more tactical flexibility in Asia.[33]

As Beijing had feared, Khrushchev's tolerance for Vietnamese and Chinese risk taking in Laos, which was never great to begin with, waned as he looked for ways to ratchet down the Berlin situation. On August 31 the Kremlin adopted measures to restrain the Chinese and North Vietnamese and promote cooperation between the Communist Pathet Lao and the neutralists led by Souvanna Phouma.[34] Throughout the summer the North Vietnamese and their Laotian clients had made a mockery of Khrushchev's and Kennedy's sole point of agreement at Vienna. Hanoi had refused to delay its policy of beefing up the military forces of the Pathet Lao and had trained the Laotians in a system of double bookkeeping to keep up the appearance of meeting Soviet demands for a coordinated policy with the neutralists.[35] The Pathet Lao concealed troops as well as ammunition from its supposed ally Souvanna. Some were hidden in the areas under Pathet Lao control in the northeast; others were across the border in North Vietnam. The effect of this effort was that the Pathet Lao's forces were actually twice as large as it declared them to be to its Lao partners.[36] Souvanna was also not told of a secret contingent of two hundred North Vietnamese military advisers in his country.

For months Moscow had been complicit in this charade, contributing two-thirds of the cost of maintaining this secret army. Despite Khrushchev's understanding with Kennedy on supporting a unified, neutral Laos, the North Vietnamese expected the Soviets to continue this covert assistance, including the allocation of funds to build a secret road from North Vietnam to Laos that could be used to supply these undeclared forces.[37] But in the third week of September the Soviets put the Chinese, the North Vietnamese, and the Pathet Lao on notice that this secret policy would have to stop.[38] Moscow was not yet ready to call for an end to the secret army, but the Kremlin advised Hanoi and the Pathet Lao to start planning for a coalition government with Souvanna, to lower the figures for the force they expected to maintain, and to rework their demands for assistance because what they had requested was unacceptable.

■

UNLIKE THE CHINESE and the Vietnamese, the Cubans lacked a history of being disappointed by Moscow, leaving them ill prepared for Khrushchev's sudden adoption of a more cautious policy toward the island in September

1961. An increase in U.S.-sponsored covert activity over the summer had prompted Castro in early September to request additional military aid and send the chief of staff of the Cuban Army, Sergio del Valle, to Moscow to negotiate a package. Included on Castro's long wish list was his first request for the best surface-to-air missiles in the Soviet arsenal. The SA-2 system had shot down Francis Gary Powers's U-2 in 1960 and the U.S. government was now flying these reconnaissance aircraft over Cuba.[39]

Initially it looked as if the Cubans would get what they wanted. On September 20 Cuban and Soviet negotiators reached an agreement for $148 million in aid, 40 percent of which would be an outright gift and the rest paid for through a ten-year loan with interest and some barter.[40] A week later the Soviet Council of Ministers approved this recommendation. But then the Presidium, the true center of Soviet power, froze the initiative.[41]

Soviet intelligence's perception of the U.S. threat to Cuba had not changed. The KGB continued to send warnings to Moscow of a possible intervention by Kennedy. "From reliable sources," cabled the KGB station chief Alekseyev, "the U.S. is preparing [an] intervention against Cuba for the end of November or the beginning of December and, from other data, for January 1962."[42] It did not matter because Khrushchev had tabled the discussion of Castro's huge military request to give negotiations with the White House a chance.

Khrushchev also kept an eye out for anything Washington might find provocative in Central Europe. In the last week of September he asked Ulbricht to show some restraint. The East Germans had already indicated their eagerness to tighten the vise around the U.S. military contingent in West Berlin. "Under the present circumstance," Khrushchev wrote to Ulbricht, "since the measures for the safeguarding and control of the GDR borders with Berlin have been implemented successfully . . . such steps which could exacerbate the situation, especially in Berlin, should be avoided."[43]

■

KHRUSHCHEV'S INITIAL efforts to defuse the superpower conflict passed unnoticed by Kennedy. By the third week of September the president was uncharacteristically pessimistic about the future. A journalist close to the Kennedy family caught a glimpse of his mood on September 22. Elie Abel had been invited to the White House to discuss the possibility of doing an authorized study of Kennedy's first term.[44] He saw Kennedy in his private study just as he was preparing to leave for a weekend at Hyannis Port. Below the window, Abel could hear the whirring of *Marine One*, the helicopter that was to take the family to Cape Cod. "What's on your mind?" Kennedy asked

Abel. When Abel told him about the book idea, Kennedy became introspective. "Why would anyone write a book about an administration that has nothing to show for itself but a string of disasters?" Kennedy started talking about what was on his mind. Such was his concern that he was about to make a huge error over Berlin that he raised the history of the Bay of Pigs debacle. The minutes dragged on, yet Kennedy was too absorbed to leave, as he was scheduled to. He shouted at his aides to tell the helicopter pilot to "turn off that thing; I'm not leaving yet." Abel later recalled what happened next: "We sat there for a while in the odd position where I, a private citizen, was busy assuring the president of the United States that his administration would not turn out to be a string of disasters and that as he got hold of the job, he and I and all his friends would be proud of his administration, that he would do great things."

As Kennedy agonized over what step to take next to avoid an armed confrontation over Berlin, Khrushchev was wondering why he had not received any response to the feeler that he had sent to Kennedy through the *New York Times*'s Cyrus Sulzberger. On September 24 the Soviet press attaché in the United States, Mikhail Kharlamov, asked the president's press secretary, Pierre Salinger, if Kennedy had received the message. "The storm in Berlin is over," Kharlamov said, "give it to him."[45]

Kennedy, who had probably not received the note from Sulzberger, got this message. Salinger passed it to him late that night in a New York hotel suite, where Kennedy was staying before a speech the next day at the United Nations. Chewing on an unlit cigar, Kennedy liked what he heard. "He's not going to recognize the Ulbricht regime—not this year, at least—and that's good news."[46]

If Khrushchev had sent the message to prevent the president from unilaterally ratcheting up the crisis another notch in his speech to the UN, he need not have worried. Kennedy had already planned to use the speech to hint that his government was rethinking the diplomatic approach to the crisis. "We are committed to no rigid formula. . . . We see no perfect solution. . . . But we believe a peaceful agreement is possible which protects the freedom of West Berlin and allied presence and access, while recognizing the historic and legitimate interests of others in assuring European security."[47] Although Khrushchev may not have viewed this as a step forward, Kennedy had also decided to send only one additional division to Europe, instead of the six that the Pentagon wanted to deploy.[48] The president was trying to avoid doing anything provocative while it was still possible to coax Khrushchev to back down from his threat to sign a peace treaty in 1961.

■

THE MESSAGE from Kharlamov was evidence that Khrushchev was getting impatient for some kind of dramatic recognition from Washington that the Berlin crisis was over. Probably aware that a note passed from one Soviet official to an American official would not be enough to end the tension, Khrushchev decided a few days later to write directly to Kennedy. He chose to make it a private letter to convey the seriousness of his concern and of his desire to reach an agreement. This would be a new tactic. He had never sent a private letter to Eisenhower, even though the leaders of their respective blocs had weathered crises over Suez, Iraq, and Berlin together.

The letter to Kennedy began with calculated insincerity.[49] Noting that the world had expected the Vienna meeting to have "a soothing effect," Khrushchev remarked, "To my regret . . . this did not happen." In the same spirit, he offered a fanciful account of how he had tried to restore a better relationship. He said that he had been prepared to send a letter, with proposals that he did not specify, in late June but that Kennedy's July 25 speech had made that impossible. Nowhere in his letter was any hint that at least until mid-August he had intentionally chosen a policy of pressure to get his way.

He now asked Kennedy to appoint a special representative for consultations. He wanted to supplement the Rusk-Gromyko talks with a conversation along a less formal channel. He again suggested George Kennan but this time added Llewellyn Thompson as a possible liaison through whom the two leaders could swap proposals directly. Khrushchev even raised the possibility of a quick summit with Kennedy in Moscow. It seemed as if the clock had been turned back to the spring, before Khrushchev had started the crisis.

Kennedy responded a few weeks later, but nothing came of this exchange of letters.[50] Khrushchev was still hung up over Western access routes to West Berlin and refused to let the United States maintain its forces in the city without a "token" Soviet contingent nearby. Meanwhile Kennedy still had nothing new to say. What the U.S. president had not mentioned in his UN speech was how much his own policy review was bogging down. The Europeans were primarily responsible for this. The French were opposed to negotiations, and the West Germans were being coy. The State Department was also having difficulties developing new ideas. With no new proposals and the possibility of further complicating Western allied diplomacy, Kennedy had no interest in using his brother or anyone else to make the kind of private approach that he had experimented with on the test ban issue before Vienna.

▪

K HRUSHCHEV DID NOT react as one might have expected when Kennedy brushed off his private letters. Intelligence from Washington may have been the reason. From sources reporting to the Soviet military intelligence service, the GRU, Khrushchev had a reasonable idea of the difficulties Kennedy was encountering in trying to alter the U.S. policy on Berlin. Georgi Bolshakov, who had served as the intermediary between Robert Kennedy and the Kremlin in May 1961, collected much of this helpful information on Kennedy's handling of the Berlin issue.[51]

Despite Khrushchev's requests to restart the back channel discussions, the Kennedy brothers had decided not to avail themselves of Bolshakov. He, however, was by now welcome to meet with members of the Kennedy policy elite, and he used this entrée to develop new sources on the Berlin policy review. From sources close to Walt Whitman Rostow, the head of State's Policy Planning Staff (perhaps Rostow himself), Bolshakov reported that Kennedy was considering a three-point plan for resolving the crisis: (1) Make West Berlin into an international city, guarantee its rights and the rights of free access to it; (2) confirm the existing borders of Germany; (3) establish a demilitarized zone in the center of Europe and, possibly, a nuclear-free zone.[52]

Bolshakov was also able to report on why the process seemed to be taking so long. His administration contacts were blaming the Western Europeans, especially the French. Washington believed that de Gaulle was choosing to be disruptive of efforts to forge an allied policy in a vain attempt to win the sympathies of West Germany.[53] The good news for the Kremlin was that according to Bolshakov, the Americans had also noticed that Adenauer's thinking on negotiations was changing. He seemed to be softening.[54]

▪

IN OCTOBER 1961 Khrushchev decided to take yet another step to create the right conditions for negotiations on Berlin with the United States. He chose the Twenty-second Party Congress of the Communist Party of the Soviet Union, scheduled for mid-October, as the occasion to announce that the Soviet Union would lift the Berlin ultimatum. Khrushchev did not intend to end the Berlin crisis—his demands and his goals remained the same—he was simply suspending it. Nevertheless, given all that he had said about the need for a resolution in 1961 (to the East Germans and, most important, to his Kremlin colleagues), this was going to be a retreat for him personally. What did Khrushchev have to show for five months of dangerous international tension other than the ugly Berlin Wall?

When making the announcement at the party congress on October 17, he tried hard to cover this defeat by exaggerating what Kennedy had given him. He had taken this step, said Khrushchev, because "the Western powers were showing some understanding of the situation, and were inclined to seek a solution to the German problem and the issue of West Berlin."[55]

Khrushchev had originally intended to use this congress to reassert Moscow's leadership over world communism. The Albanians were still in ideological rebellion from the Soviet party, and the Asian parties were unhappy with Moscow's new caution in Southeast Asia. As a sign of their displeasure, the Laotian, Vietnamese, and Chinese Communists had refused to back Khrushchev in his criticisms of the Albanians. Even the Indonesians, who had echoed Khrushchev's criticisms of Stalin in 1956, refused to provide any rhetorical support in his crusade against the Albanians.

Khrushchev encountered a contradiction between his hopes to ease the Berlin crisis and his goal of pulling the socialist world closer together. Abandoning the pledge to resolve the Berlin situation in 1961 would further weaken the Kremlin's credibility as the beacon of socialism and incite even more criticism of Khrushchev's pet idea of peaceful coexistence.

The Chinese, masters at Communist semiotics, led the criticism. They knew well how to annoy fellow Marxist-Leninists. A few days after giving his own report at the party congress, Chinese Premier Zhou Enlai announced he would return to Beijing before the end of the conference. Never before had the Chinese left in the middle of a major international Communist gathering. To make sure that Khrushchev felt the slap personally, Zhou made a solitary pilgrimage to the Lenin-Stalin Mausoleum in Red Square on the day of his departure. In spite of Khrushchev's destalinization campaign, the mummified Stalin remained on display next to Lenin. On Stalin's sarcophagus, Zhou left a telling wreath: "To Josif Vissarionovich Stalin—the great Marxist-Leninist."[56]

The most bitter response came from the East Germans. Ulbricht avoided open disagreement with Khrushchev in Moscow. Instead he chose even more dramatic means to vent his own displeasure. A year earlier the East German leader had followed willingly as Khrushchev set out to achieve his maximum objectives. Ulbricht's primary concern had been to close the gates in Berlin, whereas Khrushchev had insisted on trying to achieve everything East Germany needed to be a fully sovereign state at once, to "draw a line under the Second World War." In November 1960 Khrushchev had assured Ulbricht that this would be possible in 1961, once the East had a good feel for Kennedy's psychology. Now, after a six-month-long propaganda campaign, the East German people had come to associate a peace treaty with domestic stability. Ulbricht too had convinced himself that the wall alone could not assure him either political legitimacy or economic security. Khrushchev's sudden abandonment of the effort, without achieving any Western concessions, left his East German ally raw and vengeful. There had been no warning from the Kremlin before Khrushchev lifted the ultimatum, so it appears Ulbricht decided to initiate some unilateral changes of his own.[57]

▪

O N OCTOBER 22, 1961, Allen Lightner, the senior American diplomat in West Berlin, tried to take his wife to the theater in East Berlin and instead found himself the star of an international incident. This was not his first visit to East Berlin. Since August 23 Lightner, like all Western allied personnel, had been restricted to the use of the border point at Friedrichstrasse known as Checkpoint Charlie to enter the Soviet zone. While the reduction of the number of entry points from seven to one had been inconvenient, Lightner had not had any trouble entering via Checkpoint Charlie and did not expect this particular evening to be any different. He had not counted on the complexities of Soviet–East German relations.

At 7:15 P.M. the East German police, the Vopos, stopped the Lightners as they attempted to enter at Friedrichstrasse in their personal car. When the Vopos requested that Lightner show identification, he refused and demanded entry, as was his right as a member of one of the four-power missions in Berlin. But the East Germans wouldn't let them in. Lightner then asked to see a Soviet officer. The East Germans stalled. This new East German tactic was directed as much at Moscow as at the West.

After waiting nearly an hour, Lightner decided to try his luck at driving around the maze of roadblocks that littered the first few yards of East Berlin territory. Luck was not with him that night. As the car cleared the maze, a group of East German guards formed a line to prevent it from going any farther. Again Lightner requested a Soviet officer. Again he was refused. The performance in East Berlin a lost cause, Lightner and his wife nevertheless refused on principle to turn around and go home.

When a Soviet officer finally reached the scene at 10:00 P.M., three hours after the Lightners had first reached Checkpoint Charlie, all he could do was apologize. The Soviet said the East German action "was a mistake and will be corrected."[58]

The East Germans, however, had no intention of correcting the error. The next morning, to the surprise of the U.S. command in Berlin and Khrushchev in the Kremlin, the East German News Agency (ADN) announced that civilians crossing the Berlin sector border had to show identification cards.[59] This new regulation cut across established four-power practice. Up to that point, so long as the vehicles they were riding in had military or government license plates, civilian representatives breezed into East Berlin. If Ulbricht's goal had been to cause a U.S.-Soviet clash, he very nearly got his wish.

General Lucius Clay, Kennedy's official representative in West Berlin since the wall went up, assumed that the new policy was the next phase in a Soviet strategy to squeeze the West out of Berlin. Although handpicked by Kennedy, Clay often operated on, in the words of one historian, "a totally different wavelength."[60]

Clay had arrived in Berlin thinking he had a mandate to prevent the loss of any additional authority in Berlin to the Communists, whatever the risks this might entail. A day after the East Germans announced the new policy, he impatiently requested instructions from Washington to challenge it. Although Clay overestimated Moscow's control of the situation at the border, he had an uncanny sense of the East Germans' objectives. "I have always believed," he wrote Secretary of State Rusk on October 23, "that the elimination of Allied rights in East Berlin is of great importance to [the] GDR and that every effort will be made to accomplish this objective before any negotiations take place."[61] Clay believed that Moscow had to be made to pay for the Vopos' actions and suggested that the United States halt all efforts at negotiations with the Kremlin on the Berlin question until the Russians were prepared "to guarantee full maintenance of the present status quo."

Clay had his admirers in the Kennedy administration, but generally there was concern in Washington that he might draw the two sides into armed conflict over the right to go to dinner and a show in East Berlin.[62] Although wary of letting the situation at the border between East and West Berlin spiral out of control, the White House did authorize a series of daily probes by civilians accompanied by an armed escort to defend the right of Western allied diplomats to cross the sector boundary. U.S. M48 tanks were also deployed as a rear guard on the western side of Checkpoint Charlie during each effort.[63] The first such probe took place on October 25, when armed military police escorted a car carrying official U.S. license plates just inside East Berlin after East German police tried to have the Americans in the car show their ID cards.[64] Clay, however, wanted an even larger demonstration of U.S. impatience with the Soviets and their allies. He requested high-level approval of a "raid in force into the Eastern sector which would tear down parts of the wall on its return." The White House was appalled. Rusk responded quickly to remind the general that "we had long since decided that entry into East Berlin [was] not a vital interest which would warrant determined recourse to force to protect and sustain."[65]

It had been four days since the incident with the Lightners at the border, and Kennedy sensed that he and Khrushchev would have to intervene to prevent their local representatives from inadvertently causing a war. The same day that Clay's request for armed escalation reached Washington, Kennedy employed two channels to convey his concerns directly to Moscow. While the State Department prepared instructions for Thompson, Kennedy asked his brother to resume his secret discussions with Bolshakov. The attorney general arranged a meeting with the GRU officer for five-thirty that evening, October 26.[66]

President Kennedy wanted Khrushchev to understand the larger implications of these border tensions, that they were derailing the ongoing process of altering the Western negotiating position on Berlin. He had Robert Kennedy tell Bolshakov directly that the White House was in the midst of hammering this out with its allies. This was an arduous process, and President Kennedy assumed it would take at least another four to six weeks. One reason for the delay, not one the attorney general mentioned to Bolshakov, was that Konrad Adenauer would have some influence over the final product, and he was not scheduled to be in Washington until late November.

Kennedy hoped Khrushchev would realize that it was in his interest to help his American counterpart during this difficult period. "[T]he Soviet and Western sides should avoid any actions in Germany or Berlin that could lead to sad incidents, similar to those that had happened recently; and which could only complicate for the U.S. the process of agreement with its allies," explained the attorney general to Bolshakov. "If Khrushchev would give similar instructions to his forces, [President] Kennedy would do the same."[67]

It is unlikely that Khrushchev received this report from Bolshakov before the situation in Berlin took its most serious turn since the construction of the wall. The next morning, October 27, ten Soviet tanks rolled along the Friedrichstrasse and positioned themselves in front of Checkpoint Charlie in anticipation of the daily U.S. armed probe. Although the East Germans had started these border tensions, the U.S. probes had provoked a Soviet counterreaction.

When the U.S. probe arrived at the checkpoint, American and Soviet tanks found themselves staring at each other across the sector boundary. The scene made for dramatic photographs, which were then carried by all of the world's newspapers. Because the tanks on the eastern side bore no identifying markings, which the Soviets had intentionally removed, the local CIA station sent a representative to the area to determine the nationality of the tank drivers.[68] As Clay had expected, they all were Soviets.

Kennedy saw little advantage in getting his ambassador out of bed in Moscow, where it was already early the next morning, to make a run to the Soviet Foreign Ministry. Earlier on October 27 Thompson had been to the ministry to complain about the tensions in the divided city and had not elicited much of a reaction. The situation in Berlin was now heating up too quickly to wait for the U.S. Embassy in Moscow to get Khrushchev's attention. Kennedy had called Clay after dinner for an update and been told that the number of Soviet tanks at Checkpoint Charlie had grown to thirty.[69] After hearing this, the president for the second time in two days sent his brother to see Bolshakov.

The attorney general and the Soviet agent met at 11:30 P.M., Washington time, on October 27. "The situation in Berlin has become more difficult," Robert Kennedy explained.[70] "Today our ambassador met with Soviet Foreign Minister Gromyko, who refused our declaration regarding the recent incidents that have occurred in Berlin. It is our opinion that such an attitude is not helpful at a time when efforts are being made to find a way to resolve this (i.e. the Berlin) problem." Once again on behalf of the president Robert Kennedy asked the Kremlin for a period of four to six weeks without headlines about Berlin: "It seems to us that it is incumbent on both sides to take the necessary measures to establish a period of relative moderation and calm over the course of the next 4–6 weeks. One more refusal of our declarations could have a negative effect on future developments."[71]

Bolshakov rushed from this meeting to cable the message to Moscow, where it was already approximately 7:00 A.M., October 28. The message was received at GRU headquarters and may well have been the cause of Khrushchev's next move, though no trace of the cable has been found in Kremlin archives. What is clear, however, is that sometime before 11:30, Moscow time, that same morning, Khrushchev decided to withdraw his tanks from the Friedrichstrasse checkpoint. "I knew Kennedy was looking for a way to back down," he explained a few days later. "I decided therefore that if I removed my tanks first, then he would follow suit; [and] he did."[72]

The Soviet withdrawal from the border confrontation exacerbated Ulbricht's sense of abandonment. The East German was in Moscow, attending the Twenty-second Party Congress, while the tense standoff occurred at

Checkpoint Charlie. On October 27 Ulbricht had sent a special message from Moscow to stiffen the backs of his colleagues in East Berlin.[73] He told them to continue requiring identification from Western military personnel in civilian clothing. The day after the Soviets backed down from the tank confrontation, Ulbricht did not hide his disappointment from his colleagues at home, though he initially avoided attacking the Soviets directly. Instead he criticized the East German Defense Ministry for not having placed antitank barriers at Checkpoint Charlie in time to have prevented U.S. tanks from approaching the border.[74]

Ulbricht did not wait much longer to share his disappointment directly with Khrushchev. On October 30 he sent Khrushchev a formal document that laid out the reasons why the Soviet leadership had been wrong to cancel the push for a German peace treaty at the party congress. The wall had not solved East Germany's fundamental economic problems. In fact, to the extent that closing the border had forced the movement of industries that were close to the border and led to increased defense expenditures, the GDR's economy was now in an even greater mess. "The nonconclusion of a peace treaty in this year," he explained, "and the exacerbation of relations between the two German states threatens the economic plan of the GDR of 1962."[75]

Ulbricht argued that he needed to establish East German sovereignty through a series of gradual faits accomplis. He asked Khrushchev not only to bless the unilateral actions that had led to the tensions at Checkpoint Charlie but also to consider issuing a warning to Washington that the U.S. Army did not have the right to send military patrols along the autobahn. Step by step he would acquire more control over the access routes to Berlin without ever forcing the West to consider going to war. Four days after sending this document, Ulbricht met with Khrushchev to make his case in person.

The Ulbricht-Khrushchev meeting of November 2, 1961, was a tough, bitter encounter that shook Khrushchev to the core.[76] The Soviet leader did not like most of Ulbricht's suggestions and hated his attitude. Khrushchev wanted Berlin to be grateful to him for the wall, which he now considered a victory of adroit Soviet policy. "Could we have closed the border sooner than August 13?" he asked Ulbricht. "No . . . the adversary could have carried out countermeasures," was the reply, "but by the time of August 13 he was already worn out." Khrushchev was now insisting that the ultimatum had been all about getting the wall. He had never made this argument before to Ulbricht. It also served Khrushchev's purposes to blame the East Germans for making it impossible for him to sustain the crisis through the signing of a peace treaty. "You see we know what they are preparing for—for an economic blockade. Really would that then be easier for you?" Khrushchev's point was that he could not force the Berlin issue given the risk that the West would impose a crippling embargo on trade with East Germany.

Ulbricht refused to accept any blame for Khrushchev's decision to end the ultimatum short of a peace treaty. But the East German was not Khrushchev's equal, and the Soviet leader let him know it in no uncertain terms. When Ulbricht said that he did not know how to explain Soviet tactics to the East German public, Khrushchev told him that he did not care what he said to his own people. "All I want to know now," he said, "is what we will say to each other. I don't agree with those who argue that the longer the signing of the peace treaty is delayed, the worse will be the economy of the GDR. It is an old conversation that we are having: So long as the GDR does not free itself from economic dependence on West Germany, Adenauer will without fail [push you around]."

Khrushchev tried to beat Ulbricht into submission. When the East German explained that without West German goods "we will not fulfill the plan," Khrushchev told him that the Soviet Union had to sell $450 millions' worth of gold at the London gold exchange to acquire the hard currency that East Germany could use to buy what it needed from West Germany. "This is impossible, this is an irrational policy," protested Khrushchev. "We live independently, neither the dollar, the pound nor the mark controls us. And here the GDR cannot make it and we must provide gold to London. . . ."

The Soviet record of this tough meeting does not mention if Ulbricht ever stood up to leave.[77] Khrushchev's bullying was relentless. The nearest the meeting came to the breaking point was when Khrushchev absentmindedly admitted that Soviet and East German interests were not the same in this crisis. For Khrushchev the only peace treaty that mattered was one that removed NATO from West Berlin. Sensing that Ulbricht just wanted a signed piece of paper, he yelled at his recalcitrant ally, "[A] Peace Treaty would provide no political advantage. . . . Of course, for propaganda purposes, but otherwise not. It is [however] advantageous for the GDR."

With this, Ulbricht blew his top. Bitterly he said, "OK, then all is clear." Khrushchev knew that he had lost a point to the East German and pressed for an explanation of Ulbricht's riposte. "What is clear? Go ahead explain what is clear and what is not clear." Ulbricht would not give him the satisfaction of a response.

Khrushchev said nothing about the ongoing negotiations with Kennedy or any expectation that he might return to the struggle for a peace treaty. Ulbricht was his subordinate and should be satisfied with at least getting the wall.

Khrushchev believed his secret diplomacy with the Americans was so important that he refused to permit Ulbricht to increase the harassment on the
Western allied military personnel in Germany. The only concessions he threw
to the East German were some suggestions for tightening civil controls at the
border. "I am for order," Khrushchev said. "Let them then see that running
away is impossible." But the rest of what Ulbricht wanted was too provocative.

■

For all his bluster, the meeting with Ulbricht had weakened Khrushchev's
self-confidence. He resented the East German demands—he had been East
Germany's stalwart ally in the Kremlin for years—but he knew that Ulbricht
had a reason to be annoyed about how the Berlin affair had turned out. The
East Germans had warned Khrushchev not to start a crisis over Berlin in 1961
unless he was willing to see it through to the signing of a peace treaty. Yet
with his October 17 statement at the Twenty-second Party Congress, it was
clear that the Soviet Union had effectively given up on getting a peace treaty
in 1961.

A few days after the tense discussion with Ulbricht, Khrushchev prepared
an unusually candid letter for President Kennedy about the Berlin issue.[78]
"Dear Mr. President, I am writing not to argue with you or to try to play better
the next fall-back position as diplomats call it." He wanted Kennedy to understand that despite the suspension of the ultimatum, the Kremlin still
regarded the achievement of a peace treaty and the end of NATO's special
rights in West Berlin as an issue of the highest importance.

"Those who cling to the occupational regime in West Berlin would like,
evidently, the Soviet Union to assume the responsibilities of traffic policemen
securing continuous and uncontrolled transportation of military goods of the
Western powers into West Berlin." He went on to complain that the West
Germans used West Berlin as a staging point for subversive operations into
East Germany. He concluded by reminding Kennedy that the German
Democratic Republic could not forever be denied its right to regulate the
access routes to West Berlin, all of which ran through or over its territory.

Amid this recitation of old positions, Khrushchev revealed to Kennedy the
irreducible minimum for him. No agreement would be acceptable that permitted free air corridors to West Berlin. Unbeknownst to Kennedy, the air corridors had been the principal point of debate between Khrushchev and
Mikoyan, his only vocal Kremlin foreign policy critic in 1961. Mikoyan had not
regarded the continued existence of the air corridors as a deal breaker.
Khrushchev saw the problem differently. Once West Berlin became a free city,

Western planes would not be permitted to fly directly into it. They would be required to land and take off at a nearby airfield in East Germany to allow the East Germans to process the passengers and to check the plane's cargo. Plaintively Khrushchev wrote, "[This] cannot be considered as [a] worsening of the conditions of access to West Berlin."

Khrushchev also decided to convey to his American adversary the difficult political situation that he had placed himself in. He had suspended the Berlin crisis without getting anything in return from the United States. "If you have something else to propose—also on the basis of a peaceful settlement—we would willingly exchange opinions with you. But if you insist on the preservation of the inviolability of your occupation rights I do not see any prospect. You have to understand, I have no ground to retreat further, there is a precipice behind."

The language was not threatening. Khrushchev was in no way renewing the threat he had only recently rescinded. In an odd and unprecedented way he was appealing for Kennedy's help in solving his Berlin problem. At the party congress Khrushchev had suspended the public bullying of the West for a new deal for Berlin in 1961. In this letter he seemed to be suspending his private bullying of Kennedy as well. For a moment, at least, Khrushchev was gambling that diplomacy would achieve what threats could not in Berlin.

CHAPTER 17

MENISCUS

N THE FALL OF 1961 a dramatic shift took place in the balance of power in the Cold War. In terms of brute force, military and economic, the United States and its allies were as far ahead of the Soviet bloc as they had always been. What changed was the balance of influence, the factor nineteenth-century imperial historians called sway and modern political scientists refer to as soft power. Khrushchev's self-inflicted wound over Berlin had an ever-widening ripple effect on the credibility of Soviet power. On one side of the ledger, it led to increased U.S. confidence; on the other, it stirred skepticism and doubt among Moscow's most significant socialist allies.

Khrushchev's decision to suspend the confrontation over Berlin strengthened the conclusion already reached by some in Washington that the United States was ahead in the strategic power game. On October 21, John F. Kennedy had Deputy Secretary of Defense Roswell Gilpatric reveal to the very wary American public that the U.S. nuclear arsenal quantitatively and qualitatively exceeded anything that Khrushchev had. Kennedy's motives for the Gilpatric speech, which was delivered four days after Khrushchev had lifted the Berlin ultimatum, were primarily domestic. Besides calming the American people, Kennedy hoped the speech would serve as a warning to the leadership of the U.S. armed services and their allies in Congress not to use scare tactics any longer to force unnecessary procurement. The air force, for example, was gearing up for a campaign to purchase an additional two thousand Minutemen ICBMs, and members of Congress were already posturing for a B-70 bomber to counter an assumed fleet of Soviet Bounder bombers.[1]

Robert McNamara had originally been supposed to officiate at this public burial of the missile gap, but when a scheduling conflict arose, it was his deputy Gilpatric who delivered the speech before a conference of business-men in Hot Springs, Virginia.[2] "Our confidence in our ability to deter communist action, or resist communist blackmail, is based upon a sober appreciation of the relative military power of the two sides. The fact is that this nation has a nuclear retaliatory force of such lethal power that an enemy move which brought it into play would be an act of self-destruction on his part. . . . The number of our nuclear delivery vehicles, tactical as well as strategic, is in the tens of thousands, and, of course, we have more than one warhead per vehicle."[3]

As the first year of the Kennedy administration came to an end, close observers noticed a more relaxed president. "It's going better," Kennedy told friendly journalist Hugh Sidey.[4] "We're making a little headway here and there." Others were not so modest in their assessment of the shift in the president's fortunes. The poet Carl Sandburg, whose signature work was a multivolume study of Lincoln's war presidency, praised Kennedy's handling of this more recent national peril. "The way he is doing is almost too good to be true."[5]

■

OUTWARDLY THE FALL of 1961 seemed to be the apex of Khrushchev's personal power. On October 30, on his instruction, the body of his predecessor, Joseph Stalin, had been removed from the Lenin-Stalin Mausoleum. The carved marble plaque above the doorway now was covered by a cloth sign reading only LENIN. For the first time it could be said that Khrushchev had indeed eclipsed Stalin in the pantheon of the gods of communism. Also, at eleven in the morning on that same day, another star burned brightly for Khrushchev. At his insistence, Soviet nuclear scientists exploded the largest nuclear device ever constructed, a fifty-megaton bomb, called the Tsar Bomba, in the atmosphere over the Arctic island Novaya Zemlya.[6] After the Vienna summit Khrushchev had ordered the creation and detonation of a superbomb— originally hoped to be the equivalent of a hundred megatons of TNT—with the intention of using it to increase the pressure on the United States to wilt before his Berlin ultimatum.

As it turned out, the Berlin ultimatum was already a dead letter by the time Khrushchev had his superexplosion. Moreover, though it was a dramatic piece of political theater, the device was not at all usable as a weapon. The only Soviet aircraft that could carry it was the slow Tu-95 Bear bomber, which could have been easily shot down by U.S. air defenses, and the bomb's yield was so great that if dropped on Central Europe, it would have poisoned the residents of Eastern Europe.

The distance between the image and reality of Khrushchev's power was even greater behind the walls of the Kremlin, where his decision to back down in Berlin had eroded some of his prestige. When Khrushchev's

Kremlin colleagues supported giving Kennedy the ultimatum at the summit, they had not expected a public retreat on the issue as in 1959. There was now no outward revolt by members of the Presidium, but Khrushchev understood that he needed to restore coherence to his Berlin policy.

Khrushchev's critics elsewhere in the Soviet bloc were not as restrained as those in Moscow. The Chinese had also given their support for the Berlin ultimatum on the assumption that the Soviet Union would not back down before Khrushchev achieved what he wanted. After the Twenty-second Party Congress, Beijing began to treat him as a weak leader. The East German ambassador in Beijing remarked at the end of 1961 that the Chinese wondered why Khrushchev had not shown the same courage as he had in 1956. "In the case of the Suez aggression," the Chinese believed, "the Soviet ultimatum, which was taken seriously, scared the imperialists and forced them to stop their aggression." Khrushchev's retreat this time would "only induce the adversary to even firmer policies, to greater demands, and to stronger provocations."[7]

Ironically, it was the Chinese who first exploited Khrushchev's retreat for their own ends when they quickly repudiated the political approach that Moscow had brokered with the local Communist parties in Southeast Asia. In November the Chinese interceded with the Pathet Lao and scuttled an agreement to form a coalition government under the neutralist Souvanna Phouma.[8] Then, a month later, Beijing sent a military delegation to Hanoi for two weeks, apparently to discuss future military operations in Laos in violation of the Kennedy-Khrushchev cease-fire.[9]

What the Chinese failed to grasp, whereas Khrushchev did, was that the abortive showdown with Kennedy over Berlin and the end of the missile gap fallacy revealed serious flaws in how Moscow had been managing disagreements with the West since 1955. The use of ultimatums backed by a nuclear bluff had never been a perfect tactic. In practice it had caused an overreaction in the American press and the U.S. Congress, which created both the impetus for more defense spending and the suspicions that made real disarmament impossible. Still, in a period in which the Americans doubted their own power, there had been a chance it might force some political compromises. Now, however, the Americans seemed to understand that at the very least they were not behind the Soviets and were perhaps ahead of them. What role could nuclear bluff play in this kind of international environment?

Passivity in the face of this new balance of power would have been out of character for Khrushchev. A more cautious leader might have responded to the new power relationship with the United States and the vulnerabilities in his own backyard by seeking a temporary strategic respite. A lull in the struggle would allow time for Soviet technology and improved agricultural practices to provide new sources of strategic and economic power for the future. But that was not his way. Besides being reluctant by nature to relinquish the offensive in international affairs, he was animated by a deep-seated concern that the West would exploit any perceived Soviet weakness to destroy the Communist system. This fear had prevented Khrushchev from accepting Eisenhower's Open Skies proposal in 1955, and it reinforced his rejection of a lull in international politics in 1962. Instead he looked to turn the tactic of the occasional bluff to achieve a specific goal into a medium-term strategy of applying continuous political pressure on Washington and its allies. Convinced that despite their strength, Americans and their president continued to fear war, Khrushchev concluded that he might be able to use these fears as the Lilliputians had used cords to restrain the giant Gulliver in Swift's book.

■

IN HIS PUBLIC STATEMENTS and later in his memoirs, Nikita Khrushchev did not reveal the story of his reaction to these discouraging shifts in the international power balance. Had he done so, much of his subsequent behavior in the dangerous year of 1962 would not have seemed so mysterious. Only with the release four decades later of the transcript of his remarks to his Kremlin colleagues at a rump meeting of the Presidium on January 8 could one see the thinking that lay behind what would be the greatest risks taken by any leader in the Cold War.[10] The immediate cause was Khrushchev's disappointment at how the Berlin negotiations were turning out. Six days before this session Andrei Gromyko and U.S. Ambassador Llewellyn Thompson had met to discuss Berlin, and the Soviet foreign minister needed new instructions. All fall Khrushchev had expected new proposals from Kennedy, who had launched a policy review and was consulting with his allies. But when the moment arrived, the administration had nothing newer to offer than an international body to oversee the access routes to West Berlin. On the all-important issue of the future of Western troops in West Berlin, Washington had been silent. Khrushchev had to admit that neither nuclear bluff nor diplomacy had worked in 1961. It was time to chart a new course.

"The enemy is strong," Khrushchev admitted. "[He is] not weaker than we are." The Kremlin leadership sometimes used the less threatening term "adversary" to describe the United States, but on this day Khrushchev was in no mood for such niceties. "That is why he could play the same trump card against us that we were trying to use against him—the position of strength card." Khrushchev's confident prediction of May 1961 that he could push the Americans farther than they wanted to go had been proved wrong. Through its handling of the Berlin crisis, the White House had demonstrated to Khrushchev that it was prepared to fight to maintain access to West Berlin. "This is why no one can predict whether this game will end in a war or not. [No one can say any longer]," he said, "that war is impossible, that war is out of the question."

Khrushchev confessed to more than just a misjudgment of U.S. resolve. His strategy had also reflected the expectation that an attractive, liberal capitalist like Kennedy would be both wise and powerful enough to accept a minor retreat over Berlin for the sake of a major détente with Moscow. "Who, as a matter of fact, decides a question like that—agreement or no agreement, and whether to go to the brink, the issue of war versus peace?" Khrushchev asked in his monologue. "Kennedy decides." But this too had proved wrong. Kennedy might want better relations, but Khrushchev had no reason to believe he was willing to do what was necessary to bring them about. Kennedy "lacks authority, moral or political," Khrushchev reluctantly concluded. "This is a young and capable man, it is necessary to give him his due," he added, "but he can neither stand up to the American public, nor can he lead it." Khrushchev now believed that the system, which in his mind meant American plutocrats, militarists, and alarmists, was directing U.S. foreign policy. Kennedy, "himself, is a person of little authority in circles that decide and give direction to the policy of the United States of America. He is of no authority to both Rockefeller and du Pont." Khrushchev did not try to hide his disappointment. "[It is impossible] to say who is better, Eisenhower or Kennedy—[they are] the same shit. . . . Both represent the same class with different shades."

Khrushchev's first two errors—his mistaken assumptions that the United States would accept his terms and that Kennedy would use his authority to contain the militarists in Washington—were compounded by the fact that the Soviet leader had expected that the Europeans would help him overwhelm American intransigence. He had assumed that Western European fears of war would have canceled out whatever interest they might have had in maintaining the status quo in West Berlin. He recalled saying to the Frenchman Reynaud and the Belgian Spaak, "[H]ere, this is the maximum we can agree to."[11] Instead, to his dismay, he found that the West was unified on the Berlin question.

"[T]hey won't agree," he discovered, "because all of this is based upon the nonrecognition of any of their rights in West Berlin, upon the nonrecognition of their rights to have an army there, that our interpretation of free access is completely contradictory to the interpretation and understanding of the West. What they consider to be depriving them of their right to free access, we understand as free access." Khrushchev's conclusion was gloomy. "Will they agree to it now?" he asked himself. "No, they won't agree."

Although there is no record of any dissension in the room during this performance, there must have been some confusion when Khrushchev revealed that in spite of these hard truths, he wished to continue the drive for an agreement with the West on West Berlin. He had no intention of altering his bottom line in the negotiations—no international corridors; no Western troops in West Berlin; East Berlin to remain part of East Germany; West Berlin to be a neutral, international city—and he was not about to stop pushing for a settlement on these terms. "In a word," he exhorted the officials before him, "it is now too early to say that we will not win. We should still press on. I take the worst case: They won't agree. But it means agreeing right now that it will bring nothing. It's too early. So it's worthwhile playing this game."

Khrushchev was not sure how long the Soviet Union would have to play the "game" to win, nor could he offer any suggestion on what self-imposed limits Moscow should observe. After all, he now understood that it was possible to push the United States to war, and he admitted that he did not want war. Nevertheless, Khrushchev believed that there was no hope of that he could get his way in the struggle with America without using pressure tactics.

He then introduced the metaphor of the liquid meniscus to explain the condition of permanent international tension that he now believed was necessary both to preserve and to advance Soviet interests in a world of U.S. strategic superiority: "We should increase the pressure, we must not doze off and, while growing, we should let the opponent feel this growth. But don't pour the last drop to make the cup overflow; be just like a meniscus, which, according to the laws of surface tension in liquid, is generated in order that the liquid doesn't pour out past the rim." The pressure, Khrushchev explained, was not designed to force change but simply to deter the Americans from taking advantage of the Soviet bloc while they remained ahead in the superpower rivalry. "If we don't have a meniscus," he said, "we let the enemy live peacefully."

Acknowledging that the earlier ultimatums had been a mistake, Khrushchev refused to set a deadline for resolving the Berlin problem. He was not about to be trapped by his own rhetoric in 1962 as he had been in 1958 and 1959 and in 1961. Those deadlines had deprived him of tactical flexibility. Instead he wanted to employ Soviet foreign policy to keep the West off-balance until Moscow was powerful enough to compel the Americans to give him what he wanted. He was still extremely eager to settle the matter; it just did not make sense to rush into another Berlin ultimatum. "[W]ith each year, our material and spiritual wealth grows as well as our armed forces. Therefore, concentrate on it now or never? Really, is such an issue on the agenda now? No, on the contrary. We don't have this issue at all, because, if not now, then it will be tomorrow." Behind this optimism, but left unsaid on this day, was Khrushchev's confidence that the imminent deployment of the next generation of Soviet intercontinental ballistic missiles, the R-9 and R-16, would do a great deal to alter U.S. appreciations of Soviet power and bring Washington's arrogance to an end.

The Soviet leader stressed the logic of this new approach: "It is necessary to conduct an aggressive policy, but we need to advance rationally, not to resemble a gambler, in this game, who bets whatever is left in his pocket and then grabs a pistol and shoots himself." But he understood that it would be perceived as weakness by those in the Soviet bloc, especially the Chinese, who insisted on continuing the ultimatums. "So our friends will blame us and will exploit us regarding this issue. . . . Those who will exploit, they know them-selves that they are putting shit in their mouths." It enraged him that Beijing was now assailing him for his prudence over Berlin. During the Iraqi crisis of 1958, he recalled, Mao had asked him, "What, are you willing to fight?" When Khrushchev said, "No way," Mao had replied, "Correct, it's not necessary." Khrushchev believed that it was Sino-Soviet tension that explained Mao's cur-rent behavior. "If we had good relations right now, then Mao Zedong would write us a friendly letter and would say, 'Do you want to go to war over West Berlin?' 'No way, what the hell do we need that for?' And he would be right."

Khrushchev wanted Soviet representatives to needle Beijing about its own lapsed ultimatums in the 1950s regarding the offshore islands Quemoy and Matzu, which remained under Chiang Kai-shek's control. He also suggested a withering attack on China's toleration of British control in Hong Kong and Portuguese control in Macao. Khrushchev reminded his audience of Soviet diplomats that the Chinese had time and again resisted using force to elimi-nate their own West Berlins.

He also proposed the explanation that should be given to the East Germans and those who wondered why the Soviets did not just go ahead and sign a separate German peace treaty. He reminded his audience that the goal of the Berlin strategy was to defend East German sovereignty and Soviet pres-tige. A treaty that did not resolve questions of access and Western military presence was of no value. In 1958 he had been eager to declare the end of Western rights in Berlin unilaterally, but he had been persuaded by Mikoyan, among others, that the costs were still too high.

Khrushchev revealed to his audience that he believed that a "final fight on the issue of West Berlin" was inevitable. But he did not want to go down that path until he was sure that the Warsaw Pact countries could withstand the Western economic blockade that he expected would be NATO's first response to a Soviet-East German peace treaty. Hopeful that this fight would not be too much delayed, however, Khrushchev added, "[I]t is necessary to speed up the transformation of the GDR's economy, so that it will be reoriented away from West Germany to the Soviet Union, mainly, and other socialist countries. This is the most important thing."

In the meantime, as part of this new policy of continuous pressure, Khrushchev urged his representatives not to allow the East or the West to assume that Moscow had given up on a Berlin settlement: "Your voice must impress people with its certainty . . . don't be afraid to bring it to a white heat, otherwise we won't get anything. . . . Because if we were now to start retreating in diplomatic relations . . . then your talks would be of no use. In your talks you must drive it with the same confidence as we have done so far."

This remarkable political sermon ended with an admonition directed as much to himself as to his foreign policy team in the hall. In a telling phrase, he counseled against allowing Berlin to hijack Soviet foreign policy. "For us, West Berlin is in no way like the drunkard's addiction for alcohol. Let it be that way, please."

■

"IT IS FRUSTRATING not to know what is really going on."[12] Kennedy's chief Soviet watcher, Llewellyn Thompson, could have been on the moon for all his ability to peer inside the Kremlin. His first meeting with Gromyko on this new round of Berlin talks had taken place on January 2, and there had been little to show for it other than a restatement of the basic stumbling blocks. Not that the American had much to offer himself. The reassessment that President Kennedy had ordered in mid-September had taken three months to complete. Despite the call for something novel and potentially interesting to Khrushchev, the process had been a personal embarrassment for Kennedy. After three months of exhaustive and exhausting allied politics, there was little in Thompson's instructions in 1962 that he could not have said on behalf of Dwight Eisenhower in 1958.

The president had discovered that his European allies were not interested in seeing any new thinking on the Western side in the negotiations. West Germany's Adenauer had used his visit to Washington in November to upset any plans Kennedy might have had to offer recognition of an independent West Berlin or of East Germany as inducements for Khrushchev finally to accept the sixteen-year-old Western access routes. Meanwhile de Gaulle refused to support negotiations of any kind. The French president was as sure as ever—and he had made this point to the untested Kennedy before the Vienna summit—that since Khrushchev would not go to war, there was no reason to alter the status quo in the two Germanys. De Gaulle's abstention did not stop allied discussions, especially since Macmillan and the British government shared Washington's eagerness to find a formula that would convince Khrushchev to stop making Berlin the source of international tension. But without active French participation the United States could not be sure if it was negotiating a deal that all the Western occupying powers would accept. These unknowns, coupled with Adenauer's steely opposition, had hampered any creative policy making on the U.S. side. The single new idea that had resulted from the entire process involved a suggestion for an international access authority that would supervise the continuation of Western access to West Berlin after a peace treaty.

On its face, this suggestion was not that imaginative. But the fact that Kennedy was thinking about access after a peace treaty was a hint that he might eventually consider West Berlin a separate entity, a major deviation from the current Western support for leaving things as they were in the German city. Not surprisingly the idea of an international access authority was the only thing that Kennedy had not passed around for allied approval before mentioning it to the Soviets. He raised it in a conversation with Nikita Khrushchev's son-in-law, Aleksei Adzhubei, in late November 1961, infuriating Adenauer when he heard about it later.

■

H AD LLEWELLYN THOMPSON known what Khrushchev was saying to his colleagues in January 1962, he would not have been surprised that the Soviet leader assumed that he would have to continue playing the Berlin game to get any interesting Western offers. His defensive tone also would not have surprised Thompson, who was one of the keenest observers of Khrushchev's inferiority complex and had divined the Sino-Soviet problem before most other American Kremlinologists. But what the U.S. Ambassador did not see or could not grasp was that there was little about the Sooviet leader's approach to Berlin that was negotiable for him. Khrushchev's bottom line was not even close to something the United States could accept without seeming to abandon its commitment to the people of West Berlin. Instead the American ambassador tended to blame his own government for missing opportunities to lower the temperature in Central Europe. In particular, Thompson believed that the administration could have maneuvered Khrushchev onto a less confrontational path when the wall in Berlin had gone up. Compromise of some sort was not out of the question, but as he confided to his friend the former U.S. ambassador to Moscow George Kennan in early January, "the difficulty here is that the Soviets will almost never reveal their side of the bargain first."[13]

The Thompson-Gromyko negotiations resumed on January 11. Gromyko rejected the international access authority as "violating GDR sovereignty and in effect creating a state within a state." The Soviet foreign minister also stressed that if Western troops remained after West Berlin became a free city, then Soviet troops would also have to be stationed in the city.[14] In addition, the Soviets demanded for the first time in these negotiations that a future agreement include a series of sweeping guarantees. These included a prohibition on nuclear weapons for both Germanys, border guarantees for East Germany, and a NATO-Warsaw Pact nonaggression treaty. After hearing what Gromyko had to say, Thompson pronounced the meeting "a step backward."[15]

■

JOHN KENNEDY had the same reaction as his ambassador. The Soviets not only were brushing off his efforts but seemed to be upping the ante. Seeing few other options, the president turned again to his brother's back channel through Georgi Bolshakov.[16] Not since the tense days at Checkpoint Charlie three months earlier had the Kennedy brothers used this method to get Khrushchev's personal attention.

Bolshakov and the attorney general met twice in mid-January.[17] Hopes that perhaps Khrushchev just needed a prod from an official higher than Ambassador Thompson were soon dashed. On January 18 Khrushchev used Bolshakov as a messenger boy to deliver a tough note to his U.S. counterpart.

"[My] proposals do not make harm to anyone," argued Khrushchev. Instead it was the U.S. side that was to blame for the stalemate. Khrushchev returned to the theme of power to explain this American intransigence. "The President of the United States has himself said and everybody knows it that now the balance of power is equal. How, then, is it possible proceeding from the equal initial conditions to attempt to conduct a policy of encroachment on the interests of the USSR and its allies—socialist countries? But what the

U.S. Government is proposing is aimed precisely against our interests."[18] At the end of his letter, Khrushchev hinted that if Kennedy did not give him what he wanted, he would force a defeat on Washington: "If on its part the United States does not display an understanding of this, some time will pass and the world will witness that this policy is suffering the same and [an] even greater defeat [than] before."

There was quite a dissonance between how U.S.-Soviet relations were perceived in Moscow and how the Kennedy brothers thought about the problem. Whereas Khrushchev was saying in the Kremlin that Kennedy and Eisenhower were the "same shit" and held out little hope that words alone could change any U.S. president's mind, Kennedy still believed that by developing a private connection to the Soviet leader he could lower the temperature of the U.S.-Soviet rivalry.

The days spent discussing Berlin in January 1962 had cemented a bond between Robert Kennedy and Georgi Bolshakov. The attorney general admired the rough-hewn physicality of the spry, squarely built Russian. Bolshakov soon found himself a regular guest at the Kennedy house at Hickory Hill. One such evening, which fellow celebrant journalist Theodore White called a "mad night at Bobby['s]," left no doubt that Bolshakov had entered the charmed circle.[19]

The Kennedys assumed that it was still possible to create such a human relationship with Khrushchev himself. The clan had gotten quite fond of Bolshakov, yet had no reason to believe that Bolshakov was close to Khrushchev, and the president wanted a similarly close connection to someone within Khrushchev's charmed circle. Aleksei Adzhubei, Khrushchev's son-in-law, was incontestably close to the Soviet leader. The White House had invited Adzhubei for an interview with the president in September 1961, which the Kremlin had delayed until late November, around Thanksgiving, before it took place. In early 1962 Adzhubei was on a lengthy tour to Latin America and could come back for a second visit. Kennedy requested that this be arranged.[20]

As Kennedy prepared to meet Adzhubei, he had more than just his brother's meetings with Bolshakov and the Thanksgiving visit with Adzhubei to draw upon. One of the lessons that Kennedy thought he had learned at Vienna was the importance of putting himself into the mind of his adversary. He had made a fundamental error in launching an ideological debate with an ideologue on that first day. Kennedy was not doctrinaire by nature, and he was too much of a pragmatist—and too ironic—to be wedded to any ideology. With Adzhubei Kennedy decided he had to try to speak in terms Khrushchev would understand; he would talk about power, interests, respect, and peace.

The president and Mrs. Kennedy invited Adzhubei and his wife, Khrushchev's daughter Rada, to lunch on January 30, 1962, in the White House. Although Rada Khrushcheva was a linguist who could speak English as well as French fluently, her husband had trouble speaking English.[21] So Bolshakov tagged along as the official Soviet translator. After the lunch and a tour of the mansion, Kennedy and Adzhubei repaired to the Oval Room in the family quarters of the White House for a more intimate conversation. There Kennedy attempted to underline his hope for negotiations on a wide range of subjects in an atmosphere of mutual respect.

The trouble began as soon as Kennedy sought to establish the ground rules for that mutual respect. He wanted the Soviets not only to understand U.S. interests but to respect them. He wanted Khrushchev to accept once and for all that the United States was in West Berlin to stay. The president stressed that access was an issue separate from the freedom of West Berlin, which needed to be assured, and that he could never accept any agreement that forced the removal of U.S. troops or required the presence of Soviet troops in West Berlin. As if this were not enough to raise Khrushchev's temperature, he then suggested a possible agreement that would freeze the status quo in West Berlin for three to five years.

Kennedy also had something to say about another point of friction between the blocs, words that would provoke Khrushchev when he learned of them. In an effort to evoke his sensitivity to events in Cuba, Kennedy likened U.S. interests on the island to those Khrushchev had in Hungary. He then awkwardly told a story of having asked Allen Dulles—Khrushchev's bête noire—why the Soviet intervention had been so successful in Hungary while the Bay of Pigs had been a fiasco. "You should learn from the Russians," Kennedy recalled having said to his DCI. "When they had difficulties in Hungary, they liquidated the conflict in three days. . . . But you, Dulles, have never been capable of that."[22] Comparing Cuba with Hungary was about the most provocative way Kennedy could have chosen to underline his determination to remove an unfriendly regime that was within his sphere of influence.

Then Kennedy offered Adzhubei insight into his personal timetable for doing something about this nearby problem. "If I run for reelection and the Cuban issue remains as it is today," Kennedy said, "then Cuba will be a major issue in the campaign and we will have to undertake something."[23] Even more than the Hungarian comment, this assertion upset the Soviet. "This is a sad and alarming statement," replied Adzhubei. When word reached Khrushchev of this conversation, the president's comments on West Berlin and Cuba suggested to the Soviet leader that Kennedy felt strong enough to challenge Soviet interests in Europe and the Caribbean and was not about to budge in negotiations.[24]

■

THE ADZHUBEI MEETING ended a monthlong period of mixed signals from the Kremlin. Up to this point Soviet foreign actions, toward either Berlin or any other regional concern, had not uniformly reflected the tough language of the secret meniscus speech. Indeed, throughout the month of January the Soviet Defense and foreign ministries had acted as though the Berlin crisis were finally over. On January 10, for example, the Group of Soviet Forces in Germany brought its alert level down from highest to normal and stopped sending Khrushchev daily reports on the status of U.S. forces and the situation in Berlin.[25] The Foreign Affairs Ministry's handling of some carping from the East Germans also reflected this assumption about a relaxation of tensions. Ordinarily an East German complaint about something—in January the protest was directed at the use of the autobahn by U.S. Army—would be followed up by a "Me, too!" response from the Soviets. In mid-January they had let the issue slide.[26]

With Adzhubei's report in hand, Khrushchev decided it was time to pour water to the edge of the wineglass. First he would remind the United States of its vulnerabilities in Central Europe, where the idea of waiting another five years for a solution was repugnant to him. Every week there were approximately six hundred flights along the three air corridors to and from West Berlin. Since 1945 the Soviets had never placed any restrictions on Western use of these corridors. There was a quadripartite Berlin Air Security Control that existed to prevent Soviet and Western aircraft from unintentionally bumping into each other, but the Western allies could fly at will. The challenge began with an unexpected Soviet announcement on February 7 that for three hours the next morning the airspace between three and eight thousand feet in the southern air corridor would be closed to all non-Soviet traffic. The Soviets had never blocked Western use of an air corridor before. Meanwhile they refused to file flight plans for their own planes, as was customary, if not required, and would not assure the safety of any Western flights in the southern corridor at the reserved altitudes. This too was unprecedented.[27] On the advice of General Clay, his personal representative in West Berlin, Kennedy ordered two unarmed military aircraft to fly along the southern air corridor at between five and six thousand feet during the time of the attempted Soviet closure.[28]

On February 8 the Soviets flew L-2 military transports along the southern air corridor as they had previously warned they would do. On February 9, the Soviet Air Force announced it was closing the northern air corridor as well. On the fourteenth and fifteenth the Soviets reverted to closing only the southern corridor for a limited time. Until February 14 there were no incidents between U.S. and Soviet military aircraft. However, on that day and the next, ten Soviet fighters began buzzing the six U.S. aircraft trying to fly in the southern corridor at the time "reserved" by Moscow.[29]

Walter Ulbricht misunderstood Khrushchev's strategy. The East German leader interpreted the Soviet harassment of Western aircraft as evidence that the Kremlin was gearing up for another Berlin crisis in 1962. This was good news for Ulbricht, who still believed that his economic and political troubles would be solved if only Moscow would sign a peace treaty with his regime. Since this was not the message Khrushchev had wanted to convey, the East German leader was summoned to the Kremlin for a February 26 meeting.

Khrushchev tried to explain his strategy of maintaining pressure on the West without an ultimatum. He said that he feared that if he tried to sign the treaty now, the result would be a Western economic blockade. Since November 1961 the East German economy had gotten weaker, and it was now absolutely certain that Berlin would not be able to meet its economic targets for 1962. Given the weakness of the East German economy and its reliance on West Germany for industrial inputs—metal pipe, specialty steel, etc.—the effect of Western economic warfare would be disastrous. "We must put pressure to get a peace treaty," said the Soviet leader. "But we must not put the question in these terms: life or death."[30]

Despite Khrushchev's efforts to persuade him to be satisfied with the gains that East Germany had already made since the Berlin Wall went up on August 13, Ulbricht pleaded not to let the wall become an excuse for delaying a peace treaty. "A wide swath of our population," he said, "is starting to think that the USSR and the GDR . . . cannot fulfill [this promise]." He also made it plain that his own patience had worn thin. "We have already carried out this propaganda [in behalf of signing a peace treaty] for many years. But how much longer will it be?"

In the hopes of triggering a new Soviet ultimatum to the West, Ulbricht suggested that there be a foreign ministers' conference at the end of the summer to draft the peace treaty. "Even if it were a bad treaty," he said, "the negotiations would settle the questions of the East German border and its capital."

Khrushchev was no longer as frank with Ulbricht as he had once been. He did not tell the East German about his new grand strategy to seek to build up Soviet power until he could force a Berlin settlement on the West. Instead he patronized the East German leader, advising him not to allow his country to remain as vulnerable to the West Germans. "Adenauer has you by the short hairs, and he is yanking at them," he said contemptuously. Khrushchev also underplayed his hopes for a future deal with the West: "I believe that all we can expect from West Berlin we received on August 13. Now our task is to work quietly."

When Ulbricht did not register satisfaction, Khrushchev stressed that going to the brink now would just deepen the Soviet bloc's economic difficulties. "It wouldn't bring war, but you would be the first to come to us with a demand for 100 million dollars, and then would come Gomulka and Novotny," said Khrushchev referring to the Polish and Czech leaders. At the end of the conversation he hinted that a shift in the correlation of forces lay behind his willingness to wait. "Today we have medium range ballistic missiles that can travel 2,000 kilometers and we are not even building any more of them. [Instead] we had accelerated the construction of powerful [inter]continental missiles and next year we will have enough." Cryptically, Khrushchev concluded by saying, "Our tactic must be to press, then to wait."

■

MARCH 1962 brought another uncomfortable reminder for Khrushchev of American power. At a secret meeting with Bolshakov arranged by Robert Kennedy, the White House informed the Kremlin on March 2 that President Kennedy would soon announce a resumption of atmospheric testing of nuclear weapons. Since Khrushchev's decision to test in the atmosphere in the summer of 1961, Kennedy had ordered the resumption of underground testing but, over the objections of his advisers, had held off resuming atmospheric testing. He believed that atmospheric testing introduced harmful airborne radioactive elements and knew that this testing would subject the United States to international criticism.

"The president sincerely wants to avoid conducting these nuclear tests and wants an agreement on this issue with Premier Khrushchev," explained Robert Kennedy.[31] Privately the White House wanted Khrushchev to know that these tests did not have to happen. The Kennedys offered Moscow a deal through Bolshakov. In a few hours the president would be telling the world that U.S. testing would resume in the atmosphere on April 15. Robert Kennedy explained that the president was ready to meet with Khrushchev "at any time" to conclude an atmospheric test ban. This partial test ban would not require any form of on-site inspection because national air sensors could easily determine cheating. The attorney general explained that his brother was "eager" to reach an agreement.

Once again President Kennedy's effort at back channel diplomacy made things worse by angering Khrushchev. The Soviet leader considered this attempt at deal making little more than blackmail and not only refused to consider a partial test ban but canceled the one minor concession on disarmament that he had presented to Kennedy at Vienna. The Soviet delegation at Geneva was told to withdraw the standing offer of two to three on-site inspections a year. Khrushchev even added a personal snub. For two months U.S. and Soviet representatives had been negotiating simultaneous television broadcasts by the two leaders in each other's country. Khrushchev informed Washington that these broadcasts were incompatible with the spirit of Kennedy's planned announcement of a nuclear test series in April.

In this period Khrushchev received some highly dramatic information from Soviet military intelligence that stirred fears that the Americans were eager to capitalize on their strategic advantage. The GRU, in two reports dated March 9 and March 11, 1962, reported to the Kremlin that days after the Vienna summit in June 1961, the Pentagon had given serious consideration to a nuclear first strike against the Soviet Union. According to the source, who was described as being in the U.S. national security bureaucracy, what had averted disaster was the U.S. appreciation of Soviet power following the resumption of nuclear testing in September.[32] Alone this intelligence would have been taken as highly doubtful, but in the context of Kremlin anxiety and disappointment over the sterility of both the Berlin negotiations and the disarmament talks, such lurid images of U.S. ambition seemed more plausible.

In his last meeting with Khrushchev before leaving in mid-March for Washington as the Soviet Union's new ambassador to the United States, Anatoly Dobrynin experienced the heat of the Soviet leader's personal anger toward Kennedy. Speaking "emotionally and at length," Khrushchev cited Berlin as the major problem dividing the two superpowers. He followed with a diatribe against Kennedy for seeking to use strategic superiority against the Soviet Union, citing some intermediate-range ballistic missiles that NATO had just deployed in nearby Turkey. The Americans are "particularly arrogant," concluded Khrushchev.[33]

In February Khrushchev had vented his disappointment with American actions by causing trouble in the Berlin air corridors. In March, though his fighters played that game again for a few days in the middle of the month, his primary effort to needle Kennedy occurred in Southeast Asia.[34] For months the Soviets had been trying to encourage the Pathet Lao and their Chinese and North Vietnamese patrons to give the peace process a chance. But the Asian Communists had been eager to wipe out U.S.-backed Phoumi Nosavan's garrison at Nam Tha, the main town in the northernmost province of the same name. Although lightly inhabited, Nam Tha was next to the principal airfield used by U.S. aircraft to supply Phoumi Nosavan's forces in the north. Moscow had been unhappy with the plan, which it considered the product of Chinese influence on the Pathet Lao and their main patrons, the North Vietnamese. To head this off, Khrushchev had invited Prince Souphanouvong, the leader of the Pathet Lao, to Moscow to meet with him in January. The Soviet Foreign Ministry, in preparing for this visit, had indicated that the Pathet Lao and the North Vietnamese had just begun "a series of offensive actions of a counterattacking character against the Boun Oum–Nosavan brigands."[35]

The Pathet Lao and the Vietnamese had told the Soviets that their operations in Nam Tha Province were designed to compel Phoumi Nosavan to the negotiating table.[36] But Moscow had had its doubts. Officials in the Kremlin had feared that the joint Communist offensive would give Phoumi Nosavan a pretext to end all negotiations with Lao's neutralist leader, Souvanna Phouma, which in turn would allow the Pathet Lao, the Vietnamese, and the Chinese "to use this as justification for their policy of a military resolution of the Laotian question."[37] The Soviets had intended to use the summit with Souphanouvong to send Mao the message that regardless of Chinese desires and Chinese dogma, "the USA and the USSR did not intend to go to war in Laos in the name of China."

The January discussions with the Pathet Lao leader seemed to have the desired effect. The Pathet Lao momentarily backed away from intensifying its military campaign in Nam Tha Province. In early February, Souphanouvong assured Ambassador Aleksandr Abramov in Laos that despite the fact that the capture of Nam Tha could be accomplished in "the course of a few hours" and was "a matter of political prestige," the Pathet Lao would not do it "in order not to give any cause for a provocation."[38]

By early March, however, Khrushchev had decided to unleash the Pathet Lao as part of the policy of increasing international pressures on the United States. This was not an official reversal of the policy of peaceful coexistence in Laos; Soviet representatives continued to encourage the Pathet Lao to work toward a coalition government headed by Souvanna Phouma. What changed was that the Soviets stopped lecturing Souphanouvong and his Asian allies on the need to avoid a military clash at Nam Tha. At a summit of the four main Communist parties in the region March 7 to 9, the Soviet representative agreed to turn a blind eye to the ongoing military preparations in northern Laos. The Soviets also agreed to continue the secret support to the Pathet Lao outside what flowed to them as part of an agreement with Souvanna Phouma.[39]

In future conversations with Pathet Lao representatives, Ambassador Abramov abstained from making any comments on the spring offensive that the Pathet Lao, the North Vietnamese, and the Chinese were evidently planning. In return, the Laotians promised that this military campaign would be reasonable. On March 20 Souphanouvong reported to the Soviet ambassador that the Pathet Lao intended to pursue a policy of "active defense" that involved attacks on enemy strongholds in the "liberated areas" of Laos. The Pathet Lao wanted Moscow to understand that these operations were conducted "reasonably, so as not to cause a widening of the military conflict."[40] The next day Abramov flew to Hanoi to tell Ho Chi Minh personally that the Soviets would let the North Vietnamese, the Chinese, and the Pathet Lao determine what practical steps were required in the region.[41]

With Khrushchev stepping back to let the Pathet Lao give the Western-backed forces in Laos a bloody nose, the Chinese proceeded with a deployment of 2,149 soldiers of the People's Liberation Army, 1,772 civilian workers, 203 motor vehicles, and 639 horses and mules to carry military supplies to the Pathet Lao.[42] These men and supplies were to come south from the Chinese military command in Kunming into the province of Nam Tha. Phoumi Nosavan's garrison in the provincial capital had grown to 5,000 men, and the Pathet Lao and its North Vietnamese military advisers believed that the reinforcements from China were required to make the future offensive a success.

■

THE ONE REGION of the world where Khrushchev did not want to test U.S. power in the spring of 1962 was Latin America and the Caribbean. Kennedy's comments to Khrushchev's son-in-law reawakened concerns that the U.S. government might attempt a second invasion of Cuba.[43] Indeed, by the end of 1961 the United States had resumed a program of covert action against the Castro regime. In late November Robert Kennedy and Richard Goodwin, the chief Latin American adviser in the White House, had successfully lobbied the president for a more active policy against Fidel Castro. Called Operation Mongoose, the program included a range of measures—subversion, espionage, and sabotage—designed to raise the political temperature on the island enough to bring about Castro's removal by coup or counterrevolution.[44]

Soviet intelligence did not pick up the exact details of Mongoose planning, but in February Khrushchev received reports of a more active U.S. program of subversion against Castro that reinforced the impression that Adzhubei had received of Kennedy's determination to solve his Castro problem.[45] While ordering the testing of the Western air corridors and giving the green light to his Asian allies to make trouble in Laos, Khrushchev chose to go on the defensive in Cuba. He revived the $133 million military aid package for Havana that had been frozen in October 1961 and placed it on the Presidium's agenda in early February for rapid approval.[46] He also ordered a review of Soviet military assistance to Castro to determine if more was needed.

The Soviet military review came not a moment too soon. While Khrushchev was distracted by the Berlin crisis of 1961, the Soviet-Cuban relationship had cooled. The held-up aid package was not the only source of tension in that relationship. Castro's efforts to consolidate his power by merging the July 26 Movement and the Cuban Communist Party (PSP) into a united revolutionary front had intensified his rivalry with the old-line Cuban Communists. The PSP and the Fidelistas disagreed over revolutionary strategy. Castro and Che Guevara found the PSP leadership staid and politically irrelevant. Most of them had been hard-line Stalinists that believed that third world countries had to pass through a stage of bourgeois capitalism to achieve communism. Castro could not forget that this type of thinking had discouraged the PSP from supporting his own efforts in the Sierra Maestre in the mid-1950s. As he confided to the KGB chief in Havana, Aleksandr Alekseyev, "With regard to the policy of peaceful coexistence, I am generally not against it, as in the cases of those countries, like Italy and France, where the peaceful path to socialism is possible. . . . But in general in Latin America there aren't the necessary conditions for such an approach."[47]

No one personified this theoretical disagreement for Castro more than Anibal Escalante, the principal organizer of the PSP. "Escalante," Castro complained to Alekseyev, "was the leader of those who believed in the peaceful coexistence approach for Latin America."[48] He was also a political threat at home. Escalante may not have been an energetic revolutionary abroad, but in Cuba he was a tireless political worker with grand ambitions for himself in the new Cuban revolutionary front, the Integrated Revolutionary Organizations (ORI). Tired of the theoretical disagreements and threatened by Escalante's ambitions, Castro purged him from the ORI and allowed him to flee the country.

Castro turned against Escalante just as the Soviet military was completing its review of its assistance to Cuba. The Kremlin had had a much longer relationship with Escalante than with Castro, and when relations between these men went from bad to worse in early April 1962, the Kremlin worried about the implications. Moscow had two major concerns. The first was that perhaps under the influence of Che Guevara, who seemed to embrace Mao Zedong's theories of permanent revolution, the Cuban regime might side with China in the struggle to define socialism. The other was that Cuba might adopt a more independent line in dealing with Moscow, much as Yugoslavia had done.

Besides Castro's handling of Communists at home, the Kremlin had other evidence that April that the Cubans were eager to show their independence of Moscow. While on a long-delayed visit to Moscow, Castro's chief of intelligence, Ramiro Valdés, asked the KGB for assistance in setting up a headquarters in Cuba for training Latin American guerrillas for revolutionary activity in the Western Hemisphere.[49] The Cubans had reason to believe that Moscow might be interested. In August 1961 the Presidium had approved a plan for working with the Cubans and the Nicaraguan Sandinistas to support revolutionary movements. Three months later the KGB authorized the formation of a training center in Honduras to prepare a group that could organize a "partisan detachment on Nicaraguan territory."[50]

Despite what it had already done with the Nicaraguans, the KGB disingenuously told the Cubans in April 1962 that it was merely an intelligence-collecting organization. "We do not help national-liberation movements," Valdés was told.[51]

Without knowing it, the Cubans were probing to the outer limits of the risks Khrushchev was prepared to take even with the meniscus strategy. He was not yet ready to challenge the United States in its own backyard. The Nicaraguan operation was very small—the KGB invested only twenty-five thousand dollars into it between 1961 and 1964—and probably stillborn, whereas what the Cubans had in mind would be more expensive and attract a lot of attention.[52] Khrushchev's Southeast Asian allies were allowed to move on a pro-Western stronghold because the balance of forces favored the Soviet bloc in the border region of Laos. Cuban provocations were a different matter altogether. The United States retained an overwhelming superiority in the Caribbean. Castro's commitment to revolutionary activity seemed suicidal in the light of Kennedy's evident preoccupation with the regime.

The strong case for prudence did not reduce the Kremlin's concern that restraining the Cuban secret services might hurt Soviet-Cuban relations and push some of Castro's inner circle closer to Beijing. To reassert the USSR's position as Cuba's chief socialist ally, Khrushchev moved rapidly to eliminate any doubts that Castro might have about his support. Moscow had permitted Anibal Escalante to enter the country as an exile, but within a week of his arrival he was denounced in *Izvestia* for his "sectarianism." Castro, as Khrushchev had hoped, read a translation of this article and was pleased. Meanwhile the Soviets indicated to Havana that they would supplement the September 1961 military package to include Soviet troops, one Sopka shore missile launcher, and ten Il-28 Beagle bombers.[53] The bombers could fly as far as Miami. The amounts of the first two items were not as large as Castro had requested, twenty-five hundred troops instead of ten thousand and only one battery instead of three. However, the gesture was designed to ensure that Castro knew that the Soviet Union would not interfere in his internal political affairs. A Soviet general was sent to Havana to discuss the regime's further military needs.

■

I N EARLY MAY Khrushchev received very discouraging military and economic information that threatened his entire foreign strategy. When he made his secret announcement in the Kremlin of the meniscus policy in January 1962, he believed that Moscow would not have to wait a long time to be strong enough to force a Berlin settlement on the United States and then agreements banning nuclear tests, achieving disarmament and perhaps a superpower nonaggression pact. Indeed, in February he had hinted to Walter Ulbricht that the corner would be turned in the peace treaty and Berlin campaigns in 1963.

Bad news about the status of work on the R-9 and R-16 long-range nuclear missile programs reached Khrushchev in the late winter. Although flight testing of the R-16 was on schedule, it was a major disappointment. The missile had been designed to provide the Soviet Union with a reliable second-strike capability in the event the United States launched a first strike. But the device turned out to be so primitive that unless the Soviets were planning to be the first to launch nuclear-tipped missiles—and in the Khrushchev period there were never enough missiles to make this feasible—the weapon was useless. In February 1962, Khrushchev had been told that the R-16 was no match for the second-generation U.S. missile system, the Minuteman, the first of which was due to be deployed sometime in 1962.[54] Soviet commanders needed a few hours to prepare a missile for launch, whereas the U.S. rocket could be prepared for launch in a few minutes. "Before we managed to move the R-16 and lift it into place, nothing would be left of us," Khrushchev was told by the chief of his rocket forces.[55]

The R-16's main weakness was the volatility of its fuel. Khrushchev's protégé Marshal Mitrofan Nedelin, the first chief of the new Soviet strategic rocket forces, was one of a hundred technicians and observers who had died in October 1960, when an R-16 caught fire and exploded during a prelaunch sequence.[56] The fuel in the R-16 was also highly corrosive. Once a missile was fueled it had to be either used immediately or drained of its contents within a few days and sent back to the factory for cleaning and recalibration. The U.S. Minuteman, however, was powered by solid fuels that allowed the missile to be deployed in a ready position for years. The progress reports on the R-9, the R-16's competition to be the next generation of Soviet ICBM, were even worse. Flight tests of this rocket were turning up a series of flaws.[57]

Quantitative comparisons were no kinder to the Soviets. The first of a few dozen R-16s were deployed in early 1962. The R-9 was not yet near deployment. In 1962, however, the U.S. ICBM deployments began to reflect the earlier overreaction to the missile gap scare. Between the fall of 1961 and the spring of 1962 the number of U.S. ICBMs more than doubled, from thirty to seventy-five. From published reports the Soviets could know that by the end of the year the U.S. arsenal, with the addition of the first Minuteman missiles, would grow to more than two hundred ICBMs. Deployment of the Minuteman system, the greatest strategic threat to Soviets, was due to begin in the fall. There was talk of eventually deploying a thousand of these solid-fuel monsters.

Meanwhile Khrushchev was also given disappointing economic news. The spring of each year brought the start of the Soviet government's budgetary cycle. Between March and the summer government planners would work with members of the Presidium to come up with the actual production numbers that would be presented to the entire Central Committee at the fall plenum as the basis for future planned production. Record keeping was never very good in the Soviet Union, but in 1962 the figures Khrushchev received indicated agricultural and industrial shortfalls. The statistics were so bad that the Kremlin had to consider raising consumer prices on domestic staples, a move never before attempted in the Khrushchev era. As if this were not enough, recent wage increases were also proving difficult to sustain.

In light of this economic shortfall, Khrushchev ordered his three top economic advisers—Frol Kozlov, Aleksei Kosygin, and Anastas Mikoyan—to review the figures for defense spending for the coming year to see if they could cut more than three billion rubles—roughly three billion U.S. dollars from defense appropriations.[58] Despite Khrushchev's belief in the nuclear missile as an equalizer of international relations, he had never agreed with those who just wanted more of them. In 1959 he had scaled down requests for launchpads because of the cost of each one, and he was prepared to make the same call again in 1962 if necessary to protect his domestic economic agenda.

The tension with the United States in Laos, Berlin, and Cuba was placing an even greater burden on the Soviet economy. This was preventing Khrushchev from reducing the workweek as he had hoped to and from increasing capital investments in agriculture and industry. His instinct was to do all he could to assist his socialist allies, but he could no longer escape the costs of these efforts.[59]

Evidently amid this torrent of domestic disappointments Khrushchev asked Malinovsky in April if there was a cheaper shortcut to becoming competitive with the Americans in ICBMs. Khrushchev was convinced that there was enormous waste in the Soviet missile program, and he could no longer predict when Soviet industry and science would produce the nuclear deterrent he craved.[60] The timing of this discussion remains vague. But it may have been prompted by news about changes in the U.S. nuclear forces. Khrushchev received weekly surveys from Malinovsky of the status of deployed U.S. forces. On April 20, 1962, the first eighteen of fifty-four U.S. Titan missiles, a first-generation ICBM, were being deployed in Colorado. Meanwhile the United States was continuing its deployment, begun in 1961, of intermediate-range Jupiter missiles pointed at Moscow, thirty in Italy and fifteen in Turkey.[61]

"What about putting one of our hedgehogs down the Americans' trousers?" Khrushchev reportedly asked Malinovsky.[62] The hedgehog was a Soviet nuclear missile, and by "down the Americans' trousers," Khrushchev meant in the Caribbean. At some point in the winter of 1962 the ever-creative Khrushchev connected the two ideas of Soviet military assistance for Cuban defense and the strategic advantages for the Soviet Union of Cuba's location. Why could it not become Moscow's Italy or Turkey? Malinovsky responded that though it was a sound idea from the military point of view, a significant political decision would be required to put a nuclear hedgehog off the coast of Florida. Khrushchev asked that for the time being Malinovsky gather a small group to consider how one might implement this idea.[63] Khrushchev had not yet made up his mind whether to take the huge risk of putting missiles in Cuba, though the idea did appeal to his love of bold improvisation.

▪

THE PATHET LAO, the Chinese, and the Vietnamese launched their much-anticipated spring offensive on May 6. As the Kremlin had hoped, it was a rout. Within a matter of days General Phoumi Nosavan's garrison in Nam Tha collapsed. Phoumi had inadvisedly deployed six thousand men inside a natural basin formed by a mountain range, a perfect setting for an ambush. Once the combined Vietnamese and Pathet Lao force surrounded the position, Phoumi and his generals fled, causing their American advisers to rate their military effectiveness as "nil." Ultimately the entire garrison retreated as far away as it could get from the battlefield. In the polite words of American observers, it was a retreat that could be characterized as "far outdistancing any pursuit."[64]

As Prince Souphanouvong had predicted in trying to sell the operation to the Soviets, the seizure of Nam Tha completely altered the balance of power in the field. The Pathet Lao and the North Vietnamese now controlled all of eastern Laos from north to south. The CIA estimated that the Pathet Lao had the strength to launch Nam Tha–like offensives to capture the remaining major centers in the interior.[65] In fact U.S. intelligence believed that though Phoumi Nosavan's forces outnumbered the Pathet Lao and Souvanna's forces two to one, they were still no match for them, and the whole of Laos could come under Pathet Lao control within two weeks. The presence of North Vietnamese forces made the difference. In the words of the CIA, the North Vietnamese were "superior" fighters who "press home coordinated attacks with great skill and disregard for losses." All that was holding them back was uncertainty over the possible U.S. reaction.

No one in the Kennedy White House advocated a wait and see attitude. From the sidelines former President Eisenhower still believed that control of Laos was the key to saving South Vietnam and Thailand from Communist domination. But he did not want any U.S. troops to be sent to Laos and promised his successor not to make any such public appeal. Instead he counseled Kennedy to put more troops into Thailand and South Vietnam to stiffen backs in Bangkok and Saigon and to free up the Thais and the South Vietnamese to engage in operational activity in Laos.[66]

It was a relief for Kennedy to hear that Eisenhower would not publicly or privately advocate putting U.S. troops into Laos. He did not want to do it either. However, like his predecessor, Kennedy believed that a show of strength was necessary to have any chance of deterring the Communists from continuing their offensive. On May 14 he ordered eighteen hundred marines plus two air squadrons, one marine and one air force, to land in Thailand the next morning. Within two weeks there would be between five and six thousand U.S. troops in Thailand.[67] Kennedy hoped that these troops would lead the Kremlin and its Asian allies to seek a cease-fire.

Khrushchev received news of the U.S. move into Thailand just after arriving in Bulgaria for a routine visit to a socialist ally.[68] The Soviet military reported that eighteen hundred U.S. marines, supported by twenty attack planes and twenty helicopters, had landed in Thailand May 16 and 17. Besides this contingent, which was between thirty-five and fifty miles from the Laotian border, the Soviets reported on another group of twelve hundred U.S.

troops that had stayed on in Thailand after recent maneuvers and was about thirty-five miles from the border. Just south of the Thai capital of Bangkok, Soviet intelligence detected a U.S. air group consisting of twenty-five fighters, some transports, and a refueling plane.[69]

The arrival of more U.S. soldiers in Southeast Asia was exactly what Khrushchev had hoped to avoid. That he had turned a blind eye to the Nam Tha operation did not mean he had forgotten his long-standing assessment of the dangers in the region. He had consistently disagreed with the Chinese over the balance of power there. While Chinese representatives, seconding the public fears of capitalist enemies, spoke of a series of dominoes that would fall from Laos to Malaysia if the senior Communist parties gave a hard enough push, Khrushchev believed that U.S. military power, if allowed to operate unchecked in Southeast Asia, would carry the day.[70] Given that the Pathet Lao and its allies were already outnumbered by Phoumi Nosavan's forces, this American force could easily tip the balance in favor of the rightists.

Khrushchev sent word to Moscow on May 17 to arrange contact with the Kennedy brothers. Concerned that the U.S. deployment to Thailand was just the beginning, he resorted to the Bolshakov back channel to explain to President Kennedy that he was not behind the assault on Nam Tha. "The trouble in Nam Tha," Bolshakov was to explain to Robert Kennedy, "was really isolated and brought about by people in the area who got fed up with Phoumi's troops. This is as far as it is going." Bolshakov was to convey the personal message from Khrushchev that he still stood by their Vienna agreement to achieve a peaceful, neutral Laos.[71]

The need for this urgent message to prevent a larger U.S. intervention was deeply humiliating to Khrushchev. Kennedy's rapid projection of additional military might into Southeast Asia in May 1962, however minor, was one reminder too many of the unfavorable balance of power and its consequences for Soviet policy. Never a patient man, Khrushchev found his frustration at these international realities nearing a breaking point. Already in March, while complaining about U.S. power to Anatoly Dobrynin, Khrushchev had vowed, "It's high time their long arms were cut shorter."[72]

The day he found out about the U.S. move into Thailand, Khrushchev spoke publicly about the role of force in U.S. foreign policy, "What logic can imperialism call upon? Only the logic of strength; and with that logic as their guide, they are trying to pursue the position-of-strength policy. The late Dulles was very frank about this."[73]

At his last Presidium meeting before leaving for Bulgaria Khrushchev had participated in yet another discussion of the lack of progress of Soviet strategic weapons programs—on land, on sea, and in the air.[74] The issue was still on his mind. So too was the idea he had kicked around with Malinovsky in April about perhaps using Cuba as a shortcut to a stronger strategic position in the superpower arms race. Just before Khrushchev flew to Bulgaria, he had signed a letter to Castro laying out the panoply of Soviet military assistance that would be coming to the island over the next year or two. Moscow, which did not anticipate a U.S. attack in 1962, sought to prepare Castro for any U.S. provocations in the runup to Kennedy's expected reelection campaign in 1964.

When he received the news about Laos, Khrushchev began rethinking his entire approach for 1962. Perhaps it was the time to act. Perhaps he should not wait until 1963 to press for a settlement that would solve the German tangle, relieve his domestic economic pressures, and eliminate his military vulnerabilities in the third world, especially in Cuba. "I paced back and forth," he later recalled, "brooding over what to do."[75] Khrushchev, who kept this "private agony" to himself, was tired of leading a second-ranked power, always concerned that its initiatives would be thwarted by the stronger superpower. Cuba became the funnel through which Khrushchev's various frustrations flowed.[76] In Bulgaria the idea for using Cuba as nuclear ballistic missile base, as a strategic stopgap, ripened. "The Americans had surrounded our country with military bases and threatened us with nuclear weapons," Khrushchev later said in explaining his thinking at the time, "and now they would learn just what it feels like to have enemy missiles pointing at you; we'd be doing nothing more than giving them a little of their own medicine."[77]

Had Kennedy not sent troops to Southeast Asia in response to the capture of Nam Tha, would Khrushchev have still decided to take the risky step of sending missiles to Cuba? It is impossible to know with certainty, but it is likely that the Cuban solution was too good an idea for the impatient and disappointment-averse Khrushchev to resist for long. By 1962 Khrushchev was in a strategic bind largely of his own creation. He had based Soviet military strategy since 1959 on the acquisition of nuclear weapons. The program for developing those weapons had been slower and more costly than expected, and he refused to pour even more money down what looked to be a black hole. At the same time, he had opted to flex what muscle he had to achieve changes in the status quo in Central Europe. The fact that the United States called his bluff in 1958 and again in 1961 made him appear vulnerable to his Communist allies, especially East Germany and China. In 1962 his lingering vulnerability after the Berlin crisis of the previous year, coupled with his inherent impatience and the ambitions of his chief foreign rivals for international influence, Kennedy and Mao, emboldened him to take additional risks.

Khrushchev worked quickly once he returned home on May 20. He shared his Cuban missile idea with Gromyko on the flight back and had instructions sent to Malinovsky so that he would be ready to support the idea at a formal Presidium meeting the next day. He also conferred with Mikoyan, who was characteristically unhappy with this latest Khrushchevian scheme. Mikoyan assured Khrushchev that the Americans would never accept Soviet missiles in Cuba. Mikoyan, who had been to the island, was very fond of the young Cuban revolutionaries, but Khrushchev's idea was potentially self-defeating. "We have to defend Cuba," Mikoyan told the Soviet leader, "but with this approach we risk provoking an attack on them and losing everything."[78]

Less than twenty-four hours after his return, Khrushchev formally presented his scheme to the Presidium for approval. He had a full house. In addition to the twelve members of the Presidium, Malinovsky, Gromyko, some Central Committee secretaries, and the chief of Soviet strategic rocket forces, Marshal Sergei Biryuzov, all were in attendance.[79] The release of additional Presidium materials in 2003 revealed for the first time how Khrushchev formally explained his idea that day. To second-tier officials, Khrushchev later emphasized the altruism of this scheme. He claimed to be purely motivated by the defense needs of Cuba. But in front of his colleagues, he said, "This will be an offensive policy." Although hinged on Castro's need to deter U.S. aggression, it was designed to do much more for the Soviet Union.[80] Khrushchev in January he had spoken confidently of the growth in Soviet power that by 1963 would force the United States to accommodate Moscow's perceived needs in Central Europe and elsewhere. The Cuba ploy would ensure that this necessary change in the balance of power occurred.

Khrushchev, who explained that the missiles would have to be delivered secretly, assumed that the United States would not willingly accept this change in the balance of power. Although it is not known when he originally expected to reveal this change to the world, in outlining his idea, he explained that he would reveal the presence of the missiles in Cuba only after their deployment. He left the timetable of deployment to Malinovsky and Biryuzov, but there is evidence that he wanted the operation to be completed quickly.[81] The missiles were to remain under Soviet command. The Cubans, however, would be given a joint defense agreement to assure them that Soviet military means would be used to defend their country.

Once Khrushchev finished his monologue, the meeting descended into discord. "The debates went on for a long time," recalled Colonel General Semyon P. Ivanov, a note taker for the Ministry of Defense. Repeating the arguments he had made privately to Khrushchev, Mikoyan led those who believed that the scheme was dangerous. It is unclear how many shared this view, though Soviet Foreign Minister Gromyko later said that he harbored similar concerns. Khrushchev's principal sparring partner opposed sending not only the missiles but also Soviet troops to Cuba. Seeing that his proposal was in trouble, Khrushchev halted the meeting and asked for a recess.[82]

Three days later they gathered again in formal session to consider the proposal. Khrushchev had used the intervening days to rally support. Malinovsky had also used the time to generate a plan of action to show the Presidium how the operation might work. Eleven members of the Presidium, Malinovsky, and Gromyko spoke at this meeting. Whatever misgivings there might have been were not in evidence on May 24. The vote was unanimous. Even Mikoyan was recorded as speaking in favor of the plan.[83]

The only realistic obstacle to the missile plan that remained was Fidel Castro. The Cubans, who assumed that conventional weapons and a solemn defense commitment from Moscow would be enough to hold off the United States, had not asked for any nuclear weapons.

When Aleksandr Alekseyev, the KGB resident who was to become Moscow's new ambassador to Havana, was told about the plan, he warned Khrushchev that Castro "[would] be scared" and doubted the Cuban leader would take the missiles.[84] Alekseyev's pessimism annoyed the Soviet defense minister, who had been mulling over the idea for nearly two months. "How could your celebrated socialist Cuba not take the missiles?" screamed Malinovsky, "I fought in bourgeois-democratic Spain, and they openly took our weapons, but Cuba, socialist Cuba, which has an even greater need to take them . . . how could they not!"[85] Despite Malinovsky's passion, Alekseyev, who understood the Castro regime better than any other Soviet official, was listened to. The Presidium decided not to implement its approved plan before receiving Castro's agreement.

Khrushchev wanted a high-level Soviet delegation to sell the missile base idea to Castro. Commandeering an agriculture mission that had already been staffed and credentialed for Cuba, he added Marshal Biryuzov and Alekseyev. On the eve of the delegation's departure to Havana, Khrushchev revealed to some of its members a little more of the complex thinking behind this risky initiative. Over tea, he intoned about the importance of the mission upon which these men were embarking. "The missiles have one purpose," he said, "to scare them, to restrain them . . . to give them back some of their medicine." He admitted that his efforts to build Soviet power had not proceeded as rapidly as he had hoped. "The correlation of forces is unfavorable to us, and the only way to save Cuba is to put missiles there."[86]

Khrushchev also explained that if the Cubans accepted his offer, he intended to keep the operation a secret until after the November 6 congressional elections in the United States. The American people were hawkish, and he would not want to give Kennedy an excuse to respond aggressively to the missiles. Once the missiles were in place and the elections were over, he intended to travel to the United States to reveal the existence of the missiles and to talk to Kennedy. Then he would visit Cuba to sign a defense agreement with Fidel Castro. This was his plan. But first he needed to know if Castro would accept the nuclear weapons.

18

"I THINK WE WILL WIN
THIS OPERATION"

T HE SOVIET OFFER of nuclear missiles surprised Fidel Castro. In the past year Moscow had been giving him less of the conventional weaponry that he and his commanders believed Cuba needed. It had taken Moscow almost a year to agree to give him the much less dramatic defensive assistance he had requested in September 1961. As of May 1962, not only had the surface-to-air missiles not yet arrived, but the Soviets were now making noises that they could not supply as many as the Cubans wanted. The story was the same regarding the Sopka shore missile system. The Soviets had balked at Castro's initial request for three batteries in September 1961, and when they finally relented in April 1962, they said they could promise only one battery. Castro had also asked for ten thousand Soviet troops to be deployed to the island. He had been careful not to describe them to the Soviets as a trip wire, but no doubt he hoped they would serve as a guarantee that any U.S. invasion would be interpreted by Moscow as an attack on the Soviet Union. The Soviets then counteroffered only three thousand men. So, with all this evidence that the Soviets were having a hard time agreeing to give Castro the defensive strength he wanted, out of the blue came an offer of offensive ballistic missiles.

Sharaf Rashidov, a candidate member of the Presidium from Uzbekistan, ostensibly led the Soviet delegation that arrived on the island in late May 1962. The Cubans, however, quickly understood that the military representative, Marshal Sergei S. Biryuzov, held the real power in the group. Castro explained to Rashidov and Biryuzov that the Soviet offer was flattering. He knew of no other instance in which the Soviets had considered deploying nuclear missiles outside their country. But he was not prepared to believe that it was concern about the defense of Cuba that had motivated the Kremlin's unexpected generosity. In his estimation, the Sopka, the SAMs, and the Soviet troops would be enough to defend the island. Repeating Khrushchev's official justification for the offer, the delegates denied that the Soviet leader had any objective in mind besides defending Castro's regime.

Castro would have been excused if he found Moscow's initiative ironic. For years the Soviets had been telling the Americans that they were wrong to fear that Cuba would become an extension of Soviet power. Just before the Bay of Pigs, Khrushchev had sent Castro a confidential snippet from a conversation with the U.S. ambassador. "We disagree with the U.S. conception of Cuba," Khrushchev had lectured Thompson. What the Soviet leader had in mind was Washington's tendency to view Cuba in the same way it viewed the countries that bordered the USSR. "The USA, for some reason, believes that it has the right to put military bases along the borders of the USSR. [Yet] we do not at the same time have a military base in Cuba, but friendly relations." As a way of ridiculing U.S. concerns in 1961, Khrushchev had even indulged in sarcasm: "And in the U.S. there has already been the criticism that the USSR is building a rocket base on Cuba."[1] A year later it now looked to Castro as if reality would replace sarcasm.

The Soviet delegation failed to persuade the Cuban leader that the missiles would be coming just to defend his revolution, but he saw no reason to reject an offer that would likely tie the Soviet Union to the defense of his country. Castro told his visitors that Cuba would accept the strategic missiles.

Once he heard the good news, Khrushchev lifted some of the veil of secrecy between the two countries. He was never completely open with the Cubans about the reasons that had prompted him to take the risk of his career, but in a letter thanking Castro, he allowed that more than the defense of Cuba was at stake. Castro's agreement, he wrote, represented "a further fortification of the victory of the Cuban revolution and of the greater success of our general affairs."[2]

■

THE RASHIDOV DELEGATION returned to Moscow on June 8, 1962, and Khrushchev convened an unusual Sunday morning meeting of the Presidium two days later to hear its reports and formally approve the Cuban missile operation.

What Khrushchev had in store for his colleagues was much more than a plan to send a couple of nuclear missiles to Cuba. At the June 10 meeting Soviet Defense Minister Malinovsky outlined an audacious plan to build a powerful Soviet military base ninety miles from the U.S. coast. Under Operation Anadyr—a cover name drawn from the name of a Siberian river to confuse the uninitiated—the Soviet Union would dispatch forty nuclear missiles divided into five nuclear missile regiments, three with medium-range R-12s and two with intermediate-range R-14s. Atlanta, Georgia, was in range of a medium-range missile launched from Cuba, whereas an intermediate-range missile could hit the U.S. strategic missile bases in the Midwest and Washington, D.C. These missiles represented a major augmentation of Soviet strategic power. As of mid-1962, the Soviets had only about twenty strategic rocket launchers with missiles that could reach the United States, and they all were intercontinental ballistic missiles (ICBMs) located in the USSR.[3]

According to Khrushchev's and Malinovsky's plan, the strategic missiles were the centerpiece of what was to become an extensive Soviet military presence in Cuba. Protecting the missiles in Cuba would be four motorized regiments, two tank battalions, and a MiG-21 fighter wing, some antiaircraft gun batteries, and twelve SA-2 surface-to-air missile detachments (with 144 launchers). Each tank battalion would be outfitted with the T55, the newest Soviet tank. The total deployment of Soviet forces would be 50,874, of which 10,000 would be deployed in the four motorized regiments. Additional nuclear striking power would come from forty-two Il-28 light bombers, which could reach Florida and were given six nuclear bombs, and two cruise missile (FKR) regiments, comprising eighty nuclear-tipped missiles positioned opposite likely U.S. landing beaches. Besides this impressive land and air component, the Soviet armed forces intended to establish a submarine base on Cuba, which would simplify the logistics of maintaining patrols of the North American coastline. A massive flotilla that would establish a naval presence for the Soviet Union around the island would accompany these submarines.[4]

"I think we will win this operation," Khrushchev exclaimed after listening to Malinovsky's description of what power the Soviet Union would soon be able to project from Cuba.[5] The Soviet leader could hardly contain his excitement, but the records left of this extraordinary 11:00 A.M. Sunday meeting of the Presidium suggest that he did not explain what "winning" meant. Was it that he assumed that with Soviet power staring Washington squarely in the face, the United States would finally have to take Moscow seriously as an adversary? It is difficult to know with any certainty how clearly Khrushchev had thought through the implications of his new Cuban base in early June.

What new, formerly top secret Soviet information reveals, however, is that by early July he had developed an increasingly ambitious sense of what the Cuban deployment could mean for Soviet strategic policy. In the three weeks since Castro's acceptance of the missiles Khrushchev thoroughly revised his foreign policy objectives for 1962. This was supposed to be the year of no new diplomatic initiatives. Now he hoped to keep the Americans off-balance, allowing international affairs to be as unstable as the meniscus on a glass, until Soviet power reached a point where deals could be struck on issues like Berlin, the test ban, and Southeast Asia.

On July 1 Khrushchev unveiled his ambitious new agenda to his Presidium colleagues. The meeting was ostensibly to discuss a Soviet-Cuban defense agreement. The Cuban defense minister, Raúl Castro, was expected in Moscow the next day, and Havana wanted to sign a pact of sorts. Khrushchev used the occasion to introduce some ideas that he had on matters in an area that had never before been linked to Cuba.[6]

The Soviet leader announced that he wanted to renew the push for a settlement on West Berlin. He proposed delaying the removal of the eleven thousand Western troops from the city in a way that would not harm Soviet prestige. Immediately upon the signature of a peace treaty between the Western powers and the two Germanys, Western garrisons would be cut in half and then remain under the UN flag. On the second anniversary of the peace treaty the remaining fifty-five hundred Western soldiers would be replaced by non-Western UN troops. Four years after that—or six years in total following the signature of the peace treaty—all UN troops would leave. Under this plan there would be nothing like the international access authority that Kennedy had suggested as a way to guarantee that Western planes and trains could continue to cut across East Germany to reach West Berlin. "An international organ is unacceptable," Khrushchev announced at the July 1 session.[7] The UN's role would be limited to providing troops to satisfy American anxieties that West Berlin might be attacked by the Soviet bloc. He wanted a letter to go out to Kennedy with these proposals.[8]

Khrushchev conveyed to his colleagues that this proposal was to be Moscow's bottom line, and the Americans were to be forced to accept it, even if it meant taking the "path of aggravating things."[9] In January the Soviet leader had disavowed making 1962 the year of Berlin. "Really, is such an issue on the agenda now?" he had asked his colleagues before answering his own question. "No, on the contrary, we don't have this issue at all, because, if not now, then it will be tomorrow. And if it's not now, but tomorrow, is this worse? What, will it undermine our foundation? No, not in the least. On the contrary, our strengths are increasing, our influence in the world is increasing, our impact is increasing. So why should we take such a drastic step?"[10]

Now Khrushchev declared to his Kremlin colleagues in secret session that it was time to take that drastic step. Why? The notes of the July 1 Presidium meeting are fragmentary, but there are clues that the prospect of a substantial Soviet missile force ninety miles from the United States, in effect tripling the number of Soviet strategic nuclear missile launchers within range of North America, was just part of the story. Equally important was Khrushchev's anger at what he considered yet another act of hubris by the Kennedy administration. Two weeks earlier Secretary of Defense Robert McNamara had given a speech on U.S. nuclear policy at the University of Michigan commencement. It was a public restatement of a revolution in Western nuclear strategy he had secretly unveiled at a NATO conference in Athens in May. Soviet intelligence had apparently missed the NATO speech, but Khrushchev could easily read about the Ann Arbor speech, which was covered around the world. What McNamara said irritated the Soviet leader because the secretary of defense explained that in the future NATO should consider targeting Soviet military installations instead of cities. The U.S. government was making this argument because it wanted to discourage the French, the British, and the West Germans from building their own nuclear forces, which were inefficient and hard to control and bred Soviet concerns. Only the U.S. force was technologically sophisticated enough to hit Soviet missile silos.[11] But what Khrushchev heard was that McNamara was somehow trying to make nuclear war seem less bloody and therefore more acceptable. Minutes after outlining a new Berlin offensive, Khrushchev railed against McNamara at the July 1 meeting: "Not targeting cities—how aggressive! What is their aim?"[12] he asked. Answering his own question, as he often liked to do, Khrushchev replied, "To get the population used to the idea that nuclear war will take place." McNamara was even suspect for having announced in Michigan that U.S. and Soviet nuclear arsenals were essentially equal. "They are not equal." Khrushchev reminded his Kremlin listeners, who, like him, knew the Soviet nuclear force to be inferior. He suspected a trick by McNamara, who might be trying to lay the ground for a rapid increase in American nuclear forces. "How many bombs do they need?" Khrushchev asked.

Khrushchev's impulse to lash out at U.S. power recalled his overreaching in November 1958. At that time the imminent deployment of Soviet nuclear missiles in East Germany had steeled his determination to do something to curb NATO's nuclear alliance with West Germany and the alliance's presence in Berlin. In 1959 he had found he lacked the power to compel Dwight Eisenhower to give in, so he dropped his ultimatum. This time, however, he expected to be powerful enough to get his way, and he hinted to his colleagues

at the form this new confrontation might take. Khrushchev mused about taking the issue to the United Nations, where either the Soviets or a neutral
country would raise the German problem once the Cuban missiles were
deployed in November. He did not spell out how this would happen, but he
assured his colleagues that this would have to occur in the midst of a crisis
atmosphere. He also seemed to assume that after scoring points in the ensu-
ing debate at the UN, Moscow could then force its way to get what it wanted.

In laying out this new Berlin strategy, Khrushchev informed his colleagues
that he intended to try out traditional forms of diplomacy before launching a
new world crisis. He would make one more direct appeal to Kennedy to accept
his reasonable proposals on Berlin before going to the UN in the fall. And
although it seems Khrushchev did not mention Southeast Asia in this discussion, there is ample evidence that on July 1 he also had in mind seeking a diplomatic agreement to neutralize Laos in Geneva, if possible, that summer. On
June 11 the princes Souvanna Phouma and Souphanouvong had reached agreement on a coalition government and called for a reconvening of the Geneva
Conference to formalize Laotian neutrality.[13] The U.S. envoy to those discussions, Averell Harriman, was due to meet with Soviet Foreign Ministry officials
on July 2 in Moscow to reaffirm Kennedy's desire to seek the peaceful demilita-
rization and political neutralization of Laos, and Khrushchev planned to assure
Washington that this remained his goal as well.[14]

The tension between Khrushchev's willingness to use diplomacy in Laos
and his taste for brinkmanship over Berlin was apparently left unexplored at
the July 1 meeting. The Presidium did spend some time discussing Cuba
before the meeting ended, though its connection to the coming confrontation
over Berlin was also left unstated. Foreign Minister Gromyko read a draft
Soviet-Cuban defense agreement to the members, which they approved. The
Presidium also formally designated Khrushchev, Malinovsky, and Gromyko to
take part in the negotiations with Raúl Castro. Meanwhile Khrushchev
assured the rest of the Presidium that all the components of Anadyr would be
shipped by November 1 and that he was working to find a way to get the
Americans to stop their close air surveillance of ships on the high seas, which
endangered the ships and the secrets of their cargo.

Khrushchev got everything that he asked for from his colleagues on July 1.
This time, unlike in 1958 and 1961, he was able to bring about a radical shift
in Soviet Berlin strategy without any debate. Mikoyan, the Presidium's resident skeptic on the wisdom of launching Berlin crises, was not at the meeting, and his absence may explain the lack of opposition on July 1. If Mikoyan
later expressed any doubts when he returned to the Kremlin, those reserva-

tions either were not noted or had no discernible effect. The confrontational course was firmly set.[15]

■

RAÚL CASTRO ARRIVED in Moscow a day or two later. It was his second time in the Soviet capital. His visit two years earlier had sealed the first Soviet commitment to defend Cuba. Back then Khrushchev could give only a rhetorical promise to use nuclear weapons if the United States dared invade the revolutionary island. The Cuban defense minister had a different mission this time. In the wake of Khrushchev's offer of strategic nuclear weapons, Castro wanted to hammer out in detail the Soviet defense commitment.

Accompanying the Cuban defense minister on the special Cubana Airlines flight from Havana was Major General A. A. Dementyev, the commander of the Soviet military mission in Cuba. Dementyev had tried to warn his superiors in Moscow that American U-2 spy planes would make it difficult, if not impossible, to keep the operation secret once the missiles started arriving on the island. He had been ignored in May but raised the issue again during Raúl Castro's visit.[16]

The details of Castro's two conversations with Khrushchev on July 3 and July 8, 1962, remain elusive. If Russian notes were taken, they cannot be found. Meanwhile, in a vestige of the Cold War more than four decades later the Cuban account remains sealed. However, Khrushchev's public statements in the days that followed and his statements in highly classified settings reveal that Castro's trip altered his planning of the Cuban facet of the 1962 strategic offensive. The Cubans and General Dementyev convinced him that the security of the operation required the shipment of surface-to-air missiles to precede the delivery of the medium-range and intermediate-range rockets. According to the original Soviet military plan, the SAMs were to be delivered in two installments, the first was that July and the second in August.[17] The Cubans apparently requested that the missiles arrive the same month.

In making their request, the Cubans had differentiated between weapons necessary for their defense and strategic weapons that Khrushchev wanted on the island for his purposes. Khrushchev accepted this distinction. In explaining the change of plan to his colleagues at the Presidium on July 6, following his first meeting with Raúl Castro, he said that the "defensive" weapons would go first and that the weapons that were part of his offensive plan, the strategic missiles, would follow.[18]

The Cuban request had a second consequence, the significance of which became apparent only in the fall. Originally Malinovsky and the planners at the Soviet Defense Ministry had projected that all the nuclear missiles would be sent to Cuba in the first part of July. They were to leave in two shipments, one carrying the medium-range missiles, the other, the intermediate-range missiles.[19] Now that the Cubans wanted their SAMs first, the missile shipments had to be delayed because of the shortage of Soviet ships to carry them. According to the Anadyr plan, the Ministry of Marine, responsible for transporting everything but the nuclear warheads, which were to be handled by the Soviet Navy, had only so many ships. The Defense Ministry still believed that the entire plan could be implemented by November 1, as Khrushchev had hoped, but instead of the missiles arriving while the launch facilities were being built, they were now expected to arrive later.

Between meetings with Raúl Castro, Khrushchev approved a threatening letter to President Kennedy on Berlin. "International developments, especially those in and around West Berlin," Khrushchev wrote on July 5, "prompt the conclusion that further delay in solving the questions connected with a German peace settlement would involve such a threat to peace which must be averted already [sic] now when it is not too late."[20] The letter contained an even stronger demand than that which Khrushchev had outlined to his colleagues on July 1. Kennedy was told that Moscow wanted an immediate 50 percent cut in the Western contingent in West Berlin, with replacement troops coming from the Warsaw Pact and from neutral and some small NATO countries like Denmark. His original proposal said nothing about putting socialist soldiers in West Berlin. In the letter Khrushchev promised that the combined NATO–Warsaw Pact–Neutral contingent of eleven thousand troops would then serve under the UN flag. Over the course of four years the entire UN contingent would gradually be phased out, with proportional reductions of the Western and non-Western portions. In his July 1 proposal to Kremlin leadership Khrushchev had shown a willingness to accept a six-year transition to a demilitarized West Berlin. Evidently his confidence in what he could soon get in the new international environment was rising.[21]

Khrushchev did not coordinate this new proposal with East Germany. Relations with Ulbricht were little improved from the difficulties of 1961, when Khrushchev rescinded the ultimatum he had handed Kennedy at the Vienna summit. Of this new effort, Ulbricht was told only that the Soviet Union and the United States were about to head into some very serious negotiations on Berlin, and Khrushchev sent along the suggestion that if the East Germans wanted to tighten border controls, now was the time to do it.[22]

■

WHEN KENNEDY READ Khrushchev's letter on July 5, he immediately foresaw serious trouble ahead. The new demands signaled an unwelcome resumption of Soviet pressure for an immediate settlement of the future of Berlin and yet another test of Kennedy's resolve in Central Europe, an issue that should have been resolved by his actions in 1961. The president knew of no international developments that might have prompted this dramatic change in tone. Complicating matters was not merely the renewed hostility of Khrushchev's letter—the Soviet leader was famous for blowing hot and cold, and now he was blowing hot—but that the terms it offered were the worst to have come out of the Kremlin since 1958. Khrushchev must have known, thought Kennedy, that these terms would be unacceptable. But if there was any doubt in the Soviet leader's mind, Kennedy wasted no time in explaining to the Soviet leadership through Ambassador Dobrynin in Washington that no U.S. president could accept this deal.[23]

In handing Dobrynin the letter containing his government's formal reply to Khrushchev on July 17, Kennedy emphasized the dangerous turn that U.S.-Soviet relations were taking.[24] Using carefully chosen language, he explained why compromise along the lines Khrushchev had suggested was impossible. Maintaining the troops in West Berlin was a "vital interest of the United States." Therefore, "none of the Soviet proposals for alternative arrangements," he said, "could be accepted." To remove the troops would be "a major retreat." Historically, great powers did not accept retreats except at the point of a knife. If he were to accept Khrushchev's terms, Kennedy added, "Europe would lose confidence in U.S. leadership. It would be a major victory for the Soviet Union and a major defeat for the West." Kennedy's rejection could not have been clearer.

Two days after transmitting his response to Moscow, the president met with his Berlin team to discuss contingency planning for the now expected crisis. He was very dissatisfied with NATO's current military plans, which would take days to initiate once a crisis started. If the Soviets or East Germans were to deny Western access to West Berlin by closing any of the routes to the city, Washington might be faced with the decision to use nuclear weapons immediately because of the glacial pace by which U.S. allies would be able to get sufficient troops to the area. The U.S. plan was no better. Known as National Security Action Memorandum 109, or Poodle Blanket, it envisioned a sixty-day diplomatic and mobilization period before U.S. forces could attack. When Kennedy had routinely asked in June for the status of any of these plans, he was told that none of them could be implemented for at least another few months.[25]

A few days after this sobering meeting Kennedy received more bad news from Moscow. On July 25 Khrushchev met for five hours with Ambassador Thompson, about to leave his post in Moscow and return to the United States to become Kennedy's chief Sovietologist. The meeting began in the morning at Khrushchev's office in Moscow and ended at his dacha outside the city. Khrushchev offered a dark assessment of the state of U.S.-Soviet relations. He admitted to having little hope of achieving any agreement to ban nuclear tests. "[H]e did not think the Pentagon wanted it," Thompson reported to Washington.[26] But this was not the section of the conversation that caused concern in the White House. As the ambassador was about to leave, the Soviet leader said that he had an unpleasant subject to discuss. He told Thompson that it was evident from Kennedy's reaction to his Berlin proposals that Washington was prepared to wait indefinitely to resolve this problem, a scenario that was not acceptable to Moscow. Khrushchev recalled that the United States often referred to issues, especially Berlin, as matters of prestige but never seemed to take Soviet prestige into account. It was a matter of Soviet prestige, he explained, that the Berlin situation be resolved very quickly and the appropriate peace treaties be signed.

Khrushchev spoke calmly and, despite the ominous topic, was remarkably cordial. Thompson sensed that he was determined to move ahead but "was deeply troubled."[27] At one point Khrushchev asked the U.S. ambassador to ask President Kennedy personally if he wanted matters to come to a head over Berlin before or after the November 6 congressional elections in the United States. Khrushchev said he wanted to "help him," presumably to win seats for Democrats; but he left his meaning unclear, and Thompson did not press him on it.[28]

Despite Khrushchev's professed interest in helping him, Kennedy was convinced that a major crisis was brewing. He had been in office eighteen months, and already he had dealt with the consequences of a failed covert action in Cuba, the seemingly unsolvable puzzle in Laos, and tension over Berlin a year before. But compared with all of these foreign policy challenges, this new one had the earmarks of something worse.

As the president confronted the likelihood of another Berlin crisis, someone, possibly his brother Robert, handed him a copy of Barbara Tuchman's latest book. *The Guns of August* detailed the tortuous path taken by the great powers before the outbreak of the First World War.[29] The story left its mark on Kennedy, who was struck by how almost casually the elite of the Edwardian age had drifted into war. An exchange involving Imperial Germany's prewar chancellor, Theobald von Bethmann-Hollweg, was what impressed him most.

To the question "Oh, how did it happen?" Bethmann-Hollweg could only answer, "Oh, if we ever knew." According to his brother Robert, John F. Kennedy was "not going to have that legacy left while he was President."[30]

John Kennedy decided he owed it to himself and to history to collect a better record of the decisions that he was about to make and the information upon which they were based. Telling Secret Service officer Robert Bouck that he was concerned about recent changes in U.S.-Soviet relations, he ordered the installation of a secret taping system in the Oval Office and the Cabinet Room and upstairs in his private quarters. Although Kennedy's very first professional ambition had been journalism, he had not kept a diary since he entered elective office. The crafty Joseph Kennedy had told his boys, "Never write it down," and Kennedy had heeded that advice.[31] The tapes were to fill that void in the record. Kennedy had correctly perceived that Khrushchev was determined to have a confrontation over Berlin in 1962, and he wanted to document the steps that he took to avoid nuclear war.

As the taping system was installed, U.S. intelligence began to notice an unsettling development much closer to home. Dozens of Soviet merchant ships with undisclosed cargoes were headed toward Cuba. NATO reconnaissance planes spotted the ships as they left the Barents Sea in the north and the Black Sea in the south. They were then picked up by U.S. planes over the Atlantic. It was the largest Soviet sealift to Cuba, and the timing seemed unusual.

Amid the growing uncertainty in Washington about Soviet intentions, Robert Kennedy heard from the GRU officer Georgi Bolshakov that he had a message to deliver from Moscow. It was only the second time that the Kremlin had used Bolshakov to send a message. When the attorney general informed him of Bolshakov's request to meet him, the president decided to participate in the meeting, which was scheduled for July 31 in the Oval Office.

Khrushchev had mentioned to the Presidium on July 1 his concern about NATO's spying on the Anadyr convoys, and he opted to use Bolshakov to ask Kennedy directly to stop the intrusive overhead reconnaissance of Soviet shipping. The NATO flights were very low-level, between 150 and 300 feet over the ships.[32] In one case the plane came so close to the ship that the pilot lost control and crashed 150 yards from the ship.[33] It was a risky request by Khrushchev, who was thereby drawing attention to the armada headed to Cuba with nuclear weapons, but Moscow wanted to see if Kennedy would unintentionally help them keep the secret.

The president agreed to Khrushchev's request and used the meeting as an opportunity to send a message to the Kremlin through the Bolshakov back channel. Concerned about the sudden urgency in the Berlin negotiations, he asked Khrushchev to put the issue "on ice" for the moment.[34]

A few days later Bolshakov sent back Khrushchev's reply. He thanked the president for his "order to curtail US planes' inspections of Soviet ships in open waters" but refused to reward Kennedy by stopping his push for a Berlin settlement. Khrushchev "would like to understand what John F. Kennedy means by 'placing the Berlin question on ice,'" Bolshakov was instructed to say.[35]

The mixed signals confused Kennedy. In late July the United States and the Soviet Union signed the multiparty Geneva Agreement to neutralize Laos, which stipulated the withdrawal of foreign forces from the country. After achieving this breakthrough in superpower relations, why was Khrushchev now making trouble in Berlin and perhaps in the Caribbean? On August 1 analysts at the CIA warned that Khrushchev had chosen to resume putting pressure on the West because "the Soviets are probably convinced that no important change in the Western position [on Berlin] can be obtained without greatly increased pressures."[36] But the agency also suggested that there was a limit to the risks Khrushchev was willing to take. It anticipated nothing more than renewed harassment of Western airplanes in the air corridors or perhaps an attempt to prevent Western military traffic from entering East Berlin under the four-power agreement. The reason, the CIA assured Kennedy, was that the Soviets "almost certainly recognize that the balance of military power has undergone no change which would justify this [abandoning the traditional Soviet caution in situations involving a direct East-West confrontation]."

Unsure of why under these circumstances Khrushchev would want a second crisis over Berlin, Kennedy turned to the American who had met with and studied Khrushchev the most, Llewellyn Thompson, who had just ended his four-year tour at the U.S. Embassy in Moscow.

At their meeting on August 8 Thompson revealed more frustration and uncertainty than insight. "It's like dealing with a bunch of bootleggers and gangsters," he said without any apparent irony to the man whose father had sold liquor during Prohibition.[37] Thompson had picked up a useful tidbit, however, before leaving Moscow. He had heard that Khrushchev was likely to plead his case on Berlin before the United Nations and suggested that the United States start working to ensure that the neutral countries did not support him.[38]

The conversation ranged over Khrushchev's recent actions. Kennedy asked Thompson to explain the Russian's behavior at the Paris summit in 1960. Thompson told the president he thought it was an effort by Khrushchev to save face after he had concluded that he would not be getting a deal on Berlin at the meeting. Kennedy also wanted to rehash his own experience at Vienna. "It was educational for me," he said, "but . . . he was so sort of tough about Berlin. . . ."[39] In response Thompson suggested that Khrushchev had taken that stand because he had to prove his toughness to the Chinese. Kennedy did not buy it. His hunch was that Khrushchev characteristically pressed forward when he perceived American weakness. "Do you think that the Cuba thing and the fact that we hadn't gone into Laos," asked Kennedy, "might have given him the impression that we were going to give way in Berlin?"[40] Thompson did not think so. "He's always felt he had us over a barrel in Berlin," said Thompson. "Yeah. I think he does," said the president with a nervous chuckle.[41]

■

I N M o s c o w the Soviet Union's German experts were preparing for a fall crisis. On July 25 the Foreign Ministry's European Department began sending out letters to Soviet ambassadors in the Middle East and the Congo for detailed information on UN forces. Bodrov in Israel and Erofeev in Egypt were each asked to report within two weeks on the deployment pattern, procedures, and mission of UN forces along the truce line in the Sinai.[42] In addition, the department, which had never shown an interest in this subject before, requested copies of all legal documents establishing the UN presence in the Middle East. The same day a similar instruction went out to the Soviet ambassador in the Congo.

Meanwhile the Foreign Ministry wrote to Soviet embassies for information about previous instances in which foreign military bases in sovereign states had been closed. On July 28 the Soviet ambassadors in Tunisia, Syria, Lebanon, Morocco, and Iraq received similar letters requesting information on the liquidation of foreign military bases in their region.[43] The Soviets lacked an embassy in Saudi Arabia, so Ambassadors Barkovsky in Damascus, Kornev in Beirut, and Vavilov in Baghdad were instructed to find out whatever they could about how the United States had dismantled its air base in Dhahran, Saudi Arabia. From the embassies in Tunisia and Morocco, Moscow wanted to know how the French had gone about removing their North African bases. In each case the Soviet ambassador was told that Moscow needed this information by mid-August but not told why.

What the Foreign Ministry did not tell its ambassadors was that this information was required to prepare background documents for Khrushchev's November initiative at the United Nations. Moscow evidently wanted to prepare a detailed proposal for the withdrawal of NATO forces and their replacement by a UN force in West Berlin.

▪

KHRUSHCHEV'S NOVEMBER strategy had the character of the classic children's game of Mousetrap: So much had to go right for it to work. Most important, not only did the missiles destined for Cuba have to reach their destination safely, but their installation had to be cloaked in secrecy. Consistent with the code name of the operation—Anadyr, a river in Siberia—the military rank and file were told they were being deployed to the Soviet north.

Maintaining the secrecy of these deployments was largely the KGB's responsibility, but the Soviet foreign intelligence service monitored the progress only of the merchant marine vessels, leaving security on the navy ships to the GRU and the military security services. Soviet intelligence devised a complicated procedure to keep the destination of the ships a secret from the captains, crews, and passengers as long as possible. The captain of the wide-hatched transport *Poltava*, for example, was to learn his destination officially only after the ship had rounded Gibraltar. At that point he opened a sealed package in the presence of the ship's KGB supervisor. Besides his destination, the captain was informed that under no circumstances was he to allow any intruders onto his vessel. If an unfriendly boarding seemed likely, the ship was to be scuttled.

Despite these precautions, the destination of the cargo became the subject of accurate speculation within the Soviet armed services. The KGB reported instances of frankly bewildered ship's captains who found when they came on board their respective billets in late July that all the male passengers were sporting facial hair and suntans, as if they expected to join Fidel Castro in the Sierra Maestre. On the troopship *Mednogorsk* the KGB officer discovered that most of the soldiers and even their officers were wearing sideburns, beards, and mustaches. The facial hair was a tipoff because the crew members were trying to fit in among Castro's revolutionary forces, who were world famous as the *barbudos*, the bearded ones. When the Soviet crews were asked why they had stopped shaving, they explained that about two months earlier, in early June, they had received an order to grow facial hair if they hadn't any already. It meant, reported the KGB officer, "that even earlier the personal staff of this command knew that they were being sent to Cuba." The same was true on the *Poltava*, where the KGB reported on an entire boat of suntanned and bearded Russian technicians, all of whom seemed to know where they were going.[44]

■

ALTHOUGH NONE of these bearded sunbathers turned out to be a covert source for the CIA, U.S. intelligence nevertheless could deliver an alarming picture of this sealift to the White House. Despite his assurances to Khrushchev in late July, Kennedy had not suspended U.S. overflights of Soviet shipping in the Atlantic. By late August the evidence was accumulating that the Soviets had initiated a major supply effort for the Castro regime. In spite of lapses in Anadyr's security, U.S. intelligence could not determine with any confidence what was on board these ships while they were on the high seas. U-2s flying high above Cuba, however, were able to photograph some of what came off the ships at Cuban ports. On August 29 the White House was informed that a large number of SAMs had reached the island.

The unknowns of the Soviet sealift to Cuba caused deep divisions in Washington over the assessment of Khrushchev's objectives. Dean Rusk and McGeorge Bundy assumed this was a conventional arms buildup, much as the Soviets had done for its other third world allies. They also believed that Berlin was currently the focus of Khrushchev's aggressive actions and should therefore be the United States' main concern in the summer of 1962. Robert Kennedy and the new CIA director, John McCone, who had replaced Allen Dulles in November 1961, however, saw something ominous in the deployment of SA-2 missiles. McCone, who had spent most of his government career studying the nuclear arms race, was convinced that the SAMs were there to protect ballistic missiles. He believed that a Soviet missile base on Cuba would make up for Soviet failures to build a competitive intercontinental force. Robert Kennedy had worried about a Soviet missile deployment to Cuba as far back as April 1961. By early September 1962 he and McCone were advising the president to issue a warning to deter Khrushchev from deploying nuclear weapons to the island. Sharing Bundy's and Rusk's concerns about Berlin, Kennedy, however, was inclined to avoid any action in the Caribbean that the Kremlin might consider provocative.

At a meeting of the national security team on September 4, the attorney general made a speculative leap in an attempt to open his brother's eyes to the possibility that there might be something big behind the developments in Cuba: "I don't think that this is just a question about what we are going to do about this [now]. I think it's a question of Cuba in the future. . . . There's going to be . . . three months from now, there's going to be something else going on, six months from now. . . . That eventually it's very likely that they'll establish a naval base there for submarines perhaps, or that they'll put surface-to-surface missiles in."[45] In view of this threat, the attorney general wanted the president to announce that the United States would never tolerate the placement of Soviet strategic weapons on the island of Cuba.

Robert Kennedy's recommendation sparked a debate in the room. Bundy rejected the attorney general's prediction of Soviet behavior. The president's assistant for national security was a brilliant analyst who nevertheless lacked a feel for the Soviet mentality. He was looking for institutional patterns instead of thinking about how Khrushchev had acted under pressure in the past. Noting that everything that the Soviets had sent to Cuba thus far "really is, insofar as you can make these distinctions, a defensive weapon," Bundy predicted more of the same. The deployment of strategic missiles, he suggested, would represent an unlikely break with past practice. "[This would be] a much larger step," he said, "than the development of the kind of thing we've seen over the last year and a half, which is fully consistent with their behavior in a lot of other countries."[46] Secretary of State Rusk shared Bundy's optimism and was concerned that overreacting to the Soviet buildup in Cuba might complicate matters in the Berlin stalemate. "If we designated ground-to-ground missiles or we specified the nuclear weapon, I think we could create a kind of panic that the facts themselves don't now justify."[47]

The issue wasn't settled that morning. Before the group broke up, the president asked that a statement on Cuba be drafted and that the group meet again in the afternoon. The attorney general was due to meet Anatoly Dobrynin at 2:15 P.M., an appointment that the Soviet had asked for a few days earlier. Despite the almost uniform skepticism of his national security experts, President Kennedy was now leaning toward adopting his brother's strategy, but he decided to wait to hear what Dobrynin had to say.

It was a very determined Bobby Kennedy who met with the Soviet ambassador. "The U.S. government," the attorney general said to Dobrynin, "was viewing with growing anxiety the increase in Soviet military supplies to Cuba and the appearance there of Soviet military specialists." The United States worried that the most technically advanced of the new Soviet weapons, the SAMs, would be turned over to the Cubans. "Who will stop the emotional Cubans," he asked, "from firing on American planes?" He then brought up his pet theory. "How do we put such supplies to Cuba in perspective, following the line of logic? Won't more powerful weapons that could reach the territory of the United States appear? Could these not ultimately carry nuclear warheads? The United States in this case definitely cannot allow its security to depend on this or that decision of the current government of Cuba."[48]

Robert Kennedy would not let go of this fear. In what seemed to Dobrynin a half-joking manner, he asked, "And what if rockets with small nuclear charges appear with the Cubans, what then?"

Dobrynin dismissed this possibility. "As [you] must . . . know well from the meetings between A. A. Gromyko with Rusk, the Soviet Union supports the nontransfer and the nonproliferation of nuclear weapons." Dobrynin knew nothing about Anadyr. So sure was he of the correctness of his denial that he added, "In future I will have this position emphasized, if the U.S. side would put it forward this way."

At that point Kennedy rose, saying that he had to get back to the White House to finish work on a presidential statement on Cuba. "I only wish that in the Soviet Union it was understood what feeling was stirred up in American society as a result of the reports of Soviet military supplies to Cuba, a distance of only 90 miles from the United States."[49]

Nothing Dobrynin said had altered Robert Kennedy's determination to get a warning out to Moscow in his brother's name. The presidential statement was ready by 6:00 P.M., and although the language was more muted than he would have liked, the attorney general had essentially carried the day. The president's warning to the Soviets about not putting missiles on the island had survived the skeptics. An hour later Press Secretary Pierre Salinger read the presidential statement: "There is no evidence of any organized combat force in Cuba from any Soviet bloc country, of military bases provided to Russia, of a violation of the 1934 treaty relating to Guantánamo, of the presence of offensive ground-to-ground missiles, or of other significant offensive capability either in Cuban hands or under Soviet direction and guidance. Were it to be otherwise, the gravest issues would arise." Dobrynin, who read the statement that night, must have thought the young Kennedys were overreacting.

■

KHRUSHCHEV LEARNED about Kennedy's statement at his summer retreat in the Caucasus. In 1961 he had used his holiday at Pitsunda to find a way to reduce tensions in the Berlin crisis. A year later Kennedy's sudden announcement elicited a different response. As of September 1, none of the strategic nuclear weapons had been installed in Cuba. The missile technicians were on the island and beginning their work, but the first shipment of missile parts was still days from landing in Havana. As for the nuclear warheads, these were under lock and key in the Soviet Union. According to the revised plan for Anadyr, the warheads were not scheduled to go to sea until early October.

Among the many decisions he had faced as Soviet leader, this would be among the most fateful. Khrushchev could still turn back the missiles and keep the defensive munitions on the island. Soon he would have more than fifty thousand Soviet troops and technicians in Cuba, and their presence could prove a powerful deterrent. After all, would the United States really take a chance on killing thousands of Soviet citizens to overthrow Castro? Furthermore, in August 1962 Castro had suggested to the Kremlin that the two countries announce the signature of a joint defense treaty. Moscow had demurred then, afraid that a treaty would awaken the Americans to Khrushchev's plans for the island. In response to Kennedy's statement of September 4, however, it might be the time to announce that a U.S. attack on Cuba would represent an attack on any member of the Warsaw Pact, with consequences that the United States understood.

But having Soviet troops on the island and a Soviet-Cuban defense treaty in place would not allow Khrushchev to achieve the larger objectives that he now associated with this Cuban missile operation. He wanted to change the international balance of power. He wanted the United States to respect him when he defined something as a Soviet interest. Canceling Anadyr now would mean giving up on the grand settlement with the United States that had been his dream since his first visit to Eisenhower in 1959. More than any member of even the Kennedy administration, Khrushchev had become a disciple of the U.S. statesman he had always feared most. He had come around to the unshakable conviction that there was no alternative to John Foster Dulles's policy of peace through strength. Once the Americans were truly afraid of Soviet military power he could get them to accept what he considered a reasonable basis for better relations.

Kennedy's September 4 statement on Cuba complicated this strategy, especially when three days later the White House seemed to give it teeth by requesting stand-by authority to call up 150,000 reservists. The Soviet leader had not expected a U.S. invasion of Cuba until just before the presidential election in 1964, if at all. The statement and the call-up, however, raised the possibility that instead of the Berlin crisis that he wanted, he might end up facing a military confrontation over Cuba in the fall. Too committed to his grand strategy to back down, Khrushchev made two decisions on September 7. First, he asked the Ministry of Defense to assign twelve tactical nuclear weapons to the Soviet motorized brigades already deployed in Cuba.[50] Unlike the strategic missiles, which could strike targets in the United States, these missiles had a range of less than forty miles and were intended solely for use on the battlefield. Also unlike the strategic missiles, these were missiles that

Khrushchev was prepared to use against the United States should U.S. Marines attack Soviet positions on the island.

Fearing that Kennedy might be planning an attack in the near future, Khrushchev asked the Ministry of Defense to send the tactical missiles by plane. But here his military advisers successfully advocated caution. Were any of the planes carrying these munitions to crash, there might be a nuclear incident. Instead these tactical nuclear weapons, known as Lunas, to the Russians and Frogs to the Americans, could go by the ship *Indigirka*, already slated to carry the warheads for the medium-range ballistic missiles.

Khrushchev's second decision on September 7 was to instruct the Soviet Navy to bolster the security of the ships carrying the nuclear missiles and to increase the firepower of the flotilla sent to protect the island. He wanted submarines with nuclear-tipped torpedoes to trail the ships carrying the warheads as they made their way to Cuba and then to be permanently stationed in the Caribbean.

As these military changes took place, Khrushchev sought to deter any rash U.S. action with words. On September 11 the TASS news agency issued an official warning to Washington that Moscow had the right to help the Cubans defend themselves and that any attack on Cuba or on the Soviet ships on their way to that island would be interpreted as an attack on the Soviet Union.[51]

The unintended consequence of Khrushchev's reaction to the Kennedy announcement and the call-up was to delay further the deployment of the long-range missiles in Cuba. The shortage in Soviet shipping meant that sending the Luna short-range missiles would delay the dispatch of the ballistic missiles. The two ships carrying the intermediate-range ballistic missiles, the R-14s, were now rescheduled to arrive in Cuba between November 3 and November 5.[52] Khrushchev was apparently not worried. He had decided not to do anything about Berlin until after the U.S. congressional elections on November 6, and he was determined to first make his case at the UN.[53] In mid-September 1962 a couple of days one way or the other did not seem to make a difference.

■

As HE MADE these momentous decisions, Khrushchev met with two distinguished Americans at Pitsunda, the poet Robert Frost and the U.S. Secretary of the Interior Stewart Udall. Khrushchev was careful not to reveal his plans to either of these men. The aged Frost was touring the Soviet Union to give poetry recitals and talk up peace. He expected to meet Khrushchev and tell him, in a crusty but grandfatherly way, that the Soviet leader would have to stop "blackguarding" to create the right climate for superpower concilia-tion. Khrushchev acted gently with the eighty-eight-year-old poet, who fell mildly ill at Pitsunda, but raised with him the question of whether Kennedy was a strong enough man to fight for peace. Frost did not understand that Khrushchev was calculating the president's reaction to a choice of war or compromise peace over Berlin.[54] With Udall, Khrushchev was tough, hinting broadly that soon Soviet power would reach a point where it could compel the United States to do things that it didn't want to do. "Now, we can swat your ass," he said.[55]

He did, however, leak to another Westerner that something very big was in the offing. Khrushchev decided to tell the West German ambassador to the Soviet Union, Hans Kroll, of his strategy for the coming Berlin crisis. Khrushchev knew that Kroll had been punished for his efforts to improve Soviet–West German relations. The pro-Washington faction in the West German Foreign Ministry had considered Kroll too friendly with Khrushchev. The only explanation for his survival was that Kroll seemed to have Adenauer's personal backing. Khrushchev had found the ambassador intelli-gent and understanding, and the fact that Adenauer kept him around had always deepened the mystery of the clever German leader. But by September 1962 Kroll's luck had run out, and he was about to replaced in Moscow.

Khrushchev had a soft spot for Kroll, who since his days as a junior foreign service officer in the 1920s had been an advocate of making better relations with the Russians a cardinal point in West German foreign policy. Kroll was not a Communist, but the Russian-speaking diplomat believed that geogra-phy and culture made Russians, whatever the ideology of their regime, essen-tial trade and political partners. Since 1958 he had figured in Khrushchev's efforts to interest elements of the West German government in a special rela-tionship with Moscow. Now that Kroll was being reassigned, Khrushchev let down his guard somewhat and talked more openly than he had with any other foreigner. Kroll went alone to the meeting, and Khrushchev was accom-panied only by a senior member of the Soviet Foreign Ministry.[56]

After some time spent discussing Kroll's difficulties with the pro-American faction in the West German Foreign Ministry, the ambassador asked an indulgence of Khrushchev. The Berlin crisis had ruined Kroll's per-sonal efforts to improve relations between Moscow and Bonn. In 1960 Kroll had told Khrushchev that West Germany could accept a number of conces-sions, including recognition of East Germany and of the new German-Polish border on the Oder-Neisse line, but it could never accept the loss of West Berlin. "And this will always be so," Kroll had insisted. "Berlin is our historical capital and Bonn is only temporary."[57] In the two years since, Khrushchev and Kroll had agreed to disagree on what to do about West Berlin. Now that he was leaving, Kroll wanted to know if Khrushchev would reveal to him Soviet intentions toward Berlin in the remaining months of 1962. Six months earlier Khrushchev had apparently told him that there was no crisis on the horizon, but now the situation seemed different. In its September 11 statement on Cuba the Soviet government had mentioned Berlin in passing. While acknowledging that no resolution of the issue could be expected during a U.S. election season, the statement called for the "earliest conclusion" of a German peace treaty.[58] "Of course, you are not obligated to answer this question now and I would understand," said Kroll. "But when I return to Bonn, the chancellor will in the first instance ask me."[59]

No doubt to Kroll's surprise, Khrushchev did not duck the question. "I have very much enjoyed our meetings," the Soviet leader explained, "and I consider you to have a realistic approach to the necessity of improving relations, to the problems confronting us. I like the energy with which you pushed for the resolution of these problems."

Khrushchev had concluded reluctantly that John Kennedy was a prisoner of domestic U.S. politics. The United States had a president who lacked the courage to lead his people to a Cold War settlement with the Soviet Union. "I have regularly said in my meetings with Americans: if only Kennedy rose to the occasion and understood his obligation before history to resolve international problems!" Khrushchev told Kroll that the U.S. president was making a grave political error: "If only Kennedy understood that in solving the Berlin problem and thus consolidating peace, 90% of Americans (and not just Americans) would carry him in their arms."

So Kennedy had to be forced into making that historic decision. "We now have the freedom to choose when to implement this act," explained Khrushchev. The Soviet Union would wait until after the congressional elections of November 6; then it would push for the establishment of a free city of West Berlin. "We have already prepared everything for this," he added.

"But aren't the Americans still against this?" Kroll asked skeptically.

Khrushchev explained the thinking behind his strategy of détente through fear: "I believe that Kennedy needs us to take the first step. Kennedy cannot be the first to say, 'I agree to take my troops from West Berlin.' Why? Because Adenauer and de Gaulle would use this against him. Kennedy is waiting to be pushed to the brink—agreement or war? Of course, he will not want war; he will concede. No rational being could not but agree with us."

There were things Khrushchev did not tell Kroll. He did not reveal that the source of his confidence was the fact that forty Soviet nuclear missiles would soon be deployed in Cuba. Yet he did not completely avoid discussing Cuba with Kroll. At the end of the conversation, only minutes after laying out the psychological game of brinkmanship he intended to play with the American president, Khrushchev of his own accord raised the issue of Cuba. He didn't give away the entire strategy, but his comment revealed that his greatest concern was not the possibility of a U.S. invasion of the island. "Kennedy claims that Cuba is threatening America. This is idiocy. For this reason we issued today's appeal to America that were they to renounce the call-up of the reserves and reestablish normal relations with Cuba, then Cuba would not need to get weapons from us."

Thanks to Khrushchev, Kroll almost had enough to connect the dots. Between the lines the Russian had revealed his plan for what he would do sometime after November 6. "I don't know on which day we will sign the peace treaty with the GDR," he said. His Foreign Ministry had prepared all the documentation required to set up the new free state of West Berlin and to structure UN participation in the removal of NATO forces from the city. Khrushchev intended this to be the final crisis over Berlin.

Kroll understood the importance of what he had been told. Perhaps because Khrushchev knew he had revealed too much, he went out of his way to tell the West German that there was "nothing confidential" about his thinking on Kennedy's likely reaction to the next crisis. "It seems I have already started talking about this," he said. But Khrushchev hadn't, and Kroll had reason to believe that his information was important. That same day, September 11, he communicated with the U.S. Embassy in Moscow and with the Canadian ambassador about his meeting with Khrushchev and warned that a major Berlin crisis was brewing. But Kroll had little credibility with his Western colleagues. He had always seemed too close to Khrushchev for their liking. The State Department received a report on Kroll's statements on September 14, and within four days this information reached the White House. It appears that only the office of the vice president took special notice. "Khrushchev stated quite emphatically to Kroll just before he left Moscow," wrote Johnson's military aide, Colonel Howard Burris, "that Soviet actions leading to a separate peace treaty will begin soon and in time to permit recourse to the UN if such an action appears appropriate or necessary."[60] He added ominously: "Khrushchev has come to the conclusion that Western leaders have proven themselves so anxious to avoid conflict that they will accept the treaty and accommodate themselves to it." Frustrated that Kroll's warning was not being taken seriously, Johnson's military aide concluded his report: "Our diplomats and certain political appointees seem unable or unwilling to accept the fact that it is impossible to negotiate politely with the Soviets on an issue like Berlin. The Russians traditionally, and especially the Communists more recently, understand and respond only to recognized strength and willingness to apply it, and to firmly and clearly stated intentions to do so in support of national policy or position." President Kennedy was already convinced that Khrushchev was seeking a confrontation over Berlin. This warning from a mistrusted West German diplomat, however, did not force Vice President Johnson and his military aide to consider why Khrushchev might have thought that an ultimatum in November 1962 could wrench concessions from United States when the very same tactic had failed miserably in 1958 and 1961. Nor did this new information force a reappraisal from the CIA. On September 13 the agency produced an update of its special estimate on Soviet tactics toward Berlin. Perhaps having heard about the Kroll conversation before the State Department heard, it noted that "the Soviets have recently encouraged rumors that they will raise the Berlin issue this fall at the General Assembly," but it did not believe a major U.S.-Soviet confrontation any more likely than it had in August.[61]

Meanwhile Kroll realized that his warnings were not being taken seriously by his own government, let alone by West Germany's allies. On September 28 he went public. FINAL FIGHT FOR BERLIN IN FOUR WEEKS was the headline in the conservative *Deutsche Soldaten-Zeitung und National-Zeitung* above a lengthy interview with the former West German ambassador to the USSR.[62] Kroll predicted that Khrushchev planned a "dramatic development" after the midterm congressional elections in the United States. He expected the Soviets to sign a separate peace treaty with East Germany and to end immediately NATO access to West Berlin. Kroll admitted that the source of his predictions was his conversation with Khrushchev.

Curiously, it appears that none of Khrushchev's socialist allies, including East Germany, received anything close to this kind of tipoff about the November strategy. In the fall of 1962 Khrushchev and Ulbricht were exchanging letters on ways to improve East German agriculture.[63] The socialist who may have received the clearest warning of the complexity of the fall offensive was Prince Souphanouvong, who visited with Aleksei Kosygin on September 28, while Khrushchev was on a tour of Central Asia. The Pathet Lao had always suspected that Moscow would trade it for some advantage in Berlin, and the Kremlin wanted to set its mind at ease. "We are in for more battles with the American imperialist in the diplomatic arena," Kosygin revealed to the Laotian partisan. "It will involve, in particular, the Berlin question, Cuba and other issues."[64]

▪

In mid-September the Soviet Navy responded to Khrushchev's request for more security for the Cuban missile operation. Khrushchev had asked for special protection for the ships carrying nuclear warheads. On September 18 the Soviet Defense Council supplied him with an ambitious plan to send a convoy to Cuba, involving seven Golf missile submarines and four Foxtrot torpedo submarines, two cruisers, two cruise missile ships, two destroyers, and a host of auxiliary ships. The goal was for most of the flotilla to reach Cuba on November 9. Given that it would take the submarines twice as long to reach Cuba as the surface ships, the submarines would leave the Kola Peninsula on October 7. Besides providing defense for Cuba, they would be responsible for protecting the ships carrying the R-14 missiles and warheads. The bulk of the surface ships would leave around October 20 and were to catch up with the submarines south of Bermuda, where the Soviet Navy wanted to hold a three-day naval exercise at the beginning of November. The ships carrying the R-14 missiles and their nuclear warheads, as well as their submarine escorts, were due to arrive earlier than November 9.[65]

The Soviet Navy knew that if the Americans detected that some of the ships had submarine escorts, Washington might discover the importance of the cargoes. Foxtrot submarines had diesel engines that required them to surface periodically to run those engines and recharge the batteries that the submarines used when submerged. Consequently, the navy recommended that they stay submerged during the day and surface only at night.

Another important change was that in the original plan the Golf and Foxtrot submarines were not intended to carry nuclear weapons. In the Defense Ministry's new plan, the submarines were to be armed with nuclear weapons, and the commanders of the Golf submarines were to receive a special target list so that "upon the signal from Moscow [they could] launch an attack on the most important coastal targets of the US."[66]

Khrushchev's level of anxiety in mid-September was far too high for him to approve Malinovsky's revised naval plan in its entirety. A few days earlier the military had reported to the Presidium that in the first twelve days of September alone, the United States had flown fifty reconnaissance flights over fifteen different Soviet ships. With the United States and NATO keeping such a tight watch on his Cuban convoys, Khrushchev feared the international reaction to the movement of two cruisers and two destroyers to Cuba. He also considered the recommended submarine force too large and instructed Malinovsky to drop the idea of sending the seven Golf submarines with their nuclear-tipped ballistic missiles to Cuba. In their place Khrushchev approved sending only the four Foxtrot-class diesel subs with nuclear-tipped torpedoes.

The *Indigirka*, with the warheads for both the Luna missiles, and the short-range FKR cruise missiles, a nuclear system that had been included in the original Anadyr plan, had left the USSR on September 16, before the revision of the Soviet Navy plan.[67] According to the previous plan, it had not been provided with a submarine escort. So that it would be protected once it neared U.S. waters, the navy suggested dispatching one of the its lone ballistic missile submarines, the Zulu-class B-75, to meet up with the *Indigirka* near Bermuda. At that moment the B-75 was on patrol along the U.S. coastline, waiting for an order to launch its two R-11f nuclear missiles against coastal targets.[68]

These military decisions allayed much of Khrushchev's concern, and by the end of September his attention had returned to ending the Cold War in November. On the twenty-eighth he sent the White House a letter proposing a new basis for a test ban treaty.[69] With agreement unlikely on how to verify compliance with a ban, Khrushchev said he would accept a treaty that banned all tests in the atmosphere, in space, and underwater that did not require inspection on Soviet soil. He stipulated, however, that the three nuclear powers—Great Britain, the United States, and the Soviet Union—would also have to observe a five-year moratorium on all underground tests while negotiations on this issue continued. If agreement on a permanent ban on underground testing could not be reached in five years, the parties would then be free to reconsider the atmospheric test ban treaty. He ended the letter with an ominous reference to the superpower disagreement over West Berlin, describing it as a "dangerous hot-bed."[70] He added: "We on our part again say to you that we will do nothing with regard to West Berlin until the elections in the U.S. After the elections, apparently in the second half of November, it would be necessary in our opinion to continue the dialogue." He then hinted that he was eager for another summit with Kennedy to discuss all these issues, perhaps as early as November. "Of great importance for finding ways to solve both this problem [Berlin] and other pressing international problems," he wrote, "are personal contacts of statesmen on the highest level."[71]

■

G EORGI BOLSHAKOV, the Kennedy family's favorite Russian, had been out of touch while visiting the Soviet Union for a few weeks. He returned to the United States with a special message for the president from Khrushchev. On October 8 he met with Bobby Kennedy to ask that a meeting be set up for him with the president.[72]

Bolshakov found his friend quite downcast that day. He "was in an unusually gloomy mood," he later reported to Dobrynin at the embassy. Robert Kennedy stressed how concerned he was by the turn taken in Soviet-American relations while Bolshakov had been away. "Speaking candidly," said Kennedy, "the Soviet Union's most recent steps regarding Cuba have angered the president, and we take them to be measures directed against us." He added that the president had to be especially sensitive to these changes because of the midterm election.

Kennedy did not ask what Khrushchev's motives were, and Bolshakov offered nothing but the remark that the Soviet leader had stressed that "in order to resolve the issues in a reasonable fashion we must proceed from the real correlation of forces, to respect the sovereign right of other countries, not interfering in their domestic affairs." Khrushchev had not revealed to Bolshakov the Anadyr secret and why by November he would be very comfortable with the "real correlation of forces."

Robert Kennedy had some bad news for the Soviets regarding the prospects for negotiations. He told Bolshakov that the president was writing a response to Khrushchev's September 28 letter that would probably disappoint the Kremlin. It was impossible for Kennedy ever to agree to remove all Western troops from West Berlin, as Khrushchev had stipulated taking place over four years after the signature of an agreement. It was also impossible for the president to agree to a five-year moratorium on underground testing in return for an atmospheric test ban.

Kennedy asked Bolshakov if Khrushchev intended to come to the United Nations that fall. It is doubtful that the go-between knew any details of Khrushchev's coming political offensive. However, his response to the attorney general left open the possibility of some kind of special visit. "Khrushchev does not intend to come to the General Assembly of the United Nations before the congressional elections," said Bolshakov. "However, if the need arises for Khrushchev to speak before the General Assembly, then he could come to New York after the elections." Kennedy refused to comment.

The next day, October 9, President Kennedy shared his concerns with the French foreign minister, Maurice Couve de Murville, about what Khrushchev might have in store for November. The question, he said, was "how much risk they [the Western powers] were prepared to take." Kennedy thought it "not unlikely" that Khrushchev would come to the United States in November "under cover of the General Assembly in order to talk over Berlin with the President." Ominously, the president concluded that "as a result of the Soviet actions on Cuba," by which he meant a defensive weapons buildup, "there was much less prospect of reaching agreement on Berlin." "Khrushchev," Kennedy added, "might try to force something."[73]

■

K HRUSHCHEV'S EXACT scenario for November, if it was ever spelled out on paper, has not been found. But the elements were coming together. By November 6 the missiles would be in Cuba and operational, and his Foreign Ministry would have prepared boilerplate for formal agreements on the establishment of a UN presence in West Berlin and the withdrawal of Western troops. In addition, he would have a draft test ban treaty that he could offer Kennedy as a sweetener once the president had swallowed the retreat from Berlin.[74] So long as the secret deployment to Cuba could hold for another five weeks, Khrushchev believed that John Kennedy would have no choice but to accept Soviet terms for ending the Cold War in 1962.

19

CUBAN MISSILE CRISIS

HE UNRAVELING OF Khrushchev's grandest ploy began with a flight of an American U-2. Once again U.S. technology proved the Soviet leader's undoing. One week after Attorney General Kennedy's meeting with Bolshakov in early October 1962, McGeorge Bundy brought bad news to John Kennedy along with his morning newspapers. Bundy had been one of those who had advised Kennedy in September that it was highly unlikely that Khrushchev would install strategic weapons in Cuba. Now, on October 16, he carried photographs of what photo interpreters at the CIA believed were medium-range ballistic missile sites in Cuba. Oleg Penkovsky, the CIA's agent in the GRU, who had proved so useful in the Berlin crisis a year earlier, had turned over manuals on the R-12s that helped the analysts make sense of the photographs. There was really no doubt in their minds. Bundy made clear to the president that there should be no doubt in his either.

Kennedy immediately decided that the United States could not accept the deployment of Soviet missiles to Cuba. Although Secretary of Defense McNamara assured him that these missiles would not erode America's advantage in the strategic balance of power, the president sensed that the missiles might tip the psychological balance in Khrushchev's favor. Just one month earlier the United States had warned of the unacceptability of any deployment of Soviet offensive weapons to Cuba and had singled out missiles as an offensive weapon. The Kremlin had subsequently promised in public and through back channels that its military supply program in Cuba did not include missiles. American allies, let alone the American people, would doubt the credibility of the U.S. president's word if he suddenly turned around and accepted the missiles as a fait accompli.

Over the next six days Kennedy met secretly with his Cuban team, a group centered on the attorney general, the vice president, McNamara, Bundy, John McCone of the CIA, Secretary of State Dean Rusk and his undersecretary, U. Alexis Johnson, Treasury Secretary C. Douglas Dillon, General Maxwell Taylor, the Chairman of the Joint Chiefs of Staff, Kennedy's speechwriter, Ted Sorensen, and his chief Sovietologist, Llewellyn Thompson. Ultimately called the Executive Committee of the National Security Council, or Excomm, this group discussed and occasionally debated how to go about removing the missiles.

Kennedy's initial preference was for a surprise air strike that cleaned out the missiles before they became a threat to the United States. U.S. intelligence believed they were not yet operational. The weaknesses of this response became apparent to Kennedy as the discussion proceeded. "How effective can the takeout be?" he asked on October 16.[1] "It'll never be a hundred percent, Mr. President, we know," replied General Maxwell Taylor. "We hope to take out a vast majority in the first strike." No military commander could promise Kennedy that all the sites that had been found could be destroyed in a single attack, and no one dared suggest that all the Soviet sites had been discovered. The other military option, a massive invasion of Cuba with ground forces, was no more attractive. The Pentagon estimated it would take a week to get all the necessary troops into position for an invasion, and it did not wish to start moving any troops until after an air strike had removed the missiles. Any earlier movement would eliminate the element of surprise.

There was an additional telling argument against a surprise attack. Robert Kennedy reminded his brother that nothing defined treachery for their generation more than the Japanese decision to launch a surprise attack on Pearl Harbor. President Kennedy, who kept pushing for some certainty that an air strike alone would work, came to agree that Moscow would have to get some kind of warning.

The risks associated with each attack scenario were so great that Kennedy also began to consider how the issue might be resolved diplomatically. On October 18 he had his favorite speechwriter, Theodore Sorensen, begin drafting a letter to Khrushchev that would offer negotiations.[2] But in the end neither Sorensen nor, more important, Kennedy found a way to begin the process diplomatically without appearing weak. Instead Kennedy became increasingly fond of a suggestion that came from his defense secretary, Robert McNamara. A naval blockade or quarantine of Cuba would put pressure on the Soviets while giving Khrushchev the opportunity to consider if he wanted to plunge the world into war.[3] Initially the blockade could do nothing about the missiles already on the island, so Kennedy believed U.S. military preparations would have to continue in the event an attack against the existing launch sites became unavoidable. The United States would meanwhile seek the support of its allies in the hemisphere and in NATO to present a united front to Khrushchev.

■

THE INTENSIVE POLICY discussions in the White House passed completely unnoticed by the Kremlin until October 22. While it was already afternoon in Moscow, both the local KGB and GRU stations began reporting on unusual activity at the White House and the Pentagon that morning.[4] A few hours later, at 1:30 P.M., eastern daylight time, Pierre Salinger announced to the press that the president would be making a speech to the nation at 7:00 P.M. about "a matter of national importance."[5] Soviet intelligence could not divine on which foreign policy problem Kennedy would speak. "The press emphasizes," wrote the GRU resident from Washington, "that the reasons for this official activity remain top secret. It is assumed that this has to do with the possibility of new measures regarding Cuba or Berlin."[6]

Khrushchev reacted quickly to the news from Washington, concluding that whatever the American president had to say would affect his grandiose plans for November. He also suspected that Kennedy would have something to say about Cuba. Just a few days earlier Khrushchev had read reports on Soviet Foreign Minister Gromyko's recent meetings with Kennedy and Rusk. These had taken place on October 18 in Washington as Gromyko made his way home to Moscow from a session at the United Nations. In these reports Khrushchev detected a hardening of the U.S. position on Fidel Castro.[7]

Khrushchev had fellow Presidium member Frol Kozlov arrange a special night session of the Presidium. Kozlov shared Khrushchev's belief that the Kremlin was about to face a crisis over Cuba. When Mikoyan asked for the reason behind this unscheduled meeting, Kozlov answered, "We are awaiting Kennedy's important speech on Cuba."[8] Both the Soviet defense minister, Marshal Malinovsky, and Colonel General Ivanov, the chief of the main operational department of the Soviet general staff, were invited to the meeting. In keeping with Khrushchev's main preoccupation, Malinovsky collected whatever information he could on the status of U.S. forces in the Caribbean, and Ivanov prepared a briefing on the status of Soviet forces in Cuba.

Despite the convictions of some of the top men in the Kremlin, the agenda item for this meeting—"further actions regarding Cuba and Berlin"— betrayed the deep uncertainty in the Kremlin about the crisis to come.[9] A month earlier Khrushchev had confidently told the West German ambassador

Hans Kroll that he would be the one to choose when the next crisis in U.S.-Soviet relations took place. With news of the impending speech by Kennedy, Khrushchev had to recognize that he had lost control of events.

■

THE PRESIDIUM MEETING that started at 10:00 P.M., Moscow time, on Monday, October 22, 1962, was arguably the most tense of Khrushchev's career. "It has become known," the Soviet leader began in opening the meeting attended by all twelve members of the Presidium, "that Kennedy has prepared some kind of speech."[10] He said he believed the coming crisis involved Cuba. The Soviet press service TASS was already reporting, inaccurately as it turned out, "a concentration of ships of the U.S. Navy with marines." It was 3:00 P.M. in Washington, with four hours to go before Kennedy was to speak.

Khrushchev gave the floor to Malinovsky, who reassured the members of the leadership that the United States was not preparing a preemptive strike of any kind. "Lightninglike actions," he said, were unlikely. "If Kennedy announces an invasion," he assured the Kremlin, "there will still be enough time for us to prepare."[11] The GRU team in Havana was responsible for watching Florida. That morning it redoubled its long-standing efforts to intercept U.S. military communications.[12] It had picked up a new concentration of forces in Florida, but there still was no evidence that an attack on Cuba was likely in the near future. Consequently, Malinovsky reported that he was quite convinced that the Presidium would have some time to deal with whatever Kennedy had to say. If anything, the Soviet defense minister seemed a little cocksure. "Kennedy's radio address will be some kind of pre-election trick." Malinovsky did not believe it was as yet necessary to put the Soviet R-12s in Cuba, which had arrived there in late September, in a higher state of readiness.

General Ivanov of the general staff followed Malinovsky to report on the status of Soviet forces in and around the island. Following Khrushchev's Pitsunda decision, Ivanov had formalized the operational procedures for the Soviet Group of Forces in Cuba. In September he instructed General Igor Statsenko, the commander of the R-12 and R-14 missile detachments, to await a signal from Moscow before launching the missiles.[13] Ivanov explained to the Presidium that some of the R-12s on Cuba were operational.[14] All their warheads had arrived on the *Indigirka* before the crisis started. However, because of the changes to the Anadyr plan in September, the missiles and warheads for the longer-range R-14 missiles were not on the island. They were still en route, and it would be some time before they could be deployed. The ships carrying the R-14 missiles, the *Kasimov* and the *Krasnodar*, were not even halfway to Cuba.

The short-range or tactical missiles that Khrushchev had requested in September were also on the island. The *Indigirka* had also delivered twelve Luna missiles and forty-two FKR cruise missiles and their nuclear warheads. By the time of the meeting on October 22 the Luna had been integrated into the Soviet infantry units, and the cruise missiles deployed to coastal sites as well as near the Cuban border with the U.S. naval base at Guantánamo. The infantry units and the coastal installations were designed to protect the island and the Soviet long-range missiles against any attempt by the United States or Cuban émigrés to invade. Moscow retained control over the Lunas' and the FKRs' nuclear warheads, which were at a special warhead facility under the control of General Nikolai Beloborodov and some miles away from the infantry units and coastal installations.

Despite this impressive display of Soviet might already on the island, Khrushchev was depressed by the prospect of Kennedy's speech. A rumor reached KGB headquarters that he had been heard saying, "Lenin's work is destroyed," much as Stalin is said to have feared the collapse of the Soviet Union in the first hours of the German attack in June 1941.[15] Khrushchev realized that his effort to alter the strategic balance might actually lead to the one thing he most wished to avoid, a nuclear war. Khrushchev betrayed his inner turmoil to the men in the room: "The point is we didn't want to unleash a war. All we wanted to do was to threaten them, to restrain them with regard to Cuba."[16] The United States had missile bases all around the Soviet Union that "have restrained us," he acknowledged. Why could the USSR not have one of its own?[17]

Although he said that he "agreed with Comrade Malinovsky's conclusions," the Soviet leader did not share his defense minister's confidence that Kennedy wasn't about to launch an attack on Cuba. Since the Bay of Pigs Khrushchev had increasingly acted on the assumption that John Kennedy was not fully in control of the U.S. government. In Khrushchev's opinion, the militarists and the imperialists swirling around the White House were able to influence Kennedy to a larger extent than, in retrospect, they had shaped Eisenhower's actions abroad. Khrushchev reminded his colleagues of Kennedy's statements to Gromyko on October 18. "Kennedy chose his words very carefully when speaking about Cuba," he concluded from reading the Soviet transcript.[18] Even more disquieting was what the U.S. secretary of state had said. "During the meeting," Khrushchev said, "[Rusk] led and got drunk on the discussion about Berlin, while actually alluding to Cuba." He added with unease, "Rusk told Gromyko that Cuba was for the United States as Hungary was for us."[19] This was exactly the same simile that had first worried Khrushchev earlier in the year, when his son-in-law, Aleksei Adzhubei, reported on his January 30 conversation with Kennedy.

Khrushchev believed that the United States had been looking for a pretext to attack Cuba for some time and that the impending speech meant the Americans had found one. "The tragedy is that they can attack, and we shall respond. This may end in a big war."[20] Khrushchev concluded pessimistically, "Our problem is that we didn't deploy everything we wanted to and we didn't publish the treaty." For reasons he did not explain at the meeting, Khrushchev believed that the twenty-four R-12 nuclear-tipped missiles that were already on the island were not enough of a deterrent to protect the Cubans. Instead of suggesting that Moscow immediately declare that it already had nuclear missiles in Cuba, a military fact that might deter the Americans from taking any further action against Cuba, Khrushchev was wringing his hands because he had not taken the advice of the Cubans in late August and published the Soviet-Cuban defense agreement. Somehow he believed that this agreement would make a deeper impression on Kennedy than the half-completed Anadyr operation. Curiously, as Khrushchev explained himself that night, he never seemed to consider using Soviet power anywhere else in the world to prevent an attack on Cuba. At no point, for example, did he suggest threatening NATO's vulnerable outpost in West Berlin.

Newly available minutes from the meeting clarify how Khrushchev viewed the alternatives that night. After expressing his anxieties, he laid out a series of options in rapid sequence. "We could announce on the radio that there is already a [Soviet-Cuban defense] agreement regarding Cuba," said Khrushchev. He then asked himself, "How would the United States react to this?" Khrushchev estimated the three most likely outcomes: "They could announce a blockade of a Cuba and do nothing else; they could seize our ships that are on their way to Cuba; or they could stop thinking about attacking Cuba."[21]

Khrushchev felt it prudent that the Kremlin prepare itself for how it would respond in case Kennedy launched an invasion of Cuba. He wondered aloud whether it would be useful, if the worst came to pass, to transfer control of the nuclear weapons to the Cubans. "In the case of an attack, all means could be with the Cubans, who will announce that they will respond."[22] Otherwise he told his colleagues that the Soviet forces would have to be prepared to use the tactical nuclear weapons to defend their position and the Castro regime, though "not for the time being the strategic weapons."[23]

With these options outlined, Khrushchev called for a five- to ten-minute break, "so that comrades could consider and express their own opinion."[24] There is no evidence that the Kremlin leadership had ever before taken the time to think through how they might use the force that had been sent on their orders twelve thousand miles to Cuba. In May they had been asked to endorse the deployment for purely political reasons. In September Khrushchev alone had decided to add the Lunas to the force. Soviet military doctrine accepted the use of tactical weapons on the battlefield—it was also accepted NATO doctrine—but there was no specific plan for how these might be used in Cuba. An order that would have assigned responsibility to the Soviet commander in Cuba to determine whether or not to use them depending on the situation had never been signed at the Soviet Defense Ministry. The other tactical weapons, the FKR cruise missiles, had belonged to the original plan in May, but it seems that here too their use was never considered by the Soviet Union's political leadership until around eleven on the night of October 22.

∎

AFTER THE SHORT RECESS the Kremlin leaders received two useful bits of information. From the Foreign Ministry came news that the U.S. State Department had informed Ambassador Dobrynin that the Soviet Embassy would receive a copy of Kennedy's remarks an hour before the speech, at 1:00 A.M. Moscow time. The Defense Ministry added that a report had just come in from Soviet military intelligence sources in Moscow of consultations taking place among the European ambassadors of the NATO countries and those of South American countries.

After hearing the reports, Anastas Mikoyan and fifty-nine-year-old Mikhail Suslov, longtime members of the Presidium, expressed anxiety about the deteriorating situation in the Caribbean and their belief that a U.S. attack on Cuba was imminent. Khrushchev did not disagree. This was the reason he had wanted his colleagues to consider what to do in extremis. It was time, he believed, to consider the instructions that Moscow would send to its commander in Cuba, General Issa Pliyev. Khrushchev already had something in mind. "Bring [the units] to a condition of military readiness," he dictated. "At first do not deploy the atomic [weapons] with all the forces." In his current frame of mind a cautious instruction like this would not be enough for him. "If there is a [U.S.] landing,"—Khrushchev continued to dictate—"[use] the tactical atomic weapons, but [not] the strategic weapons until [there is] an order."[25] He then had the defense minister read the draft instruction to the group.

Once more, as he had done at key moments since 1958, Mikoyan stood up to Khrushchev and pleaded for moderation. Mikoyan did not like what he was hearing. "Doesn't using these missiles mean the start of a thermonuclear war?" he sternly asked Malinovsky.[26] The defense minister stumbled in his reply and failed to satisfy Mikoyan that he appreciated the seriousness of the situation.[27]

Mikoyan also criticized the option of transferring control of the missiles to the Cubans, either now or later in the crisis.[28] "If the Americans were to understand that the missiles are under our control, they would proceed from the assumption that we would not attempt some kind of [nuclear] adventure since we know what the consequences would be." But this would not be so if Washington thought Castro had his finger on the button. "If they found out that the missiles belonged to the masters of the island, then they would take it as some kind of provocation." Mikoyan believed Washington might calculate that the Cubans were capable of firing off the missiles. In this moment of maximum peril, Mikoyan wanted to eliminate any doubt the Americans might have that the missiles were and would remain under Soviet control.

With the elevation of many of his protégés in the late 1950s and early 1960s, Khrushchev had grown more powerful than he had been in November 1958, when Mikoyan had forced him to back down from unilaterally ending U.S. occupation rights in West Berlin. Nevertheless, the wily forty-year Kremlin veteran still commanded respect, especially on matters of foreign policy. In 1961 he had successfully discouraged Khrushchev from shooting down a Western airplane over East Germany to demonstrate his impatience at the slow progress of negotiations over Berlin. Mikoyan's words this night put Khrushchev on the defensive.

"We'll keep the missiles as Soviet property under our exclusive control," said Khrushchev, who accepted Mikoyan's point about not provoking Washington by handing them over to Castro. However, he refused to give in on the larger issue of whether Moscow's nuclear weapons should be used at all to save the Castro regime. "If we do not use nuclear weapons," said Khrushchev, "then they could capture Cuba."[29] If Khrushchev had hoped for backing from his handpicked defense minister at this crucial moment, he did not get it. "The forces that the Americans have in the Caribbean," said Malinovsky, "are not enough to seize the island."[30] Even given this more optimistic assessment from his defense chief, Khrushchev was not prepared to concede the point on using tactical nuclear weapons. "The Americans could shell from their rocket carriers [destroyers and missile sites in Florida]," he argued, "without sending any airplanes."[31]

At this point in the discussion another senior Presidium member, First Deputy Premier Aleksei Kosygin, intervened. His contribution appears lost to history. Neither of the Presidium scribes at that meeting, Vladimir Malin and Aleksandr Serov, noted it down. However, after Kosygin spoke, the focus of the discussion shifted dramatically. Whatever he said had persuaded the group to stop thinking about when to use nuclear weapons and to start thinking about how to control events so that the situation did not escalate into a nuclear war. Even if the strategic missiles were not used, nuclear war could begin after Moscow fired its tactical force to defend against a U.S. landing. Each of the Luna tactical missiles deployed with the Soviet military in Cuba had a range of thirty-one miles and a 2-kiloton nuclear warhead, enough to irradiate an area a thousand yards from the center of the blast. The thirty-six FKR cruise missiles already deployed to the island were even more powerful. These missiles, which pointed out to sea and were designed to destroy invasion armadas, had a hundred-mile range and carried warheads that varied in destructive power between 5.6 and 12 kilotons of TNT. The Soviets already had enough of them on the island to blow apart a U.S. carrier group.[32]

Khrushchev gave in to the concerns of his colleagues. Vowing that nothing would be done to provoke "the use of nuclear weapons against Cuba," he called for a revision of the instructions to the Soviet commander on the island. This time they read that in the event of a U.S. attack, the Kremlin authorized Pliyev to use "all means except those controlled by Statsenko [Major General Igor D. Statsenko, the commander of the rocket units] and Beloborodov [Colonel Nikolai K. Beloborodov, the controller of the atomic warheads]."[33] Pliyev could use the short-range Luna and the FKR cruise missiles, but only with conventional warheads. Moscow had backed down from using all means at its disposal to fight a battle in Cuba. Once again the cautious Mikoyan had helped prevent the Cold War from turning hot.

Fearful that if U.S. intelligence intercepted this order, the Pentagon might exploit Soviet weakness, Malinovsky suggested that perhaps the instruction not be sent to Pliyev until the Kremlin had had a chance to look at a copy of Kennedy's speech, which the U.S. government had promised to hand over to the Russians at 1:00 A.M. "Otherwise," he said, "they might be given a pretext to use the atomic weapon."[34]

Despite Malinovsky's reservations, the Kremlin decided not to wait to see the text of Kennedy's speech. At five minutes to midnight the Defense Ministry sent the order to Cuba. For the next hour the Presidium held its collective breath. Then, at 1:15 A.M., V. V. Kuznetsov of the Foreign Ministry brought the leadership a Russian translation of Kennedy's speech. In it, the

U.S. president demanded that the Soviet Union withdraw its nuclear missiles from Cuba and announced a naval blockade of the island, but for the moment no other military action. "It seems to me that by its tone," said Khrushchev, who had quickly scanned his copy, "this is not a war against Cuba but some kind of ultimatum."[35] The room relaxed. Khrushchev then suggested that the session be suspended until the morning, so that they all could get some sleep. He decided to stay in the Kremlin, where he would sleep on a couch in his office and be available for any emergency.

The Presidium broke for the night before making any decision on what to do about the Soviet ships and submarines heading toward the U.S. Navy. Kennedy had not established a blockade zone or line in his speech, vowing only that "all ships of any kind bound for Cuba from whatever nation or port will, if found to contain cargoes of offensive weapons, be turned back."[36] There was some very valuable Soviet offensive weaponry on the high seas. The ships with the R-14s and their warheads were in the North Atlantic steaming south, while the four Foxtrot submarines, which had left their home port on October 1, were nearing Cuba. Each diesel-electric Foxtrot carried a nuclear-tipped torpedo.

The submarines were a little behind schedule. They all had been expected to arrive at the Cuban port of Mariel between October 21 and October 23. The closest to its destination was the Foxtrot later designated C-23 by NATO, which was north of the Bahamas, a two-day sail away.[37] The others were spread in an arc that extended south from Bermuda. The C-18 and C-19 were both more than three hundred miles south of Bermuda, a hard three-day journey away from Cuba, and C-26 was trailing behind the Soviet ship *Aleksandrovsk*, more than two hundred miles northeast of Cuba near the Turks and Caicos Islands. C-26 was protecting the *Aleksandrovsk*, which carried nuclear warheads.[38]

■

KENNEDY HAD NO IDEA of the discussion going on in Moscow. He spent the hours before his speech gathering political support for a step-by-step approach to getting the missiles out of Cuba. Having ruled out a military attack as an opening move, he needed to still any domestic concerns that he was not doing enough while assuring his European and Canadian allies that he was not doing too much. His aides arranged a meeting for him with the leaders of Congress just before he was to appear on television and radio.

The meeting with the congressional leadership took a toll on Kennedy. Senator Richard Russell, the legendary power broker and the formidable chairman of the Armed Services Committee, questioned the administration's decision to buy time at this stage. "My position is that these people have been warned," said Russell. The words brought a tense exchange with the president. "[By waiting to attack,] you will only make it sure that when the time comes, when if they do use these MiGs to attack our shipping or to drop a few bombs around Miami or some other place, and we do go in there, that we'll lose a great many more men than we would right now—" Kennedy responded: "But, Senator, we can't invade Cuba. . . . [I]t takes us some while to assemble our force to invade Cuba." And just so neither the senator nor anyone else in the room doubted his determination, the president added, "We are now assembling that force, but it is not in a position to invade Cuba in the next 24 or 48 hours."[39] Kennedy now made a dire prediction: "Now, I think it may very well come to that before the end of the week."[40]

■

THE SPEECH ITSELF had been ready for a day. Sorensen had incorporated phrases from the State Department and the attorney general. A barometer of the twists and turns in the debate among Kennedy's advisers, the drafting process had taken the better part of a week.

At 7:00 P.M. on October 22, 1962, President Kennedy began a speech that an entire generation later remembered as the start of a week filled with fear and concern. "Good evening, my fellow citizens. This government, as promised, has maintained the closest surveillance of the Soviet military buildup on Cuba." Kennedy was adamant that the missiles could not stay in Cuba. Calling the deployment "a deliberately provocative and unjustified change in the status quo," Kennedy took a page from history to demonstrate his determination. "The 1930s taught us a clear lesson: Aggressive conduct, if allowed to grow unchecked and unchallenged, ultimately leads to war." In announcing a blockade against all ships that were carrying "offensive military" cargoes to Cuba, Kennedy cautioned that this was probably only the first step in what might turn out to be a protracted and bloody crisis. "No one can foresee precisely what course [the crisis] will take or what costs or casualties will be incurred. . . . But the greatest danger of all would be to do nothing."[41]

■

KENNEDY'S CODE BREAKERS in the National Security Agency were soon scanning the airwaves in search of information about the Soviet response to Kennedy's speech. They did not have to wait long. At 11:15 P.M., Washington time, on October 22 (or 6:15 A.M., October 23, in Moscow), less than four hours after Kennedy's speech, the Soviet ships on the high seas were sent what appeared to be an alert telling them to prepare for a special instruction. The messages were sent in a cipher the NSA could not break; however, because the call signs of the message were in the clear, the NSA figured out that something special had been sent. Up to that point the southern port of Odessa had been the originating point for all the messages sent to the Soviet ships plying their way to Cuba. But this time the call sign for Moscow was substituted for Odessa. The American listeners straining to hear these sounds therefore understood that something important was coming. The instruction came in at 12:05 A.M., October 23 (or 7:05 A.M. in Moscow). It seemed to be sent to individual ships and the first dispatch was directed at seven of them. The message went unbroken by the United States. But within less than two hours, through analysis of call signs, the NSA started detecting the ships responding one by one.

It was just a few minutes past dawn on the first day of this international crisis. The first light allowed U.S. ships and airplanes to see what the code breakers could not determine on their own: whether the Soviet ships were staying on course or turning around.[42]

Electronic and aerial snooping was Kennedy's most reliable guide to the developing crisis. On the eve of the crisis the CIA had lost its only mole in the Soviet defense administration. Just before the Presidium met on October 22, the KGB had pounced on Oleg Penkovsky. The day after his arrest Penkovsky signed a letter promising full cooperation. He undertook to provide every detail of his meetings with MI6 and the CIA and offered to work on behalf of the KGB in a sting operation to entrap the Western intelligence services.[43]

As a free man Penkovsky would have been very useful to the Americans in this crisis. There might have been less tension in Washington in the days that followed had the Kennedy administration known that Khrushchev was already looking for a way to avoid war.

■

THE PRESIDIUM RESUMED its discussions at 10:00 A.M., Moscow time, on October 23 with the mood still tense but the leaders relieved that the most dire scenario, a U.S. invasion of Cuba, had not yet played out. Overnight the Soviet Foreign Ministry had studied Kennedy's speech very carefully and then drafted three documents for consideration by the leadership.[44] The first was a general declaration by the Soviet government on the situation in Cuba; the second, a set of instructions for the Soviet ambassador to the United Nations, Valerian Zorin; and the third, a resolution to present to the Security Council condemning the

U.S. action. Soviet representatives were instructed to rally the third world by denying the U.S. charge that there were nuclear missiles in Cuba.

After the Presidium approved these drafts, its first order of business was to draft something to send directly to President Kennedy. Khrushchev took the floor and suggested they offer Kennedy a chance to reconsider the blockade. The U.S. president should be invited to "show prudence and renounce actions pursued by you, which could lead to catastrophic consequences for peace throughout the world."[45] Khrushchev also decided that he would take a slightly different position in his dealings with Kennedy from that which the Soviet Union took publicly. Rather than deny that there were nuclear missiles in Cuba, he suggested language that would assure Kennedy that the weapons were there only for defensive reasons. "Regardless of the weapon's class," Khrushchev dictated, "it has been delivered. [And] it has been delivered to defend against aggression."[46] In July, before this very group, Khrushchev had described the missiles as offensive weapons. Now he hoped that he could convince Kennedy and the world that their only purpose in Cuba was to defend Castro's revolution.

Despite his relief that Kennedy had not announced an attack on Cuba, Khrushchev believed that the Soviet Union would have to revise the Anadyr operation. He was not inclined to test the U.S. blockade for two reasons. Besides wanting to avoid a confrontation that might escalate, he did not want to give the United States the opportunity to capture any of the strategic technology loaded on some of the ships. The two large-hatch ships bearing the R-14 missiles, the *Kasimov* and the *Krasnodar*, were still very far from Cuba.

Khrushchev wondered aloud whether all the ships carrying weapons should not be ordered to return immediately. In the end he decided that the ships already in the Atlantic should go no farther than the approaches to Cuba until the situation was clearer.[47] Ships still in the Mediterranean were to return to their Black Sea ports immediately. But there remained the question of the *Aleksandrovsk*, the ship carrying warheads for the R-14s and some of the shore-based FKR cruise missiles. It was a day away from Cuban shores. The Presidium decided to take a risk on bringing it to shore as quickly as possible.[48]

Aware that these changes in the operation might upset the Cubans, Khrushchev recommended telling Castro that the operation "was halfway successful." He wanted to let the crisis die down, and then, "if necessary, it will be possible to send the [R-14] missiles again." Khrushchev wanted Havana to understand that his immediate priority was to stabilize the situation in the area and establish, through the UN, Cuba's right to have whatever weapons it deemed necessary to defend itself.

Khrushchev thought the submarine escorts were a different matter from the surface ships. He believed the submarines might still be of use in defending Cuba, and he also believed they could travel undetected to the Cuban port of Mariel. The records of the October 23 meeting are fragmentary.[49] From these fragments and Mikoyan's recollections it appears that the Soviet leadership had not been briefed on even the basics of U.S. antisubmarine capabilities. As almost every Soviet submariner knew, even the quietest submarine in 1962—and they were veritable jukeboxes compared with what was to be commissioned by both navies later—emitted an array of sounds and impulses, from the dropped teaspoon on board to the grinding of the propulsion screws to the electric impulses of the batteries that kept everything working. On any given day, specially outfitted U.S. Navy Orion planes crisscrossed the Atlantic and the Caribbean, listening for these sounds, using sensors dropped into the water. Whenever they thought they heard something, they reported it to a ship, which began using sonar, a process called pinging by U.S. sailors and throwing peas by their Soviet counterparts. The sonar was very effective at locating the noisy Foxtrots.

Indeed, after October 16 the Soviet submarines had begun reporting home that they could hear a lot of ship activity.[50] Although the Soviets did not yet know why, the discovery of the missiles by the U-2s on October 14 had led to a massive increase in the U.S. Navy presence in the very waters the Foxtrots had to navigate. By October 23 the sustained presence of U.S. naval vessels had forced at least one of the Foxtrots to stay underwater so long that its batteries were running very low.

It appears that Malinovsky reported none of this to the Presidium. If he had told Khrushchev about it beforehand, the Soviet leader had chosen to ignore the information in the meeting. However, Khrushchev's chief foreign policy critic, Anastas Mikoyan, worried that letting the submarines test the U.S. blockade would be a mistake. Khrushchev did nothing but watch as Mikoyan tried to put Malinovsky on the spot.[51] The defense minister refused to give an inch when Mikoyan insisted that it was risky to let these submarines into the blockade zone. He was convinced that the U.S. Navy could detect them. Moreover, the Kremlin had to assume, Mikoyan explained, that since the United States would be able to detect these four noisy diesel submarines, it would interpret their continued movement into the blockade zone as a hostile act.

Malinovsky refused to accept the premise of Mikoyan's argument. Despite the fact that some of the Foxtrots had likely been detected, the Soviet defense minister still insisted in front of the Soviet leadership that the subs would be able to approach Cuban shores without being seen or heard. In reply, Mikoyan told his colleagues that this was nonsense and would simply create a new danger for the Soviet Union, but this time he had no seconders. Khrushchev, Kozlov, Brezhnev, and the rest of the Presidium either decided that Malinovsky knew what he was talking about or at least chose to remain silent. When Mikoyan proposed that the group order the submarines to hold at the approaches to the island, he was overruled. Then the group broke for lunch.

During the lunch break Mikoyan approached Khrushchev to make a private appeal that the Presidium revisit the submarine issue in the afternoon. "I strongly believed [in my concerns]," he told Khrushchev, "and I consider that we must return to this question of the submarines because I consider that it was a mistake to turn down my proposal."[52] Khrushchev promised to raise the question again after lunch.

■

Two hours later the Presidium reconvened to hear Mikoyan's plea. Once again he warned his colleagues that these old Soviet submarines would be detected as soon as they violated the U.S. blockade. Once again Malinovsky insisted that the four boats could "reach the shores of Cuba undetected." The Soviet defense minister prevailed a second time.

Unwilling to give up, Mikoyan opted to play one last card. As the group prepared to leave for supper, he suggested that the commander in chief of the Soviet Navy, Admiral Sergei Gorshkov, the country's specialist on submarine warfare, be invited to address the group on the submarine issue. Mikoyan was a shrewd operator. He knew that tensions existed between the Ministry of Defense and the Soviet Navy, and here he was offering Admiral Gorshkov an opportunity to show up Malinovsky in front of the Presidium. It meant that the admiral would have to admit that the U.S. Navy could easily detect Soviet Foxtrots, but Gorshkov could add that the Foxtrot was not the latest in Soviet submarine technology.

At the evening session, the third time the Presidium met on October 23, Gorshkov played his part magnificently. A map of the waters around Cuba was placed in front of the Presidium. Gorshkov very carefully explained that it was extremely difficult to bring submarines close to Cuban shores. The waters got very shallow the nearer you came to Cuba. There were also a great number of tiny islands that you would have to maneuver around. "To approach the main island, the vessel must follow a very narrow channel, which is under the control of the radars from [nearby] U.S. naval bases . . . in other words it would be impossible to negotiate this channel undetected."

Just as Mikoyan hoped and expected, Gorshkov recommended keeping the four Foxtrot submarines at a perimeter, a two- to three-day sail from Cuba.

Mikoyan thought he had won. "With his incompetence revealed," Mikoyan recalled later, "Malinovsky could not possibly object." Khrushchev seemed to agree and supported a new instruction to the submarine captains ordering them to stay a distance of two days' sail away from Cuba.

■

CAPTAIN NIKOLAI SHUMKOV knew nothing about the debate in the Kremlin over his orders. He had a crew of about seventy-five men on his Foxtrot C-19. At three hundred feet long and just twenty-six feet wide, the boat could travel eighteen knots on the surface and sixteen knots when submerged. Designed for cold-water running, these submarines were neither air-conditioned nor battery-cooled. If the batteries became too hot, they would release hydrogen gas, a real hazard in a confined space.[53]

Besides the crew, food, and fuel, each Foxtrot was equipped with twenty-two torpedoes, one of which carried a nuclear warhead. Commanders were told to use their weapons only in self-defense. As Shumkov recalled, "we couldn't use our weapons independently." But all the submariners knew that in a battle situation, it might be impossible to check with Moscow. "We could only get in touch with our commanders at certain times," Shumkov recalled. "The Americans were on the surface and could keep in touch with their base all the time. . . . So it could have happened that the Americans were ordered to use arms and we would not have known anything about it . . . that was our disadvantage."

Late on October 23, C-19, like the other Soviet submarines, surfaced for the day's news. Chebrasov, the chief radioman on C-19, said, "We found out about the American blockade from the commander." Shumkov announced to his crew that "in our path stood an American fleet, in particular antinaval boats, but we were going to continue to carry out our mission that we would carry on through to Cuba."[54]

Despite the impression that Mikoyan had received in the Kremlin, none of the submarines received an order to abort its course. Either Khrushchev and Malinovsky had decided to ignore Gorshkov and Mikoyan, or the Soviet Navy could not communicate with its own submarines. Either finding underscores a flaw in Khrushchev's effort to reduce the risks of war in the crisis.[55] Were there any doubt that the United States intended to intercept submarines, this should have been dispelled on October 23. While the Presidium was debating what orders to give its submarines, the U.S. Embassy delivered to the Soviet

Navy a note from the U.S. Department of Defense that detailed its procedures for identifying submarines that attempted to violate the blockade.[56]

At 10:00 A.M., Washington time, October 24, the U.S. blockade went into effect. A line of U.S. ships was strung along the outer edge of the West Indies. And Soviet submarines were still steaming toward them.

■

WASHINGTON PICKED UP early on October 24 that Soviet surface ships were stopping. At 2:30 A.M. the NSA had intercepted another urgent message from Odessa directed at all Soviet ships. Still another indicated that all future messages would come from Moscow.[57] Eight hours later, during the late-morning Excomm meeting, Kennedy was told that the Office of Naval Intelligence had detected that all six Soviet ships in Cuban waters had "either stopped or reversed course."[58] For some time the White House was unsure whether these ships had been outbound from Cuba and were just returning their Cuban cargo or were part of the Soviet weapons buildup. While this was being cleared up, Defense Secretary McNamara explained to Kennedy the procedure the U.S. Navy planned to follow if it had to intercept a Soviet submarine. The navy had detected three Soviet submarines and thought it had found a fourth. After the State Department had sent its message to Moscow the night before, McNamara had decided to alter the rules of engagement for U.S. destroyers. "Here is the exact situation," he said. "[W]e have depth charges with such a small charge that they can be dropped and they can actually hit the submarine, without damaging the submarine." Asked if these were "practice depth charges," he replied that because it was assumed the Soviets would not be able to pick up any warnings sent in sonar, "it is the depth charge that is the warning notice and the instruction to surface." When President Kennedy heard that his secretary of defense had unilaterally ordered the U.S. Navy to deviate from standard international practice for surfacing unidentified submarines, which did not involve dropping depth charges, he experienced what Robert Kennedy later called "the time of greatest worry by the President." The president's hand, his brother noted later that day, "went up to his face & covered his mouth and he closed his fist. His eyes were tense, almost gray, and we just stared at each other across the table."[59]

"At what point do we attack him?" Kennedy asked moments later. "I think we ought to wait on that today. We don't want to have the first thing we attack as a Soviet submarine. I'd much rather have a merchant ship."[60] McNamara disagreed: "I think it would be extremely dangerous, Mr. President, to try to defer attack on this submarine in the situation we're in.

We could easily lose an American ship by that means." Faced with McNamara's concerns, Kennedy decided not to alter the navy's instructions.[61] But he worried about what Khrushchev's reaction would be if the Soviets lost a submarine or a ship. He expected the Soviets to respond where they enjoyed a geographical advantage: "[T]hey would say that there's no movement in or out of Berlin—a blockade."[62] The prospect was deeply worrying to him, "What is then our situation? What do we do then?" This was not the last time in those difficult days that Kennedy worried that forceful action by the United States in the Cuban crisis might be met by a Soviet reprisal against Berlin.

Just as he was contemplating a possible confrontation in Central Europe, John McCone, the CIA director, returned with reassuring news about the ships that the navy had spotted turning around: "These ships are all westbound, all inbound for Cuba." When Kennedy asked for clarification, McCone added, "[T]hey either stopped them or reversed direction." These ships were in the mid-Atlantic, west of the Azores. Not all Soviet ships turned, but among those that did were all those with seven-foot hatches, which U.S. intelligence associated with missile cargoes.

The news brought some relief and may have been the moment when Dean Rusk turned to McGeorge Bundy and whispered, "We are eyeball to eyeball, and I think the other fellow just blinked." Kennedy reminded the group that the United States would not touch any ship that had stopped or reversed course.[63] Soviet submarines, however, had not reversed course.

The United States was also receiving good news on the diplomatic front. On October 23 the Organization of American States had unanimously passed a resolution supporting a quarantine of Cuba. At the United Nations the Kremlin's decision to deny categorically that there were missiles in Cuba put Valerian Zorin into an increasingly untenable position. When the U.S. permanent representative to the United Nations, Adlai Stevenson, asked Zorin on October 25 if Moscow had placed missiles in Cuba, the stage was set for what would be one of the most famous exchanges in the Cold War:

ZORIN: I am not in an American courtroom, and therefore I do not wish to answer a question that is put to me in the fashion in which a prosecutor puts questions.

STEVENSON: You are in the courtroom of world opinion right now, and you can answer yes or no.

ZORIN: You will have your answer in due course.

STEVENSON: I am prepared to wait for my answer until hell freezes over.[64]

Stevenson then displayed overhead photography of the Soviet missile sites. The spectacle was carried live on American television.

▪

THE MOOD WAS sober in the Kremlin on Thursday, October 25. A day earlier Khrushchev had sent a strong letter to Kennedy that described the U.S. naval blockade as illegal and suggested that the only way for the United States to avoid a military confrontation was to back down. "Naturally," he had written, "we will not simply be bystanders with regard to piratical acts by American ships on the high seas."[65] This day, however, Khrushchev viewed the situation around Cuba differently. He had become convinced that he should take the initiative before events spiraled out of control. Zorin's humiliation at the UN had not yet happened when Khrushchev reconvened the Presidium to propose a way out of this crisis. The Soviet leader believed the time had come for tactical flexibility, and he suggested a straight trade.[66] If Kennedy would offer a pledge not to invade Cuba, Khrushchev would order the removal of the ballistic missiles.

Khrushchev tried to explain the retreat as a Soviet success. "There is no doubt the Americans have turned into cowards," he said.[67] Referring to an old Russian proverb, he added, "Apparently Kennedy slept with a wooden knife." His reference was too obscure even for wily old Mikoyan. "Why a wooden knife?" Mikoyan asked. "When a person goes bear hunting for the first time," Khrushchev explained, "he brings a wooden knife with him, so that cleaning his [soiled] trousers will be easier." The tension in the room broke with this exchange.

The joke was really on Khrushchev. It was he who was afraid at this point in the crisis and needed the protection of a fake weapon. But there was an element of truth to his hopefulness that Kennedy might take the trade. Although Khrushchev had started out with a much broader agenda than saving Fidel Castro, if Kennedy took the deal, it could be said that at least the missile scheme had prevented a future U.S. attack on Cuba. Khrushchev tried to convince his listeners that removing the R-12s from Cuba would also come at no cost to Soviet security. "We can [still] defeat the USA from USSR territory," he said without fully believing it. About the consequences for his dream of starting a crisis over Berlin in the fall, he made only one vague, passing reference: "[We] have succeeded in some things and not in others." Afterward discussion of the Berlin tie-in immediately became taboo.

Khrushchev found it hard to sustain his bravado. As he continued talking, he came to admit the terror that he and the others had felt since Kennedy's

October 22 speech. "The initiative is in our hands; there is no need to be afraid. We started out and then we got afraid.

"[But] this is not cowardice," Khrushchev said defensively about the proposed deal; "it is a prudent move." Cuba was not a good enough reason for the Soviet Union to wage war with the United States, he argued, because "the future does not depend on Cuba, but on our country." Nevertheless, he was not suggesting that Moscow abandon Havana. He recommended that in return for a noninvasion pledge from the United States the Soviet Union offer only to remove the R-12 ballistic missiles—the R-14s had not yet arrived—but to leave "the other missiles," presumably the nuclear-tipped Lunas and cruise missiles to protect the Cubans in the future. "This way we will strengthen Cuba and save it for two to three years. Then in a few years it will get even harder for [the United States] to deal with it."

Khrushchev's colleagues voted unanimously that night to approve this diplomatic retreat. None of them, including Mikoyan, forced Khrushchev to take personal responsibility for this calamity. His call for prudence must have rung hollow to those who had watched how since Vienna he had repeatedly advocated brinkmanship—creating a meniscus—to achieve Soviet foreign policy goals. On this most difficult night, however, his colleagues left it to his judgment when to make the offer to Kennedy. They should "look around," he said, and find the right time to suggest the trade.[68] The offer would be made in a letter to the U.S. president that Khrushchev would dictate. In the meantime, to lessen the risk of war, he recommended that the last ship on the high seas carrying "special cargo," a euphemism for nuclear materials, be returned to Soviet shores.

In light of Khrushchev's ambitious plans for the fall of 1962, the collapse of Anadyr represented a major personal defeat. The defense of Cuba had not been Khrushchev's sole concern and certainly was not the principal reason why he had opted to send nuclear missiles to the island. Nevertheless, it was a good fallback position that in the eyes of the world and his Cuban allies the trade would be consistent with the ostensible goals of his policy toward the island regime. "The rockets have served a positive role," he assured his colleagues, "[and] if need be, the rockets can appear there again."

That night, after the meeting, Khrushchev may have also asked that feelers be sent to the Americans in advance of his letter.[69] Soviet intelligence had been reporting that Kennedy wanted some kind of diplomatic settlement. But all this was vague, and as yet the Kennedy administration had avoided talking directly to the GRU's Bolshakov or Ambassador Dobrynin. Despite the Kremlin's security precautions, Khrushchev's interest in a diplomatic settlement may have reached the headquarters of the KGB. Vladimir Semichastny, the chairman of the KGB, had not been invited to the October 25 meeting.[70] But his patron, Aleksandr Shelepin, the former chief of the KGB, who was now a full-fledged member of the Presidium, had been there. To the end of his days Semichastny denied receiving any special request that night to test the White House's interest in a diplomatic settlement. Nevertheless, the next morning the KGB station chief in Washington did propose to an American journalist the very same deal discussed hours earlier in the Kremlin.

Since his arrival in Washington in early 1962 on his current mission, Aleksandr Feklisov had considered ABC News's John Scali a useful contact. "He came from Boston, and I thought he knew the Kennedys," Feklisov later remembered.[71] Feklisov was a legendary case officer in Soviet intelligence, having once handled the famous atomic bomb spy Julius Rosenberg. Scali, a balding spark plug, was among the generation of serious journalists who had made their start in print journalism before he became pioneer of television news. Scali was more accustomed to cultivating sources than being one himself, but after the FBI suggested it was a good thing for the country that he get to know Feklisov, the two had started meeting regularly.[72]

On October 26 Feklisov called to arrange an urgent meeting with Scali. They met for lunch at the Occidental, tucked beside the Willard Hotel. The restaurant was not the place for a secret rendezvous. It was the favorite hangout of many Washington political stars and even of those less known to newspaper readers. The high-level intelligence professional and future director of central intelligence Richard Helms had a designated table.

The conversation between Scali and Feklisov that day became a source of controversy. Kremlin records suggest that the version later recounted by Scali was the more credible one.[73] Feklisov asked Scali what he "thought" of a three-point approach to ending the crisis:

1. The Soviet missile bases would be dismantled under UN supervision.
2. Fidel Castro would promise never to accept offensive weapons of any kind, ever.
3. In return for the above, the United States would pledge not to invade Cuba.

This was almost word for word the scheme that Khrushchev had proposed to his colleagues in Moscow the night before. Scali rushed the plan to his contact in the State Department.[74]

Whatever the Kremlin's role in this feeler, Khrushchev had already decided not to wait for any further word from Kennedy before sending his letter. He had a green light from his colleagues to concede whenever the time was right. That moment came the next day. Early on Friday, October 26, Khrushchev received a stream of information indicating the likelihood that the Americans were readying an attack for October 27. None of this was hard evidence. The best was some barroom gossip that a Russian émigré who worked as a bartender picked up at the National Press Club. Late on October 25 the *New York Herald Tribune*'s Warren Rogers and his editor Robert Donovan were blowing off some steam after a tense day. Rogers had just been selected for the Pentagon's pool for any invasion of the island and thought he might be called down to Florida the next day. The Reuters correspondent in Washington, P. Heffernan, and an agent code-named Gam told the GRU and the KGB roughly the same thing.[75] Finally, Osvaldo Dorticós, the Cuban president, shared his anxieties with Soviet military intelligence at about the same time.[76] Swayed by these shards of information about the thinking in the White House, Khrushchev decided it was time to seek his diplomatic out.

The U.S. Embassy received Khrushchev's long personal letter to Kennedy just before 5:00 P.M., Moscow time, on October 26. Khrushchev offered to remove the missiles in return for a U.S. pledge not to invade the island. "We, for our part, will declare that our ships, bound for Cuba, will not carry any kind of armaments. You would declare that the United States will not invade Cuba with its forces and will not support any sort of forces which might intend to carry out an invasion of Cuba. Then the necessity for the presence of our military specialists in Cuba would disappear."[77] To make sure Kennedy understood that he meant removing the missiles, Khrushchev wrote, "[I]f there is no threat, then armaments are a burden for every people. Then, too, the question of the destruction, not only of the armaments which you call offensive, but of all other armaments as well, would look different."[78]

▪

A VERY NOISY tin can armed with a nuclear torpedo posed a threat to Khrushchev's efforts to get out of the Cuban mess without a catastrophe. By October 26 the batteries on Nikolai Shumkov's submarine were running low. A submarine could stay underwater only three or four days before the batteries had to be recharged. Shumkov had not been able to recharge for days, and two of his motors did not have enough power to work. It would take a whole day on the surface, running the diesel engines on a mixture of oil and air, to recharge the batteries. He knew he was not going to get anywhere near twenty-four hours of peace on the surface to recharge, but he had to try to get some recharging done. He prepared to take his chances whenever he had the cover of night. An attempt late on October 25 had failed when he had seen a U.S. ship, so he tried again at about 10:00 P.M. East Coast time (2:25 A.M., Zulu time) on October 26. "We went up and managed to recharge for about two or three hours. [Then] I was told that from four directions U.S. antisubmarine warfare ships were approaching me."[79] Neither the submarine nor its pursuers were using floodlights, a violation of the rules of international navigation, but this was a moment of possible combat, not commerce.

The Americans had detected the surfaced submarine with night vision goggles and radar. C-19 was a sitting duck. "When I heard that they had detected us," Shumkov recalled, "I ordered the recharging to stop and for the submarine to submerge." Sluggish because of its weakened power plant, C-19 began its dive only just in time to miss an onrushing U.S. destroyer that sliced the water above its conning tower. "That night nearly became catastrophic for us." To alert the Soviet sub that it had been caught in this game of high-stakes tag, the U.S. ship dropped three grenades on C-19. "When they blew up those grenades," Shumkov said, "I thought they were bombing us."

Refusing to surface, Shumkov ordered the dive to continue, but soon there was another emergency. He received word that a leak had developed in one of the submarine's compartments. The textbook answer to this kind of problem was to surface. If too much water leaked in, the submarine might sink uncontrollably. Shumkov knew surfacing was no option with U.S. ships still prowling above. Fortunately it turned out to be a microfracture that his crew was able to repair. Shumkov nearly died twice in one day. It is not known if the Kremlin ever learned of this encounter before the crisis was over.

■

WHEN THEY MET in Vienna, John Kennedy had teased Khrushchev for having enough time for long visits with American columnists like Walter Lippmann.[80] Although he never learned English—his wife and his children did learn the language—Khrushchev always made time to read in translation what the prominent U.S. columnists were saying about him. To the extent he could approve of any bourgeois views, he appreciated Lippmann's realism. The columnist, who had known the famous American Bolshevik John Reed at Harvard, seemed to understand what was and was not possible in international relations. Often his knowledge seemed to indicate some inside information.

At some point late Friday, October 26, or early Saturday, October 27, Khrushchev was given Lippmann's October 25 column. The writer recommended a different variation on the diplomatic deal to end the crisis from that which Khrushchev had just sent to Kennedy. Equating the Soviet missile base in Cuba with the U.S. Jupiter missile base in Turkey, Lippmann suggested that the superpowers dismantle both to end the missile crisis.

Lippmann's idea hit Khrushchev just as he was beginning to doubt his own fears about what Kennedy would do.[81] It had been more than four days since Kennedy had given his quarantine speech, and nothing had happened. The U.S. president probably knew that some of the Soviet ships had turned around, but Khrushchev in protest of the blockade continued to send to Cuba innocuous freighters and tankers, which were about to be boarded. Why had the White House not used force by now? Then there were the shards of intelligence information about an invasion that he had received. According to Rogers and the others, the attack should be occurring. Yet it hadn't.

Could it be that Kennedy was making him an offer through Lippmann? That was a new idea for Khrushchev. But even if Lippmann's proposal was solely the product of his creative mind, the fact that the administration seemed paralyzed meant that Khrushchev could probably get a better deal to end the whole affair. Flush with the most confidence he had felt since the dreadful night of October 22, Khrushchev decided to up the ante.

In the Presidium he recommended sending yet another letter to Kennedy. This one demanded that Kennedy promise the withdrawal of the Jupiter missiles *in addition* to the conditions outlined in the letter of October 26. Thus the famous second letter of the missile crisis was born. "If we did this," Khrushchev said enthusiastically, "we could win."[82]

Excited about the prospects suggested by this new offer, Khrushchev wanted it sent immediately. Kennedy had yet to respond to his October 26 proposal; perhaps this could forestall his accepting the less advantageous offer. Instead of using a confidential channel, as he had done with his previous letters, Khrushchev instructed that this one be read by Radio Moscow. That was how Fidel Castro learned that Moscow was trying to negotiate away its Cuban nuclear base.

■

PRESIDENT KENNEDY'S Excomm met continuously throughout the crisis, and the appearance of the two letters from Khrushchev confused him and his advisers. First, Khrushchev seemed to be prepared to remove the missiles with merely a noninvasion pledge in turn. Then on the morning of Saturday, October 27, the Excomm received Khrushchev's public letter calling for the removal of the Jupiters from Turkey. Opinions differed on why the change had occurred. There was some thought that perhaps the hard-liners around Khrushchev had forced him to demand a higher price for removing the missiles from Cuba. No one near Kennedy could imagine that it was Khrushchev himself who was desperately trying to save face by achieving at least a small shift in the nuclear balance of power.

The news later on October 27 that a U-2 piloted by Colonel Rudolf Anderson had been shot down on a photographic mission over Cuba increased the tension. For many in Washington this seemed to be a deliberate ploy by Moscow to keep the heat on Kennedy as he wrestled with the two letters. Ultimately the president chose to send a formal response only to the first letter. He and his advisers differed on how to finesse Khrushchev's Jupiter demand in the second letter. Accepting it would require the participation of the Turks, who were already signaling that they did not want the Jupiters to be part of any trade, and many in the Excomm were solidly against giving Khrushchev this concession.

Kennedy, however, was sure that the Jupiters were not worth the price of a nuclear war. He sent his brother to make a private offer to the Soviets. Bolshakov had by this time been superseded by Dobrynin, who now seemed to be a better channel to the Kremlin. Late Saturday evening Robert Kennedy met with the Soviet ambassador. Kennedy announced that the president found Khrushchev's offer to withdraw the missiles in return for a U.S. commitment not to invade "a suitable basis for negotiating the entire Cuban affair."[83] Asked about Khrushchev's additional demand that the Jupiter missiles be removed, Kennedy replied, "If that is the only obstacle to achieving the regulation I mentioned earlier, then the president doesn't see any insurmountable difficulties in resolving this issue." He promised the missiles would be removed in "four to five months" and asked that the Soviet understand that "the greatest difficulty for the president is the public discussion of the issue of Turkey." Moscow got the message. The Jupiter concession would have to be kept secret.

■

KHRUSHCHEV GATHERED his advisers and the entire Presidium at his dacha outside Moscow around noon on October 28. It was early in the morning in Washington, where the White House had known about his Jupiter demand for less than twelve hours. Nevertheless, Khrushchev sensed that he could wait no longer to end the crisis, even if that meant missing the opportunity to get the Americans to dismantle their missile base in neighboring Turkey. The recent intelligence from Cuba was, if anything, even more threatening than the invasion rumors he had received on October 26. A Soviet commander had used a SAM to shoot down an American spy plane without specific authorization.[84] It also appeared that Castro was becoming irrational. Khrushchev knew that the Cuban leader had spent the night of October 26–27 dictating a letter to Ambassador Alekseyev. In it he advocated a nuclear war, if necessary, to defend the honor of Cuba and the socialist cause. "[I]f they actually carry out the brutal act of invading Cuba," he wrote, "that would be the moment to eliminate such danger forever through an act of legitimate defense, however harsh and terrible the solution would be."[85]

Until the opening of the Kremlin's archives, it had been assumed that Kennedy's decision to give in to Khrushchev's last-minute request for the removal of the missiles in Turkey had clinched the diplomatic settlement. Vladimir Malin's Presidium notes, however, leave no doubt that Khrushchev had decided to agree to the first proposed deal well before he received word that John Kennedy, through his brother Robert, had offered to dismantle the Jupiter missiles in Turkey.[86] Khrushchev had actually dictated his concession speech, which was to take the form of a letter to the U.S. president, before he knew of Kennedy's own concession. When news of Robert Kennedy's talk with Dobrynin reached the meeting hall, Khrushchev was delighted and likely relieved, for he knew that the removal of the Jupiter missiles symbolized a grudging American acceptance of a parallel between what he had attempted to do in Cuba and what the Eisenhower administration and its successor had sought to achieve in the lands around the Soviet Union. Perhaps sweeter because it had been so unexpected and unnecessary, the concession was for Khrushchev a form of justification.

Khrushchev did not change his dictated letter. Robert Kennedy had asked that the concession be a secret held between the world's two most powerful leaders, and Khrushchev agreed. His greatest concern was to get the general message that the crisis was over to the U.S. government as quickly as possible, and a radio broadcast would be the best means to do this.

The Cubans had played no role in Khrushchev's negotiations with Kennedy. In the final days of the crisis Khrushchev had not bothered to confer with Castro, even as he vacillated between feeling he had gained the upper hand and depths of anxiety over the imminent approach of war. Castro later described this lack of consultation and Khrushchev's sudden decision to remove the ballistic missiles as one of the great "betrayals" of the Cuban Revolution. What most irked Castro was that Khrushchev had been willing to deal away a measure of Cuban sovereignty to save his own skin. The Soviets knew that Castro would not allow inspectors into his country, yet Khrushchev had unilaterally offered Kennedy in his letters of October 26 and October 27 some form of inspection of the missile bases to assure the Americans the weapons were gone. At the October 28 meeting where he assembled the final package to resolve the crisis, Khrushchev discussed the possibility of involving the Red Cross in the inspections without even giving a thought to the possibility that the idea of inspection would be unacceptable to his Cuban ally. This was the kind of brazen disregard of the interests of an ally that Khrushchev had criticized Stalin for, and now he had committed the same sin himself.

Curiously, Khrushchev did find time during the crisis to assuage the concerns of one important ally. Walter Ulbricht apparently was not party to the preparations that had been made for Khrushchev's November trip to the United Nations and in all likelihood had not been told about Anadyr. Relations with East Germany had gotten frosty as the fall progressed. Once again the East Germans had proposed what the Soviets considered an irresponsible five-year economic plan. In the midst of everything else on October 23, the Kremlin had considered a report on the East German economic situation.[87] The story was not unfamiliar. Yet again Ulbricht wanted to buy more abroad and cause the Soviets to sell gold and spend hard currency to make this possible. Khrushchev blamed his ambassador in East Germany, Pervukhin, for the East German unwillingness to see economic reason. Probably worried about what concessions Kennedy might be able to wring out of Khrushchev on Berlin to end the Cuba crisis, Ulbricht had requested a visit with Khrushchev for October 27.[88]

Agreeing to the request, Khrushchev and quite a few of his Kremlin colleagues met with a large, high-ranking East German delegation, led by Ulbricht. It is unknown what the men said to each other, but Ulbricht left satisfied. Unlike Castro, Ulbricht was able to settle his concerns with Khrushchev face-to-face. With the failure of Khrushchev's Cuban bid for strategic gains, economic reforms were even more important as a guarantee of East Germany's future.

■

KHRUSHCHEV'S AGREEMENT to settle the Cuban crisis was greeted with relief in Washington on October 28. The news had reached the White House by midmorning, East Coast time.[89] John Kennedy assumed that it was the Turkish offer that had sealed the agreement. Not wishing to let on that he had made this last-minute concession, the president and the attorney general confined this knowledge to a small group of advisers.

Unaware that the missile gambit had been a crucial element of a larger

Kremlin offensive, Kennedy had no idea of the extent of his success in the crisis. Khrushchev's effort to alter the balance of power in one stroke had failed. He had taken this risk to make future gains in Central Europe and Southeast Asia more than he had done this to protect Fidel Castro. Since the Suez crisis of 1956, Khrushchev had believed that only the projection of nuclear power could bring the political settlement he sought throughout the world. He had harbored no real desire to fight to remove Western troops from West Berlin, to bring Jordan, Iraq, and Syria to the Soviet side or to end U.S. support for the Phoumi Nosavan group in Laos. In each case he had hoped to scare the United States into accepting the Soviet conception of an equitable outcome. After some confusion in January 1962 over when to make his move, by the late spring Khrushchev had decided that this would be the year of what he called the final fight.[90]

The negotiated settlement of October 28 was not the outcome he had intended. Once the missiles left Cuba, what had he gained from this operation? Was he any closer to strategic parity with the United States? Did he get a disarmament agreement or Kennedy's acquiescence to a free city of West Berlin? No. What he got was a U.S. promise not to invade Cuba, an invasion Khrushchev had not really expected until at least 1964, and a secret U.S. promise to remove some missiles from Turkey.

The Soviet leader could rejoice in the fact that John Kennedy for a few days had seemed worried. But the U.S. president had not panicked. It was Khrushchev who had been forced to admit to colleagues that his foreign policy initiative had become too risky. Events had confirmed the wisdom of Mikoyan's concerns in May and his continued caution in October. Khrushchev now better understood that there were limits to how much the Kremlin could control events in a crisis. A disastrous encounter between the Foxtrot submarines and the U.S. Navy had been only narrowly averted. On the tensest day of the crisis, when Moscow was hoping for a diplomatic settlement, a local Soviet commander had shot down an American U-2 over Cuba without authorization.

Although Kennedy worried on October 28 about the political costs of his Jupiter concession if the secret ever got out, it would be Khrushchev who had greater reason to be concerned about the lingering effects of this crisis on his ability to lead. The Cuban missile crisis proved to be a turning point in Khrushchev's handling of Soviet foreign policy and, as a result, the Cold War.

CHAPTER 20

"LEAVING FEAR ASTERN"

N THE WAKE of the Cuban missile crisis Nikita Khrushchev would have to rethink his entire approach to contesting U.S. power in the Cold War. November 1962 was supposed to bring an end to the foreign policy reversals that had plagued him since 1958. Instead he faced the challenge of negotiating a dignified retreat from his missile base in Cuba.

The exchange of letters between Kennedy and Khrushchev at the end of October had lowered the temperature considerably, ending the tensest period of the missile crisis, but the agreement between the leaders was incomplete. All that Khrushchev had in return for his promise to withdraw the strategic missiles was what Kennedy had written in his letter of October 27, 1962. "We, on our part, would agree—upon the establishment of adequate arrangements through the United Nations to ensure the carrying out and continuation of these commitments—a) to remove promptly the quarantine measures now in effect and b) to give assurances against an invasion of Cuba."[1] The president's language was more conditional than Khrushchev would have liked, but he had accepted it. Besides this written promise, Khrushchev had extracted an oral agreement conveyed by Robert Kennedy on October 27 that within four to five months the United States would withdraw the fifteen Jupiter intermediate-range missiles that it had stationed in Turkey earlier in 1962. With the crisis subsiding, the Kremlin wanted to nail down these U.S. commitments.

Khrushchev had no choice but to involve Castro in this diplomacy. Up to now the Soviet leader had excluded the Cubans from the crisis negotiations. But in his letter of October 27 Khrushchev had promised Kennedy "to reach agreement to enable United Nations representatives to verify the dismantling of these means."[2] Cuban approval of some kind of on-site inspection regime would be required to satisfy this promise. While Khrushchev had his own phobias about letting foreign inspectors into the Soviet Union, he believed the Cubans had to accept a violation of their own sovereignty for the sake of a peaceful end to the crisis.

From the Americans, Khrushchev sought a formal pledge not to attack Cuba ever, which could be submitted to the United Nations in the form of a treaty. He also wanted the United States to curtail the high- and low-altitude reconnaissance flights that violated Cuban airspace several times a day. Settling these points held Khrushchev's attention for the next three weeks.

Neither Castro nor Kennedy made this process easy for the Kremlin. On October 28 Castro publicly announced five demands that the United States had to accept before he would consider the Cuban crisis over: The United States had to end its economic sanctions against Cuba, including the trade embargo; it would have to cease all subversive activities; Washington would have to prevent all "piratical attacks" from the continental United States and Puerto Rico; U.S. planes would have to stop violating Cuban airspace and territorial waters; and the hardest of all, the United States would have to withdraw from its naval base at Guantánamo and cancel its perpetual lease. If these demands were not troubling enough for the Soviets, who had assumed the Cuban leadership would accept the diplomatic settlement arranged by Khrushchev, Castro added that he would not allow UN inspectors into Cuba under any circumstances.

Castro was lashing out at both superpowers. He felt betrayed by Khrushchev and deeply mistrusted Kennedy. Ambassador Alekseyev, who had visited the Cuban leader after the superpower deal was announced on October 28, told Moscow that he had never seen him look so depressed and irritated.[3] The Soviet ambassador had the sense that Castro believed that the withdrawal of the Soviet strategic missiles was just the first step and that ultimately Khrushchev would abandon the defense of Cuba. The Cuban feared that despite Kennedy's promises, the Americans would take advantage of any weakness in the Soviet commitment to Cuba to attack the island. Especially offensive to Castro was the Soviet offer to permit international inspection of the withdrawal of their missiles. Castro believed Khrushchev should never have put that promise in his letters to Kennedy without at least checking with Havana first.

On October 31 Castro told Alekseyev that "it is not that some Cubans cannot understand the Soviet decision to dismantle the missiles, but all Cubans."[4] Meanwhile Moscow was receiving worrisome evidence from Soviet intelligence representatives on the island that this was not an exaggeration, that the anger and suspicion within the regime extended to the Cuban military and intelligence services.[5] Without exception Cuban officials were telling the Soviets they had been naive to accept any deal from John Kennedy.

To manage the Cubans, Khrushchev sent Mikoyan, the only Presidium member ever to have visited Cuba, to Havana on November 2. His task was extremely difficult. Somehow he would have to talk Castro down from these demands while enlisting his support for a verifiable agreement with the Americans.

On the day Mikoyan flew to Cuba the U.S. government further complicated the picture for the Soviets. Kennedy sent word to Khrushchev through his UN ambassador, Adlai Stevenson, that the ballistic missiles were not the only weapons that he expected the Soviets to remove from Cuba. When Khrushchev promised on October 27 to withdraw "the means which you regard as offensive," he had meant only the medium-range ballistic missiles.[6] Stevenson explained that his government also considered the Il-28s, called Beagle bombers by NATO, offensive weapons because they were capable of dropping nuclear bombs on southern Florida. The military value of these airplanes, which were not the latest generation of Soviet medium-range bombers, was slight compared with the missiles, but the addition of another weapons system to withdraw complicated Khrushchev's effort to nail down the final diplomatic settlement. It also seemed a gratuitous effort to magnify his humiliation.

Two days after Kennedy raised the issue of the bombers, Khrushchev tried to discourage the president from pressing too hard for this Soviet concession. This demand, he wrote privately to Kennedy "can lead not to the betterment of our relations but, on the contrary, to their new aggravation."[7] The effort failed. "I assure you," Kennedy replied on November 6, "that this matter of the Il-28s is not a minor matter for us at all."[8]

■

A s   I F   A N   E M B O L D E N E D   Kennedy and an irritated Castro were not enough of a challenge for the Kremlin in the immediate aftermath of the Cuban missile crisis, the Chinese had decided to make themselves a nuisance. Initially the Chinese had maintained an official silence after the announcement of the Khrushchev-Kennedy deal, though their displeasure was thinly veiled. Chinese publications reported Khrushchev's offer to dismantle the missiles in small type, while quoting Chinese leaders lavishly praising Castro's resistance to imperialist forces.[9]

On October 31, Mao Zedong and the Chinese leadership changed tactics and started using the front page of the chief Communist newspaper, the *People's Daily*, to assail Khrushchev for giving in to "the United States' imperialist attempt to browbeat the people of the world into retreat at the expense of

Cuba."[10] According to Beijing, Kennedy's noninvasion pledge was "nothing but a hoax." In the days that followed, Chinese newspapers kept up a drumbeat of criticism of Khrushchev's handling of the crisis, describing it as a betrayal of Marxist-Leninist principles. At the same time, Beijing endorsed Castro's five demands as the only acceptable bases for ending the crisis.[11]

To further dramatize its opposition to the proposed Cuban settlement, the Mao regime sponsored four days of massive demonstrations in Beijing. Each day tens of thousands people marched to the Cuban Embassy in a show of solidarity.[12] By November 6 Chinese newspapers were comparing Khrushchev's actions to Neville Chamberlain's efforts to appease Adolf Hitler at Munich. "The attempt to play the Munich scheme against the Cuban people who have already stood on their own feet," editorialized the *People's Daily*, "is doomed to complete failure."[13] When the Soviet ambassador tried to toast Khrushchev on November 7 at a party to celebrate the anniversary of the Bolshevik Revolution, his Chinese guests stayed silent.[14] China's little ally in the Balkans added to the pressure. Albania's official radio station attacked Khrushchev for "contemporary revisionism" and asserted that communism could not prevail over capitalism "by bargaining and making concessions to imperialism."[15]

■

CASTRO'S INDIGNATION, Chinese criticism, and even new demands from Washington did not shake Khrushchev's determination to formalize his settlement with Kennedy. In Havana, Mikoyan paid lip service to Castro's five points and pressed the Cuban leadership to accept some form of inspection. At his first meeting with Castro on November 3, Mikoyan tried to sugarcoat the concession that Moscow wanted from Havana. "What we are speaking of," he said, "is not a broad inspection, but a verification of the sites known to the Americans due to aerial photography and which have been the locations of the strategic missile launchers."[16] Mikoyan assured Castro that the USSR was not expecting Cuba to accept any permanent or general inspection, something Khrushchev himself would never have accepted on Soviet soil.

Castro continued to refuse. "I want to tell you, Comrade Mikoyan," Castro told Khrushchev's surrogate on November 5, "and in this, what I say reflects the decision of the Cuban people: We oppose this inspection." For Castro nothing less than the prestige of his regime and his people was at stake. "We have the right to defend our dignity," he told the Soviet representative.[17] He also expected Moscow to support his five points, as the Chinese had done.

Castro's stubbornness only increased Khrushchev's frustration with the

Chinese, who seemed to be going out of their way to encourage the Cubans to reject Moscow's leadership. "Of course, the least amount of assistance to Cuba," he told his colleagues on the Presidium in November, "came from the Chinese. What did they do at the moment of greatest tension? The workers in the Chinese Embassy in Cuba went to a blood donation center and announced, 'We are giving our blood for Cuba.' What demagogic, cheap assistance!"[18] It irritated him that the Chinese, who were never willing or able to make a significant military contribution to the defense of Cuba, were now publicly assailing him for seeking security through diplomacy. "Cuba didn't need the blood of some men," he complained, "but real military and political assistance so that human blood and flesh should not be spread across the land."[19]

Khrushchev had good reason to expect some Chinese generosity, rather than contempt. Since mid-October he had supported Beijing's territorial claims along its border with India at some cost to Moscow's relationship with New Delhi.[20] Soviet support had continued even when the Chinese Army invaded Kashmir, in western India, on October 20. Besides giving rhetorical support to the Chinese, Moscow had also canceled an Indian order for twelve MiG-21 jet fighters that were to be delivered in early December.[21] As Chinese criticisms of the Cuban deal surfaced, the Soviets had used the press to remind the Chinese that they continued to enjoy the Kremlin's support in the border dispute.[22] In early November, still hopeful of maintaining a good relationship with Beijing, Khrushchev sent the Indian prime minister a public letter that explained why Moscow would have to continue supporting the Chinese position.[23]

The demonstrations in Beijing and the Chinese propaganda campaign so angered Khrushchev that he decided on an abrupt shift in Moscow's position in the Sino-Indian dispute. On November 5 *Pravda* announced a reversal in the Soviet position. The officially sanctioned article dropped any reference to the validity of Chinese claims. "It is necessary," wrote the editors of *Pravda*, "to cease fire and sit down at the round table of negotiations without setting any terms."[24] Khrushchev also decided to give the Indians the Soviet fighters that they had ordered and to honor a previous promise to supply India with 1.5 million tons of refined petroleum.[25]

■

WHEREAS KHRUSHCHEV urged hard-line policies to put the Chinese in their place in November 1962, he decided to treat John F. Kennedy very differently. An important change was occurring in Khrushchev's perception of the struggle with the United States, and the first signs were evident in the days after the climax of the missile crisis. The hot-tempered, impatient Khrushchev had reason to be annoyed with Kennedy. The ongoing negotiations in New York charged with hammering out the noninvasion pledge were not going well because of American insistence on the removal of the Soviet bombers. Yet Khrushchev decided not to blame the U.S. president. Instead he chose to make an even greater political investment in the American leader.

Even though his elaborate strategy for gaining diplomatic concessions from the United States in November 1962 had collapsed, Khrushchev saw signs that the missile crisis might have created an opportunity for agreement on disarmament and possibly on Berlin with Kennedy. The results of the U.S. congressional and gubernatorial elections that took place on November 6, 1962, were a source of some of this hope. Kennedy's Democrats lost fewer seats in the House than usual in a midterm election and actually gained seats in the Senate. Particularly satisfying to Khrushchev was the defeat of "my old friend Nixon" in the gubernatorial race in California. "All aggressive U.S. candidates," Khrushchev later told a British diplomat, "have been rejected by the wise U.S. electorate."[26] At a reception the day after the election, Khrushchev told the new U.S. ambassador, Foy D. Kohler, that "we may not love each other, but we have to live together and may even have to embrace each other, if the world is to survive."[27]

The more important cause of Khrushchev's future actions, however, was the favorable assessment he had developed of his counterpart in the White House. Kennedy's handling of the crisis suggested to Khrushchev not only that this U.S. president preferred diplomatic solutions but that he was strong enough to rebuff extreme domestic pressures to use military force. In the immediate aftermath of the crisis Khrushchev had received additional evidence of how close the U.S. government had come to launching a military action in the Caribbean. On November 1, Khrushchev's favorite U.S. journalist, Walter Lippmann, confirmed to Ambassador Dobrynin that a superpower conflict had been hours away when Khrushchev's message was broadcast by Radio Moscow on October 28.[28] Lippmann mistakenly believed that Kennedy had already ordered an air strike against Cuba for October 29 or 30. This dovetailed with some Soviet intelligence reports of the relief on Capitol Hill when what had been expected did not happen.[29]

In the second week of November Khrushchev perceived a similar pattern of activity in Washington. While the administration maintained a tough public line on the unconditional removal of the Soviet bombers, Moscow began to get confidential feelers from the Kennedys that suggested the president might be looking for something less than the unconditional removal of the Soviet Il-28 bombers from Cuba.

Before dressing for a formal dinner on November 9, Robert Kennedy met quickly at his home with Georgi Bolshakov to share "his personal opinion" about solving the Il-28 problem. The attorney general had not seen the Russian go-between directly since before the crisis, although some of his friends and associates had kept up the channel for the White House. Robert Kennedy had been disappointed that Bolshakov had been used to pass misinformation about Soviet military supplies to Cuba, but he still trusted him more than he did the Soviet ambassador, whom he suspected of not always accurately portraying the president's words to Khrushchev. RFK asked Bolshakov to tell his superiors that the United States would probably be satisfied with one of two developments: Either Khrushchev would give a gentleman's agreement to withdraw the bombers within a reasonable amount of time, or the Soviets could just assure the United States that so long as the bombers stayed in Cuba they would be flown by Soviet airmen. Just the day before, the *New York Times* had reported that the Cuban representative at the United Nations, Carlos Lechuga, told other delegates that the bombers were Cuban property and would not be returned.[30]

After making this offer, the White House or someone close to President Kennedy developed cold feet. An hour after their brief meeting Robert Kennedy called Bolshakov to retract part of the offer. He claimed to have misspoken when he said that the bombers could stay if they were always under Soviet control; nothing less than the complete removal of the Il-28s would satisfy his government. Although the Soviets were disappointed that the White House had retracted this offer, what Robert Kennedy told the Soviets strengthened Khrushchev's belief that though under severe domestic pressure to get the bombers out, the U.S. president was looking for a diplomatic solution.

The image of John Kennedy as an embattled leader was not something the Kremlin was picking up by accident. The White House through Robert Kennedy was consciously promoting this image in Soviet minds as a way of facilitating a settlement of the last remaining issues of the missile crisis. "Bobby's notion is there's only one peace-lover in the [U.S.] government," explained National Security Adviser McGeorge Bundy in describing the information going through the back channel to the Kremlin in November, "and he's entirely surrounded by militarists and it's not a bad image. Well, Bobby's feeding him that stuff, Mr. President."[31] The White House hoped to co-opt Khrushchev into helping Kennedy manage his domestic critics.

Khrushchev bought the argument that it was in the Soviet Union's interest to help Kennedy. On November 10, the day after the conversations between Bolshakov and Robert Kennedy, Khrushchev told his Kremlin colleagues that it was time to consider removing the bombers.[32] Despite Robert Kennedy's apparent retraction of an offer to settle the Il-28 issue, Khrushchev believed the Kennedys would ultimately make a side deal for the bombers as they had done to remove the missiles. Besides what the Kremlin had learned from Bolshakov, Moscow had received reports that Washington might be satisfied by a Soviet promise never to increase the number of their bombers in Cuba or perhaps would accept a Soviet promise to withdraw the planes, just not immediately. Khrushchev believed he had the luxury of haggling with the United States to get the bombers out. If Washington pressed hard, and if Kennedy seemed about to ratchet up the crisis, Moscow would concede. The Soviets did not need the bombers in Cuba; they had belonged to the plan for an offensive Soviet military base on the island, and that base no longer seemed politically useful to Khrushchev. Moreover, the Soviet leader had a sense that the gesture might firm up Kennedy's domestic position. In a letter sent the same day to Kennedy, he tried to revive the abortive offer received the previous day from the president's brother: "[B]ecause you express apprehension that these weapons can be some sort of threat to the U.S. or other countries of Western Hemisphere which do not possess adequate defensive means, we state that those planes are piloted by our fliers." But then he added: "We will not insist on permanently keeping those planes on Cuba. We have our difficulties in this question. Therefore we give a gentleman's word that we will remove the Il-28 planes with all the personnel and equipment related to those planes, although not now but later." Khrushchev explained that the conditions had "to be ripe to remove them."[33]

By "ripe" Khrushchev meant that he would have the approval of the Cubans for this concession. He had kept Castro at arm's length on October 26, 27, and 28 when faced with the possibility of war with Washington, and although Mikoyan's difficulties were irritating, Khrushchev had some understanding for Castro's insistence on being consulted.

Khrushchev also hinted at a possible price for the bombers. The acting secretary-general of the United Nations, U Thant, had suggested establishing UN observer posts throughout the Caribbean to guard against an aggression in the region. The Soviets endorsed that proposal and added one of their own. Recalling a Soviet proposal from the 1950s, Khrushchev suggested that the two superpowers place inspectors at railroads, airports, and other communications nodes in the southern United States and the western USSR as part of the first phase of mutual disarmament.

The same day Khrushchev sent an explanation of his strategy to Mikoyan in Havana. He told his colleague that though the Kremlin was prepared to give in on the bombers, it made sense to wait a bit to see whether the United States would accept something short of a complete withdrawal. Khrushchev stressed that Kennedy faced so much domestic pressure that it was in the Soviet interest to help him with his bomber problem. He believed that Kennedy on his own would never have demanded the withdrawal of the Il-28s.[34]

■

I N WASHINGTON, Kennedy was not aware that Khrushchev was trying to help him out politically. Robert Kennedy responded to Khrushchev's letter on behalf of his brother on November 12. President Kennedy could not accept a vague Soviet promise to remove the bombers. However, he would be satisfied if Khrushchev gave an order to remove the bombers within thirty days. The response also contained one concession for Khrushchev, who the Americans knew from intelligence evidence was having trouble in Havana. The United States pledged to remove the naval quarantine without UN confirmation that the Soviet missiles had been removed. On November 12 Robert Kennedy conveyed this offer to the Soviet ambassador in an oral message from the president.[35]

Khrushchev then decided to make his haggling more explicit. On November 13 the Presidium agreed to tell the White House that the Soviet government could remove the Il-28s within thirty days but would prefer to take two to three months. In his personal response to the president, sent the next day, Khrushchev said he would probably accept specific dates for the removal of the Il-28s "even closer than those which I name and maybe even closer than those which were named by you" if Kennedy would agree to a Soviet proposal to establish a UN inspection regime throughout the Caribbean region, including observer posts along the Florida coast and in Cuba.[36]

Meanwhile Khrushchev was losing patience with Castro. Moscow assumed that it could reach a diplomatic settlement on Cuba with Washington only if there were some guarantee of on-site inspection in Cuba, and Castro continued to oppose any foreign inspection. In informing Mikoyan of the Presidium decision to haggle with Kennedy, Khrushchev betrayed his disappointment with the Cuban leader. "[B]ecause of his youth," complained Khrushchev, "[Castro] cannot behave himself properly" and "cannot understand the difficulties" that the Kremlin was trying to manage.[37]

Soviet haggling came to an abrupt end when Moscow received intelligence information that suggested Kennedy was about to lose control of the U.S. military. On November 15 Khrushchev read a report from the KGB station in New York that drew on conversations with *New York Times* UN correspondent Thomas Hamilton and a journalist from the *New York Herald Tribune*. Both journalists stated that at a meeting in White House on November 12 "Pentagon chiefs" had demanded that Kennedy issue an unconditional ultimatum to the Soviet Union calling for both the withdrawal of the Il-28 bombers and UN inspections of the Soviet missile sites and air bases in Cuba. If these demands were not met, the Pentagon wanted the United States to launch an immediate invasion of Cuba.[38] Moscow took this report seriously enough that on November 16 it requested corroboration of this information from the KGB station in New York.

The U.S. military was indeed prepared to strike. Air Force Chief of Staff Curtis LeMay told Kennedy on November 16 that a U.S. air attack could easily wipe out the Soviet Il-28s. "The operation is fairly simple," he told the commander in chief. "It would be accomplished in a few minutes."[39] U.S. intelligence had spotted nine airplanes in crates at Holguin Airport in southeastern Cuba and thirty-two at San Julián in the western part of the island. The U.S. attack force would involve forty-eight planes, twenty-four of them bombers and the rest for fire suppression and to handle any attempts by MiG fighters to disrupt the attack. The U.S. Navy was equally ready to tighten the blockade to prevent any petroleum or industrial lubricants from reaching the island. "We're ready to put the screws on at any time," said Admiral George Anderson. But the U.S. military, which remained under tight civilian control, could not launch a strike without a presidential order, and Kennedy had not yet ordered any kind of military attack.

Although inaccurate, this alarming information from the United States altered Khrushchev's assessment of the risk of waiting for Kennedy to accept a negotiated withdrawal of the Il-28 bombers. So too did reports from Cuba that Castro was about to initiate a conflict with the United States. Eager to force the United States to curtail its low-level reconnaissance flights, which had continued despite the lowering of tension after the exchange of letters by Moscow and Washington, Castro instructed the Cuban soldiers manning antiaircraft units that by November 17 or 18 they would have the right to open fire on U.S. reconnaissance planes. The Soviets still controlled the SAMs, which could reach the high-altitude U-2s, but the defensive units under

Cuban control could threaten low-level U.S. flights. To communicate his resolve to Washington, Castro also warned Acting UN Secretary-General U Thant that he intended to attack planes that violated Cuban airspace.

On November 16 Khrushchev declared before the Presidium that the Il-28s should be removed immediately. Once again he did not blame Kennedy for the increased danger in the Caribbean. This time he directed his anger at Castro's threat to start shooting down U.S. planes. "It is just shouting and unreasonable," Khrushchev said, complaining about Castro's position on ending the confrontation in the Caribbean.[40] The Cuban leader's actions since October 28 had shown him to be far less trustworthy than Khrushchev had believed. "It is a lesson to us," Khrushchev admitted to his colleagues. He did not believe the Cubans deserved any more Soviet patience. "The affair is coming to a head: Either they will cooperate or we will recall our personnel." The last thing Khrushchev wanted was to see a return to the tense days of late October. But his colleagues convinced him to give Castro one last chance to agree to the Il-28 concession, and the Soviet announcement of its concession to Kennedy was delayed.

In light of the risk of a Cuban-U.S. conflict, Khrushchev made another major decision to help calm the situation. The Soviet Union would remove all the defensive nuclear weapons it had sent to the islands. Initially the Soviet military had planned that the Lunas, at least, would eventually be transferred to Cuban control still armed with nuclear warheads. In his fury at Castro, Khrushchev called off even that small act of nuclear proliferation. The Luna short-range missiles would stay on the island, as would some of the FKR cruise missiles, but without nuclear warheads.[41]

The patience that the Kremlin had shown Cuba began to pay off. On November 17 and 18 Castro did not order his gunners to shoot down any U.S. low-level reconnaissance aircraft (the high-level U-2s remained vulnerable only to the SAMs, which remained under Soviet control in Cuba). Then, following an all-day meeting with his closest advisers, Castro told Mikoyan on November 19 that his government would swallow the loss of the bombers, but there could not be any independent inspection of the island.

On November 20 Ambassador Dobrynin informed Robert Kennedy that the Il-28s would be out of Cuba within thirty days. In return, the president announced the lifting of the blockade on November 20, only a few hours after receiving the news of the Soviet concession. U.S. and Soviet negotiators had yet to reach an agreement on formalizing Kennedy's pledge not to invade the island. Moscow's inability to persuade Castro to accept on-site inspection had made this impossible. To satisfy American concerns that the missiles were in fact leaving, the Soviets improvised an inspection system that didn't require

Cuban participation. The ships taking the R-12 medium-range ballistic missiles back to the Soviet Union were instructed to remove the tarpaulin covers on the missiles to reveal them to U.S. planes taking photographs above. The next day the Soviet military reduced its level of readiness, and the U.S. armed forces began to demobilize. The Cuban missile crisis was finally over.

■

CURIOUSLY, THE SETTLEMENT of the Il-28s, which had involved yet another U.S. demand followed by a Soviet retreat, did nothing to weaken Khrushchev's basic assumption that the missile crisis as a whole, especially the shared experience of a near-nuclear disaster at the end of October, had convinced Americans that they had to take Soviet needs seriously. In this climate the Soviet leader was optimistic about future superpower negotiations to lessen the cost and dangers of the Cold War.

On November 12 Khrushchev had tried out some new ideas for the next round of talks at a farewell audience with the outgoing British ambassador Frank Roberts.[42] He told Roberts that in view of an apparent swing in U.S. public opinion, he thought a comprehensive nuclear test ban possible, and that to meet some of Kennedy's domestic concerns, he would permit international inspectors to supervise the operation of automatic seismic stations on Soviet soil. He mentioned that the Soviets were about to complete their most recent series of nuclear tests, and he believed that no further tests would be required. What he did not reveal to Roberts was that to sweeten the deal, he was even beginning to contemplate allowing a few symbolic on-site inspections of suspicious seismic activity.

Once he had piqued the British ambassador's interest, he raised the Berlin problem, reiterating that it remained a barrier on the road to better East-West relations through a test ban and eventual disarmament. He did not push too hard but did indicate that the issue remained important to him. Berlin was one of three areas that he thought were "ripe" for a settlement at that point. The other two were a Chinese seat at the United Nations, which Khrushchev thought was inevitable, and the signature of a NATO and Warsaw Pact non-aggression treaty.

Khrushchev did not mention the ongoing intramural struggle with China to the British ambassador. Yet the Soviet leader understood that any new efforts he would be making to enhance the prospects of peaceful coexistence with the West would anger the Chinese. This no longer seemed to matter to him. The day after Kennedy lifted the naval blockade of Cuba Khrushchev launched a new policy in Southeast Asia that was sure to strengthen relations with Washington at the expense of the Sino-Soviet relationship. In early November the Pathet Lao had shot down a U.S. supply plane bound for the neutral government of Souvanna Phouma. The Pathet Lao's formal announce-ment of this attack on November 21 coincided with a Kremlin discussion of yet another request from the Lao Communists for secret assistance. Since July Khrushchev had looked the other way as Soviet aircraft violated the spirit, if not the letter, of the July 1962 neutrality agreement in Laos. The Pathet Lao maintained a undeclared force in the border regions with China and North Vietnam, a force that China and the Soviet Union had been provisioning since late 1960 without telling Laos's neutralist prime minister, Souvanna Phouma. Now Khrushchev believed he needed to end the Soviet violations. The July 1962 agreement in Laos could serve as a model for international cooperation in West Berlin. Even if it was not an effective model, at the very least any Soviet failure to meet its obligations in Laos would be used by Soviet enemies in the West to scuttle any future Berlin agreement.

At the November 21 meeting of the Presidium Khrushchev exploded when he read the Pathet Lao's request for more secret assistance. "We will not do it!" he instructed his colleagues. For years the Soviets had tried to discourage the Pathet Lao from taking unnecessary risks, advice that usually contradicted what the Lao Communists were hearing from their supporters in Hanoi and Beijing. The one exception to this Soviet policy of caution had come during the meniscus period of Soviet foreign policy, when Khrushchev had turned a blind eye to the Chinese- and North Vietnamese–supported invasion of Nam Tha in May by the Pathet Lao. That invasion caused the deployment of additional U.S. troops in Thailand and nearly precipitated an American military intervention in Laos. In the after-math of the missile crisis Khrushchev was no longer prepared to sit back and watch socialist allies take those risks. "Peace is the major issue [now]. Peace has been made [in the Caribbean] without winners and losers. If we continue pursu-ing the same policy," said Khrushchev, "then it will not be in the interests of the leftists." He wanted Abramov's successor in the embassy in Vientiane to warn the Pathet Lao that if it chose to ignore Moscow's guidance and went to war against Souvanna, it would be a war it would have to fight on its own. Believing there were bigger issues at stake, Khrushchev was prepared to wash his hands of the Lao Communists: "We did everything we could."[43]

■

Mikoyan stopped in Washington on November 29 on his way home from Havana. Khrushchev wanted the Kremlin's envoy to reinforce his mes-sage that the time was right to move toward more substantial superpower agreements. Mikoyan was also expected to reinforce Khrushchev's new explanation for why the Cuban crisis had happened. "[T]he Soviet Union does not deserve any reproach. No one can believe that the arms build-up in Cuba was offensive and intended against the United States."[44] Mikoyan, who had opposed the entire operation, knew that Khrushchev had considered the missiles offensive weapons. The deployment to Cuba had been the logical consequence of Khrushchev's dangerous meniscus approach, his strategy of concerted pressure on the United States. Mikoyan had hated that policy, but in front of President Kennedy he was happy to sweep it under the carpet and pretend it had never existed.

The talk was important for other reasons. Kennedy was eager for Khrushchev's help in eliminating the entire Soviet military presence in Cuba. Although U.S. intelligence had lowballed the actual size of the Soviet military contingent in Cuba by a factor of three, Kennedy still believed that the seventeen thousand military personnel the CIA thought Khrushchev had on the island were too many. The Soviet record of the meeting has Kennedy at one point saying, "I know that Khrushchev did not promise this in his letters to me, but I am hopeful that the Soviet Union will withdraw those troops."[45] Mikoyan's response, which appears in both the Soviet and U.S. records of this meeting, was succinct: "We will do what we promised, nothing more and nothing less."[46]

Mikoyan returned to Moscow and was hailed by the entire leadership for his stalwart effort in Cuba. Khrushchev employed the first Presidium session after Mikoyan's return to provide a postmortem for his colleagues on the Cuban missile operation, in which he claimed it had been a tremendous success. "Cuba has been maintained," he asserted, "as a center of the revolutionary movement."[47] Even more important than that, the crisis had demonstrated once and for all that the United States respected Soviet interests and power. "The United States was forced to acknowledge that we have our own interests in the Western Hemisphere." Moreover, Khrushchev crowed, "We are members of the World Club. They themselves got scared."

Creating a kind of parity in the balance of terror between the superpowers had been Khrushchev's primary motivation for putting the missiles in Cuba. He now believed that even with them removed he had achieved that objective. In front of Mikoyan and his colleagues, he complimented himself for knowing when to withdraw the missiles: "If we had maintained our position longer, perhaps none of this would have happened."

Khrushchev did not employ the meeting of December 3 to announced formally a new approach to foreign affairs in light of America's newfound respect for Soviet powers. But at the tail end of the meeting he hinted that for the foreseeable future the Soviet use of pressure tactics was dead. Wherever possible Moscow would seek compromises with Washington. The hinting had come when Mikoyan reported Kennedy's request that the Soviets remove all their remaining soldiers in Cuba. Without prompting or complaining, Khrushchev announced to his colleagues that he and the defense minister would be looking into how this might be achieved.

Over the first week of December Khrushchev continued to mull over ways to interest the United States in serious discussions. The first step, he knew, would be to remove what was left of his July threats to reissue an ultimatum on the Berlin question. The second step involved offering something to Kennedy that might make a comprehensive test ban agreement possible.

Since the very first back channel discussions between Robert Kennedy and Georgi Bolshakov in May 1961, the Kennedys had impressed upon Khrushchev the reality that a comprehensive test ban treaty would have to be independently verifiable for it to be approved by the U.S. Senate, which under the U.S. Constitution had to ratify all treaties. In practice this meant that there would have to be on-site inspections of a certain percentage of the unexplained seismic activity that was detected every year in the Soviet Union. The U.S. position in January 1961 was that there had to be twenty of these inspections a year. By the time of the Cuban missile crisis that number had fallen to twelve.

On October 30, at the talks in Geneva the U.S. disarmament negotiator Arthur Dean had left Soviet Deputy Foreign Minister Vasily Kuznetsov with the distinct impression that Washington could go much lower. Indeed the U.S. position had been changing. Kennedy, who wanted an agreement, was already privately considering bringing the number down to eight. But Kuznetsov misunderstood or Dean misspoke. Somehow Kuznetsov took from this conversation that the U.S. Senate would accept a treaty so long as the Soviets undertook to provide three inspections a year.[48]

After he received this information from the Soviet Foreign Ministry, Khrushchev decided to give the United States the right to make three unannounced inspections of Soviet territory to verify unexplained seismic activity. "When we gave our agreement," he later explained, "we considered it to be a symbolic one. This was a concession for the president, taking his situation into consideration."[49]

■

I N EARLY DECEMBER Khrushchev revealed to an important foreign visitor that the debate with the Chinese was playing some role in his willingness to compromise with Kennedy to achieve a test ban agreement. Noted peace activist Norman Cousins, whose day job was editor of the *Saturday Review*, arrived in Moscow in early December 1962 carrying a message from Pope John XXIII to Khrushchev. From men in Khrushchev's inner circle, Cousins learned that the Soviet leader was intent on proving to the Chinese that the policy of peaceful coexistence could bring détente and benefits to the Soviet bloc.[50] A few days later Khrushchev himself made that point to Cousins. "The Chinese say I was scared," the Soviet leader told the American in a private meeting. "Of course I was scared. It would have been insane not to have been scared. I was frightened about what could happen to my country—or your country or all the other countries that would be devastated by a nuclear war. If being frightened meant that I helped avert such insanity then I'm glad I was frightened. One of the problems in the world today is that not enough people are sufficiently frightened by the danger of nuclear war."[51] Khrushchev then made a dramatic gesture to show that he believed there were at least two other world leaders who shared his understanding of the inherent destructiveness of nuclear weapons. Going over to his desk, Khrushchev pulled out some stationery. Then in his characteristic scrawl he wrote individual Christmas greetings for John Kennedy and the pope.[52]

In the week after meeting Cousins, Khrushchev sent two more confidential messages to Kennedy. In these letters he explicitly dispelled the threat of a renewed Berlin ultimatum and handed the president a new proposal for a test ban agreement. He had waited to make the test ban concession until the Soviet military had started its final previously scheduled series of atmospheric tests.[53] Among his colleagues at the Kremlin Khrushchev claimed that allowing for three on-site inspections was "a very big concession because it allows for spies."[54] But he thought he needed to meet Kennedy "half way."[55] Khrushchev believed the stage was set for 1963 to be the year of international achievement that the downing of Francis Gary Powers's U-2 in May 1960 had denied the Soviet Union three years earlier.

■

JOHN KENNEDY's third State of the Union address in January 1963 projected a sense of confidence about the direction that international events were taking. A lifelong sailor, the president drew upon seafaring language to suggest what lay ahead in the Cold War. "My friends, I close on a note of hope. We are not lulled by the momentary calm of the sea or the somewhat clearer skies above. We know the turbulence that lies below, and the storms beyond the horizon this year. Now the winds of change appear to be blowing more strongly than ever, in the world of communism as well as our own. For 175 years we have sailed with those winds at our back, and with the tides of human freedom in our favor. We steer our ship with hope, as Thomas Jefferson said, 'leaving fear astern.' "[56] The American leader sensed that something had changed in Khrushchev's assessment of the world, or at least the Soviet leadership seemed to have abandoned the use of brinkmanship in foreign affairs. This was certainly the message he discerned in the letters that Khrushchev had been sending him secretly since the lifting of the blockade around Cuba. A third letter had arrived from Moscow just a week before that reiterated the same points. Kennedy reminded his listeners that the world was experiencing a "pause" that was no basis for smugness. "[C]omplacency or self-congratulation can imperil our security as much as the weapons of our adversary. A moment of pause is not a promise of peace. Dangerous problems remain from Cuba to the South China Sea. The world's prognosis prescribes not a year's vacation, but a year of obligation and opportunity."[57]

Kennedy saw the growing estrangement between China and the Soviet Union as the greatest variable in the international system. "Now I think that we ought to keep in mind what's happening between the Soviet Union and China," he had told his foreign policy advisers in November. "Indeed, Khrushchev is attacked daily for a Munich and appeasement and is under bitter attack from the Chinese. Whether this will result in a break between them, I don't know." Kennedy had also noticed a shift in the tone of Khrushchev's comments on Berlin. "He was more forthcoming about Berlin than he's ever been the other day," the president had remarked to his advisers. "Whether it means anything, I don't know. But I think we should be . . . I completely agree that he's a liar and Castro is impossible and I don't have any view that Khrushchev is better than someone else in the Soviet Union and that we should be at all generous with Khrushchev because he's under attack from the Chinese. But at least we should keep in mind that there's a major collision going on here, and what result it will bring, whether helpful to us or not, I don't know."[58] In his more optimistic moments Kennedy had reason to believe these tensions among the two Communist giants might move the Cold War out of the dangerous pattern of crisis and relaxation that had defined every year since his inauguration.

The day after Kennedy outlined the state of the American Union, Khrushchev gave a similarly significant address in Berlin. The Soviet leader had already concluded that 1963 would be a year, as Kennedy put it, of "obligation and opportunity." Khrushchev used the occasion to call off publicly his threat of a new ultimatum on Berlin, the threat that he had withdrawn privately in his letter to Kennedy a month earlier. He indicated that Berlin would not be the cause of a crisis in 1963. Instead he presented the building of the Berlin Wall in 1961 as "a most important step" and said that now the signing of a Soviet-East German peace treaty was "no longer the problem it was before the protective measures."[59] Khrushchev repeated his desire to put U.S. troops under the UN flag in West Berlin, but this idea was presented as a hope instead of a demand.

The spurt of activism continued. The next day the Kremlin published the texts of Khrushchev's December letters to the White House. A week later Foreign Minister Gromyko visited the U.S. ambassador Foy Kohler to tell Kennedy that the Soviet leadership was prepared to resume talks on Berlin. Gromyko's tone wasn't insistent, nor was there any promise that the Soviet position had changed. Still, the manner in which the request came was a sign of a different climate from the summer of 1962.[60]

Khrushchev also believed it was time to extend an olive branch to the Chinese. For some reason, he had convinced himself that he could bring Mao around and achieve good relations with Beijing and Washington simultaneously. In December 1963 he called on Beijing to put an end to the daily criticism of the Kremlin in its newspapers, and he said that Soviet newspapers would do the same. His attempt to ease Sino-Soviet tensions did not mean that all was forgiven. He was still very angry at Mao and the Chinese leaders. "The Chinese are dimwits," Khrushchev said candidly to his Kremlin colleagues at the end of January.[61] Nevertheless, he preached to his colleagues the forgiveness that he now wanted to see reflected throughout Soviet foreign policy: "[T]he attitude should be more tolerant, it is not obligatory to drag them to the cross. . . . We should contribute to the process of releasing [them] from erroneous positions, should help them to get rid of [their] shortcomings."[62]

■

THE WHITE HOUSE greeted these signs of a renewed Soviet peace offensive with a mixture of disappointment and hope. There was nothing new in Khrushchev's December letters despite their welcome tone. The Berlin letter repeated old nostrums, and the test ban message signified merely a revival of the Soviet position of the late Eisenhower period, which was still unacceptable to the United States.

Kennedy nevertheless seized upon the change in the Soviet position on test ban inspections as a reason to rethink the official U.S. position yet again. The most enthusiastic advocate of a test ban in his administration, the president worked to persuade his advisers that the U.S. demand could come down to six inspections. He acknowledged that cutting the old official position of

twelve inspections in half would entail taking a greater risk that some secret
Soviet tests might not be detected. But at a meeting with his key arms control
advisers on February 8, 1963, the president outlined the logic behind any further concessions to the Soviets in the test ban negotiations. Freely admitting
that he expected the Soviets to try to cheat, he explained that he assumed that
any danger that this cheating might pose would be outweighed by the benefit
to the United States of hampering the development of a Chinese nuclear
force by getting Moscow to help him conclude a comprehensive worldwide
nuclear test ban.[63] Kennedy did have doubts he could sell six inspections to
the Senate, but he was determined to try. He knew, however, that he could
never sell three annual inspections.[64]

■

THE WORLD DID NOT stand still as Khrushchev and Kennedy looked for
points of superpower agreement. On February 8, 1963, elements of the Ba'ath
Party had overthrown and murdered 'Abd al-Karim Qasim. The CIA had
been scheming to remove Qasim since the late 1950s, and its precise role in
orchestrating the events of February 1963 remains murky. "We did not stage
this coup . . . [though] we covered it very well," recalled James Critchfield,
who was running the CIA's operations in the Middle East at the time.[65] But a
main Iraqi participant, Ali Saleh Sa'adi, the secretary-general of the Ba'ath
Party, described a very different role for U.S. intelligence: "[W]e came to
power on a CIA train."[66] Besides using its station in the U.S. Embassy in
Baghdad as a point of contact with the leaders of the coup, the CIA apparently operated a secret radio station in Kuwait to send its instructions.[67] The
CIA certainly had agents among the plotters; however, Abdel Salam Aref, the
most active of the lot, who would soon become the Iraqi president, was not
among them.[68] Whatever the role of the CIA in the coup, it was extremely
bloody, and the United States was pleased with the outcome. Qasim, whose
lifeless body was dumped into the Tigris, ceased being a threat to American
interests in the Middle East.

At first Moscow knew nothing of the new regime's connections to the
United States and held out hope that this political upheaval would not mean a
complete loss of its investment in that country. Qasim had not been a perfect
client. Although he had gladly accepted an enormous amount of Soviet aid—
Iraq was the third-largest recipient of aid after Cuba and Egypt—he had main-
tained a much tougher line against the Iraqi Communist Party than the
Soviets had expected. In April 1960 the Kremlin had sent Mikoyan to
Baghdad to remind Qasim that Iraqi Communists were among his strongest

supporters. The Iraqi had responded with a barely polite admonition that the Soviet Union should not meddle in Iraqi internal affairs.[69] The Kremlin leadership knew that the new government would repair relations with Nasser, but the real question was whether a government that portrayed itself as neutral, nationalist, socialist, and anti-Communist would be any different from the Egypt that had developed good relations with Moscow in 1955. Willing to take a chance, the Soviet Union joined the Western powers in recognizing the new government only days after the coup.[70]

Within ten days, however, horrific reports reached Moscow that the new regime was violently anti-Communist. With Iraqi tanks rolling through the streets to create panic, the Aref government hunted down the country's Communists. Seven thousand people, alleged to be Communist, were arrested, and it is estimated that an equal number were killed.[71] The Kremlin felt powerless to do anything about the Ba'athist attack. On February 19 the Soviet Red Cross appealed to the International Red Cross to "use its prestige and authority to stop the blood bath."[72] Soviet composer Dmitri Shostakovich, poet Ilya Ehrenburg, and other members of a Soviet Peace Committee also demanded an international crusade against the killing. At the Patrice Lumumba University in Moscow (originally the Freedom University) students protested the action and carried signs denouncing "Fascism in Iraq." These appeals went unheeded.

It was troubling to Moscow that Egypt said nothing as the Ba'ath Party continued its persecution of Iraqi Communists. On February 23, Iraq accused "some socialist states" of attempting to provoke the Kurdish tribes in northern Iraq to overthrow their regime.[73] The next day the Iraqis arrested the first secretary of the Iraqi Communist Party, Husain Ahmad ar-Radi, and two other top leaders, killing a fourth leader who resisted arrest.[74] With the Iraqi party decimated and Nasser an apparent accomplice, there seemed to be nothing left of Khrushchev's Middle East policy.

Khrushchev had not expected the bloodshed in Iraq, and it took some time for the foreign policy debacle there to become apparent to him. He seemed his buoyant self on February 9, when he sat for an interview with the international press baron Roy H. Thomson (later Lord Thomson of Fleet). When Thomson presented Khrushchev with a battery-powered watch for himself and a diamond wristwatch for Mrs. Khrushchev, the Soviet leader joked: "Thank you very much. It looks like some infernal machine that the capitalists have dreamed up to blow up the Communist world. I will tell my wife to try them on first." Then he added, "The Yugoslavs have a saying that they are all in favor of equality for women, so when they cross a minefield they let the women go first."[75] Privately, however, Khrushchev was sickened by the reports from Iraq. "The Ba'athists borrowed their methods from Hitler," Khrushchev later told a visiting Egyptian military delegation. "In Iraq they are persecuting not only communists and other progressive elements," he added, "but even Arab nationalists and peace advocates." Thinking back to Soviet motives for supporting the fallen Qasim regime, Khrushchev lamented, "we hoped that the revolution would develop in a progressive way."[76]

■

ORDINARILY KHRUSHCHEV responded to major events in the third world by striking out at the United States or the international system in one form or another. In 1956 and again in 1958 he had challenged Anglo-American power in the Middle East to provide some shelter to both the Egyptian and the Iraqi revolutions. In 1960 he had threatened Washington and demanded huge structural changes at the United Nations to ensure the survival of the Castro and Lumumba regimes. In 1962 the U.S. deployment near Laos had added significantly to his sense of encirclement and may have been the ultimate trigger for the decision to put missiles in Cuba. When the Iraqi Revolution turned sour in February 1963, however, Khrushchev did not react with his usual fire. The loss of Iraq and the suspicions Nasser was helping Aref move Iraq away from Moscow might well have provoked an earlier Khrushchev to do something. Instead there was a hint of passive acceptance in the Kremlin.

In the winter and spring of 1963 Khrushchev received reminders at home that it was not the right time to go on the offensive against the United States. In the first months of 1963 there was new evidence that the Soviet economy was even weaker than the Kremlin had been led to expect at the end of 1962. On February 27, in a speech to an audience in Kalinin, a city northwest of Moscow, Khrushchev tried again to prepare the Soviet people for the likelihood that their standard of living would not rise as rapidly as promised. He hinted that the cost of keeping up with the United States in the Cold War was largely to blame and asked that Soviet citizens "give us time" to provide consumer goods.[77] In early March the Soviet government published a collection of Khrushchev's speeches on agriculture that did not include any reference to the catch and surpass campaign of 1957. Having just issued data showing that meat production in 1962 was only 40 percent of what he had called for by the early 1960s, the Kremlin had no desire to remind Soviet citizens of the promises that had been made.[78] In mid-March Khrushchev fired his minister of agriculture.

Khrushchev was deeply concerned about the effect of his regime's inability to satisfy domestic needs. In the first three months of 1963 he gave three major addresses on ideology.[79] In openly expressing his concerns about the effect of bourgeois influences on Soviet life, he was certainly speaking to his left-wing critics in Beijing, in Tirana, and elsewhere in the socialist bloc, whom he wanted to reassure that any search for compromise with Washington did not mean a weakening in Communist discipline. But his main focus was at home.

Nothing dramatized this concern as much as the sudden shift in Khrushchev's position on the space program. Earlier in the year he had indicated to the visiting Roy Thomson that the Soviet Union might be dropping out of the space race. To Thomson's question about which year the Soviet Union would put a man on the moon, Khrushchev had replied with disarming candor, "Quite sincerely I'd say I don't know—I don't want to pose or indulge in empty chatter. . . . [It is] not imminent. Neither is it the main theme of our life. Let those make haste to get to the moon who lead a bad life on this earth. We have no intentions of doing so."[80] With the Soviet economy in a downward spiral, it made no sense to be pouring money into the moon bid.

In March Khrushchev decided the Soviet people and the socialist bloc needed a psychological lift, whatever the cost. The space program was an area where the Soviets were equal to the Americans, and in those days of Sino-Soviet tension it was also useful as a way to show up the Chinese. Mao would not have his own space program for some years. "It is not right to stop the construction of the Vostok [the Soviet manned spacecraft]," Khrushchev announced at a Presidium meeting on March 21 before he left for the south.[81] He also insisted that the Soviet space program in 1963 include a female astronaut, the first woman to go into space.

■

YET FOR ALL these troubles at home and the challenge in Iraq, Khrushchev had decided not to undermine his post-Cuban effort to lessen tensions with the United States. In mid-March, as he had promised, the Soviet military withdrew additional troops from Cuba. Khrushchev's desire to help Kennedy was not the sole reason why these troops were removed. The Cubans had complained about the lack of discipline among some of the men, and incidents of drunkenness had grown to an alarming number.[82] But the Soviets understood the benefits for Kennedy and the need to reduce right-wing pressures on him. Recent reports from the KGB conveyed the by now familiar picture of an American president who was being pressured to resume the U.S. crusade to overthrow Castro.[83] The Soviets also wanted to ensure that Kennedy would make good on his promise to remove the Jupiter missiles from Turkey.

Later in March Khrushchev's faith in Kennedy seemed to be rewarded. Since Robert Kennedy made the offer on behalf of his brother in October, the Soviet government had kept a close watch on the status of the Jupiter missiles in Turkey. The KGB had reported in February that the Turkish government strongly opposed the removal of missiles, which were near Izmir.[84] Nevertheless, by late March all the missiles had been removed, and the U.S. government informed Moscow that it had fulfilled its obligation. The Turks also made a point of inviting the local Soviet ambassador to visit the abandoned missile bases. "Only goats roamed that vacant land," Ambassador N. S. Ryzhov later recalled, "and the concrete structures that remained had been taken apart by the local peasants."[85] Ryzhov, who visited the site with the Soviet military attaché, was nevertheless concerned by the presence of some metal rods that had presumably served some purpose at the dismantled U.S. missile base. Upon his return to the Turkish capital that night, he asked the Turkish prime minister if these rods indicated a plan to reintroduce ballistic missiles at a later date. The next day the Turkish government ordered the rods destroyed.[86]

At the end of March Khrushchev went south to his home at Pitsunda for some rest. Before he left, he prepared something for the Chinese. On March 9 Beijing had finally responded to Khrushchev's olive branch by suggesting that Khrushchev himself visit Beijing. It would be the Soviet leader's first visit in four years.[87] Khrushchev did not want to go to China, however, although he was prepared to see Mao in Moscow if the Chinese leader would make the trip. Khrushchev instructed his Foreign Ministry to prepare his response to Mao carefully. "Not in a polemical form," he warned.[88] Even in their letter offering a truce, the Chinese had seemed to want to pick a fight over Soviet policy toward Yugoslavia, which Mao considered too permissive of Tito's violations of Communist orthodoxy. Khrushchev wanted his own letter to remind the Chinese, respectfully, that Moscow viewed Belgrade as an ally and Beijing should accept it.

In his first days at Pitsunda Khrushchev signed off on a new letter to Kennedy. With the Jupiter missiles out of Turkey, Khrushchev decided to apply a little pressure on the U.S. president to pay more attention to the outstanding issues between the two superpowers. This was not a return to the brinkmanship of 1962. He merely wanted to remind Kennedy of the December initiatives and provoke some creativity in Washington. His lack of subtlety meant that the tone of this letter ultimately seemed more threatening than insistent. Despite this, Khrushchev was determined not to have another crisis with Kennedy.

■

IN THE SPRING OF 1963 the Kennedy administration wondered if the sixty-nine-year-old Khrushchev was on the verge of retirement. A CIA source in Moscow reported in late March that Khrushchev would resign as chairman of the Council of Ministers on his birthday, April 17. "The reason suggested by the source," explained the report, "was that Khrushchev's colleagues felt that it would be embarrassing for him to conduct in person the forthcoming talks with the Chinese."[89] The U.S. government considered this information signifi-cant enough to share it with the British, who had nothing to add. "We have no certain knowledge of anything that goes on inside the Soviet Praesidium," a British official noted in a paper that was sent to Prime Minister Macmillan.[90]

Although CIA analysts in Washington and the diplomatic staff at the embassy in Moscow downplayed the rumors of Khrushchev's impending retirement, arguing that he was not the type to leave when he was on the defensive, the White House received reports from various additional sources suggesting that "a quiet but deep crisis was under way in the USSR."[91] A high-level paper substantially written by Walt Rostow, chairman of the State Department's Policy Planning Staff, looked to a post-Khrushchev Soviet Union. Rostow was not a Soviet expert, however, and the administration's chief Kremlin watcher was much less optimistic. Llewellyn Thompson wor-ried that in response to Chinese pressure, Khrushchev might embrace a harder line toward the West. "I am becoming increasingly concerned," Thompson wrote Rusk in the first days of April, "that the Soviets may be tempted to shoot down one of our many flights along the periphery of the Soviet Union."[92]

In the midst of this Washington discussion over Khrushchev's future, Soviet Ambassador Dobrynin unexpectedly requested a private meeting with Robert Kennedy on April 3.[93] The same afternoon Dobrynin arrived at the Justice Department with a message from Khrushchev wrapped in a newspa-per. Not only was the way it was delivered unusual, but the document itself was twenty-five pages long and lacked the formalities of a letter between lead-ers. The Russians called it a "talking paper," and it was clear from the style who had done the talking. As the attorney general read the message, his con-cern grew. "It was full of poison," he later confided to his brother.[94] The mes-sage appeared to be a tough reiteration of Khrushchev's standard arguments against U.S. positions on the test ban, Berlin, and Cuba. Robert Kennedy was startled at how little the Soviet understanding of the United States had changed in the two years that he and his brother had been dealing with Khrushchev. "It was as if a person had come down from Mars and written this," Kennedy believed.[95]

The brothers met privately to discuss this message before consulting the rest of the government. The president saw the document as the clearest sign to date that the Cold War was at a tipping point. As early as November 1962, he had asked his advisers to think through the possibility that because of Sino-Soviet tensions, Khrushchev had a choice to make between confrontation and coexistence with the West. Now Kennedy considered a dramatic gesture to influence Khrushchev's decision. He plotted with his brother for Robert to take an urgent trip to Moscow and meet Khrushchev. The attorney general's mission would be to try to correct the Soviet leader's misunderstanding of the White House's intentions.[96]

The mission never happened. When the president raised the idea in discussions with his foreign policy advisers three days later, it found no takers. Rusk and Bundy politely, but firmly, discouraged a special mission by the attorney general. The president tried hard to persuade them that his brother would make a useful emissary but then gave in and approved Rusk's suggestion that former U.S. Ambassador to the USSR Averell Harriman be the one to make the trip to Moscow. Harriman was expected to leave by the end of the month.[97]

Norman Cousins, the independent peace activist, was already scheduled to make a return trip to Moscow in a few days, and President Kennedy decided to use him to send a personal message to Khrushchev. "Dean Rusk has already spoken to you of our hope that we can get the test ban unblocked," the president told Cousins on the eve of his departure.[98] Kennedy wanted Khrushchev to understand that the United States would never be willing to accept an agreement that specified only three on-site inspections. "I believe there's been an honest misunderstanding. See if you can't get Premier Khrushchev to accept the fact of an honest misunderstanding." Cousins left the United States on April 10.

■

"**W**HENEVER I HAVE a big egg to hatch," Khrushchev told his American visitor, "this is where I come." Khrushchev had brought Cousins to Pitsunda on April 12 after only a night in Moscow. He told Cousins that he had worked on his speech to the Twentieth Party Congress and his proposals for the Twenty-second Party Congress at Pitsunda, and now, he said, "I've got something else growing inside me." He said he planned to announce whatever it was at the party plenum in mid-May.[99]

"When I come here to hatch eggs, this is all I do." Khrushchev told Cousins that in the three weeks he had already spent at Pitsunda he had seen only three guests. His life followed a comforting routine: He exercised in the morning, played badminton with his trainer or his doctor, then went for a massage and a long walk and took a swim in the pool. "Then I go out to think for a bit, come back and dictate, then I get tired, go out again, and dictate again." At the end of the day Khrushchev got another massage.

Cousins, a trained physician, noted the state of Khrushchev's health. There were rumors in Moscow that his blood pressure was high. Cousins did not know for sure. "I can only say," he later told President Kennedy, "that after ten or twelve minutes of badminton, he didn't seem unduly out of breath for a sixty-nine-year-old man. He is agile, his reflexes were good, [and] his skin tone seems fine. When he sat down to talk, he is perfectly focused." What Cousins thought unusual was that Khrushchev seemed able to drink a lot of alcohol. "I was astounded at his capacity." At lunch the Soviet leader had two glasses of vodka, two glasses of wine, and a glass and a half of brandy.

Khrushchev warned Cousins that he was ready to end the negotiations with the West on a nuclear test ban treaty. Repeating his belief that he had given Kennedy what he needed to get a treaty through the U.S. Senate, he stated that he could make no further concessions. "We held out our hand, it was not accepted . . . and now I've got to look after the national security." Khrushchev asserted that his scientists and military people had been pressuring him hard to resume testing. They had refinements that they hoped to work out. Moreover, the United States, they said, had undertaken 70 percent more nuclear tests than the Soviet Union. If Khrushchev were to keep these domestic opponents in line, he would have to sign a treaty that was not harmful to Soviet security. For this reason there would be no more concessions. "Take my word for it, I went as far as I could go; this is the end of the line for me."

Khrushchev was planning to return to Moscow in a week or so, and he left Cousins with the distinct impression that the Soviets would probably withdraw the offer of on-site inspections and resume testing. "Mr. Chairman," said Cousins, "you've broken my heart. If this opportunity is missed, there may never be another." The Soviet leader replied: "That's right, maybe not for twenty years, maybe we'll go on for twenty years this way, but tell the president I tried. . . . You're not the only one who's had a broken heart." He warned Cousins, thereby signaling to Washington, that he would have something to say in mid-May.

■

Aᴌᴛʜᴏᴜɢʜ Kʜʀᴜꜱʜᴄʜᴇᴠ had not conspired to ratchet up the pressure in the third world, events thousands of miles away in Laos in April 1963 seemed to give credence to his warnings to Norman Cousins. An uneasy cease-fire in that troubled land had collapsed earlier in the month. A pro–Pathet Lao faction had split from Kong Le's command and was now attacking the armed forces of the Souvanna government. Then, on April 8, the Pathet Lao leader, Prince Souphanouvong, left the Lao capital, Vientiane, for an area under Pathet Lao control, dramatizing the split in the coalition government. Although there was some question in Washington on whether the Soviets had any real control over the Pathet Lao, the administration had no doubt that the North Vietnamese and their Lao ally had launched an offensive in the region.

Kennedy met with his foreign policy advisers on April 19, 20, and 22 to discuss ways of putting pressure on Moscow and Hanoi to restrain their Lao ally. The president worried that the Geneva agreement on Laos was collapsing along with the neutralist forces in that country.

Unsure whether to respond with force or diplomacy, the president asked the Pentagon to outline U.S. military options, including the reintroduction of U.S. Marines in Thailand (they had been withdrawn in 1962), launching some kind of action against the North Vietnamese, or even applying some pressure on Cuba to get the Kremlin's attention. Meanwhile Kennedy wanted Averell Harriman, who was already scheduled to go to Moscow, to raise his concerns about Laos directly with Khrushchev. The president still believed that Soviet world policy was at a tipping point and could be influenced.[100]

Cousins reported to Kennedy on his meeting with Khrushchev as the president weighed his options in Southeast Asia. In an Oval Office meeting secretly taped by the president, Cousins warned that Khrushchev would probably make a tough statement at the May plenum and advocated that the United States should do something to prevent that. Cousins made two proposals. First, he suggested that the United States accept a comprehensive test ban on Soviet terms for a six-month trial period. Kennedy turned this down. Cousins also suggested that Kennedy give a major address on peace. Recalling the president's September 25, 1961, speech to the UN General Assembly, in which Kennedy had spoken of the need to replace the arms race with a peace race, Cousins argued that it was time to remind the Soviets of the U.S. commitment to peace. Kennedy listened with interest, agreeing when Cousin admitted that his greatest concern was that if the hard-liners grew stronger in the Kremlin, it would bring "a reaction to it, strengthening the hand of the Nixons over here."[101]

In the first week of May the president's principal speechwriter, Ted Sorensen, called Cousins with news that Kennedy had taken to heart his suggestion of giving a major address on peace. It seemed to the White House that a commencement address at the American University in Washington, D.C., which the president was expected to give on June 10, presented an excellent opportunity. Sorensen asked Cousins to send his ideas.

■

TANNED AND APPARENTLY buoyant, Khrushchev returned to Moscow on April 20.[102] Three days later he met with U.S. Ambassador Kohler and British Ambassador Sir Humphrey Trevelyan, who carried identical test ban proposals from their governments. "There's no substance to this message," Khrushchev said to the ambassadors. Washington and London still insisted on an agreement with more than three on-site inspections. "You want the right to position your spies who will get instructions from the intelligence agency," said Khrushchev. "We are not willing to go along with this. We will not tolerate any spies." Once more raising Berlin, he reminded the two governments that there was no hope of an arms control agreement without progress on that issue. "You don't want to decide the German issue, but it's the most important one. This is not what's important, but the German question is, while you don't want to resolve it."[103] It was the last time that this lecture represented Soviet foreign policy.

John Kennedy had been right to see the spring of 1963 as a turning point in the Cold War. On April 25 Nikita Khrushchev invited his defense minister, Rodion Malinovsky, to attend the meeting of the party Presidium. The Soviet leader wanted to outline a new course for Moscow and prepared Malinovsky to convince his colleagues that this new approach would not harm Soviet national security.[104]

Khrushchev had brought back with him from Pitsunda two new convictions: first, that the Berlin issue should no longer be a roadblock to serious U.S.-Soviet agreements and second, that if a comprehensive test ban would be impossible to achieve with the West, Moscow should accept a partial ban that outlawed tests in the atmosphere, in space, and underwater. Only underground testing would continue. Since November Khrushchev had shied away from the pressure tactics that had characterized his foreign policy strategy since 1958. Since then he had also toned down the rhetoric on Berlin. Over the course of a Presidium discussion on April 25 Khrushchev intended to formalize these tendencies as a new approach to dealing with the United States.

After recounting his sterile talk with the Western ambassadors, Khrushchev proposed a new arms control policy. Explaining that his military advisers were telling him that the country would not need to test in the atmosphere any longer, he suggested seeking a partial test ban agreement without any conditions attached. In September he had offered a partial test ban treaty to Kennedy but then stipulated that the Americans would also have to agree to a five-year moratorium on underground testing. He had also made plain that the Soviet Union would consider abrogating the partial test ban if after five years there was no agreement on a permanent ban on underground tests.[105] Now Khrushchev made no reference to underground testing and stressed instead the propaganda advantages of eliminating the major source of radiation poisoning in the water and the air. In announcing that Moscow should be prepared to offer this treaty to the West, Khrushchev said nothing about the Berlin negotiations. Kennedy and Macmillan would get a partial test ban without paying the Berlin price.

As he had done on October 25, 1962, when he sought his colleagues' approval to offer the swap to Kennedy that would end the missile crisis, Khrushchev reserved for himself the timing of this offer to the Americans and the British. "I think that on this issue we may reach an immediate agreement . . . it is only a matter of drawing up a draft. . . . [W]e can now just develop the tactics and the timing, when it is most advantageous for us."[106]

Khrushchev revealed nothing of this sea change in Soviet foreign policy when he met Kennedy's special envoy Averell Harriman to discuss Laos the next day. Khrushchev merely tried to convey to Washington that though he still believed in the Geneva settlement, the superpowers really had better things to worry about than tiny Laos. With a population of only two million, he told Harriman, there was "nothing really serious going on in Laos." He thought that the U.S. and the USSR should try hard to "ignore it."[107] Khrushchev's American guests found his lack of interest in picking a fight with Kennedy over recent events in Southeast Asia puzzling and quite comical. "Khrushchev impatiently exclaimed that he did not know all those silly Laotian names or the individuals to whom these names belonged," NSC staffer Michael Forrestal, who made the trip with Harriman, later reported to the White House.[108] In just a matter of weeks, however, Khrushchev would exploit an unexpected opportunity to reveal to Kennedy and the world his new priorities.

▪

THE WEST GERMAN chancellor took the Soviet ambassador to one side at the diplomatic reception in Bonn. It was late May 1963, and eighty-eight-year-old Konrad Adenauer had only a few months left before retirement, but there was something he wanted to do before leaving office. Adenauer told Ambassador Andrei Smirnov that he hoped for a broad normalization of relations with Moscow. The chancellor explained that he had long wished for such an arrangement but that for domestic and foreign reasons, this had not been possible.[109]

Adenauer tried to convey to the Soviets that he had often had to fight alone for better relations. In 1955, when he decided to reestablish diplomatic relations with Moscow, he had faced opposition not only from his foreign minister, Heinrich von Brentano di Tremezzo, and the secretary of state in the German Foreign Office, Walter Hallstein, but also from many others in his government. Von Brentano and Hallstein, however, had continued their opposition to an Eastern policy. It was they who had chosen the first German ambassador to Moscow, a man who had proved supremely unsuitable, and when the second, Hans Kroll, succeeded in establishing a direct line to Khrushchev, the enemies of good relations with Moscow did everything they could to have him recalled. "In the end," Adenauer said, "Kroll was placed in such a position that remaining in the post of ambassador to Moscow became impossible." Adenauer described himself as almost a passive participant in Kroll's removal. "And of course all of this could not have turned out this way without the advice of our allies."

Adenauer designed his comments to have maximum effect on the Soviets. He told Smirnov that the Soviet Union should not pay too much attention to reports that he would retire in October. "The date of my resignation is up to me alone," he said, "and I have not stopped and do not intend to stop fighting for the realization of my plans." He also took credit for the recent positive discussions that former Ambassador Kroll had been having with Soviet representatives in Bonn.

In April and early May Kroll had visited Smirnov with Adenauer's approval. At these meetings Kroll not only complained about his treatment at the hands of the pro-U.S. lobby in the West German Foreign Ministry, which feared a better relationship with the USSR, but tried to encourage the Kremlin to make use of the dying moments of the Adenauer era to do something dramatic. Kroll explained that Adenauer was hinting that he should return to Moscow. "Don't you usually go to Russia for your holiday?" the chancellor had asked Kroll. The former West German ambassador told Smirnov that he wouldn't go back to Moscow unless the Soviets offered a new proposal. He also dropped a hint that Adenauer might not resign in 1963 if there was some movement with Moscow.[110]

The West German chancellor's decision to talk to the Soviets directly transformed these tentative feelers coming from Kroll into a serious opportunity. Khrushchev had long believed that an alliance with West Germany was possible, that despite the huge ideological differences, the two countries shared geographical and economic interests. Although he had not expected Adenauer to be the German leader who would acknowledge these mutual interests, he did not dismiss the possibility that the chancellor had had a late conversion. In 1955 Adenauer had surprised the Americans by establishing diplomatic relations with the Soviet Union despite years of promising not to do this.

Adenauer and Kroll met on June 4 to discuss how to stoke Soviet interest further. On June 11 the Soviet ambassador met with Kroll. Adenauer had nothing new to offer, but he was prepared to send Kroll to Moscow to negotiate some kind of agreement before he left office. He spoke of achieving "civil peace" and told Moscow he could accept freezing the situation as it was—with two Germanys, a divided Berlin, and no change to the postwar Polish-German border—for thirty years.[111]

■

A T T H E S A M E T I M E that Adenauer was making his secret approach to the Soviets, the Kennedy administration was well along in preparing an eloquent case for superpower peace to be given at American University on June 10. In late May McGeorge Bundy asked Arthur Schlesinger and other thoughtful liberals on the president's staff to send some ideas to Theodore Sorensen, who had already been in contact with Norman Cousins.[112] Sorensen dug up some fragments of an address that Kennedy was supposed to have given on Soviet television in the spring of 1962.[113] The broadcasting of speeches by the two leaders had fallen victim to Kennedy's decision to resume nuclear testing and Khrushchev's meniscus strategy. What the president had in mind would go much further than the ideas of mutual understanding that he had considered espousing a year earlier. The Cuban missile crisis allowed a new rhetoric. "He may well have believed the key elements of his American University speech before 1963," Bundy later recalled, "but he did not feel he could say them publicly."[114] After nearly two decades of Cold War, the American people were extremely skeptical of politicians who argued that the Soviets were not demons. Kennedy was not naive about the repressive nature of communism, but he had learned something very important about Khrushchev in the past year. Khrushchev's behavior in the crisis, after his deception had been exposed, showed a prudent respect for U.S. power and a mature concern about the possibility of accident and misjudgment. In the last years of his administration Dwight Eisenhower had tried to educate the U.S. public about the reality of the Soviet threat. Ultimately unsuccessful, Eisenhower had given way to a young man who had won in part on fears that the old World War II general had allowed the wily Khrushchev to sneak past him while he was playing golf. The young man, after nearly a thousand days in office, now understood his misjudgment of the Soviet threat. He also believed that in the wake of his success over Cuba he enjoyed enough public credibility to use the Oval Office as what Theodore Roosevelt had called the bully pulpit early in the century.

In front of the class of 1963 Kennedy suggested that the world they were joining might be a much happier place than the one into which their fathers had graduated in the late 1930s. He believed that enduring peace was possible but it could not be dictated by one side. "Not a Pax Americana," he said, "enforced on this world by American weapons of war . . . not merely peace for Americans, but peace for all men: not merely peace in our time but peace for all time."[115] Kennedy spoke beyond the students to the rest of the country and the world. "Some say it is useless to speak of world peace . . . until the leaders of the Soviet Union adopt a more enlightened attitude. I hope they do. I believe we can help them to do it. But I also believe that we must reexamine our own attitude."[116] In his inaugural address Kennedy had challenged Americans to "bear any burden" for the cause of justice at home and freedom abroad. Now he called on Americans to cast off their intellectual isolationism, to stretch their minds to imagine how their adversaries thought. Appeasement was not the goal; just understanding was. "We must conduct our affairs in such a way that it becomes in the Communists' interest to a agree on a genuine peace . . . to . . . let each nation choose its own future, so long as that choice does not interfere with the choice of others."[117] Kennedy accepted the premise that the two superpowers could peaceably coexist. "[In] the final analysis our most basic common link is the fact that we all inhabit this planet. We all breathe the same air. We all cherish our children's future. And we are all mortal." Kennedy committed himself, and with hope the nation, to put an end to this dangerous moment in the Cold War. "Confident and unafraid, we labor on—not toward a strategy of annihilation but toward a strategy of peace."[118]

▪

Three days later Khrushchev gathered his colleagues to initiate his own strategy of peace. He did not mention the speech that President Kennedy had just given at the American University, but it had had a strong effect on the Soviet leader. He told his staff that Kennedy's speech was the best given by any American president since Roosevelt.[119] In explaining his reasons for détente to the Presidium, Khrushchev did not refer to the new climate with the United States. Instead he discussed the meaning of Adenauer's secret approach.

The Soviets had been hoping for something like this from the West Germans since 1955. Although there were reasons to doubt Adenauer's sincerity, the West German initiative finally gave Khrushchev a pretext to kill off the Kremlin's unsuccessful Berlin policy. "Let's change the tactic," he said at a formal Presidium session on June 13. "We will not get an agreement from the Americans." He recalled the failed logic of the Berlin crises. The United States always held in its hand the weapon of an economic embargo that would have damaged East Germany severely. For that reason Khrushchev could press the Americans for only so long. Now the West Germans were providing a possible way around the Americans.

Khrushchev believed there were reasons why an agreement with the Germans was possible. He had long understood that economic ties could bring the two countries much closer together. He remembered fondly the extensive economic cooperation between Weimar Germany and Stalinist Russia that took its name from the Treaty of Rapallo signed by these two states in 1922. More recently West German trade with the Soviet Union had increased, and in 1962 the Soviets had turned to German manufacturers to buy steel piping. "We really are partners," Khrushchev explained to his Kremlin colleagues on June 13. "The Americans, the British, the French, they are the rivals." Khrushchev believed that a special relationship with West Germany would be possible. "Rapallo is advantageous for both the Federal Republic and the Soviet Union."[120]

Khrushchev instructed the Foreign Ministry to prepare directives for negotiations with Adenauer's representatives. It would be up to them to decide whether to come as an official delegation or as Germans on a holiday in the Soviet Union, as Kroll had done in the past. Khrushchev told his colleagues that he expected the Americans to accept closer West German–Soviet relations. They would not be threatened by this development. He anticipated resistance only from the French, who would be upset to lose their special relationship with Bonn.

The removal of the Jupiter missiles in late March, Adenauer's initiative, and Kennedy's American University speech all strengthened Khrushchev's belief that 1963 was the time to make his biggest political investment in détente with the West. In April Khrushchev had said that the Kremlin should be prepared to offer a partial test ban to the Americans and the British at a moment of Moscow's choosing. Now he believed that moment had arrived.

On July 2, 1963, Khrushchev announced he was prepared to accept a partial test ban treaty. Appropriately enough, he delivered this announcement in a hall in East Berlin. The death of his four-year Berlin strategy had liberated the test ban issue.

Washington and London greeted the announcement with enthusiasm. Both rushed negotiators to Moscow. Within three weeks an agreement was drafted and signed by the three governments. The signature of the treaty marked for many the start of a détente in the Cold War. What Kennedy and Macmillan could not know was that Khrushchev had run out of ideas for additional confidence-building measures. There was no newfound Soviet flexibility on the issue of general disarmament or, if discussion returned to it, Berlin. Even more disappointing would have been the realization that having agreed to a partial test ban, Khrushchev was no less committed to competing with the West for new allies in the third world and the industrialized world. As it had been since 1955, Khrushchev's goal remained a better climate for this competition, where the weapons would be ideas and the major benefit would be reduced military budgets. That is what he had always meant by peaceful coexistence.

■

KHRUSHCHEV HAD no illusions about the effect that signing the test ban would have on Soviet relations with Beijing. Besides the Chinese ideological aversion to agreements with the United States, Beijing wanted a nuclear device of its own, which would be more difficult to achieve under international pressure to accept a test ban. But in Khrushchev's eyes his efforts to improve relations with China since the start of the year had been so unproductive that he had little to lose. In January he had told his colleagues that if Moscow allowed the split with China to continue, what he called pursuing a policy of severance, this would only encourage nationalism in the Communist movement. "Severance is not the Communist route."[121] He believed that the Soviet Union had to show the patience expected of a world leader. "We are paving the way to the future . . . [and we should] have a tolerant attitude." Later, in May 1963, when Castro visited the Soviet Union, Khrushchev admitted that he really did not understand the bases of Sino-Soviet tension. "Look, I am asking myself," he told Castro, "what are the divergences? We are for peace and they are for peace. We are for coexistence and so are they. What's the problem?"[122]

He did acknowledge that the Chinese were jealous of the Soviet Union's preeminent position in the bloc. "They want to be first violin," said Khrushchev.[123] Beijing had to accept that it could not be. Since the Chinese said that they followed Lenin, Khrushchev assumed that any ideological differences should ultimately be resolved in Moscow's favor, the home of Leninism. To his dying day, Khrushchev never appreciated the imperialism inherent in that thinking.

Within days of Khrushchev's speech in East Berlin proposing a partial test ban, a bilateral meeting between the Chinese and Soviet Communist parties took place in Moscow. The two sides had been hammering out the agenda items for these discussions for months. In the end neither Khrushchev nor Mao was prepared to visit the other's capital. Their places were taken by Mikhail Suslov and the chiefs of the International Department of the Soviet party's Central Committee and a Chinese delegation led by Deng Xiao Ping. The talks were a failure. After a five-hour opening speech by Deng, the two delegations immediately began trading barbs. The Chinese attacked Moscow for its "nonrevolutionary" line. Since 1956 the Soviets had indulged in vicious attacks on Stalin at the expense of a clear-eyed assessment of their own mistakes. Deng blamed Khrushchev's zealous anti-Stalinism for the instability in Eastern Europe in 1956. He criticized Khrushchev's efforts to reach an accommodation with the United States: "The United States of America is an imperialist country—the Soviet Union is a socialist country. How can these two countries, which belong to two fundamentally different social systems, coexist; how can they exercise general cooperation? . . . This is completely unthinkable and in this relationship one cannot submit to illusions."[124]

He also attacked Khrushchev's efforts to spread the doctrine of peaceful coexistence to the third world. In 1958 the Cuban Communist Party, the PSP, had opposed Castro's revolution as "putschism" and "terrorism." Had matters been left to Anibal Escalante and the other PSP leaders, Cuba would never have become a Communist country. Similarly, the Chinese found fault with Moscow's handling of the Algerian and Iraqi Communist parties. Under pressure from Moscow, the Algerian party had renounced armed struggle in 1957 "and in doing so wasted its place in the political life of the country." The Chinese blamed Moscow for the ease with which the Ba'ath Party had taken over Iraq in February 1963. By pushing the Iraqi Communist Party to cooperate with Qassim, Moscow had effectively defanged the movement, laying it open to the Ba'athists.[125]

Although not a complete surprise, the talks opened a more difficult chapter in Sino-Soviet relations. "The time has come to publicly cross swords with the Chinese," Khrushchev announced at one of the first Kremlin meetings after the Chinese delegation had returned home.[126]

■

IN THE EIGHT MONTHS since the end of the Cuban missile crisis there had occurred in international politics a seismic shift, largely caused by a change in Khrushchev's international strategy. In midsummer 1963 the Soviet Union was on better terms with the United States than it was with the People's Republic of China. With a series of unilateral gestures, Khrushchev had removed the Berlin issue from the top of the international agenda, where he had placed it in November 1958. Faced with a series of setbacks at home and abroad in the spring of 1963, he had chosen the path of concession and discussion, instead of tension. He had allowed himself to change his mind, and the world was a safer place, though the Kremlin leader now had to worry that the Soviet bloc seemed to exist more in theory than in fact.

CHAPTER 21

LEGACY

KHRUSHCHEV BEGAN TO THINK of his own mortality after Frol Kozlov suffered a major stroke in the late spring of 1963. Kozlov was a controversial figure who had once been viewed as a possible successor to Khrushchev. But it was the fact that this comparatively young man—he was fifty-five to Khrushchev's sixty-nine—had fallen ill that concerned Khrushchev. "I've gotten old," he admitted to his son sometime after hearing the news, "and the rest of the Presidium are old enough to retire as grandfathers. I was forty-five when I joined the Politburo. That's the right age for matters of state; you have the strength, and there's lots of time ahead of you."[1]

Khrushchev had been tossing around the idea of retirement for some time. After his first trip to the United States in 1959 he had shocked his colleagues by revealing that he did not intend to follow Lenin's and Stalin's examples by dying in office. "[I]t is impossible to use a person until he is worn out,"[2] Khrushchev had said. "If the bourgeois and capitalists are not afraid that their foundations will be destroyed because after two terms the elected president changes, then why should we be afraid?"[3]

But the robust sixty-nine-year-old was not thinking in 1963 of an imminent departure. He told his son that he planned to continue in his job until the Twenty-third Party Congress, expected in a little over two years. Besides the détente with Kennedy, Khrushchev had launched major domestic economic reforms in 1963. Earlier in the year he had rammed through a massive reorganization of Soviet industry over the objections of Mikoyan, who had oppposed dismantling the republic-level industrial groups in his native Caucasus.[4] In particular, Khrushchev had reason to want to stick around long enough to see some returns on the huge investments that he had ordered in the chemical industry. There was a messianic quality to Khrushchev's crusade for chemicals that mirrored how he had oversold the importance of growing corn in the mid-1950s. A first-rate Soviet chemical industry would create reservoirs of fertilizer to improve crops and to increase Soviet textile production by substitut-ing man-made for natural fibers.

For the first time since 1955, Khrushchev now lacked a similar sense of mission in foreign policy. Sino-Soviet relations had displaced the superpower struggle as the Kremlin's most difficult international problem. In his rela-tions with the United States Khrushchev had reached a plateau of sorts by the fall of 1963. On September 30 the United States had tried to open a new back channel to Khrushchev. Kennedy had recommended to the Kremlin that his press secretary, Pierre Salinger, start meeting privately with Colonel G. V. Karpovich, an officer at the KGB station in Washington.

The Salinger-Karpovich channel had not yet been established when events in Dallas, Texas, on November 22, gave Khrushchev a shocking reason to con-front the finality of human mortality. Upon hearing of Kennedy's assassina-tion, Khrushchev believed that a conspiracy had killed the president. The KGB tried its best to find evidence that the right-wing militarists and oil barons had been responsible but could do no more than present the Kremlin with disconnected, uncorroborated fragments of information. Khrushchev refused to let the lack of evidence get in the way of a confirmation of his dark-est suspicions of American society. Ten years of negotiations and some sum-mitry with Americans had not altered his fundamental belief in the existence of two Americas. Kennedy represented the better America, which, though anti-Soviet, was prudent, mildly progressive, and antiwar. The other America was bellicose and profiteering. Khrushchev considered the latter his enemy and was now convinced that this sinister America had killed Kennedy.

He showed his concern about the loss of the youthful American leader by appearing at the U.S. Embassy to sign a book of condolences. Mikoyan went to the funeral to represent Khrushchev and the entire Soviet Union and to meet the new president, Lyndon B. Johnson.

The loss of Kennedy was yet another reminder for Khrushchev of the fragility of his apparent successes abroad. In late 1963 and early 1964 he tried once again to improve relations with the People's Republic of China but with little success. The Chinese reopened border disputes with Russia that pre-ceded the foundation of the two Communist states. In January 1964 Khru-shchev sent his own version of an encyclical to most world leaders, calling for the peaceful settlement of boundary disputes. China simply ignored it, and no negotiations followed between the Chinese and the Soviets on their dis-pute. Moscow also witnessed a cooling of relations with North Vietnam, which not only was following China's lead but disliked Moscow's increasingly hands-off approach to the struggle for communism in Southeast Asia.

Khrushchev continued to travel the world in search of friends. In May he attended the inaugural ceremony for the Aswan Dam project in Egypt, and in June he went to Scandinavia. The ceremony in Egypt, which symbolized the positive achievements of the Soviet-Egyptian relationship that Khrushchev had worked hard for almost a decade to create, also brought reminders of the failures of Soviet policy in the region. Khrushchev found himself seated next to Iraq's anti-Communist leader Abdel Salam Aref, and it was all he could do to maintain his composure. In their private sessions with the Egyptians, the Soviet delegation raised the awkward subject of Nasser's persecution of Egyptian Communists. "How is it possible," asked the Soviets, "to pursue a policy of anticommunism in a country that is building socialism?" Nevertheless, Khrushchev returned from the Middle East hopeful that the Soviet Union could continue to broaden its influence in that region. He reported to the Presidium on May 26 that Nasser seemed prepared to help Moscow with Aref. Soviet Foreign Minister Gromyko, who accompanied Khrushchev, noted that Nasser was "a serious political figure," who could be "unyielding on a number of issues, but he tried to understand our views." Still, Khrushchev cautioned that future gains depended on the Kremlin's being smarter about how it responded to Arab nationalism. Local Communists, like the Syrian Communist leader Khalid Bagdash, railed against Arab unity, which they saw as antithetical to a socialist revolution. Although Moscow was sympathetic to these concerns about nationalism, Khrushchev brought back from this trip a sense that Moscow needed to be more pragmatic in the region. "[B]y keeping to this slogan [against Arab nationalism]," he said, "we will not find our way to the Arabs. . . . There is no reason we should be against Arab unity. This issue should be developed." The Soviet leader was convinced that Moscow should consider getting more involved in the Middle East. He believed that Nasser was a true progressive and that there were others like him in the region. Ideology was not the only attraction. Khrushchev's competitive instincts were flowing, and he came home ready to suggest that the Kremlin should find additional weapons systems to sell to the Arabs. If Moscow did not do more in the Middle East, he cautioned his colleagues in the Presidium, "the Chinese might interfere [there]."[5]

The Chinese were not Khrushchev's greatest political threat, however. While he was abroad, a group of his Presidium colleagues began to coalesce against him. By all accounts, neither the sterile relationship with Washington nor the confrontation with Beijing had inspired this opposition. Khrushchev had lost favor because of his increasingly authoritarian management of the Kremlin.

Education, specifically the number of years Soviet children had to spend in grade school, was the issue that brought the resistance to him out in the open. Khrushchev, who equated general education with freethinking, wanted to limit the standard Soviet education to eight years. In 1958 he had spear-headed an overhaul of Soviet education. To eliminate those he called loafers, Khrushchev had called for adding an extra year to the ten-year Soviet system of primary and secondary education.[6] The extra year was largely devoted to vocational education. Soviet students were sent to factories two days a week to prepare them for manual labor. Six years later Khrushchev believed the exper-iment a failure. But instead of deciding to eliminate the vocational training and add an extra year of science and liberal arts, Khrushchev sought to reduce the number of hours that Soviet students spent in the classroom.

This scheme stirred deep opposition in the Presidium. The discussion, which started in December 1963 and lasted until July 1964, pitted men like Mikoyan, who believed that the Soviet Union needed more scientists to be able to compete with the West, against Khrushchev, who feared the expansion of the country's intelligentsia.[7] It was in discussions like these that Khru-shchev bared an orthodox commitment to Marxism-Leninism and a deep anti-intellectualism. "Those who support the idea of an eleven-year education system," he said in December 1963, "support a politically wrong trend."[8] He wanted young Soviets to start working after grade eight. "The main thing," said Khrushchev in restating his familiar argument, "is to inure [the student] to work."[9] Despite his insistence, as of July 30 the leadership could not agree on what to do.

Trouble began for Khrushchev in August, when he unilaterally announced the elimination of the eleventh grade in Soviet schools.[10] With the Presidium still undecided on educational reform, his action represented a cavalier disre-gard of Soviet ritual. Even at the height of his power, just before the Cuban disaster, he had shown respect for the principle of decision by majority vote in the Presidium. The forces arrayed against Khrushchev were too strong in 1964 for him to be forgiven this indiscretion.

■

THE PLOT BEGAN with the man who stood to gain the most by removing Khrushchev, Soviet President Leonid Brezhnev. A onetime protégé of Khrushchev's who had also been born in the Ukraine, Brezhnev was a decade younger than the first secretary and had grown in stature since becoming Soviet president in 1960. Brezhnev shared Khrushchev's fascination with missiles and space, and for some time Brezhnev had been allowed to give reports to the Presidium on those matters. Most recently he had vowed that the Soviet Union would be second to none in space. By his side was Nikolai Podgorny, a member of the Presidium since 1960. Like Brezhnev, Podgorny had also benefited from Khrushchev's patronage.

Needing the support of the Soviet secret services, Brezhnev turned to Aleksandr Shelepin, a secretary in the Central Committee who until 1961 had been chairman of the KGB and retained special ties there. Shelepin required no persuasion to sign on. Unlike colleagues who were dissatisfied with Khrushchev because of his domestic failures, Shelepin was determined to oust Khrushchev because of his foreign policy maneuvers, especially the fledgling détente with the United States. Shelepin believed that compromise with the United States was at best temporary, and Khrushchev's vision of a general abandonment of the military competition seemed to him a pipedream. He was also uncomfortable with Khrushchev's efforts to mold Soviet foreign policy to fit the promotion of nationalist regimes in the third world. He did not share Khrushchev's optimism that postcolonial regimes would always serve Moscow's interest of spreading communism far and wide.

The trigger for Shelepin may have been Khrushchev's visit to Egypt. Shelepin believed that Khrushchev was trying too hard to be liked by anti-Communist third world leaders and, as a result, was sacrificing Soviet dignity. The idea of Khrushchev and a man like Iraq's Aref together on a ceremonial stage nauseated him.

One area where Shelepin did not disagree with Khrushchev was the Soviet policy toward Beijing. He viewed Mao as a menace. Still, he blamed Khrushchev for the falling-out with Hanoi, which he attributed not to Moscow's mistakes in its handling of the Chinese but to Khrushchev's single-minded drive to reach an accommodation with the Americans in Laos.

Shelepin was able to bring to the plot the assistance of his long-time protégé Vladimir Semichastny, who had replaced him as chairman of the KGB in 1961. Semichastny owed a great deal to Khrushchev, but he owed even more to Shelepin. The move to the KGB was only the most recent instance of Shelepin's handing posts off to Semichastny as he himself rose even higher on the Kremlin's ladder of success. Semichastny had served first as Shelepin's deputy, then succeeded him as leader of the Soviet Communist youth organization, Komsomol. The two men symbolized a new generation of Soviet administrator, the "Komsolets," to whom the baton of the aging Stalinist generation was to be passed in the 1960s.

Sometime in 1963 Brezhnev, Podgorny, and Shelepin began to use Khrushchev's many absences from Moscow to begin their plotting. There is scattered evidence that the group had a hard time deciding how best to remove Khrushchev. Sometime in the spring of 1964 Brezhnev approached Shelepin and Semichastny with the request that they consider ways of assassinating Khrushchev. Perhaps his airplane could suffer an accident on one of his trips abroad. For a while planning had centered on Khrushchev's long-delayed trip to Scandinavia. In the end the idea was dropped. The circle of conspiracy was widening enough that the key plotters had reason to believe that Khrushchev would lose a vote in the Central Committee.

Remarkably, the conspiracy continued for months before any of it leaked to Nikita Khrushchev. The Khrushchev family first caught wind of the plot just after the old man returned from Egypt. A loyalist in the bodyguard of N. I. Ignatov, a longtime Central Committee member, revealed to Khrushchev's son, Sergei, that his boss was traveling the country lining up support for Khrushchev's removal.[11] The source, Vasily Galyukov, named the key conspirators, including Shelepin, Brezhnev and Podgorny, and stated that the planning had been going on for some time. The coup was slated for October, before the party plenum in November.

Khrushchev mishandled the warning. "When I told Father about Galyukov's disclosures," Sergei Khrushchev later recalled, "he both believed them and didn't believe them." Khrushchev was still very confident of his hold over the party and the Soviet state. He had defeated a serious attempt to unseat him in 1957, and he just doubted that a conspiracy that dangerous could be organized against him now. "Brezhnev, Shelepin, Podgorny—such different people. . . . Unbelievable!"[12]

The only person Khrushchev turned to was his old comrade Mikoyan. Since Cuba their relationship had improved. Khrushchev was grateful to Mikoyan for his superb handling of the Cubans in November 1962, when it seemed that Castro was spoiling for a fight with both the Americans and the Soviets. More important now was Mikoyan's own renewed respect for Khrushchev. The submarine dispute of October 1962 had been forgotten. Khrushchev's decision to end his quixotic Berlin policy in June 1963 was a signal to Mikoyan that Soviet foreign policy was finally proceeding in the proper direction. For five years Mikoyan had agitated from within to tame Khrushchev's wilder instincts, while supporting the leader's innate belief in the possibility of accommodation with the West. Khrushchev asked Mikoyan to meet the bodyguard Galyukov to assess the tip.

Khrushchev also let the conspirators know that he was watching them. He confronted Podgorny, who issued an immediate denial. No doubt within hours Shelepin and Brezhnev knew that either they had to move fast or give up the attempt.

Watching his father's reaction to the tip, Sergei Khrushchev was disappointed. He found that his father behaved in "a strange, illogical and inexplicable way." Khrushchev did not allow the rumors of a plot to alter his plans for a vacation in Pitsunda in the first week of October. The only change was that he invited Mikoyan to visit after talking to Galyukov.

The Soviet leader believed he could defeat whatever plan his enemies had prepared. It is not known for sure what, if any, advice Mikoyan offered. His later behavior strongly suggests that he advised Khrushchev to relinquish at least one of his posts as a way to preserve his line in foreign policy.

Khrushchev also brought Mikoyan along when he visited Gagra on October 12 to witness the launching of the world's first three-man space mission. For all its economic difficulties, the Soviet Union was once again committed to besting the United States in outer space. Khrushchev was scheduled to meet with a personal representative of Charles de Gaulle's the next day. The schedule allowed for a one-hour meeting and then a formal lunch for Gaston Palewski, a longtime ally of the French president's. News from Moscow upset that schedule.[13]

While Khrushchev witnessed the launch of the Vostok 3 spacecraft, Brezhnev assembled almost the entire Presidium in Moscow to plan for his dismissal. In recent weeks the Kremlin's chief ideologist, Mikhail Suslov, and Khrushchev's chief economics adviser, Aleksei Kosygin, had been brought into the conspiracy. It was decided to summon Khrushchev for a meeting the very next day at the Kremlin. Brezhnev made the call to Pitsunda. He told Khrushchev that the Presidium planned to meet to discuss a "variety of questions" and he should be there.[14]

Khrushchev was in no rush to leave Pitsunda. "What's the hurry? I will be there. I will arrive and [then] we can work things out."[15] It was natural for the Presidium to meet without the first secretary to settle second-tier matters. On October 8 Suslov had chaired a meeting on forming a drafting committee for the forthcoming Communist Party plenum.[16] Khrushchev said he would think about coming back for the next day's meeting. Brezhnev was always considered an excellent sycophant. Soon he would no longer need these talents. But on this day he shamelessly stroked Khrushchev to get him to return: "We can't decide without you. . . . We are asking you to come."[17]

Khrushchev did not bother to call Brezhnev back. He thought about the request and decided he had to return. He had word sent to Palewski on the evening of October 12 that the lunch was off—the excuse being that he had to return to Moscow early to organize a reception for the Vostok cosmonauts—and that he would only be able to meet him briefly at 9:30 A.M.[18]

The next morning, October 13, there was no panic in the Khrushchev camp. The leader himself left a strong impression on his French visitor during their brief meeting. He was "in excellent form and gave no sign of suffering from age or ill health," Palewski later reported.[19] Khrushchev, who seemed at peace, told Palewski that the USSR could live with the status quo in Germany. "We can wait," he said. "We have patience."[20] There was only an oblique reference to what Khrushchev thought he might be facing later that day in Moscow. He told Palewski with approval that statesmen like de Gaulle left office only when they died.[21]

Brezhnev had learned from the KGB at about midnight that Khrushchev would be coming to Moscow after all. Vladimir Semichastny's service controlled the general secretary's plane as part of its protective responsibilities. Soon after the Khrushchev family ordered the plane to be ready, Semichastny had been on the telephone with Brezhnev to alert him that the plan was back on track. Brezhnev ordered Semichastny to be at the airport in Moscow to escort Khrushchev and Mikoyan to the Kremlin. Everyone else who mattered in this drama, ultimately twenty-five people including Khrushchev, would then gather in the meeting room of the Presidium on the second floor of the old Czarist Senate to try to sentence Khrushchev to political oblivion.[21]

Khrushchev noticed on the plane that something was amiss. The KGB had replaced his regular bodyguards with new men. As he left the airplane, he also noticed that there were only two waiting to greet him, Semichastny and M. P. Georgadze, a Georgian ally of Mikoyan's. Probably suspecting the answer, Khrushchev asked the waiting KGB chief, "Where are the rest?" Semichastny replied: "Everybody's at the Kremlin waiting for you." With a momentary lapse into some human feeling, he then asked, "Do you want to have lunch at home first or eat at the Kremlin?" Khrushchev had lost his appetite: "Let's go to the Kremlin."[22]

Once in Moscow, Khrushchev rode with Mikoyan to the Kremlin in the long black Zil limousine that he customarily used. It is now impossible to know what, if any, strategy they cooked up during this car ride. Did Mikoyan hide his knowledge of the seriousness of the plot from Khrushchev? Or was it only at that point that both men understood how serious all the plotting had become? Mikoyan recommended to Khrushchev that he be prepared to relinquish the post of chairman of the Council of Ministers to Kosygin as a way of preserving his control over the party. Khrushchev would have no part of it. "I am not going to fight," he told Mikoyan. The two men then took the elevator to the second floor, where the Presidium meeting was already in session. Unseen by the two as they stepped into the elevator, Khrushchev's guards, who had stayed on the first floor, were disarmed and told to go home. They would no longer be required to protect Nikita Khrushchev.[23]

Brezhnev, who was in Khrushchev's usual spot when Khrushchev arrived, set the tone for what followed by enumerating instances where the Soviet leader had acted unilaterally.[24] One after the other, Khrushchev's other colleagues, most of whom had once been his protégés, piled on criticisms of his leadership. They emphasized that Khrushchev had failed to respect the system of collective leadership, exactly the same charge he himself had once made against Lavrenti Beria and then Georgi Malenkov.

The most articulate of Khrushchev's opponents, Aleksandr Shelepin, attacked the fallen leader for spreading myths about Soviet achievements. "When did you get the idea that things are going well?" he asked.[25] He rattled off the domestic disappointments. Economic growth had slowed over the decade. Annual growth in national income had dropped from 11 to 4 percent. Agriculture had become a "merry-go-round" with uncoordinated production, stockpiles, and shortages. Khrushchev's efforts to reinvigorate industry through administration reorganization had "detached science from production." Shelepin then took aim at the basic tenet of Khrushchev's foreign policy. He believed peaceful coexistence was dangerous. "We should be on guard when it comes to imperialists. You," he said to Khrushchev as if he had been alone in supporting this policy, "are diverging from the main line." Shelepin listed Khrushchev's foreign errors. He blamed Khrushchev for taking Moscow unnecessarily to the brink of war in 1956 over Suez. On the Berlin question, he said that Khrushchev's position had "caused damage." His assessment of the Cuban missile crisis was even harsher. Operation Anadyr had been "a risky enterprise," and during the crisis that ensued in the Caribbean, Khrushchev had "juggl[ed] with people's fates." Shelepin rejected the idea that it had been necessary to risk so much to force the United States to accept Soviet positions. "The slogan—'If the USSR and the United States reach an agreement, everything will be all right'—is wrong." Shelepin saved his only good word for Khrushchev's handling of the Chinese problem. That policy was "correct," he said, though it should have been carried out "in a more flexible manner." The critique was seconded by others who blamed Khrushchev for taking the country down the wrong path because of his "morbid competition with America."

The discussion continued into the next day, when Khrushchev and his one defender, Anastas Mikoyan, were given a chance to speak. Mikoyan directed criticism as well as praise toward Khrushchev. "In foreign policy," Mikoyan explained, "at first Khrushchev did not understand very much, but he quickly became proficient in it."[26] He reminded the group that he had opposed Khrushchev's Berlin Policy. "In general," he added, "I was right." He also recalled how he had tried to reduce the risk of war in the Cuban missile crisis. "I argued," he said, "that sending the submarines verged on adventurism." Yet in the end Mikoyan refused to blame Khrushchev for all these mistakes. He wanted Khrushchev to lose some of his posts but not be dropped from the Presidium altogether. Mikoyan's was the lone voice suggesting a future political role for Khrushchev. "I cannot make bargains with my conscience," said Brezhnev, setting the tone for what came next. "Dismiss Comrade Khrushchev from the posts he holds and divide them."

Khrushchev was resigned to losing everything. "You gathered together and splatter shit on me, and I can't object to you," he said, his earthiness intact.[27] Although he understood that he was not primarily being fired because of his foreign policy, he issued a defense of what he had done abroad. He said that the risk he took in the Cuban missile crisis was "inevitable" and asked his colleagues to think rationally about the problem that he had faced. He also requested understanding for his Berlin policy, which he believed had been "very well carried out." But these were the last gasps of defiance. "I do not ask for mercy," he concluded; "the question is solved." With remarkable insight, Khrushchev found the energy to remind his colleagues that though he was the victim of this event, the fact that the event occurred signaled one of his greatest achievements as first secretary of the CPSU. "Finally the party has grown," he attested, "and is able to control anyone." In true Bolshevik style, he then requested his own dismissal. When he left the meeting room, Khrushchev found that his bodyguard had already been dismissed and his Zil limousine been replaced by a Volga sedan. In an instant his once-immense power and all its trappings were history.[28]

■

KHRUSHCHEV'S OUSTER came as a surprise to the West when TASS reported the news on October 15, 1964. The Soviet press ascribed the change to "reasons of age and health," but no one bought that.[29] Describing the event as "a political coup," the British ambassador explained to London that "whatever preparations were made for his removal were secret from us, from the great majority of the population and, presumably, from the victim himself."[30] In recent years rumors of Khrushchev's retirement had become an annual event at the time of his birthday celebration. Khrushchev himself fed some of the speculation. In April 1963 he was quoted in *Pravda* as saying, "Everyone understands that I cannot occupy forever the post which I now occupy in Party and State."[31] A visiting Italian dignitary had asked Khrushchev in February 1964 if he had any plans to write his memoirs. "Perhaps," Khrushchev had responded playfully but with unintended clairvoyance, "when they send me away."

The U.S. government interpreted Khrushchev's ouster as primarily a repudiation of his domestic leadership and not as the harbinger of new trouble in the Cold War.[32] President Lyndon B. Johnson met with the inner circle of his national security team on October 16 to discuss the change.[33] Secretary Rusk and Ambassador Thompson stressed that Washington should not project any anxiety about this change in leadership. It might well bring less tension in the Cold War. "After all," Rusk argued, "it was Khrushchev who brought on the Berlin crisis and the Cuban missile crisis in 1962." Johnson agreed with his advisers' view that the approach should be "watchful but steady."

Later that day TASS announced the elevation of Leonid Brezhnev to first secretary of the CPSU and Aleksei Kosygin to the post of chairman of the Council of Ministers (Soviet premier). Soviet Ambassador Dobrynin then visited Johnson to convey directly an assurance from the new Kremlin chieftains that Soviet foreign policy would not change. It remained "the pursuit of peaceful coexistence and the relaxation of tensions."[34] This settled any remaining American concerns.

Soviet allies reacted in different ways. The North Vietnamese representative in Paris told a French representative that Soviet policy had long been misinformed in Southeast Asia because of Khrushchev's "lack of interest" in the region.[35] The North Vietnamese thought that the Soviets had not properly discharged their socialist responsibilities and with Khrushchev's departure there was a chance that Moscow would become fully committed to Hanoi's struggle to control South Vietnam. Eastern European reaction was muted.

■

THE PRESIDIUM SESSIONS of October 13–14, 1964, turned out to be the opening salvo of a debate that shaped Soviet foreign policy in the post-Khrushchev years. Since the Cuban missile crisis Khrushchev had moved closer to Mikoyan's thinking on matters of war and peace. In so doing, he had alienated some of the men that he had promoted from within the party apparatus. These men identified with only one-half of Khrushchev's strategy. They approved of efforts to force Washington to accept Soviet interests and welcomed the development of new allies in the third world. Shelepin and Suslov, however, viewed with suspicion anything resembling a global partnership with Washington. For the next few years the Kremlin set aside Khrushchev's complex strategy for reshaping the Cold War and concentrated on accumulating more strategic weapons. Only with the departure of Shelepin in the late 1960s and the deepening of Sino-Soviet tensions did Leonid Brezhnev revive the Khrushchev formula: cooperation on the strategic plane, competition in the developing world.

■

Henry Kissinger captured the dilemma for superpower leaders in the middle years of the Cold War. "[A]s power has grown more awesome," he wrote as a Harvard professor before entering government, "it has also turned abstract, intangible, elusive."[36] Although Khrushchev never attended an institution of higher learning, he instinctively understood this problem. Throughout the years in which he directed Soviet foreign policy, the Soviet leader had attempted to make power less abstract, more tangible and accessible.

The international position of the USSR when Khrushchev rose to the top could hardly have been worse. It controlled an expensive and restive empire in Eastern Europe, which had already started to splinter, and Stalin's errors had pitted once-friendly Yugoslavia against Moscow. On the positive side of the socialist balance sheet was the Kremlin's strong relationship with the People's Republic of China. Yet nationalistic tensions between Beijing and Moscow lay not far beneath the surface. Beyond Eastern Europe, China, and its allies in Southeast Asia, Moscow had few friends. Looking westward, the Kremlin faced a united and self-confident enemy. In 1955 the United States was far ahead of the Soviet Union militarily and economically. Washington led a military alliance that was both well aware of Soviet inferiority and eager to exploit it for diplomatic gains.

Khrushchev had refused to accept the world on these terms. From the moment he stepped onto the world's stage, he sought to alter the status quo. Enthralled by his colorful gestures and barnyard humor, observers of this impetuous and erratic man generally missed the strategist within. For all the bluster, there was a consistency of goals. Over the course of his time at the top Khrushchev sought to avoid war with the United States while seeking American respect, to shore up existing socialist states while cultivating new allies abroad, and to provide a better standard of living to his own people while building a sufficient strategic force. Convinced of the benefits of Marxism-Leninism, he blamed his country's difficulties abroad on Stalin's excesses and the military competition with the West. Khrushchev imagined a grand settlement with the United States that would demilitarize the Cold War, allowing him to redirect resources to the Soviet civilian economy and restrict the East-West struggle to the ideological and economic level, where he was convinced history would ultimately prove him right.

What varied was his strategy for attaining this settlement. Bobbing as he so loved to do in his pool at Pitsunda, Khrushchev alternated between trying to seduce the West and scheming to scare it. The carrots he offered were promises of mutual disarmament, a comprehensive test ban, and a world-wide nonaggression pact. When these concessions, as he saw them, did not work, he sought to get his way by impressing Washington with the dangers inherent in Soviet power.

He never wavered in his belief that because of the overwhelming nature of U.S. power, the key to attaining his goals was to alter Washington's behavior. Khrushchev had known little about foreign policy when he reached the top rung of the Kremlin ladder. What he saw in the 1950s was that American leaders were relying increasingly on nuclear weapons as both a means of defense and an instrument of influence in world affairs. President Eisenhower understood that the cost of defense could cripple the country's economy and introduced the new look strategy, which relied on nuclear forces as a cheaper deterrent than large armies. Meanwhile the combative John Foster Dulles hailed the political utility of nuclear weapons. U.S. strategic power—or, as Dulles called it, this position of strength—could be used to compel the Soviets to accept concessions, to roll back the gains Stalin had made in World War II.

Having learned from his American tutors that under the right circumstances nuclear weapons could be source of tangible, usable political power, Khrushchev made himself synonymous with playing the nuclear card. "The purpose," he explained to his colleagues in 1957, "is to give a rebuff, to steer to détente."[37] Adopting what political scientists call coercive diplomacy, Khrushchev sought to make the United States fear the consequences of not accepting Soviet positions in international negotiations. The stick that he wielded in 1956, 1958, 1960, 1961, and for the last time in 1962 was the threat to use nuclear weapons unless Soviet interests were respected.

Ultimately none of his strategies resulted in immense gains for the Kremlin. The mistrust between the superpowers was too great to permit the United States to accept disarmament on Khrushchev's terms. He did not help his cause by resolutely opposing any real verification regime. This too was a by-product of his fear of the United States. He was convinced that allowing on-site inspectors or overhead reconnaissance would give the United States the chance to look behind the curtain of Soviet power and, like the protagonists in the *Wizard of Oz*, see the true weakness of the Kremlin. Although both Dwight Eisenhower and John Kennedy would have agreed to verifiable arms reductions, neither was prepared to submit to the U.S. Senate a treaty that rested on blind faith. Moreover, even though Khrushchev did offer cuts in Soviet conventional forces, they were never enough to remove completely the threat posed to West Germany by the frontline Soviet divisions in the western USSR. Although Khrushchev promised a nonaggression pact, this could not bridge the gap in trust, especially as it had been enlarged by the Soviet crackdown in Hungary in 1956. The West was unprepared to trade its advantage in strategic weapons for a piece of paper. Similarly, the pursuit of a comprehensive test ban treaty foundered on the issue of verifiability.

Khrushchev's political antennae also failed him in his efforts to negotiate a way out of the Berlin impasse. Khrushchev was never prepared to allow the West to retain its special relationship to West Berlin. Although he had witnessed the first Berlin crisis and had blamed Stalin for so clumsily maneuvering the Soviet Union into an unnecessary and futile crisis, he discounted the lingering effects of that crisis on Western politicians. From 1948, whether Moscow liked it or not, the defense of West Berlin became a barometer for U.S. commitment to European security. Khrushchev never accepted that this was one concession that Washington could not deliver short of war.

The explosion of nationalism in the third world made whatever trust that was possible between the superpowers even more elusive. Khrushchev and his American rivals were hostages to fortune in these countries where a few planeloads of weapons and one charismatic leader could install new regimes. One of the great myths of the Cold War was that the superpowers orchestrated events in these regions through handmade puppets. Qasim, Castro, Nkrumah, Touré, Lumumba, Souvanna, and Nasser were nobody's puppets. Indeed, most skillfully played the superpowers off each other. Nevertheless, Washington and Moscow competed for these leaders' favor, and the competition consistently undermined any gains made in discussions over the main issues dividing the superpowers in Europe or at home.

Khrushchev's resort to coercive diplomacy was equally problematic. He managed to transform the years between 1958 and 1962 into the most dangerous period of the Cold War without achieving a grand settlement. The threat of nuclear war was useful only if your enemy truly believed you were suicidal. Instead, with the United States aware of its strategic advantage, these standoffs turned into games of chicken that Khrushchev always called off first.

It was Khrushchev's propensity to risk war to make peace that bedeviled U.S. presidents. Eisenhower was self-confident enough to dismiss these challenges. He refused to get into a lather over Berlin in November 1958 or to bemoan a collapse of the Paris summit in 1960. Until the Cuban missile crisis, the younger, less tested Kennedy was more vulnerable to Khrushchev's pressure tactics. More than Eisenhower he worried about the possibility of miscalculation in the nuclear era and was concerned about the impression that his actions made on foreign leaders, especially those in the Kremlin. This was what prompted him to ask Llewellyn Thompson in August 1962, "Do you think that the Cuba thing and the fact that we hadn't gone into Laos might have given him the impression that we were going to give way in Berlin?"[38] In retrospect we can see that the answer was no. Khrushchev wanted the U.S. president to stand up to the Pentagon and the CIA, which the Soviet leader believed were at the center of U.S. militarism. But if the president was weak —and he assumed until the Cuban missile crisis that Kennedy was weak— Khrushchev believed that there was no alternative but to use nuclear threats to move the Americans in the right direction. "We are not afraid of German aggression. . . . Germany that will not start a new war. The most dangerous [country] is America," he had asserted before heading off to Vienna in a foul mood in the spring of 1961.[39]

Would any successor to Stalin have handled the problem of Soviet strategic inferiority the same way? Certainly, there were structural reasons for why the Soviet Union was so far behind the United States. The Soviet command economy began a slow death spiral in the late 1950s that would be delayed only by the dramatic increase in the price of oil in the 1970s. But Khrushchev made critical decisions that further widened the military power gap and deepened Moscow's economic difficulties. He chose to implement a Soviet new look policy without building as many rockets as Moscow could afford; he decided not to build aircraft carriers, thus excluding the possibility of rapidly and reliably projecting force into other regions of the world; he repeatedly cut the number of Soviet citizens under arms. Yet at the same time that he consciously reduced the defense burden on the Soviet civilian economy, Khrushchev increased the number of Soviet commitments overseas, providing weapons at cost or below to Iraq, Egypt, Syria, Afghanistan, Indonesia, India, Laos, North Vietnam, Congo, and Cuba. The effect was to make him increasingly reliant on the appearance rather than the reality of Soviet power.

This strategy, though dangerous, was not entirely barren. By 1960 Khrushchev's nuclear arsenal did include a handful of missiles that could reach the U.S. homeland. His willingness to brandish those missiles raised an uncomfortable uncertainty in the minds of Western politicians who could not take the risk that Khrushchev would finally act on his impulses. It did not get him the deal he wanted on West Berlin or an arms reduction agreement, but it did deter John Kennedy from considering an invasion of Cuba at the height of the Cuban missile crisis and forced the U.S. president and his successors to accept the existence of East Germany. The Kennedy-Khrushchev agreement of 1962 held, and the Castro regime no longer had to be concerned about a U.S. military intervention. Never again would the West attempt to compel the Soviets to accept general elections in a reunified Germany as a precondition for a European security agreement. By the 1970s NATO was acknowledging the existence of East Germany and the United States had joined the countries of Europe, including the USSR, in signing the Helsinki Agreement, which created a standard for the protection of human rights throughout the continent.

When Khrushchev abandoned coercive diplomacy in April 1963, the world witnessed what it thought was a superpower détente. Khrushchev delinked the stubborn Berlin question from progress in arms control and accepted a partial test ban. In July 1963 Kennedy said that "a shaft of light cut into the darkness."[40] The reason for the enthusiasm was an underappreciation of Khrushchev's basic objectives and an exaggeration of his willingness at any time since 1958 to use force to get his way.

The costs to Khrushchev of his pressure tactics had been very high. His rhetoric and his actions served to confirm worst-case assumptions about his objectives, spurring a great American military buildup and complicating the efforts of U.S. presidents to seek some form of coexistence. The specter of the Soviet Union's backing down from its threats three times in five years betrayed a weakness in the Kremlin that at the very least emboldened the Chinese to take their own path in international affairs. At home these reverses undermined Khrushchev's credibility as a leader.

Ironically, Khrushchev disappeared just as he had decided to abandon pressure tactics altogether for patient diplomacy. Mikoyan's lament in those final hours of Khrushchev's leadership that he was being forced out when he was finally good at foreign policy suggests that had he been given time, Khrushchev might have come closer to achieving his wider goal of demilitarizing the Cold War. His successors accelerated the Soviet defense buildup to prevent a humiliation like the Cuban missile crisis from ever happening again. Given the dynamics of the Cold War and the nature of Khrushchev's personality, however, it is equally likely that had he stayed, something might have triggered yet another Berlin ultimatum in 1965 or 1966. Moreover, it is hard to imagine that despite his uneasiness with the North Vietnamese, he would have countenanced Lyndon Johnson's expansion of the war in Vietnam without again seeing Soviet prestige at risk and then trying to do something about it.

What is indisputable is that once Khrushchev abandoned brinkmanship in the wake of the Cuban missile crisis, the superpower struggle became more predictable and less dangerous. From 1963 to the Soviet invasion of Afghanistan in 1979, Beijing, Havana, and Hanoi were the main centers of international change. In 1973 the Soviet Union and the United States found themselves in a tense but very short standoff over the Middle East, but Moscow's sense of vulnerability and alarm was then much less than in 1956. Once Khrushchev was gone, no Soviet leader would again make the argument that to get peace, one had to go to the brink of war. Until Mikhail Gorbachev, who ended the Cold War, no Soviet leader—arguably no leader of any country—would so hold the world in his thrall.

ACKNOWLEDGMENTS

This book would have been impossible without the kind assistance of many colleagues, friends, and institutions. We are very grateful for the assistance of the University of Virginia's Miller Center of Public Affairs, which facilitated the first Russian publication of the minutes of the Presidium of the Central Committee of the Communist Party of the Soviet Union in the Khrushchev period and made it possible for Naftali to assist Fursenko, the editor in chief, and the Russian team in annotating those documents. And without Aleksandr Fursenko's perseverance, these materials would never have been declassified. Philip D. Zelikow, then the director of the Miller Center, was a stalwart supporter of our work, as were the members of the center's Governing Council; the director of the Miller Center Foundation, B. Wistar Morris; Professor Zelikow's chief of staff, Robin Kuzen; Tim's administration assistant, Lorraine Settimo and Olga Riukin, who assisted with the translations for the Kremlin Decision-making Project. In addition, we wish to thank Ambassador Piotr V. Stegni, formerly the director of the archive of the Russian Foreign Ministry, for his assistance and Natalia Y. Tomilina, the director of the Russian Archive of Contemporary History (RGANI), and her colleague Mikhail Prozumenshikov. We both benefited enormously from the research that we were able to do at these fine Russian institutions. Interviews were also an important part of our work and we wish to make special mention of the patient assistance of Sergo Mikoyan and Nikita Khrushchev's son, Sergei, his daughter Rada and his grandson Nikita Khrushchev, Jr. We are also grateful to Ernest R. May, who with Philip Zelikow invited us to participate in Harvard University's Suez project, and to Vitali Afiani, a superb archivist, formerly of RGANI and now at the Russian Academy of Sciences. Finally, we wish to thank our agent, John Hawkins, and our devoted editor and friend, Drake McFeely, and his able young editor, Brendan Curry, at Norton.

Aleksandr Fursenko wishes to single out V. N. Jakushev, A. S. Stepanov, and S. N. Mel'chin at the Archives of the President of the Russian Federation; his fellow editors of the Archives of the Kremlin series, A. K. Sorokin and V. A. Smirnov, and his colleagues B. V. Anan'ich. R. Sh. Ganelin, N. L. Korsakova, L. M. Mlechin, V. V. Noskov, V. N. Pleshkov, and V. O. Pechatnov. In the United Kingdom he received the kind assistance of Peter Brown and Jane Lyddon at the British Academy, Lawrence Freedman, and Christopher Andrew. Aleksandr's research in France benefited from the assistance of Maurice Aymard and Sonia Colpart at La Maison des Sciences de l'Homme, Maurice Vaisse, and Jean Soutou and Isabelle Neuschwander at the Archives Nationales. Timothy Naftali also wishes to thank Zachary Karabell, Fred Logevall, Marc Trachtenberg, Irv Gellman, Mel Leffler, and David Coleman for insightful comments and suggestions on the manuscript. He also thanks his mom and Robert Feldman, Kent Germany, Gerry Haines, Hope Harrison, Serge and Debbie Lacroix, Gloria Naftali, Jean René Scheffer, Gordon Knowles, Neil Hultgren, Matt Waxman, and Andy Tompkins for their friendship. This book would not have been possible without Tim's muse, Laura Moranchek, who remained a dear friend and helpful editor in spite of all the challenges. In addition, he received assistance from the expert staff at the Sterling Memorial Library at Yale University, the Nixon Library and Birthplace, the National Archives facility at Laguna Niguel, the Manuscripts and Archives Division of the Library of Congress, the Hoover Institution, and the John F. Kennedy Presidential Library. In particular, he wishes to thank David Haight and Kathleen A. Struss at the Dwight D. Eisenhower Presidential Library, Regina Greenwell at the Lyndon B. Johnson Library, Robert Hamilton at the Roy H. Thomson Archive, Tom Blanton at the National Security Archive, Maryrose Grossman at the John F. Kennedy Presidential Library, and Joseph Lelyveld for allowing him to use the New York Times Archive.

NOTES

INTRODUCTION

1. Jerrold L. Schecter with Vyacheslav V. Luchkov, ed. and trans., *Khrushchev Remembers: The Glasnost Tapes* (Boston: Little, Brown, 1990), p. 3.

2. The original transcripts of Khrushchev's recorded reminiscences are preserved at Columbia University's Low Library. Between 1970 and 1990 three edited volumes of English translations appeared. Strobe Talbott translated and edited the first two, *Khrushchev Remembers* (Boston: Little, Brown, 1970) and *Khrushchev Remembers: The Last Testament* (Boston: Little, Brown, 1974). Schecter with Luchkov translated and edited the third volume, *Khrushchev Remembers: The Glasnost Tapes*.

3. Schecter, ed., loc. cit., p. 3.

4. Kotkin, *Armageddon Averted: The Soviet Collapse 1970–2000* (New York: Oxford University Press, 2001), pp. 32–33.

CHAPTER 1: RED STAR ASCENDANT

1. Interview (1963), Sir William Hayter, NBC Death of Stalin Collection, Hoover Institution. This comes from research materials prepared for a television documentary marking the tenth anniversary of Stalin's death.

2. Ibid.

3. Ibid. Clifton Daniel, "Bulganin Is Premier as Malenkov Resigns, but Khrushchev Is Viewed as Real Leader; Moscow Shake-Up; Malenkov Avows Guilt for Shortcomings in Agriculture," *New York Times*, February 9, 1955.

4. Hayter to London, "Mr. Molotov's Speech on Foreign Affairs to the Supreme Soviet," February 14, 1955, Prem 11/1015, National Archives—UK.

5. Memorandum of discussion, 236th meeting of the NSC, Washington, February 10, 1955, *Foreign Relations of the United States* [hereafter *FRUS*], *1955–1957* (Washington D.C.: Government Printing Office, 1989), vol. 24, p. 27.

6. "Harriman Terms News Disturbing; Governor, former U.S. Envoy to Moscow, Sees Return to Stalin Arms Policy," *New York Times*, February 9, 1955.

7. "Bedell Smith Worried; Ex-Envoy Says He Can Find No Comfort in Soviet Shake-up," *New York Times*, February 9, 1955.

8. "London Sees End of 'Coexistence'; Malenkov's Fall Viewed Also as Return to One-Man Rule—Bulganin called 'Front'; Effect Held Domestic; Paris Feels Shift Is No Reply to Western Policy—Rome Fears 'Tough Course,' " *New York Times*, February 9, 1955.

9. Diary entry by the president's press secretary (Hagerty), February 8, 1955, FRUS, 1955–1957, vol. 24, p. 24.

10. Memorandum of discussion, 236th meeting, NSC, February 10, 1955, ibid., pp. 25, 27.

11. James Reston, "Private memorandum, conversation with John Foster Dulles, July 6, 1955, Carlton Hotel, Washington, D.C.," Dulles File, A. H. Sulzberger Papers, New York Times Archives.

12. Steno, June 7, 1963, AOK. For full citation, see the Abbreviations section.

13. Felix Chuev, ed., *Molotov Remembers: Inside Kremlin Politics* (Chicago: Ivan R. Dee, 1993), pp. 337–38.

14. The other full members were Stalin, Lev Kamenev, Leon Trotsky, and Nikolai Krestinskii. G. E. Zinoviev, N. I. Bukharin, and M. I. Kalinin were the candidate members of the first Politburo. Richard Pipes, *Russia under the Bolshevik Regime* (New York: Vintage Books, 1995), p. 439; Leonard Shapiro, *The Communist Party of the Soviet Union* (New York: Vintage Books, 1971), p. 647.

15. The Central Committee numbered fewer than one hundred people in 1919 and comprised representatives of local, regional, and republic Communist organizations as well as representatives from the Soviet armed services. Formally elected at the huge party congresses, the membership of the Central Committee could be changed between the congresses by the general secretary. By 1955 there were approximately three hundred people in the Central Committee. Shapiro, op. cit., pp. 587–93.

16. Full members: Malenkov, Khrushchev, Molotov, Bulganin, Anastas Mikoyan, Lazar Kaganovich, Maksim Z. Saburov, Mikhail Pervukhin, and Kliment Voroshilov. Ibid., p. 649.

17. Protocol [104], January 22, 1955, AOK.

18. These rumors were spread by Ralph Parker, the *London Daily Worker* correspondent, who was suspected of being a KGB agent by the CIA. See Charles E. Bohlen, *Witness to History, 1929–1969* (New York: Norton, 1973), p. 369.

19. Protocol [104], January 22, 1955, AOK. Besides the nine full members, the Presidium in early 1955 included candidate members Aleksei Kirichenko, Nikolai Shvernik, and Mikhail Suslov.

20. There are two reasons to believe this. First, just after Khrushchev made his recommendation, Voroshilov expressed some doubt about the arrangement—"I was for Comrade Bulganin, but a nonmilitary [may be necessary]"—implying that he had been party to earlier discussions. Second, Molotov is described as providing a set of arguments in support of Bulganin that may have been rehearsed.

21. Hope Harrison, *Driving the Soviets up the Wall* (Princeton: Princeton University Press, 2003), pp. 34–38.

22. Besides the United States, Canada, Great Britain, France, Iceland, Denmark, Norway, Portugal, Belgium, the Netherlands, Luxembourg, and Italy were charter members.

23. Cited in William Taubman, *Khrushchev* (New York: Norton, 2003), p. 332.

24. CIA, Berlin Handbook, December 27, 1961, NSF, Kissinger, Box 462, JFK Library.

25. Christopher Andrew and Vasili Mitrokhin, *The Sword and the Shield, The Mitrokhin Archive and the Secret History of the KGB* (New York: Basic Books, 1999), p. 357.

26. Ibid., p. 358.

27. Interview (1963), Sir William Hayter, NBC Death of Stalin Collection, Hoover Institution.

28. Bohlen to Department of State (DOS), November 8, 1954, *FRUS, 1952–1954*, vol. 8, p. 1260.

29. Allen Dulles, "A Current Intelligence Appreciation of Soviet Policy," April 30, 1954, CIA/Dulles—Freedom of Information Act Collection. Dulles's mistaken reference to Khrushchev's nationality indicates the limits of U.S. knowledge of major Soviet personalities. Khrushchev was not a Ukrainian. He grew up in a Russian-speaking family in the Ukraine. The authors wish to thank Max Holland for the opportunity to look through the vast amount of Dulles material released to him by the CIA through FOIA.

30. Ibid.

31. Ibid.

32. Oleg Troyanovsky, "Through Space and Time: History of One Family," Moscow, 1997, p. 176. The Malin notes for the January 24, 1955, and February 7, 1955 (the last meeting before the new Austrian policy was announced), do not show any evidence of a debate between Molotov and Khrushchev over the new Austrian policy.

33. This is the argument made by Vladislav Zubok in "The Case of Divided Germany, 1953–1964," *Nikita Khrushchev*, ed. William Taubman, Sergei Khrushchev, and Abbott Gleason (New Haven: Yale University Press, 2000).

34. Khrushchev's memoirs are strong on the substance of debates and less good on the chronology of events. However, it seems from the Malin notes, the timing of Molotov's introduction of the end of linkage, the date of the invitation to the Austrians to start negotiations, and the events later recounted by Khrushchev that he put pressure on Molotov to sign a treaty after the February 8 speech. See also Jerrold L. Schecter with Vyacheslav V. Luchkov, *Khrushchev Remembers: The Glasnost Tapes* (Boston: Little, Brown, 1990), pp. 72–80.

35. Ibid., p. 76.

36. Ibid., pp. 72–80. Although there is no reason to doubt Khrushchev's recollection on this point, no minutes have been found for meetings 107 through 119, February 8–May 18, 1955. See AOK.

37. This story of these negotiations and their immediate aftermath is narrated very well by Gunther Bischof in "The Making of the Austrian Treaty and the Road to Geneva," *Cold War Respite: The Geneva Summit of 1955*, ed. Bischof and Saki Dockrill (Baton Rouge: Louisiana State University Press, 2000).

38. The *Pravda* article was cited in *Documents Diplomatiques Français* [hereafter *DDF*], *1955*, vol. 1, note to Record No. 243, Ministère des Affairs Étrangères, Commission de Publication des Documents Français (Paris: Imprimerie Nationale, 1987), p. 561.

39. Harrison E. Salisbury, "Zhukov: Rising Star in the Kremlin," *New York Times Magazine*, May 8, 1955.

40. Record of the July plenum of 1995, Istoricheskii Archiv 1999, no. 5, S. 43. Cited in Protocol 120, May 19, 1955, note 4, AOK.

41. Ibid.

42. Protocol 120, May 19, 1955 note 3, AOK.

43. Protocol 120, May 19, 1955, AOK.

44. Schechter, ed., op. cit., p. 76.

45. Protocol 120, May 19, 1955, AOK.

46. Protocols 121 and 122, May 23 and 25, 1955, AOK.

47. Strobe Talbot, ed., *Khrushchev Remembers* (Boston: Little, Brown, 1970), p. 379.

48. Interview (1963), Edward Crankshaw, NBC Death of Stalin Collection, Hoover Institution.

49. Interview (1963), Philippe Ben, NBC Death of Stalin Collection, Hoover Institution.

50. Protocol 125, June 6, 1955, AOK.

51. Protocol 121, May 23, 1955, AOK.

52. Protocol 125, June 6, 1955, AOK.

53. Protocol 126, June 8, 1955, AOK.

54. Years later a retired Molotov pointed to the fight over Yugoslavia as the moment when Khrushchev turned Soviet policy upside down. Chuev, op. cit., p. 351.

55. Record of the July plenum of 1995, Istoricheskii Archiv 1999, no. 5, S. 43. Cited in Protocol 120, May 19, 1955, note 4, AOK.

CHAPTER 2: GENEVA

1. Klaus Larres, *Churchill's Cold War: The Politics of Personal Diplomacy* (New Haven: Yale University Press, 2002), passim.

2. "Reds Offer West Germany New Status," *Washington Post and Times Herald,* January 16, 1955.

3. Hollis W. Barber et al., *The United States in World Affairs, 1955* (New York: Harper & Brothers, 1956), p. 35.

4. Ibid., p. 37.

5. Lincoln P. Bloomfield, Walter C. Clemens, Jr., and Franklyn Griffiths., *Khrushchev and the Arms Race: Soviet Interests in Arms Control and Disarmament, 1954–1964* (Cambridge, Mass.: MIT Press, 1966), pp. 22–25.

6. Oleg Bukharin et al., *Russian Strategic Nuclear Forces* (Cambridge, Mass.: MIT Press, 2001), Table 8.1, pp. 485–87. The figure for U.S. testing is as of May 10, 1955. The Soviets issued their disarmament proposals during a U.S. test series.

7. Carlo D'Este, *Eisenhower: A Soldier's Life* (New York: Henry Holt, 2000), p. 693.

8. Robert Caro has written a brilliant discussion of the battle over the Bricker Amendment, as this legislative initiative was called. See Robert A. Caro, *The Years of Lyndon Johnson: Master of the Senate* (New York: Knopf, 2002), pp. 527–41.

9. Robert A. Divine, *The Sputnik Challenge* (New York: Oxford University Press, 1993), p. 18.

10. In an off-the-record press briefing, Allen Dulles alluded to his brother's estimate by way of saying that he was less sanguine about an early Soviet collapse. W. H. Lawrence, memorandum of conversation [hereafter memcon], July 14, 1955, A. W. Dulles File, A. H. Sulzberger Collection, New York Times Archives.

11. Cited in Richard Immerman, "Trust in the Lord but Keep Your Powder Dry," Günter Bischof and Saki Dockrill, *Cold War Respite: The Geneva Summit of 1955* (Baton Rouge: Louisiana State University Press, 2000), pp. 48–49.

12. Ibid., p. 46.

13. W. H. Lawrence, memcon, July 14, 1955, A. W. Dulles File, A. H. Sulzberger Collection, *NYT.*

14. Memorandum of discussion, National Security Council, October 20, 1955, *FRUS, 1955–1957,* vol. 5, p. 618.b.

15. Cited in David L. Snead, *The Gaither Committee, Eisenhower and the Cold War* (Columbus: Ohio State University Press, 1999), p. 39.

16. William Taubman, *Khrushchev* (New York: Norton, 2003), pp. 43–44.

17. Protocol 99, December 20, 1954, AOK; Protocol 106, February 7, 1955, AOK.

18. Gerald Haines and Robert E. Leggett, eds., *Watching the Bear: Essays on the CIA's Analysis of the Soviet Union* (Washington, D.C.: Center for the Study of Intelligence, CIA, 2003), pp. 142–43.

19. C. L. Sulzberger, "Molotov Proposes 4 Powers Reduce Forces in Germany," *New York Times*, February 5, 1954; "East German Army Put at 80,000 in White Paper Issued in Britain," *New York Times*, July 14, 1954; Hanson W. Baldwin, "Is Time on Our Side—or Russia's?," *New York Times Magazine*, August 1, 1954.

20. Robert C. Albright, "Symington Seeks Aerial Arms Probe," *Washington Post and Times Herald*, May 18, 1955.

21. Lawrence Freedman, *US Intelligence and the Soviet Strategic Threat*, 2nd ed. (London: Macmillan, 1986), pp. 66–67; John G. Norris, "Red Warplanes Strides Revealed by Pentagon," *Washington Post and Times Herald*, May 14, 1955.

22. Protocol 120, May 19, 1955, AOK.

23. Clifton Daniel, "Khrushchev Sees Fruitful Parley If West Is Honest; Attends U.S. Fete; Denies Any Weakness Calling Soviet Solid as Never Before," *New York Times*, July 5, 1955,

24. William Galbraith, "U.S. Accepts Soviet Offer to Pay Plane Damage," *Washington Post and Times Herald*, July 8, 1955.

25. Protocol 130, Meeting, July 12, 1955, AOK.

26. Elie Abel, "Dulles to Insist on German Unity as Big Four Topic," *New York Times*, June 29, 1955.

27. "TASS Statement of Soviet Views on Big Four Parley," *New York Times*, July 13, 1955.

28. Sergei N. Khrushchev, *Khrushchev and the Making of a Superpower* (University Park: Pennsylvania State University Press, 2000), p. 83.

29. Charles E. Bohlen, *Witness to History* (New York: Norton, 1973), p. 382.

30. Strobe Talbott, ed., *Khrushchev Remembers* (Boston: Little, Brown, 1970), p. 397.

31. Ibid., p. 398.

32. The Soviet memcon of this meeting is in Fond 5 at RGANI; the U.S. memcon can be found in *Foreign Relations of the United States* [hereafter *FRUS*], 1955–1957, vol. 5, pp. 408–18.

33. Memcon, DDE and Zhukov, July 20, 1955, ibid., vol. 5, p. 409.

34. Ibid.

35. Ibid.

36. Ibid.

37. Ibid., pp. 412–13.

38. Protocol 106, August 6, 1957, AOK.

39. Bohlen, op. cit., pp. 384–85.

40. Ibid.

41. Clifton Daniel, "Russians See End of 'Cold War' and a Milder Line in Their Press," *New York Times*, July 25, 1955.

42. "Mikoyan Hails Parley; Says Result Was 'Good,' as It Changed Atmosphere," *New York Times*, July 24, 1955.

43. "Nixon Bans Umbrellas as Reminders of Munich," *New York Times*, July 25, 1955.

44. Harry Gabbett, "Found Evidence of New World Friendliness, Says President," *Washington Post and Times Herald*, July 25, 1955.

45. "Conference Views of U.S. Editors," *Washington Post and Times Herald*, July 25, 1955.

46. Ibid.

47. "What Happened at Geneva," *New York Times*, July 24, 1955.

48. Gerald Haines and Robert E. Leggett, eds., *Watching the Bear: Essays on CIA's Analysis of The Soviet Union* (Washington, D.C.: Center for the Study of Intelligence CIA, 2003), pp. 142–43.

49. Memcon, NSK and Berthold Beitz, January 1960, Ministry of Foreign Affairs (herafter MFA). A leading West-German industrialist, Beitz was chief executive of the Krupp business conglomerate.

50. T. Kuprikov, chief, First Department, Committee of Information, MFA September 2, 1955, "Chancellor of the Federal Republic of Germany (Political Characteristics)." V. Zdorov, chief, Information Bureau of the Foreign Intelligence Service of the KGB, "Spravka on the Chancellor of the Federal Republic of Germany, Konrad Adenauer," September 6, 1955. Both documents, SVR.

51. V. Zdorov, chief, Information Bureau of the Foreign Intelligence Service of the KGB, "Spravka on the Chancellor of the Federal Republic of Germany, Konrad Adenauer," September 6, 1955, SVR.

52. Ibid.

53. T. Kuprikov, Chief, First Department, Committee of Information, MFA September 2, 1955, "Chancellor of the Federal Republic of Germany (Political Characteristics)," SVR.

54. Dulles to Adenauer, August 15, 1955, FRUS, 1955–1957, vol. 5, p. 548.

55. Ibid., p. 550.

56. Khrushchev's statement to the East Germans of September 17, 1955, excerpted in Armstrong to Secretary of State, "Recent Communist Statements," December 13, 1955, RG 59, INR, 1945–1960, Box 14, NARA-II.

57. Drew Middleton, "Geneva Opening; A Pallid Revival; Lines Familiar, July's Stars Have Left Cast and Famed 'Spirit' Seems Harsher," New York Times, October 28, 1955.

58. Protocol 168, November 6, 1955, note 2, AOK, citing document at Fond 3, Opis 8, Delo 327, pp. 2–5, RGANI.

59. Protocol 168, November 6, 1955, AOK.

60. Protocol 168 (continuation), November 7, 1955, AOK.

61. Ibid.

62. Welles Hangen, "Molotov Flying to Geneva, Carrying 'Better Baggage,' Remark Made in Moscow Held by Some to Mean He Will Offer Plan to End Stalemate on German Unity," New York Times, November 8, 1955.

63. Chalmers M. Roberts, "Closes Door on German Settlement; Unexpected Stand Could Reopen 'Cold War'; Big 3 Recess Conference," Washington Post and Times Herald, November 9, 1955. Drew Middleton, "Soviet Bars German Unity Except on Its Own Terms; West Is Shocked by Stand; Atmosphere Grim; Molotov's Implications So Wide Dulles Halts the Sitting," New York Times, November 9, 1955.

64. Chalmers M. Roberts, "'Geneva Spirit' Broken, Dulles Tells Molotov," Washington Post and Times Herald, November 10, 1955.

65. Drew Middleton, "Big 4 Conference Drops Discussion of German Unity; Geneva Step Taken on West's Insistence after Molotov Bars Negotiation of Issue; Soviet Stand Assailed; Macmillan Says Attitude May Gravely Affect Other Items— Dulles Sees Injustice," New York Times, November 10, 1955.

66. Walter Lippmann, "The Geneva Gamble," Washington Post and Times Herald, November 10, 1955.

67. Walter Sullivan, "Soviet Says Rule in Berlin Is Over; Commandant Asserts City Is East German Capital Now—Rejects U.S. protest," New York Times, November 30, 1955.

68. M. S. Handler, "East Germans Put on West Frontier; Soviet Said to Withdraw Troops into Interior—Political Link Implied," New York Times, November 23, 1955.

CHAPTER 3: ARMS TO EGYPT

1. The rumor appeared in the *New York Times*, June 3, 1955; Molotov's "joking" was reported by the same newspaper, July 10, 1955.

2. Excerpt of Khrushchev, November 26 speech, at Bangalore, in W. Park Armstrong to Secretary of State (hereafter), "Recent Communist Statements," December 13, 1955, RG 59, INR 1945–1960, Box 14, NARA-II.

3. Grigorii Zaitsev, "K Poyezde Tov. Shepilova v Egypte" [For Comrade Shepilov's Visit to Egypt], July 18, 1955, 5/30/123, pp. 194–200, RGANI.

4. Quoted in Keith Kyle, *Suez* (New York: St. Martin's Press, 1991), p. 55.

5. Salim Yaqub, *Containing Arab Nationalism: The Eisenhower Doctrine and the Middle East* (Chapel Hill: University of North Carolina Press, 2003), pp. 25–26.

6. Memcon, Solod and Nasser, July 8, 1954, 087, 17/5/34, pp. 206–10, Ministry of Foreign Affairs. When Moscow indicated that it might be willing to assist Egypt with the dam project and was not opposed to selling Nasser weapons, the Egyptian leader suddenly seemed to lose interest. In July 1954 he stopped talking with the Soviet ambassador about weapons.

7. D Zhukov to Molotov, "Situation in Guatemala," April 14, 1953, 06 (Molotov Files), 129/2050/284, MFA; "Chronicle of Events: June 1954—November 1954," 110 (Mexican desk, Latin American department), 14/30/8, MFA. For evidence that Washington also knew this, see Zachary Karabell, *Architects of Intervention: The United States and the Third World and the Cold War, 1946–1962* (Baton Rouge: Louisiana State University Press, 1999), p. 103. See also Stephen Schlesinger and Stephen Kinzer, *Bitter Fruit: The Story of the American Coup in Guatemala* (Garden City, N.Y.: Anchor Books, 1982).

8. Cited in Karabell, op. cit., pp. 111–12.

9. Ibid., pp. 128–31.

10. Nick Cullather, *Operation PBSUCCESS: The United States and Guatemala, 1952–1954* (Stanford, Calif.: Stanford University Press, 1999), p. 58.

11. Ibid.

12. Cited in Piero Gleijeses, *Shattered Hope: The Guatemalan Revolution and the United States, 1944–1954* (Princeton: Princeton University Press, 1992), p. 299.

13. Richard Bissell, quoted in Cullather, op. cit., p. 52.

14. Ibid., p. 61.

15. Molotov to Soviet UN mission, June 24, 1954, 06 (Molotov Files) 129/250/289, MFA. We were unable to see any 1954 KGB materials on Guatemala, which would likely have come from the station in Mexico City. However, in a report distributed to the Presidium, the Foreign Ministry described its inability to establish reliable communications with the Guatemalan government. As we shall see elsewhere, the Presidium regularly used intelligence channels to communicate with foreign leaders, if necessary and available.

16. Ibid.

17. Foreign Minister Guillermo Toriello to Molotov, June 25, 1954, received 12:15 P.M., 06, 129/250/289, MFA.

18. Ariel Sharon with David Chanoff, *Warrior: The Autobiography of Ariel Sharon* (New York: Simon and Schuster, 1989), pp. 102–9. Palestinian guerrillas and Egyptian military personnel had indeed been infiltrating into Israel from the Gaza Strip, but the Nasser government denied that these were authorized missions. Following this raid in February—which left thirty-eight Arabs dead—and another in the summer of 1955, the

Egyptians later said that they formally authorized commando operations. Yaqub, op. cit., p.39.

19. Khrushchev and Nasser meeting, April 30, 1958, 10:00 A.M., MFA.

20. Walter Z. Laqueur, *The Soviet Union and the Middle East* (New York: Praeger, 1959), pp. 199–200.

21. Daniel Solod, memcon of meeting with Nasser, May 21, 1955, 087, 18/3/36, pp. 176–180, MFA.

22. Khrushchev reported on this conversation to the Presidium. Protocol 125, June 6, 1955.

23. Representative was the information received from the Romanian chargé d'affaires in Cairo, Ion Gheorgescu, who said in June 1954 that Nasser needed U.S. weapons to satisfy his own military. According to the Romanian diplomat, the Indian ambassador to Egypt was trying to convince Nasser that taking U.S. weapons would be a mistake. Memcon, Solod and Gheorgescu. June 16, 1954, 087 17/34/5, MFA.

24. Peter Hahn, *the United States, Great Britain, and Egypt, 1945–1956: Strategy and Diplomacy in the Early Cold War* (Chapel Hill: University of North Carolina Press, 1991), pp. 184–85.

25. Byroade to DOS, June 9, 1955, *FRUS, 1955–1957*, vol. 14, pp. 237–40.

26. Byroade to DOS, June 17, 1955, ibid., pp. 255–56.

27. Ibid., pp. 165–79.

28. Ibid., pp. 188–92.

29. Memcon, DOS, June 8, 1955, *FRUS, 1955–1957*, vol. 14, pp. 231–33.

30. Telegram 2214, DOS to Egypt, June 17, 1955, ibid., p. 256, n. 2.

31. Telegram, Cairo to DOS, July 2, 1955, ibid., p. 274.

32. Memcon, San Francisco, June 24, 1955, ibid., pp. 265–66.

33. The other two secretaries added in July 1955 were A. Aristov and Nikolai Belayev. They played important roles in the run-up to the Twentieth Party Congress in 1956.

34. Shepilov, memcon, 1956, MFA.

35. D. T. Shepilov, "Vospominaniia," 1998, p. 171.

36. Memcon, Solod and el-Kouni, July 18, 1955, 087, 18/4/37, pp. 4–5, MFA. Nasser had Ambassador Mohammed Awad el-Kouni who was back in Cairo, deliver this message to Solod.

37. Jean Lacouture, *Nasser: A Biography* (New York: Knopf, 1973), pp. 45–47.

38. Laqueur, op. cit., pp. 199–200.

39. Solod, memcon of meeting with Major Salach Salem, 087/18/3/36, pp. 201–7, MFA.

40. Memcon, Solod and Ali Sabri, August 22, 1955, 087, 18/4/37, pp. 40–44, MFA.

41. Eisenhower Oral History, interview with Andrew Goodpaster, [by Dr. Thomas Soapes], October 11, 1977.

42. Dulles to Byroade, August 23, 1955, *FRUS, 1955–1957*, vol. 14, pp. 382–83.

43. Byroade to DOS, August 24, 1955, ibid., pp. 387–88.

44. Solod, memcon, meeting with Ali Sabri, September 4, 1955, 087/18/4/37, p. 6, MFA.

45. DOS to Secretary of State, New York, September 19, 1955, *FRUS 1955–1957*, vol. 14, p. 481. Dulles's staff repeated the Cairo cable to him and informed him of instructions for Byroade.

46. DOS to Cairo, September 20, 1955, ibid., p. 482; Cairo to DOS, September 20, 1955, ibid., pp. 483–84.

47. Editorial note, ibid., p. 483.

48. Telephone conversation [hereafter telcon], Eisenhower and John Foster, Dulles

[hereafter JFD] September 23, 1955, ibid., pp. 509–10; telcon, Allen W. Dulles [hereafter AWD] and JFD, Dulles, September 24, 1955, ibid., pp. 511–12.

49. One of Nasser's closest aides, Mohamed Heikal, later presented himself as Nasser's biographer and the keeper of Nasser's state papers after the Egyptian leader's death in 1970. But time and again Heikal's account differs so dramatically from the facts in Soviet, American, and British accounts that one must suspect it. Nowhere does the Heikal account diverge more from the truth of Nasser's relations with the great powers than in 1955.

50. Roosevelt sent two cables on this meeting, which CIA rerouted to the secretary of state in New York. See DOS (Washington) to U.S. UN mission, September 27, 1955, *FRUS, 1955–1957*, vol. 14, pp. 320–22. For information on the number of MiG-15s sold to Egypt, see memcon, Solod and Nasser, December 10, 1955, 087, 18/4/37, pp. 304–07, MFA.

51. Allen Dulles's cable to Kermit Roosevelt was repeated to Foster Dulles in New York as telegram, Hoover to JFD (NY), September 27, 1955, ibid., pp. 522–23.

52. Memcon, Solod meeting with Ali Sabri, September 26, 1955, 087, 18/4/37, pp. 117–21.

53. Ibid.

54. Mohamed Heikal, *The Cairo Documents: The Inside Story of Nasser and His Relationship with World Leaders, Rebels, and Statesman* (New York: Doubleday, 1973), p. 51.

55. Memcon, Solod and Nasser, September 29, 1955, 087, 18/4/37, pp. 124–28, MFA.

56. Ibid.

57. Ibid., October 1, 1955, pp. 135–41.

58. Ibid., September 29, 1955, pp. 124–28.

59. Ibid., October 5, 1955.

60. Ibid., September 29, pp. 124–28, October 5, 1955.

61. Solod, meeting with Nasser, October 18, 1955, 087/18/4/37, pp. 167–74, MFA.

62. Memcon, Solod and Nasser, October 5, 1955, 087, 18/4/37, MFA.

63. Solod told Nasser about the expected arrival of the *Krasnodar* on October 20 or 21 at their meeting on October 18. See memcon, Solod and Nasser, October 18, 1955, 087, 18/4/37, pp. 167–74, MFA.

64. The *Giulio Cesare* with its ten 12.6-inch guns, was the largest ship awarded to the Soviet Union from the captured navies of Italy, Nazi Germany, and Imperial Japan; the closest challenger, the damaged German aircraft carrier *Graf Zeppelin*, could never be exploited by Moscow. See Donald W. Mitchell, *A History of Russian and Soviet Sea Power* (New York: Macmillan, 1974), p. 473.

65. Ibid., p. 387.

66. Protocol 169, November 16, 1955, AOK.

67. Ibid.

68. Robert Kerrick, "Soviet Naval Strategy and Missions, 1946–1960," in *The Sources of Soviet Naval Conduct*, ed. Philip S. Gillette and Willard C. Frank, Jr., (Lexington, Mass.: Lexington Books, 1990), p. 181.

69. Mitchell, op. cit., p. 476.

70. Solod, meeting with Nasser, December 10, 1955, 087/18/4/37, pp. 304–7, MFA. At this meeting the Soviets informed Nasser of their response to his request.

71. Protocol 169, November 16, 1955, AOK. The Presidium first discussed sending additional arms to Egypt on November 7, after a telegram was received from Cairo. Protocol 168, November 7, 1955, AOK.

72. Protocol 169, November 16, 1955, AOK.

73. I. Turgarinov, August 2, 1956, "O Proyekte Stroitlstva Asuanskou Plotinii [Regarding the Aswan Dam Construction Project]," 087 19/14/40, pp. 48–65, MFA.

74. Torgovloye Soglashenye mezhdy SSSR u Egyptom," March 24, 1954, MFA.

75. Turgarinov, op. cit.

76. The Soviets were well aware that the Egyptians were doing this. Ibid.

77. Editorial note, *FRUS, 1955–1957*, vol. 14, p. 797.

78. Eden to Eisenhower, November 27, 1955, ibid., pp. 808–9.

79. Kyle, op. cit., pp. 82–85.

80. Zaitsev, Short report on Soviet proposals to Egypt to finance the building of the Aswan Dam, January 5, 1956, MFA.

81. Protocol 175 (continuation), December 22, 1955, AOK.

82. Ibid.

83. Protocol 122, December 16, 1955, AOK.

84. Protocol 122 (continuation), December 22, 1955, AOK.

CHAPTER 4: SUEZ

1. Abd Allah Imaam, "Ali Sabri Yatadhakir [Ali Sabri Remembers]" (Beirut: Dar al-Wahdah, 1988), p. 20, cited in Jon Alterman, "The View from Cairo, Developments to July 31, 1956," in "The Suez Crisis and Its Teachings: Case Studies for a conference at the American Academy of Arts & Sciences, February 15–16, 1997" [hereafter May and Zelikow Suez compilation]." The authors are grateful to Ernest May and Philip Zelikow, the conference directors, for the opportunity to consult this important compilation of excellent papers on the Suez crisis.

2. Peter Hahn, *The United States, Great Britain and Egypt: Strategy and Diplomacy in the Early Cold War, 1945–1956* (Chapel Hill: University of North Carolina Press 1991), pp. 202–4.

3. Abd Allah Imaam, op. cit., p. 20.

4. Zachary Karabell, *Parting the Desert: The Creation of the Suez Canal* (New York: Knopf, 2003), p. 269; Goodpaster, memorandum of conversation with the president, July 27, 1956, *Foreign Relations of the United States* [hereafter *FRUS*], *1955–1957*, vol. 16, p. 6. On Nasser's risk calculations, see Mohamed Heikal, cited in J. A. Sellers, "Military Lessons: The British Perspective," in *The Suez-Sinai Crisis 1956: Retrospective and Reappraisal*, ed. S. Troen and M. Shemesh, (New York: Columbia University Press, 1990), p. 24.

5. Keith Kyle, *Suez* (New York: St. Martin's Press, 1991), pp. 132–34.

6. Mohamed Haikal, "Milafaat al-Sulways," pp. 460–63, cited in Alterman, op. cit.

7. Kyle, op. cit., pp. 132–34.

8. Nasser did not promise to let Israel use the canal.

9. Memcon, Shepilov and Amer, June 18, 1956, 6/1956/1A/13/3, MFA. On behalf of the Kremlin, Shepilov explicitly turned down the Egyptian request for T-54 tanks and MiG-19s with the explanation that they were still undergoing testing in the USSR and could not be exported.

10. Yevgeni Kiselev to MFA, July 26, 1956, MFA. Kiselev had replaced Daniel Solod as Soviet ambassador in the spring of 1956.

11. Turgarinov, August 2, 1956, "O Proyekte Stroitlstva Asuanskou Plotinii [Regarding the Aswan Dam Construction Project]," 087 19/14/40, pp. 48–65, MFA.

12. Memcon, Shepilov and Amer, June 18, 1956, 6/1956/1A/13/3, MFA. On behalf of the Kremlin, Shepilov explicitly turned down the Egyptian request for T-54 tanks and

MiG-19s with the explanation that they were still undergoing testing in the USSR and could not be exported.

13. [Protocol 185], February 1, 1956, AOK.

14. Protocol 187, February 9, 1956, AOK.

15. Ochab cited in William Taubman, *Khrushchev* (New York: Norton, 2003), p. 290.

16. Ibid., pp. 288–89; William J. Thompson, *Khrushchev: A Political Life* (New York: St. Martin's Griffin, 1997), pp. 166–67.

17. Memcon, Shepilov and el-Kouni, July 27, 1956, 087 1956, 19/38/2, pp. 2–11, MFA.

18. Ibid.

19. Nuri al-Said quoted in David Nickles, "The View from London, Developments until August 1, 1956," May and Zelikow Suez compilation. Selwyn Lloyd refers to this discussion in *Suez 1956: A Personal Account* (London: Coronet, 1980), p. 74.

20. Diane Kunz, *The Economic Diplomacy of the Suez Crisis* (Chapel Hill: University of North Carolina Press, 1991), p. 130.

21. Julian Amery, "The Suez Group: A Retrospective on Suez," in Troen and Shemesh, op. cit., pp. 117–18.

22. Robert Rhodes James, *Anthony Eden: A Biography* (New York: McGraw-Hill, 1987), pp. 456–57.

23. This was not a formal meeting of Eden's cabinet. It appears that only those cabinet ministers who happened to be at the state dinner for the Iraqis were invited. Ibid., p. 454.

24. Foster [London] to DOS, July 27, 1956 [5:00 A.M.], *FRUS, 1955–1957* (Washington, D.C.: Government Printing Office), vol. 16, pp. 3–5.

25. Mollet cited in Charles G. Cogan, "The View from Paris, Developments until July 31, 1956," May and Zelikow Suez compilation.

26. On the French investment in Algeria, see William Hitchcock, *The Struggle for Europe: The Turbulent History of a Divided Continent, 1945–2002* (New York: Doubleday, 2002), pp. 184–92.

27. Ely, cited ibid.

28. Jean Chauvel, French Embassy (London) to Joxe personally, July 28, 1956, Secretariat General, Suez 82, Suez Crisis 1956–1957, French Diplomatic Archives.

29. Rhodes James, op. cit., p. 458; Sellers, op. cit., p. 24.

30. Jean Chauvel, French Embassy, (London) to Joxe personally, July 28, 1956, Secretariat General, Suez 82, Suez Crisis 1956–1957, French Diplomatic Archives. On August 1 Albert Thomas, the director-general of the French Defense Ministry, told the Israeli Defense Ministry official (and later prime minister) Shimon Peres: "The English and the French have decided in principle on a joint military operation to conquer the Canal." The operation was to occur in three weeks, and Britain had stipulated that Israel not be involved. David Ben Gurion's Diary, August 3, 1956, ed. and trans. Selwyn Ilan Troen, in Troen and Shemesh, op. cit., pp. 291–92.

31. Dulles cited in Robert R. Bowie, "Eisenhower, Dulles, and the Suez Crisis," *Suez 1956: The Crisis and Its Consequences*, ed. Wm. Roger Louis and Roger Owen (New York: Oxford University Press, 1989), p. 191.

32. Ibid.

33. Dwight D. Eisenhower, *The White House Years, Waging Peace: 1956–1961* (Garden City, N.Y.: Doubleday, 1965), p. 39.

34. Telcon, JFD–DDE, July 29, 1956, *FRUS, 1955–1957*, vol. 16, pp. 38–39.

35. Murphy [London] to DOS, July 29, 1956, *FRUS, 1955–1957*, vol. 16, pp. 35–36.

36. June 28, 1956, on the basis of el-Kouni's recommendations, Shepilov's deputy

Vladimir Semenov and the chief of the Near East Department, Grigorii, Zaitsev crafted a set of suggestions for the Presidium, 19/39/8, p.1, MFA.

37. Semenov and el-Kouni meeting, August 1, 1956, 19/13/7, MFA.

38. Ibid.

39. Bohlen to SecState, August 1, 1956, RG 89, State Department Decimal File 974.7301/8-156, NARA-II.

40. Ibid.

41. Semenov and el-Kouni meeting, August 1, 1956, 19/13/7, MFA.

42. V. I. Afiani and N. S. Ivanov, "Sovyetskii Soyuz u Sueskii Krisis 1956 g. (po materialam TskSD) [The Soviet Union and the Suez Crisis 1956 (according to the materials at the TskSD)]." The authors are grateful for this remarkable work by two archivists, which refers to classified materials summarized on cards kept by the Secretariat of the Communist Party of the Soviet Union. [This source will hereafter be referred to as Afiani-Ivanov, op. cit.] Although Afiani and Ivanov list several intercepted U.S. Embassy cables that were distributed to the Presidium, they do not claim that the KGB acquired all of the embassy's cable traffic. The State Department, which discovered the Soviet surveillance system in the early 1960s, concluded that Soviet intelligence had the capability of acquiring all embassy cables until the system was removed. The damage assessment of this penetration can be found attached to: memo, Jacob Beam to Mr. Henry, May 27, 1964, in Records of Llewellyn E. Thompson, 1961–1970, State Department Records, Box 10, RG 59, NARA-II. The United States believed the penetration dated back to 1953, but the Afiani-Ivanov compilation suggests it started only in 1956.

43. Semenov and El-Kouni meeting, August 1, 1956, 19/13/7, MFA.

44. Ibid.

45. Murphy [London] to DOS, July 31, 1956, *FRUS, 1955–1957*, vol. 16, p. 61.

46. Memcon, July 31, 1956, ibid., p. 63.

47. Memcon, August 1, 1956, ibid., p. 95.

48. Ibid.

49. Sellers, op. cit., pp. 28–29.

50. Protocol 30, August 3, 1956, AOK.

51. Ibid.

52. Ibid.

53. Ibid.

54. "Aircraft Carriers Prepare to Sail; Merchant Ships Taken Over," *Times* (of London), August 4, 1956.

55. "Precautionary Army Measures," Ibid., August 3, 1956.

56. Meeting, Nasser and Kiselev, August 3, 1956, APRF.

57. The reference to Kabul was puzzling. Afghanistan of course had no oil to sell. Nasser probably said Kuwait.

58. Nasser was grandstanding to force the Soviets to act. He never threatened the United States with a reign of terror.

59. Protocol 31, August 5, 1956, AOK.

60. Ibid.

61. Nehru had decided to attend the conference even before hearing from Moscow. Just after midnight, August 8, Moscow received a letter from Nehru, explaining India's decision. India believed that participation would not symbolize approval of Western actions in this crisis. Nehru told the Soviets that though it was in India's interest to attend the conference, he fully supported Nasser's decision not to send anyone from Cairo. India also fully supported the nationalization of the canal. It was a matter of the

sovereign right of Egypt. But Nehru added that India had its own interests too. In London, India's approach reflected its support for the principle of free use of the canal, as enshrined in the 1888 convention. August 8, 1956, New Delhi to Moscow, 01/02/15, MFA.

62. Protocol 31 (continuation), August 9, 1956, AOK; Protocol 32, August 11, 1956, AOK.

63. Protocol 169, November 16, 1955, AOK.

64. Protocol 32, August 11, 1956, AOK.

65. Ibid. To ease the concerns of his colleagues, Khrushchev also suggested that in London Shepilov be quite open about Nasser's mistakes. His Alexandria speech had been "provocative, excited." Khrushchev also wanted Soviet diplomats to coordinate with their counterparts from India and Indonesia.

66. Afiani and Ivanov, op. cit.

67. KGB report, August 14, 1956, APRF. The authors were unable to corroborate in U.S. or Israeli state archives that this meeting took place.

68. Memcon, August 14, 1956, FRUS, 1955–1957, vol. 16, pp. 198–99.

69. "Shepilov Says 'No,' Too, but Not Harshly; His Manner Is Not So Stiff as Molotov's," New York Times, August 24, 1956.

70. "Delegates' Arrival in London of Suez Conference; Mr. Shepilov on equality of States," Times (of London) August 15, 1956.

71. Compare Kuznetsov's draft of "Soviet Declaration on the Question of the Organization of an [International] Conference," August 14, 1956, in 01/02/20, to Shepilov's draft, 01/02/19, MFA. Shepilov redrafted this document on or about August 20.

72. Telegram 10107, JFD to Washington, August 16, 1956, RG 59, State Decimal File, 974.7301, NARA-II.

73. Telegram 10119, JFD to Washington, August 16, 1956, RG 59, State Department Decimal File, 974.7301, 8-1656, NARA-II; also FRUS, 1955–1957, vol. 16, pp. 206–09

74. Ibid.

75. Ibid.

76. Telegram, August 17, 1956, FRUS, 1955–1957, vol. 16, pp. 216–18.

77. DDE, August 17, 1956, ibid., pp. 218–19.

78. Memcon, August 18, 1956, ibid., pp. 221–26.

79. Ibid.

80. JFD to DDE, August 18, 1956, ibid., p. 227.

81. DOS to JFD (London), August 18, 1956, ibid., pp. 230–31.

82. DDE to JFD, August 19, 1956, ibid., pp. 232–33.

83. "Khrushchev Warns West on a Suez War," New York Times, August 24, 1956.

84. Ibid.

85. Dmitri Shepilov, Pravda, August 5 and 10, 1996.

86. Edwin L. Dale Jr., "Suez Committee Asks Quick Reply by Egypt on Talk," New York Times, August 25, 1956.

87. Dmitri Shepilov, Pravda, August 5 and 10, 1996.

88. Protocol 37 of August 27, 1956, AOK.

89. Kiselev to MFA, August 29, 1956, APRF.

90. Protocol 38, Presidium meeting of August 31, 1956, APRF.

91. Ibid.

92. Ibid.

93. Central Committee [hereafter CC] instruction, August 30, 1956, APRF.

94. Afiani and Ivanov, op. cit.

95. On February 24, 1956, Andrei Gromyko forwarded to Suslov and Molotov a request by Elliot and Frazer (Burgess and Maclean) to meet with two British Communist leaders who were coming to Moscow and with S. Russell, a correspondent for the *Daily Worker*, who was also expected in the Soviet capital, Fond 5, Microfilm Reel 4581, Delo 162, pp. 37–38, RGANI. On October 26, 1956, Khrushchev received a report on Burgess's subsequent meeting with Tom Driberg and with Labour, MP Konni Zilliacus, Fond 5, Microfilm Reel, 4582, Delo 163, pp. 119–27, RGANI.

96. I. Tugarinov to Nikita Khrushchev [hereafter NSK], August 14, 1956, Fond 5, Microfilm Reel 4581, Delo 162, pp. 114–16, RGANI.

97. Afiani and Ivanov, op. cit.

98. Ibid. On September 6 a transcript of this conversation was distributed to the Presidium.

99. Afiani and Ivanov, op. cit.

100. Ibid. In early October the Presidium voted to authorize the KGB to send this security detail to Nasser because of the threat of assassination.

101. Percy Craddock, *Know Your Enemy: How the Joint Intelligence Committee Saw the World* (London: John Murray, 2002), p. 117.

102. Ibid., pp. 117, 124.

103. Spravka, "O Voennyx Meropriyatiyax Zapadnix Derzhav v Cviyazi s Nastionalizyiei Egyptom Kompanii Suezskovo Kanala [On Military Measures of the Western Powers in Connection with the Nationalization of the Suez Canal Company]," GRU, September 1956. From internal evidence it appears to have been written after September 27, 1956. Regarding eventual U.S. participation, the report stated that "the military forces of England, France and the United States in the Mediterranean are training for the carrying of landing operations."

104. Tugarinov, "The Alignment of Political Forces in England on the Suez Question," September 25, 1956, 087, 19/39/8, pp. 60–66, MFA.

105. Tugarinov, "On the Alignment of Political Forces in France on the Suez Question," September 29, 1956, 19/39/8, pp. 69–75, MFA.

106. Shepilov cited in Kyle, op. cit., p. 272.

107. Afiani and Ivanov, op. cit.

108. Roosevelt, report of conversation on Suez, Cairo, October 9, 1956, RG 59, 58D776, INR, 1945–1960, Box 11, NARA-II.

109. Although not conclusive, it is suggestive that there is no evidence in Malin's notes for the Presidium meeting of October 11 or in the Foreign Ministry archives that the Presidium acted on this request in early October. Also significant is that in their discussions of the Egyptian problem on November 4 and 5, 1956, the members of the Presidium made no reference to any direct Soviet military assistance offered in October. See Protocol 41 (continuation), November 4, 1956, and Protocol 52, November 5, 1956, AOK. For the U.S. response to this request, see *FRUS, 1955–1957*, vol. 16, pp. 674–75, 678–81. The United States interpreted Nasser's initiative as a welcome sign of Egyptian interest in negotiating a peaceful end to the crisis. But the administration did not apply any additional pressure on the British in the days that immediately followed. Indeed, Eisenhower did not believe what Nasser had said about his relationship with Moscow. On October 11 the president wrote to Eden that the Soviets had "developed quite a hold on Nasser." Letter, DDE to Eden, October 11, 1956, ibid., p.694.

110. During a meeting with the Egyptian ambassador on October 11 Shepilov got the impression that to achieve agreement, Cairo would accept a Western proposal to

exclude Moscow from the Suez Canal users' association. Shepilov to CC, October 11, 1956, APRF.

111. Television broadcast, *The People Ask the President*, October 12, 1956, *Public Papers of the Presidents of the United States Dwight D. Eisenhower, 1956* (Washington, D.C.: Government Printing Office, 1958) pp. 903–21.

CHAPTER 5: TWIN CRISES

1. Protocol 36, August 24, 1956, AOK.

2. Protocol 44, October 4, 1956, AOK. Khrushchev did not attend this meeting.

3. Ibid.

4. Ibid., p. 365.

5. Wayne G. Jackson, "Allen Welsh Dulles as Director of Central Intelligence, February 26, 1953–November 29, 1961," vol. 5, Intelligence Support for Policy, unpublished CIA history July 1973, declassified 1994.

6. Ibid.

7. W. Scott Lucas, *Divided We Stand: Britain, the U.S., and the Suez Crisis* (London: Nodder & Stoughton, 1991), p. 215.

8. Percy Craddock, *Know Your Enemy: How the Joint Intelligence Committee Saw the World*, (London: John Murray, 2002), p. 121.

9. Khrushchev quoted in William Taubman, *Khrushchev* (New York: Norton, 2003), p. 293.

10. Ibid.

11. Taubman quotes from an autobiographical note on the Polish events of 1956 dictated by Mikoyan on May 28, 1960. Taubman, op. cit., p. 294, n. 86.

12. Protocol 47, October 21, 1956, AOK.

13. Keith Kyle, *Suez* (New York: St. Martin's Press, 1991), p. 317.

14. Ultimately the Anglo-French attack took place forty-eight hours after the Israeli attack. At the last minute the British delayed a little.

15. Spravka, "Military Actions by the Western Powers in Connection with the Nationalization of the Suez Canal Company by Egypt," September 1956, GRU.

16. Spravka, "On Syrian President Shukri Quwatly," October 1956, GRU.

17. Semyonov to el-Kouni, October 16, 1956, 087, 19/38/2, pp. 78–84, MFA.

18. Ibid.

19. Gromyko to NSK, with memcon of D. A. Elliot (G. Burgess) with Thomas Driberg, October 26, 1956, f. 5 (rolliki 4582), opis 30, D. 163, ll. 119–23, RGANI.

20. This is clear from Khrushchev's statements at the November 5, 1956, Presidium meeting, AOK.

21. Note 3, Document 73, "Sovyetskii Soyuz i Vengrii Krisis 1956 r.: Documenti [The Soviet Union and the 1956 Hungarian Crisis: Documents]" (Moscow: Russian Political Encyclopaedia, 1998).

22. Protocol 48, October 23, 1956, AOK.

23. Ibid.

24. Mark Kramer, "New Evidence on Soviet Decision-making and the 1956 Polish and Hungarian Crises." CWIHP, issues 8–9 (Washington, D.C.: Woodrow Wilson International Center for Soldiers, Winter 1996–1997), pp. 366–67.

25. This information comes from Protocol 81, October 28, 1956, AOK. In the notes Suslov is said to have reported that 600 Soviet soldiers had died and only 350 Hungarians, but this appears to be an error.

26. Ibid.

27. Chaim Herzog, "The Suez-Sinai Campaign: Background," Selwyn Ilan Troen and Moshe Shomesh, eds., *The Suez-Sinai Crisis 1956: Retrospective and Reappraisal* (New York: Columbia University Press, 1990), pp. 8–9.

28. Cited in Kyle, op. cit., p. 358.

29. Ibid., p. 359.

31. Cited in Diane Kunz, *The Economic Diplomacy of the Suez Crisis* (Chapel Hill: University of North Carolina Press, 1991), p. 120.

32. Edward L. Merta, "The View from Washington, October 14–November 30, 1956," May and Zelikow Suez compilation.

32. The letter was sent on October 30. See DDE to Eden, October 30, 1956, *FRUS, 1955–1957* (Washington, D.C.: Government Printing Office, 1990), vol. 16, pp. 848–50.

33. Merta, op. cit.

34. The late Richard Neustadt made this insightful point at the Harvard-sponsored conference on Suez at the American Academy of Arts and Sciences, February 15–16, 1997.

35. Memcon, October 29, 1956, 7:15 P.M., *FRUS, 1955–1957*, vol. 16, p. 835.

36. Kiselev to MFA, October 31, 1956, MFA.

37. Nasser to NSK, undated [probably early November 1956], APRF.

38. Shetemenko (GRU) to Zhukov, October 30, 1956, GRU.

39. Protocol 49, October 30, 1956, AOK.

40. Protocol 49 (continuation), October 30, 1956, AOK.

41. S. Shetemenko to Zhukov, November 4, 1956, GRU.

42. Protocol 49 (continuation), October 31, 1956, AOK.

43. Kiselev to MFA, October 31, 1956, MFA.

44. Carol R. Saivetz, "The View from Moscow: October 14–November 30, 1956," May and Zelikow Suez compilation.

45. Taubman cites a figure of twenty thousand Hungarian casualties and fifteen hundred Soviet casualties. See Taubman, op. cit., p. 299.

46. S. Shetemenko to Zhukov, November 4, 1956, GRU. For an excellent discussion of Nasser's movements during this period, see Jon Alterman, "The View from Cairo: October 14–November 30, 1956," May and Zelikow Suez compilation.

47. Protocol 52, November 5, 1956, AOK.

48. Oleg Bukharin et al., *Russian Strategic Nuclear Forces* (Cambridge, Mass.: MIT Press, 2001), pp. 177–79.

49. The Presidium approved the deployment of the R-5 only in late 1957. See Protocol 128, December 7, 1957, AOK.

50. Protocol 52, November 5, 1956, AOK.

51. Memcon, with the president, November 5, 1956, 5:00 P.M., *FRUS, 1955–1957*, vol. 16, pp. 1000–01.

52. Cable, Paris to DOS, November 6, 1956, 2:00 A.M., ibid., p. 1012.

53. Kunz, op. cit., pp. 116–52.

54. Patrick Reilly Memoirs, Bodleian Library, Oxford.

55. Timothy Naftali interview with Chester Cooper, April 2005.

56. *FRUS, 1955–1957*, vol. 16, p. 1029, note 1.

CHAPTER 6: "KHRUSHCHEY'S COMET"

1. Naftali interview with Dino Brugioni, Havana, October 13, 2002. Brugioni was the CIA photo analyst who brought the briefing board to Eisenhower.

2. Keith Kyle, *Suez* (New York: St Martin's Press, 1991), p. 545.

3. "Egyptian Proposal to Cooperate with U.S.," November 8, 1956, *Foreign Relations of the United States*, [hereafter *FRUS*], *1955–1957* (Washington, D.C.: Government Printing Office), vol. 16, p. 1087.

4. See Eisenhower's comments at the 303rd Meeting of the National Security Council, November 8, 1956, *FRUS*, vol. 16, pp. 1070–86.

5. Dwight Eisenhower, *Waging Peace, 1956–1961; The White House* (Garden City, NY.: Doubleday, 1965), p. 180. In response to the executive branch's request for joint action, the U.S. Congress passed a joint resolution on the Middle East that the President signed into law on March 9, 1957.

6. Ibid., pp. 182–83.

7. For a concise discussion of the background to the Eisenhower Doctrine, see Robert D. Schulzinger, "The Impact of Suez on United States Middle East Policy, 1957–1958," in *The Suez-Sinai Crisis 1956: Retrospective and Reappraisal*, ed. Selwyn I. Troen and Moshe Shemesh (New York: Columbia University Press, 1990).

8. Protocol 58, November 20, 1956, AOK.

9. Protocol 61, November 29, 1956, AOK; Protocol 62, December 6, 1956, AOK.

10. KGB statistic quoted in Anne Appelbaum, *Gulag: A History* (New York: Doubleday, 2003), p. 579.

11. Khrushchev cited ibid., p. 514.

12. Protocol 62, December 6, 1956, AOK.

13. Ibid.

14. On the basis of her research in former prisoners' accounts, Appelbaum writes that Hungarian sympathizers started showing up in the gulag in 1957. See Appelbaum, op. cit., p. 529.

15. For Mikoyan's criticism of Khrushchev's conduct of the Suez crisis, see meeting of October 14, 1964 [no protocol number], AOK. His critical comments on Suez in October 1964 were tame compared with those of Aleksandr Shelepin, who lambasted Khrushchev's risk taking in the crisis. A general criticism of Khrushchev's handling of that crisis appeared in the document prepared by the leaders of the coup that successfully removed him in October 1964. Many of the coup leaders were his protégés in 1957. See "The Presidium of the Central Committee of the CPSU to the October Plenum of the CC of the Communist Party of the Soviet Union," "Not Later than October 14, 1964" (draft), RGANI.

16. Protocol 68, January 11, 1957, AOK. Perhaps because he was vulnerable to criticisms that he had invested too much Soviet prestige in Egypt, Khrushchev did ask his colleagues if giving this support would "draw us into giving [further] assistance to Egypt." But with the exception of some grumbling by Molotov support for this arms package was strong.

17. Instruction, Moscow to Damascus, March 27, 1957, MFA.

18. Protocol 89, April 13, 1957, AOK.

19. Protocol 90, April 18, 1957, AOK.

20. Protocol 89, April 13, 1957, AOK.

21. Ibid., Protocol 91, April 23, 1957, AOK.

22. U.S. Department of State, *United States Participation in the United Nations: Report by the President to the Congress for the Year [1957]* (Washington, D.C.: Government Printing Office, 1958), p. 17.

23. The trio disagreed over Khrushchev's economic management reform. Kaganovich supported them; Molotov did not. Malenkov was cautiously supportive, almost neutral. See Protocol 85, March 27, 1957, AOK.

24. Martin McCauley, *Khrushchev and the Development of Soviet Agriculture: The Virgin Land Program, 1953–1964* (London: Macmillan, 1976), p. 80.

25. Ibid., p. 91.

26. William Taubman, *Khrushchev* (New York: Norton, 2003), p. 305.

27. Cited in "Nikita Sergeevich Khrushchev, Major Speech Chronology," Joseph Alsop Collection, Box 46, Library of Congress. This document is found among materials apparently prepared by the U.S. government and given to Alsop before his 1958 trip to the Soviet Union.

28. Ibid.

29. Cited in Taubman, op. cit., p. 305.

30. At a Presidium meeting in February 1961, Khrushchev disdainfully recalled Molotov's, Malenkov's, and Kaganovich's reaction to his catch and surpass campaign: "[T]hey got frightened by the call to catch up with America. I was certain though that it [was] possible to catch up with America quickly." Steno, February 16, 1961, AOK.

31. Ibid.

32. Protocol 88, April 6, 1957, AOK.

33. There were eleven full members of the Presidium in June 1957: Khrushchev, Bulganin, Voroshilov, Kaganovich, Kirichenko, Malenkov, Mikoyan, Molotov, Pervukhin, Saburov, and Suslov.

34. Taubman, op. cit., p. 312.

35. Pervukhin, Malenkov, Molotov, and Kaganovich all disagreed with Khrushchev. See Protocol 98, June 15, 1957, AOK.

36. Taubman, op. cit., pp. 310–24; William J. Thompson, *Khrushchev: A Political Life* (New York: St. Martin's Griffin, 1997), pp. 179–84. See also N. Kovalena, ed. Molotov, Malenkov, Kaganovich, 1957: Stenogramma iyun'skogo plenuma CK KPSS i drugie dokumenty [Stenographic Account of June Plenum of the Central Committee of the CPSU and other documents] Moscow: International Foundation "Democracy," 1998.

37. Cited in Thompson, op. cit., p. 184. Thompson has written a very useful summary discussion of the politics of the 1957 coup.

38. Paul Dickson, *Sputnik: The Shock of the Century* (New York: Walker & Co., 2001), pp. 94–95.

39. Dickson writes that the CIA and the Defense Department competed to see who could decipher the beeps first. Ibid., p. 113.

40. Ibid., pp. 105–6.

41. Sergei N. Khrushchev, *Khrushchev and the Creation of a Superpower* (University Park: Pennsylvania State University Press, 2000), p. 259.

42. Ibid., pp. 88–89.

43. Cited in Dickson, op. cit., p. 11.

44. Ibid., p. 24.

45. Ibid., p. 117.

46. Geoffrey Perret, *Eisenhower* (New York: Random House, 1999), pp. 557–61.

47. Dickson, op. cit., p. 119.

48. Ibid.

49. John S. D. Eisenhower, *Strictly Personal* (Garden City, N.Y.: Doubleday, 1974), p. 199.

50. Protocol 116, October 10, 1957, AOK.

51. Protocol 117, October 17, 1957, AOK.

52. Protocol 106, August 6, 1957. See Khrushchev's discussions of this disagreement as part of the indictment against Zhukov, Protocol 121, October 26, 1957, AOK.

53. Protocol 176, December 24, 1955, AOK. Zhukov stated in a discussion on the navy, "We need floating bases."

54. Protocol 103, July 26, 1957, AOK.

55. Protocol 117, October 17, 1957, AOK.

56. Ibid.

57. Protocol 118, October 19, 1957, AOK.

58. Protocol 120, October 25, 1957, AOK.

59. Protocol 121, October 26, 1957, AOK.

60. Protocol 117, October 17, 1957, AOK.

61. Richard P. Stebbins, *The United States in World Affairs, 1957* (New York: Harper & Brothers, 1958), p. 138.

62. Protocol 122, November 2, 1957, AOK.

63. For a detailed description of U.S. and Soviet proposals and counterproposals for aerial inspection zones, see U.S. Department of State, *Documents on Disarmament, 1945–1959* (Washington, D.C., Government Printing Office, 1960), vol. 2, Documents 213 and 215 and Maps 1 and 2.

64. Ibid.

65. Protocol 116, October 10, 1957, AOK.

66. Protocol 126, November 15, 1957, Fond 3, Opis 12, Delo 1008, pp. 30–30a.

67. Aleksandr Fursenko interview in September 2005 with a former Kremlin guard, who had worked in this building at the time.

CHAPTER 7: COUP IN IRAQ

1. 'Abd al-Karim Qasim's name is transliterated in various ways. It also appears as Qassim and Kassem. We have chosen the transliteration that is currently preferred by scholars.

2. Negotiations between the USSR and the United Arab Republic (UAR), minutes, April 30, 1958, at 10:00 A.M., MFA. See also Negotiations between the USSR and the UAR, minutes, May 14, 1958, MFA.

3. Khrushchev revealed this to the Egyptian government in a meeting with Field Marshal Amer in June 1963. See memorandum of conversation, Khrushchev and Amer, June 9, 1963, 52-1-561, APRF.

4. In the late 1960s Khrushchev recalled that the Kremlin knew of the contacts between Qasim and the Communists and that he had been told that Qasim considered himself a Communist. See Strobe Talbott, ed. *Khrushchev Remembers* (Boston: Little, Brown, 1940), p. 438. Contemporaneous information is fragmentary but is not incompatible with Khrushchev's later recollection. See steno, August 4, 1958, CC and Khrushchev's meeting with Amer in June 1963. In the latter conversation Khrushchev discusses the deal between Qasim and the Communists but assures the Egyptians that he did not know about it. It is fair to assume Khrushchev had an interest in deceiving the anti-Communist Nasser government on that point. Memcon, Khrushchev and Amer meeting, June 9, 1963, 52-1-561, APRF.

5. See Syria File, 0128, 1958, 21/28/4, MFA.

6. This was said to Nasser on July 17, 1958. See Mohamed Heikel, *The Sphinx and the Commissar: The Rise and Fall of Soviet Influence in the Middle East* (New York: Harper & Row), 1978, p. 98.

7. Protocol 116, October 10, 1957, Fond 3, Opis 12, Delo 1008, pp. 8–11.

8. On the United States in that crisis, see David W. Lesch, *Syria and the United States: Eisenhower's Cold War in the Middle East* (Boulder, Colo.: Westview Press, 1992),

passim. In May 1958 Khrushchev discussed with Nasser the importance of deterrence in the Syrian crisis. See memcon, USSR and UAR negotiations, May 14, 1958, MFA.

9. Protocol 126, November 15, 1957, AOK.

10. The timing of this crisis is clear from the fact that at the first meeting of the Presidium following the Iraqi Revolution the only substantive foreign policy discussion concerned the handling of the Chinese problem. Protocol 163, July 15, 1958, AOK.

11. CIA, Special National Intelligence Estimate, 30-2-58, "The Middle East Crisis," July 22, 1958, *Foreign Relations of the United States* [hereafter *FRUS*], *1958–1960*, vol. 12, p. 88.

12. Memcon, Bryce Harlow, July 14, 1958, 2:35 P.M., *FRUS, 1958–1960*, vol. 11, microfiche supplement 278/2.

13. Nigel John Ashton, *Eisenhower, Macmillan and the Problem of Nasser: Anglo-American Relations and Arab Nationalism, 1955–59* (London: Macmillan, 1996), pp. 165–81.

14. For an excellent introduction to the politics of Lebanon before and during the crisis of 1958, see Zachary Karabell, *Architects of Intervention: The United States and the Third World and the Cold War 1946–1962* (Baton Rouge: Louisiana State University Press, 1999), pp. 136–72.

15. Ashton, op. cit., p. 113.

16. Memcon, Robert Cutler, July 14, 1958, 10:55 A.M.–12:05 P.M., *FRUS, 1958–1960*, vol. 12, microfiche supplement, 274. Saeb Salaam was the leader of the rebel forces in Beirut. In a meeting with the CIA's Miles Copeland on July 27, 1958, Nasser admitted that he assumed Salaam's telephone calls to Damascus were being tapped. Nasser said that he was now urging restraint on Salaam. Telegram, Cairo to SecState, July 28, 1958, *FRUS, 1958–1960*, vol. 12, microfiche supplements, 545.

17. Department of state Memcon "Lebanon," June 15, 1958, cited in Douglas Little, "His Finest Hour? Eisenhower, Lebanon, and the 1958 Middle East Crisis," *Diplomatic History*, vol. 20, no. 1 (Winter 1996). pp. 41–42.

18. Memcon, July 14, 1958, 2:35 P.M., *FRUS, 1958–1960*, vol. 11, p. 220.

19. Memcon, Robert Cutler, July 14, 1958, *FRUS, 1958–1960*, vol. 11, microfiche supplement, 274.

20. Memcon, July 14, 1958, 10:30 A.M., ibid., pp. 211–15.

21. As originally conceived, the operation was to involve two army battle groups from Europe and three marine battalions, two attacks carriers, and an assortment of other surface ships, as well as a Tactical Air Corps composite air strike force, which was deployed to Adana, Turkey. One of the battle groups was later dropped from the operation. Situation Report on Lebanon (1), July 16, 1958, Records of White House Staff Secretary Subject Series, Department of Defense subseries, Joint Chiefs of Staff, vol. 2 (I), DDE Library. The authors are grateful to Eisenhower library archivist David Haight for bringing this series to their attention.

22. Eisenhower discussed his assumption about "mob-like actions" by the Iraq revolutionaries in a letter to George Humphrey, July 22, 1958, ed. note, *FRUS, 1958–1960*, vol. 12, p. 331.

23. Memcon, July 17, 1958, 2:30 P.M., *FRUS*, ibid., pp. 776–77. Telcon, Dulles and Nixon, July 15, 1958, JFD Telcons, microfilm, University Publications of America.

24. Ibid.

25. Memcon, July 14, 1958, 10:50 A.M., *FRUS, 1958–1960*, vol. 11, p. 213.

26. Ibid., p. 226.

27. William Roger Louis, "Harold Macmillan and the Middle East Crisis of 1958," *Elie Kedomie Memorial Lecture, Proceedings of the British Academy*, vol. 94 (Oxford,

U.K.: Oxford University Press, 1997), pp. 207–28. The authors are indebted to Dr. Taylor Fain for drawing our attention to this important article.

28. Ibid., p. 211.

29. Harold Macmillan, *Riding the Storm, 1956–1959* (London: Macmillan, 1971), p. 523, cited in W. Taylor Fain, "The United States, Great Britain, and Iraq: Confronting Radical Arab Nationalism in the Persian Gulf Region, 1958–1959," unpublished manuscript.

30. Memo from Board of National Estimates to AWD, "The Outlook for Kuwait," March 16, 1959, *FRUS, 1958–1960*, vol. 12, p. 784, n. 3.

31. Telcon, July 14, 1958, 5:43 P.M., ibid., vol. 11, 232–33.

32. Report of Eisenhower and Macmillan telephone call, July 14, 1958, 5:43 P.M., *FRUS, 1958–1960*, vol. 11, microfiche supplement, 284. JFD memo for the record, July 14, 1958, ibid., microfiche supplement, 285.

33. Heikal, op. cit., p. 98. Heikal heard Khrushchev say this to Nasser at their July 17 meeting.

34. "Text of Soviet Statement on Mideast," *Washington Post and Times Herald*, July 17, 1958. No notes have been found for the Presidium meeting of July 16, 1958, Protocol 164. However, in his diary entry for July 16, 1958, the Yugoslav ambassador, Veljko Micunovic, describes two meetings with Khrushchev in which the Soviet leader discussed these Presidium decisions. Micunovic was meeting with Khrushchev to plan for Nasser's secret visit. See Veljko Micunovic, *Moscow Diary*, trans. by David Floyd (Garden City, N.Y.: Doubleday, 1980), pp. 409–11.

35. V. V. Kuznetsov to CC, July 16, 1958, APRF.

36. Ibid.

37. For accounts of Nasser's trip, see Heikal, op. cit., pp. 76–102; Talbott, ed., op. cit., pp. 438–39; and Khrushchev's comments to Marshal Amer in June 1963, APRF.

38. Micunovic, op. cit., pp. 409–11.

39. See Aleksandr Fursenko and Timothy Naftali, *"One Hell of a Gamble": Khrushchev, Castro and Kennedy, 1958–1964* (New York: Norton: 1997), pp. 109–11.

40. "Holeman," Box 347, General Correspondence, Richard M. Nixon Pre-Presidential Papers, Vice President [hereafter RMN], NARA-LN.

41. Strobe Talbott, ed., *Khrushchev Remembers: The Last Testament* (Boston: Little Brown, 1974), pp. 366–67.

42. Richard Nixon to Frank Holeman, November 12, 1955, "Holeman," Box 347, General Correspondence, RMN, NARA-LN. They had gotten to know each other in 1948, when Nixon was grabbing headlines in his pursuit of the truth about Alger Hiss, a suave former State Department staffer alleged to have been a Soviet agent, and Holeman was just getting his start. In 1952 the *Daily News* assigned Holeman to the press corps that followed Nixon around the country. By the end of the campaign he and the future vice president had developed an easy relationship and were soon on a first-name basis. In 1956, when the National Press Club invited Harold Stassen, a man vying to replace Eisenhower whenever he decided to retire, Holeman made a point of sending word to the Nixon camp that he "just wanted to make it clear off-the-record that we invited him merely because he is in the news and for that reason only!" Frank Holeman to RMN, July 24, 1956, Box 347, General Correspondence, RMN, NARA-LN.

43. "Bulgarian Maneuvers with Russians Reported," *Washington Post and Herald Tribune*, July 18, 1958; "Bulgarian Maneuvers with Russians Reported," ibid., July 20, 1958.

44. Heikal, op. cit., p. 98.

45. Ibid.

46. Osgood Caruthers, "Nasser, in Moscow, Cautions Khrushchev Imperiling Peace," *New York Times*, July 19, 1958.

47. Memcon, USSR and UAR negotiations, May 14, 1958, APRF.

48. Khrushchev described this dramatic meeting in a letter he sent to Nasser in April 1959, at a time when the USSR, dragged into the middle of a struggle between Egypt and Iraq, was being criticized by Nasser for having failed to provide sufficient military assistance to Cairo. NSK to Nasser, April 12, 1959, Fond 087, 22/12/49, pp. 45–64, MFA.

49. Extract from Protocol 169, Presidium meeting of July 26, 1958, APRF. At this meeting, where the leadership discussed the first plan for sending arms to Baghdad, the Soviets reviewed the history of Iraqi requests for military supplies.

50. Protocol 170, July 18, 1958, APRF; Qasim to Khrushchev, July 18, 1958, APRF.

51. Russell Baker, "Dulles Doubtful of Soviet Action," *New York Times*, July 19, 1958.

52. Chairman of the Joint Chiefs Twining requested that the 101st Airborne also be prepared for dispatch. Eisenhower turned down that request because the lack of sufficient navy transport meant that this would involve chartering private vessels, an act that would reveal the movement and add to international tension. Memcon, DDE and Twining, July 15, 1958, 11:25 A.M., *FRUS, 1958–1960*, vol. 11, p. 246. Twining estimated it would take ten days to load the marine division and its equipment.

53. Memcon, July 16, 1958, ibid., p. 75.

54. Memcon, DDE and Selwyn Lloyd, July 17, 1958, ibid., p. 321.

55. Ibid., Memcon, JWD and Lloyd, ibid., pp. 319–20.

56. *FRUS, 1958–1960*, vol. 12, p. 93, n. 1.

57. Memcon, July 17, 1958, ibid., p. 326.

58. Viscount Hood to Foreign Office, July 15, 1958. Prem 11/2368, National Archives—UK.

59. Michael Wright to FO, November 24, 1958, from Baghdad, Prem 11/2368, National Archives—UK.

60. "Proclamation by Brigadier Kassem, prime minister of Iraq, on oil policy," Baghdad, July 18, 1958, Gillian King, ed., *Documents on International Affairs, 1958* (London: Oxford University Press, 1962), p. 300.

61. J. Bowker to FO, July 17, 1958, 71/134199, National Archives—UK.

62. Macmillan and Lloyd, July 18, 1958, National Archives—UK, 11/2408, quoted in Ashton, op. cit., p. 178.

63. Dulles told Lloyd that he thought the moderate language coming from Iraq was "part of a façade to deceive the West." Memcon, Dulles and Lloyd, July 19, 1958, 6:00 P.M., *FRUS, 1958–1960*, vol. 11, p. 342.

64. The UAR's guarantee of Iraqi territory was reported to President Eisenhower on July 18, 1958. Note, Andrew Goodpaster, July 1958, *FRUS, 1958–1960*, vol. 11, microfilm, 446.

65. Alphand to Paris, Juillet (July) 18, 1958, *Documents Diplomatiques Français* [hereafter *DDF*], *1958*, vol. 2, Record No. 56, Ministère des Affaires Étrangères Commission de Publication des Documents Diplomatiques, Français (Paris: Imprimerie Nationale, 1993), p. 110, n. 2. The telegram in question is summarized in the note.

66. On July 20 Dulles reported that it had been agreed with the British and approved by the president "not to back a military effort to retake Iraq." Memcon, meeting with DDE, July 20, 1958, 3:45 P.M., *FRUS, 1958–1960*, vol. 12, p. 83.

67. Telegram, SecState to London Embassy, July 18, 1958, 8:30 P.M., *FRUS,*

1958–1960, vol. 11, p. 325. Memcon, Lloyd to Dulles, July 19, 1958, 6:00 P.M., ibid., Alphand to Paris, July 19, 1958, *DDF*, 1958, vol. 2, Document 56.

68. Memcon, July 20, 1958, 3:45 P.M., *FRUS, 1958–1960*, vol. 11, p. 349.

69. U.K. consul-general (Istanbul) to FO, July 17, 1958, Prem 11/2368, National Archives–UK.

70. Alphand to Paris, July 19, 1958, *DDF, 1958*, vol. 2, Document 56. In the July 19 Presidium meeting Mikhail Suslov made a direct reference to Paris's disagreements with London and Washington over the handling of the crisis in the Middle East, steno, July 19, 1958, AOK.

71. The British concluded that Turkish intervention "would almost lead the new Iraqi regime to invite the Russians to intervene. This would alter the whole military situation in the Middle East to our extreme disadvantage." FO to U.S. State Dept, July 18, 1958, Prem 11/2368, National Archives—UK.

72. *Krasnaya Zvezda*, July 17, 1958, quoting an interview with Brown that appeared on July 16 in the *New York Journal-American*.

73. Steno, July 19, 1958, AOK.

74. In a letter to Nasser, Khrushchev explained by inference that he had been most concerned about an intervention by Pakistan, Iran, or Turkey into Iraq. NSK to Nasser, April 12, 1959, MFA.

75. Steno, July 19, 1958, AOK.

76. Walter Lacqueur, *Stalin: The Glasnost Revelations* (New York: Scribner's, 1990); Appendix 3, "Voroshilov," Talbott, ed., op. cit., pp. 554–55.

77. It was the old marshal who had sounded the death knell for Zhukov's Kremlin career when he denounced him in full view of his colleagues as "not being much of a party man." Protocol 121, October 26, 1957, AOK.

78. Protocol 157, June 7, 1958, AOK.

79. Steno, July 19, 1958, AOK.

80. "Text of Khrushchev Message on Summit Parley," *New York Times*, July 20 1958.

81. *FRUS, 1958–1960*, vol. 11, p. 56, n. 5.

82. Joint Chiefs of Staff, sitrep, July 22, 1958, Records of White House Staff Secretary, subject series, Department of Defense sub series, Joint Chiefs of Staff, vol. 2 (1), DDE Library.

83. Editorial note, *FRUS, 1958–1960*, vol. 11, p. 372.

84. Sokolovskii and Skatchkov to CC, July 25, 1958, APRF.

85. Protocol 169, July 26, 1958, APRF.

86. Gerasimov (Cairo) to CC, July 28, 1958, APRF.

87. Ibid.

88. Gerasimov (Cairo) to CC, August 11, 1958, APRF.

89. Protocol 169, July 26, 1958, APRF.

90. See Strobe Talbott, ed., *Khrushchev Remembers: The Last Testament* (Boston: Little Brown, 1970), p. 472, loc. cit., pp. 19–34; also memcon, Khrushchev and Mao, July 31, 1958, Volkogonov Papers, Library of Congress.

91. Protocol 163, July 15, 1958.

92. See Khrushchev's comments at the July 31 meeting with Mao and his later recollections in *Khrushchev Remembers: The Last Testament*, loc. cit., pp. 19–34. See discussion of the fall of Admiral Kuznetsov in chapter 3, "Arms to Egypt."

93. R. Pikhoia, *Sovietskii Soyuz: Istoria 'Vlast, 1945–1991* [Soviet Union: History of Power, 1945–1991] (Moscow: R.A.A.S. Publishing House, 1991), pp. 203–8.

94. See memcon, NSK and Nasser, May 14, 1958, 51/1/561, APRF.

95. On July 15 the Presidium had decided to have Mikoyan draft the letter (See

Protocol 163, July 15, 1958), but Khrushchev intervened. See Khrushchev's discussion of this decision to send his own private message in memcon, NSK and Mao, July 31, 1958, Volkogonov Papers, Library of Congress.

96. See their exchange, ibid.

97. See Chen Jian, *Mao's China and the Cold War* (Chapel Hill: University of North Carolina Press, 2001), pp. 163–205.

98. Protocol 168, July 24, 1958.

99. Khrushchev told the story of how he decided to go to Beijing in the midst of the Middle East crisis at his August 3 meeting with Mao. See memcon, August 3, 1958, Volkogonov Papers, Library of Congress.

100. Editorial note, *FRUS, 1959–1960*, vol. 11, pp. 406–7.

101. Memorandum, July 28, 1958, Pavel Yudin, China Referentura 0100, 51/432/6 1958, MFA.

102. Ibid.

103. Soviet memorandum of conversation between Mao and Khrushchev, July 31, 1958, Volkogonov Papers, Library of Congress.

104. "Peiping Hits U.S.," *Washington Post and Times Herald*, July 17, 1958.

105. Nigel John Ashton, *Eisenhower, Macmillan and the Problem of Nasser: Anglo-American Relations and Arab Nationalism, 1955–1959* (London: Macmillan, 1996).

106. Memcon, NSK and Mao, August 3, 1958, Volkogonov Papers, Library of Congress.

107. Steno, August 4, 1958, AOK, on the second question.

108. Ibid.

109. Ibid. At the Security Council, China sat next to CCCP, the English transliteration of the Russian abbreviation of Union of Soviet Socialist Republics.

110. Khrushchev believed that it was also time to bring the military exercises to an end in the southeastern border region and in Bulgaria. He ordered the broadcast of a public report announcing the end of the exercises and that the commander for those exercises, Marshal Andrei Grechko, be described as having returned to Moscow to deliver his report. Meanwhile the Bulgarians were to be told that they could stop their exercises.

111. Zaitsev to CC, August 24, 1958, APRF.

112. Ibid.

113. This had happened a few days earlier, July 31, 1958.

114. " 'Tough Line' May Gain," *New York Times*, August 7, 1958.

CHAPTER 8: "A BONE IN MY THROAT"

1. Khrushchev made these points to the Presidium on August 4, 1958. See Steno, August 4, 1958, AOK.

2. Memcon, NSK and Nasser, May 1958, APRF.

3. Memcon, Andrei Gromyko with Ambassador Tarazi, October 21, 1958, 087, MFA. Tarazi accompanied Amer on his visit to the USSR.

4. Many fine historians have worked on this issue. The most thoughtful student, however, remains Marc Trachtenberg, who analyzed the crisis first in his essay "The Berlin Crisis," in *History and Strategy* (Princeton: Princeton University Press, 1991), and then in his important book, *A Constructed Peace: The Making of the European Settlement, 1945–1963* (Princeton: Princeton University Press, 1999). The authors found that despite his not having Soviet materials to work with, Trachtenberg ably captured Khrushchev's anxieties over the rise in strength of the West German Army,

especially Adenauer's efforts to acquire nuclear weapons. Although this turned out not to be the main reason for the Soviet ultimatum policy in 1958, it was a very significant contributing factor.

5. Charles Williams, *Adenauer: The Father of the New Germany* (New York: Wiley, 2000), pp. 23–24. Williams notes that the first mention of this story came in Adenauer's authorized biography, written by Paul Weymar and published in 1955.

6. James Critchfield, *Partners at the Creation* (Annapolis, Md.: Naval Institute Press, 2003), pp. 131–50.

7. The SPD chief, Erich Ollenhauer, was not a neutralist, but he opposed the possession of nuclear weapons by NATO troops in Germany and advocated a more concerted effort at negotiating with Moscow. To blunt SPD attacks on West German foreign policy, Adenauer made sure to emphasize his government's support for the ongoing general disarmament talks at the United Nations.

8. Memcon, May 1, 1957, U.S. Delegation to the Ministerial Meeting of the North Atlantic Council. Conference Files 1949–1963, Entry 3051B, CF 878, RG 59, NARA II. The authors are grateful to Laura Moranchek for finding this document.

9. Memcon, Adenauer visit, May 26, 1957, Conference Files, 1949–1963, Entry 3051B, CF 888, RG 59, NARA II. Soviet belief in these assurances comes out in the text of Mikoyan's meetings with Adenauer in April 1958. See 0757, FRG 1958, 3/17/3, pp. 30–51, MFA.

10. Hans-Peter Schwarz, *Adenauer: Der Staatsmann: 1952–1967* (Stuttgart: Deutsche Verlages-Anstalt, 1991). Schwarz, Adenauer's authorized biographer, describes this as the zenith of Adenauer's power.

11. Cable, DKE Bruce to secretary of state, March 24, 1958, 662a.00/3-2458, RG 59, NARA-II.

12. This was the general view of the Kremlin and the Soviet Ministry of Foreign Affairs. See "Results of Mikoyan's Visit to Bonn," May 1958, and "An Account of Soviet-FRG Relations," August 1958, MFA.

13. Protocol 146, March 29, 1958; Protocol 147, March 31, 1958, AOK.

14. Memcon, Mikoyan and Adenauer, April 26, 1958, 0757, FRG 1958, 3/17/3, MFA; Soviet Embassy in Bonn, "Results of Mikoyan Visit to FRG," May 13, 1958, 0757, FRG 1958, 3/18/16, MFA.

15. In November 1958 Khrushchev hinted at his assumptions about U.S. acceptance of a West German nuclear force. See Protocol 190, November 6, 1958, AOK. Marc Trachtenberg argues that U.S. policy toward nuclear sharing with its allies, including West Germany, was indeed "extraordinarily liberal" in this period, but apparently the Eisenhower administration either delayed consideration of Adenauer's May 1957 request for tactical nuclear weapons or found some particular reason not to approve it. By 1960 the administration had shifted to a policy of preferring the establishment of a single European nuclear force over fostering national nuclear arsenals by its allies. Trachtenberg, op. cit., pp. 204–15.

16. CIA, Berlin Handbook, December 27, 1961, NSF, Kissinger, Box 462, John F. Kennedy Presidential Library.

17. Vladislav Zubok and Constantine Pleshakov, *Inside the Kremlin's Cold War: From Stalin to Khrushchev* (Cambridge, Mass.: Harvard University Press, 1996), p. 196.

18. Hope Harrison, "Ulbricht and the Concrete Rose: New Archival Evidence on the Dynamics of Soviet–East German Relations and the Berlin Crisis," Cold War International History Project [hereafter CWIHP], Working Paper 5, pp. 8–21.

19. Ibid.

20. Gromyko to CC, November 3, 1958, 3-64-718, p. 185, APRF.

21. Ibid.

22. Protocol 188, October 23, 1958, AOK.

23. Protocol 190, November 6, 1958, AOK.

24. The authors are grateful to German historian Matthias Uhl for his counsel and assistance. Dr. Uhl and Vladimir I. Ivkin unearthed documents in Moscow and Koblenz that revealed the Soviet medium-range ballistic plan in 1955 and the much-delayed Soviet deployment to East Germany in 1958. See Matthias Uhl and Vladimir I. Ivkin, "'Operation Atom': The Soviet Union's Stationing of Nuclear Missiles in the German Democratic Republic, 1959," CWIHP *Bulletin*, issue 12/13 (Winter–Spring 2001), pp. 299–307. The Malin notes confirm that R-5ms were not deployed in 1956 during the Suez crisis, but they do not refer to any decision in 1958 to proceed with the East German deployment.

25. Hope Harrison, *Driving the Soviets up the Wall, Soviet–East German Relations, 1953–1961* (Princeton: Princeton University Press, 2003), p. 128.

26. Max Frankel, "Consumer Wooed at Moscow Fete," *New York* Times, November 7, 1958.

27. The reconstruction of this event is based on Malin's notes for the meeting and Mikoyan's later recollections. See Protocol 190, November 6, 1958, AOK.

28. The description of Gromyko's fear of Khrushchev comes from Andrei Aleksandrov-Agentov, a former Gromyko assistant, cited in William Taubman, *Khrushchev* (New York: Norton, 2003), p. 398.

29. John W. Wheeler-Bennett and Anthony Nichols, *The Semblance of Peace: The Political Settlement after the Second World War* (New York: St. Martin's, 1972), pp. 278–79.

30. Ibid.

31. Johannes König, "Comments on the Preparation of the Steps of the Soviet Government Concerning a Change in the Status of West Berlin," December 4, 1958, GDR Foreign Ministry Archives, trans. Harrison, in *CWIHP Bulletin*, vol. 4, pp. 36–38.

32. Cited in Harrison, *Driving the Soviets Up the Wall*, loc. cit., p. 107.

33. CWIHP *Bulletin*, "Minutes from the discussion between the Delegation of the PRL [People's Republic of Poland] and the Government of the USSR," October 25–November 10, 1958," from Douglas Selvage, "Khrushchev's November 1958 Berlin Ultimatum: New Evidence from the Polish Archives; Introduction, Translation and Annotation by Douglas Selvage," www.wilsoncenter.org (accessed February 20, 2006). Dr. Selvage did groundbreaking research in Polish sources for his unpublished doctoral dissertation, "Poland, the German Democratic Republic and the German Question, 1955–1967," Yale University (December 1998).

34. Ibid.

35. Khrushchev address, November 10, 1958, U.S. Department of State, *Documents on Germany, 1944–1985*. Office of the Historian, Bureau of Public Affairs (Washington, D.C.: Government Printing Office, 1985), pp. 542–546.

36. Reilly to London, November 11, 1958, Prem 11/2715, National Archives—UK.

37. Foreign Relations of the United States [hereafter *FRUS, 1958–1960*] (Washington, D.C.: Government Printing Office, 1993), vol. 8, p. 69, n. 1.

38. Telcon, Dulles and McElroy, November 17, 1958, ibid., p. 81; telcon, Dulles and McElroy, November 18, 1958, ibid., p. 85. On November 16 Norstad formally requested permission to send a convoy of military trucks up the autobahn.

39. In a telephone call to Eisenhower, Dulles called these views "extreme." Telcon, November 18, 1958, ibid., pp. 84–85.

40. In his memoirs, Mikoyan writes that Khrushchev made his November 10 speech without a preliminary discussion in the Presidium. In fact there had been a discussion, which Mikoyan attended. But Mikoyan objected to the fact that the Soviet leader had proceeded with the speech without any instruction from the Presidium. See Anastas Mikoyan, *Tak B'ilo* (Moscow: Vagrius, 1999), pp. 604–05.

41. "Soviet to Submit Plan," *New York Times*, November 15, 1958.

42. The men took pains not to speak of these truths where they could be overheard. Serov let his guard down once among Khrushchev's family, and it was an event that remained indelibly printed on the minds of those who were there. It had happened during a lunch when Khrushchev was away from the dacha. Serov was being entertained by Khrushchev's son-in-law, the editor of *Pravda*, Aleksei Adzhubei. Adzhubei was interested in recent requests from the Poles for the truth about what had happened in the Katyn Forest. For Khrushchev's children, Rada, Adzhubei's wife, and Sergei, the story was Cold War propaganda, fabricated to blame Moscow for something that Hitler's henchmen had done. Serov's response was as unexpected as it was disturbing. He stammered that the Belorussian chekists, secret service men, had been lamentably ineffectual: "They couldn't cope with such a small matter." Sergei Khrushchev then recalled how Serov "let the cat out of the bag": "There was a lot more in the Ukraine when I was there. But not a thing was said about it, nobody even found a trace." How many had Serov killed? How many had Khrushchev ordered Serov to kill? The Khrushchev children never asked their father. They were too afraid. Sergei Khrushchev, *Nikita Khrushchev and the Creation of a Superpower*, (University Park: Pennsylvania State University Press, 2000), pp. 165–66.

43. See Protocol 188, October 23, 1958, AOK.

44. Notes by James Reston, November 19, 1958. Allen W. Dulles File, A. H. Sulzberger Collection, New York Times Archives.

45. Ibid.

46. Brooks Richards to Philip de Zulueta, November 19, 1958, Prem 11/2715, National Archives—UK.

47. Ibid.

48. Protocol 191, November 20, 1958, National Archives—UK.

49. Mikoyan, op. cit., p. 605.

50. Gromyko's suggestion of an approach to the West German ambassador appears in a memorandum to the Central Committee dated November 20. It does not appear to have been prepared for discussion at the Presidium meeting of that day. There is no mention of it in Malin's notes for that meeting. Moreover, the Presidium accepted the proposal on November 21 and assigned it the next protocol number. For the acceptance, see extract from Protocol 192, November 21, 1958, 3-64-718, p.212, APRF, or References to Presidium decision 192/9 of November 21, 1958, in the Bischoff initiative materials at the MFA, 0757, FRG 1958, 3/18/14, and 065, Third European Department, 1958, 42/224/3, MFA.

51. Background on the initiative can be found both in the Russian Foreign Ministry Archive and in the Presidential Archive. In the MFA, see Briefing note for Bischoff, November 20, 1958, 0757, FRG, 1958, 3/18/14; in the APRF, see Gromyko to CC, November 20, 3-64-718, p. 197.

52. Gromyko to the CC, November 20, 1958, 3-64-718, p. 185, APRF.

53. Hans Kroll, *Lebenserinnerungen eines Botschafters* (Cologne: Liepenheuer U. Witsch, 1967), pp. 15–17.

54. Ibid., p. 19.

55. Extract from Protocol 192, November 21, 1958, 3-64-718, p. 212, APRF.

56. Memcon, Gromyko and Bischoff, November 22, 1958, 065, Third European Department, 1958, 42/224/3, MFA.

57. Memcon, Gromyko and Bischoff, November 24, 1958, 065, Third Department 1958, 42/244/3, MFA. This is how Bischoff described the meeting to Gromyko. This memorandum was distributed to Presidium members on November 27. A copy is in 3-64-719, p. 3, APRF.

58. Aleksandrov-Agentov, *Ot Kollonthai do Gorbacheva*, pp. 71, 103, cited and trans. Harrison, *Driving the Soviets up the Wall*, loc. cit., p. 109.

59. The Foreign Ministry's draft of the note containing the free city proposal is dated November 22. See Gromyko to CC, November 22, 1958, 3-64-719, pp. 65–79, APRF. Khrushchev's intervention may well have occurred on November 21 or 22.

60. Uhl and Ivkin, "'Operation Atom,'" loc. cit.

61. Harrison, *Driving the Soviets up the Wall*, loc. cit., p. 129.

62. Protocol 73, February 6, 1957, AOK.

63. Extract from Protocol 192, November 24, 1958, 3-64-719, p. 5, APRF.

64. Mikoyan, op. cit., p. 605.

65. Telcon, DDE and JFD, November 24, 1958, *FRUS, 1958–1960*, vol. 8, p. 119.

66. The British thinkpiece is summarized in Cable, DOS to Bonn, November 17, 1958, ibid; pp. 82–83. Selwyn Lloyd's comments are in London to DOS, November 19, 1958, ibid., pp. 86–88.

67. Editorial note, ibid., p. 134; telcon, JFD, and DDE, November 30, 1958, ibid., pp. 142–43.

68. Embassy in Bonn to DOS, November 28, 1958, ibid., pp. 136–37.

69. This message was conveyed back to the Soviets by Bischoff, who met with Kroll after he returned from Bonn after the new note was published. See Memcon, Gromyko and Bischoff, December 3, 1958, Third Department, 065 1958, 42/224/3, MFA.

70. This final act in the Serov drama can be reconstructed from Mikoyan's memoirs, op. cit., pp. 607–8, and Malin's notes on the December 3 Presidium session: Protocol 194, "O Serova," AOK.

71. Embassy in Moscow to DOS, December 3, 1958, *FRUS 1958–1960*, vol. 8, pp. 148–52.

72. Ibid.

73. Uhl and Ivkin, "'Operation Atom,'" loc. cit., Harrison, *Driving the Soviets up the Wall*, loc. cit., p. 128.

74. Editorial note, *FRUS 1958–1960*, vol. 10, Part I, p. 207. The Soviet note was dated November 16, 1958.

75. December 18, 1958, Holeman File, General Correspondence, RMN, Box 347, NARA-LN.

CHAPTER 9: KHRUSHCHEV IN AMERICA

1. Mikoyan may have learned something about canneries, but it was his discovery of ice cream that had a profound effect on Soviet life. After tasting his first cone, Mikoyan received permission to license American ice-cream machinery. For the next thirty years, until the end of the Soviet Union, the standard Soviet style of ice cream imitated what Mikoyan had tasted in the United States.

2. Dwight Eisenhower, *Waging Peace 1956–1961: The White House Years* (Garden City, N.Y.: Doubleday, 1965), p. 340.

3. John S. D. Eisenhower, *Strictly Personal* (Garden City, N.Y.: Doubleday, 1974), p. 218.

4. Ibid.

5. Note, Protocol 203, January 24, 1959, AOK.

6. William Taubman, *Khrushchev* (New York: Norton, 2003), p. 409.

7. In his fine biography of Nikita Khrushchev, Taubman relies on the recollections of Sergei Khrushchev to conclude that the Soviet leader was disappointed by Mikoyan's visit (see pp. 409–10). In fact, the opposite was true, and this would help explain Khrushchev's actions throughout the year.

8. Note, Protocol 203, January 24, 1959, AOK. Mikoyan returned on January 21.

9. See the *New York Times* front-page coverage of the press conference, January 25, 1959. At his press conference Mikoyan said that "the main thing was not the deadline but to have talks."

10. Note, Protocol 204, February 11, 1959, AOK.

11. Soviet Draft Peace Treaty with Germany, January 10, 1959, Department of State, *Documents on Germany, 1944–1985* (Washington, D.C.: U.S. Department of State, office of the Historian, Bureau of Public Affairs, 1985), pp. 594–607.

12. Memcon, August 1, 1956, *Foreign Relations of the United States* [hereafter *FRUS*], *1955–1957* (Washington, D.C.: Government Printing Office, 1992), vol. 16, p. 108.

13. SecState to DOS, February 5, 1959, *FRUS, 1958–1960* (Washington, D.C.: Government Printing Office, 1993), vol. 8, pp. 321–22.

14. Note from the United States to the Soviet Union Proposing a Foreign Ministers Meeting on Germany, February 16, 1959, U.S. Department of State, *Documents on Germany, 1944–1985*, pp. 607–8. The basic model used by the CIA and State Department to understand Soviet politics placed Khrushchev as a captive of the hawkish members of the Soviet hierarchy and the Berlin issue as a Soviet ploy to undermine the unity of NATO. Under those circumstances, negotiations were really not possible. All one could hope for was that the Soviets would be dissuaded from continuing to pressure for these radical changes to the status quo in Germany. The note was an effort at dissuasion.

15. This is evident from Mikoyan's comments at the February 21, 1959, Presidium meeting. See Protocol 206, February 21, 1959, AOK.

16. Ibid.

17. Ibid.

18. Protocol 206, February 21, 1959, AOK.

19. Sir Patrick Reilly to Macmillan, August 25, 1958, Prem 11/5115, National Archives—UK. Evidence that Macmillan absorbed this view comes from a note from his assistant Philip de Zueleta to D. C. Tebbitt at the Foreign Office, September 1958, also Prem 11/5115, National Archives—UK.

20. Alistair Horne, *Macmillan, 1957–1986* (London: Macmillan, 1989), p. 122.

21. Ibid., p. 125.

22. Patrick Dean (Moscow) to Hoyer Millar (London), February 26, 1959, Prem 11/2715, National Archive—UK.

23. Horne, op. cit., p. 126.

24. Protocol 219, May 24, 1959, AOK. On May 23 one Grishin cabled from Geneva requesting instructions for the use of one Libich. Grishin is not listed as one of the key Foreign Ministry officials accompanying Gromyko, and Libich has not been identified. However, from the Kremlin discussion it appears that Libich, who was possibly a European diplomat or journalist, was in contact with the Americans on behalf of the Soviet intelligence services.

25. Protocol 219, May 24, 1959, AOK. At the same time, the Soviets decided to send Presidium member Kozlov to the United States to open the Soviet National Exhibition of Science, Technology and Culture in New York City in late June.

26. Hope M. Harrison, *Driving the Soviets up the Wall: Soviet East German Relations, 1953–1961* (Princeton: Princeton University Press, 2003), p. 122.

27. "Protocol on the Guarantees of the Status of the Free City of West Berlin," undated, but submitted to the conference by the Soviet delegation on May 30, 1959, *FRUS, 1958–1960*, vol. 13, pp. 810–11.

28. Herter to DOS, June 9, 1959, ibid., vol. 8, pp. 865–67.

29. DDE to NSK, June 15, 1959, ibid., pp. 901–3.

30. NSK to DDE, June 17, 1959, ibid., pp. 913–17.

31. Khrushchev cited in Harrison, op. cit., p. 127.

32. Ibid., p. 122.

33. Telcon, Herter and DDE, July 8, 1959, *FRUS, 1958–1960*, vol. 10, pp. 308–9.

34. Dwight Eisenhower, op. cit., p. 405.

35. Ibid.

36. Gregory W. Pedlow and Donald E. Welzenbach [CIA History Staff], *The CIA and the U-2 Program, 1954–1972* (Washington, D.C.: Center for the Study of Intelligence, CIA, 1998), pp. 144, 162–63.

37. Ibid., p.122.

38. Quoted by Dwight Eisenhower, op. cit., p.46.

39. Once it became clear that Khrushchev would be coming to the United States, Eisenhower again placed a freeze on U-2 overflights of the USSR. Still concerned about Soviet missile development, he permitted the CIA to fly fourteen electronic intelligence-gathering missions along the Soviet border. These picked up the emissions from Soviet rockets during testing. Pedlow and Welzenbach, op. cit., p. 163.

40. Memcon, July 8, 1959, *FRUS, 1958–1960*, vol. 10, pp. 306–7.

41. See *FRUS, 1958–1960*, vol. 10, pp. 307–19.

42. Receiving the invitation from Kozlov on July 13, on the eve of a trip to Poland, Khrushchev formally accepted a week later. NSK to DDE, July 21, 1959, ibid., pp. 324–25.

43. H. S. Foster, "American Opinion on Khrushchev's Visit," October 8, 1959, RG 59, Office of Soviet Union Affairs, Subject Files, 1957–1963, Box 4, NARA-II.

44. Strobe Talbott, ed., *Khrushchev Remembers: The Last Testament* (Boston: Little, Brown, 1974), p. 372.

45. Ibid.

46. The remarkable story of the Khrushchev family and their rickety *Air Force One* is told in Sergei Khrushchev, *Nikita Khrushchev and the Creation of a Superpower* (University Park: Pennsylvania State University Press, 2000), pp. 328–30.

47. Cited in Hitchcock, *The Struggle for Europe: The Turbulent History of a Divided Continent, 1995–2002* (New York: Doubleday, 2003), p. 200.

48. Sergei Khrushchev, op. cit., p. 324.

49. Memoir of a member of this security detail, Nixon Library and Birthplace, Yorba Linda, California. The authors are grateful to Irwin Gellman for pointing this document out to them.

50. Talbott, ed., op. cit., p. 376.

51. Mrs. Llewellyn D. Thompson, [memorandum], RG 59, Office of Soviet Union Affairs, Subject Files 1957–1963, Box 4, NARA II.

52. "Khrushchev Pays Lincoln Homage," *New York Times*, September 17, 1959.

53. Memcon, September 15, 1959, POF "USSR-Vienna Meeting, Background Documents, 1953–1961 (c), Reading Material," Box 126, JFK Library.

54. Henry Cabot Lodge, "Train Trip from Los Angeles to San Francisco," September 21, 1959, RG 59, Office of Soviet Union Affairs, Subject Files 1957–1963, Box 4, NARA-

II. Khrushchev had similar recollections of his reaction to Victor Carter. See Talbott, ed., op. cit., p. 385.

55. Hollywood Greets Premier in Star-Studded Welcome," *Los Angeles Times*, September 20, 1959.

56. The Café de Paris had been swept with a Geiger counter the day before. The L.A. policeman undertaking the investigation explained, "We're just checking for 'hot spots.' It's not that we fear an explosion but we're just taking precautions against the secretion of any radioactive poison that might be designed to harm Khrushchev in his food or drink." "Film Studio Checked for Any Radiation," *Los Angeles Times*, September 20, 1959.

57. "Mme. K Talks Children with Sinatra at Lunch," *Los Angeles Times*, September 20, 1959.

58. Ibid.

59. Henry Cabot Lodge, *The Storm Has Many Eyes: A Personal Narrative* (New York: Norton, 1973), pp. 166–67.

60. Talbott, ed., op. cit., p. 389.

61. Lodge, op. cit., p. 168.

62. "The Scatology and Ribaldry of N. S. Khrushchev," December 1959, RG 59, Office of Soviet Union Affairs, Subject Files, 1957–1963, Box 5, NARA-II.

63. Naftali interview with Sandor Vanocur, a journalist on the trip, in March 2001.

64. Talbott, ed., op. cit., p. 390.

65. Roswell Garst to NSK, September 9, 1959, *Letters from an American Farmer: The Eastern European and Russian Correspondence of Roswell Garst*, ed. Richard Lowitt and Harold Lee (De Kalb: Northern Illinois University Press, 1987), pp. 148–51.

66. Ibid., p. xii.

67. Harold Lee, *Roswell Garst: A Biography* (Ames: Iowa State University Press, 1984), pp. 153–215, passim.

68. Cited in *Letters from an American Farmer*, loc. cit., p. xiii.

69. Lee, op. cit.,

70. Steno, December 16, 1960; steno, February 16, 1961; steno, April 25, 1963, AOK.

71. Lee, op. cit., p. 219.

72. Steno, December 16, 1960, AOK.

73. Memcon, Lodge, "Train Trip from Los Angeles to San Francisco," September 21, 1959, RG 59, Office of Soviet Union Affairs, Subject Files, 1957–1963, Box 4, NARA-II.

74. Steno, December 16, 1960, AOK.

75. Henry Cabot Lodge, "Car Trip to Garst Farm," September 23, 1959, *FRUS, 1958–1960*, vol. 10, pp. 442–43.

76. Mrs. Llewellyn Thompson (memorandum), RG 59, Office of Soviet Union Affairs, Subject Files 1957–1963, Box 4, NARA-II.

77. Eisenhower and Khrushchev meetings, September 26, 1959, 9:20 A.M., 1:00 P.M.; September 27, 1959, 11:45 A.M., POF, "USSR—Vienna Meeting, Background Documents 1953–1961 (c) Reading Material," Box 126, JFK Library.

78. Talbott, op. cit., p. 412.

79. Thompson to Foy Kohler, "Observations Gained during My Tour of the United States with Chairman Khrushchev," September 28, 1959, RG 59, Office of Soviet Union Affairs, Subject Files 1957–1963, Box 4, NARA-II.

80. Peregovorii N. S. Khrushcheva s Mao Tszedunom 31 Iul'ï'a–3 Avgusta 1958 i 2 Okt'ï'abr'ï'a 1959 ["N. S. Khrushchev's Conversations with Mao Zedong, July 31–August 3, 1959," and October 2, 1959"], *Nova'ï'a i Nove'ï'sh'ï'a Istoria* no. 2. (2001).

81. Protocol 240, September 25, 1959, and Protocol 242, October 2, 1959, AOK.

CHAPTER 10: GRAND DESIGN

1. Nikita S. Khrushchev, "Speech by N. S. Khrushchev, Moscow Airport, September 28, 1959," *Khrushchev in America: Full texts of the Speeches Made by N. S. Khrushchev on His Tour of the United States, September 15–27, 1959* (New York: Crosscurrents Press, 1960), pp. 228–31.

2. Meeting with a group of U.S. businessmen, September 24, 1959, reproduced ibid., p. 182.

3. Matthew Evangelista, "Why Keep Such an Army?: Khrushchev's Troop Reductions," Working Paper 19, CWIHP *Bulletin*, December 1997, pp. 25–26. Evangelista cites the estimates of Jutta Tiedtke.

4. Steno, December 16, 1960, AOK.

5. Ibid.

6. Sergei Khrushchev, *Nikita Khrushchev and the Creation of a Superpower* (University Park: Pennsylvania State University Press, 2000), p. 281.

7. Meeting, NSK with Nasser, May 14, 1958, 52-1-561, APRF.

8. Khrushchev, op. cit., pp. 282–83.

9. Ibid., pp. 280–82.

10. *Pravda*, May 29, 1960, cited in Evangelista, op. cit., p. 39.

11. NSK memo to CC, CPSU Presidium, December 8, 1959, trans. Vladislav Zubok, in CWIHP *Bulletin*, Winter 1996–1997.

12. Steno, "Discussion at the Session of the Presidium of the CC Regarding the Question of the Party Program," December 14, 1959, AOK.

13. Ibid.

14. Ibid.

15. Ibid.

16. Ibid. Khrushchev's statements met with an enthusiastic response. Mikoyan, Aristov, and Koslov understood that there was no real threat to their jobs. They appreciated, however, Khrushchev's call for additional emphasis on social services and individual standards of living.

17. The stenographer did not stay for the military discussion, "Regarding further steps with regard to the struggle for relaxing international tension." Malin, however, did produce minutes for this discussion. Protocol 253, December 14, 1959, AOK.

18. The only quibble was a comment by Malinovsky that the Soviet force in East Germany be exempt from the cuts. "Our forces there," argued the marshal, "effect a significant amount of influence on our adversaries."

19. At the time Moskalenko was military commander of the Moscow Military District.

20. Protocol 253, December 14, 1959, AOK.

21. NSK, memo to CC, CPSU Presidium, December 8, 1959, trans. Vladislav Zubok, CWIHP *Bulletin*, Winter 1996–1997.

22. The Presidium decided that Khrushchev's memorandum of December 8 would be read to all military commanders on December 18.

23. Protocol 253, December 14, 1959 AOK.

24. Gregory W. Pedlow and Donald E. Welzenbach [CIA History Staff] *The CIA and the U-2 Program, 1954–1974* (Washington, D.C.: Center of the Study of Intelligence, CIA, 1998), p. 160.

25. Ibid., p. 164.

26. Memcon, Eisenhower meeting with McNamara, Dulles, and Lemnitzer, July 15,

1961, Memoranda of Conferences (1961–1963), Post-Presidential, Augusta-Walter Reed Series, Box 2, DDE Library.

27. On February 2, 1959, the CIA sent the president a briefing on the seven-year plan. Two days later, the president's son, John, called the CIA to say that the president had read the memorandum with "a great deal of interest," Document 9-0693, Allen W. Dulles Collection, Holland-Freedom of Information Act.

28. Ibid. For two years, analysts working in the usually unrewarding area of manpower studies, had been warning their superiors that the Kremlin did not have the labor force required to meet the seven-year plan objectives. See CD-ROM supplement to Gerald K. Haines and Robert E. Leggett, eds. (Washington, D.C.: Center for the Study of Intelligence, CIA, 2001). [CIA History Staff] *CIA's Analysis of the Soviet Union 1947–1991*. What the CIA did not know was that the Kremlin colleagues had been discussing a plan to reduce the number of hours that Soviets had to work per week, making the manpower shortage an even more significant political issue for Moscow.

29. Joseph Alsop to Lucius Clay, February 28, 1959, "General Correspondence," Box 15, Joseph and Stewart Alsop Papers, Library of Congress.

30. "Truman Would Not Have Dared Invite Stalin, Symington Says," *New York Times*, September 28, 1959.

31. Wayne A. Jackson, "Allen Walsh Dulles as Director of Central Intelligence, 26 February 1953–29 November 1961," vol. 5, *Intelligence Support for Policy*, unpublished CIA history, July 1973, declassified 1994, p.70.

32. Ibid.

33. "The Great Debate over to Adequacy of Our Defense," *New York Times*, February 7, 1960.

34. "United States Military and Diplomatic Policies—Preparing for the Gap," *Congressional Record*, August 14, 1958, Pre-Presidential Papers, "60 Campaign—Press & Publicity," "Defense + Disarmament, Missile Gap," Box 1029, JFK Library.

35. Jackson, op. cit., vol. 5, p. 62.

36. Jackson, op. cit., vol. 5, p. 70.

37. Memcon, 432rd Meeting of the NSC, January 14, 1960, *Foreign Relations of the United States* [hereafter *FRUS*], *1958–1960*, vol. 10, pp. 498–99.

38. Ibid.

39. Discussion at the 433rd Meeting of the NSC Thursday, January 21, 1960, NSP Fiche 249/1, *FRUS*, supplement, Document 235.

40. Ibid., vol. 5, p. 94.

41. Ibid.

42. Russell Porter, "S.A.C. Chief Urges Defense Speed-up," *New York Times*, January 20, 1960.

43. "The Great Debate over the Adequacy of Our Defense," *New York Times*, February 7, 1960.

44. Joseph Alsop, "The Missile Gap: Basic Facts," *New York Herald Tribune*, January 25, 1960, "Alsop" File, RMN, NARA-LN.

45. Joseph Alsop, The Missile Gap: The Bridge," January 25, 1960, *New York Herald Tribune*, ibid.

46. Steno, February 1, 1960, AOK.

47. Ibid.

48. Khrushchev explicitly contrasted the spirit of this approach with the tactics of his fallen nemesis Vyacheslav Molotov, who had been fond of trying to trap the West into bad propaganda positions by making proposals that the Kremlin never intended

to accept. To drive home how different a negotiator he was, Khrushchev reminded the Presidium of how Molotov used to insist publicly on all-German elections.

49. Memcon, DDE and Herter, February 2, 1960, *FRUS, 1958–1960*, vol. 3, p. 834.

50. Memorandum of discussion, NSC meeting, February 18, 1960, ibid., p. 840.

51. "Transcript of Eisenhower's News Conference on Domestic and Foreign Matters," *New York Times*, February 4, 1960.

52. Lodge (Moscow) to SecState, February 9, 1960, *FRUS, 1958–1960*, vol. 10, pp. 507–9.

53. See "Entretiens de Général de Gaulle et M. Khrouchtchev," March 23–25, and April 1–2, 1960, *Documents Diplomatiques Français* [hereafter *DDF*], 1960, (Paris: Imprimerie Nationale, 1995), vol. 1, record no. 146.

54. Memcons, Macmillan and de Gaulle, 6:00 P.M., April 5, 1960, and 9:45 A.M., April 6, 1960 (with their foreign ministers present), Prem 11/3001, National Archives—UK. The British Foreign Office distilled de Gaulle's depiction of his talks with Khrushchev into a "top secret" report, "Khrushchev's visit to France," which presumably became the basis for briefing the Americans, [undated], Prem 11/3001, National Archives—UK.

55. Memcon, Macmillan and de Gaulle, 6:00 P.M., April 5, 1960, Prem 11/3001, National Archives—UK.

56. Ibid.

57. Jackson, op. cit., vol. 5, pp. 88–89.

58. Pedlow and Welzenbach, op. cit., pp. 170–72.

59. Ibid., p. 167.

60. Ibid.

61. Memcon, DDE and Macmillan, *FRUS, 1958–1960*, vol. 9, pp. 258–62.

62. In his memoirs, Bissell fudges the presidential instruction, so that it appears he was authorized to carry out a U-2 mission with the sole restriction that "no operation [was] to be carried out after May 1." Richard M. Bissell, Jr., with Jonathan E. Lewis and Frances T. Pudlo, *Reflections of a Cold Warrior: From Yalta to the Bay of Pigs* (New Haven: Yale University Press, 1996), p. 125.

CHAPTER 11: THE CRASH HEARD ROUND THE WORLD

1. Protocols of witness statements: P. E. Asabin, May 2; V. N. Glinskich, May 3; M. N. Berman, May 4; V. P. Pankov, May 17; I. A. Ananyev, May 17, 1960, Central Archive, FSB.

2. Ibid.

3. This account is based on protocols of witness statements: P. E. Asabin, May 2; V. N. Glinskich, May 3; M. N. Berman, May 4; V. P. Pankov, May 17; I. A. Ananyev, May 17, 1960, Central Archive, FSB, and on Francis Gary Powers recollections, *See Operation Overflight* (New York: Holt, Rinehart and Winston, 1970), pp. 89–90.

4. Ibid. Also, Michael Beschloss, *Mayday: Eisenhower, Khrushchev and the U-2 Affair* (New York: Harper & Row, 1986), p. 15.

5. Strobe Talbott, ed., *Khrushchev Remembers: The Last Testament*, (Boston: Little, Brown, 1974), p. 443.

6. Gregory W. Dedlow and Donald E. Welzenbach, p. 176. Sergei Khrushchev, *Nikita Khrushchev and the Creation of a Superpower* (University Park: Pennsylvania State University Press, 2000), p. 368.

7. Sergei Khrushchev, op. cit., p. 369.

8. Ibid.

9. Ibid., p. 370.

10. Ibid., pp. 379–80.

11. Richard M. Bissell, Jr., with Jonathan E. Lewis and Frances T. Pudlo, *Reflections of a Cold Warrior: From Yalta to the Bay of Pigs* (New Haven: Yale University Press, 1996), p. 127.

12. Pedlow and Welzenbach, op. cit., pp. 89–90.

13. Ibid., p. 80.

14. Ibid.

15. Powers, op. cit., p. 99.

16. CIA, Operations Policy Letter No. 6, December 9, 1957, Attachment C to CIA, Report of the Board of Inquiry into the Case of Francis Gary Powers, February 27, 1962, CIA Electronic Reading Room [hereafter ERR], www.ucia.gov (accessed February 20, 2006).

17. Protocol of Interrogation of Francis Gary Powers, May 1, 1960, Central Archive, FSB.

18. CIA, Report of the Board of Inquiry into the Case of Francis Gary Powers, February 27, 1962, CIA ERR, www.ucia.gov (accessed February 20, 2006).

19. Powers recalled warning the Soviets about the needle at his first interrogation in Moscow. Powers, op. cit., p. 102.

20. On May 2, after a less rigorous interrogation, Powers's captors gave him a car tour of some of Moscow. Ibid., pp. 107–8.

21. Pedlow and Welzenbach, op. cit., p. 176.

22. Beschloss, op. cit., p. 39.

23. There is a brief discussion of the tax plan in Protocol 266, February 25, 1960, AOK, but the best summary of Khrushchev's May 5 plan is in William J. Thompson, *Khrushchev: A Political Life* (New York: St. Martin's Griffin, 1997), p. 222.

24. The letter was dated March 5, 1960. See Protocol 274, April 7, 1960, AOK.

25. Ibid. The Presidium session was on April 7.

26. This description of the event is derived from the discussion of the incident at the Presidium session of April 15, 1960. Protocol 275, AOK.

27. Voroshilov made this comment at the Presidium session of April 28, 1960. Protocol 277, AOK. At this meeting he also attacked the policy of granting incentives to encourage the recycling of scrap metal, calling it a gross mistake. Since the beginning of the year, Voroshilov had increased his attacks on Khrushchev. In January he had taken aim at the new residential construction, widely associated with Khrushchev, describing it as unpopular with the citizens because it was of such low quality. Protocol 259, January 13, 1960. In February, during a trip to India, Voroshilov made no attempt to hide his contempt for the Soviet Foreign Ministry. He publicly called Deputy Foreign Minister Kuznetsov a bootlicker, and he also managed to offend his Indian hosts by spitting as he left a burial vault. During the same trip he happily flouted Presidium protocol. During a diplomatic reception he went over and talked with the Chinese ambassador without prior authorization from his colleagues in the Kremlin. Protocol 263, February 9, 1960, AOK.

28. William Taubman, *Khrushchev* (New York: Norton, 2003), p. 449.

29. Memcon, NSK and Dejean, May 3, 1960, 4-64-736, APRF.

30. There are two reports on the important Khrushchev and Dejean conversation of May 3. The French version is dated May 4, 1960, in *Documents Diplomatiques Français* [hereafter *DDF*], 1960 (Paris: Imprimerie Nationale, 1995), vol. 1, record 198; the Soviet version is dated May 3 and is in 4-64-736, APRF.

31. Charles de Gaulle to Nikita Khrushchev, April 30, 1960, *DDF*, vol. 1, record 191.

32. Osgood Caruthers, "Premier Is Bitter," *New York Times*, May 6, 1960.

33. Ibid.

34. Protocol, May 4, 1960, AOK.

35. Editorial note, *Foreign Relations of the United States* [hereafter *FRUS*], *1958–1960*, (Washington, D.C.: Government Printing Office, 1953), vol. 10, part 1, p. 511. Sergei Khrushchev, op. cit., p. 382.

36. Editorial note, *FRUS*, *1958–1960*, vol. 10, part 1, p. 511.

37. Ibid., pp. 510–11.

38. Dwight D. Eisenhower, *Waging Peace, 1956–1961: The White House Years* (Garden City, N.Y.: Doubleday, 1965), p. 549.

39. Ibid.

40. Protocol of interrogation of Francis Gary Powers, May 6, 1960, Central Archive, FSB.

41. Ibid.

42. "Excerpts From Premier Khrushchev's Remarks on U.S. Jet Downed in Soviet," *New York Times*, May 8, 1960.

43. Memcon, NSC discussion, May 24, 1960, *FRUS*, *1958–1960*, vol. 10, part 1, p. 524. In fact that detail had come from a map hidden in the cockpit that survived the crash. Powers had not even known about that map. CIA, Report of the Board of Inquiry into the Case of Francis Gary Powers, February 27, 1962, FOIA, ERR. This characterization of Powers persisted in the Eisenhower and Kennedy administrations, causing Allen Dulles's successor as DCI, John McCone, to resist efforts to rehabilitate Powers. In February 1962 an internal CIA review found that Powers had followed orders and done nothing wrong under Soviet interrogation. The Soviet-era records reviewed for this book not only confirm this but reveal how Powers cleverly deceived his interrogators to protect both national security and his own skin.

44. Thompson to SecState, May 7, 1960, *FRUS*, *1958–1960*, vol. 10, part 1, p. 515.

45. Ibid.

46. The British called their program Oldster. See Alistair Horne, *Macmillan, 1957–1986*, (London: Macmillan, 1989), pp. 225–26.

47. Interrogation of Francis Gary Powers, May 8 and May 10, 1960, Central Archive, FSB; Powers, op. cit., p. 133.

48. Beschloss, op. cit., p. 262.

49. Khrushchev describes his strategy in Talbott, ed., op. cit., pp. 446–47. Excerpts from Khrushchev's statements at the informal press conference in Gorky Park appeared in the *New York Times*, May 12, 1960. Soviet censors tried to tone down these comments about Eisenhower. Beschloss, op. cit., p. 263.

50. Taubman, op. cit., cites Sergei Khrushchev, p. 459.

51. "The Presidium of the CC of the CPSU to the October Plenum of the CC of the CPSU," "Not Later than 14 October 1964" (draft), RGANI.

52. Extract from Protocol 280, May 12, 1960, 3-64-737, APRF, pp. 1–79. Besides Khrushchev the official delegation included Gromyko, Malinovsky, V. V. Kuznetsov, V. A. Zorin, S. A. Vinogradov, A. A. Soldatov, M. A. Melnikov, G. A. Zhukov, L. F. Ilichev, P. A. Satyukov, A. I. Adzhubei, G. G. Shuisky, V. S. Lebedev, O. A. Troyanovsky, A. F. Dobrynin, V. F. Grubyakov, A. A. Krochin, Colonel General A. A. Gryzlov, and S. M. Kudryavstev.

53. Extract from Protocol 280, May 12, 1960, 4-64-737, APRF.

54. Ibid.

55. Telcon, Paris and SecState, May 13, 1960, *FRUS*, *1958–1960*, vol. 9, pp. 395–79; memcon, heads of government meeting, May 15, 1960, ibid., p. 418.

56. Memcon, with President Eisenhower, May 15, 1960, *FRUS*, *1958–1960*, vol. 9, p. 415; memcon, foreign ministers' meeting on disarmament, April 13, 1960, ibid., p. 318.

57. Dwight Eisenhower, op. cit., p. 553.

58. Tom Wicker, *Dwight D. Eisenhower* (New York: Times Boots, 2002), p. 80.

59. DDE, president's news conference on May 11, 1960, *Public Papers of the Presidents, Dwight D. Eisenhower, 1960–1961* (Washington, D.C.: Government Printing Office, 1961), pp. 403–14.

60. Talbott, ed., op. cit., p. 447.

61. Oleg Troyanovsky, "The Foreign Policy of Nikita S. Khrushchev." Taubman, op. cit., p. 460. Khrushchev recalled making this decision on the plane, not in the airport before the flight. Talbott, op. cit., pp. 450–51. This difference is minor. What matters is that he made it after the May 12 meeting, and this required long-distance approval from the Presidium on May 14.

62. NSK (Paris) to CC, May 14, 1960. The cable was five pages long. 3-64-738, APRF.

63. Oleg Troyanovsky, *Cherez Godu Rasstovanya* [Through Space and Time] (Moscow: Vagrins, 1997), p. 226.

64. These conditions appeared in Khrushchev's formal statement. See *New York Times*, May 17, 1960.

65. Talbott, ed., op. cit., p. 452.

66. Ibid.

67. Steno, February 1, 1960, AOK.

68. The French record for the May 15, 1960, meeting between de Gaulle ans Khrushchev (11:30 A.M. to 12:45 P.M.) is in *DDF, 1960* (Paris: Imprimarie Nationale 1995), vol. 1, record 221, document II, pp. 645–48, The Russian record is in 3-64-738, pp. 33–43, APRF.

69. Memcon, Khrushchev with Macmillan, May 15, 1960, 3-64-738, APRF.

70. Memcon, May 15, 1960, 2:30 P.M., *FRUS, 1958–1960*, vol. 9, pp. 417–22. Memcon, May 15, 1960, 6:00 P.M., ibid., pp. 426–35.

71. Talbott, ed., op. cit., p. 454.

72. Ibid.

73. Ibid., pp. 454–55.

74. Khrushchev told this story to Averell Harriman, who repeated to John F. Kennedy in 1962. Harriman told JFK that Bohlen had denied this had ever happened. See Timothy Naftali, ed., *Presidential Recordings: John F. Kennedy*, vol. 1, *The Great Crises* (New York: Norton, 2001). August 8, 1962, Meeting on China and the Congo, pp. 280–81. In *Waging Peace*, Eisenhower makes no mention of his even considering an apology.

75. Protocol 121, October 26, 1957, AOK.

76. Khrushchev to the CC, May 16, 1960, 3-64-738, APRF.

77. Memcon, Khrushchev and Macmillan, 2100 hours, May 16, 1960, ibid.

78. Ibid., p. 101.

79. Talbott, ed., op. cit., p. 458.

80. Curiously, Khrushchev's memoirs do not mention his being in the embassy in the afternoon or sending a cable to Moscow. In Ibid., p. 459, he speaks of returning to Paris in the evening.

81. Khrushchev to the CC, May 17, 1960, 3-64-738, APRF.

82. Memcon, May 17, 1960, 3:00 P.M., *FRUS, 1958–1960*, vol. 9, p. 468.

83. Quoted in Horne, op. cit., vol. 2, p. 228.

84. Transcript of Powers interrogation, June 10, 1960, FSB.

85. Thompson discussed these theories with the *New York Times* correspondent C. L. Sulzberger before leaving Paris. C. L. Sulzberger, *The Last of the Giants* (New York: Macmillan, 1970), pp. 669–70.

86. DDE to Lleras Camargo, May 19, 1960, No. 1541, *The Papers of Dwight David Eisenhower*, vol. 20, *The Presidency: Keeping the Peace*, ed. Louis Galambos and Daun Van Ee (Baltimore: Johns Hopkins University Press, 2001).

87. Editorial note, *FRUS, 1958–1960*, vol. 10, part 1, pp. 540–42.

88. Pedlow and Welzenbach, op. cit., pp. 184–87.

89. [Soviet Union], "Basic Provisions of a Treaty on General and Complete Disarmament," submitted to the Geneva Conference on June 7, 1960, *Documents on International Affairs, 1960*, ed. Richard Gott, John Major and Geoffrey Warner (London: Oxford University Press, 1961),

CHAPTER 12: CASTRO AND LUMUMBA

1. The Presidium approved the Friendship University plan on February 5, 1960, RGANI, Fond 4, Opis 16, Dela 783, pp. 12–15, cited in A. B. Davidson and S. V. Mazov, eds., *Rossiya i Afrika: Dokumenti i Materiali VIII v.—1960 g.* [*Russia and Africa: Documents and Materials 18th century—1960*], vol. 2, p. 313. To ensure that this school not be considered a ghetto for Africans, the Soviets decided that 20 to 30 percent of the student body would include Soviet citizens or individuals from other countries in the socialist bloc. V. P. Yeliotin, minister of special higher and middle-level education in the USSR, and S. M. Rumyantsev, rector of the Friendship University, to NSK, April 12, 1960, ibid., pp. 312–13.

2. Alvin Z. Rubinstein, "Friendship University," *Soviet Survey: A Quarterly Review of Cultural Trends*, no. 34 (October–December 1960), pp. 8–10.

3. Strobe Talbott, ed., *Khrushchev Remembers: The Last Testament* (Boston: Little, Brown, 1974), p. 317.

4. Rubinstein, op. cit., pp. 8–10.

5. NSK to Nasser, April 12, 1959, 0507, MFA.

6.Memcon, NSK and el-Kouni, May 22, 1959, 52-1-561, APRF.

7. Meeting, Zaitsev and Mahdavi, February 18, 1960, MFA. In 1959 Gromyko described Mahdavi as "one of the most prominent progressive statesmen" in Iraq. Mahdavi's children were studying in the Soviet Union, and in August 1959 he asked to visit the USSR for rest and some medical care. The Soviets checked with a member of the Politburo of the Communist Party of Iraq who liked the idea of Mahdavi's going to the Soviet Union. The Presidium approved the visit on August 26, 1959. See Gromyko to CC, August 24, 1959, 24/22/12, p. 41, MFA, with a marginal note about the Presidium's approval.

8. Meeting, Zaitsev and Mahdavi, February 18, 1960, MFA.

9. Ibid.

10. Excerpt from Protocol 274, Presidium Meeting of April 7, 1960, "Aide-Mémoire for A. I. Mikoyan for his meeting with A. K. Qasim," APRF.

11. Mikoyan encountered a difficult Qasim when the Iraqis finally allowed him to visit in early April. When Mikoyan complained about the treatment of Iraqi Communists, many of whom were in jail facing the death penalty, Qasim brushed him off: "This is an internal matter." Meeting, Mikoyan and Qasim, April 14, 1960, APRF.

12. Davidson and Mazov, eds., op. cit., report by Soviet Ambassador Gerasimov on Trip to Guinea, December 1–13, and December 20, 1958, Document 123.

13. Extract from Protocol 198, Presidium meeting of December 27, 1958, Folio 3, List 65, File 871, APRF. Details of the covert operation comes from a memorandum of the same date that was distributed at the meeting and is the file alongside the extract.

14. Fursenko interview in 1995 with veteran of the Soviet military intelligence service, the GRU, who described Raúl Castro's recruitment by Raúl Valdes Vivo, the head of the youth wing of the PSP.

15. Naftali interview with Vilma Espín, wife of Raúl Castro, Havana, October 2002. Ms. Espin spoke of her husband as having joined the party and not just the youth wing.

16. Anibal Escalante to CC, April 3, 1962, Folio 3, List 65, File 903, pp. 39–42, APRF. Escalante, a longtime and high-level PSP leader, told the Soviets how Fidel Castro "learned" of Raúl Castro's and Che Guevara's hitherto secret memberships in the PSP at a stormy meeting in March 1962. A year later the KGB repeated this version of events in its general study of Fidel Castro prepared on the eve of his first visit to the USSR. Semichastny to CC, April 25, 1963, "Spravka on Fidel Castro," File 88497, vol. 1, pp. 361–75, SVR. Raúl Castro's best friend in the KGB, Nikolai Leonov, however, believed that the Kremlin knew that Escalante did not have the full story. He recalled Fidel's knowing that Raúl was a Communist. He endorsed the spirit of Espín's version, though he doubted Raúl had had time to join the PSP (as opposed to just the youth wing) before the Castros led an attack in 1953 on the Cuban Army's Moncada barracks, were jailed and then exiled to Mexico. Naftali interview with Leonov, Havana, October 2002.

17. Anibal Escalante to CC, April 3, 1962, Folio 3, List 65, File 903, pp. 39–42, APRF.

18. Ponomarev and Mukhitdinov to CC, April 15, 1959, Folio 3, List 65, File 874, APRF.

19. Resolution, Presidium, Protocol 214, April 23, 1959, Folio 3, List 65, File 871, APRF.

20. Kobanov (International Department of the CC) to the CC, September 30, 1959, Folio 3, List 65, File 874, p. 16, APRF.

21. Fursenko interview with Aleksandr Alekseyev, February 16, 1994.

22. Resolution, Presidium, January 29, 1960, APRF. This may have been from Protocol 261 or 261. This decision is not noted in the Malin note for either protocol.

23. Mikoyan cited in Max Frankel, *High Noon in the Cold War: Kennedy, Khrushchev and the Cuban Missile Crisis* (New York: Presidio Press, 2004), p. 63.

24. Fursenko interview with Alekseyev, February 16, 1994.

25. Cable, Alekseyev (Havana) to Center, February 7, 1960, File 78825, pp. 108–12, SVR.

26. In January 1959, the general secretary of the Communist Party of Belgium, while attending the Twenty-first Party Congress in Moscow, discussed with Soviet officials the possibility of sending Congolese students to Moscow.

27. Memcon, meeting with Patrice Lumumba, Soviet Ambassador to Guinea P. I. Gerasimov, April 28, 1959, APRF, Fond 0590, 1/1/1, in Davidson and Mazov, eds., op. cit., Document 135.

28. Ibid.

29. Ibid.

30. Memcon, meeting with "De Coninck on the Situation in the Congo," B. A. Kavinov, first secretary of Soviet Embassy in Brussels, April 27, 1959, in Davidson and Mazov, eds., op. cit., Document 136.

31. John Reader, *Africa: A Biography of a Continent* (New York: Vintage Books, 1997), p.651.

32. Ibid., pp. 637, 651.

33. Memcon with Pierre Muhlele, Antoine Kingotolo, and Rafael Kinki, December 28, 1959, Davidson and Mazov, op. cit., Document 137.

34. Memcon, Savinov and De Coninck, April 27, 1959. Ibid., Document 136.

35. Aleksandr Fursenko and Timothy Naftali, *"One Hell of a Gamble": Khrushchev, Castro, and Kennedy, 1958–1964* (New York: Norton, 1997), pp. 5–10.

36. Jeffrey J. Safford, "The Nixon-Castro Meeting of 19 April 1959," *Diplomatic History*, 4 (1980), pp. 426–31.

37. Memorandum for the president, November 5, 1959, Bay of Pigs Collection, National Security Archive.

38. J. C. King, chief, Western Hemisphere Division, to Dulles, December 11, 1959, Bay of Pigs Collection, National Security Archive. The document carries the notation that Dulles approved the proposal the next day.

39. Memcon, Burden and Lumumba, February 25, 1960, *Foreign Relations of the United States* [hereafter *FRUS*], *1958–1960* (Washington, D.C.: Government Printing Office, 1992), vol. 14, p. 263.

40. Ibid.

41. Ibid.

42. Alekseyev (Havana) to CC, March 8, 1960, File 78825, pp. 164–66, SVR. Khrushchev received a copy of this report. It appears in Folio 3, List 65, File 871, pp. 42–45, APRF.

43. Memcon, March 7, 1960, *FRUS*, *1958–1960*, vol. 6, p. 823.

44. Protocol 270, March 12, 1960; CC to Alekseyev, March 12, 1960, Folio 3, List 65, File 871, APRF.

45. A. Sakharovskii, the chief of the KGB's First Chief Directorate, to Deputy Foreign Minister V. S. Semenov, July 18, 1960, File 84124, vol. 12, SVR.

46. Archive of the Secretariat of the CC, Folio 4, List 16, File 954, p. 169, RGANI.

47. Telegram March 8, 1960, 7:00 P.M., *FRUS*, vol. 6, pp. 824–25.

48. Editorial note, ibid., pp. 826–27.

49. Memo from Rubottom to SecState, March 9, 1960, "NSC Discussion of Cuba, March 10, 1960," ibid., p. 829.

50. Memcon, 436th Meeting of the NSC, March 10, 1960, ibid., pp. 832–37.

51. 5412 Committee, "A Program of Covert Action against the Castro Regime," March 16, 1960, ibid., pp. 850–51.

52. Ibid.

53. U.S. Senate, *Alleged Assassination Plots Involving Foreign Leaders, An Interim Report of the Select Committee to Study Government Operations with Respect to Intelligence Activities*, November 20, 1975 (Washington, D.C.: Government Printing Office, 1975), p. 72.

54. KGB Chief Aleksandr Shelepin to CC, June 18, 1960, File 86447, pp. 319–320, SVR. Paco Ignacio Taibo II, *Guevara Also Known as Che*, trans. Martin Michael Roberts (New York: St. Martin's Press, 1997), p. 305

55. Shelepin to CC, June 24, 1960, Folio 3, List 65, File 893, pp. 33–34, APRF.

56. Fursenko and Naftali, op. cit., pp. 49–50.

57. A. Sakharovskii, the chief of the KGB's First Chief Directorate, to Deputy Foreign Minister V. S. Semenov, July 18, 1960, File 84124, vol. 12, SVR.

58. U.S. State Department, "Principal Soviet Public Statements on Defense of Cuba," Cuban Missile Crisis Collection, National Security Archive.

59. Memcon, NSK and Raul Castro, July 18, 1960, APRF.

60. Ibid.

61. Fursenko interview with Boris Ponomarev, 1994.

62. Fursenko and Naftali, op. cit., p. 55.

63. *Public Papers of the Secretaries-General of the United Nations*, vol. 55: *1960–1961*,

Dag Hammarskjöld, ed. Andrew Cordier and Wilder Foote (New York: Columbia University Press, 1975).

64. Catherine Hoskyns, *The Congo since Independence, January 1960–December 1961* (London: Oxford University Press, 1965), pp. 95–96.

65. *Public Papers of the Secretaries-General*, vol. 5, p. 19.

66. Davidson and Mazov, op. cit., Document 138.

67. Thomas Hamilton, "U.S. and Soviet Asked to Supply Vehicles and Food for New Unit," *New York Times*, July 15, 1960.

68. Seymour Topping, "Khrushchev Tells the West to Keep Its Hands off Congo; Replies to New Republic's Appeal for Intervention by Soviet If Needed; U.S. Accuses Russian; Says 'Irresponsible' Charge Is Part of Current Attempt to Inflame Atmosphere," *New York Times*, July 16, 1960. The Russian original is Document 140 in Davidson and Mazov, op. cit.

69. Hoskyns, op. cit., p. 129.

70. Editorial note, *FRUS*, vol. 14, p. 280.

71. Ibid.

72. Telegram, Timberlake (Leopoldville) to DOS, August 29, 1960, ibid., p. 448.

73. Madeleine G. Kalb, *The Congo Cables: The Cold War in Africa—from Eisenhower to Kennedy* (New York: Macmillan, 1982), p. 35.

74. Dillon cited ibid., p. 37.

75. Ibid., pp. 36–37.

76. Ibid., pp. 37–41.

77. Ibid., p. 42.

78. NSK to Lumumba, August 5, 1960, Davidson and Mazov, eds., op. cit., Document 141.

79. Gromyko to CC, August 9, 1960, Davidson and Mazov, op. cit., Document 119. The date of Nkrumah's request is mentioned in the draft text of Khrushchev's reply, dated August 6, ibid., document 120.

80. Hoskyns, op. cit., pp. 161–65, 167.

81. Ibid., p. 169.

82. Ibid., pp. 169–70. Kalb, op. cit., p. 44.

83. MID [MFA] to CC, draft letter, August 9, 1960, Davidson and Mazov, eds., op. cit. Document 120. note 1 indicates that this draft was approved on April 11.

84. Spravka MID SSR [MFA USSR] on the supply of Soviet airplanes to African countries in connection with the provision of assistance to the republic of the Congo (June–August 1960), Davidson and Mazov, eds., op. cit., Document 143.

85. Hoskyns, op. cit., p. 174.

86. Document 191, note 3, *FRUS, 1958–1960*, vol. 14, p. 447.

87. Spravka MID SSR [MFA USSR], on the supply of Soviet airplanes to African countries in connection with the provision of assistance to the republic of the Congo (June–August 1960) Davidson and Mazov, eds., op. cit., Document 143.

88. Ibid.

89. Memo from the director of the Bureau of Intelligence and Research to SecState, July 25, 1960, *FRUS, 1958–1960*, vol. 14, p. 356.

90. Memcon with DDE, August 1, 1960, ibid., p. 377.

91. U.S. Senate, *Alleged Assassination Plots*, pp. 13–16, 73–74.

92. Memorandum of discussion, 456th Meeting of the NSC, August 18, 1960, *FRUS, 1958–1960*, vol. 14, p. 424.

93. CJCS (Twining) to SecDef, August 18, 1960, ibid., pp. 425–27.

94. U.S. Senate, *Alleged Assassination Plots*, p. 73.

95. Ibid.

96. Gerald K. Haines, "CIA History Staff Analysis: CIA and Guatemala Assassination Proposals 1952–1954" (Washington, D.C.: CIA, June 1995).

97. Ibid.

98. U.S. Senate, *Alleged Assassination Plots*, pp. 74–79.

99. Ibid., p. 60.

100. Editorial note, *FRUS, 1958–1960*, vol. 14, p. 443.

101. Telegram, Henry Lodge, Cabot Lodge [New York] to DOS, August 26, 1960, ibid., pp. 444–46.

102. Ibid.

103. Hoskyns, op. cit., pp. 219–21.

104. Ibid.

105. Kalb, op. cit., pp. 71–75.

106. Hoskyns, op. cit., p. 194.

107. Kalb, op. cit., p. 75.

108. Talbott, ed., op. cit., p. 482.

109. Hoskyns, op. cit., p. 214.

110. Kalb, op. cit., pp. 92–93.

111. Hoskyns, op. cit., p. 214.

112. Taubman, op. cit., p. 477.

113. Kalb, op. cit., pp. 103–104.

114. Protocol 306, October 15, 1960, AOK.

115. Hoskyns, op. cit., p. 248.

116. Kalb, op. cit., p. 104.

117. U.S. Senate, *Alleged Assassination Plots*, p. 24.

118. Ibid., pp. 24–25.

119. See Lawrence Devlin's comments at Cold War International History Project's Critical Oral History Conference, "The 1960–1961 Congo Crisis," September 22–24, 2004. The authors are grateful to Christian Ostermann, the director of the CWIHP, for allowing us to see the edited transcript of this event.

120. Kalb, op. cit., p. 111.

121. Ibid., p. 112.

122. Protocol 306, October 15, 1960, AOK.

123. Kalb, op. cit., p. 135.

124. Ibid., p. 136.

125. See Devlin, "The 1960–1961 Congo Crisis," loc. cit.

126. Kalb, op. cit., p. 133.

127. Taubman, op. cit., pp. 475–76.

128. Protocol 306, October 15, 1960, AOK.

129. Fursenko and Naftali, op. cit., p. 63.

130. Ibid., pp. 65–70.

131. "Pravda Charges Plot by U.S.," *New York Times*, October 15, 1960.

132. Fursenko and Naftali, op. cit., pp. 65–70.

133. Ibid.

134. Ibid., p. 161.

CHAPTER 13: SOUTHEAST ASIAN TEST

1. Diary of Soviet Ambassador Aleksandr Abramov, meeting with Kong Le, October 17, 1960, 0570, 6/3/2. MFA.

2. He visited Burma and Indonesia in the spring of 1960. It was Khrushchev's second visit to Burma.

3. Strobe Talbott, ed., *Khrushchev Remembers: The Last Testament* (Boston: Little, Brown, 1974), p. 315.

4. Ibid., p. 480.

5. William J. Duiker, *Ho Chi Minh: A Life* (New York: Theia, 2000), pp. 493–95.

6. Ibid., pp. 510–13.

7. Memcon, Soviet Ambassador to the People's Republic of China. S. Chervonenko with the ambassador of the Democratic Republic of Vietnam to the People's Republic of China, Chan Ti Bin, October 13, 1960, 0570, 6/3/5, MFA.

8. Draft Paper on Soviet-Laos Relations [no date] 0570 6/3/5, MFA.

9. This note was handed to the Laotian ambassador to Thailand on October 23, 1956. 0570/6/3/5, MFA.

10. Spravka, Laos, 0570, MFA.

11. S. Chervonenko, meeting with North Vietnamese Ambassador Chan Ti Bin, October 13, 1960, 0570 6/3/5, MFA.

12. North Vietnamese sources stated that the Soviets provided no assistance to Laos of any kind until December 1960. It is hard to believe that in the 1940s and 1950s the International Department of the Central Committee of the Communist Party of the Soviet Union ignored the Indochinese Communist Party and its Lao successor.

13. Memcon, Soviet ambassador to the PRC, S. Chervonenko, with DRV ambassador to China, Chan Ti Bin, October 13, 1960, 0570, 6/3/5, MFA.

14. Cited in Chen Jian and Yang Kuisong, "Chinese Politics and the Collapse of the Sino-Soviet Alliance," *Brothers in Arms: The Rise and Fall of the Sino-Soviet Alliance 1945–1963*, ed. Odd Arne Westad (Stanford, Calif.: Stanford University Press, 1998), p. 272.

15. Ibid., p. 273.

16. Talbott, ed., op. cit., p. 464.

17. See George Eliades, "United States Decision-making in Laos, 1942–1962," unpublished Harvard dissertation, pp. 333–372, for a superb discussion of these debates in the Eisenhower administration in the second half of 1960.

18. Dwight D. Eisenhower, *Waging Peace 1956–1961: The White House Years* (Garden City, N.Y.: Doubleday, 1965), p. 607.

19. Eliades, op. cit., p. 256.

20. Eisenhower, op. cit., p. 608.

21. Ibid.

22. Ibid.

23. Diary of Ambassador Aleksandr Abramov, meeting with Indian Ambassador Patnom, October 13, 1960, 0570, 6/3/2. MFA.

24. Memcon, Souvanna and Abramov, October 27, 1960, 0570, 6/3/2, MFA.

25. "New Laos Drive Ordered," *Washington Post and Times Herald*, November 15, 1960.

26. "U.S. Urges Laos Drop Attack Plan; Fears Move on Right-Wing Force in Luang Prabang Would Aid Pro-Reds," *New York Times*, November 16, 1960.

27. Jacques Nevard, "Laos to Seek Ties with Red Chinese; Missions Going to Peiping and North Vietnam—A Top General Defects to Rebels," *New York Times*, November 18, 1960.

28. "Reds Taken into Laos Cabinet," *Washington Post and Times*, November 19, 1960.

29. Memcon, Abramov and Souvanna Phouma, November 23, 1960, 0570, 6/3/2, MFA.

30. "Laos Regime Hints at Call for Red Aid," *Washington Post and Times Herald*, November 23, 1960.

31. "Soviet Aid to Arrive in Laos in Few Days," *New York Times*, November 24, 1960; "Reds to Fly Supplies to Laos," *Washington Post and Times Herald*, November 24, 1960.

32. Eliades, op. cit., p. 349.

33. "Laotians Report Rightist Attack; Premier Says 3 Battalions and Armor Are Striking 100 miles from Capital," *New York Times*, December 1, 1960.

34. Roy Essoyan, "Laos Leftists Protest Inclusion of Rightists in All-Party Coalition," *Washington Post and Times Herald*, December 3, 1960.

35. Jacques Nevard, "Laos Calls on US to Halt Rebel Aid; Premier Also Discloses Bid for Cease-fire Agreement with Attacking Rightists," *New York Times*, December 6, 1960.

36. Jacques Nevard, "Laos Confirms Rightist Attack; Premier Tells of Fighting 100 Miles from Capital—Sends Reinforcement," *New York Times*, December 4, 1960.

37. Jacques Nevard, "Rightist Troops Advance in Laos; Cross River at Scene of Fighting 100 Miles East of Neutralist Capital," *New York Times*, December 5, 1960.

38. Jacques Nevard, "Soviet Says U.S. Fans War in Laos; Envoy in Vientiane Hints of Intervention If Neutralist Regime Is Imperiled," *New York Times*, December 6, 1960. Arthur Dommen, *Conflict in Laos: The Politics of Neutralization*, rev. ed. (New York: Praeger, 1971), p. 164.

39. Resolution, December 7, 1960, APRF. Some of the Soviet supplies were carried by rail across the Soviet-Chinese border to Nanjing and then flown to Hanoi and Vietienne. Eleven railway cars of weapons and thirty-five cars of petroleum products arrived at the Soviet-Chinese border on December 10, 1960. See Memcon, N. G. Sudarikov, and Li Xian, December 10, 1960, 0100, 53/455/13, p. 53, cited in Ilya V. Gaiduk, *Confronting Vietnam: Soviet Policy toward the Indochina Conflict, 1954–1963* (Washington, D.C.: Woodrow Wilson Center Press, 2003), p. 143.

40. "On Laos," March 14, 1961, 0570, 7/6/19, pp. 1–3, MFA.

41. Memcons, Aleksandr Abramov and Quinim Pholsena, December 9 and 10, 1960, 0570, 6/3/2, MFA.

42. Arthur Dommen, "Laotian Army Chief Proclaims Military Rule," *Washington Post and Times Herald*, December 11, 1960.

43. Jacques Nevard, "Soviet Guns Sent into Laos by Air; Pro-Red in Power; Artillery Bolsters Vientiane Defense against Pro-West Forces outside City," *New York Times*, December 12, 1960.

44. Memcon, V. V. Kuznetsov and Polish Ambassador B. Yashchuke, January 9, 1961, 0570, 7/5/14, MFA.

45. Aleksandr Abramov, Diary, December 2–20, 1960, 0570, 6/3/2, MFA.

46. Madeleine G. Kalb, *The Congo Cables: The Cold War in Africa—from Eisenhower to Kennedy* (New York: Macmillan, 1982), pp. 184–89.

47. Herbert S. Parmet, *Jack: The Struggles of John F. Kennedy* (New York: Dial Press, 1980), pp. 226–29.

48. Robert Dallek, *An Unfinished Life: John F. Kennedy, 1917–1963* (Boston: Little, Brown, 2003), pp. 222–23.

49. Parmet, op. cit., p. 227.

CHAPTER 14: "HE IS A SON OF A BITCH"

1. Charles Bohlen, *Witness to History, 1929–1969* (New York: Norton, 1973), p. 475.

2. American Legion Convention, Miami Beach, Fla., October 18, 1960. U.S. Senate,

The Speeches, Remarks, Press Conferences and Statements of Senator John F. Kennedy, August 1 through November 7, 1960, Committee on Commerce, 87th Congress (Washington, D.C.: Government Printing Office, 1961), 1961.

3. Ibid., passim.

4. Fresno, California, September 9, 1960. Ibid.

5. Cincinnati, Ohio, October 6, 1960. Ibid.

6. Ibid.

7. Gromyko to NSK, August 3, 1960, 5/30/335, pp. 92–108, TsKhSD, reproduced in Cold War International History Project [hereafter CWIHP] *Bulletin*, no. 4 (Fall 1994), pp. 65–67. Information Department (Department 16) to chief of D Department, May 31, 1961, pp. 96–109, SVR.

8. Gromyko to NSK, August 3, 1960, 5/30/335, pp. 92–108, TsKhSD, reproduced in CWIHP *Bulletin*, no. 4 (Fall 1994), pp. 65–67.

9. Information Department (Department 16) to chief of D Department, May 31, 1961, pp. 96–109, SVR.

10. Khrushchev's view of the leadership of the United States comes through clearly in two stenographic accounts of Presidium meetings, May 26, 1961, and January 8, 1962, AOK.

11. See memcon, Ulbricht and Khrushchev meeting (East German version), November 30, 1960; Ulbricht to Khrushchev, September 15, 1961; Ulbricht to Khrushchev, October 31, 1961 in "Khrushchev and the 'Concrete Rose,'" trans. Hope Harrison, *Papers*, appendices. Memcon, NSK and Ulbricht (Russian version), November 30, 1960, APRF.

12. Ibid.

13. Ibid.

14. Shelepin to NSK, December 3, 1960, SVR.

15. NSK to Ulbricht, January 30, 1961, "Khrushchev and the 'Concrete Rose,'" loc. cit.

16. Remarks in Madera, California, September 9, 1960, U.S. Senate, *Speeches, Remarks, Press Conferences and Statements of Senator John F. Kennedy*, loc. cit.

17. JFK press conference, July 28, 1960, ibid.

18. Cited in David G. Coleman, "The Greatest Issue of All: Berlin, National Security and the Cold War," unpublished dissertation (University of Queensland, 2000), pp. 236–37. The authors are grateful to Professor Coleman for sharing his cogently argued and thoroughly researched dissertation.

19. Ibid.

20. John Helgerson, *Getting to Know the President: CIA Briefings of Presidential Candidates 1952–1992* (Washington, D.C.: Center for the Study of Intelligence, CIA, 1996), ch. 3, passim.

21. Harrison Salisbury observed the prices in early 1962. Harrison E. Salisbury, *A New Russia?* (New York: Harper & Row, 1962), p. 120.

22. Steno, February 16, 1961, AOK.

23. Salisbury, op. cit., p. 120.

24. Ibid. Regarding the consequences of the decision to expand the height of these buildings, see Steno, June 17, 1961, AOK.

25. Protocol 320, March 23, 1961, AOK.

26. Steno, February 16, 1961, AOK.

27. Ibid.

28. Protocol 321, March 25, 1961, AOK.

29. William E. Griffith, *Albania and the Sino-Soviet Split* (Cambridge, Mass.: MIT

Press, 1963), p. 81. At their party congress in February the Albanians had launched a verbal attack on Khrushchev in the presence of a Soviet delegation headed by Presidium member Pyotr Pospelov. Hoxha's regime in Tirana shared the view in Beijing that Khrushchev was too soft on Western capitalists.

30. Protocol 316, February 24, 1961, AOK.

31. Spravka, situation in Laos, March 14, 1961, 0570, 7/6/19, MFA.

32. Ibid.

33. Telegram, JFK to Rusk (Bangkok), March 27, 1961, *Foreign Relations of the United States* [hereafter *FRUS*], *1961–1963*, vol. 24, pp. 105–7. This cable, in which the president described his meeting with Gromyko, is the only U.S. record that has been found. A Soviet memcon was not found among the Foreign Ministry's Laos records.

34. Memcon, Soviet Deputy Foreign Minister G. Pushkin with Nguyen Zui Chinya, deputy prime minister, DRV, April 1, 1961, 0570, 7/5/14, MFA.

35. The Soviets announced their support for a cease-fire on April 7. See statement of Pathet Lao in response to the Soviet position, April 7, 1961, 0570, 7/5/14, MFA. Telephonogram, Soviet Ambassador Chervonenko (Beijing) to Moscow, April 12, 1961, 0570, 7/5/14, MFA. Assessment of Chinese aide-memoire, May 12, 1961, 0570, 7/5/14, MFA.

36. Sergei Khrushchev, *Nikita Khrushchev and the Creation of a Superpower* (University Park: Pennsylvania State University, 2000), p. 431.

37. Ibid., pp. 433–34.

38. Fursenko, in Leningrad at the time, recalls the spontaneous pride of those in the USSR's second city who came out to celebrate Gagarin's achievement.

39. Sergei Khrushchev recalls his surprise at the scale of the celebration.

40. At a Presidium meeting in June 1961, Khrushchev discussed the problem of collapsing balconies. See Steno, June 17, 1961, AOK.

41. Canadian Embassy, Havana, to Ottawa, April 26, 1961, "Bay of Pigs 40 Days After: Briefing Book of International Documentation from Brazilian, British Canadian, Czech and Russian Archives," International Conference, Havana, March 22–24, 2001.

42. KGB (Mexico City) to Center, April 12, 1961, SVR.

43. See Aleksandr Fursenko and Timothy Naftali, *"One Hell of a Gamble": Khrushchev, Castro and Kennedy, 1958–1964* (New York: Norton, 1997), pp. 47–92.

44. Thompson to SecState, April 1, 1961, Record Group 59, State Department Central Decimal File, 611.61, NARA-II.

45. The President's News news conference of April 12, 1961, *Public Papers of the Presidents of the United States: John F. Kennedy Containing the Public Message, Speeches, and Statement of the President January 20 to December 31, 1961* (Washington, D.C.: Government Printing Office, 1962) pp. 258–59.

46. Fursenko interview of Aleksandr Alekseyev, 1993. See also Fursenko and Naftali, op. cit., p. 89.

47. Memcon, Ernesto Guevara and S. M. Kudriavtsev, April 14, 1961, Bay of Pigs Collection, National Security Archive.

48. Canadian Embassy, Havana, to Ottawa, April 26, 1961, "Bay of Pigs 40 Days After: Briefing Book of International Documentation from Brazilian, British Canadian, Czech and Russian archives," International Conference, Havana, March 22–24, 2001. Evidence that Castro did not know the date of the Bay of Pigs invasion ahead of time comes from a speech he made to the Cuban people on April 23; see Canadian Embassy, Havana, to Ottawa, April 27, 1961, ibid.

49. Havana to Center, April 17, 1961, File 88631, pp. 169–70, SVR. See Fursenko

and Naftali, op. cit., pp. 93–94, for the story of how the Soviet intelligence service mobilized to handle this unexpected development.

50. Athens to the Center, April 28, 1961, 87701 (March 1961–August 1962: Internal and Economic Politics of USA), p. 31, SVR; Washington to the Center, April 30, 1961, 87701, p. 33, SVR; London to the Center, April 29, 1961, 87701, p. 32, SVR. Kennedy did indeed undertake an internal review of the role of intelligence in the disaster. Soviet information on this internal review of the Bay of Pigs was quite poor. First, it was reported that Telford Taylor, former U.S. prosecutor at the Nuremberg trials, was in charge of this study. In fact the chief was General Maxwell Taylor, military assistant to President Kennedy and later chairman of the Joint Chiefs of Staff. Paris to the Center, June 3, 1961, p. 49, SVR.

51. The source was a journalist named Wald, a correspondent of the *New York Herald Tribune*. London to the Center, April 29, 1961, 87701, p. 32, SVR.

52. See Fursenko and Naftali, op. cit., pp. 92–97; Canadian Embassy, Havana, to Ottawa, April 27, 1961, "Bay of Pigs 40 Days After: Briefing Book of International Documentation from Brazilian, British Canadian, Czech and Russian Archives," International Conference, Havana, March 22–24, 2001.

53. April 25, 1961, 3/65/900, p. 119, APRF.

54. Evan Thomas, *Robert Kennedy: His Life* (New York: Simon & Schuster, 2000), photo insert commentary.

55. Naftali interview with Edwin O. Guthman, July 14, 1994.

56. Timothy Naftali interview with McGeorge Bundy, November 1995.

57. Ibid.

58. For evidence of Kennedy's commitment to a comprehensive nuclear test ban, see Timothy Naftali, ed., *The Presidential Recordings: John F. Kennedy The Great Crises* (New York: Norton, 2001), vol. 1, pp. 132–86.

59. Kennedy told his closest associates that had it not been for his experience in Laos, he would have sent men into Laos in April 1961. For a discussion of how close he came, see Lawrence Freedman, *Kennedy's Wars: Berlin, Cuba, Laos and Vietnam* (New York: Oxford University Press, 2000), pp. 299–304.

60. May 9, 1961, summary, Kratkoye Soevershanye: Besed G Bolshakova s R Kennedy (9 Maya 1961 goda–14 Dekabria 1962 roga), GRU [summaries of meetings between G. Bolshakov and R. Kennedy (May 9, 1961–December 14, 1962), GRU. Hereafter this document will be referred to as Bolshakov-RFK general meeting summaries (May 9, 1961–December 14, 1962)]. No American account of this meeting has been found.

61. NSK to JFK, May 12, 1961 (delivered May 16, 1961), *FRUS, 1961–1963*, vol. 6, pp. 18–21.

62. Khrushchev discussed military pressure on him at the May 26, 1961, Presidium meeting. Steno, May 26, 1961, AOK. He mentioned the Soviet delay in developing the ability to test underground at a Presidium meeting in April 1963. Steno, April 1963, AOK.

63. Protocol 329, May 18, 1961, instructions regarding Bolshakov meeting with RFK, 3-66-311, APRF.

64. Pervukhin to MFA, May 19, 1961, cited in "Ulbricht and the Concrete 'Rose,'" loc. cit., p. 36.

65. The basis for our knowledge of the May 21, 1961, meeting comes from two synopses of the RFK-Bolshakov conversations prepared by the GRU, the Russian military intelligence service. The first, prepared in 1995, we have referred to as the Bolshakov-RFK general meeting summaries (May 9, 1961–December 14, 1962) and the second,

which was prepared in 1999, deals only with conversations related to the German question: Kratkoye Sovershanye: Besed G. N. Bolshakova s R Kennedy i blizhaishim okruzheniem evo i presidenta J. Kennedy no Germanskimi voprosu (21 Maia 1961–13 Aprelia 1962) [summaries of meetings between Georgi Bolshakov and Robert Kennedy and with his inner circle and that of President J. Kennedy on the German Question (May 21, 1961–April 13, 1962). Hereafter these will be referred to as the Bolshakov German Question summaries (May 21, 1961–April 13, 1962)].

66. Summary, May 21, 1961, Bolshakov German Question summaries (May 21, 1961–April 13, 1962), GRU.

67. Ibid.

68. Thompson to SecState, May 24, 1961, *FRUS, 1961–1963*, vol. 14, pp. 66–69. Thompson did not report any direct quotations. These come from what Khrushchev told the Presidium on May 26. See Steno, May 26, 1961, and for Robert Kennedy's responses to Georgi Bolshakov, see summary, May 24, 1961, Bolshakov-RFK general meeting summaries (May 9, 1961–December 14, 1962), GRU.

69. Thompson, who knew nothing of the discussions going through Robert Kennedy, had been ill prepared by the president for this meeting. He should have been warned that Khrushchev was stonewalling on the test ban and trying to force a dialogue on Berlin. Kennedy did use the Bolshakov channel to find out what Khrushchev had meant by the comment about U.S. forces tightening their belts, but Bolshakov could add nothing to that phrase, and the Kremlin gave him nothing else to work with. See Fursenko and Naftali, op. cit., pp. 123–24.

70. Thompson to SecState, May 27, 1961, *FRUS, 1961–1963*, vol. 14, pp. 77–78.

71. He had not invited a stenographer to the November 7, 1958, meeting at which he unsuccessfully tried to unilaterally end the Potsdam Agreement. But at the height of the Iraqi crisis and during the discussions over the Twenty-first Party Congress, there was a stenographer at hand. The fact that this was a surprise to the Soviet Foreign Ministry is suggested by the materials which the ministry had prepared for the May 26 meeting. Deputy Foreign Minister V. V. Kuznetsov wrote a memorandum that suggested possible areas for discussion without saying anything about the delivery of an ultimatum on Berlin. Kuznetsov, May 26, 1961, 3/66/311, pp. 58–61, APRF. There is also no indication in the Presidential Archive file on the Vienna meeting that the aide-mémoire on Berlin suggesting a six-month ultimatum, which Khrushchev handed Kennedy on June 4, was prepared in advance of the May 26 meeting.

72. The stenographer did not note Mikoyan's rebuttal. From Malin's notes of the meeting and Khrushchev's response to Mikoyan, which was transcribed, Mikoyan's argument can be inferred. See Steno, May 26, 1961, and Protocol 331, May 26, 1961, AOK.

73. Protocol 331, May 26, 1961, AOK.

74. Anatoly Dobrynin attended this meeting as head of the American Department of the Soviet Foreign Ministry. His brief memoir account of this meeting supplements the Malin note and the stenographic account. Dobrynin, *In Confidence: Moscow's Ambassador to America's Six Cold War Presidents (1962–1986)* (New York: Times Books, 1995), pp. 44–45.

75. Khrushchev added that he was prepared to spend money on conventional forces in Germany to signal his resolve: "[M]aybe we have to add armaments if reinforcements are needed there. It needs to be thought through in order to do it with no hurry. First, we have to deliver artillery weapons and basic weapons, and afterward to bring in troops so that we will have strong positions there in the event of provocation. You have a deadline of half a year to do it. So there is no hurry, think about it now and

report your conclusions afterward, in about two weeks' time. If additional mobilization is necessary, it can be carried out without declaring it. It requires reinforcement
here because one has to match one's words with reality."

76. The Central Committee officially approved the list of gifts on May 27. "List,
commemorative gifts and souvenirs for possible delivery at the time of N. S.
Khrushchev's stay in Austria," May 27, 1961, APRF.

77. Memcon, May 31, 1961, 12:30 P.M., *FRUS, 1961–1963*, vol. 14, p. 81.

78. Ibid., p. 82.

79. Memcon, 2:50 P.M., ibid., p. 86.

80. Memcon, June 3, 1961, 12:45 P.M., *FRUS, 1961–1963*, vol. 5, pp. 172–78.

81. Moscow to SecState, May 24, 1961, 8:33 A.M., State Department Central Decimal
File, 1960–1963, 611.61, NARA-II.

82. Memcon, June 3, 1961, 3:00 P.M., *FRUS, 1961–1963*, vol. 5, pp. 182–97.

83. Memcon, June 4, 1961, 10:15 A.M., ibid., pp. 206–25.

84. Edwin O. Guthman and Jeffrey Shulman, eds., *Robert Kennedy in His Own
Words: The Unpublished Recollections of the Kennedy Years* (New York: Bantam, 1988), p.
258.

85. Evidence of the content of Bolshakov's statements comes from two different
archives. Khrushchev's reaction to Kennedy's test ban proposals can be found in a
third. See Steno, May 26, 1961, AOK.

86. This aide-mémoire is an unusual document. It bears the signs either of haste
or of a minor rebellion against Khrushchev's risk taking in the Soviet Foreign
Ministry. The six-month ultimatum is buried in a discussion of the odds of the two
Germanys' ever reaching an agreement. See U.S. Department of State, *Documents on
Germany, 1944–1985* (Washington, D.C.: U.S. Department of State, Office of the
Historian, Bureau of Public Affairs, 1985), pp. 729–32. Despite the woolly language of
the document, in his comments to Kennedy and later in public speeches from East
Berlin to Moscow Khrushchev left no doubt he was talking about a December 1961
deadline.

87. Memcon, June 4, 1961, 3:15 P.M., *FRUS, 1961–1963*, vol. 5, pp. 229–30.

88. Strobe Talbott, ed., *Khrushchev Remembers: The Last Testament* (Boston: Little,
Brown, 1974), p. 499.

89. Ibid., p. 501.

90. Khrushchev's appearances are described in Robert M. Slusser, *The Berlin Crisis
of 1961: Soviet-American Relations and the Struggle for Power in the Kremlin,
June–November 1961* (Baltimore: Johns Hopkins University Press, 1973), pp. 5–15, and
William Taubman, *Khrushchev* (New York: Norton, 2003), p. 590.

91. The CIA obtained a copy of this resolution, dated June 17, 1961, RG 59, Lot
74D379, Bohlen Papers, Box 26, NARA-II.

92. Steno, June 17, 1961. All quotations regarding Khrushchev's decision to rein-
state capital punishment for additional crimes come from this source.

93. Maria Los, *Communist Ideology, Law and Crime* (New York: St. Martin's Press,
1988), pp. 93–94; Peter H. Solomon, Jr., *Soviet Criminologists and Criminal Policy:
Specialists in Policy-Making* (New York: Columbia University Press, 1978), pp. 68–69.

94. The July 8 speech is cited in Slusser, op. cit., pp. 51–57.

95. He had done so most recently on May 26, when he told the Presidium that the
Soviets should wait to let the Americans break the moratorium. Steno, May 26, 1961,
AOK. In an interview with Vladislav Zubok, Yuri Smirnov, a member of Andrei
Sakharov's research team, recalled Khrushchev's alerting the nuclear community on
July 10, 1961, that he intended to end the test moratorium. See Zubok and Constantine

Pleshakov, *Inside the Kremlin's Cold War: From Stalin to Khrushchev* (Cambridge Mass.: Harvard University Press, 1996), pp. 253 and 333, 64.

CHAPTER 15: IRON RING

1. The *New York Times'* James "Scottie" Reston was allowed to see Kennedy in the U.S. Embassy as he relaxed after the last session with Khrushchev. Kennedy opened up to him about why everything seemed to have gone so wrong. James Reston, *Deadline: A Memoir* (New York: Random House, 1991), p. 299. The quotation comes from Robert Dallek, *An Unfinished Life* (Boston: Little Brown, 2003), p. 413.

2. Summary, May 9, 1961, Bolshakov-RFK general meeting summaries (May 9, 1961–December 14, 1962), GRU.

3. Dallek, op. cit., pp. 413–14.

4. Charles Bohlen, *Witness to History* (New York: Norton, 1973), p. 483.

5. Kennedy suffered from Addison's disease, which produced a chronic adrenaline deficiency. On the president's many ailments, see Dallek, op. cit.

6. Veteran White House correspondent Hugh Sidey was part of the group. See Sidey, *John F. Kennedy, President* (New York: Atheneum, 1964), pp. 173–74.

7. Dallek, op. cit., p. 418.

8. Hanson W. Baldwin, "Soviet Air Power Rouses Congress," *New York Times*, July 23, 1961.

9. Seymour Topping, "Soviet Says Navy Has Atomic Edge," *New York Times*, July 22, 1961.

10. James Chace, *Acheson: The Secretary of State Who Created the American World* (New York: Simon & Schuster, 1998), pp. 381–94, passim; Douglas Brinkley, *Dean Acheson: The Cold War Years, 1953–71* (New Haven: Yale University Press, 1992), pp. 108–53, passim.

11. Cited in Herbert Parmet, *Jack: The Struggles of Jack Kennedy* (New York: Dial Press, 1980), p. 208.

12. Theodore White, "JFK-2," Notebook, Box 80, Theodore White Papers, Harvard University.

13. Dean Acheson to Harry S. Truman, August 4, 1961, Truman Post-Presidential Papers: Name File: Acheson, Dean – Correspondence, 1960–1963, HST Library.

14. See memcon, ICC Group on Germany and Berlin, July 12, 1961, *Foreign Relations of the United States* [hereafter *FRUS*], *1961–1963* (Washington, D.C.: Government Printing Office, 1992), vol. 14, pp. 187–91. Memcon [Bundy], NSC meeting, July 13, 1961, ibid., pp. 192–94. Notes on NSC meeting [Lemnitzer], July 13, 1961, ibid., pp. 194–96.

15. For the president's mindset on the eve of seeing this intelligence, see memcon (Bundy), NSC meeting, July 13, 1961, ibid., p. 194. For the timing of his decisions on Berlin, see Theodore C. Sorensen, *Kennedy* (New York: Harper & Row, 1965), pp. 587–91.

16. Jerrold L. Schecter and Peter S. Deriabin, *The Spy Who Saved the World: How a Soviet Colonel Changed the Course of the Cold War* (New York: C. Scribners' Sons, 1992), pp. 188–89.

17. Ibid., p. 186.

18. The memcon of Secretary of Defense Robert McNamara's meeting with Dwight Eisenhower confirms that this information reached the White House before Kennedy's July 17 Berlin decision. See memcon, July 15, 1961, memorandum of conference, 1961–1963, Post-Presidential, Augusta—Walter Reed Series, Box 2, DDE Library.

The effect of this Corona satellite program intelligence does not show up in formal national intelligence estimates, however, until September 1961. See *National Intelligence Estimate*, 11-8-61, September 21, 1961, Kevin C. Ruffner, ed., *Corona: America's First Satellite Program* (Washington, D.C.: Center for the Study of Intelligence, CIA, 1995), pp. 127–56. This version of NIE 11-8-61 reflects the additional releases possible after the declassification of the Corona program in 1995.

19. See memcon, July 15, 1961, memorandum of conference, 1961–1963, Post-Presidential, Augusta—Walter Reed Series, Box 2, DDE Library.

20. Kennedy later mused about his mistaken belief in the missile gap in a wide-ranging defense budget conversation that he taped on December 5, 1962. The authors are grateful to David G. Coleman of the Miller Center's Presidential Recordings Program for sharing the draft transcript of this conversation.

21. For information on McNamara and the missile gap, see Deborah Shapley, *Promise and Power: The Life and Times of Robert McNamara* (Boston: Little Brown, 1992), pp. 97–99.

22. NIE, 11-8-61, June 7, 1961, Donald P. Steury, ed., *Estimates of Soviet Military Power 1954 to 1984* (Washington, D.C.: Center for the Study of Intelligence, CIA, 1994), 1994.

23. Peter J. Roman, *Eisenhower and the Missile Gap* (Ithaca, N.Y.: Cornell University Press, 1995), p. 184.

24. Memcon, July 15, 1961, memorandum of conference, 1961–1963, Post-Presidential, Augusta—Walter Reed Series, Box 2, DDE Library.

25. McGeorge Bundy explains how he and Theodore Sorensen, at least, understood this to be the thinking behind Kennedy's July decisions. McGeorge Bundy, *Danger and Survival: Choices about the Bomb the First Fifty Years* (New York: Random House, 1988), pp. 374–75.

26. Memo, Bundy, June 10, 1961, *FRUS, 1961–1963*, vol. 14, pp. 107–9.

27. Memcon, July 17, 1961, *FRUS*, ibid., pp. 209–12. Kennedy also made sure that neither Acheson nor LBJ sat on the steering group that he formed that day to supervise the day-to-day management of the crisis.

28. Dallek, op. cit., p. 417.

29. NSK to JFK, September 29, 1961, *FRUS, 1961* vol. 6, p. 25.

30. Aleksandr Fursenko and Timothy Naftali, *"One Hell of a Gamble": Khrushchev, Castro, and Kennedy, 1958–1964* (New York: Norton, 1997), p. 208.

31. Khrushchev describes the drain as a "major threat" to the GDR in Strobe Talbott, ed., *Khrushchev Remembers* (Boston: Little Brown, 1970), p. 456.

32. Honore M. Catudal, *Kennedy and the Berlin Wall Crisis: A Case Study in U.S. Decisionmaking* (Berlin: Berlin-Verlag, 1980), p. 164.

33. Memcon, NSK to Ulbricht, November 30, 1960, APRF.

34. Steno, May 26, 1961, AOK. Strobe Talbott, ed., *Khrushchev Remembers* (Boston: Little, Brown, 1970), p. 57.

35. Jerold L. Schecter, ed., *Khrushchev Remembers: The Glasnost Tapes* (Boston: Little Brown, 1990), p. 168.

36. Statement by the president concerning the U.S. reply to the Soviet government's aide-mémoire on Germany and Berlin, July 19, 1961, *Public Papers of the Presidents of the United States: John F. Kennedy, January 20–December 31, 1961* (Washington, D.C.: Government Printing Office, 1962), Document 292, pp. 521–23.

37. At a later meeting with Ulbricht, Khrushchev hinted at the importance that this information had in his thinking in late July 1961. Memcon, NSK and Ulbricht, August 3, 1961, APRF.

38. Shelepin to NSK, July 20, 1961, APRF. Khrushchev did not need the KGB for this. The July 3 issue of *Newsweek*, which appeared on newsstands in late June, outlined much the same steps that the Pentagon had suggested to Kennedy.

39. See steno, May 26, 1961, AOK, for a discussion of this intelligence.

40. Ibid.

41. Pervukhin to Gromyko, May 19, 1961, in Hope M. Harrison, *Driving the Soviets up the Wall: Soviet-East German Relations, 1953–1961* (Princeton: Princeton University Press, 2003), pp. 170–71.

42. "Measures to effect the strengthening of control and the protection of the outer ring and sectoral borders of Greater Berlin," signed July 21, 1961, by the GDR's deputy minister of internal affairs, Major General Seifert; the chief of staff of the MVD Colonel Zide; and the chief of staff of the German border police, Major General Boruvko, and approved by the chief of staff of the Soviet Forces in Germany, Lieutenant General Ariko, 3-64-744, pp. 53–56, APRF.

43. Gromyko to CC, July 22–23, 1961, 3-64-744, p. 21, APRF.

44. Soviet Ambassador Patsuro (Warsaw) to Moscow, July 27, 1961, 3-64-744, pp. 121–22, APRF. Patsuro described his meeting with Gomulka on July 26, as instructed by the Central Committee.

45. James Reston, "Kennedy to Speak on Berlin Tonight," *New York Times*, July 25, 1961.

46. Sorensen, op. cit., pp. 591–92.

47. "Kennedy: 'A Wider Choice,'" *Newsweek* (August 7, 1961).

48. Ibid.

49. Radio and Television Report to the American People on the Berlin Crisis, July 25, 1961, *Public Papers of the Presidents of the United States: John F. Kennedy*, loc. cit., pp. 533–40. Sorensen, who wrote most of the speech, credited Maxwell Taylor with the lines comparing the defense of West Berlin with that of Bastogne, which he knew from personal experience, and Stalingrad, which Khrushchev knew from personal experience. See Sorensen, op. cit., p. 591.

50. Cable, McCloy to Rusk, July 29, 1961, *FRUS, 1960–1963*, vol. 14, p. 235.

51. No record was found of Khrushchev's communication to Pervukhin in the Presidium materials for the crisis. The authors assume that Khrushchev used his special telephone to convey the information to Ulbricht. Pervukhin's cabled response is in the files. That cable and Khrushchev's retelling of this story to Ulbricht in August are the basis for this reconstruction. Cable, Pervukhin NSK, July 27, 1961, 3-64-744, APRF; memcon, NSK and Ulbricht, August 3, 1961, APRF.

52. On July 24, the East German Politburo had approved a draft of Ulbricht's speech that mentioned only increasing control of the Berlin border, not closing it. It appears that the East Germans had not yet decided that the border sector should be closed before the signing of a peace treaty. They were awaiting a green light from Moscow. See Harrison, op. cit., pp. 189–90, for information on the July 24 East German Politburo discussion and the language in Ulbricht's draft speech.

53. Schecter, ed., op. cit., 169; Soviet Foreign Ministry veteran Yuli Kvitsinsky recalled that Khrushchev informed Ulbricht in the first week of July that he was prepared to allow the East Germans to build the wall. The tone of Pervukhin's July 27 report, however, suggests that the final approval from Khrushchev came later, on July 26. On Kvitsinsky, see Harrison, op. cit., pp. 186–87.

54. Pervukhin to NSK, July 27, 1961, 3-64-744, APRF.

55. The Malin collection is no help on the choreography of Presidium activities around the building of the Berlin Wall because there are no notes for any meetings

between Protocol 334 of June 17, 1961, and Protocol 349 of October 7, 1961, AOK. By using Pravda, Robert Slusser determined that Khrushchev did not return to Moscow until July 31 [see Robert Slusser, *The Berlin Crisis of 1961: Soviet-American Relations and the Struggle for Power in the Kremlin, June–November 1961* (Baltimore: John Hopkins University Press, 1973), pp. 95–96]. A formal Presidium meeting at Pitsunda can also be ruled out. Had Khrushchev been able to gather the leadership at Pitsunda before making the call to Pervukhin in East Berlin on July 27, McCloy would have noticed this activity.

56. Mikoyan and Gromyko to CC, July 29, 1961, 3/14/947, pp. 26–42, RGANI, cited in David Murphy, Sergei Kondrashev, and George Bailey, *Battleground Berlin: The CIA vs. KGB in the Cold War* (New Haven: Yale University Press, 1997), p. 499.

58.Vladislav Zubok, and Constantine Pleshakov, *Inside the Kremlin's Cold War: From Stalin to Khrushchev* (Cambridge, Mass.: Harvard University Press, 1996), pp. 253–54.

59. Christopher Andrew and Vasili Mitrokhin, *The World Was Going Our Way: The KGB and the Battle for the Third World* (New York: Basic Books, 2005), pp. 40–43.

60. Ibid.

60. Memcon, NSK and Ulbricht, August 3, 1961, APRF.

61. Ibid.

62. Strobe Talbott, ed., (Boston: Little, Brown, 1974), p. 506.

63. Gomulka to CC, July 30, 1961, APRF.

64. Murphy et al., op. cit., pp. 373, 499, n. 32.

65. Ulbricht to the CC, CPSU, July 29, 1961, 3-64-744, p. 130, APRF.

66. For a superb description of this Warsaw Pact meeting see pp. 194–205 of Harrison, op. cit.

67. Khrushchev quoted ibid., p. 201.

68. Ibid.

69. On the "hand wringing" by the socialist allies on the issue of economic assistance to East Germany, see ibid., pp. 199–202. For evidence that they passed a resolution in support of closing the sectoral boundaries, see Pervukhin to Khrushchev, August 10, 1961, 3-64-745, p. 125, APRF.

70. Harrison, op. cit., p. 205.

71. Pervukhin to Khrushchev, August 10, 1961, 3-64-745, p. 125, APRF.

72. Ibid. The information about the distribution of barbed wire comes from Peter Wyden's *Wall*, cited in Murphy et al., op. cit., p. 377.

73. Talbott, ed., *Khrushchev Remembers*, loc. cit., p. 457; also *Khrushchev Remembers: The Last Testament*, loc. cit., p. 505.

74. Curtis Cate, *The Ides of August: The Berlin Wall Crisis, 1961* (New York: M. Evans, 1978), pp. 178–81.

75. CIA, Current Intelligence Weekly Summary, August 17, 1961, in Donald P. Steury, ed., *On the Front Lines of the Cold War: Documents on the Intelligence War in Berlin, 1946 to 1961*, CIA History Staff (Washington, D.C.: Center for the Study of Intelligence, 1999).

76. Pervukhin, Konev, Chuikov to Khrushchev, August 10–12, 1961, 1961, 3-64-745, pp. 133–35, APRF.

77. Harrison, op. cit., p. 205.

78. www.wall-berlin.org, German Historical Museum (Berlin) Web site (accessed June 17, 2003).

79. Ulbricht gave this account to Khrushchev at their November 1961 meeting, NSK and Ulbricht, November 2, 1961, APRF.

80. Marshal Konev and General Ariko to NSK, August 13, 1961, 3-65-745, pp.

140–41, APRF. They also reported that the East German police had handled themselves well and that the majority of the people had accepted the measures.

81. Bundy, op. cit., p. 398.

82. Sorensen, op. cit., p. 593. On August 18, Kennedy formally announced that the U.S. government would not use force to tear down the wall. Chace, op. cit., pp. 393–94.

83. Dallek, op. cit., p. 426; After Joseph Alsop explained the utility of the wall in his column, Kennedy sent him a handwritten note saying privately how he agreed. Alsop with Adam Platt, *"I've Seen the Best of It": Memoirs* (New York: Norton, 1992), p. 446.

84. Dallek, op. cit., pp. 425–27. See also Sorensen, op. cit., pp. 593–95.

85. Ann Tusa, *The Last Division: A History of Berlin, 1945–1989* (Reading, Mass.: Addison-Wesley, 1997), pp. 282–86; Murphy et al., op. cit., pp. 378–81.

86. The CIA reported Adenauer's announcement. Donald P. Steury, ed., *On the Front Lines of the Cold War*, loc. cit., Current Intelligence Weekly Summary, August 17, 1961, pp. 525–26.

87. Ibid., p. 530.

88. Schecter, ed., *Khrushchev Remembers: The Glasnost Tapes*, loc. cit., p. 170.

89. Seymour Topping, "Russia Exhibits Atomic Infantry," *New York Times*, August 18, 1961.

90. Gromyko and Malinovsky to the Central Committee, July 7, 1962 (this report recounts the events of 1961), 0742, 7/28/54, pp. 10–13, MFA.

91. Ulbricht to Khrushchev, October 31, 1961, APRF. In this letter Ulbricht rehearsed the story of the August decision. Pervukhin had opposed the idea of reducing the number of access points, but Ulbricht did it anyway.

92. Gromyko and Malinovsky to the Central Committee, July 7, 1962, 0742, 7/28/54, pp. 10–13, MFA. In mid-1962 Ulbricht again tried to get a security zone, and the Soviets again said no.

93. A few days later Khrushchev recalled these words for Ulbricht. Memcon, NSK and Ulbricht, August 1, 1961, APRF.

94. See letter, NSK to JFK, November 9, 1961, *FRUS*, vol. 6, pp. 45–57.

95. Acheson to Truman, September 21, 1961, Harry S. Truman Library. The authors are grateful to archivist Randy Somell for turning up this document.

96. Arthur Schlesinger, Jr., *A Thousand Days: John F. Kennedy in the White House* (Boston: Houghton, Mifflin, 1965), p. 397.

97. Ibid., pp. 397–98.

CHAPTER 16: "THE STORM IN BERLIN IS OVER"

1. Robert M. Slusser, *The Berlin Crisis of 1961: Soviet-American Relations and the Struggle for Power in the Kremlin, June–November 1961* (Baltimore: Johns Hopkins University Press, 1973), pp. 190–210; Cyrus Sulzberger, *The Last of the Giants* (New York: Macmillan, 1970), p. 786.

2. Editorial note, *Foreign Relations of the United States* [hereafter *FRUS*], *1961–1963*, (Washington, D.C.: Government Printing Office, 1993), vol. 14, p. 387.

3. Rusk to Kennan, August 14, 1961, reproduced in Rolf Steininger, *Der Mauerbau: Die Westmächte und Adenauer in der Berlinkrise 1958–1963* (Munich: Olzog, 2001), pp. 267–68.

4. John Kennedy believed Spaak had shown "great courage and restraint" in reversing Belgium's support for Moise Tshombe and Katangan separatism in the Congo. Theodore C. Sorensen, *Kennedy* (New York: Harper & Row, 1965), p. 637.

5. Memcon, Deputy Soviet Foreign Minister Nikolai Firyubin and Polish Ambassador Yastuka, July 29, 1961, 7/5/14, 0570, MFA. The Poles asked for this meeting with the Soviet Foreign Ministry in Moscow to report on feelers from the Belgians on West Berlin. Initially a Belgian official named Lambiotte approached the Polish Embassy in Brussels. Then Spaak himself went directly to the Polish Embassy to outline his ideas on a possible settlement. He was the first former NATO official to indicate support for a free West Berlin.

6. Ernest May, *Strange Victory: Hitler's Conquest of France* (New York: Hill and Wang, 2000), p. 325.

7. "Talk with Khrushchev encourages Reynaud," *New York Times*, September 16, 1961, "M. Paul Reynaud: M. Khrushchev a jugé en homme d'Etat la Vraie Valeur du Problème de Berlin," *Le Monde*, September 19, 1961.

8. May, op. cit., p. 337.

9. Steno, May 26, 1961, AOK. The one bright spot in the July 20 report from the KGB was that though NATO seemed unified, the Europeans were far less committed to using force to defend the access routes to West Berlin than were the Americans. Shelepin to NSK, July 20, 1961, APRF.

10. Memcon, Kuznetsov, meeting with Kroll, 3-64-746, August 29, 1961, APRF.

11. Ibid.

12. Sulzberger, op. cit., pp. 801–02.

13. This presidential initiative most likely preceded Washington's receipt of Khrushchev's private note. Sulzberger managed to mail his note to Kennedy only on September 10. Editorial note, *FRUS*, 1961–1963, vol. 14, pp. 401–2.

14. See *National Security Action Memorandum* 92, September 8, 1961, *FRUS, 1961–1963*, vol. 14, pp. 398–99.

15. Memo, Maxwell Taylor to JFK, September 8, 1961, ibid., vol. 7, pp. 168–70.

16. Rusk to Thompson, September 3, 1961, ibid., vol. 14, pp. 388–89.

17. Thompson to Rusk, September 7, 1961, ibid., pp. 394–95.

18. Memo, JFK to Dean Rusk, September 12, 1961, ibid., pp. 402–3.

19. Hugh Sidey, *John F. Kennedy, President* (Greenwich, Conn.: Fawcett Publications, 1964), p. 178.

20. JFK to Rusk, Berlin negotiations, September 12, 1961, *FRUS, 1961–1963*, vol. 14, p. 402.

21. See the daily reports from the Ministry of Defense (signed by Malinovsky and Zakharov) to the Central Committee, September 15 and 16, 1961, Fond 89, Microfilm, Hoover Institution Library and Archives, Palo Alto, CA. For the response of the Soviet command in Germany, see the speech from early October 1961, probably given by Marshal Konev, to the Communist Party leadership in the military, Fond 89, Microfilm, Hoover. At his meeting with Reynaud on September 16, Khrushchev asked, "Do you think the West Germans want war?" Moscow (Dejean) to Paris, September 16, 1961, *DDF*, no. 111, 1961, vol. 11.

22. Walter Lippmann, "Nuclear Diplomacy," *New York Herald Tribune*, September 14, 1961.

23. Moscow (Dejean) to Paris, September 16, 1961, *DDF*, no. 111, 1961, vol. 11.

24. Moscow (Dejean) to Paris, September 16, 1961, *DDF*, no. 111, 1961, vol. 11 (Paris: Imprimerie Nationale, 1998).

25. Memcon, Firoubina meeting with Polish Ambassador Yastuka, July 29, 1961, 7/5/14, MFA.

26. Paul-Henri Spaak, Combats inachevés: De l'espoir aux deceptions (Paris:

Inyard, 1969), vol. 2, pp. 334–42. Although providing a good account of his trip to Moscow, Spaak left out of his memoir his July initiatives via the Poles. Instead he claimed that Khrushchev called on him in August because as NATO secretary-general he had had a good relationship with the Soviet ambassador in Paris, Sergei Vinogradov.

27. "M. Paul Reynaud: M. Khrouchtchev a jugé en homme d'Etat la Vraie Valeur du Problème de Berlin," *Le Monde*, September 19, 1961; Seymour Topping, "Moscow Suggests the U.N. Be Moved to West Berlin," *New York Times*, September 20, 1961.

28. Memcon, Allen Dulles, August 22, 1961, NSF, Box 82, "Germany Berlin— General 8/22/61," JFK Library. Eisenhower had recounted this story to Dulles at a Berlin briefing on August 20 organized by the Kennedy administration.

29. Sydney Gruson, "Spaak Says Soviet Backs Wide Talks with No Deadline," *New York Times*, September 25, 1961; Spaak, op. cit., vol. 2, p. 338.

30. Telegram from DOS to Paris, summarizing September 21 Rusk and Gromyko conversation, *FRUS, 1961–1963*, vol. 14, pp. 431–33.

31. Gromyko to Central Committee, October 22, 1961, cited in Hope M. Harrison, *Driving the Soviets up the Wall: Soviet–East German Relations 1953–1961* (Princeton: Princeton University Press, 2002), p. 209.

32. See Chen Yi meetings with Gromyko, July 5 and 6, 1961, 0570, 7/5/14, pp. 157–71, MFA.

33. Memcon, Chen Yi and Gromyko, July 5, 1961, 0570, 7/5/14, MFA.

34. These instructions were sent to the Soviet ambassador to North Vietnam, Suren Tovmasyan. See Hanoi (Ambassador Tovmasyan) to Moscow, November 14, 1961, report on meeting called at the request of the North Vietnamese in Hanoi, September 22–25, 1961, 0570 7/5/15, MFA.

35. Ibid.

36. Assistance requested by royal government and Pathet Lao—last half of 1961 and 1962, 0570, 7/5/15, pp. 132–59, MFA. The Pathet Lao's declared size was 8,100 men in Laos, with 400 legally in training in North Vietnam. In fact, in addition to those men, the Pathet Lao had a secret army of 13,324, with 1,100 Lao fighters in training in North Vietnam.

37. Ibid.

38. See Hanoi (Ambassador Suren Tovmasyan) to Moscow, November 14, 1961, report on meeting called at the request of the North Vietnamese in Hanoi, September 22–25, 1961, 0570, 7/5/15, MFA. The North Vietnamese were not merely lying to Souvanna Phouma but were preventing much of the Soviet aid from reaching the Pathet Lao. To weaken the Pathet Lao's support for Moscow, the Vietnamese military switched Soviet rifles for 1903 U.S. Enfield rifles that they had picked up in the field at the end of World War II. The Pathet Lao had no idea that the rusty, old weapons they were receiving were war booty. Presumably the Vietnamese shipped the better Soviet weapons south to assist the insurgency in South Vietnam. At the September conference it seemed to the Soviets that the Chinese had stage-managed the Lao and North Vietnamese presentations. But in the end, once Moscow promised to continue some assistance to the Pathet Lao, the Chinese chose to show solidarity with the Soviets, despite their fundamental disagreement over tactics.

39. Regarding this activity, see cable, Havana (Alekseyev) to Moscow, July 19, 1961, SVR; cable, Havana (Alekseyev) to Moscow, July 22, 1961, SVR. Regarding the letter, Castro to NSK, September 4, 1961, 3-65-872, pp. 136–38, APRF.

40. The Cubans requested eight divisions of surface-to-air missiles (a total of 360 SA-2 missiles), 412 tanks, 100 transports, and 282 Zenith cannons.

41. The only assistance agreed to in late 1961 were four antitorpedo and antisubmarine devices sent aboard the ship *Tbilisi*. Cable, Alekseyev to Moscow, January 21, 1962, SVR.

42. Cable, Alekseyev to Moscow, November 11, 1961, SVR.

43. NSK to Ulbricht, September 28, 1961, SED Archives, Hope Harrison, trans., "Ulbricht and the Concrete 'Rose': New Archival Evidence on the Dynamics of Soviet–East German Relations and the Berlin Crisis, 1958–1961," CWIHP, Working Paper No. 5.

44. Elie Abel Oral History, March 18, 1970, pp. 3–4, JFK Library. Abel had been offered a job as Pentagon press secretary in January but had turned it down to earn a little money for his family. His relations had nevertheless remained close. See Elie Abel, "Kennedy after 8 Months Is Tempered by Adversity," *Detroit News*, September 23, 1961.

45. Pierre Salinger, *With Kennedy* (Garden City, N.Y.: Doubleday, 1966), p. 191.

46. Cited in Robert Dallek, *An Unfinished Life: John F. Kennedy, 1917–1963* (Boston: Little, Brown, 2003), p. 431.

47. Address in New York City before the General Assembly of the United Nations, September 25, 1961, *Public Papers of the Presidents of the United States: John F. Kennedy Containing the Public Messages, Speeches, and Statements of the President, January 20 to December 31, 1961* (Washington, D.C.: Government Printing Office, 1962), p. 625. Dallek, op. cit., p. 431.

48. Memcon, JFK and Taylor, September 18, 1961, *FRUS*, vol. 14, pp. 428–29.

49. NSK to JFK, September 29, 1961, ibid., vol. 6, pp. 25–38.

50. JFK to NSK, October 16, 1961, ibid., pp. 38–44.

51. The extent of KGB reporting in the fall of 1961 is unknown. The GRU seemed to have better-placed informants.

52. Bolshakov meeting with source, October 8, 1961, Bolshakov German Question summaries (May 21, 1961–April 13, 1962), GRU.

53. For an insightful summary of actual French policy in the Berlin crisis, see Marc Trachtenberg, *A Constructed Peace: The Making of the European Settlement, 1945–1963* (Princeton: Princeton University Press, 1999), pp. 267–74.

54. Bolshakov meeting with source, October 21, 1961, Bolshakov German Question summaries (May 21, 1961—April 13, 1962), GRU.

55. Arthur Schlesinger, Jr., *A Thousand Days: John F. Kennedy in White House*, (Boston: Houghton Mifflin, 1965), p. 400.

56. Slusser, op. cit., p. 342.

57. Moscow sent a high-level delegation to attend the GDR's twelfth anniversary celebrations, October 5–8, but there is no evidence that any warning was given at that time. Harrison, *Driving the Soviets up the Wall*, loc. cit., p. 210. Ulbricht's behavior at his November 2 meeting with Khrushchev indicates that he was not warned.

58. Allen Lightner to DOS, October 23, 1961, *FRUS, 1961–1963*, vol. 14, pp. 524–25.

59. Note 1, ibid., p. 532. On October 25, Soviet Foreign Minister Gromyko and Defense Minister Malinovsky suggested to Khrushchev that he "request that Comrade Ulbricht take measures to halt such actions of the police and the GDR authorities which create tensions not corresponding with the requirements of the given moment." Harrison cites research by Brice W. Menning in the archives of the Soviet general staff. Harrison, loc. cit., p. 213.

60. Norman Gelb, *The Berlin Wall: Kennedy, Khrushchev, and the Showdown in the Heart of Europe* (New York: Times Books, 1986), p. 238.

61. Clay to Rusk, October 24, 1961, *FRUS, 1961–1963*, vol. 14, pp. 532–34.

62. Foy Kohler, the assistant secretary of state for European affairs, who headed the Berlin task force, was upset when Clay did not sent a probe into East Berlin on October 24. Clay had decided to await further instructions before proceeding. Kohler considered Clay's momentary restraint "a tactical mistake." Ibid., p. 535.

63. Ann Tusa, *The Last Division: A History of Berlin, 1945–1989* (Reading, Mass.: Addison-Wesley, 1997), pp. 335–36.

64. E. W. Kenworthy, "German Ride Act," *New York Times*, October 26, 1961.

65. Rusk to Clay, October 26, 1961, *FRUS, 1961–1963*, vol. 14, p. 540.

66. This meeting was arranged by Edwin Guthman. See RFK Date Diary, RFK Papers, JFK Library.

67. Report from Bolshakov, October 26, 1961, Bolshakov German Question summaries (May 21, 1961–April 13, 1962), GRU.

68. Tusa, op. cit., p. 336.

69. Editorial note, *FRUS, 1961–1963*, vol. 14, p. 544.

70. Bolshakov German Question summaries, GRU. There is no record in RFK's Date Diary for this meeting. In 1964, as part of the JFK Oral History Program, Robert Kennedy recalled that at his meeting with Bolshakov on October 27 he had requested on JFK's behalf that Khrushchev remove the tanks within twenty-four hours. This request has subsequently became part of the lore of the standoff at Checkpoint Charlie. In the GRU record, however, there is no specific mention of the tank confrontation or of any presidential request that the Soviet tanks be withdrawn in twenty-four hours. No Bolshakov report or cable from October 27 has been found in the Presidential Archives subject file for Berlin in 1961. For information on the time that Soviet tanks began to withdraw (10:30 A.M., Berlin time), see editorial note, *FRUS, 1961–1963*, vol. 14, p. 544.

71. Ibid.

72. Memcon, Khrushchev and Kroll, November 9, 1961, APRF.

73. Harrison, *Driving the Soviets up the Wall*, loc. cit., p. 214.

74. Ibid.

75. Ulbricht and the Socialist Unity Party of Germany (SED) Central Committee delegation to the CPSU Twenty-second Congress in Moscow to NSK, October 30, 1961, Appendix K, Harrison, "Ulbricht and the Concrete 'Rose,'" loc. cit. In machine tools, the GDR would be 2.5 percent under plan in 1961; in the construction industry, about 5.3 percent below. As a result, Berlin expected imports to increase by 13 percent in 1962. The Soviet Union had provided an emergency supply of raw materials in 1961 to offset what East Germany could not get from West Germany or buy from the rest of the world. These supplies could last only through mid-1962. "Due to the dragging out of the conclusion of the peace treaty," Ulbricht added, "this term will no longer suffice."

76. Memcon, NSK and Ulbricht meeting, November 2, 1961, APRF.

77. Ibid. An East German record of this important meeting has not been found. See Harrison, *Driving the Soviets up the* Wall, p. 306, n. 338.

78. NSK to JFK, November 9, 1961, *FRUS, 1961–1963*, vol. 6, pp. 45–57.

CHAPTER 17: MENISCUS

1. O'Brien interview with Roswell Gilpatric, June 30, 1970, JFK Library. The air force ultimately got an order for a thousand Minutemen.

2. For background on the speech, see the June 30, 1970, Gilpatric Oral History at the JFK Library and John Lewis Gaddis, *We Now Know: Rethinking Cold War History*

(New York: Oxford University Press, 1997), pp. 256–57. Defense and State worked on the speech before Kennedy personally reviewed it

3. Cited in Hugh Sidey, *John F. Kennedy, President* (New York: Atheneum, 1964), p. 218.

4. Ibid., p. 220.

5. Ibid., p. 218.

6. www.nuclearweaponarchive.org/Russia/Tsarbomba (accessed November 28, 2005). See also Viktor Adamsky and Yuri Smirnov, "Moscow's Biggest Bomb: The 50-Megaton Test of October 1961," Cold War International History Project [hereafter CWIHP] *Bulletin*, issue 4 (Fall 1994), pp. 3, 19–21.

7. Memcon, GDR Ambassador to Beijing Josef Hengen with the Polish minister counselor of the Polish Embassy in Beijing, December 1, 1961, cited in Hope M. Harrison, *Driving to Soviets Up the Wall: Soviet-East German Relations, 1953–1961* (Princeton: Princeton University Press, 2003), p. 240.

8. Superb testimony on the change in China's policy in Southeast Asia comes from Marek Thee, Poland's member on the tripartite International Control Commission. Marek Thee, *Notes of a Witness: Laos and the Second Indochinese War* (New York: Random House, 1973), pp. 180–205. See also Spravka (preceding the visit of Souphanouvong to the USSR), January 26, 1962, 0570, 8/8/15, MFA.

9. Spravka (preceding the visit of Souphanouvong to the USSR), January 26, 1962, 0570, 8/8/15, MFA.

10. Protocol 11, January 8, 1962, AOK. The most significant absentee was Mikoyan, Khrushchev's debating partner on Berlin, who in 1961 had openly predicted trouble. Shelepin and Brezhnev were also not in their chairs. Instead the visitors' banks were filled with Gromyko and some of the key second-tier foreign policy specialists from the Central Committee and the Ministry of Foreign Affairs.

11. He also recalled having said this to the Italian prime minister Antonio Fanfani and the Norwegian foreign minister Halvard Lange.

12. Thompson to Kennan, January 5, 1962, *Foreign Relations of the United States* [hereafter *FRUS*], *1961–1963*, (Washington, D.C.: Government Printing Office, 1998), vol. 5, p. 347.

13. Ibid., pp. 346–48.

14. Thompson to Rusk, January 12, 1962, *FRUS, 1961–1963*, vol. 14, pp. 751–55.

15. Moscow (Thompson) to State, January 12, 1962, ibid., pp. 751–55.

16. Summary, January 12, 1962, Bolshakov-RFK general meeting summaries (May 9, 1961–December 14, 1962), GRU.

17. Ibid.

18. NSK to JFK, January 18, 1962, *FRUS, 1961–1963*, vol. 14, pp. 763–66.

19. Theodore White, "Friday, the 26th," Theodore White Papers, Box 193, Binder "May 1961–December 1962," Harvard. The authors are grateful to Laura Moranchek for discovering this item.

20. The White House did not involve U.S. Ambassador Thompson in the invitation to Adzhubei. Thompson heard about the invitation from Moscow Radio on January 25, 1962. Thompson to Bohlen, January 25, 1962, *FRUS, 1961–1963*, vol. 5, p. 353.

21. Pierre Salinger, *With Kennedy* (Garden City, N.Y.: Doubleday, 1966), pp. 213–14.

22. Adzhubei to CC, March 12, 1962, APRF.

23. Adzhubei to Moscow, January 30, 1962, APRF. No U.S. memorandum of conversation for the postlunch conversation has been found. All that exists is a memorandum by an official who did not attend the meeting that was based on information given to him after the fact by President Kennedy. Akalovsky, January 30, 1962, *FRUS, 1961–1963*, vol. 5, pp. 356–60.

24. Ibid.

25. Malinovsky and Zakharov to CC, January 10, 1962, Berlin Report, Roll 4640, Fond 5, Opus 30, Delo 399, RGANI. That same day the Soviet Defense Ministry, which had been sending daily reports to the Central Committee on the situation in Germany, reduced the regularity of these reports to one a week.

26. January 20, 1962, MFA. The Foreign Ministry rejected a recommendation from Pervukhin that Moscow lodge a protest against the Americans for the use of the autobahn by the U.S. military. The Soviet ambassador in East Berlin was told that this protest was unnecessary.

27. CIA, Current Intelligence Weekly Review, February 16, 1962, *FRUS, 1961–1963*, vol. 5, pp. 369–70.

28. Foy Kohler, memorandum for the record, February 7, 1962, ibid., vol. 14, p. 792.

29. CIA, Current Intelligence Weekly Review, February 16, 1962, loc. cit. Zakharov and Malinovsky to the CC, February 17, 1962, F. 5, Opis 30, Delo 399, p.57, RGANI. This document describes the Soviet action as having been ordered by the headquarters of the Group of Soviet Forces in Germany and indicates that the Kremlin knew of the decision and presumably approved it.

30. Memcon, NSK and Ulbricht, February 26, 1962, APRF.

31. Aleksandr Fursenko and Timothy Naftali, *"One Hell of a Gamble": Khrushchev, Castro and Kennedy* (New York: Norton, 1997), pp. 154–55.

32. Spravka (summary), GRU. This was also the period that Kennedy seemed to indicate in an interview with Stewart Alsop, published in the *Saturday Evening Post*, that he would be the first to use nuclear weapons in a war, if need be. See Fursenko and Naftali, op. cit., p. 177.

33. Anatoly Dobrynin, *In Confidence: Moscow's Ambassador to America's Six Cold War Presidents (1962–1986)* (New York: Times Books, 1995), p. 52.

34. Rusk to Dept. of State, March 13, 1962, *FRUS, 1961–1963*, vol. 15, pp. 40–41.

35. Spravka (preceding visit of Souphanouvong to USSR), January 26, 1962, 0570, 8/8/15, MFA.

36. Memcon, Abramov and Souphanouvong, February 3, 1962, 0570, 8/7/5 MFA.

37. Spravka (preceding visit of Souphanouvong to USSR), January 26, 1962, 0570, 8/8/15, MFA.

38. Memcon, Abramov and Souphanouvong, February 3, 1962, 0570, 8/7/5 MFA.

39. Memcon, March 29, 1962, Abramov meeting with Liu Chuna of the Chinese economic and cultural mission in Laos. Memcon, March 31, 1962, Abramov meeting with the deputy chief of the State Planning Committee of North Vietnam, Le Van Huan. Liu Chuna and Le Van Huan both described to Abramov the agreements reached at the quadripartite meeting earlier in the month, 0570, 8/7/5, MFA.

40. Ibid.

41. Thee, op. cit., pp. 241–42. Abramov shared with his Polish colleague a copy of the letter that Moscow had given to Ho.

42. Lifeng Deng, *Jianguohou junshi xingdong quanlu* [Complete Records of Military Operations since the Founding of the People's Republic of China] (Taiyuan: Shanxi renmin, 1994), p. 355, cited in Han Zhao, *"China's Policy* toward Laotian Neutrality, 1961–1975," unpublished paper. The authors are grateful to Mr. Zhao, a graduate student at the University of Virginia, for sharing this paper. See also Qiang Zhai, *China and the Vietnam Wars, 1950–1975* (Chapel Hill: University of North Carolina Press, 2000), p. 104.

43. Fursenko and Naftali, op. cit., p. 153.

44. Ibid., pp. 143–45.

45. Ibid., pp. 159–60.

46. It was approved February 8, 1962. Ibid., p. 154.

47. Memcon, Alekseyev and Castro, February 6, 1963, APRF.

48. Ibid.

49. Fursenko and Naftali, op. cit., pp. 167–68.

50. Christopher Andrew and Vasili Mitrokhin, *The World Was Going Our Way: The KGB and the Battle of the Third World* (New York: Basic Books, 2005), p. 43.

51. Fursenko and Naftali, op. cit., pp. 167–68.

52. For information on the Nicaraguan operation run by Andara y Ubeda (code name Prim), see Andrew and Mitrokhin, op. cit., p. 43.

53. April 9, 1962, decision of the Presidium, APRF.

54. Sergei Khrushchev attended this briefing. See Sergei N. Khrushchev, *Khrushchev and the Making of a Superpower* (University Park: Pennsylvania State University Press, 2000), pp. 468–82.

55. Ibid., p. 474.

56. For technical information on the R-16, see Oleg Bukharin et al., ed., *Russian Strategic Nuclear Forces* (Cambridge, Mass.: MIT Press, 2001), pp. 189–92.

57. On the R-9, see Sergei Khrushchev, op. cit., p. 474; Bukharin et al., op. cit., pp. 192–95; James Harford, *Korolev: How One Man Masterminded the Soviet Drive to Beat America to the Moon* (New York, Wiley, 1997), pp. 117–20.

58. Steno, May 31, 1962, AOK.

59. Ibid.

60. Protocol 30, May 4, 1962, AOK.

61. Philip Nash, *The Other Missiles of October: Eisenhower, Kennedy and the Jupiters, 1957–1963* (Chapel Hill: University of North Carolina Press, 1997).

62. The only record of this conversation comes from historian Colonel General Dmitri Volkogonov, *Autopsy for an Empire: The Seven Leaders Who Built the Soviet Regime* (New York, Free Press, 1998), p. 236. As adviser to President Boris Yeltsin, Volkogonov had exclusive and extensive access to Soviet-era political and military records.

63. Ibid. The Russian Defense Ministry's official history also argues that some staff work for this operation had to have been done before Khrushchev's visit to Bulgaria. *Na Kraiu Propasti* [On the Brink] (Moscow: 1994), pp. 35–40.

64. Secretary of Defense Robert S. McNamara briefing summarized in memcon, "Meeting with Congressional Leaders," May 15, 1962, 9:15 A.M., *FRUS, 1961–1963*, vol. 24, p. 770.

65. Message to DCI McCone, May 13, 1962, ibid., p. 763. Memcon, May 15, 1962, ibid., p. 770.

66. Memcon, May 13, 1962, ibid., p. 760.

67. Memo, Forrestal to JFK, May 14, 1962, ibid., pp. 767–68.

68. Khrushchev said this in a speech near Pleven, Bulgaria, on May 18. The *Current Digest of the Soviet Press*, vol. 14, no. 20 (June 13, 1962), p. 4. Khrushchev was in Bulgaria from May 14 to 20.

69. Zakharov and Malinovsky to the CC, May 26, 1962, F. 5, Opis 30, Delo 399, RGANI.

70. Steno, May 26, 1961. On Chinese assessments of the situation in Southeast Asia, see Deputy Foreign Minister Ko Bang Fi's September 23, 1961, presentation at the quadripartite socialist summit on Laos in Hanoi, 0570, 7/5/15, MFA, and memcon, Gromyko and Chen Yi, July 6, 1961, 0570, 7/5/14, MFA.

71. The gist of Bolshakov's message was preserved in a memcon produced by Dean

Rusk after speaking with RFK, *FRUS, 1961–1963*, vol. 24, p. 782, n. 2. A Soviet account was not found. However, the fact that Bolshakov and RFK met twice on May 17 to discuss Laos was noted by the GRU the list prepared of RFK and Bolshakov meetings.

72. Dobrynin, op. cit., p. 52.

73. *Current Digest of the Soviet Press*, vol. 14, no. 20 (June 13, 1962), p. 4.

74. Protocol 30, May 4, 1962, AOK.

75. Strobe Talbott, ed., *Khrushchev Remembers* (Boston: Little, Brown, 1970), p. 494.

76. John Lewis Gaddis uses this elegant concept to describe the Cuban missile crisis. It is equally useful in thinking about how the resolution of the Cuban problem eventually became bound up with Khrushchev's efforts to resolve all his problems. Gaddis, op. cit., p. 261.

77. Talbott, ed., op. cit., p. 494.

78. Anastas Mikoyan, *Tak Bylo* [As It Was] (Moscow: Vagrius, 1994), p. 606.

79. Protocol 32, May 21, 1962, AOK.

80. Ibid. This note is cryptic on how he described the offensive nature of the plan. It is only through the study of associated materials and the later Malin notes that it becomes clear that he saw the strategic nuclear missiles as offensive weapons primarily deployed to establish a balance of terror with the United States.

81. Malin noted Khrushchev saying, "Comrade Malinovsky and Biryuzov should make calculations, consider the time issue." Protocol 32, May 21, 1962, AOK.

82. Protocol 32, May 21, 1962, AOK and Dmitri Volkogonov, *Sem Vozhdei* [Seven Leaders] (Moscow: Novosti, 1995), pp. 421–22. For our reconstruction in *"One Hell of a Gamble"* of how the Kremlin considered Khrushchev's proposal to send missiles to Cuba, we drew upon information from an apparent May 21 Defense Council meeting described in Volkogonov's book *Sem Vozhdei*, as well as on Colonel General Semyon P. Ivanov's brief notes from the Presidium meeting of May 24, 1962, and the short description of the resolution passed by the Presidium on May 24. We did not then have Malin's notes for the May 21 and May 24 Presidium meetings where the proposal was discussed. The Malin notes showed that it took two Presidium meetings for the proposal to be adopted, and even then the operation was not to be formally approved by the leadership of the Soviet Communist Party until the Cubans said yes. It now appears that the May 21 meeting was a joint session of the Defense Council and the Presidium (the Defense Council included military commanders). It is not clear from the Malin note for the May 24 Presidium meeting whether it was also considered a joint Defense Council–Presidium meeting. See Protocol 32 (continuation), May 24, 1962, AOK.

83. Protocol 32 (continuation), May 24, 1962, AOK.

84. Fursenko interview with Aleksandr Alekseyev, February 16, 1994.

85. Ibid.

86. Fursenko and Naftali, op. cit., p. 182.

CHAPTER 18: "I THINK WE WILL WIN THIS OPERATION"

1. Resolution, April 11, 1961, APRF.

2. NSK to Castro, June 12, 1962, Folio 3, List 65, File 872, pp. 58–59, APRF.

3. Raymond L. Garthoff, *Reflections on the Cuban Missile Crisis*, rev. ed. (Washington, D.C.: Brookings Institution, 1989), p. 206. Garthoff cites General Dmitri Volkogonov.

4. *Na Krayu Propasti* [On the Brink] (Moscow: 1994), pp. 54, 73–74.

5. Protocol 35, June 10, 1962, AOK.

6. Protocol 39, July 1, 1962, AOK.

7. Ibid.

8. Ibid.

9. Ibid.

10. Steno, January 8, 1962, AOK.

11. Deborah Shapley, *Promise and Power: The Life and Times of Robert McNamara* (Boston: Little, Brown, 1993), pp. 140–46.

12. Protocol 39, July 1, 1962, AOK.

13. Memorandum from Michael V. Forrestal to McGeorge Bundy, June 11, 1962, *Foreign Relations of the United States* [hereafter *FRUS*] *1961–1963* (Washington, D.C.: Government Printing Office, 1994), vol. 24, pp. 837–39. See also note 1.

14. Telegram, Averell Harriman to secretary of state, July 3, 1962, *FRUS, 1961–1963*, vol. 19, pp. 860–62. In this cable, Harriman described his meeting on July 2 with Soviet official Georgi M. Pushkin, who had read a personal message from Khrushchev.

15. Kennedy's envoy, Averell Harriman, who knew nothing about the substance of the Presidium's July 1 meeting, nonetheless reported Mikoyan's absence from the Kremlin that day. Harriman to Washington, July 3, 1962, ibid., vol. 24, p. 860.

16. Aleksandr Fursenko and Timothy Naftali, *"One Hell of a Gamble": Khrushchev, Castro and Kennedy* (New York: Norton, 1997), p. 191.

17. Malinovsky and Zakharov, "In connection with your instructions, the Defense Ministry Recommends . . . ," May 24, 1962, Volkogonov collection, Library of Congress.

18. Protocol 40, July 6, 1962, AOK. Although the switch in plan was evident from other materials available in the 1990s, the authors did not have access to this note (and Khrushchev's differentiation between the different kinds of weapons) when writing *"One Hell of a Gamble."*

19. Ibid.

20. Ibid.

21. NSK to JFK (undated), *FRUS, 1961–1963*, vol. 15, pp. 207–12.

22. NSK to Ulbricht, July 11, 1962, APRF.

23. Even before this latest release of Soviet documents a few astute scholars noticed the sharp change in Soviet rhetoric on Berlin in July 1962 and concluded there might be a link to Khrushchev's May decision to send missiles to Cuba. See Ernest R. May and Philip D. Zelikow, *The Kennedy Tapes: Inside the White House in the Cuban Missile Crisis*, concise ed. (New York: Norton, 2001, 2002); and Graham T. Allison and Philip D. Zelikow, *Essence of Decision: Explaining the Cuban Missile Crisis*, 2nd ed. (New York: Longman, 1999). We think it unlikely that Khrushchev had West Berlin in the front of his mind when he decided to put missiles in Cuba during his visit to Bulgaria. Khrushchev's plans for 1962 were characteristically dynamic. In May the Cuban operation had unfocused goals, reflecting the fact that the operation stemmed from a general impatience with the worldwide balance of power. By July, however, Khrushchev was clearly working out a more specific strategy for a major political offensive in 1962, one that would take final form only after Kennedy turned down Moscow's last effort at a diplomatic settlement over West Berlin.

24. Memcon, JFK and Dobrynin, July 17, 1962, *FRUS, 1961–1963*, vol. 15, p. 223.

25. Memcon, "Meeting with the President on Berlin Planning, 1000 hours, 19 July 1962," Timothy Naftali, ed., *Presidential Recordings: John F. Kennedy, The Great Crises* (New York: Norton, 2001), vol. 1, pp. 203–26.

26. Cable, Thompson to DOS, July 26, 1962, 1:00 P.M., *FRUS, 1961–1963*, vol. 5, p. 465.

27. Cable, Thompson to DOS, July 26, 1962, 1:00 P.M., *FRUS, 1961–1963*, vol. 15, p. 254.

28. Cable, Thompson to DOS, July 25, 1962, 4:00 P.M., ibid., pp. 252–53.

29. Naftali, "Introduction: Five Hundred Days," *Presidential Recordings: John F. Kennedy*, op. cit., pp. xli–iv.

30. Edwin O. Guthman and Jeffrey Shulman, eds., *Robert Kennedy, in His Own Words: The Unpublished Recollection of the Kennedy Years* (New York: Bantam, 1988), p. 168.

31. Cited in Evan Thomas, *Robert F. Kennedy, His Life* (New York: Simon & Schuster, 2000).

32. Zakharov and Ivanov to Kosygin, September 12, 1962, APRF.

33. Ibid.

34. Instructions to Soviet ambassador (Dobrynin), (n.d., but clearly in response to RFK and Bolshakov meeting of July 31, 1962), Folio 3, List 66, File 316, pp. 194–95, APRF.

35. Ibid.

36. CIA, Special National Intelligence Estimate, "Soviet Intentions with Respect to Berlin," August 1, 1962, NSF, Box 100, LBJ Library.

37. Naftali, ed., Meeting with Llewellyn Thompson on Khrushchev, August 8, 1962, *Presidential Recordings: John F. Kennedy*, loc. cit., vol. 1, p. 270.

38. Thompson to SecState, July 28, 1962, *FRUS, 1961–63*, vol. 15, p. 255.

39. Naftali, ed., Meeting with Llewellyn Thompson on Khrushchev, August 8, 1962, *Presidential Recordings: John F. Kennedy*, loc. cit., vol. 1, p. 266.

40. Ibid., p. 267.

41. Ibid.

42. Vladimir S. Lavrov, Third European Department, to Mikhail F. Bodrov, July 25, 1962, "Materialyi o politicheskom i ekonimicheskom polizhenii v Zapadnom Berlinye," [Materials on the Political and Economic Situation in West Berlin], 1962, 7/54/29, MFA; Vladimir S. Lavrov to Vladimir J. Erofeev, July 25 1962, ibid.

43. Moscow (Third European Department) to Tunis; Moscow to Damascus; Moscow to Beirut; Moscow to Rabat; Moscow to Baghdad, July 28 1962, "Materialyi o politicheskom i ekonimicheskom polizhenii v Zapadnom Berlinye," [Materials on the Political and Economic Situation in West Berlin], 1962, 7/54/29, MFA.

44. Report of the responsible KGB officer from the Ukrainian KGB in the Nikolaiyevsky region, August 24, 1962. Report of the KGB officer to the Council of Ministers of the Azerbaijian SSR, August 30, 1962, FSB.

45. Timothy Naftali and Philip Zelikow, eds., *Presidential Recordings: John F. Kennedy: The Great Crises* (New York: Norton, 2001), vol. 2, p. 25.

46. Ibid., p. 27.

47. Ibid., p. 29.

48. Dobrynin, From the Diary of the Soviet Ambassador to the United States, September 13, 1962, APRF.

49. Ibid.

50. Malinovsky to Khrushchev, September 6, 1962, Volkogonov Collection, Library of Congress. Khrushchev scribbled his decision on this memorandum.

51. CIA memorandum, September 12, 1962, *FRUS, 1961–1963*, vol. 10, p. 1055, n. 1.

52. Ivanov, Spravka-Doklad, "On the Correction of a Section of Operation 'Anadyr' in September–October 1962," September 13, 1962, Volkogonov Collection, Library of Congress.

53. Memo, from the vice president's military aide (Burris) to LBJ, "Khrushchev Moves toward Berlin Showdown," September 18, 1962, *FRUS, 1961–1963*, vol. 15, p. 119. In late August Khrushchev told UN Secretary-General U Thant that he intended to

involve the UN in his effort to get the United States to withdraw its forces from West Berlin. U Thant advised him to use the existing four-power framework, not the UN, to settle this issue.

54. Fursenko and Naftali, op. cit., p. 211; F. D. Reeve, *Robert Frost in Russia* (Boston: Little, Brown, 1964).

55. Stewart Udall, report on trip to Pitsunda (undated) Cuban Missile Crisis Collection, National Security Archive.

56. Memcon, NSK and Kroll, September 11, 1962, 0757, 7/33/2, MFA.

57. Memcon, NSK and Kroll, January 8, 1960, 0757, 7/33/2, MFA.

58. Cited in CIA memorandum, September 12, 1962, *FRUS, 1961–1963*, vol. 10, pp. 1055–56.

59. Memcon, NSK and Kroll, September 11, 1962, 0757, 7/33/2, MFA.

60. Memo from the vice president's military aide (Burris) to LBJ, "Khrushchev Moves toward Berlin Showdown," September 18, 1962, *FRUS, 1961–1963*, vol. 15, pp. 324–25.

61. CIA, Special National Intelligence Estimate, "Current Soviet Tactics on Berlin," September 13, 1962, NSF Box 100, LBJ Library, Austin, Texas.

62. "Endkampf um Berlin in 4 Wochen," *Deutsche Soldaten Zeitung und National-Zeitung*, September 28, 1962. The authors are grateful to David Coleman for finding this evidence of Kroll's public campaign.

63. Protocol, October 14, 1962, AOK.

64. Memcon, Kosygin and Souphanouvong, September 28, 1962, 0570, 8/7/3, MFA.

65. Zakharov and Fokin to Defense Council, "(to show to NSK, only)," September 18, 1962, Volkogonov Collection, Library of Congress.

66. To the commander of the Soviet Forces in Cuba, September 8, 1962, ibid.

67. Zakharov to Kosygin, September 16, 1962, APRF.

68. Zakharov and Fokin to NSK, September 25, 1962, Volkogonov Collection, Library of Congress.

69. NSK to JFK, September 28, 1962, *FRUS, 1961–1963*, vol. 6, pp. 151–62.

70. Ibid.

71. Ibid.

72. Dobrynin to NSK, October 9, 1962, Volkogonov Collection, Library of Congress.

73. Memcon, MFK and Couve de Murville, October 9, 1962, *FRUS*, vol. 15, pp. 351–55. The French record is in *Documents Diplomatiques Français*, 1962 (*DDF*) (Paris: Imprimerie Nationale, 1999), vol. 2, pp. 283–86.

74. Khrushchev revealed the relationship between the test ban treaty and Berlin in a top secret Presidium discussion in 1963. See steno, April 17, 1963, AOK. On October 14, 1962, Khrushchev raised the need to prepare new language for a test ban treaty. Protocol 59, October 14, 1962, AOK.

CHAPTER 19: CUBAN MISSILE CRISIS

1. Timothy Naftali and Philip Zelikow, eds., *Presidential Recordings: John F. Kennedy, The Great Crises* (New York: Norton, 2001), vol. 2, p. 413.

2. Ibid., pp. 512–72.

3. Ibid., pp. 464–66.

4. Chizhov to Center, October 22, 1962, GRU.

5. Summary (prepared 1994), GRU reports through October 22, 1962.

6. Chizhov to Center, October 22, 1962, GRU.

7. Notes, A. K. Serov, October 22, 1962, RGANI.

8. This reconstruction of the meetings of October 22 and October 23 is much fuller than that which we could present in 1997. Supplementing Malin's notes are sections from Mikoyan's unpublished memoirs. In 1999 a portion of Mikoyan's memoirs was published in Russia as *Tak Bylo* (As It Was). The section of the memoir dealing with the Cuban missile crisis, however, was not published. It consists of a dictation made by Mikoyan on January 19, 1963, in the A. I. Mikoyan Archive of the State Archive of Social-Political History [hereafter RGASPI]. The other new source is the memorandum of record prepared by A. K. Serov, a Central Committee staffer who attended the meeting. His notes are on deposit at RGANI. Unless otherwise indicated, all references to protocol minutes refer to Malin's notes.

9. Protocol 60, October 22, 1962, AOK.

10. Notes, A. K. Serov, October 22, 1962, RGANI.

11. Protocol 60, October 22, 1962, AOK.

12. Havana to Center, October 23, 1962, GRU.

13. The rules of engagement for the Lunas are listed in Ivanov's military plans. See Dmitri Volkogonov Collection, Library of Congress.

14. Protocol 60, October 22, 1962, AOK.

15. Aleksandr Fursenko and Timothy Naftali interview with Vladimir Semichastny, June 1994.

16. Protocol 60, October 22, 1962, AOK.

17. Notes A. K. Serov, October 22, 1962, RGANI.

18. Ibid.

19. Ibid.

20. Protocol 60, October 22, 1962, AOK.

21. Ibid. Notes, A. K. Serov, October 22, 1962, RGANI.

22. Protocol 60, October 22, 1962, AOK.

23. Ibid.

24. Notes, A. K. Serov, October 22, 1962, RGANI.

25. Protocol 60, October 22, 1962, AOK.

26. Mikoyan's unpublished memoir, RGASPI.

27. Ibid.

28. Ibid.

29. Notes, A. K. Serov, October 22, 1962, RGANI.

30. Ibid.

31. Ibid.

32. *Na Krayu Propasti* [On the Brink] (Moscow: 1994), pp. 58, 73; Dmitri Volkogonov, *Sem Vozhdei* [Seven Leaders] (Moscow: Novosti, 1998), p. 423.

33. The cable was sent by KGB channels to Cuba, Folio 16, Inventory 3753, File 1, Box 3573, Historical Archive and Military Memorial Center of the General Staff of the Armed Forces of the Russian Federation (AGSRF).

34. Protocol 60, October 22, 1962, AOK.

35. Notes, A. K. Serov, October 22, 1962, RGANI.

36. "Radio and Television Report to the American People on the Soviet Arms Buildup in Cuba," October 22, 1962, *Public Papers of the Presidents: John F. Kennedy, 1962; Containing the Public Messages, Speeches and Statements of the President, January 1–December 31, 1962* (Washington, D.C.: Government Printing Office, 1963), p. 807.

37. For convenience we are using the U.S. designations for the four Foxtrots as they were detected by the U.S. Navy. C-18 was the first detected. Shumkov's C-19 was next, then C-20 (later renumbered as C-26), then C-23. The Soviet designation for C-18 was

B-130. The other designations were B-4, B-36, and B-59, but the authors were unable to establish the correlation between these designations and the NATO designations. For documents on the U.S. antisubmarine warfare operations in the Cuban missile crisis, see the National Security Archives Submarine file.

38. The authors are grateful to William Burr and Thomas Blanton of the National Security Archives for sharing information on the locations of the Soviet submarines during the crisis.

39. Ernest May and Philip Zelikow, *The Kennedy Tapes: Inside the White House during the Cuban Missile Crisis*, concise ed. (New York: Norton, 2001, 2002), p. 173.

40. Ibid.

41. "Radio and Television Report to the American People on the Soviet Arms Buildup in Cuba," October 22, 1962," *Public Papers of the Presidents: John F. Kennedy, 1962*, loc. cit., p. 809.

42. Information to Timothy Naftali from the National Security Agency.

43. Interrogations of Oleg Penkovsky, Central Archive FSB.

44. Protocol 60 (continuation), October 23, 1962, AOK.

45. NSK to JFK, October 23, 1962, *Foreign Relations of the United States* [hereafter *FRUS*], *1961–1963*, vol. 6, p. 166.

46. Protocol 60 (continuation), October 23, 1962, AOK.

47. These ships were not ordered to turn around until October 25. See Protocol 61, October 25, 1962, AOK.

48. Protocol 60, October 22, 1962, AOK. This note begins on October 22, but internal evidence suggests that it includes the deliberations at the two meetings on October 23.

49. Serov treats the October 23 discussions as a continuation of Protocol 60 (the meeting of October 22).

50. Naftali interview with Second Captain (ret.) Vadim P. Orlov, Havana, Cuba, October 2002. During the crisis Orlov was an intelligence officer on Submarine B-59.

51. Mikoyan's unpublished memoir, RGASPI.

52. Ibid.

53. Transcript, interview with Nikolai Shumkov, BBC Scotland. The authors are grateful to Jacqui Hayeth and Ross Wilson for sharing to BBC Scotland Cuba Missile crisis interviews with them.

54. Transcript, interview with "Albert" Chebrasov, BBC Scotland.

55. Mikoyan was sure that the order had been sent. Not only in his memoir but later, in the contemporaneous account of the October 1964 meeting at which Khrushchev was dismissed, Mikoyan noted the importance of ending the submarine mission during the crisis. (Protocol 162, October 8, 1964, AOK.) However, U.S. records of the positions of the submarines and the recollections of the surviving Soviet commanders all dispute Mikoyan's belief that this order was sent. Instead of a general order, the submarine captains were ordered one by one to return as they were surfaced by the U.S. Navy or as their batteries died. But these orders were sent after October 27, the climax of the crisis.

56. Deputy Undersecretary of State for Political Affairs U. Alexis Johnson discussed this message at a meeting of the Excomm on October 24. See Philip Zelikow and Ernest May, ed., *Presidential Recordings: John F. Kennedy, The Great Crises* (New York: Norton, 2001), vol. 3, p. 192.

57. Ibid., p. 184.

58. Ibid., p. 191.

59. Ibid., p. 193. For Robert Kennedy's notes on the meeting, see Arthur Schlesinger, Jr., *Robert Kennedy and His Times* (New York: Random House, 1978), p. 514.

60. Zelikow and May, eds., op. cit., vol. 3, p. 194.

61. Ibid.

62. Ibid., p. 195.

63. Ibid., pp. 196–97.

64. Quoted in Robert Dallek, *An Unfinished Life: John F. Kennedy, 1917–1963* (Boston: Little, Brown, 2003), pp. 564–65.

65. NSK to JFK, October 24, 1962, *FRUS, 1961–1963*, vol. 6, p. 170.

66. Protocol 61, October 25, 1962, AOK.

67. Memcon, A. K. Serov, October 25, 1962, RGANI.

68. That quotation does not appear in the Serov memcon. It comes from Malin's record of the meeting. See Protocol 61, October 25, 1962, AOK.

69. The Serov note was not available to us when we wrote *"One Hell of a Gamble."* It shows that the decision to end the crisis through diplomatic means was made on the night of Wednesday, October 25. This suggests that the Scali and Feklisov discussion of the next day may well have been a peace feeler initiated by Khrushchev or someone close to him once the Presidium had set the new line. The similarity of the language of this decision and Feklisov's language on October 26 seems too strong to be merely a matter of coincidence.

70. Indeed the KGB chief was not invited to any of the Presidium meetings during the crisis. Fursenko and Naftali interview with Semichastny, 1994.

71. Fursenko and Naftali interview with Aleksandr Feklisov, September 1994.

72. Naftali interview with John Scali, July 1994.

73. Kallistrat (Feklisov) to Center, October 26, 1962, File 116, vol. 1, pp. 1062–64, SVR.

74. "John Scali's notes of first meeting with Soviet Embassy counselor and KGB officer Aleksandr Fomin, October 26, 1962," Document 43, in Laurence Chang and Peter Kornbluh, eds., *The Cuban Missile Crisis, 1962* (New York: New Press, 1992).

75. Markov to Serov, October 26, 1962, GRU; Kallistrat (Feklisov) to Center, October 25, 1962, File 116, vol. 1, p. 1034, SVR. Heffernan spoke to representatives of both the KGB and the GRU. Gam was a KGB source.

76. Murov (from Havana) to Serov, October 24, 1962, GRU.

77. NSK to JFK, October 26, 1962, *FRUS, 1961–1963*, vol. 6, pp. 176–77.

78. Ibid., p. 176.

79. Transcript, interview with Nikolai Shumkov, BBC Scotland.

80. Memcon, June 3, 1961, 3:00 P.M., *FRUS, 1961–1963*, vol. 5, p. 182.

81. Mikoyan told the Cubans that Lippmann's column had been Khrushchev's inspiration. Memcon, Mikoyan, November 4, 1962, APRF.

82. Protocol 63, October 27, 1962.

83. Dobrynin to MFA, October 27, 1962, MFA, p. 171. This document is the source of all the quotations from this meeting.

84. On October 26, the Soviet commander in Cuba had received permission to use force against an aerial attack but not against an isolated U-2 flight. See Fursenko and Naftali, *"One Hell of a Gamble": Khrushchev, Castro, and Kennedy, 1958–1964* (New York: Norton, 1997), pp. 277–78.

85. Ibid., p. 272.

86. Protocol 64, October 28, 1962, AOK.

87. Protocol 60 (continuation), October 23, 1962, AOK.

88. Ulbricht to NSK, October 1962, APRF.

89. For the chronology of this day in Washington, see Fursenko and Naftali, op. cit., pp. 287–89; Zelikow and May, op. cit., vol. 3, pp. 512–25.

90. Steno, January 8, 1962, AOK.

CHAPTER 20: "LEAVING FEAR ASTERN"

1. JFK to NSK, October 27, 1962, *Foreign Relations of the United States* [hereafter *FRUS*], *1961–1963*, vol. 6, p. 182.
2. NSK to JFK, October 28, 1962, ibid., p. 184.
3. Alekseyev to Moscow, October 29, 1962, APRF.
4. Alekseyev to Moscow, October 31, 1962, APRF.
5. KGB (Havana) to Center, October 29, 1962, SVR. The KGB reported on Castro's discussion with Cuban military leaders and the comments of the head of Cuban intelligence, Manuel Piñero. KGB (Havana) to Center, November 1, 1962, SVR. The KGB here reported on dissatisfaction with the Soviets in Cuba's ministry of the interior and other ministries, and the Cuban armed forces.
6. NSK to JFK, October 27, 1962, *FRUS*, *1961–1963*, vol. 6, p. 179.
7. NSK to JFK (undated), ibid., p. 200.
8. JFK to NSK, November 6, 1962, ibid., p. 201.
9. "China Press Sees K as Weak Man," *Washington Post and Times Herald*, October 31, 1962.
10. Robert Trumbull, "Peking Criticizes Russians on Cuba; Party Warns Soviet Must Back It in India Dispute," *New York Times*, November 1, 1962.
11. "Castro Defended in Crisis," *New York Times*, November 3, 1962. Seymour Topping, "Red-Bloc Conflict Seen on Cuba and War in India," *New York Times*, November 2, 1962.
12. The demonstrations were large, though it is difficult to determine how large. The British news agency Reuters reported tens of thousands marching on November 3, whereas the official Chinese count was three hundred thousand. "Chou Reaffirms Support of Cuba; Gives Impetus to Anti-US Drive in Peking Speech," *New York Times*, November 4, 1962. "Chinese Marchers Back Cuba" (Reuters), *New York Times*, November 4, 1962. "Peking Condemns 'Appeasing' of US; Red Paper Pledges Support of Castro's Defiant Stand," *New York Times*, November 6, 1962; John Roderick, "Chinese Liken Soviet Action on Cuba to Munich Appeasement," *Washington Post*, November 6, 1962.
13. Roderick, "Chinese Liken Soviet Action on Cuba to Munich Appeasement," loc. cit.
14. Adam Kellet-Long, "Soviet Envoy's Praise of Khrushchev Meets Silence at Peking Celebration," *Washington Post and Times Herald*, November 7, 1962.
15. "Soviet Policy on Cuba Is Attacked by Albania," *Washington Post and Times Herald*, November 8, 1962.
16. Memcon, November 4, 1962, Cold War International History Project [hereafter CWIHP] *Bulletin*, no. 5 (Spring 1995).
17. Mikoyan to NSK, November 6, 1962, Folio 3, List 65, File 908, p. 184, APRF.
18. Protocol 65, Presidium Meeting of November 15, 1962, Folio 3, List 65, File 911, APRF.
19. Ibid.
20. Protocol 58, October 11, 1962, AOK, Protocol 59, October 14, 1962, AOK.
21. Ibid.
22. "MiG Deal with India Appears Off; Russian Official Supports Peking in Border Clash," *Washington Post and Times Herald*, October 30, 1962.
23. A. M. Rosenthal, "India's Hope for Support by Soviet All but Ended; Khrushchev Letter to Nehru Speaks of Friendship, but Says Moscow Will Continue Backing Red China," *New York Times*, November 4, 1962.

24. Seymour Topping, "Soviet Indicates a Return to Neutrality on India," *New York Times*, November 6, 1962.

25. "Nehru Says Soviet Jets Will Arrive; MiGs are expected Next Month Despite Conflict with China," *Washington Post and Times Herald*, November 1, 1962; "India Says Soviet Union Will Honor Oil Commitment," *New York Times*, November 14, 1962; "Soviet Again Promises MiGs," *New York Times*, November 19, 1962.

26. Moscow to secretary of state, November 13, 1962, 9:00 P.M. (Section 1 of 2), NSF, JFK Library.

27. Sir Frank Roberts to Lord Home, November 19, 1962, Prem 11/3996, 83827, National Archive—UK.

28. Cable, Dobrynin to Moscow, November 1, 1962, APRF.

29. Cable, KGB (Washington) to the Center, October 31, 1962, Delo 90238, vol. 1, SVR. The KGB quoted three congressional staffers.

30. Thomas J. Hamilton, "Cuba Bars Return of Soviet Planes," *New York Times*, November 9, 1962.

31. Excomm meeting, November 14, 1962, 5:45 to 6:02 P.M., unpublished draft transcript by David G. Coleman, The authors are grateful to David Coleman for the use of this transcript.

32. NSK to Mikoyan, extract from Protocol 65, November 10, 1962, 3-65-909, 44–45, APRF.

33. NSK to JFK (undated), *FRUS, 1961–1963*, vol. 6, p. 207.

34. NSK to Mikoyan, extract from Protocol 65, November 10, 1962, 3-65-909, pp. 44–45, APRF.

35. Editorial note, *FRUS*, vol. 6, p. 209.

36. NSK to JFK, November 14, 1962, ibid., p. 211.

37. NSK to Mikoyan extract from Protocol 65, November 13, 1962, 3-65-909, APRF.

38. KGB (New York) to the Center, December 15, 1962, Delo 90238, SVR, "Copies to Khrushchev, Kozlov, Gromyko, Malinovsky."

39. President's Office Files, Presidential Recordings, tape 60, JFK Library.

40. Protocol 66, November 16, 1962, AOK.

41. David Coleman, "The Missiles of November, December, January, February: The Tactical Missiles in Cuba," unpublished manuscript.

42. Roberts to London, November 12, 1962, National Archive—UK.

43. Protocol 68, November 21, 1962, AOK.

44. Memcon (by Edward S. Glenn), Kennedy and Mikoyan, November 29, 1962, *FRUS, 1961–1963*, vol. 11, pp. 545–62.

45. Memcon (by Y. Vinogradov and I. Bubnov), Mikoyan and Kennedy, November 29, 1962, APRF.

46. Ibid. Memcon (by Edward S. Glenn), Kennedy and Mikoyan, November 29, 1962, *FRUS, 1961–1963*, vol. 11, pp. 545–62.

47. Protocol 71, December 3, 1962, AOK.

48. There is no memorandum of conversation in U.S. archives regarding the October 30 discussion, and none has yet been found in Russian archives. Regarding U.S. efforts to figure out what Dean might have said, because he was not under instructions to offer three inspections, see Editorial note, *FRUS, 1961–1963*, vol. 7, pp. 623–25.

49. Steno, April 25, 1963, AOK.

50. Norman Cousins, *The Improbable Triumvirate: John F. Kennedy, Pope John, Nikita Khrushchev* (New York: Norton, 1972), pp. 32–33.

51. Ibid., p. 46.

52. Ibid., p. 57.

53. This last series, which took place at the northern test site in Novaya Zemlya, lasted from December 18 to 25, 1962.

54. Steno, April 25, 1963, AOK.

55. Ibid.

56. John F. Kennedy, Third Annual Message, January 14, 1963, *The State of the Union Messages of the Presidents, 1790–1966*, vol. III, *1905–1966*, ed. Fred L. Israel (New York: Chelsea House, Robert Hector, 1966), pp. 3144–54.

57. Ibid.

58. Transcript, meeting, 4:05–4:55 P.M., November 16, 1962. The authors are grateful to David Coleman for sharing this draft transcript, which he worked on as primary transcriber. The transcript will appear in its final form in volume 4 of the Miller Center's Presidential Recordings Series, John F. Kennedy. The "Munich" reference is to the 1938 Munich meeting at which the French and British acquiesced in allowing Nazi Germany to swallow the Sudetenland region of Czechoslovakia.

59. CIA, Current Intelligence Weekly Review, January 18, 1963, *FRUS, 1961–1963*, vol. 5, p. 609.

60. Telegram, Moscow to DOS, 6:00 P.M., January 26, 1963, ibid., vol. 5, pp. 480–81.

61. Protocol 80, January 29, 1963, AOK.

62. Ibid.

63. Editorial note, *FRUS, 1961–1963*, vol. 7, pp. 644–47.

64. Kennedy outlined his thinking in a conversation he taped with Norman Cousins on April 22, 1963. See Tape 82, Presidential Office Files, Presidential Recordings, JFK Library.

65. Naftali, telephone interview with James Critchfield, November 25, 2002. As chief of the CIA's Near East desk between 1960 and 1968, Critchfield oversaw U.S. activities in Iraq.

66. Cited in Andrew Cockburn and Patrick Cockburn, *Out of the Ashes: The Resurrection of Saddam Hussein* (New York: HarperCollins, 1999), p. 74.

67. Ibid.

68. Naftali interview with James Critchfield, August 18, 2001.

69. Meeting, Mikoyan and Qasim, April 14, 1960, APRF; aide-mémoire, Mikoyan for negotiations with Qasim, Protocol 274, April 7, 1960, APRF.

70. Tad Szulc, "U.S. and Britain Recognize Iraq; Soviet Also Acts; Speedy Decision Is Made by Washington, Which Finds New Regime Stable; Anti-Nasser Bloc in Middle East Moves to Counter Any Links to Cairo," *New York Times*, February 12, 1963.

71. Batatu Hanna, *The Old Social Classes and Revolutionary Developments in Iraq: A Study of Iraq's Old Landed and Commercial Classes and Its Communists, Ba'athists, and Free Officers* (Princeton: Princeton University Press, 1978), pp. 985–89.

72. "Soviet Bloc Campaigns against Iraqi Regime," *Washington Post and Times Herald*, February 20, 1963.

73. "Iraqi Accuses Red Bloc of Plotting Overthrow," *Washington Post and Times Herald*, February 24, 1963.

74. "High Iraqi Red Killed, Others Arrested," *Washington Post and Times Herald*, February 25, 1963. Ar-Radi was eventually killed by the new Iraqi regime. See Batatu Hanna, op. cit., p. 675.

75. Interview (with NSK) conducted Saturday afternoon, February 9, 1963, at the Kremlin, unpublished transcript, Roy H. Thomson Archive, Toronto. The authors are grateful to the current Lord Thomson for his permission to consult and quote from

this document. They also appreciate the assistance of the archivist Robert Hamilton and David Thomson and Professor Wesley Wark.

76. Memcon, Khrushchev with Marshal Hakim Amer, June 9, 1963, 52-1-561, APRF. In this interesting conversation, Amer denied any Egyptian involvement in the Ba'athist coup of February 1963 and added that Nasser later warned Aref that any persecution of communists would complicate Iraq's relations with the Socialist world. The Egyptians gave a higher number for the number arrested by the Iraqis (16,0000). Meanwhile Khrushchev reminisced about Soviet support for Qasim, mentioning that in July 1958 the Kremlin responded to fears of an imminent attack on Iraq by Turkey, Pakistan, and Iran by giving military assistance without the need for a formal agreement. When Qasim later revealed himself to have "dictatorial ways," the Kremlin sent Anastas Mikoyan to urge him to alter his methods. Although Qasim refused to change, the Ba'athists, Khrushchev concluded, were even worse for Iraq.

77. "Sir H. Trevelyan's interview with Khrushchev of March 6," Prem 11/4498, National Archives—UK. Lincoln Broomfield, Walter C. Clemens, Jr., and Franklyn Griffiths, *Khrushchev and the Arms Race: Soviet Interests in Arms Control and Disarmament 1954–1962* (Cambridge, Mass.: MIT Press, 1996), pp. 230–31.

78. Harry Schwartz, "Soviet Wipes Out Promise to Raise Meat Allowances," *New York Times*, March 4, 1963.

79. Harrison E. Salisbury, "The Khrushchev Line; Premier Stiffens His Ideology at Home before Risking It in Conflict with China," *New York Times*, March 12, 1963.

80. Interview, February 9, 1963, unpublished transcript, Roy H. Thomson Archive, Toronto, Canada.

81. Protocol 89, March 21, 1963, AOK.

82. Memcon, Alekseyev and Castro, February 6, 1963, MFA.

83. KGB, cable (New York) to Center, February 21, 1963, SVR; KGB, cable (Washington) to Center, March 1, 1963, SVR.

84. Report, KGB to MFA and GRU, February 19, 1963, APRF.

85. Fursenko interview with Ambassador N. S. Ryzhov, January 4, 1995.

86. Ibid.

87. Seymour Topping, "Chinese Suggest Khrushchev Visit and Party Truce; Willing to Receive Another Russian or Send Official of Their Own to Moscow; Neither Side Retreats; but Notes Are Conciliatory—Peking Insists on Rebuke to 'Yugoslav Revisionism,' " *New York Times*, March 14, 1963.

88. Protocol 87, March 12, 1963, AOK.

89. Washington (Sir David Ormsby Gore) to FO March 28, 1963, Prem 11/4496, National Archives—UK. This was a priority, top secret cable that passed on the information received in Washington at 4:00 A.M. that day.

90. Harold Caccia to Philip de Zulueta, April 3, 1963, Prem 11/4496, National Archive—UK.

91. Ibid., for the view of CIA analysts, which was described by British Ambassador Ormsby Gore. Regarding the thinking at the U.S. Embassy in Moscow, see Memo to Philip de Zulueta, March 29, 1963, Prem 11/4496, National Archives—UK. For evidence of the contrary indicators coming to the White House, see "Highlights from the Secretary of State's Policy Planning Meeting," March 26, 1963, *FRUS, 1961–1963*, vol. 5, p. 654.

92. Thompson to Rusk, April 3, 1963, ibid., p. 663.

93. RFK to JFK, April 3, 1963, vol. 6, p. 262.

94. Tape 79-2, Meeting, April 6, 1963, President's Office Files, Presidential Recordings, JFK Library.

95. Ibid.

96. Ibid. This behind-the-scenes activity is evident from the president's and the attorney general's statements in this meeting.

97. Ibid.

98. Cousins, op. cit., p. 79.

99. Tape 82, President's Office Files, Presidential Recordings, JFK Library.

100. Meeting on Laos, April 19, 1963; NSC Meeting on Laos, April 20, 1963; NSC Meeting on Laos, April 22, 1963, Tape 82, President's Office Files, Presidential Recordings, JFK Library.

101. Meeting with Norman Cousins, April 22, 1963, Tape 82, President's Office Files, Presidential Recordings, JFK Library.

102. "K Back at Work Ignores Attack in Albania Press," *Washington Post and Times* April 21, 1963.

103. Khrushchev described his April 23 meeting with the British and American ambassadors to the Presidium on April 25. See Steno, April 25, 1963, AOK.

104. Protocol 94, April 25, 1963, AOK.

105. NSK to JFK, September 28, 1962, *FRUS, 1961–1963*, vol. 6, pp. 152–61.

106. Steno, April 25, 1963, AOK.

107. Memcon, Khrushchev and Harriman, April 26, 1963, *FRUS, 1961–1963*, Vol. XXIV, pp. 1000–1005.

108. Memorandum for the Record, April 30, 1963, *FRUS, 1961–1963*, Op cit., p. 1006.

109. Smirnov to MFA, May [29?,] 1963, 0757 1963, 8/35/5, MFA.

110. Smirnov to MFA, April 6, 1963, and May 17, 1963, 0757 1963, 8/35/5, MFA

111. Smirnov to MFA, June 14, 1963, 0757 8/35/4-5, MFA. Kroll did come to the Soviet Union in the summer of 1963 and was given a personal letter from Khrushchev to deliver to Adenauer. But Adenauer never responded to the letter. On October 10, 1963, Adenauer told Soviet ambassador Smirnov that "he hadn't the time [to respond]." Smirnov to MFA, October 10, 1963, 0757, 8/35/4-5, MFA.

112. Arthur Schlesinger, Jr., *A Thousand Days: John F. Kennedy in the White House* (Boston: Houghton Mifflin, 1965), p. 900; Theodore C. Sorensen, *Kennedy* (New York: Harper & Row, 1965), p. 730.

113. Sorensen, op. cit., p. 730.

114. Naftali interview with McGeorge Bundy, November 15, 1995.

115. Sorensen, op. cit., p. 731.

116. Ibid.

117. Ibid., p. 732.

118. Ibid.

119. William Taubman, *Khrushchev: The Man and His Era* (New York: Norton, 2003), p. 602.

120. Protocol [102], June 13, 1963, AOK.

121. Protocol 80, January 29, 1963, AOK.

122. Steno, June 7, 1963, AOK.

123. Memcon, NSK and Castro, May 5, 1963, APRF.

124. Translated and cited in Odd Arne Westad, "The Sino-Soviet Alliance and the United States," *Brothers in Arms: The Rise and Fall of the Sino-Soviet Alliance 1945–1963* (Washington, D.C.: Woodrow Wilson Center Press, 1998), p. 180.

125. Records of Meetings of the CPSU and CCP Delegations, Moscow, July 5–20, 1963, Appendix 17, ibid., pp. 385–86.

126. Protocol 107, July 23, 1963, AOK.

CHAPTER 21: LEGACY

1. Sergei Khrushchev, *Khrushchev on Khrushchev: An Inside Account of the Man and His Era*, trans. William Taubman (Boston: Little, Brown, 1990), pp. 30–32.

2. Steno, December 16, 1959, AOK.

3. Ibid.

4. William Taubman, *Khrushchev* (New York: Norton, 2003), p. 613.

5. Protocol 145, May 26, 1964, AOK.

6. "Soviet School Retreat," Editorial, *New York Times*, August 14, 1964.

7. Protocol 126, December 23, 1963, AOK.

8. Ibid.

9. Protocol 152, July 30, 1964, AOK.

10. "Soviet School Retreat," Editorial, New York Times, August 14, 1964. At the special session of the Presidium where Khrushchev was dismissed, the other members severely criticized his unilateral education reform. Protocol (no number), October 13, 1964, AOK.

11. Sergei Khrushchev, op. cit., pp. 725–26.

12. Ibid.

13. The chronology of Khrushchev's last days in office was compiled by the British Embassy in Moscow. Trevelyan to FO, October 16, 1964, FO 371/177665, National Archive—UK.

14. "How They Removed Khrushchev," interview with Vladimir Semichastny, *Argumenti i Facti*, May 1989, p. 5.

15. Ibid.

16. Protocol 162, October 8, 1964, AOK.

17. Taubman, op. cit., p. 5.

18. "How They Removed Khrushchev," interview with Vladimir Semichastny, *Argumenti i Facti*, May 1989, p. 5. Regarding the call to Palewski, see H. A. F. Hohler, British Embassy in Moscow, October 21, 1964, FO 371/177665, National Archives—UK. Hohler had a conversation with Palewski.

19. Cited in Trevelyan, "The Circumstances of Mr. Khrushchev's Downfall," paper to the British Foreign Office, November 2, 1964, FO 371/177666, National Archives—UK.

20. Baudet to Couve de Murville, October 16, 1964, *Documents Diplomatiques Français (DDF)*, *1964*, vol. 2, Record No. 136 (Brussels: P.E.I.—Peter Lang, 2002).

21. Cited in Trevelyan, "The Circumstances of Mr. Khrushchev's Downfall," paper to the British Foreign Office, November 2, 1964, FO 371/177666, National Archives—UK.

22. "How they removed Khrushchev," interview with Vladimir Semichastny, *Argumenti i Facti*, May 1989, p. 5; Taubman, op. cit., p. 10.

23. Fursenko interviews with veterans of Kremlin guards, October 2005.

24. Protocol (no number), October 13, 1964, AOK.

25. Ibid.

26. Protocol (no number, continuation), October 14, 1962, AOK.

27. Ibid.

28. Fursenko interviews with veterans of the Kremlin guard, October 2005.

29. Telegram, Moscow to Washington, October 16, 1964, *Foreign Relations of the United States* [hereafter *FRUS*], *1964–1968*, vol. 14, pp. 122–23.

30. Trevelyan to FO, "The Circumstances of Mr. Khrushchev's Downfall," November 2, 1964, FO 371/177666, National Archive—UK.

31. Quoted in dispatch by Thomas Brimelow, British Embassy (Moscow), March 6, 1964, FO 371/177165, National Archive—UK.

32. Intelligence note, Bureau of Intelligence and Research to SecState, October 15, 1964, *FRUS, 1964–1968*, vol. 14, pp. 119–21. Memcon, meeting of executive group of NSC, October 16, 1964, ibid., pp. 124–25.

33. Memcon, Meeting of Executive Group of NSC, October 16, 1964, ibid.

34. Memcon, Dobrynin and LBJ, October 16, 1964, ibid., pp. 127–30.

35. H. A. F. Hohler, British Embassy in Paris, October 24, 1964, FO 371/177667, National Archive—UK.

36. Henry A. Kissinger, "Central Issues of American Foreign Policy" (1968), reproduced as Document 4 in *FRUS, 1969–1976*, vol. 1, p. 26.

37. Protocol 73, February 6, 1957, AOK.

38. Timothy Naftali, ed., *The Presidential Recordings: John F. Kennedy*, vol. 1, *The Great Crises* (New York: Norton, 2001), p. 267.

39. Steno, May 26, 1961, AOK.

40. John F. Kennedy, July 26, 1963, quoted in editorial, *Life* (August 9, 1963).

ABBREVIATIONS

AOK Archivii Kremlya: Prezidium TsK KPSS, 1954–1964, Tom. 1, *Chernovive protocolniye zapici zacedanii; Stenogrammi* [*Archives of the Kremlin: Presidium of the Central Committee of the Communist Party of the Soviet Union, 1954–1965*] vol. 1, Notes of State Meetings; Stenographic Accounts], editor in chief Aleksandr A. Fursenko, (Moscow: Rosspen, 2004)

APRF Archives of the President of the Russian Federation

AWD Director of Central Intelligence Allen W. Dulles

CC Central Committee of the Communist Party of the Soviet Union

CWIHP Cold War International History Project

DDE President Dwight D. Eisenhower

DDF *Documents Diplomatiques Français*

DOS U.S. Department of State

ERR Electronic Reading Room

FO British Foreign Office

FRUS *Foreign Relations of the United States*

FSB Archive of the (Russian) Federal Security Service

GRU Glavnoye Razvedyvatelnoye Upravlenie (Main Intelligence Administration of Russian General Staff)

JFD Secretary of State John Foster Dulles

Memcon memorandum of conversation

MFA Archives of the Foreign Ministry of the Russian Federation (AVPRF)

National Archives—UK British National Archives, Kew, UK

NARA-II National Archives and Records Administration, College Park, Maryland

NARA-LN National Archives and Records Administration, Laguna Niguel, California

NSK Nikita Sergeyvich Khrushchev

RGASPI Russian State Archive of Socio-Political History

RGANI Russian State Archive of Contemporary History

RMN Vice President Richard Milhous Nixon

SVR Archive of the (Russian) Foreign Intelligence Service

Telcon telephone conversation

INDEX